D1562708

Choice and Democratic Order applies theories of group conflicts within political parties in a discussion of the internal politics of the French Socialist Party (SFIO) from the late 1930s to the 1940s. Having analysed the formal and informal structure of the party in 1937, Professor Graham gives a detailed account of the clash which took place between the leadership and two dissenting groups, the Gauche Révolutionnaire and the Bataille Socialiste, prior to the Royan Congress of June 1938. This conflict is compared with that which occurred in the post-war party during 1946, when Guy Mollet led a successful revolt against the party leaders and became General Secretary of the organization after the 38th National Congress. Mollet began with the intention of preserving the existing alliance with the Communists, but as the latter moved into opposition he accepted the necessity of the centre alliance, the so-called 'Third Force' in French politics.

Choice and Democratic Order provides much important new information on a confused but compelling episode in modern French history, and will appeal to both historians and political scientists. Professor Graham emphasizes the continuities between the pre- and post-war periods, and his chosen approach enables the reader to observe major figures like Léon Blum and Guy Mollet working within the complex party structures of French socialism.

Choice and Democratic Order

Choice and Democratic Order

The French Socialist Party, 1937–1950

B. D. Graham
University of Sussex

CAMBRIDGE
UNIVERSITY PRESS

Published by the Press Syndicate of the University of Cambridge
The Pitt Building, Trumpington Street, Cambridge CB2 1RP
40 West 20th Street, New York, NY 10011–4211, USA
10 Stamford Road, Oakleigh, Melbourne 3166, Australia

First published 1994

Printed in Great Britain at the University Press, Cambridge

A catalogue record for this book is available from the British Library

Library of Congress cataloguing in publication data
Graham, Bruce Desmond, 1931 –
     Choice and democratic order: the French Socialist Party,
     1937–1950 / B. D. Graham.
         p.   cm
     Includes bibliographical references (pp. 404–18).
     ISBN 0-521-41402-4 (hc)
     1. Parti socialiste-S.F.I.O. – History. 2. Parti socialiste
(France) – History. 3. France – Politics and government – 20th century.
4. France – History – 20th century. I. Title.
JN3007.S6A49 1994
324.244′074′0941 – dc20   93–20995   CIP
ISBN 0 521 414024 hardback

wv

To the memory of
Saul Rose
this book is dedicated
with gratitude and affection

Contents

Figures

Tables

Preface

The origins of this book lie in the study of the French Socialist Party which I undertook as a postgraduate student at St Antony's College, Oxford, under the able direction of Mr Philip Williams. It was also my good fortune to have as a neighbour in Winchester Road Dr Saul Rose, Fellow of St Antony's, who had previously been the International Secretary of the Labour Party and whose work with the French Socialists had given him a sensitive understanding of their outlook and their characteristics as a party. Both then and later he was unfailingly generous with help and advice and he remained an intellectual stimulus and good friend until his untimely death in 1992.

My initial research was carried out between 1958 and 1962, first at St Antony's College and then as a member of the Cycle Supérieur d'Etudes Politiques at the Fondation Nationale des Sciences Politiques in Paris, where I received invaluable advice from Professor René Rémond, M. Serge Hurtig and M. Jean Touchard. At the time I was mainly concerned with the Socialist Party's involvement in *tripartisme* at the levels of parliament and government, but I became increasingly aware of the readiness of the Socialists of the post-war period to compare the internal difficulties which they were experiencing with those which had beset the party in 1938. This earlier conflict has always fascinated me and the present study stems from the pursuit of this interest in recent years.

I owe a considerable debt to the following institutions and their staffs: in Paris, to the Library of the Office Universitaire de Recherche Socialiste, whose rich and well-organized collection of books and papers has been of great assistance to me, to the Bibliothèque de Documentation Internationale et Contemporaine, to the Archives d'Histoire Contemporaine and the Library of the Fondation Nationale des Sciences Politiques, to the Archives Nationales and to the Bibliothèque Nationale; in Nantes, to the Centre de Documentation du Mouvement Ouvrier et Travail; and in Brighton, to the Library of the University of Sussex.

Several friends have encouraged me in this work and I would like to thank in particular Dr John Gaffney, Dr David Bell, Professor Sian Reynolds, Mrs Annette Morgan and M. Frédéric Cépède for their support and criticism. Above all, I am indebted to Dr Christophe Jaffrelot and to Mme Christine Bronnec for the help they have given me in innumerable ways and for their warm hospitality during my visits to France.

My thanks must also go to the University of Sussex, which provided me with study leave and research funds at various points in the project, and to the Nuffield Foundation, which gave me a grant for a final round of interviews and library research in the summer of 1992.

I am also very much indebted to Mr Richard Fisher of the Publishing Division of Cambridge University Press for his advice about organizing and presenting the material contained in this book, and to Dr Margaret Deith, who has seen the text through publication with expert skill, sensitivity and efficiency.

B. D. GRAHAM
October 1993

Abbreviations

AN	Assemblée Nationale
ANC	Assemblée Nationale Constituante
CAP	Commission Administrative Permanente
CAS	Comité d'Action Socialiste
CASR	Comité d'Action Socialiste Révolutionnaire
CD	Chambre des Députés
CFLN	Comité Français de la Libération Nationale
CGA	Confédération Générale de l'Agriculture
CGT	Confédération Générale du Travail
CGTU	Confédération Générale du Travail Unitaire
CNC	Commission Nationale des Conflits
CNM JS	Comité National Mixte des Jeunesses Socialistes
CNR	Conseil National de la Résistance
Déb.	*Débats parlementaires*
Doc.	*Documents parlementaires*
FGE	Fédération Générale de l'Enseignement
JAC	Jeunesse Agricole Chrétienne
JO	*Journal Officiel de la République Française*
JOC	Jeunesse Ouvrière Chrétienne
LD	*Lois et décrets*
MLN	Mouvement de Libération Nationale
MRP	Mouvement Républicain Populaire
MURF	Mouvement Unifié de la Renaissance Française
OCM	Organisation Civile et Militaire
OURS	Office Universitaire de Recherche Socialiste
PCF	Parti Communiste Français
PRL	Parti Républicain de la Liberté
PSF	Parti Social Français
PSOP	Parti Socialiste Ouvrier et Paysan
SDN	Société des Nations
SDP	[German] Social Democratic Party
Sén.	*Sénat*

SFIO	Section Française de l'Internationale Ouvrière
TPPS	Toujours Prêts Pour Servir
UDSR	Union Démocratique et Socialiste de la Résistance
USR	Union Socialiste et Républicaine

1 The internal politics of political parties

This book deals with an unusually turbulent chapter in the history of the French Socialist Party, the period from the beginning of 1938 until the summer and autumn of 1946. During the late 1930s, the party was still tolerating the activities of two dissident groups within its ranks, the Gauche Révolutionnaire and the Bataille Socialiste, both of which wished to see the organization take a new direction. The intense competition between them as each tried to gather support for its own views on strategy produced a series of major crises within the party during the first six months of 1938 and threatened to undermine the leadership group, which had some difficulty in maintaining its position at the party's Royan Congress in June that year. No sooner had order been restored than the party found itself divided again, this time over foreign policy and the question of whether it should favour conciliation as a means of avoiding war or should come out in support of a firm policy towards Germany and Italy. The outbreak of the Second World War put an end to normal political activity in France but throughout the period of German occupation and the Vichy regime, a new generation of Socialists played a prominent part in the Resistance movement and looked forward to the re-emergence of the party, freed from disagreements and structural weaknesses, when hostilities ended. With the liberation of most of France in the autumn of 1944, Charles de Gaulle's Provisional Government re-established the basic conditions for democratic life and the restored Socialist Party made a vigorous attempt to regain its former position in French society. However, in the difficult political circumstances which surrounded the First and Second Constituent Assemblies of 1945–6, it found itself allied to and competing with two powerful neighbours, a robust Communist Party and a surprisingly strong Christian Democratic group, the Mouvement Républicain Populaire. Frustrated by this situation, many Socialists again became dissatisfied with the policies being pursued by their leadership, with the result that the party's 38th Congress of August 1946 became the occasion for a fierce debate about strategies and ideas. Although the party was to face many difficulties in the years which followed, it was never again to be so divided.

The whole of this period was one of rapid change and conflict for the Socialist Party, but the crises of 1938 and 1946 bring out most clearly its vulnerability to sustained outbursts of discontent on the part of its ordinary members. However, although the two episodes are in many respects comparable, they differ both in the nature of the dissent expressed and in the response of the party's authorities to it. In 1938, in spite of the fact that two dissident groups were able to exploit the widespread rank-and-file dissatisfaction at the party's inability to restore the fortunes of the Popular Front, a well-entrenched leadership managed to maintain its position and to carry the day at the annual congress. In 1946, by contrast, a generalized and largely uncoordinated revolt took shape at the annual congress with devastating effect and it was only at the last minute that it could be checked and partially controlled. Because in each case the people who took part in these events have left good records of what happened, it is possible to build up a narrative of each crisis with reference to the terms used by the actors themselves. Moreover, because the episodes raise interesting questions about the nature of the internal politics of social democratic parties, discovering the abstract patterns of conflict underlying them can provide us with a useful basis for comparative studies. We shall therefore analyse the two crises with reference to three ideal-typical models of conflict, namely sectarianism, sectionalism and factionalism, each characterized by distinctive modes of leadership, structure and activity.[1] These models are set out below.

Sectarianism entails conflict about moral values underlying a group's organization and goals. Where parties are concerned, a dissident group

[1] The theoretical literature on the internal conflicts of parties belongs to the much larger body of literature on factionalism (see in particular, Raphael Zariski, 'Party factions and comparative politics: some preliminary observations', *Midwest Journal of Political Science*, 4, 1 (February 1960), pp. 27–51; Norman K. Nicholson, 'The factional model and the study of politics', *Comparative Political Studies*, 5, 3 (October 1972), pp. 291–314; Frank P. Belloni and Dennis C. Beller, 'The study of party factions as competitive political organizations', *The Western Political Quarterly*, 29, 4 (December 1976), pp. 531–49; Belloni and Beller (eds.), *Faction Politics: Political Parties and Factionalism in Comparative Perspective* (ABC-Clio, Santa Barbara, Calif., 1978) and it has been heavily influenced by the notion that informal conflict groups within parties are purely power-seeking in nature, and that their claims to philosophical and sectional identities can usually be reduced to underlying interests in power and position. However, the value of distinguishing between factions and tendencies has been successfully demonstrated by Richard Rose ('Parties, factions and tendencies in Britain', *Political Studies*, 12, 1 (1964), pp. 33–46) and by David Hine ('Factionalism in West European parties: a framework for analysis', *West European Politics*, 5, 1 (January 1982), pp. 36–53). For my own approach, see Graham, 'The play of tendencies: internal politics in the SFIO

adopts a sectarian approach when it accuses the established leadership of a moral failing, perhaps because it has not acknowledged the normative implications of its policies, perhaps because it is ignoring or trying to water down the principles embodied in the party's charter or founding document, or because it cannot appreciate the significance of new ideas which the sect wishes to promote. Whatever its claim, a sect must both consolidate the beliefs of its own members and use the techniques of proselytization, conversion, witness and revivalism to convert sceptics and opponents to its way of thinking. With whom does a sect see itself in conflict? Not with the party's rank-and-file members who are assumed to have a natural sympathy for the new or revived morality, but rather with the established leadership which may have prudent reasons for ignoring matters of faith, or with rival sects whose 'mistaken' views it regards as evidence of backsliding, ignorance or even apostasy. Sectarian conflict is not, therefore, necessarily binary; at any one time a sect may find itself at odds with one or more rival sects as well as with the established leadership.

A sect is homogeneous and exclusive, accepting as members only those who are convinced of the truth of its philosophy and the importance of its mission. It can remain in being for relatively long periods of time, sustained by its conviction that the transformation of the party into a body of true believers will remain a possibility for as long as idealists continue to proclaim their faith. The leaders of a sect are expected to be selfless and inspirational, solely concerned with conveying to ordinary members a clear vision of the party's moral purpose. A sect tends to have a complex structure, reflecting the division of labour needed to develop and disseminate its essential message. Although the leader of a sect may have unusual gifts of insight and understanding, he must work with a group of close disciples to organize his special knowledge into a coherent body of doctrine, just as they in their turn must co-operate with those activists who have the task of spreading the basic precepts and articles of faith to the circle of believers and to potential converts.

The second mode of conflict, sectionalism, occurs when a group within a party claims to speak on behalf of a particular section of society, whether the section concerned is based on an occupational category (such as industrial workers or agricultural labourers) or a regional, ethnic, religious or linguistic sentiment. Such a group may wish the

before and after the Second World War', in David S. Bell (ed.), *Contemporary French Political Parties* (Croom Helm, London, 1982), pp. 138–64; and Chapter 8 ('Conflict and competition within parties') in Graham, *Representation and Party Politics* (Basil Blackwell, Oxford, 1993), pp. 141–62.

party to identify itself exclusively with the outlook of the section, or it may simply urge the party to frame its policies to discriminate in that section's favour. Frequently the members of a sectional group will signify their external loyalty by adopting the style of dress, behaviour and speech associated with the outside body which they aspire to represent. Such an expression of separateness is, at a deeper level, a rejection of the party's claim to be an association in its own right. Whereas a sect acknowledges the validity of the party's inherited morality, a sectional group claims either that the party is a derivative organization, a projection into electoral and parliamentary politics of its main supporting group, or that it is simply an arena in which various sectional delegations come to terms with each other and co-operate to press their combined demands upon the government. In either case, members of a sectional group are subject to conflicting loyalties, and they may try to resolve this conflict by claiming that the section concerned is a passive constituency rather than an organized force aiming to manipulate the party for its own ends.

The third type of conflict is factionalism, which occurs when an established leader or leadership group is challenged by a group of dissidents intent on taking control of the organization. Factionalism, in this sense, is a simple power struggle between those in authority and challengers aiming to provoke a succession crisis which will enable them to take office by regular means. The challengers are intent not on usurping authority but on gaining it according to the rules, using the pressure of a membership revolt to compel the incumbent officers to retire from their posts for the sake of a settlement and the preservation of party unity. Leadership contests arising from factionalism must be settled quickly, for a factional venture is always a limited operation. In forming a faction, a dissident leader need only demonstrate that he has a reasonable chance of taking office and that he will honour his obligations to those who have supported him in his bid for power; he therefore recruits his followers individually, asking for their personal loyalty in return for the promise of some future benefit. As a result, the members of a faction may be drawn from a variety of backgrounds and persuasions. For their part, potential followers know that any commitment they make to the faction leader will be conditional. Their only shared interest is in their leader's bid for power and, should he fail in his attempt, the faction will usually dissolve.[2]

Although sectarianism, sectionalism and factionalism can be specified thus as ideal types, actual conflicts within parties combine the character-

---

[2] On factionalism generally, see F. G. Bailey, *Stratagems and Spoils: A Social Anthropology of Politics* (Basil Blackwell, Oxford, 1969), esp. pp. 51–5.

istics of all of them to varying degrees. As a result, conflict groups within parties are also multifaceted and complex in their structure and behaviour: a predominantly sectarian group may have factional and sectional features; a group which begins life as a faction may choose to participate in sectarian and sectional disputes to establish its legitimacy; and a sectional group may justify its existence on sectarian grounds. The ideal types provide a means of studying regularities in the process by which conflict groups acquire particular mixtures of characteristics; they also allow us to ask why certain combinations occur more frequently and last longer than others do, and how a group suited to one type of conflict – say, sectarianism – adapts itself to another – perhaps factionalism – should the need arise.

Our immediate concern is with the patterns of conflict which existed within the French Socialist Party in the pre-war and post-Liberation periods when it essentially conformed to the model of a mass party with a fee-paying membership, an active branch life and a considerable degree of democracy in its organizational affairs, and when its internal groups had to work within special conditions. Of these conditions, the most important was the dominance of the party's membership by a body of activists with a strong attachment to the party as a time-honoured institution (*la vieille maison*, as they often called it) who regarded the leadership as the trusted custodian of its traditions.[3] Dissident groups had to take account of this sentiment and to tread warily in criticizing the leaders and their policies but, providing they were cautious, they had opportunities to gain support for their views by stimulating and manipulating sectarian conflict. The activists, despite their loyalty to the party, were willing to tolerate wide-ranging debate about the nature and goals of socialism, with the result that dissent from settled policies was usually expressed in sectarian terms. If the leaders of a dissident group were tempted to challenge one of the party's central officers, thus giving their opposition the appearance of factionalism, however, they generally found themselves the object of considerable disapproval and subject to disciplinary action.

The party's organizational culture also inhibited the expression of sectional conflict. Socialists had inherited the view that the functions of trade unions were quite separate from those of political parties and that each should respect the organizational and political autonomy of the other. It was therefore difficult for dissident groups to claim to represent the trade unions as a whole, or even a particular category of unionists

---

[3] Cf. Angelo Panebianco's distinction between believers and careerists in party life, in Panebianco, *Political Parties: Organization and Power*, trans. Marc Silver (Cambridge University Press, Cambridge, 1988), pp. 25–30.

such as coalminers or railwaymen. The party did devote some attention to agrarian issues and a number of its leaders became expert in farming and land tenure matters, but dissident groups seldom claimed to speak on behalf of the farmers, confining themselves to general statements on agricultural policies. As far as religious matters were concerned, the party was still strongly opposed to the political and social influence of the Roman Catholic Church and in favour of the principles of *laïcité*, especially with regard to the maintenance of a system of state schooling. At party congresses, representatives of units from those parts of France where the Church's influence was strongest – the Brittany and Normandy regions, for example – would sometimes band together to press for a stronger statement of the party's policy towards secular schooling, but in this area too, views were expressed in general terms and dissident groups seldom gave great prominence to the cause of *laïcité*.

Under these circumstances, active and organized dissent from the leadership's strategies was usually expressed within the prescribed forms of sectarian conflict, and the party became adept at keeping it within bounds. However, in the two crises of 1938 and 1946, the matching systems of conflict and control were severely disrupted. In both cases, the clash between the party's officers and their main opponents rapidly became factional in nature. We shall look in some detail at the phases of activity which led to the outcome in each instance, and examine the changes in form and content of the conflict patterns which occurred.

The crucial information for studying these crises is contained in the many documents which were written during the events by the protagonists themselves. As we shall see, the cycle of organizational activity which took place each year within the French Socialist Party was accompanied by a considerable output of special resolutions, motions and tracts. Taken very seriously by leaders and members alike, these deserve much more attention than they have so far received. In the detailed narratives which follow we shall be discussing the principal texts at some length; in spite of certain shortcomings, they are the best surviving evidence of the meaning which the people concerned ascribed to the various activities in which they were involved.

2   The French Socialist Party in 1937

In order to analyse the conflicts which affected the French Socialist Party in the first six months of 1938, we need to understand the context of tradition and custom within which they occurred. This chapter is intended to establish this context in three stages: first, it discusses the history of the party (the SFIO, Section Française de l'Internationale Ouvrière) from its origins to 1937, identifying the main problems of doctrine and strategy which it encountered in the 1920s and 1930s; secondly, it reviews the ideas which formed the background to the party's internal discussions in these two decades; and thirdly, it describes the organizational, social and geographical factors which influenced the competition for power between the party's internal groups.

The Origins and History of the SFIO, to 1937

The SFIO was formed in 1905 as a result of a merger of several existing groups, including the Parti Socialiste de France, headed by Jules Guesde (1845–1922), and the Parti Socialiste Français, led by Jean Jaurès (1859–1914). The new organization was expected to co-operate with other parties belonging to the Second Socialist International with the aim of solving the problem of how social and political revolution could be achieved in the existing system of capitalist states. The French Socialists were already at odds over the prior question of whether they should have any dealings at all with the existing state, the Third Republic; they had differed in their reactions to the Dreyfus affair, the public controversy surrounding claims that Captain Alfred Dreyfus, of the French army, had been guilty of espionage, some agreeing with Jaurès that Dreyfus was innocent and that the Republic should be defended against the forces of reaction, and others refusing to take sides, on the grounds that the dispute was simply one between two factions of the bourgeoisie and therefore to be ignored. Jaurès had also defended the decision of Alexandre Millerand, a fellow Socialist, to accept a post in

7

the government formed in June 1899 by Pierre Waldeck-Rousseau but others considered that Millerand had betrayed a principle by agreeing to help in the administration of the bourgeois state.

These differences lingered on within the newly formed SFIO. Whereas Jaurès took the view that the French Republic embodied liberal and humanist ideals which should be defended and that Socialists could gain benefits for their supporters by co-operating to a limited extent with bourgeois parties in parliament and in government, Guesde stressed the need for the party to retain its independence and its revolutionary ambitions. The weight of opinion within the party was finely balanced between the two men; although Jaurès was an effective and popular leader, he was handicapped by the fact that there was no sectional pressure on the party to achieve specific policy objectives through parliamentary action. At this time, for example, the national organization of trade unions, the Confédération Générale du Travail (CGT) was still strongly influenced by the theories of revolutionary syndicalism and therefore showed no interest in working through constitutional channels.

The Socialists remained in opposition in the French parliament until the middle of 1914, when their position changed dramatically. Just after his return to Paris after attending a meeting in Brussels of the Bureau of the Second International which had tried to find ways of preserving the peace, Jaurès was assassinated on 31 July 1914. The Socialists now agreed to join the broad-based coalition, the Union Sacrée, which governed France during the early stages of the First World War. Guesde, Marcel Sembat and later Albert Thomas accepted ministerial posts but a peace movement within the party eventually forced the parliamentary group to dissociate itself from the administration and in 1917, when Thomas, the only remaining Socialist minister, finally resigned his post, the brief period of participation in government came to an end. With peace came further changes; the general elections of 1919 produced a right-wing majority, known as the Bloc National, in the Chamber of Deputies and laid the foundation for a succession of conservative governments which held office in the early 1920s. Meanwhile, the SFIO was attracting large numbers of new members, many of whom had been inspired by the Russian Revolution and now believed that a wave of revolutionary change was about to sweep through western Europe. When the Socialists met for the 18th National Congress at Tours in December 1920, a majority of the delegates agreed that the party should join the Third International, based in Moscow. The minority which had opposed this decision then broke away and set about reconstructing the SFIO according to the original design while the majority went on to found the French Communist Party. In 1921 a similar division occurred within the trade union movement, when a minority left the CGT to form the pro-Communist Confédération Générale du Travail Unitaire (CGTU).

The rebuilt SFIO quickly established a secure place for itself in post-war politics under the leadership of Paul Faure, its General Secretary, and Léon Blum, the secretary and subsequently the president of the party's parliamentary group. The first sign of its rehabilitation was its impressive showing in the general elections of 1924, when its candidates fought alongside those of the Radical-Socialist Party in an alliance known as the Cartel des Gauches and the left as a whole greatly increased its representation in the Chamber of Deputies. This result enabled Radical and liberal leaders to form a series of governments in the period between June 1924 and July 1926 but the Socialists did not use this opportunity to form a close working relationship with the Radicals. Although some members of the SFIO were prepared to commit their party to participation in coalition governments alongside the Radicals, others believed that it should restrict itself to providing conditional support to governments whose policies were acceptable, and yet others considered that the party should remain permanently in opposition. In an attempt to specify the conditions under which Socialists might accept a limited responsibility for government, Blum distinguished between the act of 'exercising power' within the framework of existing political institutions and that of 'conquering power' in a revolutionary situation. He envisaged the party's 'exercising power' only when it could ensure that one of its members would be Premier and that it could determine the content of the government's policies. In line with his views, the party's 23rd National Congress of January 1926 adopted a resolution declaring that the party was prepared to take power either alone or with representatives of other parties, but only if it had a majority and 'the preponderant voice in decisions'.[1]

By this stage, however, the balance of power in the Chamber of Deputies had shifted towards the right. A conservative government under Raymond Poincaré held office from July 1926 until the end of the legislature. The 1928 general elections weakened the left-wing parties in the Chamber and confirmed the extent of the support which his policies

---

[1] On Blum's distinction between the exercise and the conquest of power, see Joel Colton, 'Léon Blum and the French Socialists as a government party', *The Journal of Politics*, 15, 4 (November 1953), pp. 517–43. See also Gilbert Ziebura, *Léon Blum et le Parti Socialiste 1872–1934*, trans. Jean Duplex (Armand Colin, Paris, 1967), pp. 283–90; Tony Judt, *La Reconstruction du Parti Socialiste 1921–1926* (Presses de la Fondation Nationale des Sciences Politiques, Paris, 1976), pp. 193–4.

had obtained in the country. Then followed a sequence of conservative governments punctuated by minor political crises in which some attempts were made to form centre or centre-left administrations. One such crisis occurred in October 1929, following the resignation of a ministry which had been headed by Aristide Briand. The President of the Republic asked Edouard Daladier, a prominent Radical, to form a government and he invited the Socialists to join a coalition under his leadership. His offer was accepted by the Socialist parliamentary group but was rejected by the party's National Council, whose decision was subsequently endorsed in January 1930 by an extraordinary National Congress.[2]

Nevertheless, the possibility of participating in power on the basis of a policy agreement was explored by the Socialists in the weeks immediately following the general elections of May 1932, when Radicals and Socialists were again returned in increased numbers to the Chamber. In advance of any offer from the Radicals, the 29th National Congress of the SFIO specified nine policy proposals (described as the Cahiers de Huyghens after the hall in which the meeting was held) which were put to the Radical leader, Edouard Herriot, as the price of the Socialists' joining any coalition government which he might form. Herriot effectively refused to give an assurance that he would accept such terms and, when invited by the President to construct a government, he went ahead and put together a ministerial team without any Socialists. His government fell in December 1932 and he was succeeded as Premier by Joseph Paul-Boncour, whose offer of participation the Socialists rejected. After this government was defeated in its turn, in January 1933, the responsibility for forming the next ministry was given to Daladier, who also found that the Socialists' attachment to policy conditions prevented him from including them in his administration.[3]

A number of the Socialist deputies were now prepared, however, to offer the Daladier government consistent rather than conditional support and in March 1933 they voted for the approval of the general budget. As this routinely contained financial estimates for the armed forces, it should have been opposed by their group on the grounds of principle, in accordance with the party's founding agreement or Charter of 1905, so their breach of discipline was referred to an extraordinary National Congress at Avignon in April. There the delegates adopted a resolution declaring that support for the government could be only conditional and that the party should oppose the budget in general and

[2] See Ziebura, *Léon Blum et le Parti Socialiste*, pp. 312–26.
[3] See ibid., pp. 336–47; Georges Lefranc, *Le Mouvement socialiste sous la Troisième République (1875–1940)* (Payot, Paris, 1963), pp. 292–4.

the military and colonial estimates in particular. Despite this, a majority of the party's deputies again voted in favour of the budget at its second reading in May 1933, causing the 30th National Congress, which met in July, to condemn what it deemed to be a defiant gesture. When their further acts of indiscipline forced the National Council to expel six of the leading rebels in November, these were joined in forming a new party by a small number of the SFIO's deputies and senators. The dissidents were described as neo-Socialists, in keeping with the claim that a disagreement about the very nature of doctrine lay at the heart of the conflict, and the rebellion was presented to the party's members as the action of men who had been tempted by the attractions of 'ministerialism'.[4]

No sooner had this crisis subsided than the SFIO was drawn into the Popular Front of the mid-1930s. The immediate origins of this movement were the reactions to the Parisian street riots of 6 February 1934, riots which were widely interpreted as the first signs of a fascist insurrection in France. For years the French Communist Party had attacked the leaders of the SFIO for dividing the working class in its struggle with the bourgeoisie, but in 1934, after some hesitation, it began talks about unity of action with its rival. Then, in 1935 the Communist and Socialist Parties made approaches to the Radicals and in January 1936 the three parties put forward a programme of economic and social reforms which they promised to implement if they were returned to power. In March 1936 the CGTU and the CGT formed a united trade union body, which also favoured a policy of working for reforms within the existing political order.[5]

By joining the Popular Front, the SFIO escaped from the isolated position which it had occupied in the 1920s and was no longer faced with the problem of choosing between office and opposition as it had been in 1932 and 1933, but its role in the new alliance was ambiguous. First, it had to explain to its members that it was now willing to participate in government, both to preserve the Republic from the threat of

---

[4] See Ziebura, *Léon Blum et le Parti Socialiste*, pp. 347–62; Joel Colton, *Léon Blum: Humanist in Politics* (Alfred A. Knopf, New York, 1966), pp. 80–8; John T. Marcus, *French Socialism in the Crisis Years 1933–1936: Fascism and the French Left* (Frederick A. Praeger, New York, 1958), pp. 7–40; Lefranc, *Le Mouvement socialiste sous la Troisième République*, pp. 295–301; 'L'identité du socialisme français: Léon Blum et les néo-socialistes', *Cahiers Léon Blum*, nos. 15–16 (1984), containing articles by Alain Bergounioux, Jean-François Biard and Marc Sadoun.

[5] See James Joll, 'The making of the Popular Front', in Joll (ed.), *The Decline of the Third Republic, St. Antony's Papers, No. 5* (Chatto and Windus, London, 1959), pp. 36–66; Marcus, *French Socialism in the Crisis Years*, pp. 46–174; Julian Jackson, *The Popular Front in France: Defending Democracy, 1934–38* (Cambridge University Press, Cambridge, 1988), pp. 17–81.

fascism and to help bring about the economic and social reforms envisaged in the agreed programme, but that it would not be possible for any Popular Front government to implement policies which were peculiarly those of the Socialist Party itself. Secondly, it had to face the possibility that a Popular Front government, given its opposition to fascism within France, would pursue a foreign policy directed against Germany and Italy but aimed at maintaining friendly relations not only with Britain and the USA but also with the Soviet Union, with which France had agreed a pact of mutual assistance on 2 May 1935; such a prospect could hardly be expected to appeal to rank-and-file Socialists, who saw the only means of achieving a lasting peace as being general disarmament under the watchful eye of the League of Nations. Thirdly, the Popular Front entailed a degree of restrained competition between its constituent parties and, although the Socialists were confident that they could better the Radicals in electoral politics, they had good reason to fear that the Communist Party, with its established system of workplace cells at the local level, would strengthen its position within the reunified CGT and in certain industrial areas such as the northern suburbs of Paris and the coalfields. Finally, the Socialists were only too aware that it would be difficult to fund the proposed reforms so long as the government was forced to rely upon orthodox financial and economic policies. The leaders of the SFIO had ideas about what could be done to introduce price, credit and exchange controls but they had neither translated these ideas into a coherent plan of action nor been able to persuade the Radicals, many of whose members were strongly in favour of financial orthodoxy, that such a plan was even necessary.

A growing awareness within the Socialist Party of the seriousness of these problems stimulated debate and enabled its internal groups, known as *tendances*, to canvass support for their own distinctive policies. The largest of these *tendances* was the Bataille Socialiste, which had been established in 1927 and which was strongly opposed to the idea that the party should participate in government and thus weaken its links with the working class. For a period it drew considerable support from the centre ranks of the party (Paul Faure, the General Secretary, and Jean-Baptiste Séverac, his deputy, wrote articles for its journal) but by the middle of 1934 it was firmly identified with the left. Its principal leaders, Jean Zyromski and Marceau Pivert, both belonged to the party's Paris-based Seine Federation and were at that stage endeavouring to develop the Popular Front as a mass movement. However, they reacted in different ways to the events of 1935 and began to follow separate paths; while Zyromski was a strong supporter of the

Franco-Soviet pact and of the policy of strengthening the French armed forces, Marceau Pivert subscribed to the doctrine of 'revolutionary defeatism', based on the idea that the best means of avoiding war was to work for revolutions which would change the social and political character of both the liberal-democratic and fascist states and thus remove the causes of war. Finally, in October 1935, Marceau Pivert and his supporters formed a new *tendance*, the Gauche Révolutionnaire, which soon became the focus for those in the party who believed that the Popular Front could be converted into a revolutionary movement. For all its appearance of hierarchy and discipline, the Gauche Révolutionnaire was a heterogeneous body but its members were generally agreed on the need to foster a revolutionary avant-garde which could interpret the ideas and aspirations of the working class while reaching out to the SFIO's large audience amongst that class, helping it to develop its capacity for revolutionary action.[6]

Unity within the SFIO was largely restored by the victory of the left in the general elections of 26 April and 3 May 1936, in which the Popular Front parties between them won 386 of the 608 seats in metropolitan France and Algeria (the full house of 618 included an additional 10 seats from the colonies) and the Socialists were credited with 149 deputies compared with 129 returned in the 1932 elections.[7] With the approval of the SFIO's National Council and of its 33rd National Congress, Léon Blum then formed a government consisting mainly of Socialists and Radicals, the Communists having adopted the policy of simply offering support to the new administration without accepting any ministerial places. The Blum government carried through a series of reforms partly based on the Popular Front programme, including the Matignon agreements for wage increases and collective bargaining (agreed following a widespread series of strikes in the summer of 1936) and measures for a National Wheat Board to regulate the marketing of

---

[6] On the origins and development of the left-wing *tendances* within the SFIO in the inter-war period, see D. N. Baker, 'The politics of Socialist protest in France: the left wing of the Socialist Party, 1921–39', *The Journal of Modern History*, 43, 1 (March 1971), pp. 2–41, and, for a more extended treatment, his 'Revolutionism in the French Socialist Party between the World Wars: the revolutionary tendances' (Ph. D. thesis, University of Stanford, 1965). Regarding the formation of the Gauche Révolutionnaire, see Jean-Paul Joubert, *Marceau Pivert et le pivertisme: révolutionnaires de la S.F.I.O.* (Presses de la Fondation Nationale des Sciences Politiques, Paris, 1977), pp. 77–85; Daniel Guérin, *Front populaire: révolution manquée: témoignage militant* (2nd edn, François Maspero, Paris, 1976), pp. 102–4; Maurice Jaquier, *Simple militant* (Denoël, Paris, 1974), pp. 91–2.

[7] Georges Lachapelle, *Elections législatives, 26 avril et 3 mai 1936: résultats officiels* (*Le Temps*, Paris, 1936), p. xi.

wheat, a 40-hour working week, a system of conciliation and arbitration in labour conflicts, and a scheme to provide for a fortnight's paid holiday each year for employees.

For different reasons, many Socialists welcomed the Blum ministry even though they had not been converted to the idea that their party should share in the responsibility for managing the French state. In his public statements Blum emphasized that his was a Popular Front government, established to carry out the Popular Front programme, rather than a Socialist government implementing a Socialist programme,[8] and many believed that it would further the cause of the Popular Front. For their part, Marceau Pivert and the Gauche Révolutionnaire considered that the Popular Front, were it to be based on the kind of spontaneous strikes which had occurred in the summer of 1936, could become a revolutionary movement and establish a new political order. Zyromski and his friends in the Bataille Socialiste considered that the Socialists, working with the Communists and the CGT, could continue to offer the mass of the people new programmes of reforms and thus ensure their continuing support for the alliance. Others placed the emphasis on the opportunity offered by the Blum government for Socialist ministers to demonstrate that they were capable of imaginative, progressive and competent legislative and administrative action and that the party therefore deserved to hold power in its own right.

Given such differences in expectation, it is not surprising that Socialists varied in their reactions to the Blum government's policies. In foreign affairs, the main focus of attention was the Spanish Civil War, which began shortly after the ministry had taken office. Blum's first instinct had been to offer active support to the Republican side in the conflict but within a short space of time, faced with British reluctance to become involved in the war and with misgivings amongst his own ministers, he adopted the position that neither France nor any other of the great powers should intervene. This was acceptable to the large number of pacifists within the SFIO's membership and, initially, to Marceau Pivert but it was strenuously attacked by the Communists and by Zyromski. An equally important cause of discord was the government's handling of economic and financial affairs. Blum had relied heavily on the theory that a stimulation of consumer demand (by wage increases, higher payments for farm produce, expenditure on public works and the release of private savings) would cause an expansion in production and thus a reduction in unemployment. However, produc-

---

[8] See, for example, his speech at Lens on 11 October 1936 (Léon Blum, *L'Oeuvre de Léon Blum, 1934–1937* (Albin Michel, Paris, 1964), pp. 443–50), and also that at Narbonne on 25 October 1936 (ibid., pp. 458–65).

tion failed to keep pace with demand and the result was a rise in inflation which even the devaluation of the franc on 27 September 1936
failed to arrest. Concerned to control inflation and to balance the
budget, the government formed the view that it would be unwise to
undertake further social reforms for the time being. In February 1937
Blum finally announced that there would be a 'pause' in the government's programme.[9]

The hazards of responsibility for public order were brought home to
the Socialists by a tragic incident at Clichy, in the northern suburbs of
Paris, on 16 March 1937. An extreme right-wing group, the Parti Social
Français (PSF), had arranged to hold a meeting in a local cinema on
that day and, the government having refused to ban the event, a left-
wing street demonstration was organized. When this clashed with a
police detachment, shots were fired; six people died (one later in
hospital) and over 200 were wounded. Members of the Socialist youth
movement (Jeunesses Socialistes) in Paris used their journal to complain about the role of the police and to suggest that the government,
and the Socialist Minister of the Interior, Marx Dormoy, in particular,
shared in the blame. Some Parisian party branches associated with the
Gauche Révolutionnaire were responsible for wall posters with a similar
message. In an attempt to restore party discipline, a meeting of the
SFIO's National Council on 18 April 1937 approved the expulsion of
several members of the Jeunesses Socialistes and dissolved the Gauche
Révolutionnaire, which was no longer permitted to continue as an
organized body within the party.[10]

Although this crisis had been brought under control, the party still
faced the problem that the weakness of the economy was preventing the
government from undertaking further reforms. A number of financial
measures had been prepared for consideration by parliament but specu-
lative pressure on the money market in June prompted Vincent Auriol,
the Minister of Finance, to bring forward a bill asking for special powers
to be delegated to the government to restore public finances and to
ensure the economic development of the country. The Chamber gave
its consent but the Senate, afraid that the delegated authority might be
used for radical purposes, rejected the proposal and adopted a more

[9] In a radio broadcast on 13 February 1937, when addressing civil servants, Blum had
said that 'un temps de pause est nécessaire' and he expanded on this remark in a
speech at Saint-Nazaire on 21 February 1937 (see Georges Lefranc, *Histoire du Front
Populaire (1934–1938)* (2nd edn, Payot, Paris, 1974), p. 229). For the Saint-Nazaire
speech, see Blum, *L'Oeuvre de Léon Blum, 1934–1937*, pp. 478–85.
[10] See Parti Socialiste (SFIO), 34ᵉ Congrès National, Marseille, [10–13 juillet 1937], *Rapports* (Librairie Populaire, Paris, 1937), pp. 24–7; Joubert, *Révolutionnaires de la
S.F.I.O.*, pp. 122–6.

restrictive bill which had been prepared by its own Finance Committee. The Chamber responded by reviving the original bill. In an effort to break the deadlock, the government agreed to present the Senate with a modified scheme which took into account some of the concerns expressed by the Senate but the upper house rejected the new proposal and adopted another text prepared by its Finance Committee. Reluctant to meet this challenge to his authority and risk a constitutional crisis, Blum resigned as Premier on 21 June.[11]

The Radical leader, Camille Chautemps, was then asked by the President to form a new ministry. In an attempt to construct another cabinet consisting mainly of Radicals and Socialists, Chautemps offered several ministerial places to his allies. His offer was considered at a specially convened meeting of the SFIO's National Council on 22 June and was adopted by 3,972 votes (73.7 per cent of the total) to 1,369 with 9 abstentions and 43 absent, on the understanding that certain guarantees would be given: the most important of these were that the government would seek no other majority than that of the parties of the Popular Front and would consider its mission to be the full realization of the Popular Front's programme.[12] Blum and a number of his colleagues therefore joined the new ministry, which took office the same day. They were given several positions of high responsibility: Blum became Vice-Premier, Paul Faure a Minister of State and others were left with the portfolios which they had held in the outgoing government – Marx Dormoy with the Interior, Georges Monnet with Agriculture, Marius

[11] See Georges Dupeux, 'L'échec du premier gouvernement Léon Blum', *Revue d'Histoire Moderne et Contemporaine*, 10 (1963), pp. 35–44; Irwin M. Wall, 'The resignation of the first Popular Front government of Léon Blum, June 1937', *French Historical Studies*, 6, 4 (Fall 1970), pp. 538–54; A. Soulier, *L'Instabilité ministérielle sous la Troisième République (1871–1938)* (Sirey, Paris, 1939), pp. 184–6; Nathanael Greene, *Crisis and Decline: The French Socialist Party in the Popular Front Era* (Cornell University Press, Ithaca, New York, 1969), pp. 102–6. See also *The Times* (London), 21 June 1937, p. 14; the accounts of developments given to the Chamber of Deputies by Jammy Schmidt, *rapporteur général* of its Finance Committee (*JO* (*CD*), *Déb.*, 15 June 1937, pp. 1963–4; 19 June 1937, p. 2040); and the report given by Vincent Auriol to the party congress on 11 July 1937 (Parti Socialiste (SFIO), 34ᵉ Congrès National, Marseille, 10–13 juillet 1937, *Compte rendu sténographique* (Librairie Populaire, Paris, n.d.), pp. 274–304, esp. pp. 291–7.
[12] Parti Socialiste (SFIO), 35ᵉ Congrès National, Royan, 4–7 juin 1938, *Rapports* (Librairie Populaire, Paris, 1938), pp. 28–9. For details of the division and for the votes cast in the name of each of the party's federations, see *La Vie du Parti* (Paris), no. 75, 5 August 1937, p. 300. When obvious errors in the list of votes by federation given in the latter source are rectified and the figures recalculated, the adjusted totals are found to be 3,966 for, 1,375 against, 9 abstentions and 43 absent. Hereafter, such differences between published and adjusted figures will be noted and highlighted in tables by means of square brackets. For details of the adjustments, see the appendix (pp. 398–9).

Moutet with Colonies and Albert Rivière with Pensions. The most significant change was the transfer of Vincent Auriol from the Ministry of Finance to that of Justice so that a Radical, Georges Bonnet, could take over his former portfolio, while André Février inherited the Ministry of Labour from Jean Lebas, who was given the Ministry of Posts, Telegraphs and Telephones instead.

The question of whether the Socialists should remain in this government was considered by the SFIO's 34th National Congress, which met at Marseille on 10–13 July 1937. Here the party's leaders effectively asked the delegates to accept participation as a defensive measure aimed at protecting the legislative gains of 1936, preserving the possibility of further reforms and providing a secure basis for France at a time of uncertainty in European affairs. This justification was accepted: following the usual debate on general policy matters, the National Council's decision in favour of joining the ministry was endorsed by 3,484 votes (64.6 per cent of the total) to 1,866 with 43 abstentions and a pro-participation motion identified with Blum and Paul Faure was approved by 2,949 votes (54.7 per cent of the total) against dissenting motions submitted on behalf of the Bataille Socialiste and the Gauche Révolutionnaire, which received 1,545 (28.6 per cent) and 894 (16.6 per cent) votes respectively, with 5 abstentions.[13]

Conflict within the party now became more intense. By the autumn of 1937 the two dissident *tendances* were much more aggressive than they had been a year earlier. Although the Gauche Révolutionnaire had been formally dissolved by the National Council on 18 April 1937 on the grounds of its lack of discipline, it had remained in being in the form of a network of activists built around Marceau Pivert and his following in Paris, and its new journal, *Les Cahiers Rouges*, was providing a forum for revolutionary intellectuals. Where strategy was concerned, this group had not accepted the decision of the Marseille Congress and was still pressing the party to leave the Chautemps ministry and form 'un gouvernement du Front populaire de combat'. Within the Bataille Socialiste, Zyromski's strong opposition to the policy of non-intervention in the Spanish Civil War had strained his relations with other members of his group and in November 1936 he had given up his position as political director of its journal. However, by the summer of 1937 he was once more to the fore; he had been one of the sponsors of the motion which the Bataille had submitted to the

[13] Parti Socialiste (SFIO), 34ᵉ Congrès National, Marseille, 10–13 juillet 1937, *Compte rendu sténographique*, pp. 307–521, 550–96 and 604–7; *La Vie du Parti*, no. 75, 5 August 1937, pp. 297 and 299–300. For details of adjustments, see the appendix (p. 399, nn. 2 and 3).

Marseille Congress and by August he had rejoined the editorial staff of its journal. He and his *tendance* also favoured a Socialist withdrawal from the Chautemps ministry, but only when there was sufficient mass support for a government which would be a true reflection of the Popular Front, that is, one which included the Communists and the CGT as well as the Socialists and the Radicals.[14]

The central leaders had often been embarrassed by the activities of the *tendances* but it was especially difficult for them to maintain the morale and coherence of the loyalists amongst the party's members when official policies were being attacked so openly and so frequently. In an effort to provide a gathering point for loyalists, a group of prominent party members, who included Paul Faure, founded a new fortnightly journal, the *Socialiste*, to be 'l'organe de ceux qui veulent défendre le parti, les décisions de ses congrès, sa doctrine, ses règles, sa discipline' and as a means of counteracting the influence of 'les tendances et leurs journaux devenus plus hargneux et plus agressifs'.[15] The implication that the *tendances* were destructive and that the moral integrity of the party had to be defended against their influence was especially resented by the Bataille Socialiste, which considered itself to be a constructive opposition group. Its journal objected strongly to the line which had been taken by its new rival:

Il n'est guère loyal, s'il paraît habile, pour conserver une majorité de 'tendance' comptée sur une motion de faire croire que l'on ne forme pas une tendance et de chercher à attirer ainsi la 'masse flottante' des militants hésitants.

Il n'est guère loyal, s'il paraît habile, d'accuser tous ceux qui sont en dehors de la majorité, de vouloir dissocier, désorganiser le Parti. Ce n'est pas aux militants de la 'Bataille Socialiste' qu'on peut reprocher de manquer de patriotisme de Parti.[16]

There was a further trial of strength between the leaders and the *chefs de tendance* at the party's National Council meeting of 6–7 November 1937 when, following a full debate on policy, a drafting committee

---

[14] On the Bataille Socialiste at this time, see Irwin M. Wall, 'French Socialism and the Popular Front', *The Journal of Contemporary History*, 5, 3 (1970), pp. 11–13; Michel Bilis, *Socialistes et pacifistes: l'intenable dilemme des socialistes français (1933–1939)* (Syros, Paris, n.d.), pp. 214–15. See also 'Pour le Conseil National du 7 Novembre, déclaration de la "Bataille Socialiste" ', *La Bataille Socialiste*, no. 103, 25 October 1937, p. 1; Jean Zyromski, 'Après le Conseil National', ibid., no. 105, 1 December 1937, p. 1; Zyromski, 'Politique de classe, politique de masse, politique active d'unité', ibid., no. 106, 1 January 1938, p. 1.

[15] *Le Socialiste*, no. 1, 15 September 1937, cited by Bilis, *Socialistes et pacifistes*, p. 230. See also André Costedoat, 'Faisons le point', *Le Populaire*, 26 January 1938, p. 4.

[16] Pierre Métayer, 'A propos d'un journal', *La Bataille Socialiste*, no. 102, 25 September 1937, p. 3. Although Métayer does not name the *Socialiste* in his article, this is clearly the journal he is criticizing.

agreed on a resolution which pressed the case for further reforms but did not question the need to continue the party's participation in the Chautemps ministry. Zyromski proposed an amendment indicating his preference for an eventual change in government and Marceau Pivert submitted an alternative motion advocating the immediate resignation of the Socialist ministers and class action by the workers to establish a Popular Front government *de combat*. When a division was called, 3,420 votes (63.1 per cent of the total) were given to the text of the drafting committee, 1,018 (18.8 per cent) for that text as amended by Zyromski, and 925 (17.1 per cent) for Marceau Pivert's motion, there being 10 abstentions and 47 absent.[17] The dissidents had thus been held in check, but the leaders were still left with the problem that the Chautemps ministry was very unlikely to satisfy the extravagant expectations of left-wing activists about the ability of the Popular Front to drive a further set of social legislation through parliament, especially given the financial problems which the government still faced.

Meanwhile, the SFIO's partners in the alliance were pulling in different directions and the body responsible for co-ordinating their relations, the Comité National du Rassemblement Populaire, was unable to resolve the matters in dispute. Whereas the Radicals, especially those in the Senate, were becoming increasingly reluctant to approve any further attempts to inflate the economy or to experiment with financial policy, the Communists and the CGT were insisting that the government should embark upon a new programme of reform measures without further delay. Now that the Popular Front had lost its momentum, the Communist Party was able to use its privileged position, that of being part of the parliamentary majority and yet free to criticize the government's policies, to demonstrate to the CGT and to the Popular Front's general following that it was more prepared than the Socialist Party to press for further reforms, even if this meant antagonizing the Radicals. The breakdown in mutual trust between the two parties impaired the effectiveness of the Comité National d'Entente, through which they had intended to prepare for joint action, and explains why the Socialists objected so strongly to a manifesto which was published by Georgi Dimitroff, the Secretary General of the Communist International, and which presented the European Social Democratic parties in

[17] Parti Socialiste (SFIO), 35ᵉ Congrès National, Royan, 4–7 juin 1938, *Rapports*, p. 35; *Le Populaire*, 7 November 1937, pp. 1–2; 8 November 1937, pp. 1–3; 10 November 1937, p. 4 (for the text of the Pivert motion); *La Vie du Parti*, no. 76, 25 November 1937, p. 302. The details of the votes by federation in the latter source show that the number of votes attributed to absent federations was 47 and not 27, the figure cited in accounts of the totals of votes in this division. For details of adjustments, see the appendix (pp. 399–400, n. 4).

a very unfavourable light, implying that their proposed fusion with the Communist Parties would be on Communist terms. On 24 November 1937 the SFIO's executive, the Commission Administrative Permanente (CAP), broke off discussions with the French Communists about the possibility of forming a united party; the reason which it gave for doing so was the issuing of this manifesto and the only one of its members to vote against the decision was Zyromski.[18]

By the end of 1937, the SFIO's relations with its allies within the Popular Front were deteriorating and its dissident *tendances* were becoming more and more confident as the weeks passed by. Faced with these external and internal problems, the Socialist leaders had good reason to fear for the stability of their party. However, before taking up the narrative of the crisis which was about to break upon them we must turn our attention to the background of beliefs and organizational structures against which the impending conflicts took place.

Leaders and ideas in the SFIO in the late 1930s

The *jeu de tendances* could not have maintained itself so successfully had it not been for the existence during this period in the party's history of a leadership hierarchy which allowed considerable freedom to dissenters, and a body of myths and doctrines which provided ample justification for disobeying authorities and decisions on the grounds of moral principle. In this section we shall consider the party's leaders and their beliefs under three main headings, even though the resultant groupings may oversimplify the complexity of the intellectual relationships involved.

The most characteristic but also the least coherent of these groupings was that of the Guesdistes, those who drew their inspiration from Jules Guesde and his particular interpretations of the writings of Marx and Engels. The Guesdistes venerated the Charter of 1905, adopted at the time of the SFIO's foundation and preserved thereafter as a basic statement of beliefs. Its text referred to the formation of

un parti de lutte de classe qui, même lorsqu'il utilise au profit des travailleurs les conflits secondaires des possédants ou se trouve combiner accidentellement son action avec celle d'un parti politique pour la défense des droits et des intérêts du prolétariat, reste toujours un Parti d'opposition fondamentale et irréductible, à l'ensemble de la classe bourgeoise, et à l'Etat, qui en est l'instrument.

[18] Parti Socialiste (SFIO), 35ᵉ Congrès National, Royan, 4–7 juin 1938, *Rapports*, pp. 124–34.

The party's purpose was described in the following terms:

Le Parti socialiste est un parti de classe qui a pour but de socialiser les moyens de production et d'échange, c'est-à-dire de transformer la société capitaliste en une société collectiviste ou communiste, et pour moyen l'organisation écono- mique et politique du prolétariat. Par son but, par son idéal, par les moyens qu'il emploie, le Parti socialiste, tout en poursuivant la réalisation des réformes immédiates revendiquées par la classe ouvrière, n'est pas un parti de réforme, mais un parti de lutte de classe et de révolution. [Parliamentary strategy was reduced to outright opposition to any bourgeois government.] Les élus du Parti au Parlement forment un groupe unique, en face de toutes les fractions poli- tiques bourgeoises. Le Groupe socialiste au Parlement doit refuser au gouverne- ment tous les moyens qui assurent la domination de la bourgeoisie et son main- tien au pouvoir; refuser en conséquence les crédits militaires, les crédits de conquête coloniale, les fonds secrets et l'ensemble du budget . . . [19]

This text can only be understood in the context of the controversies which were disturbing the European Socialist movement at the turn of the century. The points at issue were posed most clearly within the German Social Democratic Party (SDP), whose Erfurt programme, approved in 1891, had assumed that the means of production would be increasingly concentrated in the hands of a small number of capitalists and large landowners and that conditions would worsen for the prolet- ariat and the intermediate classes – the petite bourgeoisie and the peas- antry. It claimed that the gap between those with and those without property would be further widened by the economic crises which were endemic in the capitalist system and portrayed the SDP as the force which would organize and guide the working class towards final victory in its struggle against capitalist exploitation.[20] 1891 was also the year in which Engels had released the commentary which Marx had written on the SDP's earlier Gotha programme of 1875 and which contained his claim that '*the revolutionary dictatorship of the proletariat*' was needed to make the transition from capitalist to communist society.[21] The idea that a Socialist party had no role in a parliamentary democracy other

[19] 'Déclaration commune des organisations socialistes adoptée le 13 janvier 1905', in J. Ferretti, *Ce qu'est le Parti Socialiste* (Parti Socialiste (SFIO), Librairie Populaire, Paris, 1928), pp. 11–14. On the background to the adoption of this declaration, see Aaron Noland, *The Founding of the French Socialist Party (1893–1905)* (Harvard University Press, Cambridge, Mass., 1956), pp. 165–87.

[20] For an English translation of the Erfurt programme, see R. C. K. Ensor, *Modern Socialism as Set forth by Socialists in their Speeches, Writings, and Programmes* (Harper and Brothers, London, 3rd edn, 1910), pp. 317–22. See also Peter Gay, *The Dilemma of Democratic Socialism: Eduard Bernstein's Challenge to Marx* (Collier Books, New York, 1962), pp. 62–4.

[21] Karl Marx, 'Critique of the Gotha Program', in Lewis S. Feuer (ed.), *Basic Writings on Politics and Philosophy: Karl Marx and Friedrich Engels* (Anchor Books, New York, 1959), p. 127.

than to prepare for an inevitable class conflict and then to take control of the state on behalf of the proletariat was challenged by Eduard Bernstein, whose book, *Die Voraussetzungen des Sozialismus und die Aufgaben der Sozialdemokratie*, published in 1899, denied that capital was being concentrated in the hands of fewer people and claimed that the trend was in the opposite direction, towards an increasing number of property owners, a lessening in the intensity of commercial crises, and more gradations within society. As regards political action, he suggested that socialism could be achieved within a democratic framework rather than through a dictatorship of the proletariat.

Within the SDP and other European Socialist parties, Bernstein's ideas were treated as if they were heretical or at best as spurious justifications for the errors of 'revisionism' and 'reformism'. The principles of orthodox Marxism were therefore reaffirmed in a series of resolutions adopted by congresses of the Socialist International in 1901 and 1904. The SFIO was founded when this reaction was still strong and its 1905 Charter simply echoed the anti-revisionist and anti-reformist themes of orthodox doctrine and provided little guidance for those in the new party who wanted to develop a realistic strategy for dealing with other political forces, and especially with the Radical Socialists, and for working constructively within the institutions of the Third Republic. Although some phrases in the text touched on these issues its main emphasis was upon a simple class struggle between the proletariat and the bourgeoisie and upon the conflict between the Socialist parliamentary group and the governing mechanism of the state.

The Guesdistes of the 1930s assumed that the Charter of 1905 embodied their creed – they believed in the reality of the class struggle, the inevitability of revolution and the need for the Socialist Party to seize control of the state. The possibility of alliances, either between the proletariat and other classes or between the Socialist and other parties, had no place in their scheme of things; they assumed that the SFIO was essentially a party of the working class and that its main function was to organize and co-ordinate the action of that class while maintaining its own discipline and strength for that purpose. Guesdistes rarely considered these principles in relation to one another, and in documents they tended to present one principle at a time, often in the form of a slogan, as a justification for a particular course of action or as a reason for opposing one. They regarded them also as a set of moral standards, against which proposals could be classified as good or bad instead of being analysed, with the result that disagreements over strategy (as in 1933, at the time of the revolt of the neo-Socialists) were often reduced to fundamental differences of outlook.

The abstract nature of their ideas enabled Guesdistes to disagree amongst themselves in their appreciation of actual events and to take up quite different, and often opposed, positions within the party. Paul Faure, the SFIO's General Secretary, Jean-Baptiste Séverac, his deputy, and Jean Lebas, the head of the party's huge Nord Federation, had no difficulty in reconciling their Guesdisme with the policy of governing the bourgeois state on the basis of the Popular Front, while the leaders of the Bataille Socialiste, such as Jean Zyromski and Bracke (A.-M. Desrousseaux), saw no contradiction between their support for dissent and the Guesdiste principle of organizational solidarity.

Each of the five leaders named above personified a different aspect of what Guesdisme represented as a philosophy of party life, as distinct from a body of ideas. Paul Faure (1878–1960) was very much a product of southern Guesdisme. Born in Périgueux, he came into contact with Socialist ideas as a student in Bordeaux and in 1901 joined the Dordogne Federation of the Parti Ouvrier Français. In 1906, after the formation of the SFIO, he and some colleagues founded *Le Travailleur du Périgord* which, renamed as *Le Travailleur du Centre*, became the official organ of the Corrèze, Creuse, Dordogne and Lot Federations of the new party. During the First World War, when he belonged to the Haute-Vienne Federation, he became the leader of a movement within the party for a negotiated peace. In 1920 he was associated with Jean Longuet and a group of members who were in favour of the party's joining the Third International, though only on certain conditions. Unable to accept the degree of control which Moscow was threatening to impose on the organization, he stayed with the SFIO after the Tours split, became General Secretary of the reconstructed party, and helped Léon Blum in the task of converting *Le Populaire* into its central newspaper. As a deputy from Saône-et-Loire, Paul Faure was a member of the Chamber of Deputies between 1924 and 1932 but he remained an opponent of the idea that the party should participate in government and therefore took a firm line against the neo-Socialists in 1933. Despite his obvious distaste for working with the Communists, he did everything possible in the mid-1930s to make the Popular Front a success and accepted Blum's invitation to join his first Cabinet as a Minister of State in 1936. This action did not mean that he had given up his objection to participation in government but simply signified his agreement with the argument that an exceptional arrangement was needed for exceptional times.[22]

[22] Jean Jolly (ed.), *Dictionnaire des parlementaires français: notices biographiques sur les ministres, députés et sénateurs français de 1889 à 1940*, V (Presses Universitaires de France, Paris, 1968), pp. 1663–5; A. Compère-Morel, *Grand dictionnaire socialiste du*

Paul Faure relied heavily on his deputy, Jean-Baptiste Séverac, to back up his own efforts to keep the party's press and organization on an even keel. A scholarly and erudite man, Séverac (born in 1879) had joined an association of Socialist students in his home town of Montpellier in 1897 but he later moved to the north and worked in the Aisne Federation of the SFIO in 1907–14 and in the Seine Federation from 1914 onwards. He was on the editorial staff of *L'Humanité*, then the party's principal newspaper, between 1916 and 1918 and after the Tours split helped Blum and Paul Faure to run *Le Populaire*.[23] Having worked so closely with Paul Faure in the rehabilitation of the SFIO in the 1920s, he was well aware of the strict limits which his friend had set on his role as General Secretary, especially where matters of doctrine were concerned. Writing in 1933, he addressed him almost as though he were a lost leader:

Maintenant – et depuis longtemps – les heures difficiles de la reconstitution du Parti sont, grâce à toi, révolues. Tu pouvais, dès lors, et dans l'intérêt du Parti lui-même, affirmer tes conceptions et . . . la 'tendance' en face des autres. Comme ce sont aussi les miennes, nous nous sommes trouvés et nous nous trouvons encore ensemble.[24]

Séverac and Paul Faure were both southerners and the chief representative in the party of the northern aspect of Guesdisme was Jean Lebas, who, like them, had accepted the Popular Front governments as an exception to the rule that Socialists should not help to administer the bourgeois state. Lebas (1878–1944) was the son of a textile worker in Roubaix, where at the age of 14 years he had heard Guesde speak and had then read some of his pamphlets. He used an abridgement of Marx's *Das Kapital* to read the full text in a French translation and made Guesde's notion of collectivism the centre-piece of his own philosophy. He joined the Parti Ouvrier Français in 1896 and in 1906 was appointed deputy secretary (later full secretary) of the SFIO's Nord Federation. In 1912 he became Mayor of Roubaix and after the First World War served as one of the representatives from the Nord Department in the Chamber of Deputies between 1919 and 1928 and between 1932 and 1940, his special parliamentary interests being labour, conditions of employment and social security. He served as Minister of

mouvement politique et économique, national et international (Publications Sociales, Paris, 1924), p. 291; Greene, *The French Socialist Party in the Popular Front Era*, pp. 34–48; Claude Willard, *Le Mouvement socialiste en France (1893–1905): les Guesdistes* (Editions Sociales, Paris, 1965), p. 623.

[23] Compère-Morel, *Grand dictionnaire socialiste*, p. 820.

[24] J.-B. Séverac, *Le Parti Socialiste: ses principes et ses tâches: lettres à Brigitte* (Editions de la Bataille Socialiste, Paris, 1933), p. 20.

Labour in the first Blum government and as Minister for Posts, Telegraphs and Telephones in the subsequent Chautemps ministry.[25]

Within the Nord Department, Lebas and his colleagues had worked as municipal Socialists, concerned to administer Lille, Roubaix and other industrial centres on progressive lines and to strengthen local co-operative institutions, but in Paris, at least until the Popular Front, they were anti-participationists, stressing the dangers of trying to work within the existing institutional framework. In a preface to an edition of early writings by Jules Guesde and Paul Lafargue, Lebas had reminded his readers how necessary it was to occupy the state

sans partage, soit à la suite d'élections générales portant par un courant populaire, le parti socialiste au gouvernement, soit à la faveur d'une situation révolutionnaire . . .

He then explained how this control should be used:

le gouvernement révolutionnaire ne remplirait sa mission que 1° s'il s'attachait immédiatement à arracher la racine du mal capitaliste en nationalisant ou socialisant tous les grands monopoles privés et concédés de production, d'échange, de transport, 2° s'il était animé d'une volonté d'atteindre rapidement ce but – son but – et décidé pour cela à briser toutes les résistances hostiles.[26]

His plea for a revolutionary dictatorship implied that a great deal would have to be done after the seizure of power, both to reshape the economic framework and to defeat any political reaction. Indeed, such Guesdiste accounts of what would be entailed in the dictatorship of the proletariat came uncomfortably close to the Communist notion, despite denials to the contrary.

While Lebas was more than thirty years younger than Guesde and knew him as a patron and mentor, someone who had worked closely with him in the rough and tumble of Socialist politics at the turn of the century was Alexandre-Marie Desrousseaux (1861–1955), commonly known as Bracke. As a young man, Bracke had embarked on an academic career, teaching Greek philology first at Lille and subsequently in Paris, where he had come to know Guesde. He was deputy secretary of the Parti Ouvrier Français and then of its successor, the Parti Socialiste de France, and served for two periods in the Chamber of Deputies, representing the Seine Department between 1912 and 1924 and the

[25] See Jean Piat, *Jean Lebas* (Editions du Parti Socialiste S.F.I.O., Librairie des Municipalités, Paris, 1964); Jean Maitron, *Dictionnaire biographique du mouvement ouvrier français*, XIII, Part 3, *1871–1914* (Editions Ouvrières, Paris, 1975), pp. 228–30; Willard, *Le Mouvement socialiste en France*, pp. 630–1.
[26] Jules Guesde and Paul Lafargue, *Pourquoi l'avenir est au socialisme* (Librairie Populaire, Paris, 3rd edn, 1933), pp. 7–8.

Nord Department between 1928 and 1936; he also served for many years as the party's chief representative at meetings of the Second International and as a member of its executive.[27] As a leader of the Bataille Socialiste, he believed in the value of constructive criticism but he was also understanding and considerate in his relations with Blum and Paul Faure.

His younger colleague, Jean Zyromski (1890–1975), was much more intransigent. Born at Nevers, he had studied law at Toulouse and had joined the SFIO in 1912. He saw military service in the First World War and afterwards settled in Paris, where he worked in the Prefecture of the Seine Department and eventually became an inspector in its welfare division. Steeped in the internal politics of the party's Seine Federation, he was strongly committed in the 1930s to strengthening the Popular Front and to bringing about the reunification of the Communist and Socialist Parties.[28] He was also an ardent supporter of the Republican side in the Spanish Civil War and was very opposed to the French policy of non-intervention in that conflict. At party gatherings he was a blunt and forceful speaker, always trying to predict the course of events and then to reduce strategies to fixed lines of action so that adequate guidance could be given to the party faithful. Of all the Guesdistes we have considered, he was the most prepared to accept the determinism of their philosophy and to translate his beliefs into practice.

The second major family of ideas within the SFIO was associated with a diverse group of intellectuals, most of them belonging to the Gauche Révolutionnaire in the late 1930s, whom we shall call the romantic revolutionaries. Whereas the Guesdistes assumed that the course of events leading towards a revolutionary crisis was predictable, and therefore placed a duty of discipline and obedience on the party and its members, the romantics believed that revolutionary situations could be created by the spontaneous actions of the masses and that the party's task was to aid this process by responding to opportunities and encouraging the individual initiatives of its members. Again, while the Guesdistes saw the state as a centre of structured power which, having

---

[27] Willard, Le Mouvement socialiste en France, p. 607; Compère-Morel, Grand dictionnaire socialiste, p. 83; Théodore Beregi, 'Bracke, socialiste et humaniste', L'OURS (Paris), no. 222 (August–September 1991), pp. 8–9.

[28] See Greene, The French Socialist Party in the Popular Front Era, pp. 48–55; Baker, 'The politics of Socialist protest in France', pp. 13–16; Lefranc, Le Mouvement socialiste sous la Troisième République, pp. 353–5. See also Zyromski, Sur le chemin de l'unité (Editions 'Nouveau Prométhée', Paris, 1936), which consists of several articles and one speech from the 1934–5 period putting the case for the fusion of the Socialist and Communist Parties. These pieces show clearly the nature of his ideas about revolution, social classes, party organization and the state.

served the ruling class, could now be seized by the party and used to effect the transition from capitalism to socialism, the romantics believed that the socialist state would be fashioned during the process of revolution, as the people explored new ways of organizing their work and their lives. Finally, whereas the Guesdistes were, at heart, determinists who believed in historical laws, the romantics were voluntarists who believed that the creative energies of the masses were the main causes of radical change.

At the turn of the century this voluntarist tradition had been identified with a number of different groups, such as the Blanquists, who looked back to the example of Louis Auguste Blanqui at the time of the 1848 revolutions, the Possibilists, whose chief theorist was Benoît Malon, and the Allemanists, named after Jean Allemane, who was strongly opposed to central control by either a political party or a state.[29] The SFIO inherited elements from many such groups but the scale and complexity of its organization forced voluntarist leaders to appeal for support on general rather than specific grounds and to encourage currents of opinions which could flow across regional boundaries. The first of their number to do so was Gustave Hervé, who built up a following in several of the party's departmental federations and established a *tendance* known as the *insurrectionnels* or the Hervéistes in the early SFIO.[30]

By the late 1930s, Marceau Pivert was making very effective use of voluntarist themes to strengthen the position of the Gauche Révolutionnaire within the party. Although he borrowed freely from the ideas of others, including those of Rosa Luxemburg, he was essentially a romantic revolutionary in the French tradition. In his speeches and congress resolutions he assumed that the mass of the people had a capacity for making revolution which depended neither on the appropriate objective conditions nor on the right degree of class consciousness. He thought in terms of a revolutionary avant-garde working in close sympathy with the masses and helping them to develop their ideas and their methods of action, and he also believed that the best means of realizing those ends was for his group to work inside the SFIO, taking advantage of its democratic structure to gather support. He evidently expected that the revolution, when it came, would take the form of a general insurrection within which the workers could create their own political structure and militia with the aim of seizing power and

---

[29] See André Philip, *Les Socialistes* (Seuil, Paris, 1967), pp. 20–7.
[30] For the place of Hervé in the anti-state movement of his time, see Madeleine Rebérioux, 'Les tendances hostiles à l'Etat dans la S.F.I.O. (1905–1914)', *Le Mouvement Social*, no. 65 (October–December 1968), pp. 21–37.

establishing a class dictatorship of the proletariat. He valued the Popular Front more as a mass movement than as an electoral and parliamentary alliance and, after the fall of the Blum government in June 1937, he argued that the time had arrived for a further advance towards a more radical and combative form of that movement. Where international affairs were concerned, he refused to accept that workers had a duty to help defend the nation state; instead, he advocated revolutionary defeatism, the doctrine which sees the best way of avoiding war as being by fomenting revolutions in those states likely to engage in military conflict.[31] He therefore had little in common with a Guesdiste who accepted the principle of national defence, believed that a revolution would not occur until the historically determined conditions were present, and placed more value on the educational than on the agitational function of the party. However, he and his colleagues did share with the Guesdistes a reverence for the Charter of 1905, which they cherished as a general affirmation of revolutionary principles.

Marceau Pivert (1895–1958), who came from a rural background in the Seine-et-Marne Department, had served in the infantry in the First World War but in 1917, after a serious illness, he had returned to civilian life to resume his profession as a schoolmaster. He taught science in a secondary school in the Yonne Department, where he joined the SFIO and helped to re-establish its local federation in the wake of the Tours split. Later he went to Paris to study at the Sorbonne, became secretary of the party's branch in the 15th *arrondissement*, and quickly established himself within the leadership hierarchy of the Seine Federation. Like Zyromski, he was committed to the success of the Popular Front in the Paris region but he saw it more as a revolutionary force in the making than a formal political alliance, and it was his insistence that the movement needed to be pushed further that made his use of the Gauche Révolutionnaire so unsettling for the party's central leaders. For a time, he remained in touch with them, advising on the use of film and other propaganda techniques and, under the Blum government,

---

[31] The clearest indication of his ideas at this time is given in his letter to Léon Trotsky of 20 August 1935, in La XVe Section du Parti Socialiste, *La Gauche révolutionnaire du Parti Socialiste S.F.I.O. et le groupe bolchevick–léniniste (trotskyste)* (Paris, [1935]), pp. 5–8, and in his pamphlet, *Révolution d'abord! La révolution avant la guerre* (Editions 'Nouveau Prométhée', Paris, [1935]). See also his speech to the National Council on 18 April 1937, in Pivert, Lucien Hérard and René Modiano, *4 discours et un programme: de l'exercice à la conquête du pouvoir* (Paris, May 1937), pp. 31–49, and his long address on 12 July 1937 to the Marseille Congress (Parti Socialiste (SFIO), 34e Congrès National, Marseille, 10–13 juillet 1937, *Compte rendu sténographique*, pp. 411–44).

working in the Premier's office in the field of media services. He resigned from that post in February 1937 and then, after the Clichy incident and the dissolution of his *tendance*, moved into a position of outright opposition to the party's authorities.[32]

One of Pivert's principal lieutenants in the late 1930s was Daniel Guérin, who had been influenced by the ideas of revolutionary syndicalism. He had met Pivert in 1930, during a first, short-lived period in the party, and he teamed up with him after renewing his membership in May 1935.[33] Guérin was particularly interested in the causes and significance of the strike movement of June 1936 and in the possibility of organizing the industrial workers in the Paris region.[34] Another of Pivert's companions was Georges Soulès (born in 1907), a young highways engineer from Toulouse, who had joined the party in 1931 while he was a student at the Ecole des Ponts in Paris. Having been appointed to an engineering post at Valence in the Drôme Department, he became the leader of the left-wing minority in the Socialist Federation there and also joined Révolution Constructive. The latter group consisted of intellectuals (including Georges and Emilie Lefranc) who were interested in the ideas of the Belgian Socialist, Henri de Man, for constructing a planned economic order which could serve as an intermediate stage in the transition from capitalism to socialism. Blum and others were sceptical of this theory and wary of those, like Soulès, who were attracted to it, but the latter nevertheless found a ready welcome in the Gauche Révolutionnaire. After his return to Paris, he was elected to the SFIO's central executive as one of the Gauche Révolutionnaire's representatives in July 1937.[35]

Several members of Marceau Pivert's entourage had belonged to the Communist Party in the early 1920s before the onset of its Stalinist phase. They included Lucien Hérard, Maurice Jaquier and Henri Goldschild. Hérard, a school-teacher, had left it in 1926 and, while living at

---

[32] For biographical details of Marceau Pivert before 1938, see Etienne Weill-Raynal, 'Marceau Pivert', *La Revue Socialiste* (Paris, NS), no. 118 (June 1958), pp. 561–6; Joubert, *Révolutionnaires de la S.F.I.O.*, esp. pp. 13–14; Baker, 'The politics of Socialist protest in France', pp. 16–22; Guérin, *Front Populaire: révolution manquée*; Greene, *The French Socialist Party in the Popular Front Era*, pp. 55–64; Georges Lefranc, 'Le socialisme français dans l'entre-deux guerres', *Information Historique*, 40 (1978), pp. 131–4 (for a review of Joubert, *op. cit.*).

[33] For membership details, see Parti Socialiste (SFIO), 35e Congrès National, Royan, 4–7 juin 1938, *Rapports*, p. 34.

[34] For Guérin's own account of his political activities in this period, see his *Front populaire: révolution manquée*, pp. 13–189.

[35] See Raymond Abellio [Georges Soulès], *Ma dernière mémoire*, II, *Les Militants 1927–1939* (Gallimard, Paris, 1975), pp. 7–281 *passim*.

Besançon, had helped to establish the Fédération Communiste Indépendante de l'Est, from which he resigned in 1933.[36] By the mid-1930s he and his wife, Madeleine, were working in Dijon, where they joined with some activists of the Fédération de l'Education Nationale to establish a Marxist *tendance* in the SFIO's Côte-d'Or Federation in 1935 and subsequently made common cause with the Gauche Révolutionnaire.[37] Other provincial figures in sympathy with Pivert were Sylvain Broussaudier of the Alpes-Maritimes Federation, Henri Midon of the Meurthe-et-Moselle Federation and Maurice Deixonne (also a leading member of Révolution Constructive) of the Cantal Federation.

Opinions have varied regarding the nature of Marceau Pivert's intellectual influence on those around him. According to Léon Trotsky, whom Pivert visited at Barbizon, near Fontainebleau, during the winter of 1933–4, the Socialist leader was 'un petit professeur de province, honnête et consciencieux, mais à l'horizon limité'.[38] While it is the case that most of Pivert's writings were occasional pieces and that they did not have a wide reference, they were sufficiently declamatory and general to appeal both to those activists who were not concerned with theoretical subtleties and to those who were sufficiently secure in their own beliefs not to feel threatened by them. Pivert's lieutenants did not treat him as a doctrinal authority but they were willing to defer to him as a brave and resourceful champion of the revolutionary cause, and he in turn gave them warm friendship and uncritical trust. For those outside the inner circle of the Gauche Révolutionnaire he represented the ideal of the selfless activist, hardworking, and an enduring optimist.

The unity of his *tendance* owed a great deal to its members' lack of ordinary political ambition (none of them were members of parliament) and to their shared obsession with what they took to be basic questions of strategy. They were agreed, first, that the masses could be roused to take revolutionary action by direct appeals to their class interest, and, secondly, that the role of a revolutionary party should be limited to that of providing advice and guidance. They did not believe that the Communist Party could serve this purpose but they considered that the SFIO, for all its weaknesses from their point of view, provided sufficient internal democracy for a revolutionary *tendance* to develop within the framework of its organization and then to communicate with the masses so that the revolutionary process could be set in motion. Once that

---

[36] Jean Rabaut, *Tout est possible! Les 'gauchistes' français 1929–1944* (Denoël/Gonthier, Paris, 1974), pp. 90 and 141; Joubert, *Révolutionnaires de la S.F.I.O.*, pp. 12 and 81–2.

[37] L. Perrein (interview, July – August 1985), 'Lucien Hérard, syndicaliste et "révolutionnaire" ', *Cahiers Léon Blum*, nos. 17–18 (1985), pp. 71–4.

[38] See Fred Zeller, *Trois points: c'est tout* (Robert Laffont, Paris, 1976), p. 124.

stage had been reached they were quite prepared to break with the
Socialists and to form a party of their own. The essential problem was
one of deciding when the moment for action had arrived. The members
of the Gauche Révolutionnaire became involved in an endless appraisal
of events such as strikes and political crises in order to identify signs
that the movement towards revolution had begun. They were equally
tireless in their search for enemies who might try to frustrate their
designs; the existence of a hostile interest in their plans at least showed
them that they were working along the right lines, whereas indifference
would have left them in a limbo of uncertainty, with no judgements
other than their own to offer them reassurance. Until the masses
answered their call to revolution their only spur to action, the only
guarantee that their knowledge was true knowledge, was the animosity
of their opponents.[39]

The third major family of ideas in the inter-war SFIO was that of
radical republicanism, distinguished by the belief that the republican
ideal had not reached its final form in the Third Republic and that
further changes would bring about a socialist order, in which economic
and social as well as political equality would be realized. According to
radical republicans, these changes could and should be brought about
within the existing political system and any attempt to destroy that
system by a violent revolt would be unnecessary and harmful. They
might differ in their opinions as to the order and urgency of reforms,
but they were generally persuaded that the Senate should be abolished
or reduced in authority, and that the Chamber of Deputies would provide a better picture of public opinion if the system for electing its
members were one of proportional representation rather than that of
the single-member, two-ballot method, known as the *scrutin d'arrondissement*, which had been reintroduced in 1927 and which encouraged
the expression of local rather than party attitudes. Once such changes
had made the Chamber more powerful and more responsive to the
electorate, it would be much easier for parties of the left to win support
for far-reaching programmes of economic and social reform. Radical
republicans nevertheless acknowledged that the Third Republic, if its
constitution were not revised, would remain vulnerable to certain forms
of political reaction. First, at a time of uncertainty the people might
turn for security to political leaders who wanted to establish a Bonapar-
tist system of personal rule, either by strengthening the presidency or
by resort to plebiscite and national rallies of opinion. Secondly,

---

[39] On the need for enemies, cf. Abellio, *Ma dernière mémoire*, II, *Les Militants 1927–
1939*, pp. 209–10.

experience had already shown that the lower-middle classes and the peasantry could be persuaded to join with the bourgeoisie in supporting a Union Nationale, a political combination of parties of the centre and right, such as that which had formed the basis of the Poincaré government of 1926–8 and of the Doumergue ministry in 1934. Thirdly, the radical republicans were deeply disturbed by the rise of fascism, seen as a technique of mass politics which could use the binding force of romantic nationalism to create authoritarian regimes with sufficient power to destroy all liberal democratic institutions and thus remove any possibility of reform.

Radical republicanism was by no means a monopoly of the Socialist Party and indeed it was much easier for left-wing Radical Socialists to proclaim this philosophy than for members of the SFIO, who had to be cautious whenever they defended the existing regime. Radical republicans amongst the Socialists distinguished themselves from their Guesdiste colleagues by calling up the memory of Jean Jaurès and by claiming that he had wanted Socialism to be the salvation of all mankind, a universalistic rather than a class-bound ethic, and a force for transforming the whole of society and not just one part of it. Whereas Guesdistes tended to assume that Jaurès and Guesde had been adversaries, and that Guesde had been vindicated, radical republicans would claim that the party had inherited a synthesis of the ideas of these two leaders and that this justified their own sympathy for the republican tradition and for the parliamentary method of government.

Without doubt, Léon Blum (1872–1950) was the main defender of radical republican ideas within the Socialist Party in the inter-war period. The second son of a Jewish business family, he grew up in Paris and studied at the Ecole Normale Supérieure before joining the Conseil d'Etat, the supreme administrative court which also gives opinions on decrees and bills. Having met Jaurès in 1897, he worked with him in the campaign in support of Dreyfus and later in the negotiations to form a united Socialist party, but he was not closely involved in the affairs of the SFIO before 1914, his main concern at that time being with writing and literary criticism. After the outbreak of the First World War, he was appointed as the *chef de cabinet* to Marcel Sembat, one of the two Socialist ministers who joined the Viviani government in August 1914, but he left this post in December 1916 when Sembat resigned from office. Blum was elected to the Chamber in 1919 and, having relinquished his position on the Conseil d'Etat, threw himself fully into the life of the Socialist Party. He opposed the idea of affiliating the party with the Third International and, after the Tours split of 1920, he played a central role in the reconstruction of the SFIO, both as an editor of *Le Populaire* and as secretary (later president) of the party's parliamentary group.[40]

Until he became Premier in 1936, Blum provided the readers of *Le Populaire* with a constant flow of perceptive articles on national and international affairs and sought by this means to provide the party's members with detailed guidance on the positions which they should adopt in public discussions. These writings were partly a commentary on current events, partly a discussion of party policies and partly an evocation of doctrinal issues. However, in this period Blum did not proceed to the next stage of organizing his doctrinal views into a systematic statement which might have brought into the open the conflict between his theory of the nature of the state and of revolution and that embodied in the Charter of 1905. Instead, he encouraged the idea that something resembling a consensus had been achieved; writing in 1946, he was to claim that:

pendant les quinze années qui ont suivi l'unité de 1905, puis pendant les quinze années qui ont suivi la scission de Tours, il s'est élaboré au sein de notre parti un corps de doctrine commune, combinant la pensée de Marx avec celle de Jaurès . . . qui ne faisait et qui ne fait l'objet d'aucune contestation, d'aucune division sérieuse.[41]

His unqualified admiration for Jaurès and his belief in doctrinal unity were really two sides of the same coin. In February 1933, referring to the part which Jaurès had played in unifying the Socialist movement, he had insisted that reform and revolution were compatible ideas:

Mais dans la doctrine socialiste, c'est le même effort et c'est le même résultat. Je pourrais vous le montrer pour deux notions, comme la notion de réforme et la notion de révolution sociale et vous faire sentir comment c'est la pensée de Jaurès qui est arrivée à les pénétrer l'une par l'autre, à les incorporer l'une dans l'autre, à montrer ce qu'il y avait de nécessairement réformiste dans l'action révolutionnaire et de nécessairement révolutionnaire dans l'action réformiste.[42]

---

[40] See the following biographies of Blum: Geoffrey Fraser and Thadée Natanson, *Léon Blum: Man and Statesman* (Victor Gollancz, London, 1937); Colette Audry, *Léon Blum ou la politique du Juste* (René Julliard, Paris, 1955); Louise Elliott Dalby, *Léon Blum: Evolution of a Socialist* (Thomas Yoseloff, New York, 1963); Joel Colton, *Léon Blum: Humanist in Politics* (Alfred A. Knopf, New York, 1966, and Duke University Press, Durham, 1987 reprint); Ziebura, *Léon Blum et le Parti Socialiste*; William Logue, *Léon Blum: The Formative Years 1872–1914* (Northern Illinois University Press, DeKalb, 1973); Philippe Bauchard, *Léon Blum: le pouvoir pour quoi faire?* (Arthaud, Paris, 1976); Jean Lacouture, *Léon Blum* (Seuil, Paris, 1977). See also, Jules Moch, *Rencontres avec . . . Léon Blum* (Plon, Paris, 1970); Louis Guitard, *Mon Léon Blum ou les défauts de la statue* (Régirex-France, Paris, 1983).

[41] From a speech given on 29 August 1946 to the 38th National Congress of the SFIO in Blum, *L'Oeuvre de Léon Blum, 1945–1947* (Albin Michel, Paris, 1958), p. 277.

[42] Blum, *Jean Jaurès: conférence donnée le 16 février 1933 au Théâtre des Ambassadeurs* (Editions de la Liberté, Paris, 1944), p. 35.

When Blum's speeches and writings took him into the field of general theory, he was cautious and restrained in developing his ideas. For example, he was prepared to discuss the applications of certain of Marx's ideas, including his theory of historical materialism, his doctrine of classes and their relations, and his analysis of value, and this led him to agree that the existing political order was in some sense a creation of the bourgeoisie and that at some point in time it would be replaced by a new collectivist order. However, Blum did not accept Lenin's extensions of these ideas and he argued that the dictatorship of the proletariat should not be an end in itself; he did not reject the idea outright but took the view that such a dictatorship could be justified only if the ground had been prepared beforehand by the education of the working classes and by anticipatory changes in the economy, so that any transitional arrangements would be short-lived. The same concern for democracy led him to reject the idea of a highly centralized vanguard party and the associated doctrine of democratic centralism; he considered that a Socialist party had to be open and democratic if it was to prepare and educate the working class for its future role in society.[43] Nevertheless, Blum did not challenge the assumption that a political revolution involving the conquest of the state would be necessary to bring about socialism; he did not in the 1930s advance the idea that socialism could be achieved by stages within the existing political framework, even though his discussion of short-term possibilities took it for granted that substantial reforms, such as those achieved by his own government in 1936, were perfectly feasible within the parliamentary institutions of the Third Republic.

It was in his analyses of contemporary politics that Blum expressed most clearly the radical republican strain in his philosophy. In the mid-1930s, for example, the threats to the state and, under his own government, the nature of the authority of the state, were matters which concerned him directly and he gave them considerable thought. In 1934 and 1935 he published a series of articles to counter proposals for strengthening the executive[44] and in 1936 he brought out a revised edition of his book, *Lettres sur la réforme gouvernementale*, which had first appeared in 1918.[45] His basic proposition was that the 1789 revolution had transferred sovereignty from the monarchy to the people and at

---

[43] See his speech on 27 December 1920 at the Tours Congress in Blum, *L'Oeuvre de Léon Blum, 1914–1928* (Albin Michel, Paris, 1972), pp. 137–60. See also Blum, *Bolchevisme et socialisme* (Librairie Populaire, Paris, 8th edn, 1936); the first edition of this brochure appeared in 1927.

[44] See Blum, *L'Oeuvre de Léon Blum, 1937–1940* (Albin Michel, Paris, 1965), pp. 419–68.

[45] Blum, *La Réforme gouvernementale* (Bernard Grasset, Paris, 1936). This edition contains a section (pp. 211–27) which corresponds in part to a set of articles published in

the same time had established a direct relationship between the community of citizens (each of whom possessed a unit of sovereignty and a set of individual rights) and the central authority of the state.[46] In an ideal republic, the citizens would elect an assembly of representatives to represent their will and to choose an executive, which would always remain responsible to the assembly. Blum accepted the constitutional laws of 1875 as an imperfect reflection of this ideal, but he also saw the Third Republic as an embodiment, in a spiritual sense, of the liberties which the French nation had won for itself in the uprising of 1789 and in the revolutions of the nineteenth century. At the level of administrative procedures and conventions, he had clear and practical ideas about how the executive and the legislature could be made into more effective instruments of government, but his main prescriptions for improving the Republic were to restrict the power of the Senate and to encourage the growth of stable, differentiated and electorally based political parties, chiefly through the introduction of proportional representation.

Underlying these ideas were abstract notions of the state, both as a system of law and as an enduring framework of authority, and a theory of consent which was much more sophisticated than that underlying the Leninist account of bourgeois democracy. In the context of the Popular Front, Blum saw the Rassemblement Populaire not as an expedient political alliance but as a coalition of social groups aiming not only to achieve a programme of reforms but also to preserve the existing structure of individual rights and democratic institutions. His familiar distinction between the exercise and the conquest of power acquired a new significance after the Parisian street riots of 6 February 1934 had indicated that the French Republic was once more in danger and he therefore placed more emphasis on the Socialists' duty to work and ultimately to govern within the existing order, not simply to carry out reforms but also to defend the parliamentary system itself.[47]

In the 1920s and early 1930s, however, the main responsibility for making the case that the Socialist Party had to play a full part in parliamentary politics, even to the extent of forming coalition governments

---

Le Populaire between 28 and 31 December 1934 (see Blum, *L'Oeuvre de Léon Blum, 1937–1940*, pp. 440–8).

[46] See his speech in celebration of Jaurès on 31 July 1937, in Blum, *L'Oeuvre de Léon Blum, 1937–1940*, pp. 480–4, and his essay on the Declaration of the Rights of Man for the Encyclopédie Quillet, ibid., pp. 497–506.

[47] *Le Populaire* editorials of 1, 2 and 4 July 1935, in Blum, *L'Oeuvre de Léon Blum, 1934–1937*, pp. 193–8. On the general question of Blum's republicanism, see Boris Mirkine-Guetzévitch, 'La République parlementaire dans la pensée politique de Léon Blum', *La Revue Socialiste* (NS), no. 43 (January 1951), pp. 10–24, and 'L'identité du socialisme français: Léon Blum et la République', *Cahiers Léon Blum*, nos. 19–20 (1986), and especially the articles by Jean-François Biard, '1934, les ligues, le fascisme',

with the Radicals, had fallen to the reformist wing of the party's parliamentary group, whose chief spokesman was Pierre Renaudel. Blum went only so far as to envisage the exercise of power within restricted conditions and the issues raised by the reformists concerning the Socialist Party's duty to work with other republicans were reduced in the rhetoric used by the party's centre and left-wing members to a simple case of 'ministerialism'. The split of 1933 removed not only outright rebels, such as Marcel Déat and Adrien Marquet, but also many genuine parliamentarians, such as Paul Ramadier, whose attachment to radical republicanism was as strong as Blum's and who would have been his natural allies in the conflicts of the late 1930s. Blum was fortunate that a handful of experienced and reform-minded parliamentarians did remain with the party in 1933 and two of them, Vincent Auriol and Marx Dormoy, provided him with valuable support during the period of the Popular Front governments.

Vincent Auriol (1884–1966) was born at Revel in the Haute-Garonne Department. He studied at Toulouse, joined the SFIO in 1907, and in 1909 became the chief editor of *Le Midi Socialiste*, a newspaper which had been established by Albert Bedouce, a Socialist deputy from the area. Auriol himself was elected to the Chamber from an Haute-Garonne constituency in 1914 and was returned in all the inter-war elections. He worked closely with Blum in the 1920s when, as a prominent member of the Chamber's Finance Committee, he gained an expert knowledge of public finance, and in 1936–7 he held the important post of Minister of Finance in the first Blum government before moving to the Ministry of Justice under Chautemps.[48] In the closing months of 1937, faced with mounting pressure from the dissident *tendances* for the party's withdrawal from the government, he argued the case for continued participation on what were really radical republican grounds. He claimed that the Blum government had intended to bring forward legislation which would have provided a transition between the Popular Front's programme and the reforms of structure which the Socialist Party had wanted, that the Senate had overthrown the government because it wanted to avoid such measures, and that the party nevertheless aimed to carry out reforms of structure and to change the role and composition of the Senate.[49] Later, writing during the period of the

---

pp. 83–95, and by Marc Sadoun, 'Mystique et politique: les ressources de la République', pp. 97–111.

[48] *L'Année politique, 1947* (Editions du Grand Siècle, Paris, 1948), p. 3; *Le Populaire*, 17 January 1947, p. 1.

[49] Vincent Auriol, *Pour les candidats aux élections cantonales de 1937: la vérité sur la gestion socialiste* (SFIO, Librairie Populaire, Paris, 1937), pp. 7–11.

wartime occupation, Auriol was still willing to grant that the constitutional laws of 1875 had provided the conditions for political democracy, even though

l'Etat était condamné, par le jeu de ses institutions, tantôt à l'inaction ou à la réaction quand les forces démocratiques se divisaient, tantôt à la résistance lorsque, coalisées, elles se faisaient menaçantes.[50]

Blum was equally fortunate to have the friendship and support of Marx Dormoy (1888–1941), who came from Montluçon in the Allier Department. His father, Jean Dormoy, had been a follower of Jules Guesde and had been the first Socialist Mayor of Montluçon. Marx Dormoy, having served in the First World War, became secretary of the Allier Federation of the SFIO in 1924, was the first editor of *Combat Social*, and was appointed Mayor of Montluçon in 1925. He was elected to the Chamber from a by-election in a Montluçon constituency in 1931 and retained his seat in the 1932 and 1936 elections. He was one of two Secretaries of State attached to the Premier's Office when the Blum government was formed, became Minister of the Interior on 24 November 1936 following the suicide of Roger Salengro and retained that portfolio in the Chautemps government which took power in June 1937. In this post, Marx Dormoy took a firm line with groups of the extreme right and pushed ahead vigorously with the police inquiries which uncovered the extent of Cagoulard activities following the bomb explosions of 11 September 1937.[51]

Although their numbers and influence were small at this stage, those members of the Socialist parliamentary group who had held office in the Blum government or were holding office in the Chautemps government had acquired first-hand experience of the workings of the executive and of the relations between ministries and sectional interests. As a result, the party was now in a much better position to judge the value of participation in government than it had been when in opposition. This was most obviously the case in agrarian politics, where Georges Monnet, as Minister of Agriculture in both administrations, had been directly involved in the work of establishing the Wheat Office. Monnet had been born in 1898 in Aurillac, in the Cantal Department, and after his war service he had taken up farming in the Chemin-des-Dames district of the Aisne Department. Following his election to the Chamber in 1928, he had played a prominent part in the affairs of its Agricultural

---

[50] Vincent Auriol, *Hier . . . demain*, II (Editions E. Charlot, Paris, 1945), p. 113.
[51] Compère-Morel, *Grand dictionnaire socialiste*, p. 226; Blum, *L'Oeuvre de Léon Blum, 1945–1947*, pp. 454–6; Jolly (ed.), *Dictionnaire des parlementaires français . . . de 1889 à 1940*, IV (1966), pp. 1470–1.

Committee.[52] The Wheat Office which he formed in 1936 had some of
the features of an independent public corporation but it also depended
heavily on the authority of the Minister of Agriculture, who, with the
Minister of Finance, was responsible to parliament for its operations.
Although the Central Council of the Office had important supervisory
powers, and contained representatives of the consumers, traders,
millers and bakers as well as those of the producers, its ability to determine policy was relatively restricted. The Office was authorized to offer
wheatfarmers a minimum guaranteed price for the purchase of their
grain but prefects and mayors continued to be responsible for fixing the
prices for flour and bread. In addition, the Office was given a monopoly
of the import and export of wheat and flour.[53] The strategy behind the
scheme was to help the small farmers, who often lacked the means to
play the market and had therefore to sell their grain for low prices,
and to restrict the economic freedom of the large farmers, the private
marketing firms and the millers. Through this reform, Monnet and his
colleagues had made an imaginative attempt to persuade a hitherto
unorganized sectional group, the small farmers, that state marketing in
foodgrains would serve their interests and that it was possible to prevent
those who were opposed to the scheme from restoring the free market.
However, to stand a chance of full success the policy needed to be
carried further, both to improve the efficiency of the Wheat Office,
especially in its administration of the guaranteed price scheme, and to
extend the principle of state marketing to other commodities, such as
milk, sugar, wine and meat. Any such moves were bound to encounter
further resistance from the conservative Chambers of Agriculture at the
level of the departments. For its part, the Socialist Party was faced with
the challenge of taking full account of the interests of small farmers in
formulating its policies, of ensuring that the Ministry of Agriculture
remained in its hands for as long as possible and, more generally, of
acknowledging that it could no longer afford the luxury of abandoning
power because of doctrinal objections to sharing in the administration
of the existing state.

Experience in government had also impressed upon the Socialist parliamentary group the importance of economic planning and therefore
the value of those of its intellectuals who had already taken an interest
in technical subjects. The most prominent of these was Jules Moch
(1893–1985), who had been educated in an Ecole Polytechnique and

[52] Jolly (ed.), *Dictionnaire des parlementaires français* . . . *de 1889 à 1940*, VII (1972),
    pp. 2493–4.
[53] 'Loi tendant à l'institution d'un office national interprofessionnel du blé', 15 August
    1936, *JO*, *LD*, 18 August 1936, pp. 8866–71.

who, after service in the First World War, had completed his training and had qualified as a marine engineer. In 1919 he was placed in charge of a programme to restore industry and agriculture in Germany and in other defeated countries but he resigned this post in 1920 to work for a railway construction company, on whose behalf he visited the Baltic states and spent several months in Moscow in 1924. On his return from the Soviet Union he joined the SFIO and was elected to the Chamber in 1928 from a Drôme constituency. He served on the Chamber's Public Works, Aeronautics and Navy Committees and was involved in the preparation and presentation of legislation in several fields. In 1934, encouraged by Léon Blum, he established a group known as the Union des Techniciens Socialistes (UTS) to go into the details of how the party's policies could be turned into specific pieces of legislation.[54] Although he was not returned to parliament in the 1936 elections he was given the post of Secretary-General to the government when the Blum ministry was formed. Elected to the Chamber in May 1937 from a by-election, he was appointed as an Under-Secretary to the Premier's Office but he was not a member of the Chautemps government which took power in June.[55]

André Philip (1902–70) shared Moch's interest in planning. He came from an old Protestant family in the Midi and, after attending secondary school in Marseille, he studied law in Paris and gained his doctorate. Following a period at the University of Columbia in the USA, he was appointed as Professor of the Law Faculty at Lyon in 1926. At this time Philip was also interested in the ideas of Henri de Man, and particularly in his view that socialism had taken from Christianity the principle that every person should be given a sense of equality and personal pride. Philip had been a member of the SFIO since 1920 and in 1936 was elected from a Lyon constituency to the Chamber, where he served on the Finance Committee and on a special committee entrusted with the task of preparing the Blum government's social legislation.[56]

By the end of 1937 the Socialists had been part of the government for eighteen months and several members of their parliamentary group had served either as ministers, or as under-secretaries or as representatives on important parliamentary committees. These members now belonged to the layer of *ministrables*, composed of those deputies and

---

[54] Moch, *Rencontres avec . . . Léon Blum*, p. 118; Jean-François Biard, 'Le débat sur le régime intermédiaire et le plan (juillet 1933 – juillet 1934)', *Cahiers Léon Blum*, nos. 15–16 (1984), p. 40.
[55] Jolly (ed.), *Dictionnaire des parlementaires français . . . de 1889 à 1940*, VII, pp. 2481–2.
[56] Ibid., p. 2683.

senators whose experience, standing and particular skills qualified them for consideration as possible ministers whenever any coalition involving their party was being formed. The Socialist *ministrables* included not only Paul Faure, Jean Lebas, Vincent Auriol, Marx Dormoy, Georges Monnet, Jules Moch and André Philip but also Charles Spinasse, who had won respect for his work as Minister for National Economy in the first Blum government, Albert Bedouce, Marius Moutet, Albert Rivière, Robert Jardillier, Henri Sellier and André Février. When next the question of participation came up at a party plenum, men such as these could be expected to argue that the SFIO, almost in spite of itself, had become a party of government, that it should accept this role and that it should now spend its energy on securing those portfolios which would best serve its supporting interests. The simple condition of being in power had thus strengthened the position of the radical republicans within the party.

How does the pattern formed by the party's three intellectual traditions help us to understand the mechanism of the *lutte de tendances*? The essential answers to this question can be given with reference to the diagram on page 41, which provides a simplified scheme of the relationships between traditions, *tendances* and parties. By 1937, the Gauche Révolutionnaire was practically coterminous with the sector of romantic revolutionary opinion in the party and enjoyed a close affinity with the various groupings and journals, mainly in the Paris area, which sustained a variety of Trotskyist, libertarian and anarchistic currents of opinion during this period. The Bataille Socialiste, by contrast, was essentially a radical version of the party's Guesdiste mainstream but was nevertheless conforming closely to the movements of the French Communist Party, especially in its policies towards the Spanish Civil War and international affairs in general. Both *tendances* were still travelling along divergent paths from their point of separation in 1935 but each one assumed that under the right conditions it could win over the bulk of the party to its point of view. In this competition the advantage lay with the Bataille Socialiste, because Zyromski's variety of orthodox Marxism, with its emphasis upon historical inevitability, the class struggle and determinism, was much more intelligible to the rank-and-file membership than Marceau Pivert's constant calls for dramatic action to exploit some dimly perceived eventuality. In one sense, the existence of the Bataille Socialiste, so insistent that mass action could revitalize the Popular Front and prepare the ground for a government which would include the Communists, made it difficult for the Gauche Révolutionnaire to put across its simpler claim that the party was betraying

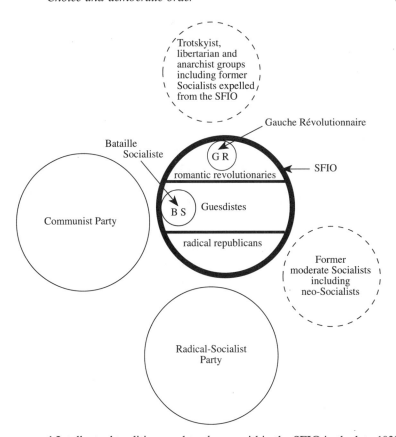

1 Intellectual traditions and *tendances* within the SFIO in the late 1930s

the Charter of 1905 by continuing to take part in the management of the bourgeois state.

Confronted by two such determined and aggressive groups, the party's central leaders had to rely mainly on appeals to organizational discipline and loyalty, knowing that their faithful majority was composed of two quite different strands of opinion. Participation in the Chautemps ministry was acceptable to the radical republicans, but they could not have justified it on grounds of principle without admitting that some of the neo-Socialists, such as Renaudel and Ramadier, had been right to take the position in 1933 that the party needed to play a more constructive part in budgetary discussions and co-operate more fully with the Radicals for the sake of the Republic. On the other hand, Guesdistes such as Paul Faure and Jean Lebas could not have attacked the evils of ministerialism and reformism without also renouncing the party's place in the current ministry and abandoning the idea of the Popular Front altogether. All that the leaders could do was to justify their policy on grounds of expediency, arguing in effect that the Popular Front and their acceptance of participation had been caused by unexpected contingencies, and most obviously by the sudden rise of fascism.

Thus far we have concentrated on those aspects of the party's beliefs which concerned the nature of the state and of revolution, and as a result we have emphasized the differentiation of intellectual traditions within the organization. However, the SFIO was also affected by powerful waves of sentiment which were capable of sweeping right through its membership, completely destroying established alignments and divisions in the process. Such a surge of emotion could easily be aroused during debates about peace and war; the party had inherited from the peace movement of the First World War period and from the antimilitarism of the 1920s a strong attachment to pacifism, and any proposal that France should envisage rearmament and defensive alliances to check the advance of the fascist powers risked provoking a reaction from a minority of the party's republicans, from a majority of its Guesdists, and from all of its romantic revolutionaries against any prospect of war. Equally powerful emotions could be aroused by the suspicion of a threat to *laïcité*, the system under which the state had excluded the Roman Catholic Church from the realms of politics and administration, and especially from state educational institutions. The Marseille Congress of July 1937 had unanimously adopted a resolution expressing the view that 'la classe ouvrière rencontre l'Eglise dans toutes les entreprises de réaction politique et de conservatisme social' and that 'la bataille laïque est une des formes essentielles de la lutte sociale'; it went on to demand more action by the government against the privileges of private Roman Catholic and congregational schools, to ensure the neutrality of teachers in religious matters, and to strengthen the state-schooling system in the three Alsace-Lorraine departments which had been returned to France after the war.[57] Anticlericalism varied in intensity from tradition to tradition and from person to person (there is a world of difference between Blum's sparing and restrained references to the question and Marceau Pivert's polemics against the influence of the clergy)[58] but it was an issue which aroused strong feelings in all

---

[57] See Parti Socialiste (SFIO), 35ᵉ Congrès National, Royan, 4–7 juin 1938, *Rapports*, pp. 10–12.

[58] See, for example, Marceau Pivert, *Tendre la main aux Catholiques? Réponse et réflexions d'un socialiste* (Editions du Parti Socialiste SFIO, Librairie Populaire du Parti Socialiste S.F.I.O., Paris, 2nd edn, 1937).

sections of the party: there was no telling in advance how a crisis in relations between church and state would affect the SFIO.

The connection between anticlericalism and freemasonry was still an important factor in French politics in the late 1930s also, but from the time of its Lyon Congress of 1912 the SFIO had decided that no account would be taken of whether its members were also attached to associations, including those of the freemasons and the League of the Rights of Man, which were concerned with philosophical, educational or ethical matters, and which were not aiming to gain political power.[59] The reputation of the Grand Orient, the largest of the Masonic orders, had been tarnished by the rumour and gossip which followed two political scandals in 1934 and its influence was weak during the period of the Popular Front, but some Socialists nevertheless placed a high value on their membership of this order. For men such as Marceau Pivert, who belonged to a lodge entitled L'Etoile Polaire,[60] freemasonry offered a setting which was partly that of a club and partly a meeting ground where matters of principle could be discussed without reference to the problems of realization and policy, and away from the political scene, where motivation was always being called into question.

The organization of the SFIO in 1937

Having considered the *lutte de tendances* as a conflict of ideas, we must now examine its place within the organizational politics of the SFIO. In this section, a review of the party's formal and informal structure is followed by a survey of the eight largest of its departmental federations and by an analysis of the balance of power between the dissident *tendances* and the party's central authorities.

The SFIO's constitution was a variant on the basic Social Democratic model, designed to ensure that ordinary members were given the maximum possible freedom of expression and that plenary institutions had sufficient powers to control the executive bodies and the parliamentary group. The principles underlying the model were those of direct democracy and assumed that the body of members possessed a general will and that delegates to higher bodies were bound to obey instructions and thus respect the dictates of that will.

[59] See Denis Lefebvre, 'Maçons et anti-maçons socialistes (1906–1912)', *Cahier et Revue de l'OURS* (Paris), no. 183 (September–October 1988), pp. 19–24; Pierre Chevallier, *Histoire de la franc-maçonnerie française*, III, *La Maçonnerie: église de la République (1877–1944)* (Fayard, Paris, 1975), pp. 139–42; Zeller, *Trois points: c'est tout*, pp. 286–8; Compère-Morel, *Grand dictionnaire socialiste*, p. 320.
[60] See Zeller, *Trois points: c'est tout*, pp. 284–5.

Throughout its history the SFIO was organized at three levels, the local area (where branches and sub-branches were the basic units), the administrative department (within which branches formed federations) and the centre (where delegates from the departmental federations would meet to decide policies and choose officers). Between 1905 and 1940 this arrangement took the following form:

Functions and units   *Levels of organization*

	Central	Departmental	Local
I Unit	SFIO	Federation	Branch
II Executive and administrative bodies	General Secretariat Bureau	Federal Secretariat Federal Bureau	Branch Secretariat Bureau
	Permanent Administrative Committee (CAP)	Executive (or Administrative) Committee	Administrative Committee
III Plenary bodies	National Council	Federal Council	Branch meetings and assemblies
	National Congress	Federal Congress	

As revised to 1929,[61] the party's rules (*statuts*) provided for the annual renewal of these bodies in the following sequence: in each department, the party's branches would elect delegates to attend their federal congress which, in its turn, would elect one delegate to be the federation's representative on the National Council and one or more (depending on the size of the party membership in the department) to attend the National Congress of the party. Once in session, the National Congress would elect the thirty-three members of the CAP, which was authorized, subject to the ratification of the National Council, to appoint the officers of a small Bureau, headed by the General Secretary. While the

[61] The *statuts* were adopted by the 1st National Congress of April 1905 and were amended by the second session of the 8th National Congress in November 1911, by a National Council in July 1913, by another National Council meeting in November 1925, and by the 26th National Congress in June 1929. They were not further amended until after the Second World War. For a discussion of the early organization, see Ziebura, *Léon Blum et le Parti Socialiste*, pp. 168–89, and for an official guide to the party's organizational conventions, see Ferretti, *Ce qu'est le Parti Socialiste*, pp. 32–49.

annual session of the National Congress was intended to be the occasion when most policy decisions were made, the National Council, meeting at least once every three months, and the CAP were able to act for it between sessions. A similar relationship obtained for the federal congress, federal council and federal executive (or administrative) committee within each department.

The party's elected representatives in parliament and in municipal, general and local councils were all subject to the authority of the organization. The parliamentary group was declared to be 'distinct de toutes les fractions politiques bourgeoises' and its members were expected to accept the founding declaration of 1905 and to conform to the party's tactical line. So far as discipline was concerned, the group and each of its members came under the control of the National Council and its participation in the activities of the organization was severely limited. Its representation on the National Congress was restricted to between two and five deputies, who were expected to reply to observations on the group's annual report but were not accorded voting rights, and only members of its executive body along with members of the CAP, all without voting rights, were entitled to attend meetings of the National Council. Furthermore, no more than twelve of the thirty-three places on the CAP itself could be occupied by parliamentarians.

Members of the party were recruited at the level of the branch, where each person joining the party would acquire a permanent card containing the text of the party's rules, and an annual card (*la feuille de cotisation annuelle*) with twelve squares in which stamps could be placed by the Branch Treasurer on payment of each monthly subscription. The numbers of permanent and annual cards issued and monthly stamps sold were reported upwards through the federation to the central office, which was therefore able to compile two series of membership statistics, a maximum (the number of annual cards distributed) and a minimum (the number of stamps sold divided by twelve, to obtain annual figures). Table 1 sets out the maximum and minimum measures of membership from 1921, immediately following the Tours split, to 1937.

Both series show a rising trend to 1932 (with perturbations in 1927 and 1928), a sharp downturn in 1933 and 1934, and sharp increases in 1936 and 1937. The pattern of membership renewal and recruitment which accompanied the latter expansion can be judged from Table 2.

These figures show that the peak enrolment of new members occurred in 1936 and 1937 and that the rate of card cancellation did not rise appreciably until 1938. As a result, the total number of cardholders,

Table 1. *SFIO: maximum and minimum membership 1921–37*

Year ending	Maximum member-ship (no. of cards distributed)	No. of stamps sold	Average of stamps per card	Minimum member-ship (stamp totals divided by 12)
1921	50,449	372,694	7.39	31,058
1922	49,174	374,805	7.62	31,234
1923	50,496	402,373	7.97	33,531
1924	72,659	605,147	8.33	50,429
1925	111,276	924,098	8.30	77,008
1926	111,368	1,018,578	9.15	84,882
1927	98,034	934,446	9.53	77,871
1928	109,892	915,339	8.33	76,278
1929	119,519	1,064,121	8.90	88,677
1930	125,563	1,167,925	9.30	97,327
1931	130,864	1,194,885	9.13	99,574
1932	137,684	1,198,667	8.71	99,889
1933	131,044	1,160,643	8.86	96,720
1934	110,000	963,423	8.76	80,285
1935	120,083	1,017,397	8.47	84,783
1936	202,000	1,604,315	7.94	133,693
1937	286,604	2,476,988	8.64	206,416

Source: For numbers of cards distributed and stamps sold, Parti Socialiste (SFIO), 35ᵉ Congrès National, Royan, 4–7 juin 1938, *Rapports* (Librairie Populaire, Paris, 1938), p. 196.

Table 2. *SFIO: numbers of cardholders 1935–8*

Year ending	Numbers of SFIO members whose cards were: New	Renewed	Cancelled	Total cardholders	Percentage of new cardholders
1935	26,726	93,357	16,643	120,083	22.3
1936	100,211	101,789	18,290	202,000	49.6
1937	101,332	185,272	16,728	286,604	35.4
1938	38,107	237,266	49,338	275,373	13.8

Sources: Based on the figures for *nouveaux adhérents*, *anciens adhérents* and *radiés* given in Parti Socialiste (SFIO), 35ᵉ Congrès National, Royan, 4–7 juin 1938, *Rapports* (Librairie Populaire, Paris, 1938), p. 204; ibid., 36ᵉ Congrès National, Nantes, 27–30 mai 1939, *Rapports* (Librairie Populaire, Paris, 1939), p. 154.

the measure of maximum membership, more than doubled between 1935 and 1937 and the proportion of new cardholders was significantly high in both 1936 and 1937.[62]

By the end of 1937, the SFIO contained 103 federations, of which 90 represented departments in metropolitan France and 13 represented overseas departments and territories. The variation in the size of membership between federations was considerable, as can be seen from Table 3, which presents the distribution in terms of minimum membership.

The numbers of federations in the membership ranges fall off rapidly from 37 (including 10 overseas units) and 35 in the two lowest categories to 2 in the 4,001–5,000 range, while the largest federations (Nord with 19,167 members, Seine with 15,783, Pas-de-Calais and Seine-et-Oise each with 8,750, and Bouches-du-Rhône with 7,867) are spread out through the higher ranges. The distribution of membership between the federations was thus very uneven, with 29.2 per cent of the total being

Table 3. *SFIO: distribution of membership by federation in 1937 (year ending)*

Membership ranges	Nos of federations	Membership totals	Per cent of total membership
0–1,000	37	22,643	11.0
1,001–2,000	35	48,654	23.6
2,001–3,000	18	44,422	21.5
3,001–4,000	6	21,554	10.4
4,001–5,000	2	8,792	4.3
7,001–8,000	1	7,867	3.8
8,001–9,000	2	17,500	8.5
15,001–16,000	1	15,783	7.6
19,001–20,000	1	19,167	9.3
Individuals		35	0.1
Totals	103	206,417	

Source: Parti Socialiste (SFIO), 35ᵉ Congrès National, Royan, 4–7 juin 1938, *Rapports* (Librairie Populaire, Paris, 1938), pp. 192–3, for stamp totals, which were divided by twelve and rounded.

[62] For detailed analyses of the membership trends of the party in the inter-war period, see Greene, *The French Socialist Party in the Popular Front Era*, pp. 161–4; I. M. Wall, 'French Socialism and the Popular Front' (Ph. D. thesis, University of Columbia, 1968), pp. 284–91 (regarding the membership increases of 1936 and 1937); Tony Judt, *Marxism and the French Left: Studies in Labour and Politics in France, 1830–1981* (Clarendon, Oxford, 1986), pp. 129–36.

concentrated in the five largest federations. The inequalities in membership were translated into similar inequalities in the distribution of voting units, or mandates (*mandats*), which federations could use for ballots at meetings of the National Council and the National Congress. Under the party's rules, each federation was entitled to one mandate by right and to additional mandates for every 25 members, calculated by dividing its minimum membership by this number. As one would expect, given the membership distribution noted above, large numbers of mandates were allocated to the units with most members, such as the Nord and Seine Federations.

The federations were the basic units of the party's organization. The rules of the SFIO were designed to ensure that they retained an important degree of control over the policies and actions of the party's central bodies through the delegates whom they sent to each national congress and to the quarterly meetings of the National Council. Decisions on these occasions could be taken by a show of hands but Article 25 of the rules specified that, should one-tenth of the delegates make such a request, voting would be by mandate; this provision ensured that the votes of federal delegations in the ballot would be registered and eventually published, so that the ordinary members of each federation would have information about how their delegate or delegates had used their mandates in that instance. Some federations were prepared to allow their delegates freedom of judgement but others insisted upon the use of *le mandat impératif*, and instructed their delegates to support particular groups or policies.

The rules also reveal an intention to preserve the rights of minorities. Thus the first paragraph of Article 19 stated that:

Chaque fois que l'entente n'aura pu se réaliser, la minorité aura droit à tous les degrés de l'organisation du Parti: section, fédération, C.A.P. et pour toutes les commissions ou délégations de ces divers organismes, à une représentation proportionnelle.

In line with this provision, Article 21 specified that a minority had the right to proportional representation in the election of delegates to the national congress by each federal congress.

Such provisions for the control of those in authority by the membership and for the organized expression of minority views were applications of a democratic theory that it was the function of the branches of the party to generate ideas and policies and the function of the federal and national congresses to transform this raw material into coherent statements of doctrine and programme. In practice, a congress would appoint a special committee, the Resolutions Committee, to evaluate the various motions and statements which it had received, and this committee was expected either to produce a single document expressing the general view (*une résolution de synthèse*) or to present the congress with a simple choice between different motions. The *tendances* were in a good position to exploit this system by using their network of supporters and sympathizers to ensure that their motions were considered at the local and departmental levels and passed on to the national congress with delegates and mandates committed to them. To balance and counteract the views set out in such motions, the party's General Secretary, Paul Faure, would work with others loyal to the central leadership to prepare and circulate texts setting out and justifying the party's agreed policies and strategies. Before a national congress, therefore, the delegates at federal congresses would find themselves dealing with the loyalist text signed by Paul Faure and his colleagues, with the motions of the dissident *tendances*, and with motions submitted by the local branches. Their responses were various: some federal congresses would decide to support the loyalist text or one of the dissident texts, possibly in an amended form or with the addition of comments and reservations; others would simply divide their mandates amongst the competing motions in proportion to the support which each had obtained either in a formal vote at the congress or in a survey of members' opinions at branch level; and yet others would attempt to produce their own motions to demonstrate both their independence and their belief in the need for party unity.

At the national congress itself, the *tendances* would come into their own on the second or third day of the proceedings when the delegates, having considered the standard reports from officers and committees, would embark upon the discussion of general policy. At this point, a resolutions committee of some 30 members would be appointed by a procedure in which the federal delegations were asked to fill in forms recording the numbers of mandates which each was authorized to assign to one or more of the motions in contention. Once the numbers had been tallied, the places on the committee were distributed proportionately amongst those motions which had attracted at least the quota of mandates required for representation. Once elected, the committee would attempt to frame a resolution which the congress as a whole could be invited to endorse, but the representatives of the main *tendances* would usually insist on maintaining their own motions, or amended versions of them, so that the congress delegates could be presented with several texts and asked to record their preferences by a ballot of mandates. By convention, the result of this ballot was used to determine the number of places on the 33-member CAP which were to be at the disposal of the central leadership (on account of the proportion of the mandates obtained by the 'unity' or loyalist motion which the Resolutions Committee had recommended) and the numbers for allocation to each of the *tendances* (depending on the proportions of the mandates gained by their respective motions). This convention could be varied (for example, by an agreement to share out places on the CAP with reference to the support demonstrated for the various motions in the appointment of the Resolutions Committee) but unless the pressures for a show of unity were overwhelming the *chefs de tendance* much preferred to confirm their standing by a vote of the full congress. In any case, once the division of places had been decided, the main signatories of the surviving motions were effectively in a position to choose the persons to represent them on the CAP although congress still had the right to approve the consolidated membership list for that body.

Although these procedures had worked satisfactorily for several years, the system on which they were based was inherently unstable. Two quite different organizational principles were in conflict within the party, at all levels, and the efforts to hold the structure together were beginning to fail; those who were attached to the idea that the party should work in a hierarchical fashion, with branches, federations and finally the national bodies striving to achieve agreement and solidarity, were at odds with those who considered that it should work like a general assembly, in which the interaction of *tendances* rather than the orderly reflection upon experience would determine doctrines and define strategies. The two ideas were mutually inimical; the partisans of hierarchy saw only a restricted role of *tendances* as temporary associations formed for the discussion phase of a meeting, whereas the partisans of the general assembly saw permanent *tendances* as the key instruments of change. Party unity had been preserved by the formulation of normative rules which were intended to define the limits of acceptable behaviour for the existing *tendances*, but the Gauche Révolutionnaire in particular was already testing those limits to breaking point. The tension was most acute at the level of the party's federations; if they were to lose their organizational integrity, and become no more than departmental arenas for the *lutte de tendances*, the party as a whole would collapse, its energy consumed by internal conflict. To form a view of how far this process had gone by 1937 we shall review the politics of eight of the largest federations before returning to the subject of the *tendances* and their relations during the congress cycle of that year.

Some writers have explored the possibility of classifying the federations of the SFIO into various categories[63] but in the 1930s at least these units are too diverse and mixed in structure to fit into a simple typology. However, in order to pursue our central enquiry into the stability of the organization at this level, we shall take account of the difference between those federations which were concerned to build up a 'local party' by encouraging ambitious men and women within their membership to make careers on municipal and general councils within the department and to influence the provision of housing, education, health and other social services for the benefit of the party's supporters, and those which preferred to foster an 'activist party' in which members could concentrate on questions of theory and general strategy, while ignoring local authorities on the grounds that they were an integral part of the bourgeois state and therefore to be shunned. These are, of course, ideal categories, but we shall proceed on the assumption that they are related to the distinction between the hierarchical and general-assembly ideas of party life, in the sense that the 'local party' strategy is likely to be associated with the former and the 'activist party' strategy with the latter.

The first of our examples is the party's federation in the Seine Department, enclosing the city of Paris and its suburbs. As the centre of French government and cultural life, the region contained unusual concentrations of people engaged in the professions, in administration and in services, but it was also a commercial and industrial area of considerable importance. By 1937 the Socialists had virtually accepted the dominance which the Communists had achieved in the industrial and outer suburbs of the capital but they were still holding their own in a handful of outlying municipalities (such as Suresnes in the west, Châtenay-Malabry in the south, and Aubervilliers in the north) and in some of the inner *arrondissements*, where their supporters included manual workers, white-collar employees, small shopkeepers and members of the liberal professions. The federation's most active branches were established in this inner-city area, and it was their intense meetings, their abiding preoccupation with theoretical issues and their relish for public demonstrations which set the style for its politics.

Under Zyromski's leadership, the Bataille Socialiste had been the strongest group in the Seine Federation for a number of years but he

---

[63] See, in particular, Marc Sadoun, 'Sociologie des militants et sociologie du parti: le cas de la SFIO sous Guy Mollet', *Revue Française de Science Politique*, 38, 3 (June 1988), pp. 358–68. See also François Lafon, 'Des principes du Molletisme', in Bernard Ménager *et al.* (eds.), *Guy Mollet: un camarade en république* (Presses Universitaires de Lille, Lille, 1987), pp. 67–72.

had drifted away from his colleagues following his decision to oppose the government's policy of non-intervention in the Spanish Civil War. However, even without his direct support, the Bataille was still in control of the federation in the summer of 1937, with Francis Desphelippon as secretary, Roger Dufour as administrative secretary, Charles Pivert (the brother of Marceau) as secretary for external relations and Robert Dupont as propaganda secretary.[64] The most serious threat to its position was the growing strength of the Gauche Révolutionnaire under the leadership of Marceau Pivert. His base was in the 15th *arrondissement*, in the southwestern part of the city, where his local branch was reported in April 1937 to have 1,600 members,[65] equivalent to the size of a respectable provincial federation. The *tendance* had the advantage of a network of experienced members extending through the branches of the various *arrondissements*, including Jacques Enock in the 5th, René Cazanave in the 7th, Charles Lancelle in the 11th, Michel Collinet in the 14th, René Rul in the 18th and Lucien Vaillant in the 20th. An overlapping network, anchored to Marceau Pivert himself, tied together a number of informal youth groups, some within the party and some outside it. In 1934, following the street riots of 6 February, Marceau Pivert had founded a youth militia, Toujours Prêts Pour Servir (TPPS), in which René Rul, André Weil-Curiel and René Cazanave had been involved,[66] and in 1935 he had given moral support to Fred Zeller and David Rousset when they and other members of the federation's youth group, Jeunesses Socialistes, had been expelled by the national conference of Jeunesses Socialistes at Lille on 28–30 July 1935. 'On vous exclut de quoi?' he wrote:

Des Jeunesses, sans aucun doute, mais pas du Parti. Les portes de la 15ᵉ section vous sont grandes ouvertes pour le Parti.[67]

Shortly after these events, Zeller went to Norway to meet Trotsky and joined a Trotskyist group when he eventually returned to Paris, but by that stage the leadership of the federation's Jeunesses Socialistes had passed to Lucien Weitz, one of Marceau Pivert's former students. He was one of those expelled from the party for demonstrating in the days which followed the Clichy incident of 16 March 1937 and had then

---

[64] Parti Socialiste (SFIO), *Fédération de la Seine, Congrès Fédéral administratif, 12 juin 1937* (Paris, n.d.), p. 3.

[65] According to Marceau Pivert, in his speech to the National Council on 18 April 1937 (he referred to *adhérents*); see Pivert *et al.*, *4 discours et un programme*, p. 33.

[66] Rabaut, *Tout est possible!*, p. 142.

[67] *La Vérité*, 2 August 1935, cited by A. Jamin, in Parti Socialiste (SFIO), 35ᵉ Congrès National, Royan, 4–7 juin 1938, *Compte rendu sténographique* (Librairie Populaire, Paris, n.d.), p. 124.

formed a group, the Jeunesse Socialiste Autonome, in the belief that the Gauche Révolutionnaire would eventually break away from the SFIO.[68] Throughout the mid-1930s, from the formation of the TPPS onwards, Marceau Pivert had been much more disposed than had other senior members of the federation to treat young activists like Zeller and Weitz as people of mature judgement rather than as novices, and they in turn gave him their ready allegiance.

To compete on even terms with the Gauche Révolutionnaire, the Bataille Socialiste had to demonstrate that its own radicalism and activism were beyond reproach and it therefore placed an increasing distance between itself and the federation's loyalists, to whom it had looked for support in the past. The loyalists reacted to isolation by becoming, in effect, a third group, with its own networks and communication lines and its own territories; it had some standing, for example, in branches in such outlying suburbs as Le Pré-Saint-Gervais, Puteaux, Pantin and Issy-les-Moulineaux and, within Paris proper, in those of the 14th and 18th *arrondissements*.[69] The leading loyalists had established a new journal, *Le Socialiste*, and thus had the pretext for building up the usual readers' clubs, in this case 'Les Amis du *Socialiste*', which had been built up around similar periodicals in the past. André Costedoat in the 14th and Suzanne Buisson in the 18th *arrondissement* were to emerge as leaders of this group.

By this stage, the *lutte de tendances* in the Seine Federation no longer conformed to the national pattern (two dissident groups pitted against the party authorities and a relatively amorphous majority) but had assumed the form of a competition between three *tendances*, each claiming to represent an exclusive set of doctrines and each refusing to compromise with its rivals. The basic competition, that between the Bataille Socialiste and the Gauche Révolutionnaire, had accentuated the federation's character as an 'activist party' and had increased its isolation from the bulk of the Parisian population. Its lack of general appeal had been evident even at the time of the 1936 general elections, when SFIO candidates won only three of the 60 seats in the Seine Department and polled only 12.95 per cent of the votes on the first ballot.[70] It had only 20 representatives on the 140-member General Council for the department, a small minority on the 90-member Municipal Council of

---

[68] Rabaut, *Tout est possible!*, pp. 248–9.

[69] Judging from the list of signatories to *Motion du 'Socialiste' pour le redressement du Parti dans la région parisienne* [Paris, January 1938] (Archives de l'OURS), p. 4.

[70] In this and the following studies of federations, the electoral data have been compiled from constituency returns in Lachapelle, *Elections législatives, 1ᵉʳ & 8 mai 1932: résultats officiels* (*Le Temps*, Paris, 1932), and *Elections législatives, 26 avril & 3 mai 1936: résultats officiels*.

Paris, and control of very few of the municipalities in the outer suburbs. Yet this was the second largest federation in the party, with 15,783 members and 98 branches in December 1937.[71]

There were close connections between the Seine Federation and its neighbour in the Seine-et-Oise Department, which, until its subdivision in 1964, completely surrounded the Seine Department and contained several units of the Paris conurbation, such as Versailles, Pontoise, Saint Germain-en-Laye and Argenteuil. The Seine-et-Oise Federation had lost many members as a result of the party split of 1920 and its recovery in the 1930s had largely been due to Eugène Descourtieux, who had become its secretary in 1929 and had been one of Zyromski's closest allies. By December 1937, its membership had risen to a level of 8,750 and its branch numbers to 282. Descourtieux had been the first secretary of the liaison committee for the anti-fascist groups in the Parisian region and agreed with Zyromski about the need for unity of action with the Communists at the local level.[72] Some of the conditions which had produced the pattern of three *tendances* in the Seine Federation were present here as well, because, despite the local predominance of the Bataille Socialiste, the Gauche Révolutionnaire possessed a strong following and the Club du *Socialiste* also had some influence. However, the leaders of the two dissident *tendances* were on good terms and there was evidently not the same pressure on members to commit themselves to one of the three organized groups as there was in the Seine Federation. The Seine-et-Oise Federation was by no means the base for a 'local party' (in the 1936 general elections, the SFIO candidates had won only one of the fifteen constituencies in the department and only 14.87 per cent of the first ballot votes) but neither had it encouraged the degree of activism which had converted the Seine Federation into a cockpit of *tendances*.

Respect for the hierarchical idea of party life was strongest in the Nord and Pas-de-Calais Federations. In the manner of the pre-1914 German Social Democratic Party, the Nord Federation encouraged its members to hold wide-ranging discussions at the beginning of the congress cycle but to close ranks once the federal congress had taken its decisions. Although it was the largest federation in the party, with 19,167 members and 379 branches in December 1937, it maintained its unity and vitality throughout the turbulence of the Popular Front

[71] In this and the following studies of federations, membership figures are minima (the number of stamps sold divided by twelve) and are taken from Parti Socialiste (SFIO), 35ᵉ Congrès National, Royan, 4–7 juin 1938, *Rapports*, pp. 192–3. The branch totals are from ibid., pp. 198–9.
[72] See *Le Populaire*, 9 January 1938, p. 4; and Zyromski's obituary of Descourtieux in *La Bataille Socialiste*, no. 111, October 1938, pp. 1 and 2.

period. Its leaders attributed its disciplined behaviour to the instinct for solidarity amongst its predominantly working-class membership; located in one of the most industrialized departments in France, its support came not only from textile workers in the Lille-Roubaix-Tourcoing conurbation but also from employees in small metallurgical firms, from white-collar workers, from civil servants and from small shopkeepers.[73] It was proud of its Guesdiste tradition, which it had inherited from the time of the Parti Ouvrier Français,[74] but it had also become a 'local party', committed to participation in municipal and departmental institutions. Of its leaders, Jean Lebas had been Mayor of Roubaix since 1912 and Roger Salengro Mayor of Lille from 1925 until his tragic suicide on 18 November 1936, after which his place had been taken by another Socialist, Charles Saint-Venant. On the departmental General Council, the size of the Socialist group rose to 31 in a house of 68 after the cantonal elections of October 1937, when Jean Lebas became president of the council.[75] This investment in local authorities gave the SFIO an edge in its competition with the Communist and Radical-Socialist Parties and in the general elections of 1936 its candidates won 13 of the 24 constituencies in the department and attracted 32.26 per cent of the votes on the first ballot.

Despite his ministerial and parliamentary responsibilities, Jean Lebas remained secretary of the federation and played a full part in its affairs, but the size of its organization required more delegation of responsibility than would have been the case in most federations. His deputy was Augustin Laurent (1896–1990), who came from a mining family and had been elected to the General Council in 1931 and to the Chamber in 1936.[76] The two of them would lead the federation's huge delegation to national congresses and would share the speech-making between them, always as men from the Nord who made no concessions to the 'general assembly' view of how the party should be run; replying to criticism of the way in which his federation had conducted its business, Lebas offered no apologies to the Marseille Congress of July 1937:

Et lorsque nous tenons notre Congrès fédéral, je vous assure que c'est un véritable régal pour tous les militants, que de participer à nos débats. Ils sont rarement passionnés, mais toutes les opinions s'expriment. Notre ami

---

[73] See Yves-Marie Hilaire, 'La vie politique du Nord sous Daladier', in Marcel Gillet and Hilaire (eds.), *De Blum à Daladier: Le Nord/Pas-de-Calais 1936–1939* (Presses Universitaires de Lille, Lille, 1979), p. 206.

[74] See Robert P. Baker, 'Socialism in the Nord, 1880–1914: a regional view of the French Socialist movement', *International Review of Social History*, 12 (1967), pp. 357–89.

[75] Hilaire, 'La vie politique du Nord sous Daladier', p. 206.

[76] Jolly (ed.), *Dictionnaire des parlementaires français . . . de 1889 à 1940*, VI (1970), p. 2155. See also an obituary by Jean-René Lore in *Le Monde* (Paris), 3 October 1990, p. 11.

Zyromski, a ses partisans. Notre ami Marceau Pivert, a aussi les siens. Ce qu'on appelle 'les tendances' trouvent tous leurs représentants. Ils développent leur thèse et je vous assure que personne ne tente de gêner un exposé quelconque. (*Applaudissements.*)

Mais le résultat de la discussion, souvent, j'allais dire depuis toujours, depuis l'origine de la Fédération du Nord – et cela remonte, si j'ai bonne mémoire, à 1880 – c'est que la Fédération du Nord est venue dans les Congrès nationaux du Parti généralement en unanimité ou en très grosse majorité. On peut le regretter. On peut souhaiter qu'il en soit demain différemment. Mais que voulez-vous! c'est ainsi. Peut-être celá tient-il au milieu économique lui-même. Peut-être cela tient-il aux conditions de vie et de travail de nos ouvriers, de nos paysans, car nous en avons, et beaucoup, que nous commençons à conquérir. Mais le fait est là. Et je tiens à vous dire, et je prie tous nos camarades de ne pas douter de mon affirmation, lorsque les délégués de la Fédération du Nord votent, ils expriment de la façon la plus exacte, l'opinion des membres de la Fédération.[77]

Based on the coal-mining region to the north of Arras, the SFIO's Pas-de-Calais Federation had also been shaped by Guesdisme and the Social Democratic tradition. With a relatively high number of members and branches, 8,750 and 185 respectively in December 1937, its electoral support, though concentrated, was sufficiently strong for it to win 6 of the 15 constituencies in the Pas-de-Calais Department in the 1936 elections and to amass 25.92 per cent of the votes on the first ballot. Its veteran leader, Raoul Evrard, had been born in Denain, in the Nord Department, in 1879, and had begun work in the mines at the age of 12. In 1895 he had joined the Lille branch of the Parti Ouvrier Français and had later moved to the Pas-de-Calais where he had worked on various Socialist newspapers and was secretary to the deputy, Raoul Briquet. After war service he became secretary of the Pas-de-Calais Federation and in 1919 was elected to the Chamber, to which he belonged until 1936.[78] There is evidence of tension between him and a later federal secretary, André Pantigny, in 1932[79] but he maintained his grip on the federation throughout the 1930s and ensured that its support for the central leadership was solid and dependable.

The large Bouches-du-Rhône Federation, with 7,867 members and 73 branches in December 1937, was also proof against the dissident *tendances* but for reasons very different from those which explain the ability of the Nord and Pas-de-Calais Federations to hold them at bay.

---

[77] Parti Socialiste (SFIO), 34ᵉ Congrès National, Marseille, 10–13 juillet 1937, *Compte rendu sténographique*, pp. 268–9.

[78] Jolly (ed.), *Dictionnaire des parlementaires français . . . de 1889 à 1940*, V, p. 1639.

[79] See letter from Pantigny to Paul Faure, from Lens, 16 December 1932, in 'Histoire du Parti Socialiste S.F.I.O., le courrier de Paul Faure (1931–1935)', *Cahier et Revue de l'OURS*, no. 111 (June – July 1980), pp. 21–2.

The politics which were generated by the city of Marseille, the heart of the Bouches-du-Rhône Department, were quite unlike those of such northern cities as Lille and Roubaix. They were industrial towns, with a developed infrastructure of co-operatives and municipal services and, above all, well-established conventions about the open and public conduct of affairs, but Marseille was a major port with a tradition of clientelism and private arrangements behind its public institutions. Its population, which numbered about 620,000 in 1936,[80] contained a large minority of people of Mediterranean origin who were often bound into protective frameworks of patronage in the crowded inner cantons of the city. Immigrants from such places as Corsica would attach themselves to earlier arrivals from their village or locality of origin and would rely on family or friends to find them jobs in agencies or departments of the Municipal Council, or on the docks and ships of the port. Patronage was provided by municipal councillors, trade-union leaders and local politicians, and by the 1920s the clientelist system in the city was so well established that the creation of an urban machine of the kind which flourished in America in the closing decades of the nineteenth century was well within the bounds of possibility.[81]

The first Socialist to gain power in Marseille was Siméon Flaissières, who was Mayor of the city from 1892 to 1902 and again from 1919 until his death in 1931; his first administration saw the introduction of electricity and tramways and his second the construction of an airport at Marignane and an improved lighting system.[82] His deputy in the 1920s was Henri Tasso (1882–1944), a businessman of Sicilian descent who, after serving in the artillery in the First World War, had formed a company in 1918 to import and refine mineral oil for use in lubricants. As deputy Mayor from 1919 to 1926, he was responsible for canals and tramways in the city and as a member of the Chamber of Deputies, which he entered in 1924, he became President of the Merchant Marine Committee and Vice-President of the Commerce and Industry Committee.[83] In the normal course of events, Tasso would probably have

[80] From Table 1.1 ('Marseilles population growth 1801–1946') in D. A. L. Levy, 'The Marseilles working-class movement, 1936–1938' (D. Phil. thesis, University of Oxford, 1982), p. 2.

[81] On Marseille politics in the 1930s, see D. A. L. Levy, 'From clientelism to communism: the Marseille working class and the Popular Front', in Martin S. Alexander and Helen Graham (eds.), *The French and Spanish Popular Fronts: Comparative Perspectives* (Cambridge University Press, Cambridge, 1989), pp. 201–12; Levy, 'The Marseilles working-class movement, 1936–1938'; Paul Jankowski, *Communism and Collaboration: Simon Sabiani and Politics in Marseille, 1919–1944* (Yale University Press, New Haven and London, 1989).

[82] Jolly (ed.), *Dictionnaire des parlementaires français . . . de 1889 à 1940*, V, pp. 1695–6.

[83] Ibid., VIII (1977), p. 3055.

succeeded Flaissières as Mayor, but in 1929 the latter won the municipal elections in association with Simon Sabiani, a former Communist who had maintained a radical reputation, and who then became his deputy. After the death of Flaissières in March 1931, Sabiani backed Georges Ribot, who became the new Mayor. The 1935 municipal elections were the occasion for a fierce contest between Sabiani's organization on the one side and the Socialists and Communists on the other, but the outcome was a majority for the Socialists on the incoming Municipal Council and the election of Tasso as the Mayor.[84]

The Socialists' return to power in Marseille was due in part to the formidable organizing ability of Jean-Baptiste Canavelli, who was the secretary of the party's Bouches-du-Rhône Federation in the 1930s. A former deputy, he had been defeated by Sabiani in the contest for the third Marseille constituency in the 1928 elections and had opposed any compromise with him in 1931 at a time when Tasso was inclined to be conciliatory.[85] In the city, the Socialists reinforced their branch system by parallel structures of informal associations, the anticlerical Amis d'Instruction Laïque, which they had taken over in the 1920s, and the Comités des Intérêts des Quartiers, through which the party's municipal councillors could keep in touch with their localities.[86] The Socialists had also enlisted the services of Pierre Ferri-Pisani, the secretary of the sailors' union, who had quite definite ideas about how trade unions should be run.[87] Tasso and Ferri-Pisani had the backing, in the Marseille underworld, of Antoine Guérini and his brothers, the key figures in a group of immigrants from the Calenzana area of north-western Corsica: the Guérinis were at this stage a minor group compared with those, headed by Paul Carbone and Lydro Spirito, which were in league with Sabiani, but they provided an important link between the Marseille Socialists and local clientelism, especially where recruitment to local services was concerned.[88] However, the Socialists had taken over the running of the city just at the point when a number of service departments had reached the limits of their ability to maintain such chronic levels of

---

[84] See Jankowski, *Communism and Collaboration: Simon Sabiani and Politics in Marseille*, pp. 32–49.

[85] Jean-Baptiste Nicolaï, *Simon Sabiani* (Olivier Orban, Paris, 1991), p. 161. On the background to Canavelli, see ibid., p. 97.

[86] See Levy, 'The Marseilles working-class movement, 1936–1938', pp. 180–1.

[87] See ibid., pp. 182–3, for a discussion of Ferri-Pisani's book, *Sur le syndicalisme maritime* (1933).

[88] See ibid., pp. 170 and 172; James Sarazin, *Dossier M . . . comme milieu* (Alain Moreau, Paris, 1977), pp. 257–82, especially 257–9; Jean Bazal, *Le Clan des Marseillais: des nervis aux caïds 1900–1974* (Guy Authier, Paris, 1974), pp. 291–3; Georges Marion, *Gaston Defferre* (Albin Michel, Paris, 1989), pp. 130–1.

overmanning and in March 1939 the parlous state of the municipality's finances forced the central government to appoint an administrator to run the city under the authority of the Premier and the Minister of the Interior. An official report revealed the extraordinary levels of recruitment which had been reached and the heavy indebtedness which had been caused by a series of budget deficits;[89] the main reason for these difficulties had been the willingness of succeeding mayors to delegate responsibility to their deputies and even to municipal councillors.[90]

Subsequent enquiries added detail to the general picture: a building programme which had cost 75 million francs and had been set in motion without approval; a councillor placed in charge of the abattoirs who had had no compunction about paying the moneys which he, in his private capacity as a wholesale butcher, owed them with 114 cheques for which there had been no provision; and a woman who had obtained *certificats d'indigence* from a civil servant, had sold them for 20 francs each, and explained that she had inherited the 'business' from her mother.[91] The decision of the administrator to dissolve the fire brigade and to bring in a team of naval firemen in its place had led one reporter to comment: 'For years past municipal employees in Marseilles have been recruited without regard to their professional qualifications. What really counted was their association with influential voters.'[92] In 1937, of course, these revelations were still in the future; in that year the Socialist administration in Marseille was still intact, though it had already been obliged to suspend job recruitment.[93]

The SFIO had also established itself in the western sector of the Bouches-du-Rhône Department, where Félix Gouin (1884–1977) had become Mayor of Istres in 1923 before winning a seat in the Chamber in 1924 from the Aix-en-Provence constituency.[94] However, the party's position had been weakened in February 1934 by the defection of Fernand Bouisson, the deputy for the eighth Marseille constituency, and

---

[89] See 'Réorganisation administrative de la ville de Marseille, rapport au Président de la République Française', 20 March 1939, by Edouard Daladier (Premier) and Paul Reynaud (Minister of Finance), in *JO*, *LD*, 21 March 1939, pp. 3671–6.

[90] 'Annexe au décret relatif à la réorganisation de la ville de Marseille: rapport déposé par les enquêteurs du Comité de Réorganisation Administrative sur l'administration de Marseille', in ibid., p. 3674.

[91] See the statement by Paul Reynaud, Minister of Finance, in *JO* (*CD*), *Déb.*, 9 June 1939, pp. 1569–71.

[92] *The Times*, 23 August 1939, p. 14.

[93] 'Annexe au décret relatif à la réorganisation de la ville de Marseille', *JO*, *LD*, 21 March 1939, p. 3674.

[94] From biographies in *Le Monde*, 25 January 1946, p. 1; and *Le Populaire*, 17 December 1946, p. 4.

by the growth of support for the Communists. Between the 1932 and 1936 general elections, the Communists' share of the first-ballot vote had risen from 9.16 to 29.10 per cent and their leader, François Billoux, had defeated Sabiani in the contest for the third Marseille constituency in the 1936 poll. The SFIO's percentage vote had fallen from 44.99 to 32.97 per cent over the same period but it still managed to return five deputies, including Gouin and Tasso, to the Chamber in 1936, and Tasso went on to become Under-Secretary for the Merchant Navy in the Blum and Chautemps governments.

Clientelism had given the Socialist Party in Marseille a social base which was predominantly lower-middle class and immigrant in character, and a social style which was quite unsuited to the task of representing the demand for radical reforms which had arisen during the mid-1930s and which eventually found an outlet through the Communist Party.[95] This failure to respond to the reform movement may explain why the dissident *tendances* failed to establish themselves in the federation; both the Gauche Révolutionnaire and the Bataille Socialiste had developed in other federations by trying to extend the Popular Front in particular directions, the former towards a mass revolution and the latter towards a more dynamic alliance in which the Communist Party would be fully involved, but in the Bouches-du-Rhône unit such opportunities were almost entirely lacking.

The federation in the Gironde Department, containing the Atlantic port of Bordeaux, had developed along quite different lines. Severely weakened by the neo-Socialist revolt of 1933, it had been largely rebuilt during the Popular Front period by a new leadership. Before 1933, the earlier federation had constructed a 'local party' under the leadership of Adrien Marquet, who had become Mayor of Bordeaux in 1925. In the 1932 general elections, Socialist candidates had polled 36.06 per cent of the first-ballot votes and won seven of the thirteen constituencies in the department. However, in 1933 Marquet became one of the leaders of the neo-Socialists and took most of the members of the 'local party' with him when he was finally expelled from the SFIO. A new and loyal federation had then to be constructed on the foundation of a small group of activists appointed by the central secretariat and headed by Robert Vielle, who became its principal secretary.[96] Their task would

[95] On this point, see Levy, 'From clientelism to communism: the Marseille working class and the Popular Front', especially pp. 205–12.

[96] See Parti Socialiste (SFIO), 31ᵉ Congrès National, Toulouse, 20–23 mai 1934, *Rapports* (Librairie Populaire, Paris, 1934), p. 27. See also letter from Vielle to Paul Faure, from Bordeaux, 27 October 1933, in 'Histoire du Parti Socialiste S.F.I.O., le courrier de Paul Faure (1931–1935)', *Cahier et Revue de l'OURS*, no. 111 (June–July 1980), pp. 33–4.

have been easier had the neo-Socialist group broken up, but Marquet managed to hold his followers together, led them to victory in the 1935 municipal elections and was then appointed for a further term as Mayor of Bordeaux. In the 1936 elections, the former Socialist vote was divided between Marquet's contingent of the Union Socialiste Républicaine, which secured the election of four deputies with 16.36 per cent of the first-ballot votes, and the new SFIO team, which polled 17.60 per cent of the votes and returned three deputies. Subsequently, the Socialist deputies attacked the policy of non-intervention in the Spanish Civil War while the local neo-Socialist organization supported it.[97] In effect, the nature of the original division of 1933 and the compulsion to distinguish itself from the Marquet group had forced the new federation to turn away from the local party model and to encourage an active life in the branches, where considerable freedom of discussion and independence of mind were encouraged. Recruitment proceeded apace during the years of the Popular Front and by the end of 1937 the membership of the unit had risen to 4,625 with 222 branches. Both of the dissident *tendances* enjoyed some support in the federation, but Robert Vielle and his fellow leaders had sufficient standing to follow independent policies in the national politics of the party, where they belonged to the left wing of the loyalist majority. They were strongly in favour of maintaining the Popular Front in being, Communists included, and of extending the programme of reforms; to that extent, their views were similar to those of the Bataille Socialiste, whose general policy resolution had attracted 110 of the federation's 117 mandates at the Marseille Congress of July 1937, but they differed radically from Zyromski in their views on foreign policy, being inclined to favour the party's traditional policy of relying on negotiations and disarmament as a means of preserving the peace.

The neo-Socialist revolt also affected the development of the Meurthe-et-Moselle Federation, and in this case too the 'activist party' rather than the 'local party' model was chosen as the best method of organization. Situated in the Lorraine region of north-eastern France, the Meurthe-et-Moselle Department contained the important iron and steel towns of Briey and Longwy in its northern sector and, in its southern part, the city of Nancy, which lay at the centre of a variety of mining and other industries. The great majority of the local Socialists had remained with the Communist Party after the split of 1920, and the formation of a new SFIO federation proved to be a lengthy and difficult process. Its first secretary was Charles-André Doley, a lawyer in the

---

[97] See Greene, *The French Socialist Party in the Popular Front Era*, p. 181.

Nancy Appeal Court, but he was succeeded in December 1930 by André Lévy, a local merchant, who in 1932 became political director and chief editor of the *Populaire de l'Est*, the party's departmental newspaper. However, before Lévy and his team could prove themselves they were caught up in the neo-Socialist crisis; Lévy and his main lieutenants supported the defiant parliamentarians and, as the tide began to turn against the Neos, they resigned from their posts in July 1933. They were replaced by a group of radical leaders, headed at first by Maurice Mathelin and then, from 1934, by Henri Midon. It was during Midon's time that the federation grew rapidly in size until, in December 1937, it could claim 3,833 members and 70 branches.

Midon was courted by the Parisian leaders of the Gauche Révolutionnaire, and the federation moved towards this *tendance* rather than towards the Bataille Socialiste. Born in Nancy in 1900, Midon had built up a business based on the making and selling of a variety of pine-flavoured confectionery while living in the small town of Neuves-Maisons, about 10 kilometres to the south of Nancy. The views which he expressed at meetings reveal a libertarian turn of mind; he was wary of both Communists and Radical Socialists and was anticlerical and pacifist in outlook. His socialism was sentimental and anti-authoritarian and it was these qualities that attracted him to the Gauche Révolutionnaire rather than any strong doctrinal sympathies. Under his leadership the Meurthe-et-Moselle Federation made little electoral progress: its anticlericalism and pacifism brought it scant respect in a regional community with a pronounced religious and nationalist outlook. The federation's political isolation was revealed most clearly by the results of the 1936 general elections in the department, when the SFIO's share of the first-ballot vote fell to 9.25 per cent from the 1932 level of 18.26 per cent while three left-wing candidates who were willing to combine support for the Popular Front with an acceptance of the need for national defence won their seats with relative ease, Pierre-Olivier Lapie in one of the Nancy constituencies and Georges Izard and Philippe Serre in constituencies in the Briey *arrondissement*.[98]

There was much more continuity and balance in the history of the last of our examples, the SFIO's Haute-Vienne Federation, which had 4,167 members and 91 branches in December 1937. Based on industrial workers in the old manufacturing town of Limoges, a centre for the making of porcelain, leather goods and paper, this federation was proud

---

[98] The above two paragraphs on the history of the Meurthe-et-Moselle Federation are based on the excellent *mémoire de maîtrise* by Jean-Marie Moine, 'Le mouvement socialiste en Meurthe-et-Moselle sous la Troisième République' (Université de Nancy, Nancy, 1973).

of its Guesdiste tradition and its independence; one of its first generation of leaders, Adrien Pressemane, had worked alongside Guesde in
the Parti Ouvrier Français and had played a leading role in the movement for a negotiated peace during the First World War. The federation
had broken the grip of the Radical Socialists over Limoges and the
surrounding rural areas before 1914 but after the Tours split of 1920
four Socialist members of the local General Council had gone over to
the Communists, taking the majority of their supporters with them.
However, Pressemane remained with the SFIO and the federation
retained its Guesdiste and pacifist spirit. Although the Socialists were
very successful in local politics, returning Léon Betoulle as Mayor of
Limoges in the 1935 municipal elections and capturing all five of the
department's constituencies in the 1936 general elections when they
polled 46.94 per cent of the votes on the first ballot, the older activists
remained strongly anti-participationist in outlook, even after the advent
of the Popular Front government. The case for participation was
defended locally by Jean Le Bail, a former member of the party's
branch in the fifth *arrondissement* of Paris, who had also been associated
with the small but influential Révolution Constructive group and was
now a teacher in a Limoges secondary school.[99] The federation had
certainly built up a 'local party' but it had also fostered traditions of
internal debate and reflection which enabled it to judge the various
congress resolutions on their merits rather than on the basis of personalities or past commitments.

The federations we have considered above were the eight largest in
terms of membership in 1937 and are to that extent unrepresentative
but, although the Seine, Bouches-du-Rhône and Gironde Federations
were in classes of their own, the other five cases do have their counterparts elsewhere in the organization. The controlled tripartism of Seine-
et-Oise was reminiscent of the situation in the Aisne and Côte-d'Or
Federations; the Sarthe resembled the Haute-Vienne Federation in several respects, not least in its independence; the Alpes-Maritimes was
just as consistent in its support for the Gauche Révolutionnaire as the
Meurthe-et-Moselle Federation; and the social-democratic style of the

---

[99] On the history of the Socialists in the Haute-Vienne Department, see Pierre Cousteix,
'Le Congrès de Tours vécu par une fédération socialiste: la Haute-Vienne', in *Cahier
et Revue de l'OURS*, no. 121 (June – July 1981), pp. 76–93; François Goguel, 'Esquisse
d'un Bilan de la sociologie électorale française', in Goguel and Georges Dupeux,
Sociologie électorale (Armand Colin, Paris, 1951), pp. 16–21; Guy Decouty, 'Introduc-
tion à l'étude de l'évolution de l'opinion politique dans le Département de la Haute-
Vienne' (Thesis, Institut d'Etudes Politiques de l'Université de Paris, Paris, [1950]);
Jean Lenoble, 'L'évolution politique du socialisme en Haute-Vienne sous la IIIme
République' (Thesis, Institut d'Etudes Politiques à l'Université de Paris, [1950]).

Nord and Pas-de-Calais Federations had also been adopted by other northern units, such as the Somme Federation. Our survey has also identified certain factors which affected several federations outside the sample, such as the tendency for national divisions within the party to have drastic local consequences (most obvious in the cases of Gironde and Meurthe-et-Moselle) and the process of building up an apparently energetic 'activist party' to the detriment of a unit's electoral standing. However, large federations, for all their variability, were much more stable and predictable in their behaviour than the small, provincial units, so dependent on the enthusiasm and administrative skill of their federal secretary and on the strength of his ties with the party's General Secretary.[100] A federal congress could be swayed by the address of a persuasive outside speaker, or by that of a veteran activist, or by the impact of a single issue, such as the policy of non-intervention in the Spanish Civil War or an alleged infringement of the principle of secular schooling.

Now that we have outlined the positions of the large federations in the organizational politics of the SFIO, we can return to the *tendances* and to their exploitation of the party's annual congress cycle. The *tendances* justified their preoccupation with philosophical and doctrinal matters by appealing to the tradition that a given problem could be solved only if the debate were conducted between opposed points of view and that a party member had either to adopt one point of view or to assume a mid-way position, to declare his persuasion, as it were. The Socialists had inherited a vocabulary in which such persuasions were described as *tendances d'esprit*, or *courants de pensée*, or *méthodes de recherche*, signifying intellectual dispositions rather than associations. The formation of *tendances d'esprit* was supposed to be a wholly beneficial process, rather than a source of discord and division. One writer explained the tradition in the following terms:

dans tout groupement politique, il y aura toujours une gauche, une droite et un centre, serait-ce que par classification des tempéraments. Lorsqu'une question de tactique est à trancher, lorsqu'il s'agit de déterminer la politique du parti pour un temps donné ou devant un événement donné, il est naturel encore que les courants d'opinion issus des tendances diverses se heurtent et se confondent. Quand la synthèse est faite ou la majorité dégagée, la discussion est finie; l'action commence dans le sens défini par cette unanimité ou cette majorité, et l'action doit se poursuivre dans la discipline fraternelle de tous.

---

[100] On the general nature of Paul Faure's administrative influence, see Greene, *The French Socialist Party in the Popular Front Era*, pp. 35–6. An excellent idea of how he maintained his network of correspondents can be gained from the collection of letters which he sent and received in the period 1929–35, published in *Cahier et Revue*

Là où les choses risquent de se gâter, c'est lorsque l'esprit de tendance est plus fort que l'esprit de parti, où la tendance se met à combattre le Parti lui-même. Ce moment arrive lorsqu'une ou plusieurs tendances s'organisent en parti distinct dans le parti, avec leur discipline propre, leurs mots d'ordre, leurs conceptions clichées.[101]

By this reasoning, a permanent *tendance d'esprit* was a contradiction in terms, because *les courants d'opinion* could vary in composition from issue to issue and from time to time, but the SFIO had tolerated the convention that differences of opinion reflected persistent and fundamental philosophical divisions within the party, and that *tendances* were the legitimate manifestations of those divisions. In practice, each *tendance* became an informal brotherhood which relied on leadership and moral sanctions to maintain its unity; this was the spirit which L. O. Frossard found amongst the Guesdistes in the period after the formation of the SFIO in 1905.

Ils s'épaulaient fortement les uns les autres. Sur toutes les questions, une sorte d'accord spontané, auquel on reconnaissait leur étroite parenté intellectuelle, s'établissait entre eux. On ne peut pas dire qu'ils formaient dans le Parti un parti distinct, mais ils constituaient, sans même avoir besoin de se concerter, une 'tendance'. Dans les Congrès, ils se rassemblaient autour du chef et de son Etat-major. Ils prenaient leurs repas ensemble. Ils se réunissaient à part, avant et après les séances, pour fixer leur attitude et choisir leurs orateurs.[102]

The *tendances* of the 1930s had inherited this pattern of behaviour. Formed in 1927, the Bataille Socialiste had taken maximum advantage of the party's tolerance of group activity; it founded its own journal, built up its own framework of supporters and its own lines of communication, but nevertheless took care to observe the party's normative rules governing the expression of dissent. These were that critics of the party's leaders or policies should not air their grievances in public or challenge the decisions of a National Council or a National Congress, nor turn for support to the party's youth wing, the Jeunesses Socialistes, or to its students' wing. The Gauche Révolutionnaire, on the other hand, began breaking nearly all of these rules within months of its creation in 1935, and it soon found itself faced with the threat of disciplinary action. Matters came to a head when the Gironde Federation complained that the Gauche Révolutionnaire had invited members of the Jeunesses Socialistes to attend a meeting at Bordeaux. The CAP

---

de *l'OURS*, no. 87 (February 1978); no. 105 (December 1979); and no. 111 (June–July 1980).

[101] 'La meilleure des tendances, SERVIR!', *La Bataille* (Lille), 7 August 1938, p. 3.

[102] L. O. Frossard, *De Jaurès à Léon Blum: souvenirs d'un militant* (Flammarion, Paris, 1943), pp. 129–30.

then examined the role of the *tendances* and decided on 13 January 1937 that the central secretariat should warn all federations and branches of the serious consequences of allowing disruptive activities and attacks on agreed policies to take place within the party; Paul Faure accordingly sent out a strongly worded circular to that effect.[103] Then came the events at Clichy, the subsequent demonstrations and finally the dissolution of the Gauche Révolutionnaire by the National Council on 18 April 1937. In a grudging and limited response, Marceau Pivert and his group simply described their resolutions as those of *la minorité de la C.A.P.* and substituted a new journal, *Les Cahiers Rouges*, for the *Gauche Révolutionnaire*.[104]

This passage of arms forced the party's central leaders and their chief opponents to specify the conventions which they thought should govern the behaviour of *tendances*. In presenting his case to the National Council on 18 April 1937, Marceau Pivert had argued that his group had simply modelled itself upon the Bataille Socialiste:

je n'aperçois pas la différence d'organisation entre notre tendance et celle de la Bataille Socialiste, à laquelle j'ai longtemps appartenu avec Paul Faure et Séverac: Des réunions de militants, des conférences d'information, des adresses de camarades, des cartes d'adhésion, un bulletin périodique, des tracts, des motions pour les Congrès; c'est avec ces moyens de propagande que j'ai travaillé près de dix années durant avec des camarades qui, aujourd'hui, semblent l'avoir oublié . . . [105]

He had also taken the line that a *tendance* should serve as an instrument of renewal and purification within the party and quoted with approval a letter which he had received from a colleague on the eve of the National Congress of 1931, justifying a decision to leave the Bataille Socialiste.

J'ai été profondément déçu de ne pas trouver *en elle un organisme de combat, discipliné, forgeant des mots d'ordre clairs, nets, directs et aussi un cercle de culture révolutionnaire vérifiant sans cesse nos vieilles doctrines par l'étude des faits, étudiant un à un les programmes d'action du Parti*; de ne pas rencontrer un noyau sans cesse plus important et plus éclairé de camarades *pourchassant impitoyablement l'équivoque là où elle se trouve. Et ce n'est pas à droite qu'elle se trouve, l'équivoque, c'est au centre, toujours au centre!* Comme le redressement du Parti ne doit pas être recherché dans une bataille systématique contre

---

[103] See Parti Socialiste (SFIO), 34e Congrès National, Marseille, [10–13 juillet 1937], *Rapports*, pp. 143–6; Georges Lefranc, *Histoire du Front Populaire (1934–1938)* (Payot, Paris, 2nd edn, 1974), pp. 233–4.
[104] Guérin, *Front Populaire: révolution manquée*, p. 158.
[105] Pivert et al., *4 discours et un programme*, p. 45.

la droite, mais *dans une réaction contre les faiblesses et les complaisances de la majorité.*[106]

Two quite different ideas of the party were now at issue. Blum and Paul Faure, and the leaders of the Nord Federation, believed that the SFIO was both a moral community, whose members shared a common faith in the values of socialism, and an association, dedicated to the task of returning members of the working class to local councils and to parliament; each purpose, in their eyes, required an open and democratic expression of different points of view so that decisions could be taken in a full knowledge of the likely consequences of particular courses of action. The opposing idea, held by Marceau Pivert and the Gauche Révolutionnaire (and, to a lesser extent, by Zyromski and the Bataille Socialiste) was that the party had been created to serve a revolutionary purpose, and that it would lose its moral basis if, by a process of accommodation it allowed itself to be diverted from that purpose by everyday events and by the politics of the here and now; just as it was inevitable that the party's established leadership would try to involve the party in the operations of the existing political system, so it was inevitable that active and radical *tendances* would arise to remind ordinary members of what they regarded as the party's essential mission. The two ideas were inimical: whereas the central leaders were striving to foster agreement, unity and solidarity by means of compromise, the permanent *tendances* wanted a continuing confrontation between what they saw as truth and untruth, so that the party could be kept to the 'correct' path. In organizational terms, the first idea favoured hierarchy, compartmentalization and regulation, whereas the second called for direct democracy, the general assembly, and freedom of action for enlightened dissidents.

By 1937, such conflicts of principle were threatening to undermine the party's stability. While the central leaders and the secretariat were trying to win approval for unpopular policies and to preserve organizational unity by appeals for loyalty and discipline, the dissident *tendances* were proclaiming the need for the party to rise above existing circumstances and return to the principles on which it had been founded, even at the risk of causing a political crisis. One way of assessing the balance of advantage between the authorities and the *tendances* is by looking at the crucial division on general policy which took place at the 34th National Congress of July 1937, bearing in mind that this meeting was held shortly after the fall of the Blum government and the formation

---

[106] Ibid., pp. 45–6. The letter had been written by Louis Lagorgette.

of the Chautemps ministry, in which Socialists had been included. The SFIO's participation in the Chautemps administration had already been approved by a National Council resolution on 22 June and this decision had been duly endorsed at the National Congress. However, the delegates had also been asked to choose between three policy resolutions, earlier versions of which had been sent out for consideration by the federal congresses. When put to the vote, a pro-participation resolution linked to the names of Blum and Paul Faure obtained 54.7 per cent of the mandates while a Bataille Socialiste motion sponsored by Bracke and Zyromski attracted 28.6 per cent and another, defended by Marceau Pivert, drew 16.6 per cent of the vote. Both of the latter motions expressed a preference for a government which would be more representative of the Popular Front, but whereas the Bracke–Zyromski text simply described the formation of the Chautemps ministry as a setback to the Front and did not propose that the party should leave the coalition at once, Marceau Pivert's motion recommended the immediate withdrawal of the Socialist ministers and argued that the party should use mass support to press for a new government under Socialist leadership.[107] The detailed figures for the aggregate vote and for the votes of the eight largest federations are shown in Table 4.

We thus have a situation in which the strategy recommended by the party's leader and its General Secretary had been approved by a bare majority, despite the strong backing that the Blum–Faure motion had received from the Bouches-du-Rhône, Nord and Pas-de-Calais Federations, which together contributed 904 (or 30.7 per cent) of the 2,949 mandates registered in favour of it. Do the votes by federation in this division reveal any significant geographical distributions? The nominal support for the Gauche Révolutionnaire was widely spread, 86 of the 96 federations represented in the vote giving at least one mandate to the Marceau Pivert motion. Apart from the large Seine and Seine-et-Oise votes for this *tendance*, it received strong support in the Lorraine region (a bloc vote from Vosges and absolute majorities from Moselle and Meurthe-et-Moselle) and votes above the 20 per cent level from groups of federations in the Paris basin and in the Poitou area of the Vendée. The vote for the Bataille Socialiste motion was also represented in most regions but the degrees of support for this *tendance* were generally higher than those obtained by the Gauche Révolutionnaire, except in the Lorraine region, and it had been given absolute majorities in several federations, including those in the Ariège, Dordogne, Eure-

[107] For the texts of these resolutions, see Parti Socialiste (SFIO), 34ᵉ Congrès National, Marseille, 10–13 juillet 1937, *Compte rendu sténographique*, pp. 551–79. For the original versions, see *La Vie du Parti*, 3 June 1937, pp. 293–5.

Table 4. SFIO: 34th National Congress, Marseille, 13 July 1937: division on motions on general policy

Federations	Mandates for the motions of:										Totals
	Blum–Faure (loyalist)		Bracke–Zyromski (Bataille Socialiste)		Marceau Pivert (Gauche Révolutionnaire)		Abstentions		Absent		
	no.	%	no.	%	no.	%	no.	%	no.	%	no.
Bouches-du-Rhône	210	100.0									210
Gironde			110	94.0	7	6.0					117
Meurthe-et-Moselle	3	7.1	9	21.4	30	71.4					42
Nord	560	98.8	7	1.2							567
Pas-de-Calais	134	84.8	22	13.9	2	1.3					158
Seine	73	17.2	178	41.9	174	40.9					425
Seine-et-Oise	44	19.9	96	43.4	80	36.2	1	0.5			221
Haute-Vienne	68	50.0	68	50.0							136
Others	[1,857]	52.8	1,055	30.0	601	17.1	4	0.1			[3,517]
Totals	2,949	54.7	1,545	28.6	894	16.6	5	0.1			5,393

Sources: La Vie du Parti (Paris), no. 75, 5 August 1937, pp. 299–300; Parti Socialiste (SFIO), 34e Congrès National, Marseille, 10–13 juillet 1937, Compte rendu sténographique (Librairie Populaire, Paris, n.d.), pp. 606–7. For details of adjustments, see the appendix (p. 399 n. 3).

et-Loir, Gironde, Ille-et-Vilaine, Nièvre, Sarthe, Seine-Inférieure and Deux-Sèvres Departments and that in Tunisia. The loyalist vote was relatively weak in the Paris basin and in the South-West, but had been sustained at reasonable levels in the North, in Alsace, in the Centre and, to some extent, in the Midi.[108] However, this pattern should be interpreted with caution; in particular, it should not be assumed that the distribution of the votes of either or both of the dissident *tendances* accurately reflected the distribution of particular philosophies or doctrines. Whereas the voting patterns in the Seine tended to provide a fair guide to the relative weight of distinct opinions, those of the smaller rural federations were much less reliable for this kind of measurement. Although each of the *tendances* had the benefit of networks of informed sympathizers amongst secondary schoolteachers and other professional groups in the provinces, each became a simpler and paler version of its Parisian self in the outlying regions; removed from its element, the Bataille often had to make do with members who still remembered with approval its earlier attacks on ministerial participation and who saw it as the true defender of Guesdisme, whereas the Gauche Révolutionnaire relied upon its reputation as a more absolute version of its rival. Finally, at the very end of the chain, the *tendances* were reduced to the images of their leaders, as when the Mayet branch of the Sarthe Federation met to consider the resolutions which were coming before the federal congress.

C'était l'époque des tendances divergentes, Paul FAURE, BLUM, ZIROMSKI, ZORETTI, Marceau Pivert étaient les chefs de file des grands courants. A cette réunion la section devait prendre position pour l'une des nombreuses motions présentées par les tendances. En général on votait pour la personnalité qui présentait la motion beaucoup plus que pour son contenu, et les hommes les plus populaires étaient BLUM et Paul FAURE.[109]

The essential aims of the *chefs de tendance* were to make certain that their resolutions reached the National Congress, that they were the subjects of the final division at this meeting, and that the shares of the votes obtained by the various texts in this ballot continued to determine the apportionment of places on the CAP. This latter

---

[108] Cf. the interpretation of the geographical distribution of the votes of the dissident *tendances* as revealed by this division and by the subsequent division at the National Council meeting of 7 November 1937 in Greene, *The French Socialist Party in the Popular Front Era*, pp. 164–7, based on detailed statistics set out in Table 9 of ibid., pp. 314–18.

[109] From a 'Rapport établi par un militant', cited in Annie Combes, 'Monographie de la Fédération Socialiste de la Sarthe' (Thesis, Institut d'Etudes Politiques de l'Université de Paris, Paris, 1953), p. 17.

convention was left unchanged at the Marseille Congress of July 1937, with the result that 18 of the 33 places on the 1937–8 CAP were placed at the disposal of the central leaders by virtue of the fact that the Blum–Faure motion had obtained 54.7 per cent of the mandates on the final division, while the Bataille Socialiste was given 9 places for 28.6 per cent of the mandates and the Gauche Révolutionnaire 6 places for its vote-share of 16.6 per cent. The final list of members was as follows:[110]

Parti Socialiste (SFIO): CAP membership 1937–8

1. *Appointed on the basis of the Blum–Faure motion* (18 members)

Paul Faure	Jean-Baptiste Séverac
Jean Longuet	Raoul Evrard
René Château	Paul Favier
Marx Dormoy (Deputy)	Maurice Paz
J. P. Granvallet	Maurice Caille
Louis Lagorgette[1]	Eugène Gaillard
Salomon Grumbach (Deputy)	André Blumel
Jean Lebas (Deputy)	Augustin Laurent (Deputy)
Louis Lévy	Sansimon Graziani

2. *Appointed on the basis of the Bracke–Zyromski (Bataille Socialiste) motion* (9 members)

Jean Zyromski	Roger Dufour
Bracke (Alexandre-Marie Desrousseaux)	Jacques Grumbach
Eugène Descourtieux	Francis Desphelippon
Robert Coeylas	Augustin Malroux (Deputy)
	Charles Pivert

3. *Appointed on the basis of the Marceau Pivert (Gauche Révolutionnaire) motion* (6 members)

Marceau Pivert	Degez
René Modiano	Georges Soulès
Lucien Hérard	Georges Floutard

[1] Louis Lagorgette was killed in a motor accident on 29 December 1937 and Alexis Mailly, one of the substitutes for the list of names associated with the Blum–Faure motion, was appointed in his place by the CAP on 12 January 1938 (*La Vie du Parti*, no. [78], 10 March 1938, p. 312).

[110] According to lists published in Parti Socialiste (SFIO), 34ᵉ Congrès National, Marseille, 10–13 juillet 1937, *Compte rendu sténographique*, p. 598; 35ᵉ Congrès National, Royan, 4–7 juin 1938, *Rapports*, p. 21.

From this membership, the following officers were chosen to compose a small executive board (*bureau*):

General Secretary	Paul Faure
General Treasurer	J. P. Granvallet
Deputy General Secretary	Jean-Baptiste Séverac
Secretaries to Subcommittees:	
Finance	Jean Lebas
Propaganda	Eugène Descourtieux
General Administration	André Blumel
External Relations	Maurice Paz
International Activities	Bracke
Publications and Documentation	Marceau Pivert

These appointments were ratified by the National Council at its meeting on 6–7 November 1937.[111]

As a member of the *bureau*, Marceau Pivert was in a good position to further the interests of his *tendance* and was considering ways of extending its influence amongst the provincial federations. It is interesting to find him, in a letter which he wrote in August 1937 to Maurice Deixonne of the Cantal Federation, reflecting on the need to make a better impression outside Paris.

Par la force des choses, les problèmes politiques sont perçus avec une sensibilité particulière dans notre région parisienne; mais j'ai assez d'expérience des milieux ruraux pour savoir que rien ne se fera de solide en dehors de l'accord, que dis-je, de l'*impulsion* de la province révolutionnaire. Moins d'improvisation de notre part, *c'est promis*.[112]

Later in this same letter he considered the question of means:

le 'relai' des équipes de province est une nécessité, pour que les éléments les plus révolutionnaires (disons aussi les plus 'impatients') restent avec nous . . . Je vois se lever, heureusement, des camarades solides et décidés, un peu partout: Allier, . . . Puy de Dôme, Lot, Charente, Deux Sèvres, Manche, Orne, Calvados, *Aisne*, Marne, Meurthe et Moselle, Alpes Maritimes, Yonne . . . Je compte sur toi pour déclencher le Nord. Je ne ferai rien que par ton intermédiaire (Fischer, de l'Aisne a aussi des relations dans le Nord)[.] Il est donc entendu que tu te charges du Puy de Dôme, de l'Yonne, du Maine et Loire, du Nord et du Cantal. Je demanderai à Floutard de te communiquer les adresses des correspondants. Nous verrons, il y a lieu de modifier ensuite la répartition des 'zones' d'influence. Mais la période de prospection et de défrichement est loin d'être terminée. Donc, au travail. Dans la mesure où je puis me déplacer et prendre un contact personnel avec les militants j'observe d'ailleurs des progrès

---

[111] Parti Socialiste (SFIO), 35ᵉ Congrès National, Royan, 4–7 juin 1938, *Rapports*, p. 30.
[112] Letter from Marceau Pivert to Maurice Deixonne, from an address in Haute-Savoie, 9 [?]August 1937 (Archives Maurice Deixonne, OURS).

rapides car nous avons à détruire préjugés et calomnies comme les pionniers du socialisme ont eu à en souffrir.[113]

Although some of the phrasing is obscure, this letter indicates that Marceau Pivert had an interest in building up a network of provincial organizers who could extend the influence of his *tendance* – intermediaries such as Maurice Deixonne himself, Georges Floutard from the Seine Federation and Raymond Fischer of the Aisne Federation; it also reveals his awareness of the limitations of his informal organization and his reluctance to confront the established forces of the party before the exploratory work had been completed. Concern about the strength and distribution of provincial dissent explains why Marceau Pivert and his colleagues paid such attention to the analysis of votes at national plena of the party, such as the vote on general policy at the National Council meeting on 7 November 1937.[114]

Blum liked to give the impression of being above the fray and either did not know how the Gauche Révolutionnaire was building up its strength or had chosen to ignore this development. Paul Faure, on the other hand, had made it his business to gather information about what was happening in the federations and for this purpose his direct lines of communication with the federal secretaries were a considerable advantage. His own freedom of action was nevertheless restricted: as we have seen, the CAP now consisted of what were in effect three separate groups, a loyal majority and two minorities, and yet this was the executive body to which he, as General Secretary, was responsible. He also lacked *cadres* who could work to his instructions; attached to his secretariat were five permanent delegates whose task was to address meetings throughout the provinces, but in order to have taken effective measures to strengthen the structure of the party he would have needed the aid of a substantial body of professional organizers.[115]

Without such assistance, Faure was not in a position to do much about the training and deployment of the huge numbers of new members who were flocking to the SFIO during the Popular Front period. As noted above, the total of party cardholders had risen to a record level of 286,604 by the end of 1937 and over 100,000 of these had

---

[113] Ibid. Raymond Fischer had been one of the Aisne delegates to the 34th National Congress at Marseille in July 1937, and Georges Floutard was a Paris activist who was helping Marceau Pivert with the informal organization of his *tendance* (see below, p. 105).

[114] See G. F. [Georges Floutard], 'Le vote du Conseil National', *Les Cahiers Rouges* (Paris), no. 5, November 1937, p. 3; B. F. [Berthe Fouchère], 'Après le Conseil National socialiste', ibid., p. 4.

[115] On the initial weakness of the party's central machinery, see Ziebura, *Léon Blum et le Parti Socialiste*, pp. 171–2.

been recruited within the previous twelve months. All that the General Secretary could do was to remind the federal secretaries to set up *petites librairies d'éducation socialiste*[116] and warn the faithful of the need to provide the newcomers with firm guidance.

On a eu beau les mettre en garde sur les excessives illusions qui les portaient vers nous, et leur montrer les limites du Front Populaire. Leur ignorance des forces de résistance du régime capitaliste et des réalités politiques les empêchait de nous croire complètement. Aussi beaucoup d'entre eux, venus à nous par les voies d'un réformisme utopique, sont-ils enclins à aller vers un extrémisme aussi peu réfléchi, quand sonne l'heure des désillusions et des désenchantements.

Attendre tout de la réforme, et comme on ne l'obtient pas, réclamer tout de suite la révolution, c'est ne savoir ce qu'on veut ni dans un cas, ni dans l'autre.

Il faut mettre le Parti à l'abri de ces crises de nerfs, de ces impulsivités, de ces colères d'enfants.

Pour cela éducation socialiste, causerie dans nos sections sur la doctrine et l'histoire du Parti, sur le capitalisme, la solidité de sa structure; vente de brochures.

Et enfin éducation 'morale' des nouveaux, s'efforcer de leur faire comprendre que, inscrits tout récemment dans un Parti, ils doivent faire un stage de réflexion et d'étude avant de frapper de grands coups de poing sur la table et casser la vaisselle.

On n'est un vrai militant que lorsqu'on a dans le cœur le patriotisme du Parti et dans l'esprit une claire conception de la doctrine du socialisme.[117]

He returned to this problem of assimilation in his annual report:

Il n'est pas douteux qu'une bonne partie des hommes venus récemment à lui [that is, to the party] n'ont pas encore une culture socialiste très profonde, ni sans doute assez le sens des responsabilités et de la discipline indispensable à la vie d'un grand parti. Tout cela ne s'acquiert qu'à la longue.[118]

For Paul Faure, the party was like a religious order whose members were bound together by strong moral ties; not only did they believe in a common doctrine and share a common outlook but they had acquired a capacity for mutual tolerance and for reflection and judgement. The *tendances*, on the other hand, represented a challenge to this order of things, exploiting the inexperience, the restlessness and the impulsiveness of the newly converted.

There were other ways of looking at the party. For the activists of the Gauche Révolutionnaire, the essential moral community was the vanguard of the developing revolutionary movement and the SFIO was

---

[116] *La Vie du Parti*, no. 77, 15 February 1938, p. 306.
[117] Faure, 'Pour devenir un bon militant', *Bulletin Socialiste* (Paris), no. 321, 14 February 1938, p. 2.
[118] Parti Socialiste (SFIO), 35ᵉ Congrès National, Royan, 4–7 juin 1938, *Rapports*, p. 3.

simply one of many institutions which would be transformed in the course of its development, while others stressed the perpetual tension between the libertarian ethic of the party's ordinary members and the disciplinarian ethic of its authorities. Writing in 1946, a former federal secretary took the *rites de passage* involved in the appointment of a branch secretary to illustrate the nature of this tension.

Une section choisit son secrétaire: la veille encore il était pour tous un bon camarade, un ami. Une fois désigné le voici subitement chargé d'un double fardeau: la bonne marche de la section et la critique automatique de beaucoup de ses camarades.

Une Fédération nomme un Secrétaire fédéral et voici désormais les yeux de tous les militants braqués sur lui, prêts à rechercher ses moindres peccadilles, à grossir ses plus petites erreurs et les critiques ne tardent pas à fuser de toutes parts.[119]

The same writer explained that the relations between activists and officers were governed by a certain number of rules which effectively specified the limits to dissenting behaviour, more for the benefit of the party as a whole than for that of its individual members. One such rule was that members should confine their criticism to party gatherings and not make their grievances public. Another was that an officer should always respect the knowledge and the opinions of the activists.

Il conviendrait que nos dirigeants ne perdent jamais de vue qu'ils demandent à l'adhérent du Parti une sorte de sacrifice: celui d'une parcelle de sa liberté.[120]

The struggle between the *tendances* and the party's central authorities was kept within bounds by these conventions, and Paul Faure's greatest advantage was that his experience had given him a sound understanding of when and how to appeal beyond the *chefs de tendance* to the rank-and-file when he considered that dissent had gone beyond acceptable limits.

Conclusion

By the end of 1937, the internal conflict within the SFIO was approaching a critical phase. The results of the divisions on general policy at the Marseille Congress in July 1937 and at the National Council in November had shown that the central leaders could count on no more than three-fifths of the mandates when challenged to defend the party's continued participation in the Chautemps government, and on

---

[119] L. Lequertier, 'Militants et responsables', *La Pensée Socialiste* (Paris), no. 3, April 1946, p. 19.
[120] Ibid., p. 20.

the CAP their share of seats had been reduced to the same proportion. At the level of the federations they could still rely on overwhelming support from the large Nord, Pas-de-Calais and Bouches-du-Rhône units but loyalists were now in a minority not only in the Seine and Seine-et-Oise units but also in several federations in the Paris basin and the South-West. It was becoming increasingly difficult for the leaders to justify their position without raising issues of principle, and arguments about expediency were losing their force – their insistence that the coalition with the Radicals was necessary to protect reforms and to check fascism invited the response that a vigilant opposition was just as capable of serving these ends. The most straightforward course would have been for Blum and his parliamentary colleagues to have taken their stand on the ground of the radical republican tradition and explained their support for participation as a considered choice of strategy. However, radical republicanism was still a covert tradition having been an indirect victim of the attacks on the neo-Socialists in 1933. The 1905 Charter remained the basis of doctrinal orthodoxy in the SFIO and could always be invoked to support a claim that the party should not be involved in the management of the bourgeois state. The moral advantage therefore lay with the dissident *tendances* because they had the freedom to appeal to that doctrine and to call for *redressement*, for a return to the true path towards socialism.

3 The internal crisis of early 1938: the preliminary phases, January to mid-March

By the end of 1937, the Popular Front was no more than a ghost of its former self, and each of its constituent parties was coming to accept that the balance of forces within the party system might alter drastically and suddenly, with only the briefest of warnings. This uncertainty weakened the internal cohesion of the SFIO and worked to the advantage of its dissident *tendances*, whose prescriptions for changes of strategy could now be recommended to the membership with much more urgency than in the past. In this chapter, we shall examine how both the Bataille Socialiste and the Gauche Révolutionnaire responded to this opportunity, and how the latter group greatly improved its organizational and moral position within the party. Its first gains were made at the National Council meeting of 17 January 1938, where the central leaders maintained their authority only by agreeing that the party should not be represented in the government which Camille Chautemps was then trying to form. Shortly afterwards, the Gauche Révolutionnaire took charge of the Seine Federation, one of the most powerful administrative units within the party's organization, and immediately launched a drive to force a change of strategy upon the next regular meeting of the National Council, which was expected to take place on 27 March. However, this campaign was cut short by a further ministerial crisis and by the convening on 12 March of another extraordinary meeting of the National Council, when Léon Blum gained approval to form a government which would have included representatives from parties of the right. The Gauche Révolutionnaire immediately accused him of wishing to create a National Union, despite the party's traditional opposition to such a formula.

We shall consider each of these events in turn and concentrate on the way in which the associated moral debate steadily damaged the authority of the party's central leadership.

The response of the Socialists to the ministerial crisis of January 1938

The government of Radicals and Socialists which Camille Chautemps had formed in June 1937 had been faced with a serious economic situation and the Finance Minister, Georges Bonnet, had had no hesitation in reverting to orthodox methods of financial management. Even so, he was forced to provide in the 1938 budget for an extraordinary expenditure of 16,000 million francs, including 12,000 million for national defence, to be financed from loan income.[1] There was no immediate prospect under these circumstances of funding further social reforms, but for months the Socialists leaders had continued to tolerate this policy, partly to keep the Popular Front in being and thus to preserve the legislative gains of the preceding government and partly because they still hoped that an improvement in circumstances might make possible a return to expansionist programmes. They were reluctant to admit that the Radicals represented, not reformism, but the conservatism of a diverse clientele of independent producers, including shopkeepers, small businessmen and artisans, who had been attracted briefly by the monetary radicalism in Popular Front propaganda but who had no interest in the proposals for increased state controls envisaged by the CGT and other organizations in favour of a further wave of reforms. By contrast, the leaders of the dissident *tendances* within the SFIO were sceptical regarding the strength of the Radicals' commitment to the Popular Front and were prepared to ignore them in any future crisis, relying instead on mass action to rally support for a further programme of reforms.

For the present, however, the alliance was still in existence in parliament and, when the Chamber of Deputies reassembled for a new session in the second week of January 1938, the Premier sought to impose greater discipline upon its members. He wanted all the units of his parliamentary majority, Communists included, to accept the principles of financial rigour, *la liberté monétaire* (that is, an avoidance of exchange controls) and public order (especially where industrial relations were concerned) and to eschew campaigns aimed at changing the government's policies by popular pressure. Having discussed this approach with his Cabinet on the morning of Thursday 13th, he gave an account of his policy objectives to the Chamber in the afternoon but, in what was clearly an improvised address, he may have placed more emphasis on the need for peaceful industrial relations and for

---

[1] See Georges Bonnet, *Vingt ans de vie politique 1918–1938: de Clemenceau à Daladier* (Fayard, Paris, 1969), p. 267.

financial stability than he had intended.[2] The session was then adjourned so that the groups could consider their response to his statement. When the Socialists met, Léon Blum and Paul Faure remarked with surprise the difference between what the Premier had told the Cabinet in the morning and what he had just said to the house. The group therefore sent a small delegation to explain to him that the Socialists could not support the government unless further statements indicated clearly that the policy of the Popular Front would be continued.[3] As a result, when the session resumed in the evening, Chautemps spoke in terms which were more measured than those which he had used in the afternoon.[4] A further adjournment was called to enable the groups of the majority to frame a formal resolution expressing their confidence in the government. The wording was first discussed at a meeting of the Délégation des Gauches, the co-ordinating body for the Popular Front; here the main issue was the Premier's insistence on including a reference to *la liberté monétaire* as a means of obliging the Socialists and the Communists to signify that they would not press for exchange controls. The Communists then decided that they would abstain when the resolution was put to the vote in the Chamber but the Socialists, now appeased to some extent, voted by 75 to 36 to support the government.[5]

The agreed wording of the resolution, expressing confidence in the government to restore the financial situation and impose order, was signed by the presidents of all the groups of the majority except the Communists and was presented to the Chamber early on the morning of Friday 14 January. In an obvious attempt to embarrass the Socialists, the opposition proposed an amendment inviting the house to confirm previous votes against exchange controls. Then a Communist deputy, Arthur Ramette, complained that the Premier had not said that he would implement further reforms, such as wage increases, retirement pensions, enhanced unemployment benefits, and further measures to assist the peasantry. In response, Chautemps indicated that he was willing to release Ramette and, by implication, his party from the obligation to support the government. At this point, it was requested that the session should be suspended and this was agreed.[6] During the

---

[2] *JO (CD)*, *Déb.*, 13 January 1938, pp. 21–3.
[3] 'Rapport sur l'activité du groupe socialiste au parlement', Parti Socialiste (SFIO), 35ᵉ Congrès National, Royan, 4–7 juin 1938, *Rapports* (Librairie Populaire, Paris, 1938), p. 314.
[4] *JO (CD)*, *Déb.*, 13 January 1938, pp. 24–5.
[5] *Le Populaire* (Paris), 14 January 1938, pp. 1 and 2; 15 January 1938, p. 2; *The Times* (London), 15 January 1938, p. 10; 'Rapport sur l'activité du groupe socialiste au parlement', Parti Socialiste (SFIO), 35ᵉ Congrès National, Royan, 4–7 juin 1938, *Rapports*, pp. 314–15.
[6] *JO (CD)*, *Déb.*, 13 January 1938, pp. 25–30.

adjournment, the Socialist group met and, judging that the exchange between Chautemps and Ramette signified that the government would break with the Communists, decided that the Socialist representatives should leave the ministry.[7] Chautemps promptly resigned from office and the President of the Republic, Albert Lebrun, found himself faced with a ministerial crisis.

This extraordinarily complicated series of events revealed not only the degree of anxiety and irresolution which was affecting the Socialists but also the great importance which they attached to their parliamentary alliance with the Communists, despite the fact that the discussions between the organizations of their two parties regarding unity of action and the possibility of fusion had completely broken down. Whereas the Socialists were evidently quite prepared to accept constraints on their freedom of manoeuvre where financial policies were concerned, they would not countenance anything which could be represented as a break with the Communists and the beginnings of a centre alliance. Had such a break been tolerated, the effect on the internal politics of the SFIO would have been considerable; the Bataille Socialiste, in particular, would have been able to attack the party's leaders for having failed to preserve an alliance which, in 1934, had created the very basis of the Popular Front and which still offered the best means of ensuring its survival. Equally striking was the Socialists' apparent assumption that the Chautemps government could be brought down without any risk that the Radicals might switch sides and join with the opposition, as if the social bonds on which the Popular Front was supposed to rest, such as the imagined alliance between the middle classes, the peasants and the workers, were still as powerful and as restraining as ever.

Evidently assuming that the political crisis would be resolved to its advantage, the Socialist parliamentary group declared in favour of a new Popular Front government under Socialist leadership, a proposal which the CAP endorsed by 26 votes to 6.[8] However, President Lebrun first tried to find a Radical leader willing to put together a government and, having failed to persuade either Chautemps or Daladier to undertake this task, he turned to Bonnet, confiding to him that it was no longer possible to form a Popular Front ministry 'dont le Sénat et le pays ne veulent sous aucun prétexte'.[9] When Bonnet met Blum early

[7] 'Rapport sur l'activité du groupe socialiste au parlement', Parti Socialiste (SFIO), 35e Congrès National, Royan, 4–7 juin 1938, *Rapports*, pp. 315–17.
[8] *La Vie du Parti* (Paris), no. [78], 10 March 1938, p. 312; *Le Populaire*, 15 January 1938, p. 1.
[9] Bonnet, *Vingt ans de vie politique*, p. 269. Bonnet has described his attempt to form a ministry on this occasion in ibid., pp. 269–73; *Défense de la paix, I, De Washington au Quai d'Orsay* (Constant Bourquin, Geneva, 1946), pp. 69–76; and *Le Quai d'Orsay sous trois Républiques 1870–1961* (Fayard, Paris, 1961), pp. 180–1.

on the morning of Saturday 15th, the Socialist leader told him that his party wanted to head the government 's'ils doivent partager ses responsabilités'[10] and on the evening of that day he received a letter from Albert Sérol, the leader of the Socialist parliamentary group, informing him that this group would neither participate in nor support his proposed government.[11] Despite this setback, Bonnet chose to continue with his mission and informed Lebrun that he intended to form a centre government which could provide the basis for a national union. However, discouraged by Lebrun's refusal to give him an undertaking that he would dissolve the Chamber in the event of another ministerial crisis and disappointed by the response of his own party to his plans, Bonnet resigned his commission in the early afternoon of Sunday 16th.[12]

Lebrun then resumed his consultations. When he met with Léon Blum, the latter raised the possibility of forming a broad administration encompassing the Popular Front and the centre right, presumably to demonstrate the extent of French political unity in the face of international difficulties. At the President's request, Blum asked Edouard Herriot whether he could assemble such a ministry but the Radical leader refused to be drawn.[13] Blum himself then tried to form a ministry based on 'un Rassemblement national autour du Front Populaire' and, as a first step, spoke to Paul Reynaud, a leading member of the Alliance des Républicains de Gauche, the largest group on the centre right of the Chamber. Reynaud favoured the inclusion of the Communists in such a government on the grounds that this would increase defence production, and he also asked for a place for Louis Marin, a leader of the Fédération Républicaine group in the Chamber. According to Reynaud, Blum then consulted his colleagues, only to find that they did not favour the idea of such a ministry;[14] Blum, on the other hand, claimed that the initiative had failed because of Reynaud's request that the combination should include Louis Marin.[15] The interest which Blum had shown in establishing connections between the groups of the left

[10] Bonnet, *Vingt ans de vie politique*, p. 270.
[11] *Le Populaire*, 16 January 1938, p. 2.
[12] Bonnet, *Vingt ans de vie politique*, pp. 272–3. Cf Bonnet, *Défense de la paix, I, De Washington au Quai d'Orsay*, pp. 72–6; *Le Quai d'Orsay sous trois Républiques*, p. 181.
[13] Blum referred to this episode on several occasions: see in particular *JO (CD)*, *Déb.*, 17 March 1938, p. 839; his speech to the opposition deputies on 12 March 1938, in Blum, *L'Oeuvre de Léon Blum, 1937–1940* (Albin Michel, Paris, 1965), p. 70; and his statement at the Riom trial on 10 March 1942, in Blum, *L'Oeuvre de Léon Blum, 1940–1945* (Albin Michel, Paris, 1955), p. 241.
[14] Paul Reynaud, *La France a sauvé l'Europe*, 2 vols., I (Flammarion, Paris, 1947), p. 435.
[15] See Blum's report to the National Council of the SFIO on 17 January 1938, Parti Socialiste (SFIO), 35ᵉ Congrès National, Royan, 4–7 juin 1938, *Rapports*, p. 40.

and those of the right reflected his concern at the deteriorating international situation; because of it he was prepared to challenge the opposition within his own party to anything which might resemble the National Union ministries of 1926–8 and 1934.

Blum then tried to form a Popular Front government but immediately faced the complication that the Communists, who had refused to share power when he had formed his first ministry in the summer of 1936, were now prepared to join a coalition government. They had offered to take part in the ministry which Chautemps had formed in June 1937 and were still prepared to consider participation seven months later. Earlier in this crisis they had agreed to form part of the proposed Rassemblement National combination and, that project having failed, considered that 'un véritable gouvernement de Front populaire' (that is, one in which they would be included) should be formed.[16] Blum was therefore obliged to establish whether or not the Radicals would be willing to accept the Communists as partners in government; his conversations with leading Radicals, however, left him with the impression that their parliamentary group at its meeting on the evening of Sunday 16th 'a manifesté une résistance certaine à l'entrée des communistes dans le gouvernement'.[17] Having discovered their views, Blum could have floated the idea of a more limited government of Socialists and Radicals under his leadership, but instead he decided to resign his commission without further delay and he conveyed his decision to the President on the morning of Monday 17th. Lebrun then asked Chautemps to form another ministry and he in turn asked Blum to convey to the Socialists an offer to take part in the proposed administration.

All the weight of the crisis now fell on the SFIO's National Council, which had been convened at the request of the parliamentary group on the assumption that the delegates would be deciding whether or not to approve the idea of a *rassemblement national*. The summons had come without much warning, and the delegates were left with little time to consult the members of their federations before setting out for Paris. The principal *chefs de tendance*, Marceau Pivert and Jean Zyromski, were in Brussels for a meeting of the executive of the Socialist International when the call came and had to hurry back to the French capital for the meeting.[18] We may assume, therefore, that they would have had very little opportunity to prepare their ground before the meeting and

---

[16] See letter from Jacques Duclos, on behalf of the Central Committee of the French Communist Party, to the National Council of the SFIO, [17 January 1938], in ibid., p. 42.

[17] See Blum's report to the National Council of the SFIO on 17 January 1938, ibid., p. 41.

[18] Ibid., pp. 224–5.

that they and their supporters amongst the delegates had to fall back on positions which they had taken up at the National Council of 6–7 November 1937 and, more remotely, at the Marseille Congress of July 1937.

The National Council began its meeting at 9.15 p.m. on Monday 17th with a report from Léon Blum on his efforts to form a ministry and on the invitation from Chautemps for the Socialists to participate in his government. The parliamentary group had requested its leader, Albert Sérol, to ask Chautemps whether it was his intention to form a tripartite government, containing representatives of the Radical, Socialist and Communist Parties, but Chautemps had replied that it seemed to him to be impossible in present circumstances. Communist participation, it was suggested,

aurait l'inconvénient, aux yeux des Etats totalitaires, et même d'une partie de l'opinion anglaise, d'accréditer la légende d'une France aux ordres de Moscou.

Chautemps is also reported to have wanted to retain Marx Dormoy and André Février, both Socialists, in their ministerial posts even were the party to decline his offer of participation.[19] Although Sérol claimed that Léon Blum had been quite justified in assuming that the Radicals did not want to collaborate with the Communists, a quite different interpretation of what had happened was given to the delegates in a letter which was then read out to them. It was from Jacques Duclos, who had written on behalf of the Central Committee of the French Communist Party and who acknowledged, without apology, that his party had agreed in principle to join a government of *rassemblement national* and that statements made by Paul Elbel, the president of the Radical parliamentary group, to the Délégation des Gauches had shown that that group had never opposed the entry of the Communists into the government. Claiming further that Léon Blum had been badly informed about the real views of the Radical group and that he should have pressed ahead with the formation of a ministry representing all parties and groups belonging to the Rassemblement Populaire, he suggested that the Socialists and Communists should discuss together

l'action commune qu'il conviendrait de mener de concert avec les organisations du Front populaire pour assurer le respect des décisions du suffrage universel.[20]

The Socialist leaders did their very best to lessen the impact of this letter. Vincent Auriol said that on the morning of that day, the 17th,

[19] Henri Guenin, delegate representing the Côte-d'Or Federation, 'Le Conseil National', *Le Socialiste Côte-d'Orien* (Dijon), no. 217, 22 January 1938, p. 1.

[20] See Parti Socialiste (SFIO), 35ᵉ Congrès National, Royan, 4–7 juin 1938, *Rapports*, p. 43.

he had talked with Elbel and that their conversation had confirmed Léon Blum's findings in all respects, while Léon Blum reacted strongly to the accusations contained in the letter, claiming that both his political and his private honour had been called into question. He subsequently complained to the National Committee of the Rassemblement Populaire, which found on enquiry that Chautemps and Daladier, while pointing out that the competent bodies of the Radical Party had not taken any decision on the principle of Communist participation in government, had acknowledged 'l'entière exactitude de l'impression de résistance' which Blum had drawn from his conversations.[21]

However, this clarification belonged to the future; on the evening of the 17th the National Council had been given a clear message that, whatever the rights or wrongs of the preceding negotiations about possible coalitions, the Communists were still prepared to participate in government. This reaffirmation of their position would have embarrassed Léon Blum and Paul Faure and it strengthened the hand of Zyromski, for whom joint action with the Communists was fully acceptable. Once the debate had been thrown open to the floor, one observer noted a significant shift in mood:

Fait nouveau, des camarades de tendances diverses font entendre . . . le même son de cloche: pas de participation sans les communistes.[22]

Marceau Pivert exploited this sentiment by declaring against any government which was not a reflection of the Popular Front and under Socialist leadership; he was for forcing the issue and breaking with the Radicals if they did not want to help in forming such an administration. One of the few leaders to fight against the tide was Salomon Grumbach, a native of Alsace and now a deputy for a Tarn constituency who was highly respected as an expert on European and especially German affairs; on this occasion he argued in favour of accepting Chautemps' offer of participation, given the gravity of the international situation. Unlike Marceau Pivert, Zyromski refused to envisage an alternative to the Popular Front, which he considered could be galvanized through the pressure of the masses; he took the view that a government representing the whole of the Popular Front could be formed if the Socialists wanted one. André Philip adopted a similar view, arguing that the Socialists should neither participate in nor support the government unless the Communists were granted entry to it, and even Jean Lebas,

---

[21] See l'ordre du jour of 28 January 1938 of the National Committee of the Rassemblement Populaire, in ibid., p. 46.

[22] Guenin, 'Le Conseil National', Le Socialiste Côte-d'Orien, no. 217, 22 January 1938, p. 1.

noting that Chautemps had not said that he wanted to preserve the Popular Front majority, gave it as his opinion that the National Council could not accept his proposals as they then stood.[23]

The general debate having concluded, the National Council adjourned so that a drafting committee could consider the various resolutions which had been tabled. When the meeting resumed at 4 a.m. on Tuesday 18th, this committee presented the delegates with four texts, one requesting approval for action already taken (this was approved unanimously, with some abstentions) and three on the question of what the party should do next. The leadership's view was contained in a resolution, presented by Albert Sérol, which expressed regret that a government reflecting the Popular Front had not been formed and proposed that the party's elected representatives should be authorized to participate in a government 'qui s'appuiera sur une majorité groupée sur le programme et dans la discipline du Rassemblement populaire'. This wording indicated a willingness to accept Chautemps' offer of participation and assumed that the resultant coalition of Radicals and Socialists would expect the Communists to revert to their former role of parliamentary support.[24] For the Bataille Socialiste, Zyromski put forward a motion which effectively endorsed the Communist Party's proposal for a government representing all units of the Popular Front and opposed the idea of the Socialist Party's either joining or supporting any other combination. This text was consistent with Zyromski's view that the Popular Front was the only means through which the working class could take concerted action and that it should be promoted with energy and vigour.[25]

The Sérol and Zyromski motions, for all their differences, were informed by similar ideas: both expressed faith in the Popular Front and both acknowledged that a tripartite government was desirable. However, the resolution submitted by Marceau Pivert on behalf of the Gauche Révolutionnaire put forward the view that the party should completely change its strategy and its methods of operation. The preamble of his text offered a very pessimistic interpretation of the recent past: it suggested that there was no longer agreement regarding the content of the programme of the Popular Front; that the parties of the parliamentary majority were at odds concerning the essential problems and the political course which a Popular Front government would have to follow; that the Radicals would not accept Communist participation

---

[23] *Le Populaire*, 19 January 1938, p. 5.
[24] Parti Socialiste (SFIO), 35ᵉ Congrès National, Royan, 4–7 juin 1938, *Rapports*, p. 44.
[25] For the text, see *La Bataille Socialiste* (Seine Regional Edition, Paris), January 1938, p. 1.

in government; and, most importantly, that Blum's offer of collaboration to Reynaud signified not an enlargement but the end of the Popular Front in its parliamentary form. The National Council was therefore advised to take a radical stand, first, by rejecting participation in any government which was neither a reflection of the Rassemblement Populaire nor a purely Socialist ministry and which did not accept as the basis of its programme the immediate imposition of foreign-exchange controls and measures of nationalization; secondly, by demanding the dissolution of the Chamber of Deputies unless a *gouvernement de combat* could be formed to fight against the banks, the trusts, the Senate, and the threat of war; and, thirdly, by launching a campaign of agitation 'pour engager immédiatement les masses sur la voie de leur libération par leur action directe et autonome'.[26] Both this and the Bataille Socialiste motion advocated the rejection of Chautemps' offer of ministerial participation, but whereas the latter defended the Popular Front ideal, Pivert's text implied that this alliance had lost its vigour and that much more adventurous action should be taken.

The three motions were submitted to a vote by mandates, and the result was a majority against participation in the Chautemps ministry; the number of mandates credited to the Sérol motion was only 4,035, whereas the combined total for the two anti-participationist texts was 4,155, composed of 2,659 for Zyromski's motion and 1,496 for that of Marceau Pivert. If certain errors of recording and addition are corrected, we arrive at the distribution of mandates by motions shown in Table 5. From the point of view of the leadership, this was a serious reverse, tantamount to a vote of no confidence, and Paul Faure immediately offered his resignation as General Secretary on the grounds that the motion which he had signed had not obtained an absolute majority of the mandates. A crisis of the first magnitude had broken, and the session was adjourned so that the members of the CAP could meet with the Bureau of the parliamentary group to take stock of the situation.

What factors explain the failure of the leadership to win a majority for the principle of ministerial participation? In the first place, a concern to avoid a break with the Communists may have persuaded many delegates who might otherwise have voted for the Sérol motion to allocate mandates to the Zyromski text; as we have seen, the parliamentary group had justified the withdrawal of Socialist ministers from the preceding government by pointing to Chautemps' apparent rejection of Communist support, and the letter from Duclos to the National Council had underlined his party's willingness to share office and its belief that

[26] For the text, see *Juin 36* (Paris), no. 1, 15 February 1938, p. 4.

Table 5. *SFIO: National Council, 17 January 1938: first division on general policy*

| Federations | Mandates for the motions of: | | | | | | | | | | |
	Sérol (loyalist) no.	%	Zyromski (Bataille Socialiste) no.	%	Marceau Pivert (Gauche Révolutionnaire) no.	%	Abstentions no.	%	Absent no.	%	Totals no.
Bouches-du-Rhône	315	100.0									315
Gironde			163	87.6	23	12.4					186
Meurthe-et-Moselle	9	5.8	30	19.5	115	74.7					154
Nord	750	97.8	14	1.8	3	0.4					767
Pas-de-Calais	298	84.9	49	14.0	4	1.1					351
Seine	141	22.3	203	32.1	288	45.6					632
Seine-et-Oise	71	20.2	153	43.6	127	36.2					351
Haute-Vienne	84	50.3	83	49.7							167
Others	[2,385]	44.4	1,974	36.8	[918]	17.1			89	1.7	[5,366]
Totals	[4,053]	48.9	[2,669]	32.2	[1,478]	17.8			89	1.1	[8,289]

Source: La Vie du Parti (Paris), no. 77, 15 February 1938, pp. 305–6 and ibid., no. [78], 10 March 1938, p. 312, for the corrected vote of the Nièvre Federation. For details of adjustments, see the appendix (p. 400, n. 5).

a tripartite ministry could be formed, but Sérol's motion appeared to have put participation above the preservation of the Socialists' alliance with the Communists. Delegates inclined by such considerations to vote for Zyromski's motion may also have been influenced by the sentiment that Blum's attempt to form a government of Rassemblement National had revealed a lack of faith in the Popular Front, and that only Zyromski was prepared to identify himself wholeheartedly with that ideal. Finally, it may have been difficult for the General Secretary and his staff to form an adequate assessment of the likely outcome of divisions; not only had the meeting been convened at short notice but there had been no time to take account of the effects on voting patterns of the redistribution of federal mandates carried out to reflect changes in the levels of minimum membership which had occurred between 31 December 1936 and 31 December 1937. From 5,420 for 97 federations at the National Council of 6–7 November 1937 the total number of mandates available for national meetings had risen to 8,289 for 98 federations, an increase of 52.9 per cent, with some federations gaining many more than others.

The Bataille Socialiste, as the middle unit in the alignment of groups, had the choice either of combining with the Gauche Révolutionnaire in order to carry the revolt further or of coming to terms with the party's leaders. The former course of action was not a serious possibility, given the narrow margin of victory in the division and the considerable differences of outlook and temperament between the leaders of the two *tendances*, and it was not surprising that Zyromski and his colleagues decided to aim at a compromise with the loyalists. At the meeting of the CAP with the bureau of the parliamentary group they therefore agreed to support a resolution which simply stated that the National Council's vote had been against participation in government and that the council had confidence that the parliamentary group would work in accord with the CAP to serve the best interests of the working class, the party and the Rassemblement Populaire. The only members of the CAP to vote against this proposal were four representatives of the Gauche Révolutionnaire, Marceau Pivert, René Modiano, Georges Soulès and Degez.[27] When the National Council resumed its session at 7 a.m. the delegates approved the compromise text, which was presented to them by Sansimon Graziani, a moderate member of the CAP, and rejected a motion from Marceau Pivert which would have denied support to any government formed outside the organizations of the

[27] See *La Vie du Parti*, no. [78], 10 March 1938, p. 312; *Le Populaire*, 20 January 1938, p. 2.

Rassemblement Populaire. On this occasion, the majority for the 'official' proposal was a substantial one (Table 6). The organizational crisis thus resolved, Paul Faure agreed to continue in office as General Secretary until the next meeting of the National Council, which was scheduled to take place on 27 March 1938.[28]

What do the two divisions at this meeting of the National Council reveal about voting patterns within the party? The first division, with its three-way apportionment of mandates, is best compared with the vote on general policy at the Marseille Congress of July 1937, when the issues were similar and when the use of bloc votes was minimal (which was not the case at the National Council meeting of 6–7 November 1937, another possible means of comparison). Between July 1937 and January 1938, judging from the data set out in Tables 4 and 5, support for the principle of participation in a Radical-led government fell from 54.7 to 48.9 per cent, whereas the vote for the Bataille rose from 28.6 to 32.2 per cent and that for the Gauche Révolutionnaire from 16.8 to 17.8 per cent of the total, with very few abstentions or absences on either occasion. The sharing out of the mandates of the eight largest federations forms a similar pattern in both divisions, with the loyalists receiving bloc votes from Bouches-du-Rhône and substantial majorities from the Nord and Pas-de-Calais Federations, the Bataille obtaining an absolute majority in the Gironde and sizeable shares of the votes from the Seine, Seine-et-Oise and Haute-Vienne Federations, and the Gauche Révolutionnaire enjoying an absolute majority from the Meurthe-et-Moselle and large votes from the Seine and Seine-et-Oise Federations. The relative importance of the individual tallies within this group of federations had been altered by the variable increases in mandate totals approved at the beginning of 1938, increases which ranged from 22.8 per cent in Haute-Vienne to 266.7 per cent in Meurthe-et-Moselle, but the basic pattern had been maintained. In aggregate, the loyalist vote in these eight federations had fallen from 58.2 to 57.1 per cent and the Bataille vote from 26.1 to 23.8 per cent while that for the Gauche Révolutionnaire had risen from 15.6 to 19.2 per cent.

---

[28] For general accounts of the Socialists' reaction to this ministerial crisis, see Parti Socialiste (SFIO), 35ᵉ Congrès National, Royan, 4–7 juin 1938, *Rapports*, pp. 40–6; *La Vie du Parti*, no. 77, 15 February 1938, p. 305; and *Le Populaire*, 15–19 January 1938. See also Jules Moch, *Le Front populaire: grande espérance* . . . (Perrin, Paris, 1971), pp. 276–8; Joel Colton, *Léon Blum: Humanist in Politics* (Alfred A. Knopf, New York, 1966, reprinted 1987), pp. 290–1; Nathanael Greene, *Crisis and Decline: The French Socialist Party in the Popular Front Era* (Cornell University Press, Ithaca, 1969), pp. 197–8; 'Histoire du Parti Socialiste S.F.I.O.', Part 17, 'La fin du Front populaire (janvier – avril 1938)', *Cahier et Revue de l'OURS* (Paris), no. 94 (November 1978), pp. 7–23.

Table 6. *SFIO: National Council, 17 January 1938: second division on general policy*

Federations	Mandates for the motions of:								Totals
	Graziani (compromise)		Mareau Pivert (Gauche Révolutionnaire)		Abstentions		Absent		
	no.	%	no.	%	no.	%	no.	%	no.
Bouches-du-Rhône	315	100.0							315
Gironde	158	84.9	28	15.1					186
Meurthe-et-Moselle	39	25.3	115	74.7					154
Nord	764	99.6	3	0.4					767
Pas-de-Calais	347	98.9	4	1.1					351
Seine	344	54.4	288	45.6					632
Seine-et-Oise	[224]	63.8	127	36.2					[351]
Haute-Vienne	167	100.0							167
Others	4,474	83.4	769	14.3			123	2.3	5,366
Totals	6,832	82.4	1,334	16.1			123	1.5	8,289

Source: La Vie du Parti (Paris), no. 77, 15 February 1938, p. 306.
For details of adjustments, see the appendix (p. 400, n. 6).

The loyalists had lost more heavily in the remaining federations, mainly provincial or overseas units, where their share of the vote had fallen sharply from 52.8 to 44.4 per cent whereas the Bataille had increased its proportion from 30.0 to 36.8 per cent and the Gauche Révolutionnaire had maintained its support at 17.1 per cent of the total vote in this category. It is difficult to relate these trends to changes in the geographical distribution of support for the different groups, but it is possible to identify some general regional patterns in what at first appears to be a patchwork quilt of results. Most obviously, there are two large areas where the loyalist vote was relatively weak: it fell below the 50 per cent level in many parts of the Paris basin and its adjacent regions and was patchy in the south-west, in the Guyenne and Gascogne regions. Loyalist votes of over 50 per cent were confined in the north to the Nord, Pas-de-Calais and Ardennes Federations and in the east to the Bas-Rhin, Haut-Rhin and Belfort Federations but there was also a broad zone of predominantly loyalist majorities extending north-westwards from the Rhône valley and the Midi through the central regions to the Vendée and Brittany. If we compare the distribution of mandates of our two divisions within this geographical framework we find that the loyalist vote was seriously eroded between July 1937 and January 1938 in both the Paris basin and the south-west. Of the dissident *tendances*, the Bataille Socialiste was the main beneficiary of this shift towards opposition and received bloc votes from seven federations, including Calvados, Landes, Basses-Pyrénées and Sarthe, but the Gauche Révolutionnaire managed to secure absolute majorities not only in its Meurthe-et-Moselle stronghold but also in the Orne, Eure-et-Loir, Loiret, Vosges and Corsican Federations while attracting substantial numbers of mandates from some other provincial federations including the Aisne, Côte-d'Or, Marne, Oise, Somme and Alpes-Maritimes units.

The division list for the second ballot of January 1938, when the National Council resolved the organizational crisis by adopting the Graziani motion, shows the extent to which mandates for the dissident groups were indirectly under the control of the *chefs de tendance*. Each federation was represented by only one official delegate, who was expected not only to take account of the balance of opinion within the unit in distributing its mandates between motions but also to ensure that dedicated mandates were used for the benefit of the *tendance* concerned, even when that *tendance* adopted a position which the federation had not foreseen. Some delegates would have enjoyed a measure of discretion, but it is evident that the majority were deploying their mandates in accordance with the rules of the *jeu de tendances*: thus,

Zyromski's support for the Graziani motion was followed by a substantial transfer of the Bataille's mandates to the loyalist account, which largely explains why the vote for the 'official' resolution rose from 4,053 to 6,832 mandates between the two divisions. Equally significant was that the vote for the Gauche Révolutionnaire held up surprisingly well, despite the heavy moral pressure to close ranks; the vote for Marceau Pivert's motion on the second division was only slightly smaller than that recorded for his text on the first, 1,334 compared with 1,478, the gross loss of 222 mandates having been partly offset by 78 gains.

Let us now return to the ministerial crisis and to the problems which faced the SFIO following the National Council's decision to refuse Chautemps' offer of participation. The party's leadership would undoubtedly have preferred acceptance, mainly because another coalition of Radicals and Socialists would have been more stable than a purely Radical ministry and would have offered more of an obstacle to conservative groups in any attempt to 'reverse' the parliamentary majority. This avenue having been closed, the best alternative was to offer parliamentary support to Chautemps in the event of his forming a purely Radical ministry. Marx Dormoy is reported to have told the CAP that when he and Sérol had seen Chautemps on the 18th, Chautemps had told them that he wanted an honourable peace with the Communist Party, that he would not take office if the Socialists were hostile, that his programme would be that of his earlier government and that it would remain on the course of the Popular Front.[29] The Socialist parliamentary group later decided by 88 votes to 25, with 6 abstentions, to welcome favourably the formation of a government by a party belonging to the Rassemblement Populaire[30] and on the 18th Chautemps was able to form a ministry which consisted mainly of Radicals but also contained several representatives of the Union Socialiste et Républicaine (USR), the smallest of the Popular Front parties.

On the 20th, the secretariat of the Socialist parliamentary group attended a meeting of the CAP to discuss the implementation of the decision of the National Council. The loyalists were in favour of endorsing the decision which the parliamentary group had taken, but Zyromski tabled a motion favouring the establishment of a true Popular Front ministry. As he had done at the National Council meeting, Marceau Pivert proposed a much more radical course of action: he put forward a text requesting that the parliamentary group should vote against Chautemps when he presented himself to parliament, calling for mass

---

[29] From a report of a meeting of the CAP on 20 January 1938, in *Bulletin Intérieur de la Gauche Révolutionnaire*, 20 February 1938, p. 1.
[30] *Le Populaire*, 19 January 1938, p. 1.

demonstrations to establish a *gouvernement de combat* with Socialist leadership and a proletarian majority, and suggesting that the *comité d'entente* should meet to co-ordinate the action of Communists and Socialists and to prepare to make contact with the CGT.[31] When members of the CAP came to a division, Pivert's motion received only 5 votes, Zyromski's text (which had been softened before the ballot) gained 8, and 16 votes were given to the loyalist resolution which simply approved the action of the parliamentary group and stated that:

En attendant que soit possible la constitution d'un gouvernement exactement conforme à la volonté exprimée par le suffrage universel, la C.A.P. fait confiance au Groupe parlementaire pour déjouer les manœuvres de la réaction et assurer la réalisation du programme du Rassemblement populaire.[32]

When Chautemps came before the Chamber of Deputies on the 21st, he made it quite clear that he would continue to respect *la liberté monétaire* and that he intended to keep public expenditure under control.[33] His government therefore remained at a point of balance between two parliamentary combinations; at one level, the ministry was ostensibly bound to the Popular Front majority composed of the Radical, Socialist, Communist and USR groups, but its orthodox financial and monetary policies were generally acceptable to the groups on the centre right, and the construction of a new majority around this core was well within the bounds of possibility. As if to acknowledge that this was so, many deputies of the right joined with those of the Popular Front in voting for the customary motion of confidence, which was passed by 501 votes to one.[34]

The ministerial crisis of January 1938 had sharpened disagreements within the SFIO. When put to the test, the party's central leaders had shown that their support for the Popular Front was qualified and that they were prepared to tolerate Léon Blum's interest in forming a government which might include representatives from the centre right. The spokesmen for the Gauche Révolutionnaire had seized on the proposal for 'un Rassemblement national autour du Front Populaire' as nothing more than a veiled attempt to form a National Union, and therefore as an act of indiscipline, a break with one of the party's basic traditions; Lucien Hérard warned that:

---

[31] See *Bulletin Intérieur de la Gauche Révolutionnaire*, 20 February 1938, pp. 1–2. For the text of Zyromski's resolution see Jean Zyromski, 'Nous voulons un gouvernement à l'image du Front populaire', *Le Populaire*, 24 January 1938, p. 4.

[32] *La Vie du Parti*, no [78], 10 March 1938, p. 312.

[33] *JO (CD), Déb.*, 21 January 1938, pp. 57–8.

[34] Ibid., pp. 79–80.

le Parti entrant dans l'union nationale, même restreinte, c'est la *scission* dans le Parti.

D'aucuns se féliciteraient de participer à l'Union sacrée; mes camarades et moi tiendrions à honneur de nous en exclure et de la combattre. En d'autres termes, *nous ne nous associerons jamais, sous quelque prétexte que ce soit, à une pareille compromission.*[35]

The party's leaders were poorly placed to counter such attacks. Although they could support the decision to back the new Chautemps ministry as part of a defensive strategy, designed to protect the social and economic reforms of 1936 and to continue the fight against fascism, they were not in a position to answer the basic questions which had been raised by the crisis: Were the Radicals prepared to accept the Communists as partners in government? Were the Radicals now too much under the influence of their conservative wing, strongly entrenched in the Senate, to contemplate further progressive measures? If a reversal of the parliamentary majority was now a possibility, why should the Socialists further delay considering an alternative strategy, such as a return to opposition? Only Zyromski and the Bataille Socialiste appeared to believe that the Popular Front could be given new life, but their approach presupposed that relations with the Communist Party could be restored.

The ordinary activist could be forgiven for thinking that the party had become a slave to the past, that the central leaders were clinging desperately to a dubious relationship with the Radicals and, through them, with the centre right, and that the Bataille Socialiste was still obsessed with the project for an understanding with the Communists. By contrast, the Gauche Révolutionnaire could recommend itself as the only force in the party capable of thinking and acting independently and therefore of exploring the means of returning to anti-participationism and to revolutionism. Lucien Hérard put the choice in the following terms:

Notre Parti arrive à un moment décisif où deux chemins s'offrent à . . . lui: celui du 'moindre mal' et de l'union nationale; celui de l'action révolutionnaire.

The old road was closed:

sous sa forme parlementaire, le Front populaire était mort et . . . son expérience se soldait par un *échec.*[36]

---

[35] Hérard, 'Originale et audacieuse', *Le Socialiste Côte-d'Orien*, no. 218, 29 January 1938, pp. 1 and 2, quotation from p. 2.

[36] Hérard, 'Nécessaire explication', ibid., no. 221, 19 February 1938, pp. 1 and 2, quotation from p. 1.

At this stage, however, the central leaders were still in a relatively secure position. They continued to enjoy a majority in the parliamentary group and the CAP and they had learnt that, although the dissident *tendances* now had the combined strength to reduce the loyalists to a minority in a division of mandates at a meeting of the National Council or National Congress, they were very unlikely to form a stable coalition capable of taking over the organization. The real danger was that the Gauche Révolutionnaire could find a means of exploiting its considerable moral advantage as the only group prepared to oppose any collaboration with the centre right and to contemplate a return to revolutionary opposition to the bourgeois regime.

The Gauche Révolutionnaire takes control of the Seine Federation and campaigns for a change in strategy

It was quite natural that Marceau Pivert should want to capture the Seine Federation of the SFIO. Although the formal dissolution of the Gauche Révolutionnaire by the National Council on 18 April 1937 had weakened neither his support nor his network of contacts within the organization, it had deprived him of the right to maintain a separate membership list for his *tendance* and to build up his own administrative structure. His best means of making good these losses was to win control of the organization of the Seine Federation and to use this base to extend his influence. The Parisian region also provided ideal conditions for trying out the social and political strategies which the Gauche Révolutionnaire was advocating; if it could strengthen the links between the party's branches and workers' associations, known as Amicales Socialistes, which the party had formed in various industrial centres, including Paris, it could then try to mobilize the working class for radical strike action and to prove that it was still possible to unify the proletariat in a revolutionary cause.

To follow the course of Pivert's campaign we need to have some idea of how the Seine Federation was organized in the late 1930s. Its formal structure resembled that of the national party: at the base were the branches, each of which was entitled to send delegates to both the Federal Council and the Federal Congress. Members at branch meetings would take part in the election of a 25-member Executive Committee which would appoint a Federal Bureau, headed by a General Secretary. There were two types of Federal Congress, one to deal with administrative matters and reports from officers, and the other to consider matters of general policy with the party's National Congress in view. Under the rules, the latter type was to be held in two sessions, the first at least fifteen days and the second no later than three days before the National Congress; the first session was intended to consider motions sent in from the branches and to elect by proportional representation a resolutions committee whose main purpose was to prepare or accept texts of motions (identified as A, B, C and so on) for consideration by branch meetings; at these branch meetings, mandates were allotted proportionately to the various texts, each branch being entitled to one mandate for each member. The second session of the congress then enabled branch delegates to vote on the approved motions and to appoint delegates to the National Congress. In the fortnight which followed this final session, an Executive Committee would be elected by proportional representation on the basis of the votes cast for the motions.[37] Thus, the competition between the *tendances* was bound to concentrate on the Federal Congress, because a majority for a motion in this body would be translated into a majority on the Executive Committee and would result, finally, in control of the Federal Bureau and its secretariat.

As noted above,[38] by the middle of 1937 the Seine Federation had developed what was virtually a three-party system in which the Bataille Socialiste held power as a centre group between the Gauche Révolutionnaire on its left and the loyalists on its right. Nevertheless, the Bataille was in serious difficulties: it had committed itself so heavily to the strategy of joint action with the Communists at the regional level and to the 1935 version of the Popular Front at the national level that it was unable to stem the offensive of the Gauche Révolutionnaire, quite prepared to exploit the feeling amongst activists that the Popular Front was finished and that the drive towards revolutionary action was being frustrated as much by the Communist Party as by the bureaucracy of the SFIO. Instead of meeting this challenge head-on, the Bataille appears to have tried to conciliate the Gauche Révolutionnaire, even at the risk of antagonizing the loyalists. For example, before the Marseille National Congress of July 1937 Zyromski and his supporters had taken the line that the Blum government should have confronted the Senate instead of resigning office and that the party's decision to participate in the Chautemps government had been misguided. Looking back on this period, the loyalist leader, André Costedoat, recalled that:

---

[37] For the rules of the Seine Federation, as amended to November 1934, see Parti Socialiste (SFIO), Fédération de la Seine, Congrès Administratif des 2 et 9 décembre 1945, *Rapports, statuts fédéraux* [Paris, 1945], pp. 22–9. See also Charles Pivert, *Le Parti Socialiste et ses hommes: souvenirs d'un militant* (France-Editions, Paris, 1950), pp. 9–11.

[38] See above, pp. 51–4.

nos amis se sont souvent lassés de soutenir nos camarades de la *Bataille Social-iste* qui, tout en acceptant notre concours généreux, n'avaient pour nous que rebuffades et pour l'ex-gauche [l'extrême-gauche] que sourires. Nous avons encore, dans nos sections, le souvenir des discussions autour du Congrès de Marseille.[39]

It was then that the loyalists decided to co-ordinate their own forces more effectively. They founded their own fortnightly journal, *Le Social-iste*, the first issue of which appeared in September 1937, and began to stand up to both *tendances* instead of supporting one against the other.

In 1937 the federation's provisional bureau consisted almost entirely of members of the Bataille Socialiste, the sole exception being Claude Just, who represented the Groupe Prolétarien Révolutionnaire, a small pro-Communist body. The distribution of administrative duties was as follows:[40]

1 *Statutory appointments* (that is, required by the Rules)

Francis Desphelippon	Federal Secretary
Roger Dufour	Administrative Secretary
Robert Dupont	Propaganda Secretary
René Jousse	Treasurer
André Joublot	Deputy Treasurer

2 *Non-statutory appointments*

Claude Just	Secretary for the Amicales Socialistes
Charles Pivert	Secretary for External Relations

However, when the Federal Council was asked to ratify these appointments on 5 November 1937 the Gauche Révolutionnaire moved that the bureau should be formed according to the rules of proportional representation and this proposal was carried by 5,282 mandates to the 4,421 cast for the ratification of the existing body, with 906 abstentions. The same meeting was asked to consider the policy issues which were to be discussed by the National Council on 6–7 November, and on this occasion the *Socialiste* tabled a motion of its own, thus forcing a three-fold division of the mandates and revealing that, although the Gauche Révolutionnaire had a larger following than either of the other two groups, it could not yet count upon obtaining an absolute majority in a ballot. The details of the result are given in Table 7.[41]

---

[39] Costedoat, 'Faisons le point', *Le Populaire*, 26 January 1938, p. 4.

[40] Parti Socialiste (SFIO), Fédération de la Seine, *Congrès fédéral administratif, 12 juin 1937* [Paris, 1937], p. 3.

[41] *Le Populaire*, 6 November 1937, p. 3; *Le Temps* (Paris), 8 November 1937, p. 2 (the total number of mandates is from the latter source). See also *Les Cahiers Rouges* (Paris), no. 5, November 1937, p. 13.

Table 7. *Seine Federation, Federal Council, 5 November 1937: division on general policy*

Motions	Mandates	% of total
Gauche Révolutionnaire	4,758	44.7
Bataille Socialiste	3,339	31.3
Le Socialiste	2,286	21.5
Epinay (associated with Gauche Révolutionnaire)	102	1.0
Abstentions	160	1.5
Unattributed	6	0.1
Total	10,651	

Although complete details are still lacking, it would appear that the bureau was reconstituted at some stage after this meeting to provide representation for all three groups, but Desphelippon and Dufour continued to serve as Federal Secretary and Administrative Secretary respectively.

Subsequently, a decision was taken to hold an extraordinary Federal Congress, with its first session on 23 January and its second on 7 February, evidently in order to produce fresh instructions for the federation's delegate to the National Council, whose scheduled meeting for 13 February was cancelled only after its extraordinary session of 17 January. This was the chance for which Marceau Pivert had been waiting; writing in *Les Cahiers Rouges*, he demanded nothing less than political control of the federation:

Nous ne dissimulons ni nos intentions, ni notre drapeau.

Tout est parfaitement clair pour tout le monde: LA CONQUETE DE LA MAJORITE DE LA FEDERATION DE LA SEINE AURA DES REPERCUSSIONS POLITIQUES CONSIDERABLES.

He also specified his social objectives:

Nous voulons procéder méthodiquement à la conquête de larges bases socialistes et internationalistes dans le prolétariat parisien en faisant des AMICALES SOCIALISTES non pas des instruments d'approbation systématique du gouvernement ou des obstacles à l'indépendance du syndicalisme. MAIS DES PEPINIERES DE RECRUTEMENT POUR LE PARTI PAR LE CHEMIN D'UNE CONNAISSANCE APPROFONDIE DU MARXISME REVOLUTIONNAIRE.[42]

Early in January, preparations began for the first session of the congress, which was due to take place at Puteaux in the suburbs of Paris

[42] Pivert, 'Et maintenant, nous prenons l'offensive', *Les Cahiers Rouges*, no. 6, December 1937, pp. 2–3.

on the 23rd. Branches were invited to meet during the preceding week to consider the various motions in circulation and to instruct delegates on the expression of preferences. The Gauche Révolutionnaire and the Bataille Socialiste published their texts promptly, both concentrating as much on national as on local issues. As the group which had been in power, the Bataille was not in a position to propose radical changes without criticizing its own record, but it offered to work for a more fraternal atmosphere within the branches, more cohesion between the different bodies of the federation, and better methods of propaganda. In line with its general political strategy of reviving the Popular Front, it proposed that unity of action (that is, with the Communists) should be strengthened in each locality and made the point that the Amicales Socialistes were expected to obey the directives of the party as well as those of the federation.[43] The motion of the Gauche Révolutionnaire was much less restrained: as regards the federation, it suggested a number of reforms, such as better communication between the Federal Bureau and the branch secretaries and improved techniques and methods of propaganda amongst the working class; instead of simple collaboration with the Communists, it advocated the creation of a *front unique* aimed at specific objectives and at 'une clarification idéologique indispensable' with regard to the Communist Party. It claimed that the Amicales Socialistes should be the responsibility of the federation rather than the national party and proposed close links between branches and the Amicales in each *arrondissement* and locality.[44]

In its motion, the *Socialiste* gave most prominence to its claim that, compared with such federations as those in the Nord, Pas-de-Calais and Gironde departments, the Seine Federation did not return enough Socialists to parliament and did not recruit sufficient adult and youth members for the party. It attributed this weakness to the *lutte de tendances*, which it claimed had sapped the fighting spirit of activists, discouraged those who were best intentioned, and produced a kind of 'défaitisme socialiste'; to the accusations, insinuations and calumnies which had been directed against members of the party and created anxiety ('jettent le trouble dans les consciences'); to the uncoordinated and unregulated action of party propagandists in public demonstrations; and to serious deficiencies in propaganda methods. Essentially, the *Socialiste* was accusing its rivals of a lack of restraint and discipline, and

---

[43] This motion was published in *La Bataille Socialiste* (Seine Regional Edition), January 1938, pp. 1 and 2; and as a brochure (La Bataille Socialiste, *Pour le congrès du 23 janvier 1938* [Paris, 1938]).

[44] 'Motion pour le Congrès extraordinaire du 23 janvier 1938 et pour le Conseil National du 13 février 1938', *Les Cahiers Rouges*, no. 7, January 1938, pp. 8–9.

the remedies which it prescribed were all directed to ensure more control over the expression of opinion within and through the federation: it thus proposed the formation of a small propaganda committee; the organization of propaganda areas; the revision of the terms of collaboration with outside organizations and a tighter control of speakers who were members of the party; pressure on the Administrative Council of *Le Populaire* to ensure that this newspaper was more sensitive to the problems of making propaganda in the Parisian region; and the establishment of a newspaper for the federation using common material within local editions. In the same spirit, the motion stressed the need to respect the decisions and directives of the party, and the related need to sustain the Popular Front and to pursue the policy aims laid down by the Marseille Congress of July 1937. It expressed a readiness to prepare for workers' unity but approved the position which the CAP had taken in dealing with the Communist Party, notably in reacting to Dimitrov's statement by refusing to continue discussions with the Communists about the possibility of joining the two parties together.[45]

Fortunately, the cyclostyled documents issued by the *Socialiste* to its supporters have survived, and they provide an important insight into the conduct of the campaign. The first circular, dated 14 January, asked members to ensure that all their friends attended the branch meeting for the discussion of motions and warned them not to be shaken by attacks and insults from 'les camarades des autres tendances'. They were told of the need to be present for the actual voting and to ensure that all their votes were credited to the *Socialiste*'s motion:

Il faut veiller également à ce que les voix que nous aurons recueillies ne soient pas subtilisées au Congrès Fédéral, comme cela c'est vu dans le passé. D'ailleurs pour déjouer cette manœuvre frauduleuse indiquez-nous, dès que votre section se sera réunie, le nombre de voix que vous avez pu recueillir sur notre motion ainsi que le nombre de mandats dont dispose votre section au Congrès Fédéral.[46]

The *Socialiste* evidently saw its followers as an honest band of the party faithful, fighting against the petty corruption of party practices which had flourished in the over-heated atmosphere of the *lutte de tendances*.

According to one account, four speeches in particular had stood out during the debates at the Puteaux session on 23 January: Zyromski clarified the position which he had taken at the meeting of the National Council on the 17th; Henri Sellier, the Mayor of Suresnes and a senator, criticized the policies of the Popular Front governments; André

[45] *Motion du 'Socialiste' pour le redressement du Parti dans la région parisienne* [Paris, 1938] (Archives de l'OURS).
[46] *Le Socialiste*, cyclostyled letter, Paris, 14 January 1938 (Archives de l'OURS).

Costedoat defended the motion from the *Socialiste*; and Marceau Pivert, claiming that the Popular Front was dead in parliament but still very much alive in the country, called for:

la mobilisation des forces prolétariennes pour imposer, par l'action du prolétariat, la capitulation des puissances financières de notre pays et de la Cité de Londres.[47]

Judging from what the *Socialiste* was saying to its followers after the event, Marceau Pivert had also spoken of the Popular Front being replaced by a revolutionary proletarian front pursuing an insurrectionary course of action. Complaining that insurrection was not, had never been, and would never be 'la *révolution socialiste marxiste* pour la conquête du pouvoir', the *Socialiste* saw this error as the best example of the crisis of a federation in which three-quarters of the activists did not know 'les premiers mots de la doctrine socialiste'.[48] André Costedoat further claimed that Marceau Pivert's following had grown because of an influx of new members, who lacked 'instruction socialiste' and were a 'proie facile pour la déclamation, la grandiloquence et le verbalisme pseudo-révolutionnaire'.[49] Such bitter remarks suggest that the *Socialiste* had been taken aback by the aggressiveness and strength displayed by the Gauche Révolutionnaire at this session, and it is significant that this *tendance* won an absolute majority of the places on the 27-member Resolutions Committee, to which were elected 14 representatives of the Gauche Révolutionnaire, 7 of the Bataille and 6 of the *Socialiste*.[50] However, the *Socialiste* suggested that the minorities had been underrepresented because many branches had sent only two delegates to the session, despite the fact that there were three texts in contention.[51]

The contest now entered its second phase. Not surprisingly, the Resolutions Committee decided that it was unable to reconcile the various motions which it had received and it therefore published amended versions of the three principal texts so that these could be considered by the branches for the final and definitive apportionment of mandates at the second session of the congress on 7 February. The general sections of the motions of the Gauche Révolutionnaire and the Bataille

[47] 'Lettre de Paris' (from a delegate representing the branch for the 11th *arrondissement*), *Le Socialiste Côte-d'Orien*, no. 219, 5 February 1938, p. 1. See also *Le Temps*, 25 January 1938, p. 3; *Le Populaire*, 24 January 1938, p. 7.

[48] See *Le Socialiste*, cyclostyled notes entitled 'Motion du "Socialiste": schéma' (Archives de l'OURS), issued in preparation for the second session of the Federal Congress of the Seine Federation on 7 February 1938, pp. 1–3.

[49] Costedoat, 'Faisons le point', *Le Populaire*, 26 January 1938, p. 4.

[50] 'Lettre de Paris', *Le Socialiste Côte-d'Orien*, no. 219, 5 February 1938, p. 1; *Le Populaire*, 24 January 1938, p. 7.

[51] *Le Socialiste*, 'Motion du "Socialiste": schéma', p. 1.

had been revised to take account of the changed situation at the national level and the Bataille had also retouched its proposals regarding local affairs, making an explicit appeal for unity of action with the Communists to bring about a true Popular Front government and warning that the Amicales Socialistes should not take the place of trade unions. However, the most important changes were those made to the *Socialiste* motion, which coupled a trenchant criticism of the conduct of affairs in the Seine Federation with a considered defence of the party's strategy in national politics, and in particular of its adherence to the Popular Front.[52]

When, at the second session of the Federal Congress held on 7 February, the branch delegations allocated their mandates, the result was a victory for the Gauche Révolutionnaire, which registered a much larger vote than either of its two rivals (for details, see Table 8). It had obviously been the major beneficiary of the end-of-yearly redistribution of mandates, whose total had increased from 10,651 at the Federal Council of 5 November 1937 to 15,225 on this occasion, and although it had failed narrowly to obtain an absolute majority of the mandates it was now in a position to dominate the future politics of the federation. The way was now clear for the election of the Executive Committee, places on which were allocated with reference to the division of the mandates, so that 12 of the 25 seats were assigned to the Gauche Révolutionnaire, 7 to the Bataille and 6 to the *Socialiste*.[53]

The balloting to fill these places was conducted at branch level in the fortnight ending 21 February, when the Federal Council formally registered the election of the members of the new committee.[54] In

Table 8. *Seine Federation, Federal Congress, 7 February 1938: division on general policy*

Motions	Mandates	Per cent of total
A (Gauche Révolutionnaire)	7,450	48.9
B (Bataille Socialiste)	4,087	26.8
C (*Le Socialiste*)	3,688	24.2
Total	15,225	

[52] The motions are printed, with lists of signatories, in Parti Socialiste (SFIO), Fédération de la Seine, *Commission des Résolutions émanée du Congrès Fédéral du 23 janvier 1938* [Paris, 1938]. The *Socialiste* also published its revised motion as a brochure with the title, *Pour le redressement du Parti dans la région parisienne* [Paris, 1938] (Archives de l'OURS).

[53] See *Le Temps*, 9 February 1938, p. 3; *Le Populaire*, 8 February 1938, p. 2.

[54] *Le Populaire*, 23 February 1938, p. 7.

accordance with the rules, this body then appointed the members of the Bureau (although Marceau Pivert had already taken over the post of Federal Secretary by at least 9 February)[55] and the new team took charge of the federation's headquarters at 7, rue Meslay, in the third *arrondissement.*[56] The composition of the full Bureau was as follows:[57]

1 *Statutory appointments*

Marceau Pivert	General (Federal) Secretary
André Weil-Curiel	Propaganda Secretary
René Cazanave	Administrative Secretary
Henri Goldschild	Treasurer
Georges Gillet	Deputy Treasurer

2 *Non-statutory appointments*

René Rul	Secretary for External Relations
Daniel Guérin	Secretary [for Amicales Socialistes]
Maurice Jaquier	[Deputy Secretary for Amicales Socialistes]

What were Marceau Pivert's intentions in February 1938? Where the Seine Federation was concerned, he undoubtedly wanted to consolidate the gains which he had made and to expand his support at the expense of the Bataille Socialiste, hemmed in on its other flank by the *Socialiste* grouping. Reflecting on the Federal Congress vote of 7 February, he wrote that:

Sans doute nous manquons de peu la MAJORITE ABSOLUE, et nous allons être placés par cela même dans une situation assez difficile. Mais cela ne nous inquiète en aucune manière, car nous savons que notre travail sera appuyé par la MAJORITE DYNAMIQUE REELLE de la Fédération et que toute tentative de sabotage de la vie fédérale sera facilement brisée.[58]

His first moves in the federation were confident and determined. As we have seen, he had put together a Bureau consisting entirely of his

---

[55] According to a convocation notice in ibid., 10 February 1938, p. 7.

[56] See Daniel Guérin, *Front Populaire: révolution manquée: témoignage militant* (François Maspero, Paris, new edition, 1976), p. 180; Maurice Jaquier, *Simple militant* (Denoël, Paris, 1974), p. 155.

[57] The appointment by the Executive Committee of all the members except Maurice Jaquier is reported in *Juin 36*, no. 2, 5–20 March 1938, p. 4. Guérin's post is described in this source as *secrétaire aux entreprises* but Guérin states that he was 'chargé des groupes socialistes d'entreprise' (*Front Populaire: révolution manquée*, p. 180). Jaquier must have been appointed subsequently, and evidently shared the responsibility for the Amicales Socialistes with Guérin (see letter from Charles Pivert to Albert Jamin, secretary to the party's Commission Nationale des Conflits, from Paris, 8 April 1938, *Le Populaire*, 18 April 1938, p. 5). See also *Les Cahiers Rouges*, special number, 22 April 1938, p. 3.

[58] 'Premiers résultats', *Les Cahiers Rouges*, no. 8, February 1938, pp. 2–3.

own close supporters, and his interest now clearly lay in anchoring that body to the Federal Council rather than the Executive Committee. While the political composition of the latter body had been set for the year, the Federal Council, if called into session at frequent intervals, could be used as a means of stimulating and organizing flows of opinion at the local level; it consisted of branch delegates appointed on the basis of a minimum of two for each branch and an additional representative for each hundred members (or a remainder of fifty or more) beyond the first 100, a formula which would favour the formation of substantial delegations from the large Parisian branches, such as Marceau Pivert's own stronghold in the 15th *arrondissement*. As a first step in their propaganda campaign, the federal leadership launched a new periodical, *Juin 36*, on 15 February under the editorship of Michel Collinet. Its first issue carried a reminder from the Propaganda Secretary that during March branch secretaries were to organize a public meeting devoted to nationalizations and the battle against the Senate.[59]

Its drive for control of the Seine Federation showed the Gauche Révolutionnaire behaving very much like 'a party within the party', appealing directly to branch opinion and striving to dominate institutions by weight of numbers, but Marceau Pivert and his lieutenants were at the same time still engaged in maintaining the covert network of supporters which had given the *tendance* so much of its striking power in the preceding year. Addressing the readers of the group's *Bulletin Intérieur*, Marceau Pivert wrote of the need to prepare for some form of crisis in the near future.

Notre mouvement se développe, mais les événements s'aggravent. Nous allons vers une exaspération des conflits de classe. Soyons prêts à faire face à toutes les éventualités: pour celà: deux conditions doivent être remplies à tout prix.
    1° Un échange incessant de nos réflexions politiques.
    2° Une amélioration constante de notre organisation socialiste.
Le moment s'approche en effet, où notre Parti Socialiste devra faire la preuve qu'il est autre chose qu'un assemblage de Comités électoraux ou qu'un troupeau affolé suivant aveuglément des pasteurs sans boussole.

In the meantime, he said that it was necessary to envisage the formation of large regions organizing their own internal liaison, exchanging speakers, and furthering contacts between the activists of the *tendance*. Such co-ordination would have been difficult to realize in the absence of a formal structure; since the ostensible dissolution of the Gauche Révolutionnaire by the Puteaux National Council of 18 April 1937, Marceau Pivert and his colleagues had not used membership cards, or

---

[59] *Juin 36*, no. 1, 15 February 1938, p. 4.

established a regular executive, or extended their publications beyond the *Cahiers Rouges*. However, they had maintained a shadow administration, whose existence Marceau Pivert acknowledged when he asked the readers of the *Bulletin Intérieur* to write to the following people regarding the topics indicated:

Georges Floutard	('Pour l'échange . . . De même vos projets de motion, suggestions politiques, etc. . . . ')
Georges Soulès	('pour toute contribution d'ordre *technique* à notre mouvement')
Jacques Enock	('pour la rédaction des Cahiers Rouges')
Anita Sauvage	('pour tout ce qui concerne la trésorerie, les souscriptions, les abonnements, le Comité des Cent . . . ')[60]

This suggests that Georges Floutard was the person expected to prepare positions for party occasions, such as a meeting of the National Council or a National Congress, that Georges Soulès was regarded as a technical expert where policy issues were concerned and that Jacques Enock was responsible for the editorship of the *Cahiers Rouges*. The tasks assigned to Anita Sauvage indicate that she was effectively the treasurer of the *tendance* at this stage, and that its financial resources were derived from donations, from subscriptions to the *Cahiers Rouges*, and from the fund of the Comité des Cent, whose members had either contributed a lump sum or had spread their payments in instalments over the year.[61]

At this time Marceau Pivert's writings and speeches were informed by an intense moralism through which differences of doctrine and outlook were frequently reduced to choices between good and evil. He offered his close companions the chance to join in a fellowship and thus to preserve their idealism while working for a party which had been corrupted by its pursuit of electoral success and office. As members of the fellowship, their duty was to support each other and prepare for the time when events would reveal the moral bankruptcy of the existing leadership and restore the party to its revolutionary form and purpose. This way of looking at the party made Pivert assume much too readily that the party's disciplinary procedures were being used to suppress legitimate dissent rather than to preserve respect for the party's rules. In circumstances which were later to cause him some embarrassment, he became involved in the case of Henri Mariette, a young man from

---

[60] *Bulletin Intérieur de la Gauche Révolutionnaire*, 20 February 1938, p. 3.
[61] The financial support received from the Comité des Cent is also referred to (all too briefly) by Degez, in *Les Cahiers Rouges*, special number, 22 April 1938, p. 5.

Tourlaville, near Cherbourg, who had been expelled from the youth group of the party's Manche Federation after having refused to apologize for propaganda which he and others had directed against Léon Blum and Marx Dormoy after the Puteaux National Council of 18 April 1937. Writing in terms which show familiarity with what had already happened, Marceau Pivert wrote to Mariette early in February 1938 to complain that he had given the 'bureaucrats' the means to exclude him from the party.

Je pense que, seule, l'expérience de la vie pourra te donner en cette circonstance une formation adaptée aux exigences de la lutte: l'essentiel est de trouver les méthodes de *liquidation du réformisme* et non de permettre la *liquidation de l'avant-garde* par lui.

Pivert asked Mariette to contact Lucien Weitz, who had been expelled from the youth group of the Seine Federation by the Puteaux National Council and who was then living in the 17th *arrondissement* of Paris.[62]

For all its emphasis on the need to bring about a revolution, the Gauche Révolutionnaire under Marceau Pivert's leadership was almost wholly preoccupied with the struggle against its opponents within the SFIO and it used every party meeting to attack them. Even before the battle for the Seine Federation had run its course, it was looking ahead to the next regular meeting of the National Council, which was to have been held on Sunday 27 March, and trying to gain support for its views on strategy. Once more the branches of the federation were presented with alternative motions about general policy. The Gauche Révolutionnaire and the Bataille Socialiste simply distributed the same texts which had been sent to the branches of the federation before the congress session of 7 February, but the *Socialiste* produced a revised motion, with more doctrinal content than its earlier document. A comparison of these three texts shows the extent to which the *tendances* were treating each other as quite separate units, differentiated from each other not only by divergent views about party strategy but also by disagreements about basic issues of doctrine and party philosophy.

The Gauche Révolutionnaire, in its text, depicted France as undergoing a crisis which had dislocated the parliamentary Popular Front and had created 'un fossé grandissant entre les états-majors des partis bourgeois républicains et les masses populaires'. It wanted acknowledgement that the new Chautemps ministry was not a Popular Front

---

[62] Letter from Marceau Pivert to Henri Mariette, 2 February 1938, in ibid., p. 4. For the background to the case, see the account by Le Corre, then Federal Secretary of the Manche Federation, in Parti Socialiste (SFIO), 35ᵉ Congrès National, Royan, 4–7 juin 1938, *Compte rendu sténographique* (Librairie Populaire, Paris, n.d.), pp. 107–8.

government but one of Union Nationale and a prelude to a Union
Sacrée. Accordingly, it called for the condemnation of the decision of
the parliamentary group to support the government and proposed that
a national congress should be convened as soon as possible. In the field
of foreign affairs, it attacked what it described as the policy of *deux
blocs* (that is, one of constructing an alliance of democratic states to
balance the power of Germany and Italy), denounced non-intervention
in Spain, and, in domestic politics, called for such measures as the
nationalization of key industries, banks and large firms; for controls on
foreign exchange and prices, and for a state monopoly over external
trade. Without actually using the term *front révolutionnaire*, the text
proposed a strategy which would have entailed a break with the middle
classes and the Radicals; it envisaged the party leading a mass movement while strengthening action not only with the Communist Party and
the CGT but also with 'les groupements démocratiques qui se refusent à
capituler devant les banques et la réaction'. The objective of such unity
of action was described as:

la liquidation de toute collaboration de classes et la constitution d'un Parti
unique capable de se déterminer lui-même grâce à la libre circulation intérieure
de tous les courants d'opinion révolutionnaires et au droit pour les minorités à
l'existence, à l'expression et à la représentation à tous les degrés.

This text alluded frequently to general and abstract issues of strategy
and orientation. One of its themes was that the party had made a mistake by persevering with the Popular Front and that it should return to
its earlier position of refusing to share in the management of the bourgeois state. At one point, it referred to the 'Charte Constitutive du
Parti et à sa mission historique', an obvious evocation of the Guesdiste
tradition of refusing to take part in the compromises of parliamentary
politics. But its second major theme, that it was possible to create a
revolutionary movement through mass action and to absorb the existing
party and trade-union organizations into a unitary party, drew upon the
voluntarist theories of the Blanquistes and the Luxemburgistes. In this
way the Gauche Révolutionnaire blended anti-participationism with
revolutionary activism, challenging both the established leadership of
the SFIO and, indirectly, that of the Communist Party.[63]

In contrast, the text produced by the Bataille Socialiste remained
firmly within the context of Popular Front rhetoric, assuming that further progress would depend upon the continued collaboration of the

[63] 'Motion pour le Congrès extraordinaire du 7 février 1938 et pour le Conseil National
du 27 mars 1938', Supplement to *Les Cahiers Rouges*, no. 6, December 1937; no. 7,
January 1938.

Socialists, the Communists and the CGT and upon a disciplined expression of mass solidarity within that collaboration. Although the motion expressed dissatisfaction with the Chautemps government and proposed that the parliamentary group should bring it to an end at a favourable opportunity, it apparently assumed that the next government could and should be 'l'expression fidèle du Front Populaire', that is, one under the leadership of the SFIO, the Communist Party and the CGT and also containing 'les partis de démocratie fidèles à leur tradition historique' (presumably the Radicals). It sketched out the tasks for such a government (including the introduction of old-age pensions, a national unemployment fund, and further nationalizations) without raising the question of whether the Socialist Party should revert to an opposition role. It envisaged such a ministry being a 'gouvernement de combat' based upon 'le vaste mouvement antifasciste qui s'exprime par de puissantes démonstrations des forces populaires', but it clearly did not consider such a movement to have an insurrectionary character. Regarding foreign policy, it combined conventional appeals for collective security and arms control with proposals for an alignment of the 'puissances démocratiques et pacifistes du monde' against the effronteries of fascism and for effective and immediate aid to the Republican side in the Spanish Civil War. Finally, it pleaded for the formation of a single party of the working class and for the resumption of negotiations between the Socialist and Communist Parties towards that end.[64]

Whereas the motion of the Gauche Révolutionnaire was essentially an appeal for undirected activism, aimed at a revolutionary insurrection, the text of the Bataille Socialiste affirmed the need for – and specified – a general line which the party could follow, and took for granted that its organization would impose the discipline needed to carry that line into effect. Although it criticized the decision of the parliamentary group to support the Chautemps government, it did not question the wisdom of the Popular Front strategy. The main sign of dissidence in the text lay in its insistence that the aim of fusion with the Communist Party was still feasible, and this at a time when Paul Faure and the central secretariat still considered that the talks had broken down irrevocably.

The *Socialiste* group, hitherto reluctant to debate issues of principle, now produced a motion which justified its strategic proposals on the grounds of doctrine. Its preamble was based on the theme that the time was not yet ripe for revolution:

---

[64] 'Notre résolution pour le Conseil National du 27 mars', *La Bataille Socialiste* (Paris), no. 107, February 1938, p. 1.

Les événements des deux dernières années confirment ce que le socialisme a toujours affirmé depuis la guerre: l'ordre social existant, grièvement atteint, s'épuise en vains efforts de redressement. Mais ils confirment aussi la thèse marxiste selon laquelle la réalisation du socialisme est conditionnée par une maturité suffisante de l'économie et du prolétariat, la seconde étant d'ailleurs fonction de la première. Ces deux éléments sont aujourd'hui en train de se créer, mais ils n'existent encore que partiellement.

Dans ces conditions, il incombe au Parti Socialiste de définir, à chaque étape de l'évolution en cours, les objectifs immédiatement réalisables tant sous l'angle de ce que la situation économique peut donner que sous celui des rapports des forces sociales en présence.

It credited the reforms of the summer of 1936 to the alliance of the proletariat and the middle classes and claimed that these reforms could be defended and enlarged only by means of that same alliance:

Il s'agit donc de maintenir et de consolider le Front populaire, expression politique de cette alliance.

Having thus justified the decision to provide temporary support to the Chautemps government, the *Socialiste* claimed that 'l'immense majorité du pays républicain' nevertheless wanted a government under Socialist leadership, and it set out in some detail the programme which it would have to realize, mentioning many of the proposals favoured by the Bataille, such as old-age pensions, a national unemployment fund, and reforms of structure. It also dealt with questions of foreign policy, advocating general disarmament, collective security, confidence in the League of Nations, the tightening of agreements with America, Britain and Czechoslovakia, maintenance of the Franco-Soviet pact, and support for the Republican government in Spain. It approved the decision of the CAP to break off talks with the Communist Party about the possibility of organic unity but nevertheless acknowledged the desirability of unity of action between the Socialist and Communist Parties.

The issue of the *Socialiste* which carried this text also set out the differences between its position and those contained in the motions of the other two groups. It accused the Bataille Socialiste of wanting organic unity with the Communists at any price, of placing an absolute confidence in the masses and therefore of underestimating the value of parliamentary action; of being frightened by the responsibility of government; and of proposing to bring down the Chautemps government without sufficient regard for the consequences. In much stronger terms, it accused the authors of the Gauche Révolutionnaire text of behaving like 'les agents d'intérêts autres que ceux du socialisme'; of trying to link up with people who had been expelled from the party and with Trotskyist and Leninist–Bolshevist groups; of wanting to take over the party; and of preferring violent methods to that of democracy.

Ils tiennent l'étape de Front Populaire pour dépassée par les événements. 'Le Front Populaire, écrivent-ils, est mort; vive le Front Révolutionnaire.' Ils orientent donc leur propagande vers des fins autres que celles que le Parti s'est données; ils tirent en direction différente.

Such an approach, the *Socialiste* argued, would weaken the proletariat and isolate it from the middle and peasant classes, thus creating conditions which would favour the victory of fascism and an intensification of 'l'action de classe du capitalisme'. By making such claims, the *Socialiste* presented itself as the only one of the three *tendances* which was attached to the party's traditions, and implied that its two rivals had drifted towards the margins of credibility, where the Bataille Socialiste had adopted a policy 'de conformisme stalinien, d'unité à tout prix, d'immobilisme et d'abdication devant le Parti Communiste' and where the Gauche Révolutionnaire was intent on breaking up the Popular Front while dividing, isolating and weakening the proletarian movement.[65]

In a similar exercise, the *Bataille Socialiste* also analysed the differences between the texts. It criticized the *Socialiste* for attaching too little importance to mass action and too much to participation in government and in parliament, and also for resisting the idea of unity of action with the Communists. These were fairly mild complaints and amounted to no more than a studied contrast of varying judgements about the nature of the Popular Front and about what means were best suited to keeping it in being, but it showed little restraint in its attack on the text of the Gauche Révolutionnaire. It claimed that the strategy of a revolutionary front would isolate the proletariat from its natural allies, weaken the working class, and divide and fragment 'l'action du mouvement prolétarien'. More significantly, it virtually accused the Gauche Révolutionnaire of scorning the party's conventions for the expression of differences by subordinating the interests of the party to those of a *tendance* and of having the intention to dominate the party.[66]

Thus, by a twofold process of self-definition and the hostile characterization of opponents, the three *tendances* were moving steadily along the line of development from fluid bodies of opinion towards coherent and stable groupings, with sharply differentiated doctrinal positions. With varying emphases, the *Socialiste* and the Bataille had both

---

[65] *Le Socialiste* (special edition, Paris), [February 1938].
[66] *La Bataille Socialiste*, no. 107, February 1938, p. 2. See also Jean Zyromski, 'Notre politique', ibid., pp. 1–2.

appealed to the Popular Front mythology (with its central epic of how the working class, the middle classes and the peasantry had formed a social alliance to take power, carry out reforms and defend the Republic against fascism) in order to buttress their claims that both the social and party alliances should be preserved. They differed in their assessment of the value of the Chautemps ministry and in their views about the Communist Party and about mass action, but they were agreed on the importance of the Popular Front strategy under prevailing circumstances. The Gauche Révolutionnaire, on the other hand, had virtually abandoned the Popular Front ideal and had turned elsewhere; appealing to the powerful myth that the party had been founded for a revolutionary purpose in 1905, it saw that purpose as having been ignored not by the working class but by the party and trade-union organizations which claimed to represent it, and maintained that a return to the masses would restore both the coherence and the will of the revolutionary movement. The revolutionary front idea was linked to the notion that a spontaneous uprising would cause the collapse of the bourgeois order and it thus evoked the central myth of the Blanquiste, Luxemburgiste and Trotskyist traditions. By alluding freely to ideas from so many contexts the Gauche Révolutionnaire was attempting to create the impression that it was not a prisoner of any orthodoxy, but rather that it was above the fray, and that it therefore valued activism for its own sake, and not as the servant of a predetermined strategy. Its rhetoric implied an ethic which was at once individualistic, libertarian and voluntarist and it portrayed the SFIO's bureaucrats as the enemies of theoretical inspiration and spontaneity in action.

In these respects, the texts of the Gauche Révolutionnaire were strongly sectarian in content. The group was asking for support not on the basis of a detailed programme nor, as would a faction, on the basis of specific transactions; it was addressing activists as if it were a radical sect within an established religion. Like such a sect, it was claiming that the orthodox leaders had departed from the true faith and that, because of this, the grounds of belief had been obscured and betrayed. Its rhetoric was intended not so much to convert unbelievers as to strengthen the conviction of believers and by this means to restore the true faith, sweeping aside the established order in the process; moreover, it was designed to set in motion flows of anxiety within the whole body of believers, to play upon their doubts and misgivings about recent events, and finally to inspire the great rally which would restore the religion to its pure, pristine state. Only then would it be possible to welcome back those exiles who had kept alive the true faith in isolated communities and to undo past schisms. In the manner of such a sect, the Gauche

Révolutionnaire claimed that its purity would show up the impurity of the party as a whole and thus prepare the way for a moral transformation.

Measured against the motions prepared for earlier occasions, such as the Marseille Congress of July 1937, these three texts reveal important shifts of position by the two dissident *tendances*, but the most significant change had been the replacement of the 'official' statement of the leadership's views, such as the Blum–Faure resolution adopted at Marseille, by the motion of the *Socialiste*, a group which had now acquired many of the characteristics of a *tendance*, such as a preoccupation with issues of doctrine and general strategy and a disposition to treat conflicts within the party as matters of great importance. Furthermore, the new *tendance* had situated itself in the Guesdiste sector of party opinion, and thus separated itself from those members of the central leadership who were close to Blum and who shared his evident, though understated, radical republicanism and his willingness to work with the progressive wing of the Radical Party. At this stage, these men were prepared to consider that the centre right could be associated with the Popular Front majority in a coalition ministry of the kind which Blum had proposed in January, and they were also inclined to the view that participation in government was something which Socialists should value for its own sake and not as a temporary expedient. These questions had not been discussed seriously in the *motions de tendance* but, in an article published in *Le Populaire* on 19 February, Marx Dormoy argued that neither a bipartite coalition of Socialists and Radicals nor a tripartite one of Socialists, Radicals and Communists was a possibility, for a while at least, and that Blum's idea of a cabinet extending from Thorez to Reynaud could soon become topical ('être bientôt d'actualité').[67]

The formula, from Thorez to Reynaud, had been accepted in Socialist circles as a sign for an unstated fourth position, distinct from those of the three *tendances*, and was treated with caution, almost as if it were a kind of land-mine. This was probably because the reasoning behind the formula had not been fully justified either at the National Council of 17 January or in the Socialist press and also because it was so difficult to distinguish from two other propositions, first, that a reversal of majorities would occur in the middle of the parliamentary term as the Radicals were drawn inexorably towards the centre right and, secondly, that exceptional circumstances, such as a financial or an international

[67] Marx Dormoy, 'A propos de la formule "de Thorez à Paul Reynaud" ', *Le Populaire*, 19 February 1938, pp. 1 and 2.

crisis, would require the formation of a national union, encompassing practically all parties in the Chamber of Deputies. Some federations ignored the fourth position altogether and simply concentrated on the latter possibilities; thus, on 26 February the Administrative Commission of the Nord Federation declared against any extension of the existing majority, noting that:

toute tentative de modifier la majorité de Front populaire sortie des élections législatives de 1936, en y faisant entrer des groupes du centre d'abord, puis de la droite, sous prétexte d'union nationale nécessaire, serait la fin non seulement de la majorité sur laquelle s'appuyèrent les deux premiers gouvernements Blum et Chautemps, mais du mouvement de Rassemblement populaire lui-même.[68]

On the other hand, the Federal Bureau of the Côte-d'Or Federation acknowledged the existence of the fourth position by deciding, at its meeting on 27 February, that a vote at branch level on the three *motions de tendance* should be accompanied by a survey of responses to three questions, first, whether the party should agree to participation in or support for a government claiming to represent the Popular Front (without being constructed in its image) and basing its policy on the programme of 1936; secondly, whether the party should take part in a government which was fully representative of the Popular Front and whose programme included the policy proposals made by the Marseille Congress of July 1937; and, thirdly, whether the party should accept a government stretching from Thorez to Reynaud.[69]

The party's leaders were caught in a dilemma: if they wanted to share in government once more, they would probably have to accept the need for an extension of the parliamentary majority to the centre right, but the party was unlikely to approve such a change in policy; on the other hand, if they agreed that the party should revert to an opposition role, they would soon find themselves under pressure from the Communists and from the dissident *tendances* to form a new social movement aimed at taking power by agitational means. In the meantime anxiety and alarm were eroding their support in the provincial federations. Justin Arnol, a deputy and a prominent figure in the Isère Federation, touched on the psychological aspect of this process when he warned that *l'esprit critique* of the activists could have a harmful effect:

le mal est que la critique, parfois, tue la réflexion. Les craintes, les angoisses font alors naître des courants dangereux au sein du socialisme, pour le social-isme lui-même. Des formules dangereuses, parce que séduisantes, circulent

[68] *La Bataille* (Lille), 6 March 1938, p. 1.
[69] *Le Socialiste Côte-d'Orien*, no. 223, 5 March 1938, pp. 1 and 2.

dans nos sections. On est las du Front populaire? Vive le 'Front révolutionnaire!'[70]

The basic problem facing the leaders was that the projected meeting of the National Council on 27 March was being treated as a dress rehearsal for the impending National Congress. The publicity given to the *motions de tendance* had persuaded some provincial federations to hold federal congresses so that their delegates to the National Council could be given fresh instructions, and the CAP therefore decided to relieve this pressure by specifying that the meeting, when it came to general business, would be asked to discuss 'la situation du Parti', with reports from the delegates of the federations, rather than 'la situation politique intérieure et extérieure', which would have been more of an invitation to a general debate and the consideration of motions. In a circular to the federations explaining this decision, Paul Faure said that the change in form was intended as a reminder that the National Council was not a national congress and that federations were not bound to hold a federal congress for each meeting of the National Council.[71]

Such procedural adjustments were unlikely to have much effect. By the end of February 1938 it had become clear that the leaders' ability to win an absolute majority of the mandates at national meetings of delegates had been severely weakened and that of the two dissident *tendances* it was the Gauche Révolutionnaire which was the better placed to exploit dissatisfaction with the policy of supporting the Chautemps government in power.

The National Council meeting of 12 March 1938 and the formation of the second Blum government

By the second week of March 1938 the conditions for another ministerial crisis were already present. A decline in economic activity had placed an inevitable strain on public finances and Paul Marchandeau, the Minister of Finance, was obliged to warn Chautemps that impending Treasury deadlines could not be met unless remedial action were taken without delay. Having formed the view that the government would need power to enact measures by decree, under the customary delegation of authority by parliament, on Monday 7 March Chautemps consulted Léon Blum, who had been absent from Paris for several weeks following the death of his second wife, Thérèse, on 22 January.[72] On Tuesday the

---

[70] Justin Arnol, 'Le front révolutionnaire', *Le Populaire*, 9 February 1938, p. 4.
[71] *La Bataille* (Lille), 6 March 1938, p. 1.
[72] Camille Chautemps, *Cahiers secrets de l'Armistice (1939–1940)* (Plon, Paris, 1963), pp. 36–7.

8th the government issued a communiqué suggesting that it was necessary that all essential measures should be taken to set right public finances and the economy, and that parliament should be requested to provide the means to carry this out. This was interpreted to mean that the government would ask for special powers and for the postponement of further social reforms. After a meeting of the Délégation des Gauches had failed to produce an agreement on how the parties of the Popular Front should respond to this announcement, the Socialist parliamentary group took its own decision to inform Chautemps that the proposed policies were incompatible with undertakings which the government had given on taking office,[73] thus signifying that the Socialist deputies would not vote for the programme were it to be submitted to the Chamber for approval. Faced with what amounted to a withdrawal of support, the Cabinet decided on Wednesday the 9th that the members of the government should submit their resignations to the President but, acting on the advice of Herriot, the President of the Chamber, Chautemps agreed first to address the Chamber on Thursday the 10th, though without calling for a vote.[74]

In his report to the Chamber on the morning of the 10th, Chautemps pointed out that the recent creation of a National Defence Fund had made it essential to ensure that the Treasury had adequate resources. He also explained why the need to take urgent financial measures obliged him to ask for complete confidence in his government, for special powers, and for a temporary postponement of legislation to introduce old-age pensions and family allowances in rural areas, and spoke of applying more flexibly the regulations governing the 40-hour week in order to increase production, especially in defence industries. He then appealed to the groups of the Popular Front majority to give him their support but there was no response.[75] He and his ministers then went from the house to the Elysée Palace and there submitted their resignations to the President, who later called upon Léon Blum to form a government.

Blum immediately set out to construct a tripartite ministry containing Socialists, Radicals and Communists. To avoid misunderstandings of the kind which had arisen in January, he asked Daladier whether the Radicals would be willing to take part in such a government. When the Radicals sought information about the programme of the proposed

---

[73] See 'Rapport sur l'activité du groupe socialiste au parlement', Parti Socialiste (SFIO), 35e Congrès National, Royan, 4–7 juin 1938, *Rapports*, pp. 321–2; *La Vie du Parti*, no. 79, 3 May 1938, p. 316; *Le Populaire*, 10 March 1938, p. 1.
[74] Chautemps, *Cahiers secrets de l'Armistice*, p. 37.
[75] *JO (CD)*, *Déb.*, 10 March 1938, pp. 815–18.

administration, especially in the fields of financial and international policy, Blum refused to be drawn; he maintained that the governmental programme of the Popular Front had been drawn up with the help of four political parties and that the matter to be settled was which of them would collaborate to carry it into effect.[76]

That was how matters stood at noon on Friday 11 March, with the various political leaders and groups testing out established positions rather than trying to take new ground. Chautemps had brought the basic policy conflict out into the open without throwing the Popular Front alliance into disarray; he had demonstrated before the Chamber that he could not increase the resources needed for defence expenditure without taking steps to balance the budget, but he had not gone to the length of calling for a vote of confidence, a move which could have caused the groups of the centre right and the right to place pressure on the Radicals to change sides. For his part, Blum had moved more carefully than he had done in January, and had established at an early stage in the discussions that, unless there were a prior agreement on policy, the Radicals were reluctant to join in a government with the Communists. If the Radicals did reject his proposal, he would be forced either to resign his commission or to explore the prospects for various other combinations, such as a bipartite ministry of Socialists and Radicals or even a broad-based coalition of the 'Thorez to Reynaud' type. In the circumstances then obtaining, he would probably have resigned his commission, and the familiar sequence of events would have been set in motion: the choice of a Radical leader, possibly Daladier, as Premier-designate; an offer to the Socialists of participation in a bipartite coalition; an extraordinary meeting of the SFIO's National Council to consider that offer; a decision by the Socialists to refuse participation; and the formation of another Radical government claiming to represent the Popular Front majority.

However, events took a quite different turn, for on the afternoon of Friday 11 March news reached Paris that Austria was under heavy pressure to agree to a union with Germany. The peace settlement of 1919 had been designed to confine Germany within strict territorial limits, and both the Treaty of Saint-Germain and the Treaty of Versailles had prohibited any joining together (*anschluss*) of Germany and Austria, except with the approval of the League of Nations. In 1920 Austria had adopted a federal constitution and laid the foundations for a liberal parliamentary system, but a political crisis in 1933–4 had ended in the

[76] Letter from Léon Blum to Edouard Daladier, 11 March 1938 (*Le Populaire*, 12 March 1938, p. 2).

abolition of democratic institutions and the promulgation of a corporatist constitution. While the country's internal politics were dominated by a tension between a strong Socialist movement, centred mainly on Vienna and the towns, and a conservative, largely Roman Catholic tradition, the National Socialist Party had also built up a following, and after the assassination on 25 July 1934 of the Chancellor, Engelbert Dollfuss, during an attempted Nazi *putsch*, his successor, Kurt von Schuschnigg, found it increasingly difficult to resist the combined pressure of Germany and the Austrian Nazis. As a result of a meeting with Hitler at Berchtesgaden on 12 February 1938, Schuschnigg admitted Arthur Seyss-Inquart, a Nazi sympathizer, to his government as Minister of the Interior, an appointment which increased fears that Germany was about to overrun Austria.

France, Britain and Italy had affirmed their joint interest in maintaining Austrian independence by signing the Stresa agreement of 14 April 1935, and Germany itself had recognized the sovereignty of Austria in a joint agreement of 11 July 1936. Subsequently, Germany had steadily increased its influence over its neighbour while at the same time consolidating its ties with Italy, now at odds with France and Britain because of its invasion of Abyssinia and its support for the nationalist side in the Spanish Civil War. By the time of the Berchtesgaden conversation some form of anschluss seemed almost inevitable, but France and Britain made no formal commitments to Austria. On 9 March 1938 Schuschnigg took a stand against Germany by announcing that a plebiscite would be held on Sunday 13th on the issue of independence, but on 11 March he received an ultimatum from Hitler instructing him to cancel the original plebiscite and arrange for one to be held at a later date. This Schuschnigg agreed to do but he was immediately faced with German demands for his resignation. Hoping to appease Germany, he gave way and announced his decision to leave office in a radio broadcast at 7.30 p.m. on 11 March, with the result that Seyss-Inquart was appointed Chancellor in his place in the late evening. On the 12th, Austria was effectively occupied by German troops and on the 13th the anschluss was proclaimed.[77]

That Germany would move at some stage to incorporate Austria into its territory had been considered likely for some time, and early reports of the Berchtesgaden conversation had simply strengthened an existing expectation.[78] The anschluss had been awaited not so much as a self-

---

[77] On the events leading up to this crisis, see Alan Bullock, *Hitler: A Study in Tyranny* (Penguin, London, revised edition, 1962, reprinted 1990), pp. 420–39.
[78] Many speakers had referred to the seriousness of the situation in central Europe during the extensive debate on foreign policy in the Chamber of Deputies at the end of

contained episode but as the first in an inevitable chain of events which would unsettle the whole of eastern Europe. Those who credited Hitler with a definite plan of expansion had formed the view that the absorption of Austria would be followed by German campaigns to seize first Czechoslovakia and later Poland. Until 11 March such predictions were made with reference to an indefinite future, but now that the Austrian crisis had come and gone the problem of protecting Czechoslovakia became a pressing concern.

With so much at stake, a move to form a national union, an alliance embracing most, if not all, of the French political parties, was only to be expected. Blum must have been aware of this but he was not prepared to see the Popular Front drawn into such a combination without adequate safeguards; instead he proposed 'un rassemblement national autour du Front populaire', that is, a combination in which the Popular Front would remain in being as a parliamentary majority while the groups of the centre right and the right were built around it, like a shell around an inner core. He was to claim that:

il est nécessaire de montrer que l'unité française n'est pas la destruction du rassemblement populaire, de sa majorité et de son programme, que les deux choses sont parvenues à se combiner l'une à l'autre ou que l'une s'est organisée autour de l'autre.[79]

Reasoning in such terms, he was able to deny that he was proposing either a Union Nationale or a Union Sacrée, both of which would normally imply the same rights for all the contracting parties and the removal of distinctions between former majorities and minorities. For this very reason, the parliamentary groups of the centre right and the right were bound to find Blum's scheme difficult to accept, both because they would be treated as a minority and also because the combination would not be based on an agreement between all the parties concerned regarding future policies.

On the afternoon of Friday 11 March, Blum asked Paul Faure to convene an extraordinary meeting of the SFIO's National Council for the morning of the 12th, having confided that his aim was to gain approval for his scheme, first from the Socialists, then from other groups of the majority (that is, the Radicals and the Communists) and, finally, from the opposition parties. According to Blum, Faure then gave him the following warning:

February (see *JO* (*CD*), *Déb.*, 25 February 1938, pp. 571–84, 586–602 and 604–16; 26 February 1938, pp. 623–35, 637–55 and 655–8).
[79] Ibid., 17 March 1938, p. 839.

Ecoutez, mon cher ami, moi je n'ose pas vous donner un pareil conseil. Quelque confiance que le Parti puisse avoir en vous, il ne vous suivra pas, et vous allez sans utilité, sans résultat pratique possible, gaspiller encore un peu du compte positif, du compte créditeur que vous aviez dans ses livres.

Blum replied that he believed that it was his duty to go ahead,[80] but he must have reckoned on the possibility of failure. He told only a few close friends, including Auriol and Sérol, about his intentions,[81] and there is an interesting echo of Faure's credit metaphor in a remark which Blum made to Louis Marin, a conservative leader, on the morning of the 12th:

Les uns et les autres, nous vivons généralement dans nos partis sur le capital de confiance que nous avons accumulé par de longues années de dévouement et de services. Puis, il arrive que, sur ce compte créditeur, on soit obligé d'opérer de gros prélèvements et, quand il a fallu tirer trop souvent, on s'aperçoit un jour que le compte est nivelé et qu'il est même devenu débiteur.[82]

Blum was using his credit within the party to gain acceptance for two important changes, one in strategy and the other in foreign policy. Where strategy was concerned, he was now prepared to go much further in defining what we have called 'the fourth position', and to translate the simple and ambiguous phrase, 'from Thorez to Reynaud', into a considered proposal for a qualified alliance with the groups on the centre right and the right of the Chamber, implicitly admitting that the parliamentary majority of the Popular Front could not now provide an adequate foundation for a strong national government. He was also taking a new line towards the European crisis. In the past, one of the things which had endeared Blum to his party had been his pacifism. From 1920 onwards, he had argued that the League of Nations would become an increasingly effective support for a comprehensive system of collective security, for a programme of general disarmament, and for the subsequent control of levels of military strength. Working on

---

[80] Parti Socialiste (SFIO), 35ᵉ Congrès National, Royan, 4–7 juin 1938, *Compte rendu sténographique*, p. 516. Maurice Deixonne referred to this reported conversation in his pamphlet, *La Vérité sur la scission de Royan* (Imprimerie du Cantal, Aurillac, 1938), pp. 49–50, and thus provoked Blum to deny that Faure had advised him to ignore the National Council ('Une étonnante erreur', *Le Populaire*, 9 July 1938, p. 1). See also Deixonne's reply in ibid., 9 August 1938, p. 5.

[81] See Blum's speech to the opposition deputies on 12 March 1938, in Blum, *L'Oeuvre de Léon Blum, 1937–1940*, p. 71; and his reference to the occasion at the Royan Congress, in Parti Socialiste (SFIO), 35ᵉ Congrès National, Royan, 4–7 juin 1938, *Compte rendu sténographique*, pp. 132–3.

[82] Blum's speech to the opposition deputies on 12 March 1938, in Blum, *L'Oeuvre de Léon Blum, 1937–1940*, p. 75.

the theory that the essential cause of the First World War had been the competition between two great alliances, each trying to outweigh the other, he had strongly criticized any attempt by French statesmen to return to the balance-of-power strategy and to the practice of military pacts. Although he had been prepared to accept that the relations which had been forged between France and the countries of eastern Europe, and its understandings with Britain and the Soviet Union, were compatible with a system of collective security, by the end of 1937 he could see that this system was breaking down, partly because of the failure of the League to prevent the Italian conquest of Abyssinia, partly because the great powers were simply trying to contain individual crises instead of acting to prevent war, and partly because the rise of Hitler and the progress of German rearmament had altered the European situation for the worse.[83] Even so, he had not prepared his fellow Socialists for the perspectives which the imminent anschluss had opened up for France, and they could justifiably have claimed that a party which had supported the ideal of collective security should not now be considering a proposal for a national government and acting as though the country were on the verge of war. The position of Faure, one of the leading figures in the pacifist movement during the First World War, was unclear: for the moment, he was behind Blum, but his convictions would set limits beyond which his loyalty, and that of his followers, could not be taken for granted.

When Blum met his party's National Council on the morning of the 12th, he explained that he wanted to form, not a Union Sacrée, but 'un rassemblement national autour du Front populaire pour empêcher la guerre et pour protéger les institutions'. There was, as we have seen, much more to this proposal than met the eye, but Paul Faure asked that a decision should be taken quickly, presumably to give Blum as much time as possible for his discussions with the Radicals, the Communists and the groups of the opposition. Zyromski then appealed to the delegates to give Blum the powers he was requesting and, despite the opposition of Lucien Hérard, within two hours the council had decided by a four-fifths majority to express complete confidence in Blum.[84] The detailed result is given in Table 9.

The distribution of mandates in this division is similar to that for the second division at the National Council meeting of 17 January 1938, when the Graziani text had been approved. In each case the 'official'

---

[83] See [Blum], 'Le recul', *Le Populaire*, 16 August 1937, p. 1.
[84] See *Le Populaire*, 13 March 1938, p. 6; Parti Socialiste (SFIO), 35ᵉ Congrès National, Royan, 4–7 juin 1938, *Rapports*, pp. 47–8; *La Vie du Parti*, no. 79, 3 May 1938, p. 315.

Table 9. *SFIO: National Council, 12 March 1938: division on motion expressing confidence in Léon Blum*

Federations	Mandates: For the motion no.	%	Against the motion no.	%	Abstentions no.	%	Absent no.	%	Totals no.
Bouches-du-Rhône	315	100.0							315
Gironde			186	100.0					186
Meurthe-et-Moselle	35	22.7	119	77.3					154
Nord	764	99.6	3	0.4					767
Pas-de-Calais	347	98.9	4	1.1					351
Seine	323	51.1	309	48.9					632
Seine-et-Oise	224	63.8	127	36.2					351
Haute-Vienne	100	59.9	67	40.1					167
Others	4,452	82.8	884	16.4	13	0.2	27	0.5	5,376
Totals	6,560	79.0	1,699	20.5	13	0.2	27	0.3	8,299

Source: La Vie du Parti (Paris), no. 79, 3 May 1938, p. 315.

motion was passed by a substantial majority made up of loyalist and Bataille Socialiste mandates aligned against a small minority consisting mainly of mandates associated with the Gauche Révolutionnaire. The composition of the votes on either side in the January ballot did not change significantly in the March ballot; the slight increase in the size of the opposition vote – from 1,334 to 1,699 – was not accompanied by much movement between the columns, the net increase of 365 mandates being the product of 557 gains and 192 losses on the opposition account. However, close examination of the votes of individual federations indicates that some delegates holding Bataille mandates had not followed Zyromski's lead in supporting the 'official' motion as they had done in January, and that his *tendance* was fraying at the edges.

The brevity of the debate at the meeting on 12 March makes it difficult to explain why certain delegates broke ranks; in the case of Robert Vielle, representing the Gironde Federation, however, his motives for independent action were firm and well considered. At the previous meeting of the National Council, on 17 January, he had allocated most of his federation's mandates on the first ballot to the motion of the Bataille Socialiste and the remainder to that of the Gauche Révolutionnaire, and had routinely cast the Bataille mandates for the Graziani motion on the second ballot. In preparing for the meeting of the National Council which was to have been held on 27 March, however, he and other members of his federation's Administrative Committee decided that, rather than endorsing one of the *motions de tendance* which were then in circulation, they would draft their own resolution for consideration by the branches, and eventually by a meeting of their Federal Council. Their published text expressed opposition to the idea of a Union Nationale or any similar formula, called for an extension of the reform programme of the Popular Front, favoured support for the Chautemps ministry (which was then still in office) only to the extent that it remained faithful to the spirit and programme of the Rassemblement Populaire, and expressed their preference for a true Popular Front government under Socialist leadership. In general terms, therefore, Vielle and his team had rejected any formula of government other than that associated with the Popular Front, and had taken up a position on domestic policy which was midway between those set out in the current motions of the *Socialiste* and the Bataille Socialiste. Although they had written their text before the anschluss, they had taken a distinctive stand on foreign policy; arguing that 'le but essentiel de l'action du Rassemblement populaire et du Parti socialiste est de sauver la paix', they claimed that France should take the lead in making a proposal to governments and peoples for peace and controlled disarmament along with a study of world-wide economic reorganization.[85] By so doing, they had placed themselves in opposition to the Bataille, which was emphasizing the need for firm action against Germany and Italy, having become increasingly sceptical that concessions to those countries would reduce the risk of war. When summoned to Paris to attend the National Council meeting of 12 March, Vielle had had no time to consult his colleagues before his departure but he felt sure enough of his ground to vote against the motion of confidence. After his return to Bordeaux, he justified the action he had taken before a meeting of the federation's Administrative Committee on 14 March.

Il donne un compte rendu très détaillé de ce qu'il a observé et fait revivre pour les membres de la C. A. les problèmes qui ont été invoqués. Il indique les raisons du vote qu'il a émis et croit être resté dans les termes des indications qu'il avait formulé et qu'il avait précisé dans le projet de motion.[86]

The loyalist vote had remained solid in this ballot partly because Blum's own credit with the party was good, partly because he still enjoyed Paul Faure's support, and partly because loyalist delegates were still inclined to vote as they had been instructed by their federal congresses. Nevertheless, the fact remained that Blum, in his vigorous response to the anschluss crisis, had taken up an exposed position within his party; in particular, he had shown that he was prepared to contemplate arrangements, however limited, with groups on the right of the party spectrum, and that he was prepared to think in terms of national resistance to the threat of German expansion, a course of action which implied the need for increased defence expenditure and for a policy of alliances and territorial guarantees. In making these choices, he had challenged the views of many party members who were deeply attached to the Popular Front and to pacifism. For the moment, however, he had the support of the Bataille Socialiste – a mixed blessing. Zyromski was strongly attached to the idea of an alliance of Britain, France and the Soviet Union in order to prevent the expansion of Germany and Italy, and he would therefore have seen Blum's proposal for a national government as a step in the right direction. After the event, his journal claimed that there had been no change of course so far as the *tendance* was concerned:

Dans le domaine intérieur, depuis la victoire du Front populaire, la 'Bataille' s'était cramponnée à un mot d'ordre auquel il lui paraissait nécessaire d'obéir si l'on voulait éviter le découragement des masses: *tout faire contre la concentration et l'Union nationale.* C'est encore cet objectif que Jean Zyromski avait

---

[85] For the text, see *Le Populaire Girondin* (Bordeaux), no. 218, 11 March 1938, p. 2.
[86] Ibid., no. 219, 18 March 1938, p. 2.

devant les yeux, quand il s'est rallié à la formule du 'rassemblement national autour du Front populaire'.[87]

The apparent convergence of the Bataille and the loyalists had created an opportunity for the Gauche Révolutionnaire to intensify its campaign to win control of the party organization. At the National Council meeting on the 12th after the declaration of the vote, Marceau Pivert had read out a statement which revealed his intention to focus his attack squarely on Blum's 'fourth position' by implying that the party leader was intent on forming a national union, that he had accepted the need for an international alliance directed against Germany, and that he was prepared to collaborate with the bourgeoisie. In his statement Marceau Pivert presented his own *tendance* as the defender of the ancient faith:

Indéfectiblement attachée aux principes de la lutte de classe inscrits dans la Charte fondamentale du Parti Socialiste, la Gauche Révolutionnaire répudie l'Union Nationale sous quelque prétexte et sous quelque forme qu'elle se présente.

Obviously referring to the *rassemblement national* proposal, he stressed the unnatural character of the relationship envisaged:

La Gauche Révolutionnaire refuse catégoriquement de s'associer à cette politique d'alliance avec une bourgeoisie égoïste et aveugle, qui a construit le monstrueux traité de Versailles, forgé de ses mains l'hitlérisme, provoqué, par suite, la course aux armements et aggravé considérablement les périls de guerre, cette sanglante duperie pour le prolétariat.

He concluded by suggesting that the Socialist tradition remained the best guide to future action, denying by implication that the Austrian crisis required a government of national solidarity:

La Gauche Révolutionnaire proclame sa volonté de demeurer attachée, quoi qu'il arrive, au socialisme international, à ses solutions révolutionnaires et aux enseignements de l'expérience ouvrière de ces vingt dernières années au cours desquelles toutes les tentatives de collaboration du prolétariat avec sa bourgeoisie se sont soldées par l'affaiblissement du mouvement socialiste, par de terribles défaites et par le triomphe inévitable de ses pires ennemis fascistes.

Shortly afterwards, this statement was published as a tract, *A bas l'Union Nationale*, and was signed not only by those who represented

---

[87] 'La B. S. dans le Parti', *La Bataille Socialiste*, no. 108, March 1938, p. 3. In the context of inter-war party politics, the term *concentration* denoted a governmental alliance between the Radicals and groups of the centre right, whereas the term Union Nationale usually implied a broader alliance which included the centre right and right groups, the Radicals and, by the late 1930s, possibly the Socialists.

the Gauche Révolutionnaire on the CAP (Marceau Pivert, René Modiano, Lucien Hérard, Degez, Georges Soulès and Georges Floutard) but also by their deputies (Levant, Henri Midon and Berthe Fouchère) and by five provincial delegates – Maurice Deixonne, Federal Secretary of the Cantal Federation; Sylvain Broussaudier, Federal Secretary of the Alpes-Maritimes Federation; Benoit, Federal Secretary of the Vosges Federation; Chevaldonné, of the Loiret Federation; and Pasquis, Propaganda Secretary of the Orne Federation.[88] Two at least of the latter group had other connections: Deixonne was still in touch with members of the Révolution Constructive and Broussaudier was also a member of the Comité Directeur of the Ligue Internationale des Combattants de la Paix, a well-established pacifist organization.[89]

Meanwhile, Blum was still exploring the prospects for a broad coalition. Confident that he would have the support of the Communists and the Radicals, he directed his attention to the opposition, but a meeting of their representatives on the morning of 12 March expressed an interest in a government of union in terms which amounted to a rejection of Blum's scheme. Despite this setback, he again spoke to each of the group presidents individually and asked whether he could address a full assembly of the opposition deputies in the Salle Colbert of the Palais Bourbon at 6 p.m. At this meeting he pressed his case strongly and tried to reach beyond the formal reservations to dispel hidden anxieties, in particular those relating to the inclusion of the Communists in the proposed government. However, he did not give specific answers to the questions about policy issues which had been posed in a memorandum given to him by the opposition; although he touched on policy matters in general terms, he avoided giving explicit undertakings and claimed that it would be impossible to reach complete agreement. The outcome was that all the opposition groups with the exception of the Popular Democrats turned down his proposal.[90] Pierre-Etienne Flandin explained later that, while the opposition would have been prepared to join in the discussion of a common programme, they were not prepared

---

[88] Parti Socialiste S.F.I.O. (Tendance Gauche Révolutionnaire), *Après le Conseil National du 12 mars 1938, à bas l'Union Nationale! La déclaration de la minorité* [Paris, 1938] (Archives Maurice Deixonne, OURS). This statement was also published in *Les Cahiers Rouges*, no. 9, March 1938, p. 2; ibid., special number, 22 April 1938, p. 1; and in *Juin 36*, no. 3, 18 March – 1 April 1938, p. 4.

[89] See Norman Ingram, *The Politics of Dissent: Pacificism in France 1919–1939* (Clarendon Press, Oxford, 1991), pp. 183, 209 and 225–7.

[90] *Le Populaire*, 13 March 1938, p. 2. The full text of Blum's speech on this occasion is given in Blum, *L'Oeuvre de Léon Blum, 1937–1940*, pp. 69–76. For the text of the memorandum setting out questions on policy matters, see Pierre-Etienne Flandin, *Politique française 1919–1940* (Editions Nouvelles, Paris, 1947), p. 240, n. 1. See also Reynaud, *La France a sauvé l'Europe*, I, pp. 435–6.

to make an agreement in principle which would soon have become ineffective 'en raison des divergences de conception dans l'action gouvernementale'. He also pointed out that the proposal for 'un rassemblement national autour du front populaire' would have meant in fact 'un ralliement de l'opposition au programme du front populaire' and was therefore unacceptable.[91]

Accepting that his attempt to win over the opposition had failed, Blum now set out to form a ministry composed of Socialists, Radicals and members of the small USR group. This time he was successful and his second ministry was sworn in on the evening of Sunday the 13th. Besides Blum, its main figures were Daladier (Radical) as Minister of Defence, Joseph Paul-Boncour (USR) as Minister of Foreign Affairs, and Marx Dormoy (Socialist) as Minister of the Interior. The Ministry of Finance portfolio was not filled on this occasion and Blum himself took charge of that of the Treasury. The other Socialist ministers were Vincent Auriol (in charge of the co-ordination of services in the Premier's office), Paul Faure (Minister of State), Marius Moutet (Colonies), Charles Spinasse (Budget), Albert Rivière (Pensions), Georges Monnet (Agriculture), Albert Sérol (Labour), Jules Moch (Public Works) and Jean Lebas (Posts, Telegraphs and Telephones).

To all appearances, the political scene in France had reverted to the situation which had obtained in June 1937, before the collapse of the first Popular Front government. Once more Blum was leading a coalition of Socialists and Radicals which depended upon the Communists for parliamentary support and on the Senate for approval of its economic and financial policies, and once more he appeared to be heading for certain defeat. What was new was his belief that it was still possible, with the aid of public opinion, to persuade the opposition to join *un rassemblement national*. In his first message to the nation after the formation of his second government, he reminded his listeners of his efforts:

de constituer un gouvernement vraiment national, je veux dire un gouvernement rassemblant autour du Front Populaire toutes les forces démocratiques et républicaines du pays.

Je suis prêt à recommencer cette tentative avec la même ténacité et le même courage dès que la pression de l'opinion publique aura fait fléchir les résistances, pour moi incompréhensibles, qu'elle a rencontrées et je reste inspiré de l'esprit qui me l'a dictée.[92]

When he came before the Chamber on 17 March to make his ministerial statement he spoke as though it were both possible and desirable

[91] *JO* (*CD*), *Déb.*, 17 March 1938, p. 840.
[92] Broadcast at 9.30 p.m. on 13 March 1938 (see *Le Populaire*, 14 March 1938, p. 1).

to attempt at some stage to convert his ministry into a broad-based coalition. He said that his government

est résolu à ne laisser perdre aucune occasion de susciter, autour de la majorité, le rassemblement nécessaire d'unité française.[93]

He later indicated that he would offer the resignation of his government to clear the way for a broad coalition on condition that the opposition voted for the procedural motion which he was treating as a test of confidence. Paul Reynaud said that he would support Blum's proposal but other opposition leaders, including Flandin, declined to do so[94] and, although the motion of confidence was eventually passed by 369 votes to 196,[95] this was well short of the margin which Blum could have accepted as a demonstration of unity.

Never again did Blum try to revive the *rassemblement national* project, though he continued to defend it as a feasible formula for government, but the stand which he had taken during the ministerial crisis of March 1938 had greatly complicated one of the most demanding tasks facing the party's leaders, that of presenting to their followers a convincing account of the party's future strategy and policy. The Gauche Révolutionnaire was already shifting the weight of its own forces from the attack on the *Socialiste tendance* to the new target which Blum's ideas had presented, and the Bataille Socialiste would inevitably revert to its former demand for a tripartite coalition, Communists included, now that Blum's venture had failed.

Conclusion

The group competition within the SFIO had intensified in the course of the events reviewed in this chapter. The meeting of the National Council on 17 January 1938 had seen the loyalists defeated in a crucial division by the combined voting strength of the dissident *tendances* and the party effectively barred from taking part in another coalition under Radical leadership. Shortly afterwards, the Gauche Révolutionnaire gained virtual control of the Seine Federation and launched a campaign for a change in the party's strategy, a move which forced the *Socialiste* group, closely associated with Paul Faure, to become a third *tendance*, and to defend its strategic views on doctrinal grounds. Finally, in March, Blum's attempt to justify the formation of 'un rassemblement national autour du Front Populaire' further defined a position on strategy and

[93] *JO (CD)*, *Déb.*, 17 March 1938, p. 836.
[94] Ibid., pp. 836–47.
[95] Ibid., pp. 865–6.

policy which was distinct from that which the *Socialiste* had been defending, and which therefore made the leadership as a whole even more vulnerable in the face of attacks from an increasingly confident Gauche Révolutionnaire.

This sequence of events had changed the basic structure of the party's internal conflicts in several respects. In the middle of 1937, at the time of the Marseille Congress, the pattern had still been one of a generalized leadership group which, while sure of the support of the majority of the federations, was being harassed from different directions by two dissident *tendances*. For their part, the spokesmen for these *tendances* maintained that the party leaders, far from being an impartial ruling group, constituted with their loyalist supporters a *tendance* in all but name. Naturally, this was a definition which both leaders and loyalists refused to accept.

The first change in this pattern was caused by the increased assertiveness of the *Socialiste* group, which had responded to the aggressiveness of the Bataille and the Gauche Révolutionnaire by offering a class analysis of the political situation in justification for its support of the Popular Front. In doing so, it acknowledged that it shared with the dissident *tendances* the same landscape of traditions and philosophies and that it was now engaged in the process of claiming territories and drawing boundaries within that landscape. Having become a *tendance*, the *Socialiste* had now to sustain itself by the usual means of increasing the circulation of its journal, organizing its supporters into clubs and drawing up motions for meetings. It was thus able to offer to the hitherto unorganized mass of loyalists a disciplined avant-garde of its own.

Had it proved possible to keep the Chautemps government in office for a long period, the tripartite pattern within the SFIO might have reached an equilibrium, but events were moving too fast for this to happen. The seriousness of the international situation persuaded Léon Blum that he should rise above party considerations and he indicated, ambiguously in January but clearly in March, that circumstances required some form of national government, that a Popular Front ministry on its own could not serve that purpose, and that the time had come for Republicans to join together in defending a regime which had done so much to maintain the liberal tradition in France. The radical republicans in the party had of course welcomed the Popular Front, in both its reformist and its anti-fascist aspects, but as that front had weakened, their natural inclination had been to value the party's connection with the Radicals more highly than its alliance with the Communists and to take seriously the possibility of a national government.

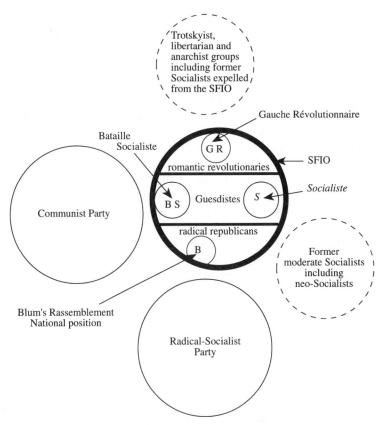

2 The competition pattern of the SFIO's internal groups, July 1937–March 1938

We thus have two changes in pattern occurring during this period, and these are set out in Figure 2.

The National Council of 12 March 1938 marks a point when the SFIO was virtually quadripartite, and it became possible to envisage quite basic realignments of the groups occurring under particular circumstances. The four-fifths majority for the motion of confidence in Blum could be regarded as a composite vote, containing mandates belonging to the Bataille, others associated with the *Socialiste* and still others which represented reasoned support for the new position which Blum had adopted in the party's politics. The Gauche Révolutionnaire was inclined to treat these elements as constituting a bloc; nevertheless, had Guesdiste antipathy to anything resembling a national union been aroused by further talk of a *rassemblement*, both the Bataille and the *Socialiste* could well have turned against Blum and the radical republicans, forcing them to renounce the idea altogether.

Much less obvious was how this structure might be affected by an intensification of the debate over war and peace, especially given the strongly held pacifist convictions of so many of the party's members, whatever the nature of their attachments to tradition. It was possible for Blum and his colleagues to play down their preference for a national government but it was becoming increasingly difficult for them to avoid taking a definite stand where foreign policy and defence matters were concerned, especially now that the anschluss had taken place. Blum, Auriol and Dormoy were very likely to support a greater emphasis on defence preparations, territorial guarantees and alliances, however much they might talk of the necessity for disarmament and collective security under the auspices of the League of Nations. In taking such a stand they could expect to receive qualified support from the Bataille and unqualified hostility from the Gauche Révolutionnaire, but what attitude would be taken by the *Socialiste*? Would it agree to represent the views of the pacifists, or would it remain loyal to Blum and his colleagues?

For the moment, however, the initiative lay with the Gauche Révolutionnaire. It could represent the positions of its rivals as false, claiming that the Bataille had simply adopted the Stalinist outlook and the national defence policy of the French Communist Party and that the *Socialiste* was nothing more than a screen for the class-collaborationist and warlike views of those who had tried to foist the plan for a national union upon the party. The Gauche Révolutionnaire could now claim that it had become, by force of circumstances, the only group concerned to revive the founding tradition of 1905 and to uphold the principles of anti-participationism and the rejection of bourgeois rule. With the Popular Front so weakened, it had become increasingly difficult for the Bataille and the *Socialiste* groups to justify their continued support for a policy which had always been represented as a contingency, a response to exceptional circumstances, rather than a course of action in keeping with the party's revolutionary tradition.

Although Marceau Pivert and his colleagues were inclined to assume that they were engaged in a moral crusade, and that shifts of allegiance towards it would be sudden and substantial, the reality was quite different. The individual federations were relatively self-sufficient, with their own established political systems and conventions, and this had given the party a segmentary structure, ensuring that a rapid change in one unit would not necessarily set off a chain reaction in neighbouring units within the same region. Where the *lutte de tendances* had permeated all aspects of politics within a federation, as in the Seine, Seine-et-Oise, Côte-d'Or and Aisne units, the Gauche Révolutionnaire had a good chance of making gains on the basis of its moral appeals, and it could also expect to win over some provincial federations with pacifist or anti-participationist backgrounds, but it could not hope to influence federations whose federal secretaries were strongly attached to the loyalist wing of the party or ones which were hardened against the influence of the Parisian intellectuals. Nor could it be sure of making much headway in units such as the Gironde Federation, which were jealous of their intellectual independence. To overcome such difficulties, the leaders of the Gauche Révolutionnaire should have prepared the ground carefully, studying the special characteristics of the provincial federations and biding their time, waiting for events to work in their favour, but patience was not one of their virtues.

4 The Royan Congress of June 1938 and the defeat of the Gauche Révolutionnaire

The SFIO's 35th National Congress, held in the town of Royan between 4 and 7 June 1938, marked the conclusion of a brief period of bitter feuding between the Gauche Révolutionnaire and its opponents. At this meeting, the delegates decided to uphold the disciplinary action which had been taken against the Seine Federation in April and approved a policy resolution which confirmed the cautious strategy which the leadership had followed in the months preceding the congress, whereupon Marceau Pivert and his close supporters left the party to form an entirely new organization.

In this chapter we shall trace the stages by which this happened, dealing first with the period extending from mid-March to mid-April 1938, which saw the imposition of sanctions on the Seine Federation and the fall of Blum's second government; then with the attempt by Pivert and his group to challenge the dissolution of the Seine Federation, and with the various policy motions produced during the preparations for the Royan Congress; and finally, with the debates at this meeting, assessing the factors which enabled the leadership to gain the upper hand in its struggle with the *tendances*.

The SFIO during the period of the second Blum government, 13 March – 8 April 1938.

The decision of the National Council of 12 March 1938 to express full confidence in Léon Blum and, implicitly, to endorse his plan for a *rassemblement national* had given Marceau Pivert an excellent opportunity to broaden support for the Gauche Révolutionnaire by claiming that Blum was intent upon forming a national union and preparing France for war. Pivert's first challenge was to persuade the majority of the members of the Seine Federation to accept his version of events and to back him in any subsequent attempt to take the matter up with the provincial federations.

For a brief period he was able to make some headway. On the evening of Monday 14 March, a hastily convened meeting of the Federal Council of the Seine Federation heard him attack the idea of a national union and call for an extraordinary national congress to discuss the issue. He further claimed that workers had no duty to defend the nation until they had taken power and he proposed a motion making the point that:

seule la lutte contre notre propre capitalisme par l'action des masses populaires peut dresser un barrage efficace contre le fascisme international et la guerre.

Zyromski had been placed in a difficult position, but he nevertheless defended the decision of the National Council and the attempt to form a broad-based ministry. He asked the delegates to approve a motion expressing faith in Blum's government:

pour entreprendre sur le plan international, une politique ferme et clairvoyante qui sauve de la domination fasciste les peuples qui veulent vivre libres: Espagne, Chine, Autriche, Tchécoslovaquie.

When the voting took place, Pivert's motion was carried by an absolute majority, and the details of the result provide an interesting comparison with the much fuller vote at the second session of the Federal Congress five weeks earlier.

Table 10. *Seine Federation: comparison of the results of the division of the Federal Congress (7 February 1938) and that of the Federal Council of 14 March 1938*

Federal Congress, 7 February 1938			Federal Council, 14 March 1938		
Motions	Mandates	%	Motions	Mandates	%
Gauche Révolutionnaire	7,450	48.9	Marceau Pivert	7,017	51.9
Bataille Socialiste	4,087	26.8	Jean Zyromski	6,379	47.2
Le Socialiste	3,688	24.2			
Abstentions				123	0.9
Totals	15,225			13,519	

The fact that fewer branches were represented on the second occasion seems to have worked to the advantage of the Gauche Révolutionnaire, which had increased its share of the mandates from 48.9 to 51.9 per cent. It is also significant that the Bataille and *Socialiste* groups appear to have worked together at the Federal Council, thus transferring to this arena the informal alliance which they had made at the National Council on the 12th.[1]

---

[1] For accounts of this meeting, see *Le Temps* (Paris), 16 March 1938, p. 2, and *Le Populaire* (Paris), 15 March 1938, p. 2. Marceau Pivert's motion is given in full in *Juin*

The Seine Federation's Federal Bureau, all of whose members belonged to the Gauche Révolutionnaire, was now intent on taking the case to the provinces and it therefore approved the distribution of a tract, dated 18 March, which had been prepared by Suzanne Nicolitch, a university graduate and a teacher at the Camille Sée lycée.[2] Entitled *Alerte! . . . Le Parti est en danger!*, the tract suggested a comparison between the current situation and that which had obtained when the party had accepted the Union Sacrée that had taken France into war in 1914.

Malgré la stupeur indignée des travailleurs de France, voici que se prépare obstinément, sous le titre *d'Union Nationale*, l'alliance monstrueuse entre les représentants les plus habiles du néo-capitalisme financier et industriel d'une part, et, d'autre part, ceux-là même que les masses ouvrières avaient délégués à la tête du pays en leur faisant confiance pour les luttes à entreprendre.

It called on activists, branches and federations to demand the immediate convocation of an extraordinary national congress and to inform the Seine Federation about decisions which branches and federations had taken for or against 'l'intégration du Parti Socialiste dans l'Union Nationale'.[3] The basic appeal for dissent was now sharply focused on the claim that the proposal for a national government was tantamount to an acceptance of a war policy.

When a copy of the tract came into the hands of Paul Faure, he seized on the fact that it had been issued under the authority of the Seine Federation. On Thursday 24 March he wrote to Marceau Pivert pointing out that:

le fait pour la Fédération de la Seine de s'adresser à toutes les sections et à toutes les fédérations du Parti en passant par-dessus la C.A.P. et le Secrétariat général du Parti constitue un acte d'indiscipline caractérisé.

He stated that he was instructing the CAP's General Administration Subcommittee to prepare a report on the question for submission to a

---

36 (Paris), no. 3, 18 March–1 April 1938, p. 1. For general accounts of the conflict between the Seine Federation and the party's central authorities, see Jean-Paul Joubert, *Marceau Pivert et le pivertisme: révolutionnaires de la S.F.I.O.* (Fondation Nationale des Sciences Politiques, Paris, 1977), pp. 137–45; Daniel Guérin, *Front Populaire: révolution manquée: témoignage militant* (François Maspero, Paris, 2nd edn, 1976), pp. 183–93.

[2] See Marceau Pivert, 'Juin 36', *La Revue Socialiste* (Paris, NS), no. 62 (December 1952), p. 538 n. 3. On Suzanne Nicolitch, see Joubert, *Révolutionnaires de la S.F.I.O.*, p. 227.

[3] *Alerte! . . . Le Parti est en danger!* (Parti Socialiste (SFIO), Fédération de la Seine, Paris, March 1938) (Archives Maurice Deixonne, OURS. Unless otherwise indicated, copies of all the printed tracts cited in the notes for this chapter are to be found in this collection of papers).

meeting of the CAP on Wednesday 30 March, and requested Pivert 'de la façon la plus formelle de ne pas mettre en circulation ces tracts'. In his reply, dispatched to Paul Faure on the same day, Pivert maintained that the General Secretary had not reacted to numerous previous acts of indiscipline and claimed that there was a political explanation for his letter.

Nous sommes prêts à nous présenter devant quelque organisme du Parti que ce soit pour répondre de notre acte.

Pour le moment, je t'indique que nous envoyons à ceux de nos camarades qui sont d'accord avec nous, et au nom desquels nous siégeons à la C.A.P., les tracts édités par la Fédération de la Seine en les priant de les faire parvenir à leurs secrétaires fédéraux.[4]

The texts of both letters, along with copies of the offending tract and other documents, were then dispatched to members of the party associated with the Gauche Révolutionnaire. At the same time, in a series of directives, Marceau Pivert stressed the need to oppose the idea of a national union and to obtain a clear reply to the question as to whether the party should join such a combination.

Il faut que tous les militants que toutes les sections, que toutes les fédérations répondent par *oui* ou par *non*, après quoi le Congrès national ayant prononcé son verdict chacun en tirera les conséquences: pour nous dès maintenant, nous pouvons dire que *nous ne resterons pas dans un Parti faisant l'Union nationale*. Reste à savoir si notre Parti socialiste est dégradé à ce point . . . Nous lui posons la question et nous dénoncerons toute tentative de manœuvre ou toute ruse pour éluder la réponse.[5]

The Bureau of the Seine Federation had quite deliberately converted a minor dispute about the proper limits of the federation's authority into an outright trial of strength with the party's central leadership. An apology from Marceau Pivert and an undertaking not to circulate *Alerte!* might not have permitted Paul Faure to drop the charges but they would have made it much easier for him to recommend leniency to the party's authorities. However, far from expressing regret, Pivert had claimed that Faure's action was politically motivated. He had fallen into the trap of failing to distinguish between his role as Federal Secretary of the Seine Federation (Paul Faure had addressed him as such) and his role as the national leader of the Gauche Révolutionnaire. His direct-ives to the members of his *tendance* revealed not only his continuing hostility to the idea of a national union but also his willingness to break

[4] *Les Cahiers Rouges* (Paris), special number, 22 April 1938, p. 2.
[5] 'Aux camarades de la tendance G.R., Paris le 24 mars 1938 ' (cyclostyled) (Archives Maurice Deixonne, OURS), p. 2.

with the party if it were to join such a combination. This was a reckless call to arms and betrayed the quite unwarranted conviction that the thinly spread network of his *tendance* was capable of undermining both the Bataille Socialiste and the central leadership. Paul Faure's task, by contrast, was a relatively easy one; all that he had to do was to insist on the observance of party discipline and wait for the Gauche Révolutionnaire to break even more of the party's conventions and rules.

Another factor was to increase the precariousness of Pivert's position. The CAP was being asked to consider a quite separate complaint from the Comité National Mixte des Jeunesses Socialistes (CNM JS), the central body entrusted with the supervision of the party's youth movement. As noted above,[6] on 2 February Pivert had written to Henri Mariette expressing his sympathy at the latter's expulsion from the Jeunesses Socialistes of the Manche Federation and had advised him to get in touch with Lucien Weitz in Paris. When this correspondence came to the attention of Raymond Le Corre, the Federal Secretary of the Manche Federation, he asked Pivert to send him a letter which he could publish as a means of calming those young dissidents who claimed to have his support. On receiving a reply from Pivert which he regarded as unsatisfactory, Le Corre decided to take his case to the National Council, which was due to meet on 27 March. However, this meeting was cancelled and in its place was held the extraordinary meeting of 12 March which was restricted to a discussion of policy. The complaint was therefore passed to the CNM JS and then to the CAP, which decided on 23 March that it should be considered by the CAP's General Administration Subcommittee.[7] Consequently, this latter body found itself dealing with two quite separate complaints directed against Marceau Pivert.

The Seine Federation attracted further criticism from the party's central leadership for the part which it was playing in the industrial unrest which affected the automobile and aeroplane manufacturing industries in the Parisian region towards the end of March 1938. Frustrated by delays in reaching agreement on new collective-bargaining contracts, the metal-workers conducted a sit-in strike in the Citroën car works on the 24th and in other factories on the following day. The Blum government was interested in arranging a settlement, but found this difficult to achieve. The SFIO itself had no direct relationship with either the

---

[6] See above, pp. 105–6.
[7] See the account given by Le Corre to the Royan Congress, in Parti Socialiste (SFIO), 35ᵉ Congrès National, Royan, 4–7 juin 1938, *Compte rendu sténographique* (Librairie Populaire, Paris, n.d.), pp. 107–10. For the CAP meeting, see *Le Populaire*, 27 March 1938, p. 7.

striking unions or with the CGT, the central trade-union organization, but the party had, shortly after the Popular Front government had taken power in 1936, formed a network of workers' associations known as the Amicales Socialistes to bring together those of its members who belonged to particular sections of the workforce.[8] The metal-workers' union of the Amicales in Paris now found itself placed in a difficult position. At the national level, the Amicales were subject to the authority of a consultative committee headed by Francis Desphelippon, a member of the CAP, but within the Federal Bureau of the Seine Federation Daniel Guérin and Maurice Jaquier had been given responsibility for relations with the Amicales in the Parisian area.

While the party's central leaders had wished the Amicales to confine themselves to spreading the party's ideas and to avoid involvement in trade-union affairs,[9] Guérin had wanted to give them a much more active role,[10] and when the strike began, the Federal Bureau of the Seine Federation issued a tract expressing complete support for the metal-workers' action. This tract declared that the Federation

est persuadée que tous ses militants, tous ses sympathisants, tous ses élus, tous les membres de ses Sections ou des Amicales Socialistes engagés ou non dans cette grande lutte sauront mettre toutes leurs forces . . . au service de l'action autonome de leur classe.[11]

On 27 March, *L'Humanité* and its companion newspaper, *Ce Soir*, carried allegations that Trotskyists and various Amicales had been trying to persuade the metal-workers to take irregular industrial action. Writing in *L'Humanité*, Marcel Gitton claimed that the Amicale in the Citroën works had issued a tract attacking not only the employers but also the trade-union leadership, and the General Secretary of the Parisian and Western Region of the Communist Party complained that the Amicales had been organizing petitions for holding strikes to support

[8] For general accounts of the origins and history of the Amicales, see D. N. Baker, 'The Socialists and the workers of Paris: the Amicales Socialistes, 1936–40', *International Review of Social History* (Assen, Van Gorcum), 24 (1979), pp. 1–33; J.-P. Rioux, 'Les Socialistes dans l'entreprise au temps du Front Populaire: quelques remarques sur les Amicales Socialistes (1936–1939)', *Le Mouvement Social* (Paris), no. 106 (January–March 1979), pp. 3–24.
[9] See the rules for the Amicales adopted by the CAP on 20 October 1937, in Parti Socialiste (SFIO), 35e Congrès National, Royan, 4–7 juin 1938, *Rapports* (Librairie Populaire, Paris, 1938), pp. 148–51.
[10] See his article, 'Où vont les Amicales Socialistes?', *Les Cahiers Rouges*, December 1937, reproduced in J.-P. Rioux (ed.), *Révolutionnaires du Front Populaire: choix de documents 1935–1938* (Union Générale d'Editions, Paris, 1973), pp. 322–4.
[11] Parti Socialiste (SFIO), Fédération de la Seine, Amicales Socialistes de la Seine, *Aux côtés des métallos* [Paris, 1938].

the Blum government against the Senate.[12] In response, *Le Populaire* published a statement by Francis Desphelippon replying to the attacks of the Communist newspapers and also a declaration by the executive committee of the metal-workers' union of the Amicales denying that the Amicales had started the strike movement, while also affirming its continued respect for the independence of trade unions.[13] Interpreting the latter article as a call to Socialists and their sympathizers to withdraw from the strike movement, the Seine Federation's Bureau sent out yet another tract claiming that Desphelippon had not been authorized to write his article and that he was consequently speaking in his own name and not that of the federation.[14]

Meanwhile, the party's administrative machinery had begun to deal with the charges of indiscipline against Marceau Pivert and his colleagues. Meeting on the evening of Monday 28 March, the CAP's General Administration Subcommittee decided to recommend to the CAP that the complaint about the distribution of *Alerte!* should be referred to the Commission Nationale des Conflits (CNC), the party's chief judicial body. News of this recommendation spread like lightning and by midnight a cyclostyled sheet signed by Pivert was ready for distribution. It claimed that what the subcommittee was in fact proposing was the referral of the twelve representatives of the Gauche Révolutionnaire on the Federation's Executive Committee to the CNC with a view to their expulsion from the party, not only for sending out *Alerte!* but also for publishing the tract attacking Desphelippon in connection with the metal-workers' strike.

C'est là le geste conscient d'hommes décidés à toutes mesures de répression bureaucratiques et autres pour se jeter dans l'union nationale en jugulant le prolétariat.

C'est là le signe avant coureur des grands effondrements: les autres sociale-démocraties ont commencé par s'en prendre à leur aile révolutionnaire avant d'être victimes de l'ennemi fasciste de plus en plus menaçant.

Nous voyons venir les événements avec maîtrise et sang-froid. Nous ne céderons sur aucun des principes socialistes qui sont en jeu. Nous faisons appel, dès maintenant, à tous nos militants de la Seine: le jeu est clair. Avec les briseurs de grève ou avec le prolétariat. Avec l'Union nationale ou avec le socialisme de classe.

---

[12] *L'Humanité* (Paris), 27 March 1938, pp. 1 and 2. See also *Ce Soir* (Paris, 6th edn), 28 March 1938, p. 3.
[13] *Le Populaire*, 28 March 1938, pp. 1 and 4.
[14] Parti Socialiste (SFIO), Fédération Socialiste de la Seine, Amicales Socialistes de la Seine, *Grèves de la métallurgie mars 1938* [Paris, 1938] (Dossier 28, 22 AS 1, Papiers des Amis de Marceau Pivert, Archives Nationales).

Alertez à votre tour et agissons tous en même temps, tous dans le même sens.[15]

The determination to treat the disciplinary charges as evidence of political motivation was as strong as ever.

The bitter confrontation between the representatives of the Gauche Révolutionnaire and the combined forces of the central leadership and the Bataille Socialiste came to a head at the meeting of the CAP on Wednesday 30 March. The General Secretariat claimed that the distribution of *Alerte!* was in breach of Article 39 of the party's rules, which stipulated that between meetings of the National Council the CAP was authorized to execute the decisions of the National Congress and the National Council. Then the CNM JS brought forward its charges against Marceau Pivert and others for the troubles in the Jeunesses Socialistes in the Manche Federation and at Cognac, in the Charente Department, and by 27 votes to nil (the six Gauche Révolutionnaire members abstaining), the meeting decided to send both dossiers to the CNC. There was also a heated exchange on the subject of the attacks on Desphelippon for his intervention in the metal-workers' strike but over this issue no complaint was sent to the CNC.[16]

It is difficult to see how Marceau Pivert and his colleagues expected to emerge unscathed from such a battery of criticism. As the *Alerte!* tract had shown, they had had high hopes of engendering within the party a substantial movement against national union and against war preparations and a subsequent tract, issued on 22 March by the Gauche Révolutionnaire rather than the federation, had actually accused the Blum government of wanting to put the country on a war footing.

L'ordre d'urgence des questions à résoudre exige *l'organisation de la nation en guerre*, c'est-à-dire la réquisition des personnes et des biens, la dictature militaire, l'instauration du fascisme à l'intérieur sous prétexte de se protéger contre celui de l'extérieur . . .
Quelle effroyable tragédie se prépare!

Referring to the decision of the National Council of 12 March to express confidence in Léon Blum when he was endeavouring to establish a government of *rassemblement national*, it asked:

[15] 'Dernière heure – 28 mars minuit. Alerte' (cyclostyled) (Archives Maurice Deixonne, OURS).
[16] 'Commission Nationale des Conflits, séance du 11 avril 1938, extrait du procès-verbal' (cyclostyled) (Archives de l'OURS), p. 1; *La Vie du Parti* (Paris), no. 79, 3 May 1938, pp. 313–14 and 316. See also the account of this meeting in *Bulletin Intérieur de la Gauche Révolutionnaire*, 16 April 1938, pp. 2–4.

Qu'en pensent les militants, machines à cotiser, chair à profit capitaliste, chair à canon, dont l'opinion compte si peu?

Se dresseront-ils enfin pour déchirer les voiles du mensonge qui, de toutes parts, cherchent à les tromper?[17]

Writing to Maurice Deixonne on 30 March, the same day as the CAP meeting which referred the cases to the CNC, Marceau Pivert still showed that he hoped for a shift of opinion in his favour.

Notre mouvement inquiète tellement la bureaucratie du Parti, qu'ils sont prêts à briser celui-ci pour donner des gages à la bourgeoisie qu'il supplie de faire l'Union Nationale. La situation va évoluer très rapidement, mais nous pouvons être réconfortés malgré la tristesse des temps par l'ampleur du mouvement qui ne fait que commencer dans tous les milieux contre le fascisme et contre la guerre. J'ai d'ailleurs l'impression que c'est plutôt maintenant l'offensive fasciste qui va se mûrir. De toutes façons nous aurons fait notre devoir et dès maintenant, nous pouvons être sûrs que cela ne sera pas en vain.[18]

Within the Seine Federation itself, the threat of disciplinary action against its officers had become the centre of attention. At a meeting of the federation's Federal Council on Monday 4 April, an absolute majority of the mandates went to a motion approving Marceau Pivert's actions in issuing *Alerte!* and the later tract criticizing Desphelippon, expressing solidarity with Pivert and declaring against his appearing before the CNC. This may be taken as the position of the Gauche Révolutionnaire but sanctions were also opposed by another motion brought forward by Henri Sellier, Pierre Commin and Andrée Marty-Capgras, all members of the Bataille Socialiste. Their text attracted just under one-fifth of the mandates while a motion proposed by André Costedoat of the *Socialiste* group and appealing for confidence in the CNC received only one-quarter of the votes.[19] The details of the ballot are given in Table 11. At this point, Marceau Pivert appeared to be gaining ground in the federation, mainly because sanctions rather than national union had become the main issue.

[17] Parti Socialiste S.F.I.O., Tendance Gauche Révolutionnaire, *Assez de ruses, assez de mensonges, qui trompe-t-on? et pourquoi?* (Paris, 1938), p. 2.
[18] Letter from Marceau Pivert to Maurice Deixonne, from Paris, 30 March 1938 (Archives Maurice Deixonne, OURS).
[19] See *Juin 36*, no. 4, 22 April 1938, p. 4; *Le Temps*, 6 April 1938, p. 2; *Le Populaire*, 5 April 1938, p. 7. Accounts of what is undoubtedly the same meeting are also given in *Les Cahiers Rouges* (no. 10, April 1938, p. 3; special number, 22 April 1938, p. 3) but they wrongly report it as having been held on 31 March. The incorrect date also appears in contemporary chronologies of the crisis (e.g. *Juin 36*, no. 5, 22–9 April 1938, p. 1; *Le Socialiste* (Paris), no. 18, 1 May 1938, p. 1) and has been carried over into secondary sources (e.g. Guérin, *Front Populaire: révolution manquée*, p. 193; Nathanael Greene, *Crisis and Decline: The French Socialist Party in the Popular Front Era* (Cornell University Press, Ithaca, New York, 1969), p. 213).

Table 11. *Seine Federation, Federal Council, 4 April 1938: division on the issue of whether the CNC should consider complaints against officers of the federation*

Motions	Mandates	% of total
From the Garenne-Colombes branch against reference to the CNC	7,514	52.0
From Henri Sellier *et al.* against sanctions	2,634	18.2
From André Costedoat expressing confidence in the CNC	3,762	26.0
Abstentions	545	3.8
Totals	14,455	

The CNC, which had already begun work on the cases against Marceau Pivert and his colleagues, was an administrative tribunal possessing considerable autonomy within the party's structure. Appointed annually by the National Congress, its members were expected to have a good knowledge of party affairs and at least ten years' party membership behind them. However, even the CNC was not exempt from the informal rule that its composition should reflect the distribution of mandates between the motions on general policy at the National Congress, and the tribunal for 1937–8 contained five loyalists, three representatives of the Bataille and one of the Gauche Révolutionnaire. That it worked so well as a unit was largely to the credit of its secretary, Albert Jamin, who had held this post since 1933, two years after first becoming a member. Until 1925, organizational disputes within the SFIO had been dealt with by a system of arbitration committees and this had led to long delays, but amendments to the rules made in that year had produced a simpler and speedier set of procedures built around federal and national committees. The powers of the CNC itself were formidable: it had virtually complete discretion to determine its own working methods and penalties and, except in the case of expulsions where the accused had the right of appeal to the National Council, its decisions were final. It was not otherwise subject to the authority of the National Council and was independent of both the CAP and the General Secretary; it reported directly to the National Congress, with evident pride in the rigour and impartiality of its work.

In dealing with the affairs of the Seine Federation, it concentrated on the question as to whether any member or members of the Federal Bureau had acted irresponsibly, and ignored the charges of bad faith and political motivation which had been levelled against the General Secretary and his colleagues throughout the controversy. On

Wednesday 6 April it interviewed Marceau Pivert, who claimed that he
had acted on a mandate from the Federal Council in distributing the
Alerte! tract and that he took full responsibility for his action. Two days
later, on the evening of Friday 8 April, the CNC interviewed members
of the federation's Executive Committee, which at the time of its election in February had been composed of 12 representatives of the
Gauche Révolutionnaire, 7 of the Bataille and 6 of the *Socialiste* group
in a total strength of 25 members. Under Article 31 of the federation's
own rules this was the body which was authorized to deal, between
meetings of the Federal Council, with all questions affecting administration, organization and propaganda and it therefore had authority over
the Federal Bureau, whose members it elected. The CNC found that
the Executive Committee had not been consulted as a body about the
Alerte! tract and that 'les membres de la minorité' (that is, the representatives of the Bataille and *Socialiste* groups) had come to know about it
only after it had been distributed.[20] Executive functions had been
usurped by the Federal Bureau, and the view that the members of this
body rather than Marceau Pivert alone were to blame for what had
been done was strengthened by a letter which Jamin received from
Charles Pivert, the brother of Marceau and one of the representatives
of the Bataille Socialiste on the Executive Committee. Unable to attend
the hearing on the 8th, Charles Pivert had set out in writing his views
on who should bear the blame:

Mon frère est un homme droit, très honnête, très désintéressé et très confiant –
trop confiant même. Il est entouré d'un certain nombre de camarades sur les-
quels je ne dirai rien mais qui prennent des initiatives sans prendre le temps
de le consulter. Initiatives que Marceau, très courageusement, couvre de son
autorité.

He asked the CNC to appreciate that there was more to the Seine
Federation than Marceau Pivert and that there was also the Bureau,
some of whose members he named.

Séparer les uns des autres serait une erreur. Je vous demande de ne pas la
commettre.
    Peut-être que Marceau ne comprendra pas le sentiment qui m'anime. Peut-
être considérera-t-il comme une injure de croire que ses collaborateurs directs
ne méritent pas la confiance qu'il leur accorde. Qu'importe![21]

The CNC met to consider its verdict on Monday 11 April, having
been informed on the Friday by Tannier, the sole representative of the

[20] 'Commission Nationale des Conflits, séance du 11 avril 1938. extrait du procès-verbal',
p. 2.
[21] Letter from Charles Pivert to Albert Jamin, from Paris, 8 April 1938, *Le Populaire*,
18 April 1938, p. 5.

Gauche Révolutionnaire among its members, that he could not be present and that he was against the imposition of any sanction. Those who were present agreed unanimously that the members of the Federal Bureau, by distributing a tract which criticized a decision of the National Council and called for replies from federations and branches had acted as if it were a veritable central body, on a level with the regular central body of the party, and that they had thus placed their federation 'en position d'insubordination à l'égard du Parti'. The CNC also found that Marceau Pivert was guilty of indiscipline for counselling Henri Mariette, the young man who had been excluded from the Jeunesses Socialistes of the Manche Federation, to get in touch with Lucien Weitz, who had himself been excluded from the Jeunesses Socialistes of the Seine Federation a year earlier. Noting that such actions could have led logically to sentences of expulsion from the party, the CNC decided to exact the lesser penalty of 'suspension de toutes délégations' with effect from Tuesday 12 April, that is, a ban on representing the party, speaking or writing in its name, standing as one of its election candidates, or occupying a post at any level in the organization. Where Marceau Pivert was concerned, the ban was for three years and in the case of the other members of the Federal Bureau – André Weil-Curiel, René Cazanave, Henri Goldschild, Georges Gillet, Daniel Guérin, René Rul and Maurice Jaquier – it was for two years.[22]

Extracts from the minutes of this meeting were sent by recorded delivery to the eight members involved, to the secretaries of their branches, to the secretariat of the Seine Federation, and to the party's General Secretariat.[23] Some in Pivert's group welcomed the result as the prelude to a split in the party. According to Maurice Jaquier:

À l'annonce de cette décision, qui en consterne certains, Daniel Guérin danse de joie.[24]

Severe though the penalties were, they offered Marceau Pivert and his lieutenants the chance of staying within the party and working from behind the scenes as their *tendance* sought to maintain its position in whatever elections became necessary to fill the eight vacant places on the Executive Committee preparatory to its appointing a new Federal Bureau for the federation. However, they were already too committed to the claim that the party's judicial process was serving a political conspiracy to accept the CNC's decision and they therefore continued

---

[22] 'Commission Nationale des Conflits, séance du 11 avril 1938, extrait du procès-verbal', pp. 2–5.
[23] Ibid., p. 5.
[24] Maurice Jaquier, *Simple militant* (Denoël, Paris, 1974), p. 157.

the confrontation. Although they had been formally suspended from office, Marceau Pivert and René Cazanave continued to act as though they were still Federal Secretary and Administrative Secretary respectively, and at very short notice they convened yet another meeting of the Federal Council for the evening of Wednesday 13 April.

This meeting adopted a resolution put forward by Pierre Commin and Andrée Marty-Capgras of the Bataille Socialiste deploring the imposition of sanctions and requesting the CAP to suspend them:

en attendant que les assises souveraines du Parti [that is, the National Congress] aient pris position sur les problèmes politiques posés. La solution de ces problèmes, qui engagera l'avenir non seulement du Parti français, mais du mouvement international ouvrier, ne peut pas être recherchée par de simples mesures disciplinaires administratives, mais au contraire dans une large confrontation idéologique, conformément aux règles démocratiques des statuts du Parti.

The Gauche Révolutionnaire rallied to this formula, which effectively invited the CAP to treat the CNC's decision as if it were subject to appeal (certainly not the case), to accept that the conflict was based upon issues of policy rather than issues of discipline, and to allow the Federal Bureau to remain in office until the meeting of the National Congress.[25] The motion was carried by an overwhelming majority, the detailed figures being as set out in Table 12.

The delegates belonging to the Gauche Révolutionnaire and the Bataille Socialiste presumably worked in concert on this occasion, but the number of mandates for the Commin–Marty-Capgras resolution was significantly larger than the combined total of the votes against sanctions at the Federal Council of 4 April. The dissidents appear to have boosted

Table 12. *Seine Federation, Federal Council, 13 April 1938: division on the resolution addressed to the CAP*

	Mandates	% of total
For the Commin–Marty-Capgras resolution	11,488	72.2
Against the resolution	204	1.3
Abstentions	1,578	9.9
Absent	2,641	16.6
Total	15,911	

[25] *Les Cahiers Rouges*, special number, 22 April 1938, p. 5. See also a brief report of this meeting in L[ucien] Hérard, 'Aux secrétaires de section de la Côte d'Or: aux membres du Parti' (cyclostyled, Dijon, n.d., but probably last week of April 1938) (Archives Maurice Deixonne, OURS); *Le Temps*, 15 April 1938, p. 4.

their vote by tactical means: the *Socialiste* leader, André Costedoat, later claimed that those delegates who belonged to his group had not attended the meeting and implied that the branches had not been asked to express an opinion except at the time of the Federal Congress of January–February 1938, with the result that the branch delegates appointed on that occasion had simply been summoned to the Federal Council on this and the earlier meetings of 14 March and 4 April without receiving fresh instructions from their units. He also alleged that those branch secretaries who belonged to the Gauche Révolutionnaire had taken advantage of the absence of *Socialiste* branch delegates to claim all the mandates at the disposal of their branches, ignoring earlier expressions of *Socialiste* views in those units.[26]

The CAP had also been in session on Wednesday 13 April but it was on the evening of Thursday 14 April that it came to grips with the situation in the Seine Federation. Observing that the latter's Federal Council, by retaining in office, even provisionally, the members of the Federal Bureau, had placed the federation 'en état d'indiscipline manifeste à l'égard du Parti', it decided to dissolve the federation and asked the General Secretary to construct a new unit in its place. Each member of the party in the Seine Department was to be asked to sign an undertaking to respect the decisions of the party (and notably those of the CNC) and each branch was to be asked to submit a declaration of loyalty to the provisional Federal Bureau.[27] This was a bold decision, and one which was bound to give the Gauche Révolutionnaire and its allies scope for attacking the General Secretary and the rest of the central leadership on the grounds that they had ignored the political dimensions of the crisis. There are indications that the politics of the meeting were affected by uncertainty and anxiety. As constituted at the time of the Marseille Congress of July 1937 the 33-member CAP consisted of 18 representatives of the Blum–Faure motion, 9 of the Bataille Socialiste and 6 of the Gauche Révolutionnaire. Marceau Pivert was dropped from its membership in keeping with the decision of the CNC to remove him from all positions of responsibility and three other members of his *tendance* (Lucien Hérard, René Modiano and Georges Floutard) were unable to attend this meeting, leaving only Degez and Georges Soulès to represent their cause. From one account, it would appear that Zyromski attacked the proposal to dissolve the federation, that the matter was put to the vote, and that it was carried by 18

[26] Parti Socialiste (SFIO), 35ᵉ Congrès National, Royan, 4–7 juin 1938, *Compte rendu sténographique*, p. 25.
[27] Parti Socialiste (SFIO), 35ᵉ Congrès National, Royan, 4–7 juin 1938, *Rapports*, pp. 159–60; *La Vie du Parti*, no. 79, 3 May 1938, pp. 314–15.

votes to 7, with Zyromski, Bracke, Girard (a replacement for Robert Coeylas), Roger Dufour and Charles Pivert of the Bataille voting in the minority alongside Degez and Soulès.[28] Bracke had been troubled by the assumption that the motion passed at the Federal Council of 13 April represented the views of the federation's members and had therefore been looking for a means (such as a referendum) other than dissolution for resolving the crisis.[29] In any case, the former Federal Bureau refused to accept the CAP's decision and continued to occupy the federation's headquarters at 7 rue Meslay in the 3rd *arrondissement*. The provisional Bureau of the new federation was therefore established in the party's central offices at 12, Cité Malesherbes in the 9th *arrondissement*.

This extended crisis altered the structure of the *lutte de tendances* in a number of ways. The core group of the Gauche Révolutionnaire had worked with very limited resources, and its margins for error were narrow. Within the Seine Federation, it had taken full control of the Bureau on the basis of a simple majority on the Executive Committee and had then embarked on an ambitious propaganda campaign, reporting only to the Federal Council. Its use of shock tactics (issuing the *Alerte!* tract without the approval of the full Executive Committee, defying the General Secretary and the CAP, and inviting opposition to the decisions of the CNC) created the illusion that the politics of the party had become a species of Grand Guignol in which deep-laid conspiracies were unveiled by an idealistic avant-garde. In the enclosed theatre of the Seine Federation, local members of the Bataille Socialiste became absorbed in the drama but party opinion in the provinces was much less affected.

The more the Seine Federation had been drawn into disputes about jurisdiction and rules of conduct, the more the Gauche Révolutionnaire was obliged to exploit one of the party's oldest and most potent myths, that the very process of organization had created bureaucratic oligarchies which had stifled the original liberties of the Socialist movement. Having presented its version of the dissolution of the federation, the journal *Les Cahiers Rouges* claimed that:

l'intention apparaît clairement: on veut réduire au silence une minorité révolutionnaire qui grandit de semaine en semaine ET QUI RISQUE DE CONQUERIR LA MAJORITE DU PARTI; on est disposé à violer toutes les garanties élémentaires de justice et de démocratie intérieure.[30]

---

[28] *Les Cahiers Rouges*, special number, 22 April 1938, p. 5. Note that the report in *Le Temps*, 16 April 1938, p. 2, gives the votes as 19 for and 6 against.

[29] Parti Socialiste (SFIO), 35ᵉ Congrès National, Royan, 4–7 juin 1938, *Compte rendu sténographique*, pp. 95–6. See also remarks by André Costedoat, ibid., p. 26.

[30] *Les Cahiers Rouges*, special number, 22 April 1938, p. 5.

By inviting its sympathizers to fight against Paul Faure and the party's central bureaucracy, the Gauche Révolutionnaire was appealing to the party's democratic ethic, which embodied the rights of ordinary members to express views without constraint and to take up vital issues without being restricted by petty rules and procedural conventions. It was always possible to build up a certain amount of support by invoking the libertarian current in the party's tradition, and the Gauche Révolutionnaire had already begun to do so, but such support was difficult to convert into a group with a coherent set of policies. An anti-bureaucratic movement could easily be set in motion, but it could just as easily be checked by firm opposition. Here, too, the Gauche Révolutionnaire was prey to illusion.

In meeting this challenge, Paul Faure could use the equally powerful myth of the party as an army, maintaining disciplined unity in the face of its enemies. In its description of the Seine crisis, the central secretariat drew a line backwards in time to the events of the spring of 1937, which had culminated in the dissolution of the Gauche Révolutionnaire and in Marceau Pivert's undertaking to respect the decisions of the Puteaux National Council of 18 April:

Que s'est-il passé depuis?
Les engagements pris n'ont pas été tenus, la parole donnée a été reniée.
La gauche révolutionnaire n'a pas été dissoute et a continué son oeuvre de désagrégation et d'indiscipline.
Elle a porté tous ses coups, toute sa propagande, contre la politique du Parti, sans tenir compte des décisions des Congrès.[31]

With indiscipline went excess, and it was at this time that the behaviour of *tendances* in general came under closer scrutiny than in previous years. According to Robert Dupont, one of the leaders of the Bataille Socialiste in the Seine:

Les frictions inévitables produites dans les groupes, dans les sections se répercutent dans la fédération et, à la faveur de la propagande dite de tendance, elles vont connaître une acuité qui atteint gravement l'Unité Morale du Parti.
Propagande de tendance? Que celle-ci hélas est souvent mal comprise! On s'amalgame autour de tel ou tel camarade, on le flatte, on lui dit qu'il est un grand homme! Il le croit, il ouvre les yeux plus grands, il regarde plus loin, il domine les 'minus habens' qui lui servent de garde du corps! Il en arrive à oublier le 'ni Dieu, ni César, ni Tribun' de son refrain favori![32]

There are a number of stories about Paul Faure's alleged antipathy to Marceau Pivert and his colleagues. Pivert himself claimed to have overheard Faure telling Louis Lévy that 'il faut mettre Marceau PIVERT

---

[31] *La Vie du Parti*, special issue, 15 April 1938, p. 1.
[32] Dupont, 'Refaire l'unité morale du Parti', *Le Populaire*, 7 April 1938, p. 4.

à la porte'.[33] There was every reason for Faure to have taken the challenge from the Gauche Révolutionnaire seriously. Until the Seine crisis became its chief concern, it had been developing a widespread network of support in the provinces and had formulated a distinctive set of policy themes – its own version of revolutionary pacifism, its revival of the spirit of the 1905 Charter and of doctrinal fundamentalism, and its warnings about the possibility of a national union. Singly or in combination, these themes could have attracted considerable sympathy within the party in the months leading up to the National Congress. In the Seine Federation, Faure had seen that the *Socialiste* group had failed to stem the growth of this *tendance*. Given this danger, he could not afford to allow his opponents to bend the party's rules governing competition between internal groups. That was why he made an issue of the Seine Federation's distribution of the *Alerte!* tract and why he referred the matter to the CAP's General Administration Subcommittee. Had he reacted less forcefully in the hope that later events would work in his favour, he could well have found himself faced with a serious rebellion at the Royan Congress. To use a military metaphor, Faure had chosen to meet his enemy at an early stage, on ground of his own choosing, rather than to wait in his fortress for a set-piece battle later in the year. From his point of view, this encounter had brought him several gains: it had diverted the energies of the Gauche Révolutionnaire to a desperate attempt to sustain a rebel federation in the Seine Department and had deflected the *tendance* from its policy objectives towards an anti-bureaucratic campaign which was bound to be diffuse and lacking in coherence.

Let us now turn to see how the second Blum government was faring, and how its policies were affecting the Socialist Party's internal divisions. A lack of resources placed limits on what the new ministry could achieve in economic policy, but a finance bill approved in late March gave it time to prepare a considered plan covering the medium-term future. At the Treasury, Blum had the assistance of Georges Boris as his *directeur de cabinet* and of Pierre Mendès-France, a young Radical deputy, as Under-Secretary of State. Both Boris and Mendès-France were conversant with the ideas set out by John Maynard Keynes in his *General Theory of Employment, Interest and Money*, first published in 1936, and were therefore prepared to think in unorthodox ways about the relationships between the various elements of the economic

---

[33] *Bulletin Intérieur de la Gauche Révolutionnaire*, 16 April 1938, p. 2. For Paul Faure's version of this story, see Parti Socialiste (SFIO), 35ᵉ Congrès National, Royan, 4–7 juin 1938, *Compte rendu sténographique*, p. 143.

system.[34] They prepared a plan for expanding the economy by increased expenditure on arms production in the expectation that this would stimulate activity in other sectors of industry. In one sense they were rationalizing what was already happening, given that French rearmament was already under way, but the merit of their scheme lay in their sophisticated appreciation of how the effects of economic growth could be controlled and directed. When Blum presented parliament with a plenary powers bill requesting the right to legislate by decree until 1 July 1938, he also submitted a preface setting out the main features of his plan and outlining various projects for future legislation and action. This preface was concerned with two general problems, the first that of obtaining sufficient funds for initial investment, and the second that of ensuring that an increased supply of money did not produce inflation, with its attendant pressure on the value of the franc, an adverse balance of payments and a reduction in the gold reserves held by the Bank of France. To free resources for public and private investment, Blum proposed a series of fiscal measures (including a non-renewable tax on capital), an extension of credit facilities, and a reduction of interest rates, but he also envisaged a greater role for the Bank of France in the regulation of the monetary system and the foreign exchange market.[35]

Throughout his parliamentary career Blum had always taken a special interest in financial and economic policy, but there was a marked difference between the theories which he had expounded in 1936 and those underlying his 1938 proposals, which were, though sketchy in some respects, the first substantial indication that the Socialist Party was prepared to translate its general preference for full employment, public controls and the reduction of income inequalities into concrete and realizable programmes of action. Blum's proposals were bound to attract the hostility of the right but, more significantly, they highlighted underlying differences of outlook within the Popular Front majority. A Radical deputy compared Blum's policy unfavourably with that which had been followed by the two Chautemps governments between June 1937 and March 1938:

De ces deux politiques, l'une repose sur un certain nombre de principes traditionnels et chers aux républicains, à la base desquels se place la liberté; l'autre

---

[34] Jean Lacouture, *Léon Blum* (Seuil, Paris, 1977), p. 428. See also Georges Lefranc, *Histoire du Front Populaire (1934–1938)* (Payot, Paris, 2nd edn, 1974), pp. 275–6; Pierre Mendès-France, 'La politique économique du gouvernement Léon Blum', in *Léon Blum, chef de gouvernement, 1936–1937* (Armand Colin, Paris, 1967), p. 239; comment by Gaston Cusin, ibid., pp. 294–5.

[35] *JO (CD), Doc., 16ᵉ législature, 1938, session ordinaire de 1938, Séance du 5 avril 1938*, Annexe no. 3936, pp. 507–13. See also Blum's speech, *JO (CD), Déb.*, 5 April 1938, pp. 1059–68.

politique, celle qui est devant nous, s'appuie sur une formule nouvelle pour les Français, formule d'intervention, sur un véritable dogmatisme de l'intervention qui admet et qui . . . implique éventuellement la contrainte.[36]

Despite the defection of a large number of Radical deputies, the bill was approved by the Chamber on 6 April by 311 votes to 250[37] but on the 8th the Senate decided by 214 votes to 47 that it would not even proceed to a discussion of the measure.[38] Blum thereupon submitted the resignation of his ministry to the President.

This ambitious attempt to develop an advanced financial and economic programme had several effects on the Socialist Party. Members of its parliamentary group became more confident about discussing specific policy problems on party occasions; one of the unusual features of the Royan Congress, held in the following June, was to be the willingness of delegates to tolerate lengthy technical explanations, such as that given by Charles Spinasse, the Budget Minister in Blum's Cabinet,[39] without raising the objection that the party should not be administering the affairs of the bourgeoisie. Furthermore, now that the party had worked out a programme derived from a close study of existing conditions rather than from an ideal and general prescription, it was possible for its experts and former ministers, such as Georges Monnet, Jules Moch and André Philip, to discuss current affairs and possibilities as though they were a kind of shadow administration, preparing themselves to manage the economy on some future occasion. In short, the Socialists had acquired a practical philosophy of government and produced their first group of *ministrables*, or potential ministers, a development which further strengthened the position of the radical republicans within the central leadership.

While the Blum government's economic and financial policy had generally served to increase party unity, its foreign policy had heightened differences within the loyalist camp over the best means of maintaining the peace. In the first two Popular Front governments, the Socialists had willingly accepted a distribution of portfolios which had left the Radicals with the major responsibility for external affairs. Edouard Daladier as Minister of National Defence and Yvon Delbos as Minister

---

[36] Georges Potut, *JO (CD)*, *Déb.*, 5 April 1938, p. 1073.
[37] Ibid., 6 April 1938, pp. 1112–13. At the time of this division, the Groupe Républicain Radical et Radical-Socialiste contained 113 full members and two associated members. Of the full members, 59 voted for the government's bill, 24 voted against it, 27 did not take part in the division and three were absent. One of the associated deputies voted against the bill and the other was absent.
[38] *JO (Sén.)*, *Déb.*, 8 April 1938, pp. 538–9.
[39] Parti Socialiste (SFIO), 35ᵉ Congrès National, Royan, 4–7 juin 1938, *Compte rendu sténographique*, pp. 424–35.

of Foreign Affairs had guided France through the difficult times of late 1936 and 1937 and both had retained their portfolios in the Chautemps government of January–March 1938. In forming his new government, Blum had retained Daladier at the National Defence Ministry but at the Foreign Ministry had replaced Delbos with Joseph Paul-Boncour, a USR Senator who had left the Socialist Party in 1931. Blum and Paul-Boncour were intent on supporting Czechoslovakia against Germany and on 14 March, his very first day in office, Paul-Boncour had informed the Czech minister in Paris that France would give immediate help to his country in the event of aggression.[40] It was partly to explore the means of making good such an undertaking that Blum agreed to Paul-Boncour's request for a meeting of the Permanent Committee of National Defence, a body chaired by Daladier which brought together the ministers and officials, top army officers included, who were responsible for defence and foreign policies.

The French commitment to assist Czechoslovakia to withstand invasion had been set down in a treaty signed on 25 January 1924 and confirmed when the Treaties of Locarno were agreed in December 1925, that is, at a time when the political and military conditions obtaining in Europe were much more favourable to France than they were in the spring of 1938. The French government had therefore inherited a treaty obligation which would not be easy to fulfil: German rearmament was already well advanced, Belgium was no longer an ally, and the only point at which France could threaten Germany on land was on their common border between the city of Basle in the south and the Moselle River in the north, with very difficult country beyond. In the east, the Czechs had an army of 35 divisions but there was no certainty that the Soviet Union, which had a separate pact with Czechoslovakia, would be permitted by Poland and Rumania to pass forces through their territories. Finally, Germany's occupation of Austria had exposed Czechoslovakia to a flanking attack from the south and in Spain the steady gains of Franco's armies were threatening to convert the Pyrenees into a hostile frontier. It was possible to envisage military operations against Germany in which the Czech forces fought defensive battles in the east while the French attacked on the Basle–

---

[40] See Joseph Paul-Boncour, *Entre deux guerres: souvenirs sur la IIIe République*, III, *Sur les chemins de la défaite 1935–1940* (Plon, Paris, 1946), p. 83; *Rapport fait au nom de la commission chargée d'enquêter sur les événements survenus en France de 1933 à 1945* (Assemblée Nationale, Première Législature, Session de 1947, Annexe au procès-verbal de la 2e séance du vendredi 8 août 1947, no. 2344) (Paris, 1951), Annexes, III, p. 801 (9 March 1948). For an excellent account of French foreign policy during this period, see Anthony Adamthwaite, *France and the Coming of the Second World War, 1936–1939* (Frank Cass, London, 1977), pp. 84–91.

Moselle line in the west, but it must have been obvious to the members of the Permanent Committee of National Defence that the result would be a general war.

When the committee met on the afternoon of 15 March it tacitly acknowledged that this was the situation by concluding that the only way in which France could support Czechoslovakia would be to mobilize troops with the aim of holding down sufficient forces on the Basle–Moselle frontier to prevent offensive action by Germany in the east. The value of Soviet aid was questioned both by General Gamelin, the chief of the General Staff, and by General Vuillemin, the chief of the Air Force. The committee was equally pessimistic about the likely effectiveness of a belated French intervention in the Spanish Civil War.[41]

Paul-Boncour had wanted a public assurance that Britain would support France should it go to the aid of Czechoslovakia in the event of a German attack[42] but the response from London was guarded. The British Foreign Secretary, Lord Halifax, instructed the British Ambassador in Paris to inform Paul-Boncour that the British government could assume no commitments in Europe other than those embodied in the Treaties of Locarno (which, in the case of Britain, entailed only an obligation to defend France and Belgium against unprovoked aggression) and those in the Covenant of the League of Nations. The memorandum of guidance, while conceding that Britain might side with France in the event of war, also touched on the possibility that Britain and France might use their good offices with the Czech government to 'bring about a settlement of questions affecting the position of the German minority', a reference to the separatist demands of the German-speaking communities in the Sudeten areas of Bohemia, adjacent to the border with Germany.[43] Very similar arguments were used by the British Prime Minister, Neville Chamberlain, when he outlined policy in a major speech to the House of Commons on 24 March; he too referred to the need to solve the problem posed by the German minority in the Sudetenland, confirmed that Britain would honour its obligations under the Treaties of Locarno and the Covenant of the League, and, while pointing out that Britain was unwilling to undertake a definite commitment to defend Czechoslovakia, indicated that it might

---

[41] Minutes of the meeting of the Permanent Committee of National Defence, 15 March 1938, *Documents diplomatiques français 1932–1939*, 2nd Series, VIII (Ministère des Affaires Étrangères, Paris, 1973), no. 446, pp. 824–31.

[42] Eric Phipps (British Ambassador in Paris) to Halifax, 15 March 1938, *Documents on British Foreign Policy 1919–1939*, 3rd Series, I (HMSO, London, 1949), no. 81, p. 50.

[43] Halifax to Phipps, 22 March 1938, enclosing memorandum of guidance, ibid., no. 106, pp. 82–6.

intervene in support of France should there be a conflict.[44] Blum saw this reassurance as a vital undertaking, and one which his government had secured by informing the British government of its intentions and obliging it to respond publicly.[45]

Paul-Boncour informed the German Ambassador in Paris that France had promised to come to the aid of Czechoslovakia 'with all the forces at her disposal' in the event of a German attack on that country; nevertheless, he declared himself ready to 'work for understanding with Germany in the same way as his predecessors had done, although at the moment the atmosphere for this was not particularly favorable'.[46] The Ambassador, writing to Berlin a few days later, advised his Foreign Ministry that France was prepared to go to war if Czechoslovakia were attacked by Germany, but he also noted that there was a reaction against this intention both in the press and in public opinion.[47]

While Blum's concern about the anschluss and his readiness to underline French commitments to Czechoslovakia indicated a willingness to stand up to Germany, even at the risk of war, Jean-Baptiste Séverac, the party's Deputy Secretary, published a series of articles suggesting that the new government's main concern was to preserve the peace and avoid war if at all possible, even though it had to accept an obligation to strengthen further the country's defences.[48] Séverac's concern to interpret the government's foreign policy in such terms was an outward sign of the underlying division between those in the party who were prepared to place an almost absolute value on peace and those who were ready to accept war as a necessary means of defending the principles of law and justice in international affairs.[49] It was a division which ran right through the loyalist centre of the party and was capable not

[44] 333 H.C. DEB. 5 S., 24 March 1938, cols. 1399–1413.
[45] See Blum, 'Action anglo-française en Tchécoslovaquie', *Le Populaire*, 27 July 1938, p. 1.
[46] Count Johannes von Welczeck (German Ambassador in Paris) to the German Foreign Ministry, 4 April 1938, *Documents on German Foreign Policy 1918–1945*, Series D, II (IIMSO, London, 1950), no. 117, p. 214.
[47] Welczeck to the German Foreign Ministry, 8 April 1938, ibid., no. 120, pp. 217–23.
[48] See Séverac, 'Non pas pour la guerre mais pour la paix!', *Le Populaire*, 15 March 1938, p. 1; 'La paix d'abord et pour le reste on verra ensuite', ibid., 16 March 1938, p. 1; ' "Une démocratie veut nécessairement la paix" ', ibid., 17 March 1938, p. 1: untitled article, ibid., 18 March 1938, pp. 1 and 2; 'Pour sauver la paix aucun sacrifice n'est trop lourd', ibid., 19 March 1938, p. 1; 'Horreur et dégoût', ibid., 20 March 1938, p. 1; 'Le temps travaille pour la paix', ibid., 22 March 1938, p. 1; 'Confiance toujours! ', ibid., 23 March 1938, p. 1; 'La force au service du droit', ibid., 25 March 1938, pp. 1 and 2.
[49] See Richard Gombin, *Les Socialistes et la guerre: la S.F.I.O. et la politique étrangère française entre les deux guerres mondiales* (Mouton and Co., Paris, 1970), especially pp. 230–1 and 256.

only of undermining the moral unity of the whole organization, but also of separating Blum from Paul Faure, whose pacifist convictions were sincere and deeply held.[50]

The tensions within the party on this and other issues directly influenced proceedings at the National Council which met in Paris at the Maison de la Mutualité, in the 5th *arrondissement*, at 9.45 p.m. on Saturday 9 April. It had been convened because Daladier, having been commissioned to form a new ministry, had offered the Socialists an opportunity of participating in his team, with Blum at the Ministry of Foreign Affairs.[51] In his speech to the council, Blum was mainly concerned to persuade the delegates that it would have been irresponsible of his government to have stood its ground against the Senate (there had been demonstrations near the Palais du Luxembourg on the 7th) and to have used the threat of a social uprising to force the upper house to accept the plenary powers bill.

Rester au pouvoir, ne pouvait avoir qu'une raison. La résolution d'imposer au Sénat notre projet. Faire appel aux forces ouvrières et républicaines, c'était possible, nous étions placés sur un terrain favorable. Pourquoi ne l'avons-nous pas fait? Le faire, je ne dis pas que c'était faire la révolution, mais c'était créer une situation révolutionnaire et de propos délibéré. Nous n'avons pas cru qu'il était possible, dans l'état présent de la France et de l'Europe, en raison de la gravité de la situation, de créer des événements de ce genre, qui auraient été amplifiés de telle sorte à provoquer ou avancer des événements dangereux dans le monde.

Blum's republicanism was always balanced by a fear of Jacobinism, by anxiety that a well-intentioned attempt to force events would set in motion a slide towards anarchy at one level and coercive force at another, but his remarks also betray a concern that the cross-pressures within the Popular Front would further weaken the party's fragile unity. He was surprisingly cautious, and did not offer the delegates any clear advice about whether or not they should accept Daladier's offer of participation.

Ce que je vous demande, c'est de ne pas vous éloigner trop de vos décisions précédentes.

Le Parti avait réclamé la formation d'un gouvernement à l'image du Front Populaire intégral. Il avait autorisé le rassemblement national autour du Front Populaire. Cette idée trouvera nécessairement un jour ou l'autre sa réalisation. Elle sera imposée tôt ou tard.

---

[50] The difference of outlook between Léon Blum and Paul Faure in the mid-1930s is discussed in Greene, *The French Socialist Party in the Popular Front Era*, pp. 13–48.

[51] According to Marcel Bidoux (*Le Populaire*, 10 April 1938, p. 1).

Elle sera l'unique moyen d'empêcher le 'bloc national'. Je voudrais que le Parti gardât sur elle son droit de priorité et le marquât de son empreinte, même si elle devait se réaliser sous une autre direction que la direction socialiste. Ce qu'on nous propose en ce moment n'est ni l'un, ni l'autre.[52]

Marceau Pivert had not as yet been sanctioned by the CNC, and his speech to the council played upon the very images which Blum had tried to dispel, those of a party committed to extra-parliamentary adventures, a party refusing to accept that there were still many ways forward in the existing political situation, and a party prepared to accept the legitimacy of class warfare. According to *Le Populaire*'s paraphrase of his remarks, he expressed the fear that a fascist dictatorship was in the making.

Il faut redresser notre politique, les conflits sont des conflits de classe, il faudra capituler ou combattre, or nous ne donnons plus l'impression de parler au nom des masses populaires, et il pense, lui, qu'au lendemain de l'échec devant le Sénat il fallait en appeler aux masses. Marceau Pivert pense qu'il faut savoir courir le risque révolutionnaire.

Aujourd'hui, nous sommes devant une tentative de pré-fascisme, le parti radical est en train de suivre le processus qu'ont suivi les partis libéraux dans d'autres pays.[53]

Speaker after speaker was recommending a refusal of Daladier's offer, but general issues of foreign policy were also being raised. Louis L'Hévéder said that he did not believe in 'l'utilité tragique de la guerre', that he did not accept the division of Europe into two antagonistic blocs, and that France should try to reach agreement with everyone. Zyromski held that the basic problem was the security of France in relation to the strategic positions occupied by fascism, by which he meant that the Spanish Civil War had to be considered against the background of Germany's absorption of Austria and its threat to Czechoslovakia, and he declared himself dissatisfied with Daladier's failure to indicate what his government would do to ensure a Republican victory in Spain. Salomon Grumbach was forced to justify his support for participation in the proposed ministry with reference to the international dimension:

il ne faut pas aller devant les masses avec un esprit de défaitisme. L'absence est une chose redoutable. Une petite cure d'opposition, et une nouvelle crise ministérielle dans trois semaines ou trois mois? . . . L'état du pays et du monde exige un gouvernement stable.

---

[52] Ibid., p. 2.
[53] Ibid.

He asked how a withdrawal from government could be justified given the international situation and, turning to Zyromski, he posed the obvious question: 'Opposition? Et alors, l'Espagne?' With L'Hévéder in view, he simply asked whether or not there was a fascist bloc in Europe and claimed that the peace could not be preserved without the union of all the great democratic powers.[54]

This debate continued until 2.15 a.m. on Sunday 10 April, when the meeting adjourned so that the Resolutions Committee could consider the seven resolutions which had been tabled. When the delegates reassembled at 3.45 a.m., Séverac reported to them on behalf of the committee and read out a long resolution which proposed that the parliamentary group should decline Daladier's offer of participation on the grounds that:

dans les graves circonstances intérieures et extérieures d'aujourd'hui, les formes d'un gouvernement bipartite, d'un gouvernement homogène ou d'un gouvernement étendant vers le centre ou la droite ses frontières à l'exclusion d'une fraction de la majorité ainsi démembrée ne peuvent pas exercer le pouvoir avec autorité et présentent une fragilité dangereuse.

On the other hand, it acknowledged that circumstances required the formation either of a government fully representing the Rassemblement Populaire or a government

groupant autour de la majorité du Front populaire toutes les énergies républicaines pour la sécurité du pays et pour la défense de la démocratie contre toutes les forces du fascisme intérieur et extérieur.[55]

This wording indicated approval of the Rassemblement National combination which Blum had tried to bring about in March 1938. Concluding his report, Séverac warned the delegates that they would have to choose between two versions of his resolution, one with an additional final section to be proposed by Marx Dormoy and one with an alternative final section to be recommended by Zyromski.[56]

Marceau Pivert then read out a motion expressing the views of the Gauche Révolutionnaire, which rejected both the notion of support and that of participation; it called for opposition to any government which did not make a direct appeal to the masses to destroy capitalist oligarch-

[54] Ibid., 11 April 1938, p. 2.
[55] La Vie du Parti, no. 79, 3 May 1938, p. 315. The original Séverac motion did not include the final paragraph ('Le Conseil national, conformément aux statuts, . . . le cadre de la présente résolution') given in this text; this paragraph was adopted as an addition to the original motion on the proposal of Marx Dormoy.
[56] Le Populaire, 11 April 1938, p. 2.

ies, to supply Republican Spain with food and arms, and to stop providing fascist countries with raw materials which would enable them to undertake modern warfare. This basic proposal was embellished with others which advocated ending the iniquities inherited from the Versailles settlement as a prelude to general disarmament, and opposed any form of national union – all likely to appeal to delegates with a pacifist or anti-participationist point of view.[57]

The case for participation had been discarded by this stage. Although Grumbach had drafted a motion proposing that Blum, Paul Faure, Vincent Auriol and Marx Dormoy should ask Daladier for further information about his governmental programme in the hope that participation would become possible, he told the delegates that he had withdrawn his text and asked them to vote for the Séverac resolution. Zyromski then proposed a conclusion for the Séverac text stating that it was impossible for the party to accept a government of the kind proposed by Daladier and to vote in favour of its being accorded plenary powers. His text further recommended that all the bodies of the party should undertake, in parliament and in the country:

une campagne vigoureuse, afin de réaliser les conditions qui permettent de constituer un gouvernement vraiment conforme à la volonté du pays.

However, although the loyalists had given away the idea of participation, they did not agree that the party should move immediately into outright opposition. Instead, they favoured a policy of waiting on events, of *attentisme*, and it was to represent this policy that Marx Dormoy proposed an ending to the Séverac text inviting the National Council to authorize the parliamentary group and the CAP:

d'arrêter l'attitude des élus socialistes au regard des décisions que commanderont les circonstances dans le cadre de la présente résolution.

He explained that his text did not at all imply the acceptance of plenary powers.[58]

The delegates were thus asked to choose between three courses of action; that proposed by Marceau Pivert, of outright opposition and a refusal to join in any ministry other than *un gouvernement de combat* (although he did not use the term on this occasion); that indicated by the Séverac text as extended by Zyromski, of an immediate move to opposition with the eventual aim of forming either a Popular Front government or a *rassemblement national* ministry; and that which would flow from the Séverac text as extended by Dormoy, of leaving the

[57] Ibid.
[58] Ibid., p. 1 (for Dormoy's proposed conclusion) and p. 2.

parliamentary group and the CAP to deal with the problems posed by a Daladier government as they arose, while also accepting the Popular Front or *rassemblement national* combinations as acceptable alternatives for any future government which the party might join. Blum asked the council to vote for the Dormoy version[59] and in the division an absolute majority of the mandates was cast in its favour. The details of the ballot are given in Table 13. The Séverac–Dormoy text had drawn strong support from the large Nord, Bouches-du-Rhône and Pas-de-Calais Federations and areas of bloc and majority votes from federations in the East, the Midi, the Centre and the West. The total vote for the Bataille Socialiste, measured in this instance by the support for the Séverac–Zyromski text, had fallen from the 2,669 (or 32.2 per cent of the total) it had gained in the first ballot at the January meeting of the council to 2,107 (25.4 per cent); in geographical terms, Zyromski's *tendance* had lost ground in the South-West while holding its own in the Paris basin. By contrast, the Gauche Révolutionnaire, despite its parallel concern with disciplinary proceedings against Marceau Pivert and his colleagues in the Seine Federation, had managed to strengthen its position; Marceau Pivert's text had attracted 1,656 mandates (19.9 per cent) on this occasion compared with 1,478 mandates (17.8 per cent) in the first division of the January meeting, and had polled exceptionally well in the Seine (353 of 632 mandates), Meurthe-et-Moselle (115 of 154), Loiret (27 of 31), Lot (all 30) and Alpes-Maritimes (52 of 83) Federations.

The party's leaders had thus succeeded in attracting an absolute majority of the mandates for the 'official' resolution and avoided another humiliating defeat of the kind which had been inflicted on them at the National Council of 17 January 1938. On that occasion, the Sérol motion had recommended acceptance of the Radicals' offer of participation but at this April meeting the Séverac text had proposed refusal of a similar offer, coming as close to an anti-participationist position as was possible under the circumstances. On the other hand, the Séverac motion did not exclude the possibility of a Popular Front government and thus avoided offending those delegates who still had hope that this alliance could be revived, and its reference to Blum's *rassemblement national* formula was sufficiently vague to avoid outright dissent (although the representatives of the Algiers, Ardèche, Doubs, Haut-Rhin (Belfort) and Yonne Federations did express reservations about this part of the text).[60] Thus constructed, the motion did not conflict

---

[59] Ibid., p. 2.
[60] *La Vie du Parti*, no. 79, 3 May 1938, p. 315.

Table 13. *SFIO: National Council, 9 April 1938: division on general policy*

Federations	Mandates for the motions of:										
	Séverac – Dormoy (loyalist)		Séverac – Zyromski (Bataille Socialiste)		Marceau Pivert (Gauche Révolutionnaire)		Abstentions		Absent		Totals
	no.	%	no.	%	no.	%	no.	%	no.	%	no.
Bouches-du-Rhône	300	95.2	15	4.8							315
Gironde			158	84.9	28	15.1					186
Meurthe-et-Moselle	9	5.8	30	19.5	115	74.7					154
Nord	753	98.2	11	1.4	3	0.4					767
Pas-de-Calais	298	84.9	49	14.0	4	1.1					351
Seine	164	25.9	115	18.2	353	55.9					632
Seine-et-Oise	70	19.9	154	43.9	127	36.2					351
Haute-Vienne	84	50.3			83	49.7					167
Others	2,642	49.1	1,575	29.3	943	17.5			223	4.1	5,383
Totals	4,320	52.0	2,107	25.4	1,656	19.9			223	2.7	8,306

Source: La Vie du Parti (Paris), no. 79, 3 May 1938, pp. 315–16.

sharply with the policy preferences of the Bataille, and some delegates normally disposed to support Zyromski may have given their mandates to the Séverac-Dormoy text on this occasion. Finally, it is possible that the Gauche Révolutionnaire could have persuaded more federations to accept its policies had its campaign against the national union not been weakened by the crisis in the Seine Federation.

What motives lay behind the central leaders' policy of *attentisme*? It is possible that they had seen the National Council of 9 April as something to be endured rather than as an occasion for taking bold decisions, and that Blum and his close advisers had formed the view that any government which Daladier formed would be fragile. If such a government were to fall, another meeting of the National Council could be called and the question of strategy reconsidered. Even then, there would have been little chance of setting up a tripartite coalition of Socialists, Radicals and Communists; although there was still talk of a further wave of Popular Front reforms, principally those which the CGT had proposed and which the Marseille Congress had approved in July 1937, both the financial means and, on the part of the Radicals at least, the will to convert them into a definite programme were lacking; the Senate had shown that it was prepared to block any financial policy which it judged to be unorthodox; and the Radical Party had made it clear that it was not now prepared to share power with the Communists.

Events moved rapidly in the days which followed. Early on the afternoon of Sunday 10 April Daladier was able to form a centre government consisting mainly of Radicals but also including three members of the USR and four representatives of the centre right. Amongst the ministerial appointments were Chautemps as Vice-Premier, Albert Sarraut as Minister of the Interior, Georges Bonnet as Minister of Foreign Affairs, Paul Marchandeau as Minister of Finance, Paul Reynaud as Minister of Justice and Georges Mandel as Minister of the Colonies. On Tuesday 12 April the Chamber of Deputies heard a brief ministerial statement from Daladier and expressed confidence in his administration by passing a procedural motion by 587 votes to 6.[61] It then approved a bill asking for plenary powers for financial purposes by 514 votes to 8,[62] but despite these almost unanimous decisions all groups assumed that, for the moment, the new ministry would rest upon the Popular Front majority in the lower house. Meanwhile, the internal crisis within the SFIO had reached its climax: the Seine Federation had tried to keep Marceau Pivert and his colleagues in office despite the sanctions which had been

[61] *JO (CD), Déb.*, 12 April 1938, pp. 1180–1.
[62] Ibid., pp. 1183–4.

imposed on them by the CNC but on 14 April it was dissolved by the CAP.

Let us now take stock of how the balance of forces within the Socialist Party had been affected by all that had happened in the five weeks following the National Council of 12 March. The formation and effective working of the Blum government had created the illusion that the clock had been turned back, at least to the middle months of the first Popular Front administration, and that the uncertainty and confusion which had affected the party's leadership in February and March had been dissipated. Only the Gauche Révolutionnaire had continued to dwell on Blum's interest in forming a national government, and the problem posed by the Communists' ambition to enter government and the Radicals' reluctance to work with them had been conveniently forgotten. With the cancellation of the meeting of the National Council which was to have been held on 27 March, the *Socialiste* group was no longer under pressure to justify its existence as a *tendance*. The economic and financial policy of the Blum government had been generally accepted by the Socialists, but its foreign policy, with its stress on the need to honour French commitments to Czechoslovakia, had threatened to revive old differences between pacifists and those who were prepared to countenance a more determined stand against Germany and Italy. With this exception, the March – April period had seen the loyalist camp restored to some semblance of unity.

The Bataille Socialiste was still locked into the relatively static position it had adopted earlier in the year. Although Zyromski had recommended opposition to the newly formed Daladier government, his *tendance* was still prepared to support the principle of participation where it applied to the tripartite version of the Popular Front, with a government composed of Socialists, Radicals and Communists, and it continued to accept the idea of a government of *rassemblement national*, which would have included Communist representatives. Yet the Bataille was a disturbing factor in the party's structure of group relations, because Zyromski's enthusiasm for a defensive alliance of France, Britain and the Soviet Union against Germany and Italy had created the impression that he and his *tendance* had accepted a European war as inevitable, whereas Blum and his colleagues were still inclined to see defence preparations as an aid to negotiations for a peaceful settlement of international relations. It was the apparent correspondence between the Blum government's foreign policy and the international outlook of Zyromski and his *tendance* which was most likely to set in motion an anti-Communist, anti-Soviet and pro-pacifist reaction within the loyalist majority.

If the relative advantage of the different groups is judged purely in terms of their policy positions, the Gauche Révolutionnaire stands out immediately as the one with most freedom of manoeuvre and the most telling normative resources. Despite its occasional references to the need for a *gouvernement de combat*, the main themes in its rhetoric were anti-participationism, anti-Bolshevism, anticlericalism and revolutionary defeatism. Its appeal in the provinces had been weakened by its association with Parisian intellectuals and by the heavy doctrinal overlay which it gave to its messages, but it remained the only rallying-point for libertarian and revolutionary dissent within the party. It could well have increased its support in the period leading up to the Royan Congress, but, as we have seen, it had become embroiled in a complicated and unpromising dispute with the party's General Secretariat over the sanctions which had been imposed on the Seine Federation.

Preparations for the Royan Congress

The arrangements for the SFIO's 35th National Congress were made by the CAP at its meetings of 23 March and 13–14 April 1938. The venue chosen was Royan, a coastal resort situated on the northern bank of the Gironde River, in the Department of Charente-Maritime, and it was decided that the meeting would extend from Saturday 4 to Tuesday 7 June 1938.[63] The CAP duly dispatched copies of the statutory reports to the federations, and they in their turn began to make arrangements for the federal congresses, while the *tendances* and other groups began to prepare motions for these meetings. In this section, we shall study this process, considering first the politics affecting the rebel federation in the Seine Department and then the main themes of the general policy resolutions produced during this period.

On Friday 15 April those members of the Executive Committee of the Seine Federation who had not followed Marceau Pivert into rebellion met at the SFIO's national headquarters at 12 Cité Malesherbes, in Paris, and nominated a provisional Federal Bureau, with Gaston Allemane as Political Secretary, André Costedoat as Administrative Secretary and René Jousse restored to his old post as Treasurer.[64] Allemane represented the fresh start not so much as a restoration of order but as a turning-point in the life of the federation, away from the culture of *tendances* and towards a new and more responsible way of conducting affairs.

---

[63] *Le Populaire*, 27 March 1938, p. 7; 15 April 1938, p. 2.
[64] Ibid., 17 April 1938, p. 5; *Le Temps*, 17 April 1938, p. 3.

Le bureau provisoire de la nouvelle fédération s'efforcera, avant toutes choses, de calmer les esprits, de faire appel au sang-froid et au 'patriotisme de parti' de tous les militants de la Seine.

Une de ses premières préoccupations sera d'attirer l'attention des nouvelles sections reconstituées, sur le jeu décevant et démoralisant des tendances cristallisées. Aucune oeuvre féconde, aucun redressement ne serait possible, si la lutte des ['clans'] devait être continuée comme par le passé. Quel temps précieux perdu pour la propagande, que ces longues heures consacrées à des mots ou à des textes souvent vides de substance, et presque toujours dépassés, dans le moment présent, par les événements nouveaux et inattendus de chaque jour.[65]

Throughout late April and early May the rival federations of the Seine waged a bitter competition to win over branches and members to their respective sides. Generally speaking, the reconstructed federation was the more successful in the suburbs and the rebel federation more successful in Paris itself, but in the end the former emerged as the stronger of the two, partly because it managed to retain the allegiance of the principal leaders of the Bataille Socialiste, including not only Zyromski but also Pierre Commin, Andrée Marty-Capgras and Henri Sellier. The party members were in any case subjected to heavy moral pressure from the authorities: the CAP decided on 27 April that those who had not signed a declaration of loyalty by 14 May would be considered to have left the party, but the Federal Congress of the reconstructed unit eventually decided to recommend to the Royan Congress that the deadline should be extended to 1 July. Of the original total of 17,000 members in the undivided federation (as of 1 January 1938), about 10,000 were reported to have signed the declaration by 15 May and by the time of the Royan Congress the figure was approaching the 12,000 mark.[66] This evidence would suggest that the rebel federation had retained about 5,000 of the original members but it would also have admitted fresh recruits from the ranks of those who had been previously excluded from the SFIO and from sympathetic groups of the non-Communist left.

The rebel federation and the Gauche Révolutionnaire were bound together, most obviously through the leadership of Marceau Pivert, but their interests were by no means identical. Whereas the rebel federation

---

[65] Allemane, 'Pour faire oeuvre utile', *Le Populaire*, 20 April 1938, p. 4, with correction from ibid., 21 April 1938, p. 4.

[66] According to figures cited by André Costedoat, Parti Socialiste (SFIO), 35ᵉ Congrès National, Royan, 4–7 juin 1938, *Compte rendu sténographique*, p. 27. These figures evidently refer to the total number of annual card-holders. The end-of-year figure for annual card-holders for 1937 for the Seine Federation was 20,200 (ibid., *Rapports*, p. 139) but not all of these would have purchased new cards at the beginning of 1938.

was a compact group of activists, concentrated largely in the branches of the Paris area, the Gauche Révolutionnaire had to maintain a link between this element and its widely dispersed provincial networks. Both the rebel federation and the *tendance* as a whole considered that the party's ordinary members would agree with them that the sanctions were unjustified; they were counting on the possibility that pressure from below would oblige the Royan Congress to reverse the disciplinary measures and allow the delegates from the rebel federation to take a full part in proceedings. However, a majority of the rebels wanted to go much further than this and to insist that the Royan Congress should reaffirm the party's revolutionary character, as defined by the founding Charter of 1905, and repudiate the ideas of national union and class collaboration. If the congress were not prepared to do this, ran the argument, the Gauche Révolutionnaire should leave the SFIO and found a new political party. However, the majority of the provincial members of the *tendance* were inclined to the view that it was more sensible to concentrate on the task of having the sanctions removed at such a crucial stage in the confrontation.

Marceau Pivert himself was a divided man. One part of him, the Parisian activist, was attracted to the idea of posing fundamental questions of doctrine and forming a new party if they were not answered to his satisfaction, while another part, the spirited orator who had won respect throughout the party for his courage and intellectual integrity, hoped that he could inspire the party's ordinary members to call for the removal of sanctions and the revival of the values of 1905. This concern to give the disciplinary issue a deep significance is evident in a circular which he prepared for dispatch to party members in the provinces; in this document, he recommended that meetings should adopt resolutions condemning the principle of national union, approving the distribution of the *Alerte!* tract, and calling not only for the withdrawal of sanctions but also for the admission of the federation's delegates to the National Congress.[67] A few days later he wrote to Maurice Deixonne asking him to write an article for *Le Populaire* in support of the rebel federation. At this stage he was quite confident that the situation could be restored.

Nous gagnerons certainement en étendue et en pénétration à la suite de cette inqualifiable et grotesque offensive bureaucratique. En tout cas, de partout

---

[67] 'La Fédération socialiste de la Seine aux camarades de province' (cyclostyled). This document is undated but is probably the enclosure described as 'une note que nous envoyons aux camarades de province qui nous demandent conseil' in a letter from Marceau Pivert to Maurice Deixonne, from Paris, 17 April 1938 (both documents are in the Archives Maurice Deixonne, OURS).

montent les témoignages de solidarité. Maintenant nous n'avons rien à perdre: Démocratie intérieure – respect de la Charte constitutive – révolte contre la faiblesse et l'impuissance incroyable des 'cadres' tout concourt à vérifier ce que contient vraiment le Parti . . . [68]

An appeal from the Gauche Révolutionnaire presented the conflict in similar terms:

il faut traquer la bureaucratie, l'obliger à rendre des comptes et restaurer au Parti sa figure de Parti de classe: cet effort doit être tenté dans l'intérêt supérieur du prolétariat, que nous plaçons au-dessus de toutes nos légitimes révoltes et qui serait la victime certaine, en dernier lieu, d'un triomphe de la dictature bureaucratique sur la base saine, démocratique et révolutionnaire de nos milliers de sections.[69]

In his private correspondence with Maurice Deixonne, Pivert continued to portray the bureaucracy as a scheming opponent but he nevertheless insisted that the membership would rally to his cause.

L'essentiel pour nous est d'informer au maximum les militants du Parti et c'est ce que nous essayons de faire avec nos propres moyens. Il s'agit de la vie même du Parti qui est mise en cause et nous avons immédiatement démontré notre souci de laisser à d'autres les responsabilités de la scission. Si en effet le Congrès de ROYAN vote la réintégration de la Fédération de la Seine avec tous ses droits pour que l'examen loyal de tous les faits soit poursuivi devant l'instance suprême du Parti, il n'y a pas de raison pour que l'unité soit menacée, mais au contraire si la bureaucratie du Parti poursuit son opération de conservation des manettes de commande par la décimation de l'opposition, alors évidemment notre responsabilité n'est plus en cause que nous le voulions ou non nous sommes obligés de défendre le socialisme . . .

Despite this faint trace of anxiety, he remained generally optimistic regarding the outcome:

on ne pourra plus dissimuler l'ampleur de la protestation démocratique et de l'opposition socialiste révolutionnaire. Nous recevons d'ailleurs de province des nouvelles réconfortantes.[70]

As the tone of this letter demonstrates, Marceau Pivert had persuaded himself that the removal of sanctions was a secondary consideration and that the main objective of the campaign should be to convince the membership that the very soul of the party was in danger. This was a major error of judgement: it would have been much easier to build

---

[68] Letter from Marceau Pivert to Maurice Deixonne, from Paris, 20 April 1938 (Archives Maurice Deixonne, OURS).
[69] From a statement by 'La tendance Gauche Révolutionnaire du Parti Socialiste', *Les Cahiers Rouges*, special number, 22 April 1938, p. 8.
[70] Letter from Marceau Pivert to Maurice Deixonne, from Paris, 25 April 1938 (Archives Maurice Deixonne, OURS).

up support by directing attention to the purely legal aspects of the affair, and appealing to the principles of natural justice rather than to major issues of doctrine. The claims about a conspiracy at the top of the hierarchy were placing too much strain on the credulity of the provincial federations. In one document, for example, the rebels revived and elaborated the charge that it was the leaders who should be on trial, and that the decision of the National Council of 12 March to support Blum in his efforts to form a national government was contrary to the principles contained in the party's foundation documents.

L'indiscipline, s'il en est une, est dans le vote par le Conseil National de décisions contraires aux principes fondamentaux du Parti. C'est sur ce fait politique essentiel que vous devez en toute franchise prendre position.[71]

In a separate circular, the leaders of the Gauche Révolutionnaire sought to demonstrate that the leaders of the party were trying to save themselves by political manoeuvres.

Nous affirmons, en effet, que de telles mesures [that is, the dissolution of the Seine Federation and the methods adopted for its reconstitution] ne peuvent s'expliquer que par le désir non pas de sauver le Parti mais de sauver sa direction actuelle, profondément inquiète devant les résultats de sa politique et l'ampleur des protestations qui montent [du] sein du Parti. Nous affirmons qu'on a voulu avant tout essayer d'affaiblir l'opposition avant le prochain Congrès National et tenter, au dépens de la Fédération de la Seine, une diversion de nature soit à impressionner les militants de province, soit à créer, on ne sait quel alibi pour détourner leurs pensées des graves problèmes politiques qui se posent aujourd'hui.[72]

Having committed themselves to such a special interpretation of recent events, the rebels and the Gauche Révolutionnaire were left with a formidable tactical problem – how were they to present such a complicated case to the Royan Congress? They decided that the best approach would be to raise a point of order at the very first session of the congress and then to generalize the discussion so that the issues of grand principle could be considered at that stage rather than piecemeal in the latter part of the proceedings. The actual plan, described in the *Bulletin Intérieur* which the Gauche Revolutionnaire issued on 27 April, involved the tabling of a preliminary motion (*une motion préalable*) before the congress had had an opportunity of considering the annual

---

[71] 'La Fédération de la Seine à toutes les fédérations du Parti S.F.I.O.' (cyclostyled) (Archives Maurice Deixonne, OURS).
[72] 'Déclaration: la minorité de la C.A.P. (tendance G.R.)' (cyclostyled) (Archives Maurice Deixonne, OURS). The signatories are Marceau Pivert, Lucien Hérard, [Georges] Soulès, [Georges] Floutard, René Modiano, Degez, Berthe Fouchère, Levant and [Henri] Midon.

report (*le rapport moral*) from the CAP, the first item on its agenda. The draft preliminary motion proposed that the congress should deal immediately with the situation which had been created by the dissolution of the Seine Federation; that the delegates of the dissolved federation should be heard in the discussion; and that immediately after this preliminary debate, the congress should embark upon a general discussion of the political situation, moving the examination of the statutory reports to the end of the agenda. Pointing out that the draft motion did not have a markedly political character, the *Bulletin Intérieur* explained that it could therefore be signed by members who did not belong to the Gauche Révolutionnaire. Recipients were asked to try out the draft on influential members of their federations and to let Lucien Hérard have their views on it. They were told that the final text would be sent to them, along with a second motion to be tabled at the end of the debate on the Seine affair which was expected to take place once the preliminary motion had been adopted.[73]

Although framed to appeal to a wide audience, this plan was much too rigid to stand any chance of success; even if members outside the Gauche Révolutionnaire were persuaded that it would be right to lift the sanctions, they were most unlikely to favour the admission to the debate of delegates from the rebel federation or to approve the idea of linking the question of discipline to the question of general policy. However, no such doubts were troubling Marceau Pivert: in a further letter to Maurice Deixonne and his wife Suzanne, he responded to the latter's apparent disquiet by reaffirming his own view of what was happening.

Je ne désespère nullement, en ce qui me concerne. Si le Parti, c'était *ça*, c'est à dire une clique de bureaucrates liés par des intérêts de caste et prêts à tout briser pour rester à la tête du Parti, qu'est ce que nous pourrions y faire? Nous avons le sentiment de représenter autre chose, de valoir autre chose et de pouvoir autre chose . . . Mais l'expérience n'est pas terminée: la tempête monte: dès maintenant notre résistance d'hommes libres suscite des réactions dont l'ampleur est imprévisible: . . .

He cited encouraging news from the Aisne Federation and continued:

mais on n'obtiendra rien sans aller au fond des choses: c'est pour l'honneur même du socialisme et pour son avenir que nous résistons à une tentative effroyablement meurtrière pour tous. Pourquoi sous-estimer la résistance des

---

[73] *Bulletin Intérieur de la Gauche Révolutionnaire*, 27 April 1938, p. 1. The draft motion, entitled 'Projet de motion préalable à faire voter immédiatement après l'ouverture du Congrès lors de la proposition de l'ordre du jour' (cyclostyled), is printed on a single sheet of paper but is obviously the document referred to in the *Bulletin Intérieur* (Archives Maurice Deixonne, OURS).

honnêtes gens du Parti? Pourquoi Suzanne considère-t-elle comme utopie l'espoir que nous avons de faire poser la question? *La question sera posée.* Quel
compromis peut on envisager? Aucun.[74]

By the middle of May the provincial federations had begun to deal
with the issue of sanctions, but generally not in the way which Marceau
Pivert and his friends had recommended. Very few of these federations
had sufficient knowledge of the background to the cases to form an
independent view of the wisdom of the decisions, and their members
tended either to accept the verdicts on trust, or to reject them on the
grounds that they offended the principles of natural justice, or to propose some form of amnesty as a convenient means of ending controversy and restoring unity. There was little sympathy for the claim that
the party bureaucracy was trying to crush the true Socialists for political
reasons. One circular presented the quite different view that party unity

est menacée d'un côté par une minorité exaltée et irritée de la Gauche Révolutionnaire qui rêve de la constitution d'un nouveau parti, de l'autre côté par une
épuration organisée et dirigée.

Its authors recommended that party members in the provinces should
seek to persuade the Royan Congress to agree to a complete amnesty
and that those in the Seine should work for the restoration of fraternal
unity.[75] Taken aback by the talk of amnesty, the Gauche Révolutionnaire made a desperate effort to salvage something of its original
plan. In its *Bulletin Intérieur* of 16 May it again recommended the device
of a preliminary motion, advising recipients of the *Bulletin* to back an
amnesty motion only as a last resort and only if two conditions were
met – they should not be alone in doing so, and the amnesty should be
justified on the grounds that it was necessary to maintain party unity.[76]
    The campaign against sanctions was further hampered by the publi-
city given to the politics surrounding the rebel federation's Federal Congress, which was held on Sunday 15 May. The committee entrusted
with the task of preparing a policy resolution for this congress had
produced a two-part motion: the first part, which the committee had
approved unanimously, called for the lifting of the sanctions and the
second, passed by a majority, actually envisaged a split in the party if
the Royan Congress refused to take such action.

[74] Letter from Marceau Pivert to Maurice and Suzanne Deixonne, from Paris, 6 May
1938 (Archives Maurice Deixonne, OURS).
[75] 'Appel aux militants du Parti Socialiste' (cyclostyled) (Archives Maurice Deixonne,
OURS). It was signed by Georges Albertini (Aube), Jacques Godard (Seine), Jean
Le Bail (Haute-Vienne), Emilie and Georges Lefranc (Seine), Paul Rivet (Seine),
Henri Sellier (Seine), Robert Viel[le] (Gironde) and Ludovic Zoretti (Calvados).
[76] *Bulletin Intérieur de la Gauche Révolutionnaire*, 16 May 1938, p. 1.

Mais s'il advenait qu'au Congrès de Royan le Parti ne réponde pas à l'appel solennel à lui adressé par la Fédération socialiste de la Seine, si par là même il ne rétablissait pas dans ses droits notre Fédération, alors la preuve serait faite que ce Parti considérerait désormais comme statutaire toute décision bureaucratique tendant à restreindre la liberté et à interdire la circulation de toutes les pensées et de toutes les opinions libres. Alors cela voudrait dire que ce Parti réviserait en fait sa charte constitutive, en y introduisant l'acceptation de l'Union nationale et de l'Union sacrée. Nous n'aurions plus devant nous un parti de lutte de classes et de révolution, mais un parti transformé dans son essence, un parti qui à aucun titre ne pourrait se réclamer des principes inscrits dans la charte de 1905.

C'est à nos délégués qu'il appartiendrait alors, et sans tarder, à Royan même, de se réunir avec les délégués des fédérations de province, afin de prendre toute décision en vue d'assurer la continuité du Parti socialiste, parti de lutte de classes et de révolution.[77]

Seizing on a version of this motion which had been included in a *Bulletin Intérieur* of the Gauche Révolutionnaire, Paul Faure and J.-B. Séverac claimed in a circular that the threat to split the party indicated that:

si le Parti déclare vouloir demeurer fidèle au Front Populaire, fidèle aux engagements contractés, fidèle aux décisions du Congrès National de Juin 1936, et aux décisions des assemblées nationales qui ont suivi, fidèle enfin à ses règles statutaires, tout cela sera considéré comme un trahison et un reniement de la pensée socialiste. On aura alors le prétexte recherché pour justifier la création d'un Parti auquel songent depuis longtemps déjà des membres influents de la G.R. et on pourra y faire adhérer des formations entières du Parti actuel. *C'est l'organisation froidement préméditée de la scission.*[78]

Seen in this light, the leaders of the Gauche Révolutionnaire were revealed not as the innocent victims of persecution but as conspirators who had long been planning to break away from the SFIO and who had now found an excuse for doing so.

On Saturday 21 May, Marceau Pivert had suffered a broken right shoulder-blade when a car in which he was a passenger had overturned near the town of Crépy-en-Valois, north-east of Paris.[79] Confined to

---

[77] *Juin 36*, 10 May 1938, cited by Paul Faure in Parti Socialiste (SFIO), 35ᵉ Congrès National, Royan, 4–7 juin 1938, *Compte rendu sténographique*, pp. 144–5, quotation from p. 145. For the division into two parts, see the version of the motion given in *Bulletin Intérieur de la Gauche Révolutionnaire*, 16 May 1938, p. 4. For detailed accounts of events within the rebel federation at this time, see Guérin, *Front Populaire: révolution manquée*, pp. 194–7; Joubert, *Révolutionnaires de la S.F.I.O.*, pp. 145–7.

[78] Cyclostyled circular signed by Paul Faure and J.-B. Séverac, Secrétariat général, Parti Socialiste (S.F.I.O.), 25 May 1938 (Dossier 31, 22 AS 1, Papiers des Amis de Marceau Pivert, Archives Nationales), p. 2.

[79] *Le Populaire*, 23 May 1938, p. 2.

bed with his shoulder in plaster, he was still undecided about what course of action he should take; he was under pressure from the freemasons, with whom Suzanne Nicolitch was connected, to pursue a moderate and conciliatory line, but he was also being advised to avoid compromise. Daniel Guérin has recalled a visit to his bedside after the accident:

Suzanne Nicolitch était assise d'un côté du lit, Michel Collinet et moi-même de l'autre. Le malheureux patient était comme écartelé entre ces conseillers antagonistes qui, l'une, l'adjurait de ne pas réduire les chances d'un compromis, les autres d'en finir avec ces chimères et d'aller jusqu'au bout.[80]

However, by the time of his departure for Royan, Pivert had made up his mind to take a definite stand. He was now predicting that after the congress the activists

s'appliqueront avec une volonté irréductible à forger soit par un 'redressement interne' que nous souhaitons de tout cœur, soit par 'un nouveau départ' si on nous y oblige, un vrai parti socialiste 'de lutte de classe et de révolution' dont les innombrables victimes de la crise attendent anxieusement les initiatives.[81]

Meanwhile, the federal congresses were dealing with motions and policy issues which were to come before the Royan Congress. The Gauche Révolutionnaire's motion was constructed around two heavily contrasted narratives, one telling the story of the Popular Front and the other relating the formation of the SFIO in 1905. The first part of the text, headed 'Nécessité d'un bilan politique', attributed the alleged failure of the Popular Front to the exclusion of proposals for reforms of structure from its original programme, to the Blum government's reluctance to build upon the mass action of 1936 by launching a bold offensive against the banks and the trusts, and its subsequent resort to economic liberalism, which entailed confidence in capitalism and the pause in policy in 1937. The Blum government was accused of denying material aid to Republican Spain, and all the Popular Front governments were blamed for not having taken a serious initiative to bring about a peaceful resolution of European conflicts in order to facilitate a reduction of armaments. In an even stronger attack on the party's leaders, the motion claimed that the decisions which had been taken at the Marseille Congress of July 1937 had not been respected; no serious attempt had been made to open the Spanish frontier, to mobilize the masses in support of the nationalization of businesses, or to arouse

---

[80] Guérin, *Front Populaire: révolution manquée*, p. 197.
[81] Cited in Michel-P. Hamelet, 'Vers une nouvelle extrême-gauche', *Le Figaro* (Paris), 1 June 1938, p. 5. See also Hamelet, 'Scission larvée chez les Socialistes', ibid., 31 May 1938, pp. 1 and 3.

popular discontent against the Senate. Yet the majority of the CAP had dissolved the Seine Federation, which had applied the Marseille decisions, and the National Council of 12 March 1938, by adopting the principle of national union:

s'est mis en contradiction avec la Charte et les décisions de tous les congrès du Parti. Ce Conseil national a, par là même, confirmé le décès du Front populaire sur le terrain parlementaire.

The Daladier government was cast in the worst possible light: it was charged with bringing about a national union in parliament and with being in itself a step towards national union at the level of government. Externally,

ce gouvernement préfasciste soumet la politique du pays aux intérêts de l'impérialisme britannique. Son abandon total de la république espagnole, son accord avec Mussolini et son accord militaire avec la Grande-Bretagne sont, en fait, dirigés contre les travailleurs. Sur le plan intérieur, il s'efforce de détruire les conquêtes sociales, militarise l'appareil de l'Etat et fait retomber sur le dos du peuple les charges écrasantes provoquées par le réarmement et la crise du régime.

The way forward was mapped out against a wider time-scale in the concluding part of the text, entitled 'Les buts du parti'. This called on the National Congress to reaffirm that the Socialist Party was a party of class struggle and revolution, in keeping with the original Charter of 1905, and to repudiate any form of national union 'avec les organisations de la bourgeoisie'. The text then outlined the need for an offensive against capitalism and fascism and set out a formidable list of slogans (*mots d'ordre*) as its basis – the nationalization of capitalist trusts, workers' control of production, the effective dissolution of fascist groups, the suppression of the Senate, the purging of the civil service and the army, political freedom for soldiers, aid to the Spanish workers, and the boycott of the export to fascist states of raw materials for use in war industries.

Ces mots d'ordre devront aboutir à l'instauration d'un gouvernement de combat, s'appuyant directement sur les masses ouvrières et démocratiques, capable de briser toutes les résistances capitalistes ou parlementaires, d'organiser la production et la répartition sur des bases collectives.

The text went on to denounce

le caractère capitaliste et impérialiste des oppositions dites idéologiques, et qui ne sont qu'une lutte pour la possession des sources de matières premières et des marchés. Il déclare que le Gouvernement de combat qu'imposeront les masses travailleuses aura parmi ses tâches essentielles et urgentes la réunion d'une Conférence internationale en vue de reviser l'inique traité de Versailles et de répartir équitablement les matières premières dans un monde enfin désarmé.[82]

By asserting that the Popular Front had failed and by depicting the Daladier government as the prelude to a national union, the Gauche Révolutionnaire had placed itself in opposition to any form of participation in government under existing conditions. To find historical justification for this stand it had reached back to the party's founding period, when a complete refusal to co-operate with the bourgeois regime and the rejection of war were the basic principles of Socialist fundamentalism. The motion's reference to an offensive against capitalism and fascism, its list of slogans and its allusions to a *gouvernement de combat* invited the reader to imagine a future time in which a revolution could be achieved by sustained activism, providing that, in the meantime, the party could preserve its moral integrity and its vision. Against this canvas, the party's leaders, with their willingness to accept compromises and even to tolerate the idea of a national union, could be represented as people who had lost touch with the party's ideals and whose faith in its essential purposes had been undermined.

Whereas the Gauche Révolutionnaire now had reservations about the Popular Front, the Bataille Socialiste still saw this alliance as the most important development in the politics of the left in the 1930s. Jean Zyromski and his followers believed that the SFIO's participation in the front had greatly enlarged its social base and brought it closer to the Communist Party and the trade unions. Where the future was concerned, they took the view that the Popular Front still had considerable capacity for renewal and growth, and that the Socialist Party would be an integral part of this process. It was for this reason that they were pressing for the formation of a government which would represent all elements of the front, including the Communists, a demand which was consistent with Zyromski's call for an international alliance of France, Britain and the Soviet Union against Germany and Italy.

In domestic politics, Zyromski's main problem was to demonstrate that it was possible to restore good relations between the Socialist and the Communist Parties. As we have seen, the SFIO's CAP had decided on 24 November 1937 to break off talks about forming a united party, given the attitude towards social democratic parties which had been

---

[82] This motion was published in *Les Cahiers Rouges*, no. 11, 13 May 1938, pp. 1–2, and was also included in a two-page supplement to this edition (there is a copy in the Archives Maurice Deixonne, OURS). The quotations above are taken from the latter text.

revealed by the Dimitroff manifesto.[83] Subsequently, the Communist Party had published two tracts, each entitled *Pour l'unité*, which claimed that the Socialists were to blame for the split in the original SFIO in 1920, that the Communists had nevertheless worked for unity of action in the years which followed the split, that their efforts had produced the agreement concluded between the two parties on 27 July 1934, and that the Communists had never considered the division of 1920 as irreversible. Such a misleading account of recent history had provoked an immediate response from the SFIO's General Secretariat, which had devoted a whole issue of *La Vie du Parti* to a fully documented account of its version of events. Party members were reminded that in 1920 it had been the Third International which had set out to exclude those judged to be reformists and centrists; that the French Communist Party had pursued a series of strategies intended to separate the leaders of the SFIO from their followers, and that it had been the Socialists rather than the Communists who had tried to bring about unity of action in the first half of 1934.[84] There were meetings of their *Comité d'Entente* on 11 March and 4 May 1938, but the two parties continued to treat each other with reserve.

On the other hand, the CGT had retained the confidence of the Socialist leaders, and Zyromski was on safe ground when arguing that the parties of the Popular Front should develop a new programme of reforms, including in it those which had been proposed by the trade-union organization. For the Marseille Congress of July 1937, the Bataille motion had set out in a special section the CGT's plans for the nationalization of insurance companies, banks and key sectors of the economy, including heavy industry and the electricity, transport, mining, chemicals, motor-fuel, water and gas industries, and for the extension of state trading to cover not only wheat but also milk, wine, fertilizer and meat production.[85] Zyromski had no difficulty in supporting such a scheme; he was a firm believer in the regulation of economic activities by the government and was not unduly concerned about the increased controls and the expenditure which they would entail.

We may assume that Zyromski was the main author of the Bataille Socialiste policy resolution, which was published early in May; it highlighted the proposals for further reform, pressed for the fusion of the

[83] See above, pp. 19–20.
[84] *La Vie du Parti*, no. 77, 10 March 1938, pp. 309–11.
[85] See Part III of the motion presented by Bracke and Zyromski to the Marseille Congress (Parti Socialiste (SFIO), 34ᵉ Congrès National, Marseille, 10–13 juillet 1937, *Compte rendu sténographique* (Librairie Populaire, Paris, n.d.), pp. 561–2).

Socialist and Communist Parties, and significantly ignored the issues which had been raised by the dissolution of the Seine Federation. This text depicted the Popular Front as having been a sound venture which had secured a certain number of gains for the working class, the peasants and the middle classes, but it complained that the successive governments of the Front had been based only upon a parliamentary majority when what was needed to overcome the forces of capitalism was a mass movement. Popular Front governments had, it suggested, completely neglected the decisive factor, 'la mise en mouvement coordonnée et disciplinée de toutes les énergies du monde du travail'. The motion expressed hostility to the Daladier government and asked the National Congress to authorize the Socialist parliamentary group to remove it from office without delay. Its place should be taken by a Popular Front government,

capable de briser la résistance des oligarchies financières, du Sénat conservateur et de l'appareil bureaucratique de l'Etat, en s'appuyant sur l'action autonome des masses, dont il favorisera les initiatives révolutionnaires . . .

The motion contained a large number of policy recommendations, including proposals for foreign-exchange and credit controls, for the structural reforms contained in the CGT's plan for nationalizations, and for action against fascist groups and a purge of the administration and the police. These parts of the text were in line with earlier Bataille motions, but the phrasing of the section on foreign policy was unusually forceful; for example, the familiar demand for the opening of the Pyrenean border was linked to a proposal to support the Spanish Republic 'par tous les moyens appropriés aux nécessités de la victoire', and there was also a reference to the need for effective aid for the peoples of Czechoslovakia and China. Other suggestions were the establishment of mutual assistance between all the democratic countries and the Soviet Union; the extension, notably in eastern and central Europe, of a system of pacts based on the Franco-Soviet example; and the strengthening of the Franco-British entente as a means of resisting international fascism. The motion stressed the need for the fusion of the Communist and Socialist Parties and called for the immediate resumption of the work of the unification committee.[86]

The first published version of the Bataille motion did not refer to the national union issue, but a revised text prepared for the second session of the Federal Congress of the regular Seine Federation did take up the question. It contained a new paragraph suggesting that a *rassemble-*

---

[86] For the full text, see *Bataille Socialiste* (Paris), no. 109, May 1938, pp. 1–2.

ment such as Blum had tried to bring about in March 1938 would be possible only if popular demands and the struggle against international fascism were given up, and that the French bourgeoisie would accept nothing but the classical form of national union.[87] Zyromski thus made it quite clear that, unlike Marceau Pivert and the Gauche Révolutionnaire, he was not prepared to equate Blum's *rassemblement national* proposal with the national union formula.

By devoting so much attention to special causes, both the Gauche Révolutionnaire and the Bataille Socialiste had weakened their ability to appeal to the full register of dissent within the Socialist Party and had therefore created opportunities for new or dormant groups to gather support by exploiting neglected issues. A significant attempt to do so was made by Révolution Constructive, a small *tendance* which, after a period of activity in the early 1930s, had been relatively quiet during the high noon of the Popular Front. It had been formed in 1930 as a study group for intellectuals who were interested in the relationship between planning and socialism, and included Georges and Emilie Lefranc, Maurice and Suzanne Deixonne and Robert Marjolin amongst its members. The name, Révolution Constructive, was adopted by the group in 1932 to signify its members' belief that contemporary capitalism was developing collective forms of organization and that Socialists should be exploring methods to regulate this process by means of systematic planning and structural reforms. They took a close interest in the ideas of Henri de Man, a Belgian Socialist who was also developing ideas about planning. In 1934 they launched a campaign to influence the policies of the SFIO but were unable to persuade the party's leaders to take their proposals seriously.[88] The announcement that Révolution Constructive was resuming its activities was made by Georges Lefranc in a brief circular letter, dated 12 May 1938, in which he recalled the group's earlier campaign for structural reforms, for going beyond the existing frameworks of parliamentary government, and for peace.

Nous irons donc au Congrès de Royan avec tous ceux qui voudront engager une action dans le même sens que nous.

---

[87] For the revised text, see Parti Socialiste (SFIO), Fédération de la Seine, *Commission des Résolutions émanée du Congrès Fédéral du 15 mai 1938* [Paris, 1938], pp. 5–7.
[88] On the early history of this group, see Stéphane Clouet, *De la rénovation à l'utopie socialistes: révolution constructive, un groupe d'intellectuels socialistes des années 1930* (Nancy, Presses Universitaires de Nancy, 1991), pp. 19–148. See also Georges Lefranc, 'Le courant planiste dans le mouvement ouvrier français de 1933 à 1936', *Le Mouvement Social* (Paris), no. 54, January–March 1966, pp. 69–89; 'Histoire d'un groupe du Parti Socialiste S.F.I.O.: révolution constructive (1930–1938)', in *Mélanges d'histoire économique et sociale en hommage au professeur Antony Babel à l'occasion de son soixante-quinzième anniversaire*, II (Geneva, 1963), pp. 401–25. See also Jean-François

Il ne s'agit pas de créer une tendance nouvelle. Mais d'associer dans un effort de recherche tous ceux qui ne se satisfont ni du jeu parlementaire, ni des intrigues ministérielles, ni d'une soumission à des conceptions contre lesquelles le Parti a toujours lutté.[89]

Subsequently, the group produced a motion signed by Georges Albertini (Aube); Jacques Godard, Ignace Kohen, Emilie Lefranc, Georges Lefranc and R. Sandoux (all five from the Seine); and Ludovic Zoretti (Calvados). Georges Lefranc, the group's main spokesman, had been the Secretary of Révolution Constructive from its inception; after an education at the Ecole Normale Supérieure in the early 1920s, he had been appointed as Secretary of the Institut Supérieur Ouvrier of the CGT in December 1932 and was a member of the Fédération Générale de l'Enseignement (FGE), the main teachers' union.[90] Apart from him, the best-known member of the group was Zoretti, a science professor from Caen University who was not only Secretary of the FGE but the virtual leader of the Calvados Federation. The motion from Révolution Constructive consisted of a brief preamble, expressing a measure of disappointment at the achievements of the Popular Front governments, followed by three sections dealing in turn with economic, foreign and political problems. Of these, the first proposed a number of structural economic reforms and the nationalization of credit institutions and key industries in order that production could be planned in the general interest. The second, on foreign relations, was an extended statement of the strong pacifist views which were to form a rallying-point for large numbers of party members later in the year.

The group was asking the National Congress to affirm that a policy of armaments and alliances intended to encircle a power, or to set one group of powers against another, was bound to lead to war. Reasoning from the premise that the treaties of 1919 were the basic cause of current problems and that peace could be secured by a new international settlement, it proposed that the party should, first, refuse to associate itself with 'campagnes néo-poincaristes d'excitation chauvine et de panique' (that is, with the kinds of policies which Raymond Poincaré had advocated in the years preceding the First World War); secondly, avoid defensive pacts so that any outbreak of war could be kept within limits; and, thirdly, demand that the French government initiate negotiations with the states concerned to work out a new economic and political

Biard, 'Le débat sur le régime intermédiaire et le plan (juillet 1933–juillet 1934)', in *Cahiers Léon Blum* (Paris), nos. 15–16 (1984), pp. 17–45.
[89] Cyclostyled letter from Georges Lefranc, from Paris, 12 May 1938 (Archives Maurice Deixonne, OURS).
[90] See Georges Lefranc, 'Le courant planiste', p. 69 n. 3.

agreement (*statut*) in Europe and a peaceful settlement (*règlement*) of the colonial question.

Seule cette voie de construction économique de la paix permettra une réalisation progressive du désarmement général.

The third section of this text was built around the theme that the party should not identify democracy with existing forms of parliamentary government. It claimed that the present regime was a false democracy because parliament could adopt an attitude contrary to that wanted by the country.

Il ne permet aucune action profonde en raison de l'incohérence des méthodes parlementaires et de la confusion trop fréquente entre le pouvoir exécutif et le pouvoir législatif.

It therefore recommended that a government, having been given the confidence of the popular house, should have, within a sufficient time-limit,

la possibilité d'agir avec toute l'énergie désirable que lui conférera l'appui et le contrôle des masses organisées.

It further argued that the delegation of powers to a government for a restricted time and for specified objectives

ne peut constituer une atteinte à la démocratie, si elle a pour but de réaliser la volonté populaire.

Although the phrasing is ambiguous, the group appears to be advocating here the creation of a powerful executive, a direct relationship between government and people, and a consequent weakening of the role of parliament. Although both the Bataille and the Gauche Révolutionnaire had proposed the abolition of the Senate neither of these *tendances* had questioned the importance of the popular house and their own views were more in line with the values of direct democracy; the Révolution Constructive was alone in its apparent preference for some form of plebiscitary democracy.

In conclusion, this motion opposed the national union formula and recommended that the Socialist Party should demand power 'en vertu du droit constitutionnel' (presumably as the largest party in the Chamber of Deputies) in order to construct an economic democracy and preserve the peace. It further proposed that the party should refuse to collaborate with or support any parliamentary or ministerial combination other than this.[91]

[91] The Archives Maurice Deixonne, OURS, contain two cyclostyled versions of this motion, both undated and both entitled 'Congrès de Royan, motion de révolution

It was very difficult for the loyalists to counter the arguments contained in these three opposition motions. Both domestic and international politics had entered a period of relative calm at this time and it was not clear whether the Daladier government would strengthen or lose its grip on power and, at the European level, whether Germany would now move against Czechoslovakia or concentrate on the absorption of Austria. All that the Socialist leaders could do was to wait upon events, but their *attentisme* was not easily justified within the form of an extended policy motion. The first statement of the loyalist case was contained in a resolution which was published on 15 May by the *Socialiste* with the explanation that it appeared to give

une réponse satisfaisante aux préoccupations qui sont les nôtres ici et de nature à donner satisfaction à nos amis. C'est pourquoi 'Le Socialiste' croit devoir conseiller à ses lecteurs de l'adopter et de le faire voter autour d'eux. Il n'y aura donc pas de motion du 'Socialiste'.[92]

However, once it reached the federations and branches, this text was described either as that of the *Socialiste* or as *la motion Paul Faure*, as if it were, in fact, the view of a *tendance* rather than a document expressing the outlook of the loyalist majority as a whole.

The *Socialiste* motion, to use its most common name, praised the achievements of the Popular Front in defending democracy against fascism and in carrying out the agreed programme of reforms for the benefit of the workers and peasants. It stressed the need to keep the front in being and proposed a second round of measures for future action: the National Congress was asked to express the view:

que le programme de 1936, en partie réalisé, ne suffit plus pour assainir les finances publiques, redresser l'économie, réaliser de nouvelles réformes sociales, comme la retraite pour les vieux et l'assurance contre les calamités agricoles, dégager l'Etat de l'insupportable chantage des puissances d'argent, restituer au suffrage universel le plein exercice de sa souveraineté.

It favoured an acceptance by the front of the policies proposed by the party's Marseille Congress of July 1937 and a revival of the financial project of the second Blum government. However, where foreign affairs were concerned, the text relied on the claim that alliances could lead to peace, and thus invited the national congress to agree

constructive'. They form a sequence and the later of the two, printed on three pages, rather than the earlier one, printed on two, has been used for the above account.
[92] *Le Socialiste*, 15 May 1938, p. 1. The resolution was reproduced in ibid., pp. 1 and 3, and published as a special two-page edition of *Le Socialiste*, and the quotations below are from the latter.

que soit poursuivie l'œuvre de paix par LE RESSERREMENT DES LIENS AVEC LES PUISSANCES DEMOCRATIQUES ET PACIFISTES ET PAR LA RECHERCHE DE TOUS LES ACCORDS INTERNATIONAUX POSSIBLES, afin d'aboutir à une limitation contrôlée des armements, préface du désarmement général, et à la sécurité collective.

The resolution referred neither to the national union formula nor to Blum's attempt to form a *rassemblement national*, and it virtually ignored the existence of the Daladier government. Although it favoured keeping the Popular Front in being to carry out a further programme of reforms, and therefore implied that the existing parliamentary majority should be maintained, it avoided a consideration of specific possibilities such as those reviewed in the Séverac resolution which the National Council had adopted on 9 April. In its closing section it declared that:

le Parti Socialiste est toujours prêt, comme l'état de ses forces dans le pays et sa représentation parlementaire lui en donnent le droit, A REVENDIQUER LES RESPONSABILITES DU POUVOIR.

It thus defended participationism, but had avoided any detailed discussion of the terms of any future bid for power.[93]

Although well-written and cogent, this text had not dealt fully with three areas of policy. First, it had skirted around the problem of explaining how the momentum of the Popular Front was to be restored, whereas the dissident texts were claiming that some form of mass action was the best means of doing so. Secondly, it had not challenged the received wisdom that defensive alliances in international affairs were akin to collective security and were therefore a method of preserving peace, but each of the dissident texts had assumed that the League of Nations had lost much of its former authority and that drastic action was needed: the Bataille favoured the construction of a chain of alliances around the fascist powers, while Révolution Constructive had proposed the quite different policy of negotiations aimed at a new international settlement and the Gauche Révolutionnaire had written of an international conference for the revision of the Versailles Treaty and an equitable sharing out of raw materials 'dans un monde enfin désarmé'. Thirdly, although the *Socialiste*'s text had called upon the National Congress to denounce the Senate it had not raised the question of constitutional reform, but both the Bataille and the Gauche Révolutionnaire had pressed for the abolition of the upper house and Révolution Constructive had raised the possibility of a strengthened executive.

However, the version of the *Socialiste*'s motion which came before the Federal Congress of the regular Seine Federation carried additional

---

[93] *Le Socialiste*, special edition [May 1938]. All quotations are from p. 2.

paragraphs which did meet some of the points raised in the rival texts. On foreign policy, it asked the National Congress to proclaim the importance of maintaining peace and to repudiate both defeatism, which might encourage invasion, and imprudent involvements (*entraînements*) which could leave France isolated. The new section also attacked the Daladier government and proposed that the Socialist Party should invite its allies to put an end to a policy 'qui ne reflète pas l'esprit du Front Populaire'. Finally, it touched on the vexed question of relations with the Communist Party, supported the CAP's decision to suspend the talks on unity and expressed the hope that the Communist Party would offer 'des explications franches sur des incidents dont aucune responsabilité n'incombe au Parti Socialiste' and thus make possible the resumption of the work towards that end.[94]

A separate statement of the loyalist position came from the large Nord Federation. Its Administrative Committee, an executive body which usually met once a month, agreed on the main lines of a policy resolution at its meeting on 30 April and its Federal Secretariat then distributed the draft to branches for their comments.[95] The final text was considered and adopted by the first session of the unit's 44th Federal Congress on Sunday 22 May. The approved resolution began with a reasoned defence of the achievements of the Popular Front and then addressed the major problems which this alliance now faced: it agreed that the programme of the Rassemblement Populaire should be extended and therefore endorsed the proposal that future policies should include the structural reforms which the CGT had recommended; noting that the two Popular Front governments under Socialist leadership had encountered opposition in the Senate, it called for the reform of the electoral college of that house and the restriction of its powers; and it also discussed the nature of the social support which the party needed when in power. Ignoring the argument that mass action was the best means of enabling the government to proceed with reforms, it praised the virtues of discipline and forbearance:

Le parti socialiste étant un parti ouvrier les travailleurs pris individuellement ou collectivement (syndicats) doivent comprendre que leur intérêt n'est pas de créer des difficultés au gouvernement dont il a la direction, ou dont il fait partie. Ce gouvernement a été et sera toujours combattu par le capitalisme et la réaction. Raison de plus pour qu'il soit défendu par les travailleurs. Il doit en résulter pour eux une certaine tactique habile parfois, courageuse toujours

---

[94] For the revised text, see Parti Socialiste (SFIO), Fédération de la Seine, *Commission des Résolutions émanée du Congrès Fédéral du 15 mai 1938*, pp. 3–5 (the additional section, entitled 'Conclusion', is on pp. 4–5).

[95] *La Bataille* (Lille), 8 May 1938, p. 3.

parce qu'elle se heurte aux manœuvres des démagogues et de ceux qui veulent nuire au parti socialiste et à ses délégués au gouvernement.

The most distinctive feature of the Nord text was its position on foreign policy. It did not look for a dramatic escape from a deteriorating situation, such as an international conference or a revision of the 1919 settlement, but implied that the way to secure peace was to behave calmly but firmly in opposing the fascist powers:

la politique extérieure de notre pays doit être empreinte d'un caractère de hardiesse et de sang-froid, de sagesse et de fermeté. La France ne doit pas céder au vertige, à la contagion, à la périlleuse idée de l'inéluctable fatalité de la guerre. Sans laisser échapper une seule chance d'accord ou de réconciliation elle doit veiller au respect de ses engagements. Elle doit maintenir, consolider, développer les pactes particuliers conclus dans le cadre général de la S.D.N. comme le pacte franco-soviétique et le pacte tchécoslovaque dont l'abandon ou le relâchement ne feraient qu'accroître les forces mauvaises déchaînées par la politique de guerre des Etats fascistes. Menacées par le fascisme international, la Tchécoslovaquie et l'Espagne sont des positions essentielles que la démocratie et le socialisme ont le devoir de conserver si elles veulent sauver la liberté et la paix de l'Europe.

While avoiding any reference to the national union issue or any explicit criticism of the Daladier government, the Nord resolution expressed a continued willingness to participate in government should the need arise. It declared that the Socialist Party should remain ready

à revendiquer les responsabilités du pouvoir pour une politique démocratique agissante de progrès social et de paix, de même qu'à soutenir tout gouvernement décidé à lutter contre les factieux, contre les oligarchies financières et à faire respecter la volonté du suffrage universel.[96]

The Nord and the *Socialiste* texts had a great deal in common. Both defended the Popular Front and its achievements, both accepted the need for the party to participate in government in appropriate circumstances, and both implicitly supported the policy of *attentisme*. Of the two, the Nord motion was the more measured and the more confident but the main contrast between them was in their treatment of foreign affairs; whereas the relevant paragraphs in the *Socialiste* motion, even in its revised version, were bland and made no allusion to concrete issues, such as the position of Czechoslovakia, the Franco-Soviet pact and the Spanish Civil War, the Nord text, as we have seen, built up its case for a consistent and balanced policy with quite explicit references to current affairs. This difference in expression was significant and showed that the *Socialiste* was having difficulty in developing a

[96] Ibid., 29 May 1938, p. 1.

consistent line of argument in this most sensitive of policy areas whereas the Nord Federation had considered the matter and made a deliberate choice of position.

The five texts we have examined above show a number of such contrasts. They were all, to a greater or lesser extent, the products of a kind of intellectual competition in which those entrusted with the task of preparing the initial drafts would use a variety of rhetorical and literary devices to convey the essential message with maximum effect. These devices included outbidding rivals in making promises, rejecting an actual or imagined government policy as a matter of high principle, or predicting a crisis or crises, usually with reference to some past period (such as the advent of the First World War) with relevant lessons of conduct. This process left the final texts sharply differentiated from each other and widely dispersed across the fields of opinion within the party. Although these motions are intensified and idealized expressions of the actual *tendances*, they do enable us to map the relative positions of the different groups and therefore to make judgements about what alignments they might have formed under differing circumstances. Another ministerial crisis, for example, would have placed most pressure on the Bataille, forcing it either to join with the Gauche Révolutionnaire in opposing another Radical-led minority government or to side once more with the loyalists in supporting such an administration. To take a second example, a major incident in European affairs, such as a German move against Czechoslovakia, was likely to impose considerable strain upon the loyalists and possibly divide them into two groups, one aligned with the Bataille for a firm stand against the fascist powers and the other with the Révolution Constructive and the Gauche Révolutionnaire for a pacifist stance. By contrast, an economic recession could have revived enthusiasm for far-reaching structural reforms of the kind favoured by the CGT and for a closer alliance with the Communist Party, even if this were to mean an open break with the Radicals, a prospect which would certainly have alarmed the loyalists and widened the gap between them and the dissident *tendances*.

Even the most casual reader of the various motions could see how the *jeu de tendances* had created a complex pattern of criss-crossing divisions within the party and thus given rise to a great deal of uncertainty about how the organization as a whole would react to future events. The Seine crisis became an example of what could happen if differences of opinion were not resolved by the usual processes of compromise and arbitration; opposed sides would become armed camps, the rival leaders would insult each other in public, and mutual suspicion and disunity would weaken the party's cohesion. Many members thought that this state of affairs could only be remedied by an act of collective will, by a general determination to transform the party and recapture the unity and fellow-feeling of an earlier time. In several federations, deliberate attempts were made to formulate motions which would generate consensus and avoid the usual division into rival *tendances*.

The best-known *texte de synthèse* had been prepared by Georges Monnet and André Philip, who saw themselves as restoring the party's freedom of thought. Monnet claimed to have said to Philip:

'Qu'il soit surtout bien entendu entre nous que nous ne voulons pas faire une nouvelle tendance; tâchons surtout de faire entendre au Parti que rien n'est plus néfaste pour la pensée même du Parti, que ces heurts brutaux et quelquefois méchants . . . qui opposent des groupements qui se sont constitués à l'intérieur même de notre Parti, et qui empêchent alors l'effort de pensée libre.'

On the grounds that the thought of the party should be a synthesis, they had encouraged friends in the federations to prepare their own texts and to be wary of 'ces courants qui s'affrontent avec la volonté préalable de ne pas se mélanger'.[97]

For all its claims to moral certainty, each *texte de synthèse* had to attribute some blame to the authorities for disunity, and the Monnet–Philip motion was no exception to this rule. It implied that the central leaders could have done more to encourage support for the Popular Front, and the National Congress was asked to invite the CAP

à adapter ses méthodes aux nécessités de la lutte présente. La propagande, la documentation, la presse du Parti, devront utiliser au maximum la bonne volonté et la compétence des élus et des militants dont le dévouement est prêt à répondre à tous les appels.

Si le Parti le veut, il ne tardera pas à reprendre tout son ascendant sur l'opinion publique.[98]

Reduced to its essentials, the text was claiming that the people could be persuaded that a new Popular Front government under Socialist leadership was desirable. It also suggested that the committee which had been entrusted with the task of exploring the possibility of reunifying the Socialist and Communist Parties could resume its work.

Let us now consider some examples of how individual federations came to terms with the motions and proposals directed towards them in the weeks immediately preceding the Royan Congress. Although the

---

[97] Parti Socialiste (SFIO), 35ᵉ Congrès National, Royan, 4–7 juin 1938, *Compte rendu sténographique*, p. 446.
[98] Ibid., p. 453. Part of the text of the motion was cited verbatim by Monnet (ibid., pp. 452–3); see also the preceding speech by Philip (ibid., pp. 435–40).

party's official journal of record, *La Vie du Parti*, did not publish the texts of the main resolutions, each of the main *tendances* used its journal to present its motion, and proposals concerning the Seine crisis were also being circulated early in the season of the federal congresses.

Strongest support for the central leaders came from the Nord Federation, whose Federal Congress met on 22 May and adopted its own loyalist motion by 800 out of a total of 861 branch mandates, giving only 48 votes to the Bataille and 13 to the Gauche Révolutionnaire texts. Subsequently, a motion from the Lille branch approving the imposition of sanctions on the Seine rebels was carried by an even larger majority of 852 mandates to 9.[99] The sense of defending a threatened code of party discipline was strong at this time, and there is a particular edge to the comments of one local writer who was looking ahead to the Royan Congress.

Sans être animé d'une sorte d'esprit de chapelle ou de beffroi, nous avons, nous dans le Nord, la fierté d'être dans le parti le centre moteur, l'axe vivant et constructif qui fait l'admiration de nos frères d'autres régions.

Notre force, notre puissance est née du combat quotidien, qu'il faut livrer dans la mine, dans l'usine, sur le chantier. Les camarades aux prises avec les magnats de l'industrie ou leurs valets à tout faire, n'ont point le temps de se livrer à des critiques de tendances à l'intérieur de leur parti.[100]

The loyalist position was much less secure in the regular Seine Federation, despite the absence of the Gauche Révolutionnaire and the hostility which the crisis had generated towards the system of *tendances* in general. In accordance with the federation's rules, its Federal Congress met for its first session on Sunday 15 May and for its second on Sunday 29 May so that the branches would have two opportunities to consider the competing motions. The first session was attended by 297 delegates representing 9,565 members[101] and the 27-member Resolutions Committee which they appointed consisted of 12 representatives of the *Socialiste* group, 8 of the Bataille, 6 of a team which had offered to produce a *motion de synthèse* and one of a new group called Combat Socialiste.[102] This result indicated, first, that the loyalists were still lacking an absolute majority amongst the delegates and, secondly, that support for a common resolution was surprisingly high. In fact, those representing this section of the delegates were now expected to produce a text which could be supported by the Resolutions Committee as a

[99] *La Bataille*, 29 May 1938, pp. 1 and 2.
[100] Gaston Leblanc, 'Autour de Royan', ibid., 5 June 1938, p. 1.
[101] *Le Populaire*, 16 May 1938, p. 2.
[102] Parti Socialiste (SFIO), Fédération de la Seine, *Commission des Résolutions émanée du Congrès Fédéral du 15 mai 1938*, p. 1.

whole. The unity team consisted of Jean Longuet, a loyalist member of the CAP and one of the party's delegates to the Executive of the Socialist International; Marcel Bloch, of the Aubervilliers branch; Robert Dupont, René Jousse and Charles Pivert, all of whom had been associated in the past with the Bataille; and Daniel Mayer, a delegate from the party's branch in the 21st *arrondissement*, who was a reporter on the staff of *Le Populaire*. However, despite their efforts, they were unable to reconcile the divergent views of the *Socialiste* and the Bataille representatives; they acknowledged that Gaston Allemane, of the former group, and Zyromski, of the latter, 'ont loyalement tenté . . . de nous faciliter la tâche', but:

Certains de leurs amis ne leur ont pas permis d'aller jusqu'au bout. Nous le regrettons profondément.[103]

The resultant text condemned the policies of the Daladier government, proposed that the latter should be brought down to clear the way for another Popular Front ministry under Socialist leadership, and recommended that domestic policies should be based on the programme of Blum's second administration. In terms of foreign policy, it proposed that the Spanish frontier be kept open, that the territorial integrity of Czechoslovakia be maintained, that the Franco-Soviet pact be strengthened, that the system of open pacts be extended to eastern and central Europe, and that everything be done 'pour résister à la volonté d'expansion et de domination du fascisme international'. On the other hand, it envisaged the promotion of greater economic co-operation and the consideration of disarmament and treaty revisions, citing with approval the speech which Blum had made on a similar theme at Lyon on 24 January 1937. It specifically referred to the desirability of including representatives of the Communist Party in the next Popular Front government, and to the need to unite the Socialist and Communist Parties.[104] It was, in fact, much closer to the position of the Bataille than to that of the *Socialiste* and it is not at all surprising that it failed to unite the two sides of the Resolutions Committee.

In the end, the branches were asked to consider the *Socialiste*, the Bataille and the synthesis texts and when the branch delegates cast their votes at the second session of the congress on 30 May the *Socialiste* group secured a relative majority of the mandates, although the Bataille may well have won but for the competition offered by the synthesis text (for details, see Table 14).

---

[103] See the declaration preceding their resolution (ibid., p. 7).
[104] Motion C in ibid., pp. 7–8. For the relevant part of Blum's Lyon speech, see Blum, *L'Oeuvre de Léon Blum, 1934–1937* (Albin Michel, Paris, 1964), pp. 379–83.

Table 14. *Seine Federation, Federal Congress, 30 May 1938:*
division on general policy

Motions	Mandates	% of total
A (*Le Socialiste*)	4,479	46.9
B (Bataille Socialiste)	3,360	35.2
C (Synthesis text)	1,573	16.5
Abstentions	139	1.5
Total	9,551	

Source: *Le Populaire* (Paris), 31 May 1938, p. 3.

The decisions taken by the federation on the sanctions issue were less clear-cut than might have been expected. Several prominent members of the Bataille, including Henri Sellier, Pierre Commin, Andrée Marty-Capgras and Zyromski, had proposed that the National Congress should be asked to proclaim a general amnesty 'pour les faits qui ont provoqué la dissolution de la Fédération de la Seine', but this was defeated by 27 votes to 9 on the Resolutions Committee and by 6,888 branch mandates to 2,172, with 333 abstentions, at the second session of the Federal Congress on 30 May. The congress further decided, by 8,443 mandates to 568, with 59 abstentions, to recommend that the deadline for signing declarations of loyalty should be extended to 1 July 1938.[105]

A further indication of the fluidity of group alignments within the party was provided by the Gironde Federal Congress, held at Talence on 22 May, for which Robert Vielle and his colleagues on the federation's Administrative Committee had prepared an independent motion. Taking the view that the Daladier government should not be supported by the Socialist parliamentary group, they declared themselves to be against a national union and for a government under Socialist leadership which fully represented the Rassemblement Populaire and was committed to an extensive programme of reforms. Reduced to essential principles, these proposals broadly corresponded to those set out in the original resolution of the Bataille Socialiste, but on two issues Vielle and his group had taken a position which differed substantially from that of Zyromski. While stating support for the ideal represented by the League of Nations and the doctrine of collective security, and for closer ties between the democratic and

---

[105] Parti Socialiste (SFIO), Fédération de la Seine, *Commission des Résolutions émanée du Congrès Fédéral du 15 mai 1938*, p. 1; *Le Populaire*, 31 May 1938, p. 3.

peaceful powers, they also claimed that the armaments race would lead to financial collapse and war and made the now familiar appeal that France should propose, to governments and peoples, peace and controlled disarmament along with a world-wide economic reorganization. On the question of how the Socialists should deal with the Communists regarding organic unity between their two parties, they had adopted a cautious approach, specifying a formidable range of preconditions for the resumption of talks and an eventual fusion.[106] In the vote on general policy, this motion received 345 of the 537 branch mandates, against 100 for one submitted by the Amis du Bataille Socialiste, 87 for an independent motion from a group aligned with the Gauche Révolutionnaire, and 5 for the *Socialiste* text. On the subject of sanctions in the Seine affair, a motion favouring an amnesty was carried by 287 out of 533 mandates.[107]

A willingness to adopt an independent stand on the questions of party discipline and foreign policy was also evident at the congress of the Allier Federation at Montluçon on 29 May. In the early afternoon, a debate on the Seine affair ended in the adoption, by 2,221 mandates out of a total of 3,454, of a motion proposing an extension to 14 July of the deadline for signing the oath of loyalty to the party and requested the CAP to consider measures of amnesty at an opportune moment, all of which reflected a much more tolerant view of the rebellion than might have been expected from such a loyalist federation. The afternoon session would normally have included a long debate on general policy but the delegates, already under firm instruction from their branches as to how their mandates were to be distributed amongst the motions, concentrated instead on discussing a resolution on foreign policy which had been written by Camille Planche, one of the deputies for the department, who had dispatched it to the federations. His text was an unusually detailed statement of the pacifist case for conciliation as a means of preserving the peace. In it, he rejected the idea that security could be achieved by an armaments race and suggested that international understanding could be improved by such means as the granting to all countries of access to raw materials and the provision of greater freedom of foreign exchange. Even Marx Dormoy, despite his reservations, gave his support to the motion, which was adopted unanimously. Finally, at the end of the proceedings it was announced that the ballot on general resolutions had produced the following result:

[106] *Le Populaire Girondin* (Bordeaux), no. 228, 20 May 1938, p. 2.
[107] *Le Populaire*, 27 May 1938, p. 4. See also *Le Populaire Girondin*, no. 230, 3 June 1938, pp. 1 and 2.

2,307 mandates for the *Socialiste* motion, 411 for that of the Bataille
Socialiste and 732 for that of the *Cahiers Rouges*, out of a total of
3,450.[108]

It was much easier for the loyalists, given the *attentisme* of their
leaders and the general and ambiguous nature of the original *Socialiste*
resolution, to gather support at the expense of the Bataille than had
been the case before the Marseille Congress of July 1937, when the
decision to participate in the Chautemps government had been difficult
to defend. Besides giving ground, the Bataille was occasionally under
pressure to agree to the adoption of unity resolutions and to come to
terms with its opponents. Sometimes, as at the Seine Congress, attempts
to produce a common motion failed because of the intransigence of the
local groups, but at the first session of the Seine-et-Oise Congress on
22 May the Resolutions Committee was able to send out a combined
Socialiste–Bataille motion for consideration at branch level.[109] In the
resultant ballot, out of a total of 9,038 branch mandates, 4,699 were
cast for the joint motion, 3,882 for that of the Gauche Révolutionnaire,
and 457 for that of the Comité d'Action Socialiste Révolutionnaire
(CASR), a group on the extreme left, and these figures were converted
into federal-mandate totals of 183, 151 and 17 respectively for the
Royan Congress.[110] Although this outcome did not mean that the
Bataille had lost its local identity, it was a further setback for Zyromski;
the creation of such a large pool of mandates for the cause of a common
front had strengthened the hands of those who wanted to persuade him
to withdraw his motion in favour of a unity resolution at the national
level.

The Côte-d'Or Federation offers an example of a unit where the
Gauche Révolutionnaire had maintained its position and where the classical tripartite pattern had continued to function. The federation's newspaper carried the full texts of the *Socialiste*, Bataille and Gauche
Révolutionnaire groups[111] and at the Federal Congress at Dijon on
Sunday 29 May each had its own spokesman. In the division, the
Gauche Révolutionnaire motion was given a relative majority of the
mandates but its margin of victory over the *Socialiste* group was a
narrow one (for details, see Table 15).

[108] *Le Combat Social* (Montluçon), no. 1263, 5 June 1938, pp. 1 and 2; *Le Populaire*, 31
May 1938, p. 4 (the voting figures have been taken from the latter source).
[109] *Le Populaire*, 23 May 1938, p. 5.
[110] Ibid., 3 June 1938, p. 4.
[111] *Le Socialiste Côte-d'Orien* (Dijon), no. 234, 21 May 1938, p. 2 (Gauche Révolutionnaire motion); ibid., no. 235, 28 May 1938, p. 2 (Paul Faure [*Socialiste*] and
Bataille Socialiste motions).

Table 15. *Côte-d'Or Federation, Federal Congress, 29 May 1938: division on general policy*

Motions	Mandates	% of total
Blum–Paul Faure [*Socialiste*]	1,060	40.3
Gauche Révolutionnaire	1,174	44.6
Bataille Socialiste	347	13.2
Absent	50	1.9
Total	2,631	

Source: Le Socialiste Côte-d'Orien (Dijon), no. 236, 4 June 1938, p. 1. The number of absences has been calculated by subtracting the total of the votes for the three motions (2,581) from the total of the votes on the Seine affair (2,631) in a division held earlier in the meeting.

Lucien Hérard, the leader of the Gauche Révolutionnaire within the federation, had earlier asked the delegates to approve a motion which requested the National Congress to consider the Seine affair before taking up any other item of business, questioned the validity of the decision to dissolve the Seine Federation, demanded the withdrawal of sanctions and proposed the admission to the congress of delegates from the rebel federation. This resolution was approved by 1,062 of a total of 2,631 mandates, while the remaining votes were distributed between a motion in favour of sanctions (716 mandates), another for an unqualified amnesty (518) and another which coupled an appeal for amnesty with approval of sanctions (335).[112]

One of the oddities of the Côte-d'Or Congress was that the *Socialiste* text had been described as the 'Blum-Paul Faure' motion, whereas in fact Blum had taken a long break from politics after the fall of his government; it was only at the end of May, in a series of articles published in *Le Populaire*, that he gave some indication of how his mind was moving. Although well aware that there would be debates at the Royan Congress on party discipline and on international policy, he concentrated almost exclusively in these essays on the problems of the party's general strategy. He argued that, were the congress to decide that the Socialist parliamentary group should oppose Daladier, the result would be either the breaking up of his ministry or the reversal of the majority in the Chamber of Deputies. Taking the outcome which he considered the more likely, the fall of the ministry, he asked what kind of government could be formed were the President of the Republic

[112] Ibid., no. 236, 4 June 1938, p. 1.

to hand this task to a Socialist. After dismissing the idea of a purely Socialist ministry, he pointed out that those who were still thinking in terms of a government representing the full range of the Popular Front, from the Communists to the Radicals, seemed to forget that he had failed on two occasions in attempts to form such an administration. He agreed that circumstances did not favour the creation of a government of French unity around the Rassemblement Populaire, but he still believed that the Socialists would, some time or other, come back to this formula.

In his view, there was only one practical solution to a ministerial crisis, namely, the formation of an administration based partly on the existing combination of the Radicals and the centre right and partly on the Socialists, who would provide the leadership. However, did those who were advocating a fresh bid for power want such a government? His own preference was to wait for a while and use the breathing space to prepare for a new stage in the development of the Popular Front; 'ne sentent-ils pas', he asked, referring to those who favoured an immediate return to opposition,

que le Parti doit se garder, autant que les circonstances le lui permettront, pour le jour où un nouveau bond en avant deviendra possible, que, d'ici là, sa tâche essentielle consiste à se préparer – *et surtout à préparer le Front populaire* – à l'accomplissement d'une nouvelle étape?[113]

Next Blum faced the problem of explaining how the Popular Front could be revived without persuading the great majority of Radical deputies and senators that another period of reforms was both socially necessary and financially feasible. Answering the claim that, instead of leaving power on 8 April, he should have confronted the Senate with the backing of a probably reduced majority in the Chamber and the support of the mass of the people, he gave two reasons for having decided against such a course: first, a confrontation with the Senate would have caused a revolutionary crisis and left the way clear for international fascism and war; and secondly, the Socialist Party would have gone into battle without the Radical Party, or at least a majority of it, just as the workers and peasants would have parted company with a considerable fraction of the middle classes.

Ce qui revient à dire que la coalition des forces démocratiques aurait été irrémédiablement rompue, et que le renversement de majorité, si âprement poursuivi,

---

[113] Blum, 'Des formules aux faits', *Le Populaire*, 28 May 1938, p. 1. The other essays in this series are: 'Le Congrès de Royan', ibid., 26 May 1938, p. 1; 'Pouvoir ou opposition?' ibid., 27 May 1938, p. 1; 'Gouvernement de combat et unité radicale', ibid., 29 May 1938, p. 1.

aurait risqué de s'accomplir, non seulement sur le plan parlementaire, mais dans le pays.[114]

He took issue with those who felt that it was necessary to divide the Radical Party. In his view, the Socialist Party should be trying to renew the agreements underlying the Popular Front, to solve the problem posed by the Senate, and to resume work on the common programme, but with the aim of strengthening rather than weakening the internal cohesion of the Radical Party.

Notre rôle est, somme toute, *de combattre l'attraction vers la Droite d'une fraction du Parti radical par une attraction plus forte, vers la Gauche, de la masse du Parti*. Nous avons rempli ce rôle en 1935 et 1936, – et c'est ce qui a permis, en fin de compte, la constitution du Front populaire. Les mêmes circonstances, les mêmes dangers nous imposent le même devoir.[115]

Although Blum had allowed himself some wishful thinking, as in his readiness to assume that a new phase in the Popular Front was about to begin, his reasoning about political possibilities was incisive and realistic. He saw clearly that an attack on the Daladier government would either precipitate a crisis or result in a reversal of the majority in the Chamber, and he was prepared to warn that the Popular Front could not be revived by a confrontation with the Senate or by a revolutionary surge, but only by patient negotiations with the Radical Party as a whole. Most obviously he was demonstrating the futility of the revolutionary strategies favoured by the Gauche Révolutionnaire and the Bataille, but he was also implicitly criticizing those in the loyalist majority who had not tried to stem the mounting tide of anti-participationism within the party. He had, as it were, sent out a clear message to his allies that the loyalist majority needed to take a stand against the sentimental Guesdisme which favoured a simple and unreflective withdrawal into the parliamentary opposition.

It had now become very difficult for observers to identify the pattern which had formed in the preparations for the Royan Congress.[116] The main cause of confusion was that two very different forms of conflict had taken shape at the same time and that their combined effect on the stability of the party was still unclear. The tripartite structure of two dissenting *tendances* challenging a loyalist coalition had remained intact, despite the late appearance of the Révolution Constructive and the

---

[114] Blum, 'Gouvernement de combat et unité radicale', ibid., 29 May 1938, p. 1.
[115] Ibid.
[116] See Raymond Millet, 'Avant le Congrès de Royan: les tendances actuelles dans le Parti Socialiste (S.F.I.O.)', III, *Le Temps*, 3 June 1938, p. 8. See also the preceding parts of this article, I, 31 May 1938, p. 6; II, 2 June 1938, p. 8.

attention which had been attracted by various *textes de synthèse*. However, cutting across these essentially sectarian divisions were lines of tension between those who intended to defend the legitimacy of the party's central authorities and those who wanted to attack them for having dissolved the Seine Federation and imposed sanctions on the former officers of that body. In some respects, this anti-bureaucratic campaign had strengthened the position of the Gauche Révolutionnaire but in other respects it had worked to the advantage of the loyalists by distracting attention from issues of doctrine and strategy; this was certainly the opinion of Germaine Degrond, one of the leaders of the Seine-et-Oise Federation and of the Bataille Socialiste:

j'ai l'impression . . . que dans nos Congrès fédéraux, on s'est battu beaucoup trop autour de la Fédération de la Seine, au lieu de se battre sur les motions de politique générale.[117]

The Royan Congress

Like the general conferences of any large political party, the national congresses of the SFIO were attempts to provide a tangible form and a sense of community to a dispersed membership. Individual delegates would travel from all over France to the congress venue; the General Secretary and his staff would leave their sanctuary at the Cité Malesherbes in Paris to travel to a distant city to reconstruct their administration in temporary accommodation; and their constant critics, the *chefs de tendance*, would enter their element, holding court at endless café meetings, talking for hours with the old hands and encouraging the novices to take part in the debates which lay ahead. Each congress would begin with an agenda, but the swirl of private conversations and mild conspiracies would inevitably create an unexpected pattern of issues and debating points.

As a result of the tensions which had been building up within the branches and federations since the spring, the 35th National Congress at Royan was an unusually stormy occasion.[118] It was attended by 500

---

[117] Parti Socialiste (SFIO), 35ᵉ Congrès National, Royan, 4–7 juin 1938, *Compte rendu sténographique*, p. 67.

[118] For accounts of the Royan Congress, see Guérin, *Front Populaire: révolution manquée*, pp. 198–202; Joubert, *Révolutionnaires de la S.F.I.O.*, pp. 147–9; Greene, *The French Socialist Party in the Popular Front Era*, pp. 216–24; Georges Lefranc, *Le Mouvement socialiste sous la Troisième République (1875–1940)* (Payot, Paris, 1963), pp. 357–61; 'Histoire du Parti Socialiste S.F.I.O.', Part 18, 'La Scission de la Gauche Révolutionnaire', *Cahier et Revue de l'OURS* (Paris), no. 99 (April 1979), pp. 1–90. See also, Maurice Deixonne, *La Vérité sur la scission de Royan* (Imprimerie du Cantal, Aurillac, 1938); Madeleine Hérard, Marceau Pivert and Lucien Hérard, *Rupture*

delegates bearing 8,296 mandates and representing 99 of the party's 100 federations. The conference centre was the main hall in the Palais de Foncillon, close to the seafront, and 100 metres away, in the Allée Maritime, the Café des Bains had been reserved by the rebel Seine Federation and the Gauche Révolutionnaire. On the balustrade of the café terrace, a banderole proclaimed to passers-by 'Ici Fédération socialiste de la Seine', while a red banner carried the words *Juin 36* along with the rebels' symbol, a clenched fist against a background of three arrows. Marceau Pivert had arrived with his arm in a sling, but since he did not have the right to attend the congress it was agreed that the chief spokesman for the *tendance* in the conference hall should be Lucien Hérard.[119]

The first item on the official agenda of the congress was the consideration of the annual reports from the CAP and other central bodies, but when the delegates assembled for the start of proceedings on the morning of Saturday 4 June Lucien Hérard presented a preliminary motion. This proposed that the congress should deal immediately with the situation created by the dissolution of the Seine Federation and that it should permit a delegation from that body to take part in the discussion.[120] Although the motion was not put to the vote, a sequence of speakers managed to prolong the debate until Paul Faure eventually had to accept that it was no longer possible to keep to the agenda. He therefore asked the delegates to settle the question.[121] Resumed after lunch, the discussion lasted well into the afternoon, when some effective speeches served to clarify the central issues. Those who favoured some form of amnesty implied that the sanctions had been inspired by political considerations whereas those defending the action taken insisted that discipline had indeed been the object and that if the congress were to reverse such decisions it would be undermining the authority of its own executive and judicial agents, the CAP, the General Secretariat and the CNC.[122]

Lucien Hérard adjusted his plea to take account of the sentiment of several provincial delegates that there had been faults on both sides and that the congress should give serious consideration to a proposal

nécessaire: réponse à Maurice Deixonne (Editions du Parti Socialiste Ouvrier et Paysan, [Paris], 1938).

[119] Guérin, *Front Populaire: révolution manquée*, p. 199.

[120] Parti Socialiste (SFIO), 35ᵉ Congrès National, Royan, 4–7 juin 1938, *Compte rendu sténographique*, p. 16.

[121] Ibid., p. 40.

[122] See the speeches by Augustin Laurent (ibid., pp. 57–63), Bracke (ibid., pp. 94–9) and Blum (ibid., pp. 125–37).

from the Haute-Vienne Federation in favour of conciliation[123] and to
another from the Doubs Federation in favour of an amnesty.[124] In one
intervention, he offered to accept the Doubs motion providing that
some changes were made to the text, and gave the assurance that even
were congress to maintain the sanctions there would be no talk of forming a new party.[125] The only motion on the subject which had been
formally submitted to the congress office had been the one from the
Nord Federation recommending approval of the decisions of the CAP
and the CNC and when the vote was taken it was approved by a three-
fifths majority. The detailed result is shown in Table 16.

The central leaders had weathered their first storm but the margin of
victory had been narrow. It was now obvious that opposition to the
imposition of sanctions had extended well beyond the ranks of the
Gauche Révolutionnaire to those of the Bataille. Although the large
Bouches-du-Rhône, Nord, Pas-de-Calais and Seine Federations had
given high proportions of their mandates in favour of sanctions, the
vote against the Nord resolution was surprisingly high in a number of
provincial federations.

The second major confrontation of the congress began on the evening
of Sunday 5 June when the delegates began the debate on general
policy. This continued throughout Monday and was completed on Tuesday morning with Blum's summing-up speech. The chairmen of the
sessions of the debate allowed each *tendance* to nominate a number
of speakers proportionate to its strength and the discussion generally
proceeded along group lines. Attention was soon centred on two related
policy questions, the strategy which the party should pursue in domestic
politics and the position which it should take in international affairs.
Where the internal situation was concerned, the loyalists were advocating *attentisme*, that is, avoiding for the time being any action which
could dislodge the Daladier government and dislocate the Popular
Front's majority in the Chamber of Deputies while leaving the CAP
and the parliamentary group with responsibility for dealing with any
contingency which might arise. This prescription was under attack from
the Bataille, which wanted to see the Daladier government removed
from office without delay and an effort made to establish a government
fully representative of the Popular Front, and from the spokesmen of
the Gauche Révolutionnaire, who were intent on persuading the congress to condemn the idea of a national union. In the field of foreign
policy, the main conflict of views was over the means of preserving

[123] Ibid., pp. 19–20.
[124] Ibid., p. 44.
[125] Ibid., p.87.

Table 16. *SFIO, 35th National Congress, Royan, 4 June 1938: division on question of discipline affecting the Seine Federation (motion submitted by the Nord Federation)*

Federations	Mandates: For no.	%	Against no.	%	Abstentions no.	%	Absent no.	%	Totals no.
Bouches-du-Rhône	250	79.4	65	20.6					315
Gironde	38	20.4	148	79.6					186
Meurthe-et-Moselle	31	20.1	119	77.3	4	2.6			154
Nord	758	98.8	9	1.2					767
Pas-de-Calais	278	79.2	64	18.2	9	2.6			351
Seine	464	73.4	146	23.1	22	3.5			632
Seine-et-Oise	169	48.1	182	51.9					351
Haute-Vienne			167	100.0					167
Others	2,916	54.2	2,133	39.6	257	4.8	78	1.4	5,384
Totals	4,904	59.0	3,033	36.5	292	3.5	78	0.9	8,307

Sources: *La vie du Parti* (Paris), no. 80, 28 June 1938, p. 319; Parti Socialiste (SFIO), 35ᵉ Congrès National, Royan, 4–7 juin 1938, *Compte rendu sténographique* (Librairie Populaire, Paris, n.d.), pp. 609–10.

peace in Europe; several loyalists, including Louis L'Hévéder and Camille Planche, favoured a policy of negotiations and concessions as the best method of producing a stable settlement which would satisfy Germany and Italy but Zyromski spoke for a system of defensive alliances and treaty guarantees designed to contain the imperial ambitions of the fascist powers.

The first major speech of the debate came from the loyalist, Jean Le Bail (Haute-Vienne), who argued that neither a national union built around the Popular Front nor the Popular Front standing alone could provide the basis for a government under existing conditions. The first alternative had been ruled out by the parties of the right and the second vitiated by policy differences within the majority. Regarding the latter point, he claimed that:

deux divorces se sont produits: un divorce dans la politique extérieure par suite d'une déviation du Parti communiste, suivie par certains éléments du socialisme. Et un divorce dans la politique intérieure par suite des glissements, des glissements naturels et connus du Parti radical, et un divorce aussi qui est peut-être plus grave, un divorce des éléments dirigeants du pays, et les masses qui se sont trouvées désabusées à certains moments, à tort ou à raison.[126]

On the grounds that the Popular Front should not be revived artificially at that stage, he claimed that the best interim arrangement was a Radical government supported by the Socialist Party. However, he emphasized that they should not abandon the alliance:

parce que deux dangers résulteraient de la dissociation du Front populaire: le désir de la constitution d'un front révolutionnaire qui serait voué à l'échec dans notre pays, et inversement certain goût pour le ministérialisme dont nous voudrions encore moins.[127]

Switching his attention to foreign affairs, Le Bail claimed that Zyromski's approach would entail a return to the policy of encircling Germany, a course which would cause fear in Europe and create the danger of war. He then tried to show that the domestic policies set out in the resolution of the Bataille were inconsistent with a foreign policy which would require a Union Sacrée rather than a Popular Front government, a war economy rather than further reforms, and the pursuit of unity with the Communist Party under inappropriate conditions ('Ils sont prêts à tout accepter, si vous acceptez comme base de l'unité, la défense de l'U.R.S.S.').[128] He went on to speak approvingly of *planisme*

---

[126] Ibid., p. 283.
[127] Ibid., p. 284.
[128] Ibid., p. 286.

and of the need to substitute a plan of structural reforms in place of the old programmes.[129]

Le Bail's reasoning illustrates how distrust of the Communists and alarm at the possible return of a system of armed blocs in Europe could produce a particular kind of *attentisme*. Ignoring the Gauche Révolutionnaire, he had concentrated his fire on the Bataille, treating it almost as a projection of Communist influence into the affairs of the Socialist Party, directed mainly to change its foreign policy and its attitude towards the Popular Front. That influence could become even stronger were the Radicals to abandon the Popular Front and join with the right, leaving the Socialists to choose between returning to opposition or joining some kind of revolutionary front in association with the Communists. Le Bail's *attentisme* thus reflected an intelligent awareness of the extent to which the party's internal balance of power was dependent on very special conditions, such as the continued existence of the Popular Front, a relatively quiet period in European affairs, and an uneasy partnership between a centre government and a left-wing majority in the Chamber.

The main advantage of *attentisme* was that it provided a generalized starting-point for a variety of excursions into future time. Jules Moch, who also spoke on Sunday evening, simply chose to assume that the party would again form part of a routine administration and accordingly examined a whole series of quite detailed policy matters, such as the need for monetary and exchange controls to prevent the costs of social reforms from causing price increases, the difficulty of relying on public-works schemes as a cure for unemployment, and the problem of ensuring that the 40-hour week did not lead to a fall in production. He proposed that the Union des Techniciens Socialistes, a group of experts, should be asked to prepare draft measures for the nationalization of various industries and suggested that the congress might place in its final motion a programme for future action along the lines of the Blum plan of April 1938. Where strategy was concerned, he stressed the need for flexibility and said that he would be happy with a vote of confidence in the party's leaders.[130]

The issue of foreign policy continued to smoulder in the background. On Sunday afternoon, during the discussion of reports, Jean Longuet had spoken on behalf of the party's delegates to the executive of the Socialist International, and had referred specifically to the need to resist the pressure which Germany was placing on Czechoslovakia and

[129] Ibid., pp. 286–7.
[130] Ibid., pp. 308–17.

generally to take a firm line with the fascist powers.[131] Once the debate on general policy had begun, Le Bail and other speakers referred to the need for caution and conciliation, but it was Louis L'Hévéder (Morbihan) who, on the Monday morning, first set out fully the case for an accommodation with the fascist powers. He said that he might not have spoken had he not felt morally obliged to do so by the letters which he had received after his intervention at the meeting of the National Council on 9 April and had he not been cited in *Le Populaire*, first by Louis Lévy and then by Blum. Claiming that the problems affecting Spain and Czechoslovakia could be solved only as part of a general settlement of all the territorial, economic and colonial differences inherited from the Treaty of Versailles, he refused to accept the view that the complexity of contemporary international problems had been caused by fascism alone. He drew attention to the number of minority problems which the 1919 settlement had created, with the result that the former allied nations were seeing

s'opérer sous leurs yeux, par le moyen de la force brutale, des révisions territoriales qui étaient dans la logique des choses et qui auraient pu s'opérer dans une atmosphère de paix et de légalité internationale.[132]

Distinguishing his position from that of those on the extreme left of the party who favoured unilateral disarmament or a general strike to prevent war, he claimed that it was dangerous to accept the inevitability of the division of Europe into two antagonistic blocs and that it should be possible to reach an agreement with the totalitarian states which would avoid war, stop the arms race and prepare the ground for general disarmament.[133]

This speech was bound to produce reactions. Louis Lévy maintained shortly afterwards that a firm and energetic policy in dealing with the fascist powers was the only way of preserving peace[134] but it was Zyromski himself, provoked beyond endurance, who insisted on the absolute necessity of alliances and containment. His case rested upon a particular view of fascism: although L'Hévéder saw Nazi Germany as totalitarian and brutal, he also believed that it would respond to reasoned appeals to self-interest, whereas Zyromski was convinced that international fascism was a further expression of capitalism, intended to check the rise of the proletariat in both the national and international spheres:

[131] Ibid., pp. 199–203.
[132] Ibid., p. 336.
[133] Ibid., pp. 332–43.
[134] Ibid., pp. 349–50.

le mouvement ouvrier, la classe ouvrière internationale n'a pas seulement à lutter contre les forces parlementaires, électorales, économiques du capitalisme; il a à lutter contre l'appareil de force des Etats totalitaires, avec tous les moyens politiques, diplomatiques et militaires.[135]

Having dismissed the idea that fascism could be checked by the use of a general strike, he fiercely attacked what he described as the 'illusionnisme pseudo-pacifique' of L'Hévéder and went on to justify his own policy, of constructing a bloc opposed to the fascist powers. He did so by bringing together a whole series of proposals as if they constituted the elements of an integrated strategy: the maintenance of the Franco-Soviet pact; the preservation of Czechoslovakia as an independent state; steps to ensure the victory of the Republican side in Spain; a policy of regional alliances in Scandinavia and eastern Europe, even if this entailed supporting anti-government movements in Rumania, Poland and Yugoslavia; popular pressure to bring England into line; and support for President Roosevelt, given his understanding of the need to contain the fascist powers. Zyromski's emotional and pugnacious address, punctuated by uproar, supplied the very image which Le Bail had sought to conjure up on the previous evening, that of a man and, indeed, of a section of the party, convinced that war was inevitable, and in his hurried closing remarks Zyromski virtually acknowledged that he was being attacked not only by members of the Gauche Révolutionnaire but also by those of the *Socialiste*.[136]

Zyromski was followed immediately by Albert Sérol, who had been Minister of Labour in the second Blum government and whose brief was obviously to rehearse the arguments in favour of *attentisme* without straying into the territory which Le Bail had explored. Sérol felt his way carefully through the thicket of issues, arguing that the mystique of the Popular Front could be restored, and that there was still scope for financial and economic reforms. While agreeing that the policies of the Daladier government were not those which Socialists would have chosen, he took the position that the party should not withdraw into opposition, first, because the result would be a ministerial crisis which could lead by degrees to a national union and, secondly, because the Rassemblement Populaire should be kept intact to protect the social legislation of the Blum governments. In any event, he asked that the parliamentary group should be given latitude to judge the government's policies and to act on its own initiative.[137]

[135] Ibid., p. 353.
[136] Ibid., pp. 351–66.
[137] Ibid., pp. 367–75.

After all the excitement of the first day of the congress, attention had shifted away from the Gauche Révolutionnaire but on Monday 6 June it was suddenly caught in a harsh spotlight. Interrupting the afternoon's proceedings, Vincent Auriol, the president of the session, announced that Marx Dormoy and others had been assaulted. Dormoy was constantly interrupted as he tried to explain how he and his companions had been set upon outside the hall by people shouting, 'Dormoy à Clichy! Dormoy au bagne!', an obvious reference to the clash between the police and a crowd at Clichy on 16 March 1937.[138] No one had said so, but it was generally assumed that the former Minister of the Interior and his friends had been attacked by people associated with the rebel Seine Federation and with the Gauche Révolutionnaire. Reconciliation between the rebels and the party was now almost out of the question, and Lucien Hérard could only cry out in frustration:

Cet incident arrive provocant! C'est une coïncidence trop singulière. C'est un incident voulu! C'est provoqué![139]

These events signified the huge gap in understanding which now separated the world of the Palais de Foncillon from that of the Café des Bains, where the course of the debates had been followed at second hand amidst rumour and speculation. There had been a closed meeting of Gauche Révolutionnaire activists on the Saturday evening after the congress had voted to maintain sanctions,[140] but no public move had been made to form a new party, despite the continued gestures of defiance.

When Lucien Hérard took the floor later in the afternoon and asked for an inquiry into the incident, he was told that the CAP would deal with the matter. He then went on to speak to that part of the Gauche Révolutionnaire's motion which dealt with foreign affairs, denying any attachment to the idea of a general strike in the event of mobilization for war and claiming that his *tendance* could combine support for the Republican side in the Spanish Civil War with opposition to the system of international blocs. He agreed with L'Hévéder that everything should be done to avoid war and said that if it became unavoidable he and his colleagues would not accept it as their duty to defend the nation within a capitalist regime. He declared that they were revolutionaries:

loin de vouloir diminuer les antagonismes de classes, loin de vouloir chercher des compromis ou des accords avec nos exploiteurs, nous voulons approfondir

---

[138] Ibid., pp. 387–90.
[139] Ibid., p. 391.
[140] Roger Dardenne was the only journalist allowed to attend this meeting (*Le Figaro*, 5 June 1938, pp. 1 and 3).

ces antagonismes de classes, nous voulons les exacerber, nous voulons arriver au pouvoir non pas par une action parlementaire dont deux ans d'exercice du pouvoir ont montré la vanité, mais par les moyens révolutionnaires, par la conquête violente, s'il le faut, du pouvoir politique et économique.[141]

The basic themes in the debate had now been established, and the later speakers were mainly concerned to consolidate and develop points made earlier. Camille Planche (Allier) read out his resolution on the need for a negotiated settlement to ensure the peace;[142] Charles Spinasse, who had been Minister for the Budget in the second Blum government, followed on from Jules Moch in discussing the lessons which could be learnt from the economic and financial proposals put forward by that administration;[143] and Philip and Georges Monnet spoke to their *texte de synthèse*, stressing the need to work for another Popular Front government.[144] Maurice Deixonne, having discussed the articles by Blum which had appeared in *Le Populaire* before the congress, proposed that, before considering any final resolution, congress should adopt a preliminary motion setting out its opposition to Socialist participation in any government which contained members of groups that were not part of the Rassemblement Populaire.[145] Had such a suggestion been approved at this stage in the proceedings, the party would have rejected any further consideration of ties with groups of the centre right while effectively vindicating the action which Marceau Pivert had taken in opposing Blum's *rassemblement national* initiative in March 1938.

On the morning of 7 June, a long speech from Léon Blum brought to an end the discussion phase of the debate on general policy. Sixty-six years old at this time, Blum was a man of considerable presence; an excellent *New York Times* photograph taken at the congress shows him standing with Marx Dormoy and André Blumel in a grassy area, dressed in a dark double-breasted suit and one of his splendid wide-brimmed hats, looking relaxed and confident. His speech to the delegates represented an intelligent and determined effort to show that the *Socialiste*, Nord and Bataille motions, as well as the statements of those delegates who had spoken to them, were based on an extensive common ground. Having defended the policy of non-intervention in the Spanish Civil War, he turned to the speeches of L'Hévéder and Zyromski, stressing their compatibility and toning down their contrasts. While agreeing with

---

[141] Parti Socialiste (SFIO), 35ᵉ Congrès National, Royan, 4–7 juin 1938, *Compte rendu sténographique*, p. 402.
[142] Ibid., pp. 422–3.
[143] Ibid., pp. 424–35.
[144] Ibid., pp. 435–40 (Philip) and 445–53 (Monnet).
[145] Ibid., p. 459.

L'Hévéder that the Versailles Treaty was unsatisfactory, he insisted that Germany and Italy did have imperial ambitions within Europe and that they had accepted war as an instrument of policy. His prescription for dealing with European problems was carefully phrased: avoiding any direct reference to Zyromski's notion of a defensive bloc, he implied that there was sufficient cohesion in the international community to preserve peace through the methods of collective security while accepting the risk of war.

Turning to domestic politics, he sought to demonstrate once again that his notion of a *rassemblement national* was quite distinct from the national union formula, and asked congress not to vote for Maurice Deixonne's preliminary motion.

Je l'adjure de ne pas se lier les mains pour des circonstances qu'il lui est impossible de prévoir.[146]

He reminded the delegates that it would be difficult to form a Popular Front government which included the Communists because the Radicals would be reluctant to join such a combination; he therefore recommended that the Daladier government should be left in office for the time being:

je vous demande de laisser votre groupe parlementaire juger comme il l'a fait toujours, et toujours à votre satisfaction, des intérêts du Parti et des intérêts de la classe ouvrière. Or, ces intérêts ne sont pas en ce moment l'ouverture d'une crise ministérielle.[147]

However, he proposed that, should the party be called on to take power again, it should seek a revision of the programme and terms of the Popular Front and that, if this were refused, a National Council meeting should be called.[148]

Attention now shifted to the work of the Resolutions Committee, whose task, as usual, was to consider the various motions which had been submitted to the National Congress from the preceding federal congresses with the aim of reaching agreement on a single text or, failing that, of deciding which texts should be put to the delegates for the final division by mandates. In accordance with past practice, the places on the committee were apportioned between the motions to reflect the degrees of support which each of them had obtained during the federal congresses, with the result shown in Table 17.

---

[146] Ibid., p. 519. For the complete text of the speech, see ibid., pp. 489–532.
[147] Ibid., p. 525.
[148] Ibid., pp. 530–1.

Table 17. *SFIO, 35th National Congress, Royan, 4–7 June 1938: numbers of members of Resolutions Committee by motion*

Motion(s)	Number of members
Le Socialiste and Nord Federation	18
Bataille Socialiste	6
Gauche Révolutionnaire	5
Monnet–Philip (synthesis)	2
Révolution Constructive	1
Seine-et-Oise Federation (synthesis)	1
Seine Federation (synthesis)	1
Total	34

This distribution of places indicates the extent to which the relative strengths of the main groups in the party had been affected by the preceding federal congresses. The *Socialiste* and Nord motions between them had gathered sufficient support to obtain a majority of the places and these were taken up both by established leaders, such as Léon Blum, Paul Faure, Jean-Baptiste Séverac, Jean Lebas, Marx Dormoy and Bracke (formerly associated with the Bataille), and by figures from the provincial federations, such as Salomon Grumbach, Fernand Roucayrol, Jean Le Bail and Louis L'Hévéder. Although the Bataille had not attracted many mandates with its own motion, it had evidently pooled resources with the Gironde group led by Robert Vielle, who was included in its delegation alongside Zyromski, Roger Dufour and Pierre Commin of the Seine Federation, Jean Pierre-Bloch, a deputy representing the Aisne Department, and Roger Veillard of the Seine-et-Marne Federation. Also on the committee were the main provincial spokesmen for the Gauche Révolutionnaire (Lucien Hérard, Georges Soulès, Maurice Deixonne, Sylvain Broussaudier and Raymond Fischer) and representatives of the minor motions – Georges Monnet and André Philip for their text, Georges Lefranc for Révolution Constructive, Pierre Métayer for the Seine-et-Oise synthesis resolution, and Jean Longuet for the Seine synthesis resolution.[149]

Early on the afternoon of Tuesday 7 June the committee held its first meeting in a room at the Royan town hall. It was then that Paul Faure proposed that Blum should be asked to prepare a *texte de synthèse*; all but the representatives of the Gauche Révolutionnaire agreed to this suggestion whereupon Blum went off and prepared an entirely new motion.[150] In this, he invited the congress to approve a foreign policy

[149] Ibid., pp. 533–4.
[150] See ibid., pp. 577–81.

based on the pursuit of peace within a framework of collective security, but, reflecting the spirit of the Nord and Bataille texts, he also called for firmness.

Le socialisme français veut la paix même avec les impérialismes totalitaires, mais il n'est pas disposé à s'incliner devant toutes leurs entreprises. S'il était réduit à cette extrémité qu'il essaiera de prévenir par tous les moyens, il saurait défendre l'indépendance du sol national, l'indépendance de toutes les nations couvertes par la signature de la France.[151]

Where the Spanish question was concerned, Blum's text noted that the policy of non-intervention in the civil war had been intended to stop the totalitarian powers from intervening to support the military rebellion and declared that the party could not accept a state of affairs in which their intervention had become public and almost lawful while international agreements continued to weigh upon the regular Spanish government. The congress was invited to authorize the parliamentary group to follow the situation with the greatest vigilance.

In his discussion of domestic politics, Blum wrote in favour of another Popular Front government but warned that ministerial instability could bring about the reversal of the parliamentary majority to the advantage of the reactionaries. Stressing the party's loyalty to the Popular Front, he proposed that the parliamentary group and the CAP should be given the responsibility

de prendre, vis-à-vis des circonstances et des difficultés de l'heure, toutes les décisions que commanderont les intérêts du Parti, ou plutôt les intérêts dont il a la charge.[152]

Looking further ahead, Blum envisaged the co-ordinating body of the alliance, the Comité National du Rassemblement Populaire, working towards a fresh programme and agreements so that a new Popular Front government could be established.[153]

This text was obviously designed to stand for all the major resolutions except that of the Gauche Révolutionnaire, and the main object of the whole exercise was apparently to force Zyromski to withdraw the Bataille motion and to make common cause with the loyalists. This would have been the signal for the representatives of the earlier *textes de synthèse* to withdraw their resolutions as well and to join in the show of solidarity. However, for some reason, probably to preserve his right to control a share of the places on the new CAP, Zyromski insisted

[151] Ibid., p. 578.
[152] Ibid., p. 579.
[153] Ibid., p. 580.

that the Bataille resolution should go before the full congress. His stand determined other reactions; Monnet and Philip decided that they would abstain when the committee came to vote on the texts and Pierre Métayer took a similar stand.

Zyromski had embarked on a difficult manoeuvre. He and his colleagues had amended their original motion in order to broaden its appeal, and the revised Bataille text[154] showed an intention not only to retain the loyalty of close allies, such as Robert Vielle and his group from the Gironde Federation, but also errant loyalists and delegates who had strayed from the Gauche Révolutionnaire. The changes to the motion had affected three subjects in particular. First, the sentences dealing with the contemporary political situation had been modified to remove the impression that the Bataille wanted the Daladier government to be dismissed from office immediately; the revised text simply stated that:

l'objectif à atteindre dans le plus court délai est de changer la formation gouvernementale actuelle.

It did, however, call for a mass movement directed towards that end.[155] Secondly, the entire foreign policy section of the original text had been replaced by a set of paragraphs taken from the synthesis motion which had been prepared by the Seine-et-Oise Federation; the borrowed material referred to the active collaboration of the democratic powers to maintain the peace but warned that socialism needed to proclaim

sa volonté de résister par tous les moyens aux attaques du fascisme, expression politique du capitalisme agonisant.

It also took a firm line on the Spanish question, declaring against the reimposition of frontier controls, for the right of the Republican government to buy war materials, and for the application of the pact of the League of Nations against aggression.[156] Thirdly, the section in the original Bataille resolution on unity with the Communist Party had been replaced by a much milder statement taken from the Monnet–Philip motion.[157]

---

[154] For the Bataille Socialiste text presented to the congress on 7 June, see ibid., pp. 565–73. This text included the paragraph on the national union question which appeared in the version of the original motion submitted earlier to the Seine Federal Congress (see above, pp. 174–5).

[155] Ibid., p. 567.

[156] For the relevant part of the text, see the section headed 'III. – Pour la défense de la paix', ibid., pp. 569–70, and for Zyromski's account of the substitution, see ibid., pp. 558–9.

[157] See the section of the text headed, 'Pour le parti unique du prolétariat', ibid., pp. 571–2, and for Zyromski's explanation, see ibid., pp. 561–4.

When he came to justify the maintenance of the Bataille text, thus revised, Zyromski expressed dissatisfaction with Blum's motion on three counts: he clearly felt that it left too much discretion to the parliamentary group to decide the fate of the Daladier government; that it should have supported freedom of trade for Republican Spain and opposed the reimposition of frontier controls; and that it lacked any reference to the question of unity with the Communists.[158] It was the third of these complaints which particularly distressed Blum, who later pointed out that the relevant section of the Monnet–Philip text had been discussed on the Resolutions Committee and that the CAP had already decided to initiate new conversations with the Communists regarding unity of action.[159]

The Resolutions Committee had also to deal with the proposal by the Gauche Révolutionnaire's representatives to use a preliminary motion as a means of persuading the delegates to vote against Socialist participation in any government containing members of groups which were not part of the Rassemblement Populaire. Lucien Hérard later revealed that the original intention had been to persuade the Bataille to join them in framing such a motion[160] but, having met with refusal, they borrowed a number of phrases from the paragraph on the national union issue which had been included in the resolution submitted by the Bataille to the Federal Congress of the regular Seine Federation.[161] The result was the following text, which the Resolutions Committee was asked to approve for submission to the full congress as a preliminary motion, separate from the original resolution of the Gauche Révolutionnaire.

Sur l'Union nationale, après l'expérience tentée par Léon Blum, mandaté par le Conseil National du 12 mars 1938, il est démontré qu'un tel Rassemblement n'est possible, en France, que dans l'abandon des revendications populaires et de la lutte contre le fascisme.

La seule Union nationale qu'accepte la bourgeoisie française, ainsi qu'elle l'a prouvé au cours des événements de mars, c'est l'union de toutes ses fractions, avec les partis ouvriers, mais contre tout progrès démocratique, contre toute véritable lutte.

Dans ces conditions, l'élargissement du Front populaire aux formations du centre et de droite ne pourra être envisagé en quelque circonstance et sous quelque prétexte que ce soit, sans consultation préalable d'un Congrès.[162]

---

[158] Ibid., pp. 555–65.
[159] Ibid., pp. 583–6. See also the statement by Jean Longuet, ibid., pp. 594–5.
[160] See Madeleine Hérard et al., Rupture nécessaire: réponse à Maurice Deixonne, p. 18.
[161] Lucien Hérard, in Parti Socialiste (SFIO), 35ᵉ Congrès National, Royan, 4–7 juin 1938, Compte rendu sténographique, pp. 553–4.
[162] Ibid., p. 553.

This text met with disapproval; Marx Dormoy complained that it questioned the authority of the National Council to take decisions in exceptional circumstances, and Paul Faure and J.-B. Séverac insisted that the *tendance* did not have the right to put two resolutions (this preliminary motion and its original resolution) before the full congress. The committee finally decided that the new text could not be submitted as a preliminary motion, and Lucien Hérard and his colleagues were therefore obliged to attach it to their original resolution, as a kind of annexe.[163]

These two events, the maintenance of the Bataille resolution and the rejection of the preliminary motion idea, had hardened the old tripartite division and distracted the Resolutions Committee from considering crucial differences of opinion which had been revealed in the course of the general debate, especially where foreign policy was concerned. The gap between the position outlined by Zyromski and that taken by Le Bail, L'Hévéder and Camille Planche was a wide one; on the one hand, the party was being asked to believe that peace could be preserved only by the threat of retaliation if the territorial integrity of Czechoslovakia were violated by Germany, and, on the other, it was being invited to believe that a crisis could be avoided if the treaties of 1919 could be revised to take account of German interests; neither approach excluded war as a last resort, but whereas the former envisaged armed conflict as a possible outcome of current international politics, the latter placed it in a remote future, beyond the definition and implementation of a new European settlement. Why, then, had this issue not produced an open division during the concluding stages of the congress? First, because Zyromski had not pressed matters to a conclusion. There is little doubt that he had agreed to substitute the mild wording from the Seine-et-Oise text for the forthright statement on foreign policy in the original Bataille motion to attract delegates who agreed with many of his views on party strategy and the Spanish question but who did not share his enthusiasm for a constricting system of alliances directed against Germany and Italy. As he himself acknowledged, the ideas which he had presented in his Monday speech were 'des conceptions personnelles' which had not been fully accepted 'par l'ensemble des camarades'.[164] Secondly, because those in the loyalist majority, such as Marx Dormoy, who shared his belief in the need to contain rather than to conciliate Germany and Italy, had not responded to the pacifist arguments used by L'Hévéder and other speakers. Many years later, Paul Faure recalled that Jean Le Bail had drawn the attention of the

---

[163] Maurice Deixonne, *La Vérité sur la scission de Royan*, pp. 17–18.
[164] Parti Socialiste (SFIO), 35ᵉ Congrès National, Royan, 4–7 juin 1938, *Compte rendu sténographique*, pp. 557–8.

Resolutions Committee to the paragraph in Blum's *texte de synthèse* which had concluded with the statement, cited above, that French Socialism, if forced to do so, 'saurait défendre l'indépendance du sol national, l'indépendance de toutes les nations couvertes par la signature de la France'. According to Faure:

Nous fûmes quelques-uns à être troublés par le trait de lumière qu'il jetait dans le débat, mais nous estimâmes qu'il était impossible, à la dernière minute d'un congrès, de créer un incident. Nous étions alertés; nous demanderions des explications et précisions dès notre retour à Paris.

En fait, c'est de ce jour que commencèrent les désaccords de politique extérieure dans les rangs socialistes. Les polémiques qui suivirent, révélèrent, en effet, ce qu'il fallait entendre par la 'Signature de la France'.[165]

In other words, the seriousness of the issue had been recognized but the advocates of conciliation had had neither the time nor the inclination to express their dissent from Blum's formulation in a separate motion. It is just possible that they might have done so had Zyromski and his colleagues withdrawn the Bataille text and accepted Blum's motion, but when this did not happen Paul Faure's main obligation was to ensure that the new *texte de synthèse* received solid support in the final division.

The members of the Resolutions Committee concluded their work on the general policy motions by voting on those texts which had not been withdrawn from consideration. The result of this division is given in Table 18.

The voting appears to have been on a group basis, with the *Socialiste* and Nord representatives voting for the Blum text, the Bataille and

Table 18. *SFIO, 35th National Congress, Royan, 4–7 June 1938: Resolutions Committee: division on texts for submission to the concluding session of the congress*

Motions	Votes
Léon Blum's *texte de synthèse*	18
Bataille Socialiste (revised version)	6
Gauche Révolutionnaire (including annexe)	5
Abstentions	5
Total	34

[165] Paul Faure, *De Munich à la Vme République* (Editions de l'Elan, Paris, [1948]), p. 55. Maurice Deixonne claimed that men such as Louis L'Hévéder 'ne se sont ralliés qu'à contre-coeur à la pseudo-synthèse de Blum' (*La Vérité sur la scission de Royan*, pp. 52–3) but it is not clear whether or not he is referring to views expressed during the meetings of the Resolutions Committee.

Gauche Révolutionnaire delegations voting for their respective motions, and the representatives of the minor texts abstaining. Finally, Blum was asked to report to the congress on his text, and Zyromski and Hérard were asked to report on the motions of their *tendances*.[166]

It was almost midnight on the evening of 7–8 June when the congress began to consider the reports from the Resolutions Committee and the discussion on the general policy resolutions soon revealed that the activities of the *tendances* and their effect on the moral unity of the party had aroused serious concern. Lucien Hérard, who reported first, actually felt obliged to defend the decision to keep the motion of the Gauche Révolutionnaire before the delegates.

C'est le texte sur lequel, dans nos sections, nos camarades ont discuté, et se sont comptés, et je crois qu'il est utile, normal – je ne voudrais pas dire moral pour ne pas choquer les camarades qui agissent différemment – que quand des motions sont présentées et ont été soumises à la discussion, il est normal que le Congrès, à des modifications de détails près, se prononce.[167]

In his commentary, Hérard maintained that the Gauche Révolutionnaire was alone in acknowledging that the experience of the Popular Front had shown that it was not possible to improve the lot of the working class within the framework of the capitalist regime and that, in consequence, the revolutionary path was opening up before the proletariat.

Zyromski adopted a quite different line of argument in his report. He presented the ideas of the Bataille Socialiste as though they were a more realistic appreciation of the party's current interests than those which Blum had put forward. He claimed that when Blum had referred to the Spanish problem in the speech which he had made in the morning, 'il semble véritablement qu'il raisonne hors du temps et hors de l'espace'.[168] With detailed comparisons, he explained why he considered the Bataille's revised motion to be a better representation of the party's general views than Blum's text and complained that the latter had ignored the question of unity with the Communist Party. He said that the Bataille had gone to the Resolutions Committee bearing

non pas un texte cristallisé et cliché, mais en tenant compte du sentiment collectif du Congrès.[169]

---

[166] Parti Socialiste (SFIO), 35e Congrès National, Royan, 4–7 juin 1938, *Compte rendu sténographique*, pp. 548–9.
[167] Ibid., p. 550.
[168] Ibid., p. 558.
[169] Ibid., p. 564.

Plainly reacting to the pressures which he must have been under not only on that committee but also in private encounters, he concluded his report with this general appeal:

Je sais bien ce que l'on va dire, que nous sommes des sectaires, que nous voulons véritablement, pour des intérêts mesquins de tendances, maintenir à toute force des textes. Nous nous élevons contre de telles prétentions, nous avons fait un effort de rapprochement, un effort pour nous tenir en harmonie avec le sentiment collectif du Congrès, j'en suis sûr.[170]

Blum then reported on behalf of the majority of the Resolutions Committee. He described how the committee had asked him to prepare the synthesis text and how he had set about his task, but his frequent references to the ritual of the occasion ('suivant la formule consacrée . . . , un petit peu traditionnel depuis de longues années . . . , ce que nous avons fait dans je ne sais combien de Congrès') implied that this was a time for spiritual renewal when members should set aside their differences and rekindle their common faith. As on previous occasions, Blum was playing on the idea that the party's capacity to transcend existing circumstances had been crucially weakened by the activities of self-seeking groups, such as the *tendances*, and that delegates had made matters worse by their slavish adherence to the rules. It was a style of rhetoric which aroused anxiety and hostility, and practically invited expressions of dissent which could then be used to repeat the basic message, as in the following exchange:

il ne faut pas que vous croyiez que ce soit votre devoir de délégués de vous en tenir ici à la lettre expresse des mandats que vous avez reçus de vos Fédérations, lorsque vous vous trouvez en présence. (*Applaudissements et quelques protestations*.) Est-ce que vous croyez que je ne connais pas les règlements du Parti et les statuts du Parti? Je les connais depuis longtemps, je vous répète que le devoir statutaire des Commissions de résolutions est de tenter des textes de conciliation et d'unanimité, car les statuts du Parti (*applaudissements, bruit dans la salle*) il est stupéfiant, quand on dit des choses qui devraient être familières à tout délégué à un Congrès socialiste, qu'on soulève un tel mouvement de surprise! C'est, je le répète, le rôle primordial, le devoir primordial de la Commission des résolutions; c'est ce qu'elle a tenté.

Almost immediately afterwards, he followed this reference to the original function of the Resolutions Committee with an appeal to the delegates to be aware of the essential purpose of their own roles:

le fait même de cet effort de conciliation et de cet effort d'unanimité place en effet les délégués au Congrès devant une situation nouvelle qu'ils ont à apprécier en pleine liberté de conscience en essayant bien entendu d'interpréter le sentiment de leurs Fédérations . . . [171]

Having read out his text to the delegates, Blum replied to the various points which Zyromski had raised and made a particular issue of the way in which the Bataille had borrowed the section on unity with the Communists from the Monnet–Philip text. He praised Zyromski's courage, but nevertheless described him as 'un chef de tendance, . . . très soucieux de questions de mandats'.[172] Zyromski tried to interrupt, but Blum was determined to make his point, claiming that he had the right 'de faire appel devant le Congrès, des résistances que j'ai rencontrées devant la Commission des résolutions'.[173]

It was as though poor Zyromski were on trial. Georges Monnet asked him to accept Blum's text to demonstrate to the public and to other parties of the Rassemblement Populaire that the Socialists were agreed on the need to prepare a new programme. He asked Zyromski for a gesture of reconciliation:

ne fausse pas, par ton attitude, ce qui doit sortir de ce Congrès, c'est-à-dire ce sentiment qu'il y a en effet cette volonté entre nous, de faire ce ralliement. Autrement, alors, il ne sortira de ce Congrès qu'une preuve: la preuve, c'est qu'il y a, qui fausse la vie de notre Parti, ces tendances qui se heurtent les unes contre les autres . . . et qui . . . finissent par ne pas aboutir à se mettre d'accord.[174]

Philip echoed Monnet's appeal to Zyromski and spoke of the need to dispel

le sentiment que les tendances sont trop souvent clichées et immobilisées à l'avance . . . [175]

Bracke held that congresses existed

pour confronter et non pas pour affronter . . . les diverses opinions, et pour essayer, bien entendu, toujours de voir s'il y a moyen de dégager une majorité.

The method of appointing the CAP

a amené ce qu'on appelle faussement des 'luttes de tendances', car ce n'est pas les tendances, ce sont les clans! (*Applaudissements*) qui se trouvent en face les uns des autres.[176]

---

[171] Ibid., p. 575.
[172] Ibid., p. 586.
[173] Ibid., p. 587.
[174] Ibid., p. 590–1.
[175] Ibid., p. 592.
[176] Ibid., p. 597.

Zyromski protested that he was not *un homme de tendance* but nevertheless refused to respond to the appeals made by Monnet and Philip.[177]

When the three motions were put to the vote, Blum's text was approved by an absolute majority. The details of the division are given in Table 19. The vote of 4,872 mandates (58.6 per cent of the total) for the Blum text was a distinct improvement on the 4,320 mandates (52.0 per cent) recorded for the Séverac-Dormoy text at the National Council of 9 April and on the 4,053 (48.9 per cent) given for the Sérol motion at the first ballot of the National Council of 17 January. The Blum text had been decisively endorsed by the large federations of Bouches-du-Rhône, Nord, Pas-de-Calais, Seine and Haute-Vienne and it had received strong support amongst the northern, eastern, southern and central federations. On the other hand, the number of mandates given to the dissident *tendances* had fallen by comparison with the levels of support registered for their motions at the National Council of 9 April, in the case of the Bataille from 2,107 to 1,735 mandates (from 25.4 to 20.9 per cent) and in that of the Gauche Révolutionnaire from 1,656 to 1,430 mandates (from 19.9 to 17.2 per cent). Although the Bataille text had been supported by decisive majorities in some federations (of over four-fifths of the mandates in Gironde, Doubs, Seine-et-Marne and Finistère), Zyromski's *tendance* had lost ground in several federations in the Parisian region (as in Seine-Inférieure, Yonne, Nièvre and Loir-et-Cher) and in Languedoc (as in Tarn, Aveyron and Lozère). However, although it no longer had any support from the regular Seine Federation, the Gauche Révolutionnaire had maintained its backing elsewhere: it had obtained 168 mandates (151 of its own and 17 from the CASR delegate, it would appear) from the Seine-et-Oise Federation and absolute majorities from a number of provincial units, including the Meurthe-et-Moselle, Loiret, Cantal, Haute-Loire, Maine-et-Loire, Orne and Calvados Federations.

Any interpretation of this result has to take account of the probable effects of the moral pressure which had been placed on the delegates to vote for the Blum text despite contrary instructions from their federations. How many of the mandates which had been given at the federal congresses to the synthesis texts, for example, were eventually given to this motion? That part of the Seine-et-Oise delegation which had been appointed to represent the federation's joint resolution simply divided into *Socialiste* and Bataille contingents[178] and the 183 mandates at its

---

[177] Ibid., p. 598.
[178] See the statement by Pierre Métayer, ibid., p. 593.

Table 19. *SFIO, 35th National Congress, Royan, 7 June 1938: division on general policy*

	Mandates for the motions of:											
	Léon Blum (loyalist)		Zyromski (Bataille Socialiste)		Hérard (Gauche Révolutionnaire)		Abstentions		Absent		Totals	
Federations	no.	%	no.	%	no.	%	no.	%	no.	%	no.	
Bouches-du-Rhône	265	84.1	21	6.7	29	9.2					315	
Gironde	2	1.1	154	82.8	30	16.1					186	
Meurthe-et-Moselle	29	18.8	16	10.4	106	68.8	3	1.9			154	
Nord	713	93.0	43	5.6	11	1.4					767	
Pas-de-Calais	319	90.9			20	5.7	12	3.4			351	
Seine	390	61.7	222	35.1			20	3.2			632	
Seine-et-Oise	56	16.0	127	36.2	168	47.9					351	
Haute-Vienne	167	100.0									167	
Others	[2,931]	54.4	1,152	21.4	1,066	19.8	224	4.2	11	0.2	[5,384]	
Totals	4,872	58.6	1,735	20.9	1,430	17.2	259	3.1	11	0.1	8,307	

Sources: *La Vie du Parti* (Paris), no. 80, 28 June 1938, p. 319; Parti Socialiste (SFIO), 35e Congrès National, Royan, 4–7 juin 1938, *Compte rendu sténographique* (Librairie Populaire, Paris, n.d.), pp. 612–14. For details of adjustments, see the appendix (pp. 400–1, n. 7).

disposal were shared out between the Blum and the Bataille texts, 56 going to the former and 127 to the latter. Where the Seine Federation's synthesis text was concerned, Charles Pivert claimed to have transferred its mandates to the Blum motion.[179] Philip had said before the division that if all but the Gauche Révolutionnaire could not agree on a single text, he and Monnet favoured abstention[180] but it is doubtful whether many of the delegates entrusted with mandates for their text (which Monnet claimed had attracted 670 votes)[181] followed this course. Another interesting question is the extent to which individual delegates decided to assign to the Blum text mandates which they had been instructed to give to the Bataille motion. One delegate from the Côte-d'Or Federation announced that he was doing so[182] and others may have followed his example.

From his point of view, Zyromski had done well to maintain his resolution until the final division; he had demonstrated that one out of every five members in the party was still prepared to support the Bataille and that most of its delegates would stand by him when the tide of opinion was running against him. Above all, he had preserved his right to representation on the CAP. As usual, the division on general policy was taken as the basis of elections to this body; the Gauche Révolutionnaire having refused to accept representation, the 33 places were therefore divided up between the remaining contenders, 24 places being allocated to supporters of the Blum text and 9 to those of the Bataille.[183]

That Zyromski's support within the party hierarchy had been reduced now became quite clear; three prominent figures who had belonged to the Bataille group in the 1937–8 CAP (Bracke, Desphelippon and Charles Pivert) had shifted to the loyalists' side (the first two to full membership and Charles Pivert to the reserve list) and Zyromski had been forced to build up his new team with such

---

[179] See Charles Pivert, *Le Parti Socialiste et ses hommes: souvenirs d'un militant* (France-Editions, Paris, [1950]), p. 63. The division on general policy at the Federal Congress of the Seine Federation (see Table 14 on p. 186 above) would have produced the following distribution of federal mandates: *Le Socialiste*, 297; Bataille Socialiste, 222; synthesis text, 104; and abstentions, 9, within a total of 632. The actual distribution in the Royan vote was: Blum text, 390; Bataille Socialiste, 222; and abstentions, 20, an outcome which indicates that 93 of the synthesis mandates were transferred to the Blum text and 11 to the abstentions column.

[180] Parti Socialiste (SFIO), 35ᵉ Congrès National, Royan, 4–7 juin 1938, *Compte rendu sténographique*, pp. 592–3.

[181] Ibid., p. 588.

[182] Vèque, ibid., pp. 599–600.

[183] Parti Socialiste (SFIO), 36ᵉ Congrès National, Nantes, 27–30 mai 1939, *Rapports*, (Librairie Populaire, Paris, 1939), p. 17. For records of attendance and replacements, see ibid., p. 107.

relatively inexperienced leaders as Robert Vielle from the Gironde, Girard from the Deux-Sèvres and Roger Veillard from the Seine-et-Marne Federations. The composition of the incoming CAP was as follows:

Parti Socialiste (SFIO): CAP membership 1938–9

1 *Appointed on the basis of the Blum motion* (24 members)

Léon Blum (Deputy)	Paul Favier
Paul Faure[1]	Maurice Paz
Bracke (Alexandre-Marie Desrousseaux)	Maurice Caille
	Eugène Gaillard
Jean Longuet[2]	André Blumel
René Château	Augustin Laurent (Deputy)
Marx Dormoy (Deputy)[3]	Sansimon Graziani
J. P. Granvallet	Gaston Allemane (Deputy)
Salomon Grumbach (Deputy)	Justin Arnol (Deputy)
Jean Lebas (Deputy)	Fernand Roucayrol
Louis Lévy	(Deputy)
Jean-Baptiste Séverac	Louis L'Hévéder (Deputy)
Raoul Evrard	Francis Desphelippon

2 *Appointed on the basis of the Zyromski motion* (9 members)

Jean Zyromski	Pierre Commin[5]
Eugène Descourtieux[4]	G. Girard
Roger Dufour	Jean Pierre-Bloch (Deputy)
Jacques Grumbach	Roger Veillard
Robert Vielle	

[1] Deputy from November 1938.
[2] Died in September 1938 and replaced by Charles Pivert.
[3] Resigned as Deputy following election to Senate in October 1938.
[4] Died in August 1938 and replaced by Germaine Degrond.
[5] Resigned in September 1938 and replaced by André Joublot.

At 4 a.m. on the morning of Wednesday 8 June, as this last session of the congress was drawing to a close, a manifesto was distributed announcing that Marceau Pivert and his group would be forming a new party, the Parti Socialiste Ouvrier et Paysan (PSOP),[184] but it soon became clear that many who had been associated with the Gauche Révolutionnaire would remain behind in the SFIO. According to his own account, Georges Soulès agreed to work with Maurice Deixonne in regrouping those members of the *tendance* who had not left the

[184] Joubert, *Révolutionnaires de la S.F.I.O.*, p. 149.

Socialist Party but he declined to do anything until October to avoid giving Marceau Pivert the impression that he was trying to entice people away from the new venture (*une tentative de débauchage*). Subsequently, he was approached by former leaders of Révolution Constructive, who proposed a pooling of resources to form a new *tendance*, to be known as *Redressement Socialiste*, and Soulès fell in with this suggestion.[185] Faced with a difficult choice, Maurice Deixonne wrote for advice to Marceau Pivert, who sent back a letter urging his friend to make the break:

La pire des choses c'est le divorce entre la *phrase* et l'*acte*. On ne peut pas être socialiste et préparer la guerre, contribuer par une sorte de complicité ouverte à l'écrasement des travailleurs.[186]

Deixonne finally decided that he would remain in the Socialist Party and published an article explaining his reasons for doing so in his local Socialist newspaper.[187] This move prompted Marceau Pivert to write to him again, regretting the choice in terms which showed how much the strong possibility of war was weighing upon his own thinking.

La crise du régime entraîne à la guerre: pour la résoudre il faut sortir du cadre des exigences de notre propre impérialisme c'est-à-dire refuser tous moyens de combat à nos adversaires de classe et faire appel à l'internationalisme prolétarien, ou bien subir la loi de notre impérialisme . . . [188]

Berthe Fouchère of the Oise Federation also stayed with the SFIO, but Lucien and Madeleine Hérard of the Côte-d'Or Federation and Sylvain Broussaudier, Federal Secretary of the Alpes-Maritimes Federation, decided to throw in their lot with the PSOP.

As at the leadership level, so at the grass-roots the defections from the SFIO were fewer than the Parisian group behind the PSOP had expected. According to Guérin, it had hoped to attract about 20,000 activists from the SFIO[189] but outside the capital the flow from the old to the new organization was minimal. Paul Faure sent a short circular to the federal secretaries at the end of June asking to be informed of the exact number of members leaving the party, and their replies

---

[185] Raymond Abellio [Georges Soulès], *Ma dernière mémoire*, II, *Les Militants 1927–1939* (Gallimard, Paris, 1975), pp. 303–4 (see also ibid., pp. 287–8).

[186] Letter from Marceau Pivert to Maurice Deixonne, 12 June 1938 (Archives Maurice Deixonne, OURS).

[187] 'Je reste!', originally published in *Le Socialiste du Cantal* on 15 June 1938 and reproduced in *Le Réveil Populaire de Saint-Quentin et de la Thiérache*, 24 June 1938, p. 1 (Archives Maurice Deixonne, OURS).

[188] Letter from Marceau Pivert to Maurice Deixonne, from Paris, 17 June 1938 (Archives Maurice Deixonne, OURS).

[189] Guérin, *Front Populaire: révolution manquée*, p. 243, n. 18.

showed that the damage had not been great.[190] In the Nord Federation, so its Administrative Committee was told on 30 July, the few individual departures recorded after Royan had not affected branch activity in any way, and those who had voted for the Gauche Révolutionnaire at the Federal Congress on 22 May had condemned the birth of the new party.[191] In Meurthe-et-Moselle, where the Gauche Révolutionnaire had enjoyed such solid support in the recent past, a number of branches adopted motions recording their intention to remain faithful to the SFIO and few activists left the party; about this same time, the federal secretary, Henri Midon, who had been one of Marceau Pivert's main supporters in the provinces, moved away from the region.[192]

Conclusion

Through its involvement in the Popular Front, the Socialist Party had found itself obliged to accept a level of governmental and parliamentary responsibility which conflicted with its anti-participationist tradition. In 1936 the party's members had been persuaded to go against that tradition and to agree that their leaders should join an administration within the framework of the Third Republic. They were told that this was necessary not only because the party had joined the crusade against fascism but also because the French people were crying out for improvements in their living standards and conditions of work. When the Blum government resigned in June 1937 some members claimed that the time had come to return to opposition, but first the National Council and then the Marseille Congress were persuaded that the party should remain in office, even under Radical leadership, both to protect the reforms which had already been enacted and to continue the fight against fascism. However, discontent was growing within the party, not only amongst anti-participationists but also amongst those members who favoured a closer alliance with the Communists. These and other currents of dissent increased support for the alternative strategies which the Bataille Socialiste and the Gauche Révolutionnaire had proposed, and by the beginning of 1938 their combined strength within the organization was equal to that of the loyalists.

We have seen how the sectarian aspect of the *jeu de tendances* had become more prominent in February 1938. The Gauche Révolutionnaire had set the pace, forcing first the Bataille Socialiste and then

[190] See Faure, 'La force du Parti', *Le Populaire*, 3 August 1938, pp. 1 and 2.
[191] *La Bataille*, 7 August 1938, p. 2.
[192] Jean-Marie Moine, 'Le mouvement socialiste en Meurthe-et-Moselle sous la Troisième République' (Mémoire de maîtrise, Université de Nancy, Nancy, 1973), p. 162.

the *Socialiste* to express differences in terms of doctrine and grand strategy. This phase of intense sectarianism fascinated and perplexed those who were most closely involved in the conflict. Lucien Hérard warned of the dangers of *tendancite*, a condition which would first manifest itself

par une espèce de polarisation, de cristallisation des camarades autour de la tendance. On pense moins au prolétariat, au parti qu'à la tendance. Puis, on organise celle-ci à la manière d'un parti dans le parti. Puis, on part à la chasse aux mandats et à la conquête de postes de direction.

Et alors se livrent des luttes intestines très préjudiciables, d'autant qu'on les complique souvent de questions de personnes.[193]

As a *tendance* developed its sectarian role and appealed to the moral sensibility of party members it threatened to expand, not by incremental gains, but by a sudden access of strength which would convert a potential into an actual majority. Hérard's telling phrase, 'une espèce de polarisation, de cristallisation des camarades', alludes to this possibility. This was what the Gauche Révolutionnaire was attempting to achieve; if it could refine its rhetoric, and dwell on the central themes of the party's anti-participationist tradition, it stood a good chance of creating a sudden and massive wave of support in its favour.

For a *tendance* to become a triumphant sect, several conditions were necessary. First, its predictions of moral danger would have to be vindicated by events. Secondly, it would have to make its appeals for support within the existing rules and avoid any action which would expose it to punishment and suppression by the party's legal and bureaucratic authorities. Thirdly, it would have to preserve the spiritual status of its leader, and to sustain the impression that he was solely interested in the moral purpose of his mission and not at all in office and organizational power. Conversely, it was in the interest of the party's authorities to avoid any actions or statements of position which could be exploited by the *tendance-secte*; to employ the party's rules as a means of constraining its activities, and even of forcing it into error; and to portray its leader as an ambitious person, prepared to use the *tendance* as a vehicle for his own advancement.

Both strategy and counter-strategy were based on an awareness that the culminating phase in sectarian conflict would involve sudden and dramatic changes of form and activity. When a generalized conflict group, in this case a *tendance*, becomes the rallying-point for a spiritual revival, it undergoes a metamorphosis; what was originally only one aspect of its character, its sectarianism, is expressed in a specialized

---

[193] Lucien Hérard, 'Tendances', *Le Socialiste Côte-d'Orien*, no. 223, 5 March 1938, p. 1.

and transcendent form, its leader expands his role as a visionary, and admission to its membership becomes a matter of simply declaring faith in the moral ideals of the preferred tradition. At the same time, the internal politics of the party are transformed; the old rules and conventions lose their relevance, and all preceding conflicts are reduced to what has become an all-absorbing contest between truth and untruth. For the French Socialists in the early months of 1938, the problem was to judge when such radical changes were about to occur; for the sectarians, it was a matter of deciding when to make the dangerous bid for spiritual ascendancy, and for the authorities the important thing was to avoid any action which could be represented as persecution.

Blum's attempt to involve the party in a 'Rassemblement National autour du Front Populaire' and the endorsement of his plan by the National Council of 12 March 1938 took the party to the threshold of such a contest. It was easy for his critics within the party to portray his scheme as nothing more than a proposal for a national union, and the Gauche Révolutionnaire thus obtained the perfect pretext for an intensified campaign against any further participation in Popular Front arrangements and for a return to the party's revolutionary traditions. However, Marceau Pivert and other officers of the Seine Federation acted precipitately by sending out a tract under the authority of their unit but without the approval of the CAP and the General Secretariat. Instead of drawing back when challenged by Paul Faure, Marceau Pivert and his colleagues continued to act in defiance of the rules and became hopelessly entangled in a web of disciplinary restrictions. In the end, they were removed from office and their federation dissolved. Now in open rebellion, they campaigned desperately for the removal of the sanctions which had been imposed upon them.

As a result, the conflict within the party shifted from a sectarian towards a factional pattern. In its efforts to sustain the Seine rebellion, the Gauche Révolutionnaire was forced to gather support wherever it was offered while stressing the opposition between *tendance* and party authority and, at the level of personalities, between the leaders of the two sides. In defending Marceau Pivert, it was forced to imply that the man himself was as important as his spiritual mission and that his clash with Paul Faure was part of a battle for the organizational headship of the party. For his part, the General Secretary had every reason to welcome the change in pattern; although he was faced with a determined and resourceful adversary, the conflict had now become a relatively intelligible affair of isolated skirmishes in different federations, where established tactics could be brought to bear, rather than the unpredictable process of sectarian revolt. The Gauche Révolutionnaire might still endeavour to exploit the national union issue, but the policy of *attentisme* had left the party's authorities much less exposed where matters of strategy were concerned, and once the Blum ministry had fallen it had been possible to pull the parliamentary group back to a less exposed position, to avoid participation in government, and to wait upon events.

The *jeu de tendances* was affected in several ways by the change from a predominantly sectarian to a predominantly factional mode of conflict. First, the reluctance of the party's leadership to adopt fixed positions and to pursue a policy of *attentisme* made it difficult for loyalists to produce a comprehensive and agreed motion for the Royan Congress; although the *Socialiste* text was widely distributed and supported, it was guarded in its statements about certain crucial issues and the decision of the Nord Federation to produce its own text was, in one respect, an attempt to remedy this deficiency. Secondly, the Gauche Révolutionnaire had lost its definition; its efforts to defend Marceau Pivert and the Seine rebels had engendered a spirit of separatism within its ranks with the result that its congress motion was treated almost like a gesture, rather than a sign of conviction. Thirdly, the Bataille Socialiste had taken advantage of the changed circumstances to move further away from the loyalists and to broaden its appeal.

Although Paul Faure had checked the Gauche Révolutionnaire's offensive, he had exposed both his office and his personal reputation in doing so and soon found himself under immense pressure from his opponents. For the first time in many years, the General Secretariat had become vulnerable and speculation about who might succeed Paul Faure and J. -B. Séverac could be taken seriously. The General Secretary himself obviously resented the fact that he had been left to shoulder the responsibility for sanctions while others pretended that it was not their concern:

je n'accepte pas, pour ma part, de me taire devant ces petites manœuvres qui consistent à charger des camarades de missions déplaisantes, et de tirer largement avantage après coup à la fois du rétablissement de la discipline, du maintien de l'autorité du Parti, et du fait qu'on n'est personnellement pour rien dans l'application des sanctions.[194]

The same point could have been made about the various *motions de synthèse* which had proliferated in the pre-congress period; Paul Faure and his officers had not only upheld the right of the party's authorities to impose disciplinary measures on recalcitrant members and units, but had also spent a great deal of time defending the party's reputation

---

[194] Faure, 'Quelques mots personnels', *La Bataille*, 22 May 1938, p. 1.

against the propaganda of the Communist Party and holding together the Popular Front alliance in very trying circumstances, only to be told, in the Monnet–Philip text in particular, that better results could have been obtained by greater skill in negotiation and a more energetic application of the Popular Front strategy. The various synthesis motions varied in content and purpose but they all hinted that the party's predicament was partly the fault of its officers and that, when the time came to replace them, there were people with independent minds and fresh ideas who were ready to fill any gaps which might appear. The manoeuvring behind these motions was a sure sign that the General Secretariat had lost some of its authority and that a succession crisis could be anticipated.

In the event, the party's officers won the crucial divisions at the Royan Congress, but their margins of victory had been narrow. They had seen one *tendance*, the Gauche Révolutionnaire, come close to persuading the delegates to annul the sanctions against the rebel federation and admit its representatives to the sessions, and they had been unable to prevent another, the Bataille Socialiste, from challenging the adequacy of Blum's *texte de synthèse* at a time when a display of solidarity to the outside world had been deemed essential. Resentment was focused on the *tendances* as institutions and Bracke's cry of anger, 'Ce sont les clans!', caught the mood of the occasion. The party had almost been broken apart by its internal dissensions.

The major weakness of the loyalists was that, while accepting that the party had to play its part in government, they had developed nothing resembling a unified set of policy proposals, nothing, in short, comparable to a detailed and comprehensive programme which could guide the parliamentary group on any future occasion when the party was required to take office, either on its own or as a member of a coalition ministry. Jules Moch had been asking for something like a working list of economic projects in his speech at Royan, and Blum's April plan was frequently cited with approval, but the main emphasis in the resolutions and in the debates at Royan had been on possible extensions of the Popular Front programme, that is, the virtual shopping list of specific reforms which had been contained in the 1936 platform. The need for planning and for systematic schemes of nationalization had been stressed both by the CGT and by Révolution Constructive, but their proposals were still being treated with circumspection. The indirectness and the diffuseness of the sectional pressures bearing upon the party were partly to blame for the weakness of its proposals; the CGT could hardly have been satisfied with the SFIO's reluctance to translate its nationalization plans into detailed technical projects, and although some delegates at Royan had pressed for more practical work in the development of agricultural policies[195] most of the general motions had discussed the farming sector of the economy in hopelessly general terms, showing no real knowledge of the complexity of the factors affecting land ownership and use, production costs, pricing, and processing industries, for example. The position was even worse where business and industry were concerned; although Blum's April plan had clearly recognized the need for a mixed economy, the basic assumption behind the various policy resolutions was that the problems of developing manufacturing, consumer-goods and service industries could be reduced to that of establishing a command economy, involving the nationalization of the main parts of the economy and the regulation of the system as a whole by tight monetary, credit and exchange controls.

Had the party established effective relationships with particular sections, it could possibly have developed a more detailed and realistic programme and at the same time achieved greater internal stability by limiting the free play of its *tendances*. It was caught in a dilemma: although it had demonstrated its readiness to help manage a capitalist economy, it had not been prepared to acquire the understanding of specific economic interests which would help it to perform that role effectively. The choice lay with the loyalist majority; it was in practice reformist and ministerialist but was as yet reluctant to justify its choice of means, preferring to act as though participation in government had arisen as a contingency.

The ambiguous relationship of the party's two main leaders, Léon Blum and Paul Faure, not only with each other but with the loyalist majority, also served to perpetuate this unsatisfactory condition. In the stable, social-democratic culture of the Nord and Pas-de-Calais Federations, these two men could be represented as an effective duumvirate, with Faure cast as the practical organizer, the model for activists, the leader with an instinctive sympathy for the ordinary party member, and Blum as the visionary and thinker, sensitive to the importance of doctrine and tradition. In federations more affected by the sectarian aspects of the *lutte de tendances*, however, or more susceptible to libertarian sentiment, the two men were seen almost as a Janus face, with Faure as the cynical manipulator, a Machiavellian figure, and Blum as a figure of wise but sad authority, only too aware that the strict application of the rules might offend the principles of natural justice. Blum's own conception of his status bore some resemblance to this caricature: as at

---

[195] See the speeches at Royan by Henry (Var) (Parti Socialiste (SFIO), 35ᵉ Congrès National, Royan, 4–7 juin 1938, *Compte rendu sténographique*, pp. 331–2) and François Tanguy-Prigent (ibid., pp. 402–6).

Royan, he saw himself as heightening the party's sense of being a moral community, as reconciling those who were in dispute, and as creating an elaborate synthesis out of apparently opposed positions. He embodied the virtues of reflection, mature wisdom and vision and could use as foils colleagues such as Zyromski whose passionate quixotism could create divisions and anxieties. His role as the author of rallying texts was an extension of this more general role.[196]

During his long silence before Royan, Blum was the subject of quite unreal expectations: there were those in the Gauche Révolutionnaire, for example, who believed that he would speak out against any expulsions when he came to the congress,[197] though when put to the test he stood out against an amnesty. Yet he was able to retain the confidence of the great majority of the delegates and at the conclusion of the debate on general policy could produce a statement which attracted a three-fifths majority of the mandates. Unhappily, his very skill at managing the party's affairs on such occasions helped to conceal its many weaknesses.

[196] Cf. the appraisal of Blum in Colette Audry, *Léon Blum ou la politique du juste* (Julliard, Paris, 1955), especially p. 60.
[197] Joubert, *Révolutionnaires de la S.F.I.O.*, p. 154.

5   The years 1938–1945: collapse and reconstruction of the SFIO

Although not altered beyond recognition, the SFIO which re-emerged after the liberation of France differed in many ways from its pre-war counterpart. Having been badly divided over questions of foreign policy between September 1938 and May 1939, it had remained on the margins of the French political scene during the first nine months of the Second World War and had virtually ceased to exist as a political force by the summer of 1940. Then, having re-established itself as an underground organization during the years of the German occupation and the Vichy regime, it had re-entered politics in 1944 as a more centralized party, determined to impose strict standards of discipline on its membership. The changes which had taken place over this period form the background to that phase of internal conflict which cast its shadow over the party between June 1945 and August 1946 and led to the appointment of Guy Mollet as General Secretary, and it is to them that we must now turn our attention.

The conflict between Blumistes and Fauristes, September 1938–May 1939

The Czech crisis of September 1938, which developed with frightening rapidity, forced political observers in the western democracies to face the fact that their efforts to restrain Germany might well involve them in a European war. A vague but menacing speech by Adolf Hitler at a Nazi rally on 12 September had been followed by widespread riots in the Sudeten border areas, arousing fears that Germany might actually invade Czechoslovakia on the pretext of defending the German-speaking minority in the Sudetenland. In an effort to find a solution to the crisis, the British Prime Minister, Neville Chamberlain, had met with Hitler at Berchtesgaden on the 15th and subsequently the British and French governments had put pressure on Czechoslovakia to surrender her border areas to Germany. Further talks between Chamberlain and Hitler at Godesberg on the 22nd and 23rd had failed to produce an agreement, and in a speech on the 26th Hitler was still speaking in terms of military action unless his demands were met. On the 29th and 30th, Chamberlain, Daladier, Hitler and Mussolini met in conference at Munich and approved the transfer of the Sudetenland to Germany, after which German troops occupied the territory on 1 October.

Throughout this month, Léon Blum had been writing in *Le Populaire* about the difficulty of preserving peace while also defending the territorial integrity of the Czech state. In an article published after Chamberlain's first visit to Hitler, when reports indicated that an adverse settlement would be imposed on Czechoslovakia, he concluded that war had probably been avoided.

Mais dans des conditions telles que moi, qui n'ai cessé de lutter pour la paix, qui depuis bien des années lui avais fait d'avance le sacrifice de ma vie, je n'en puis éprouver de joie et que je me sens partagé entre un lâche soulagement et la honte.[1]

At first the party's whole parliamentary group had expressed disapproval of what was happening but at the height of the crisis, on 29 and 30 September, its meetings were marked by bitter exchanges between the supporters of Blum and those of Paul Faure, for the latter were now prepared to endorse the Munich agreement without reservation. The Fauristes carried the day and on the 30th the group adopted a resolution which expressed its gratification that the Munich conference had halted the movement towards war.[2] When the Chamber of Deputies met on 4 October to discuss the international crisis, Blum, as leader of the Socialist group, was obliged to explain the position which the party had adopted,[3] but only one Socialist deputy (Jean Bouhey) voted with the Communists against a motion of confidence in the government's foreign policy, which was approved by 537 votes to 75.[4]

In spite of this, the disagreement had opened up a division within the ranks of the Socialist Party's leadership hierarchy. Aligned with Paul Faure in defence of the Munich agreement were his deputy, Jean-Baptiste Séverac, and several of the party's provincial leaders, including Louis L'Hévéder, Fernand Roucayrol, Justin Arnol and Maurice Paz,

---

[1] *Le Populaire*, 20 September 1938, in Blum, *L'Oeuvre de Léon Blum, 1937–1940 (Albin Michel, Paris, 1965)*, p. 221.
[2] 'Rapport sur l'activité du groupe socialiste au parlement', Parti Socialiste (SFIO), 36ᵉ Congrès National, Nantes, 27–30 mai 1939, *Rapports* (Librairie Populaire, Paris, 1939), pp. 231–6.
[3] See Blum, *L'Oeuvre de Léon Blum, 1937–1940*, pp. 224–7.
[4] 'Rapport sur l'activité du groupe socialiste au parlement', Parti Socialiste (SFIO), 36ᵉ Congrès National, Nantes, 27–30 mai 1939, *Rapports*, pp. 241–2. See also Jules Moch, *Rencontres avec . . . Léon Blum* (Plon, Paris, 1970), pp. 250–2; and letter from Jean Pierre-Bloch in *Le Monde* (Paris), 2 October 1968, p. 2.

while Léon Blum was supported by his close friends, Marx Dormoy and Vincent Auriol, by a group of younger men who included Jules Moch, Georges Monnet, Léo Lagrange and Daniel Mayer, and by Jean Zyromski and his colleagues of the Bataille Socialiste. The basis for a similar cleavage had existed at the time of the anschluss, in March 1938, but on that occasion there had been less danger of war and, whatever his private reservations may have been, Paul Faure had supported Blum. Now the differences between the two were out in the open, however, and there was a distinct possibility that the split might develop into a *lutte de tendances* which could spread downwards to the party's federations and branches.

For all that, despite their disagreement over foreign policy, the two sides were as one in their opposition to the domestic policy of the Daladier government. In a radio broadcast on 21 August, the Premier had announced that firms engaged in defence industries were to be exempt from the law which provided for a 40-hour week, and in November his government approved financial policies which represented a decisive break with those of the Popular Front administration. On 12 and 13 November, Paul Reynaud, who had been appointed to the post of Minister of Finance on the 1st, published a series of decrees which weakened the labour laws, increased direct and indirect taxation and removed the controls on wholesale prices. In protest, the CGT called for a general strike to take place on 30 November but this was not strongly supported and the authorities were able to contain it. On 9 December a motion of confidence in the government was carried by 315 votes to 256 in a division which signified that the Popular Front was breaking apart as a parliamentary force; while the Socialists and the Communists had voted together in the minority, over two-thirds of the Radical Socialists had aligned themselves with the groups of the centre right and the right in support of the government.[5] Thereafter, the Socialist group became one of the points of opposition to the new economic and financial policies, a role which did not require from it the same degree of discipline as it had had to accept when it had been part of the governing coalition. Paradoxically, therefore, the Daladier ministry's shift towards the centre right had left the Socialists with greater freedom to express their internal differences over foreign policy.

By November 1938 the debate within the SFIO over the Munich agreement had developed into a much more general dispute about the nature of the European crisis and the means of preserving peace. A

---

[5] 'Rapport sur l'activité du groupe socialiste au parlement', Parti Socialiste (SFIO), 36ᵉ Congrès National, Nantes, 27–30 mai 1939, *Rapports*, pp. 248–62; and Jean-Pierre Azéma, *De Munich à la Libération, 1938–1944* (Seuil, Paris, 1979), pp. 25–7.

study group appointed by the CAP had discussed the specific issues in a series of meetings between 11 and 25 October and had cleared the ground to a certain extent. Apart from Séverac and Zyromski, who adopted fixed and opposing positions, the members of the group tried to treat the various questions on their merits and to avoid controversy, but in the end the boundary between the two sides remained intact. The Blumistes held to their view that Germany and Italy represented a threat to peace and should be opposed by a rival force consisting of the Western powers and the Soviet Union; for their part, the Fauristes saw the basic conflict as one between totalitarian and democratic states (not necessarily involving the Soviet Union) and refused to accept the proposition that it was essentially a confrontation between 'ideological blocs'. Other differences flowed from this divergence of perspective. While neither side claimed that war was inevitable or denied the value of defensive alliances under certain circumstances, the Fauristes were more inclined than the Blumistes to believe that peaceful coexistence could be achieved between democratic and totalitarian states, and that an international conference could prepare the way for a return to stability and peace in Europe.[6]

The report of the working group was considered by the National Council, which met on 5–6 November and decided to refer it to an extraordinary national congress to be held at Montrouge, in the southern suburbs of Paris, between 24 and 26 December. When the policy motions for this congress were published on 29 November, they revealed an unusual configuration of group and personal interests. Blum, breaking his habit of avoiding fixed commitments during the formulation of pre-congress resolutions, had actually written and signed a text of his own; Paul Faure had joined with a group of his senior colleagues to produce a motion designed to express the party's traditional ideas on the question of peace and war; the Bataille Socialiste, for the first time in many years, had not submitted a motion – Zyromski had simply called upon his supporters to back Blum's text, given that there was no perceptible difference between Blum's position and his own; while the other dissident *tendance*, the Redressement, despite the fact that it was in broad agreement with the Fauristes, had put forward a resolution signed by Maurice Deixonne and Ludovic Zoretti. The array of texts was completed by a motion signed by Nadia Gukowski on behalf of the *pacifistes intégraux*, and by a text prepared by Etienne Weill-Raynal.

---

[6] See the report of the working group written by Etienne Weill-Raynal, in *La Vie du Parti* (Paris), no. 81, 29 November 1938, pp. 321–3.

While there was considerable common ground between all these documents, substantial differences remained between the positions of the Blumistes and the Fauristes, who used contrasting terms to describe the European balance of power and the underlying structure of inter-state agreements. The Blum text identified the policy of domination and proselytism being pursued by the totalitarian dictatorships as the immediate threat to peace and took the line that French security neces-sarily implied the existence of contracts of mutual assistance with other peaceful states; those contracts which already existed and which France was not prepared to honour should, it declared, be terminated but those which remained, principally the Anglo-French *entente* and the Franco-Soviet pact, should be courageously observed. The Fauriste motion rested on the assumption that the danger of war had arisen from the unsatisfactory peace settlement of 1919 and the disorganization of the European system of states which it had caused. For this reason it called upon the party to condemn anything which resembled an ideolo-gical crusade, for it claimed that the maintenance of peace required a constant search for conditions which would facilitate the coexistence of the democratic and totalitarian powers rather than the setting up of one bloc in opposition to the other. Only disarmament, it argued, would ensure peace, and it advocated the holding of an international confer-ence to deal with the problems posed by frontiers, trading relations, access to raw materials, commercial outlets and colonial mandates.[7]

These texts, having been considered by the usual round of federal congresses, were placed before the delegates at the Montrouge Con-gress on 24 December.[8] Past precedent would have dictated that there should be a general debate lasting for a day or more before the refer-ence of issues and motions to a resolutions committee, but on this occasion the delegates agreed almost immediately to appoint such a committee and give it the task of preparing a resolution which could command, if not unanimous support, at least the support of the great majority of the delegates. The committee, duly appointed, met behind closed doors without being able to reach agreement. On the 26th, there-fore, it came back to the congress with the request that the delegates themselves should be asked to choose between the Blum, Fauriste and Gukowski texts, the Redressement group having withdrawn its motion. The Blum text, which now included elements from the resolution of the Nord Federation, had been recommended by a majority of the

[7] *Le Populaire* (Paris), 29 November 1938, p. 6.
[8] For a detailed account of the Montrouge Congress, see Nathanael Greene, *Crisis and Decline: The French Socialist Party in the Popular Front Era* (Cornell University Press, Ithaca, New York, 1969), pp. 240–51.

Table 20. *SFIO, Extraordinary National Congress, Montrouge, 26 December 1938: division on foreign policy resolutions*

Motions	Mandates	% of total
Léon Blum	4,322	52.0
Paul Faure	2,837	34.1
Nadia Gukowski	60	0.7
Abstentions	1,014	12.2
Absent	79	1.0
Total	8,312	

Source: La Vie du Parti (Paris), no. 82, March 1939, p. 8.

Resolutions Committee while the minority had favoured the Fauriste text, which had also been expanded.[9] Both texts were still expressed in general terms but it was now reasonably clear that, whereas the Blumistes believed that German expansion in eastern Europe could be prevented by a firm defensive alliance which included the USSR, the Fauristes were essentially concerned with the security of France in western Europe, a matter where the support of Britain and the United States was of considerable importance. After the failure of a move to have Blum, Paul Faure and Jean Lebas draft a common resolution, the texts were put to the vote. The outcome was an absolute majority for Blum's motion but over one-third of the mandates were cast for Faure's text and a large number of abstentions were recorded. The details of the result are given in Table 20.

This conflict, ending in Blum's decisive victory, had severely strained the relationship between him and Paul Faure, but the two men were still able to work together at the apex of the party and neither had yet made any attempt to remove the other from office. Blum had described his action in preparing a motion as being a response to a moral imperative, a kind of personal witness, rather than as a call to arms.

J'ai rédigé une motion. Je l'ai rédigée seul après de longs jours de réflexion et de méditation. Je ne l'ai communiquée à personne. Je n'en ai parlé à personne. Je n'ai demandé l'avis de personne. Elle ne porte aucune autre signature que la mienne. J'ai agi ainsi pour éviter rien qui ressemblât à un groupement de forces, à la constitution d'une 'tendance', même précaire et éphémère, dans le Parti.[10]

However, the fact remained that there was a growing feeling that what may have begun as a difference of opinion between the two leaders was

[9] See *Le Populaire*, 27 December 1938, pp. 1 and 4.
[10] Ibid., p. 4.

now becoming something that resembled a *lutte de tendances*. It had been open to each federal congress to refuse to become involved in the conflict and to instruct its delegates to press for a common resolution or to abstain from voting if separate texts were maintained. In the event, although there was on this occasion an unusually high abstention rate, the majority of the federations did express a clear preference. Of the 96 federal delegations which took part in the ballot at the National Congress, 80 gave over 50 per cent of their mandates to one or other of the two main texts, 51 (including those for the Nord, Seine, Seine-et-Oise, Bouches-du-Rhône and Gironde Federations) to the Blum motion and 29 (including those for the Haute-Vienne and Meurthe-et-Moselle Federations) to the Fauriste motion.

Could the conflict have been ended at this point? The party had at its disposal procedures and rituals which might have been used in an attempt to reconcile the two sides. Had the Blum text been accepted as a reasonable, if rather ambiguous, statement of the party's foreign policy, and had the harsh words spoken before and during the congress been pushed into the background, the CAP and the parliamentary group might well have regained their solidarity and composure. What kept the tension alive was partly the fact that the European crisis showed no sign of abating; the Spanish Civil War was now in its final stages and the position of Czechoslovakia continued to deteriorate, with the result that foreign policy issues remained high on the party's agenda. Partly, too, the fact that certain groups were unwilling to abandon the positions which they had taken up during the autumn made compromise unlikely: the ultra-pacifists among the Fauristes were determined to fight the Montrouge policy and to ensure that France was not drawn into a war against Germany in support of either a Soviet or an East European cause; the committed Blumistes were equally determined to press home their advantage and to hold the party to a policy of firmness so that it would never again accept anything resembling the Munich agreement; and the Bataille Socialiste was concerned to persuade others that the European crisis was indeed a battle between the forces of peace and those of international fascism. Besides the backing of his own followers, Zyromski now had that of a number of former Communists who were associated with André Ferrat and the journal, *Que Faire?*, and who were in sympathy with the views of the Bataille, favouring French intervention in the Spanish Civil War, the unification of the Socialist and Communist Parties, and an alliance between the western democracies and the USSR. According to one of their number, André Thirion, the division in the SFIO after the Munich agreement had given the Bataille hope that at some future congress it could combine with

Blum's supporters to take over the leadership of the SFIO and, if necessary, expel 'les capitulards et les droitiers' from the party. Thirion and
his friends were convinced that an alliance would be concluded between
France, Britain and the Soviet Union by the end of the summer of 1939
and that war would not break out until 1940, by which time Thirion
confidently expected that he himself would be playing a leading role in
the Seine Federation and that either Zyromski or a *'blumiste' de gauche*
would have become the General Secretary of the party.[11]

Although the Blumistes and the Bataille had achieved ascendancy at
the Montrouge Congress, however, the Fauristes subsequently
improved their position by broadening the grounds of conflict. In particular, they created confusion amongst their opponents by suggesting
that co-operation with the Communists should be ended. While the
Bataille was still in favour of close ties between the SFIO and the PCF,
those Blumistes who had learned from experience how difficult it was
to work with the Communists at the local level were inclined to sym-
pathize with the idea of a break. Nevertheless, they were afraid that to
admit this preference would lay them open to the charge of inconsist-
ency – for how could they defend a pact with the Soviet Union in
international affairs while opposing the continuation of an alliance with
the PCF in domestic politics?

The Fauristes first tried out their new tactic at the meeting of the
National Council in Paris on 4–5 March 1939,[12] when Justin Arnol presented a resolution stating that, although the principle of unity of action
with the Communists could be a useful means of defending the Republic
when it was in peril (as it had been in 1934), under current circumstances the Socialist Party should stand alone and be as clear as possible
in its policy and action; no advantage could be gained from holding
joint public meetings with any other party, and the federations should
devote all their energy to the recruitment and education of activists,
and to the party's own propaganda. Zyromski put forward an opposing
motion but the National Council, having rejected a preliminary resolution proposed by Marx Dormoy, endorsed Arnol's text by a relative
majority. The exact figures are given in Table 21.

[11] André Thirion, *Révolutionnaires sans révolution* (Robert Laffont, Paris, 1972), pp.
441–3. See also Victor Fay, *La Flamme et la cendre: histoire d'une vie militante*, prepared with the assistance of Evelyne Malnic (Presses Universitaires de Vincennes,
Paris, 1989), pp. 137–41 and 151–7.
[12] See *La Vie du Parti*, no. 82, March 1939, pp. 11–13; 'Histoire du Parti Socialiste
S.F.I.O.', Part 20, 'De janvier à mai 1939', *Cahier et Revue de l'OURS* (Paris), no.
121 (June–July 1981), pp. 7–13; Greene, *The French Socialist Party in the Popular
Front Era*, pp. 254–8.

Table 21. *SFIO, National Council, Paris,
4–5 March 1939: division on relations with the
Communist Party*

Motions	Mandates	% of total
Justin Arnol	3,376	44.5
Jean Zyromski	1,377	18.2
Abstentions	2,534	33.4
Absent	293	3.9
Total	7,580	

Source: *La Vie du Parti* (Paris), no. 82, March 1939, pp.
14–15.

Table 22. *SFIO, National Council, Paris,
4–5 March 1939: division on motions concerning
foreign policy*

Motions	Mandates	% of total
Jean Lebas	4,025	53.1
Charles Spinasse	[3,133]	41.3
Abstentions	237	3.1
Absent	185	2.4
Total	7,580	

Source: *La Vie du Parti* (Paris), no. 82, March 1939, p. 15.
For details of adjustments, see the appendix (p. 401, n. 8).

When the meeting went on to consider foreign policy, the delegates
were asked to choose between a Blumiste text presented by Jean Lebas
and a Fauriste motion proposed by Charles Spinasse. While the Lebas
resolution condemned French recognition of the Franco regime in
Spain, insisted that France should honour its international agreements
(most notably the Anglo-French *entente* and the Franco-Soviet pact),
and specified that the liberation of Spain should be the essential condition for holding an international conference, the Spinasse motion made
the case for holding a conference without such a stipulation. In the
division the Lebas motion was adopted by an absolute majority; the
voting figures are shown in Table 22.

The details of the votes by federation in these two ballots reveal
several interesting things about the evolution of the conflict. In the first
place, the Fauristes had increased their share of the vote in the foreign
policy field from the 34.1 per cent which they had obtained in the

Montrouge division to 41.3 per cent, while the Blumiste vote had risen only slightly from 52.0 to 53.1 per cent. In the second place, the division on relations with the Communist Party had shown that the Fauristes could summon up a substantial anti-Communist vote at the level of the federations, that support for the maintenance of close ties with the Communist Party was relatively weak, and that the Blumistes were inclined to abstain rather than to take sides on this issue. In other words, by varying their angle of attack, the Fauristes had demonstrated that the *anti-munichois* grouping was in fact a single-issue coalition which could be subjected to considerable cross-pressure whenever the centre of controversy shifted to the question of the Communist connection in domestic politics.

The weeks which followed this National Council meeting saw a steady deterioration in the European situation. On 15 March, German troops moved into western Czechoslovakia and shortly afterwards the German Protectorate of Bohemia and Moravia was set up, while Slovakia was left with a form of independence. On 31 March, the British Prime Minister gave assurances to Poland, which was being subjected to increasing pressure from Germany, that Britain would come to her assistance in the event of any threat to her independence, and France associated herself with this undertaking. For those French Socialists who, like Blum, believed that only a firm alliance between France and the major states of eastern Europe could restrain Germany, it became more important than ever to come to terms with the Soviet Union.[13]

As these events unfolded, the working relations between members of the SFIO's CAP were placed under increasing strain. A particular point of contention centred on Paul Faure's right to address the party through the *rapport moral*, the customary annual report. The practice of submitting this report to the national congress had lapsed in the late 1920s, but the 1929 Congress had decided that it should be revived, provided that it was the CAP as a body rather than the General Secretary which was being called to account for the year's activities. In practice, however, the successive reports to the national congresses of the 1930s had been treated as communications from Paul Faure. Consideration of the *rapport moral* had usually been the first item on the congress agenda and delegates had sometimes taken advantage of this arrangement to raise matters of general policy prematurely. To deal with this problem, the Administrative Committee of the Nord Federation had decided in July 1938 to ask the CAP's General Administrative Subcommittee to consider a proposal for dispensing with the *rapport moral*

---

[13] See Blum, 'La coalition pacifique', *Le Populaire*, 3 April 1939, in Blum, *L'Oeuvre de Léon Blum, 1937–1940*, pp. 283–4.

altogether when it came to review the party's constitution.[14] This review was to have been submitted to an extraordinary National Congress in November 1939, but at the National Council meeting of 4–5 March 1939 during the discussion of preparations for the next regular National Congress (the 36th, to be held in Nantes between 27 and 30 May), Bracke and Jean Lebas had raised the question of doing away entirely with the *rapport moral*. No clear decision had been taken but the chairman of the session, amidst distracting interruptions, had indicated that the matter could be considered by the CAP and subsequently referred to the congress.[15]

When, on 12 April, the CAP came to discuss the various reports for the Nantes Congress, it decided by 15 votes to 13 that no *rapport moral* should be sent out, despite the fact that Paul Faure had come to the meeting with a text which he wished to submit for approval. Angry and upset, Faure then left the meeting abruptly, but those who remained, under the chairmanship of Zyromski, made no attempt to reconsider the decision or to search for a means of reconciliation.[16] It is difficult to discover the motives which prompted those involved in this incident to act as they did, but the way in which Faure had been treated caused deep resentment amongst his supporters. For the first time since the rift over the Munich crisis, an attempt had been made to undermine the authority of one of the party's elder statesmen. The implication was that Faure had been too committed to his group and to its cause to carry out his duties as General Secretary with the objectivity and even-handedness expected of someone in that office; in effect, his opponents had come very close to calling for his resignation.

Paul Faure reacted in a characteristically robust manner, sending out his report to the federations and branches without waiting for the approval of the CAP, as if to assert that, as General Secretary, he was independently responsible to the body of federal and branch secretaries and, at a further remove, to the membership in general. In his report he argued that the party should be completely independent of all other political groups and that it should abide by the conditions for unity with

---

[14] See *l'ordre du jour* proposed by Jean Lebas for the CAP meeting of 10 May 1939, in *S.F.I.O., réunions de la C.A.P., 12 avril 1939–6 juin 1940* (Archives de l'OURS).

[15] See extracts from the *Compte rendu sténographique* of the first session of the National Council of 4–5 March 1939, in *Le Populaire*, 13 May 1939, p. 4.

[16] See Parti Socialiste (SFIO), 36ᵉ Congrès National, Nantes, 27–30 Mai 1939, *Rapports*, pp. 3–4, and accounts of the event given to the Nantes Congress by Bracke (Parti Socialiste (SFIO), 36ᵉ Congrés National, Nantes, 27–30 Mai 1939, *Compte rendu sténographique* (Conservation film of original typescript, Bibliothèque de Documentation Internationale Contemporaine, Universités de Paris), 27 May 1939, pp. 32–49), Salomon Grumbach (ibid., pp. 88–102) and Paul Faure (ibid., pp. 105–15).

the Communist Party which had been specified by the Marseille National Congress in July 1937. In foreign affairs he called for a world conference to examine the problem of apportioning raw materials and to consider all means for avoiding war. These appeals were accompanied by an exhortation to work for party unity but the underlying message was that the Montrouge Congress had not produced a policy on which agreement was possible.[17]

The federal congresses which preceded the Nantes National Congress were presented with policy resolutions in which the issues of peace and war were once again those given most prominence. The Fauristes and Blumistes both put forward separate texts, as did the much smaller Redressement group and the *pacifistes intégraux*. On this occasion the Bataille Socialiste did not publish a motion of its own, Zyromski and others of its leaders having signed that of the Blumistes. The two main resolutions covered the same ground but with significant differences of emphasis. In discussing foreign affairs, both texts acknowledged that a threat of war existed, but whereas the Fauristes implied that the imperfections of the European order were to blame and that these could be remedied by an international conference, the Blumistes (while not excluding the possibility of such a conference) took the line that the nature of fascism, with its drive to expand, was the real problem. As they saw it, the only means of preserving the peace was the construction of a system of mutual-aid agreements amongst the peaceful states. With regard to domestic policy, while both texts expressed hostility towards the policies of the Daladier government and approved of the idea that the parties and groups which had belonged to the Rassemblement Populaire should maintain relations, the Fauristes stressed the need for the SFIO to be independent and the Blumistes the need to preserve the capacity for concerted action should circumstances require it.[18]

The Nantes National Congress of 27–30 May 1939 was attended by 458 delegates representing 100 of the party's 101 federations.[19] While in general it dealt with its business efficiently, its proceedings were marred by frequent displays of ill-feeling; very often chairmen had to call for order and speakers had difficulty in making themselves heard

[17] *La Vie du Parti*, no. 84, May 1939, pp. 1–4.

[18] *Le Populaire*, 5 May 1939, p. 4. For the resolutions of the Redressement Socialiste and the *pacifistes intégraux*, see ibid., 6 May 1939, p. 4.

[19] For the proceedings of the congress, see Parti Socialiste (SFIO), 36ᵉ Congrès National, Nantes, 27–30 mai 1939, *Compte rendu sténographique*, and for decisions and votes, see *La Vie du Parti*, no. 84, May 1939, pp. 1–13. See also Greene, *The French Socialist Party in the Popular Front Era*, pp. 259–72, and 'Histoire du Parti Socialiste S.F.I.O.', Part 20, 'De janvier à mai 1939', *Cahier et Revue de l'OURS*, no. 121 (June–July 1981), pp. 44–62.

above the hum of private conversation. These were the signs of dead-lock: each of the two main groups was strong enough to inflict damage on the other but not strong enough to take complete control of the party organization. Although the Blumistes had won a technical victory over the matter of the *rapport moral*, they knew that, given the extent of the loyalty which Paul Faure inspired amongst the party's ordinary members, there was no possibility of having him censured for having sent the report out on his own authority. Equally, the Fauristes knew that none of their senior parliamentarians possessed Blum's gifts as an orator or could match his public reputation, assets which had been of such importance in the party's struggle to win popular backing for its policies. The essential drama of the Nantes Congress lay in the way in which it revealed, amidst much bitterness, that each side was incomplete as a party and that each needed the other. By the closing sessions this was clear to all but the most obtuse.

On the first day of the congress, Saturday 27 May, the delegates decided to begin by discussing the *rapport moral* and then, after Paul Faure had accepted Blum's suggestion that one paragraph should be deleted from the text, the document was adopted by an overwhelming majority.[20] This decision represented a minor victory for the Fauristes, who returned to the attack at the morning session of Monday, 29 May, when they backed the Loire Federation's proposal that the existing ban on party members' belonging to another party or political grouping should be extended to include bodies which were essentially the front organizations of other parties, such as the Communist-inspired Paix et Liberté and Amis de l'Union Soviétique. This idea had been under consideration for several months: acting on the advice of its Resolutions Committee, the Royan Congress of June 1938 had referred the proposal to the National Council, and the National Council of 4–5 March 1939 had decided that it should be considered at the Nantes Congress. A special report prepared by the Loire Federation had been published in *La Vie du Parti*,[21] and the resolution had been referred by the CAP to two of its specialized subcommittees. These had then held a joint meeting at which they were unable to reach agreement, whereupon the CAP decided that the question should be aired in *Le Populaire*. In one statement, André Blumel made the point that the party's existing disciplinary procedures were capable of dealing with the kinds of indiscipline which the Loire proposal was intended to remedy and that the Nantes Congress need therefore only reaffirm the permissive

---

[20] See Parti Socialiste (SFIO), 36ᵉ Congrès National, Nantes, 27–30 mai 1939, *Compte rendu sténographique*, 27 May 1939, pp. 12–71 and 75–121; and *La Vie du Parti*, no. 84, May 1939, pp. 1–4.

[21] *La Vie du Parti*, no. 83, April 1939, pp. 5–7.

statement contained in the political resolution which had been adopted by the 1936 Congress; in a second, Maurice Paz defended the Loire Federation's proposal and advocated a return to the more restrictive provisions which had been in force before the 1936 Congress.[22] The war of words played into the hands of the Fauristes who, having already tapped a reservoir of anti-Communist feeling in the party, were in a position to exploit this issue to the full.

When the Nantes Congress came to discuss the question, the spokesman for the Loire Federation began the debate by calling for a vote by mandates on its motion. The Blumistes, fighting a rearguard action, were trying to avoid tactical errors: they would have been in difficulty had their adversaries been able to make an issue of Zyromski's well-known liking for anti-fascist associations, but he at least reduced the effectiveness of such a move by defending openly his membership of the national committees of both Paix et Liberté and Amis de l'Union Soviétique.[23] The Blumistes then tried to persuade the delegates that the Loire motion should be referred to the Resolutions Committee along with other motions but, after a series of speeches for and against this proposal, Paul Faure insisted that the question should be put to the vote there and then. Marx Dormoy, angered, declared that if the matter were to be settled in this way his people would not take part in the meetings of the Resolutions Committee.[24] However, when the procedural question was put to the vote, the Fauristes saw their opponents soundly defeated for the congress decided by an absolute majority against referring the motion to the Resolutions Committee. The detailed result can be seen in Table 23.

Table 23. *SFIO, 36th National Congress, Nantes, 29 May 1939: division on proposal to refer the Loire motion to the Resolutions Committee*

	Mandates	% of total
For	3,299	43.5
Against	4,054	53.5
Abstentions	197	2.6
Absent	30	0.4
Total	7,580	

Source: *La Vie du Parti* (Paris), no. 84, May 1939, pp. 11–12.

[22] *Le Populaire*, 14 May 1939, p. 4.
[23] Parti Socialiste (SFIO), 36ᵉ Congrès National, Nantes, 27–30 mai 1939, *Compte rendu sténographique*, 29 May 1939, p. 483.
[24] For the full debate, see ibid., pp. 453–532.

Table 24. *SFIO, 36th National Congress, Nantes, 29 May 1939: division on the methods of regulating participation in political bodies outside the party*

Proposals	Mandates	% of total
Motion of Loire Federation	5,490	72.4
Text approved by the 33rd National Congress (1936)	1,761	23.2
Abstentions	264	3.5
Absent	65	0.9
Total	7,580	

Source: *La Vie du Parti* (Paris), no. 84, May 1939, p. 12.

The delegates were then asked to choose between the alternative methods of dealing with front organizations and they voted in favour of the Loire motion by a large majority (see Table 24).

This encounter bears comparison with that concerning relations with the Communist Party which had taken place at the National Council of 4–5 March 1939. On both occasions the Fauristes had forced the anti-Communist wing of the Blumiste group to part company with the Bataille Socialiste and had revealed the fragility of their alliance in the process. At the Nantes Congress, in the ballot over whether to refer the Loire motion to the Resolutions Committee, bloc votes or large majorities for doing so were cast by the delegates from such Blumiste federations as Aisne, Nord, Pas-de-Calais and Seine-et-Oise, whereas mandates from the Bouches-du-Rhône, Meur-the-et-Moselle, Seine and Haute-Vienne delegations provided the solid base for the negative vote of the Fauristes. In the subsequent ballot, however, most of the mandates from the anti-Communist Blumiste federations, such as Allier, Côte-d'Or, Nord and Pas-de-Calais, went to the Loire motion while the majority of those from federations sympathetic to the Bataille, such as Seine-et-Oise, Seine-et-Marne and Deux Sèvres, or from federations of a liberal persuasion such as Aisne, were cast for the 1936 formula.

The mood of the congress had changed by the time of the debate on general policy. It was almost as though the antagonists had expended their emotional energy in the early exchanges and could not face the prospect of another long-drawn-out contest. In any case, both sides had made an effort to tone down their arguments in order to win the support of moderate elements in the party's membership, and this had had the effect of narrowing the gap between them. A reconciliation now seemed possible, providing that the Fauristes were prepared to acknowledge the value of defensive alliances and the

Blumistes willing to concede that, under some circumstances, conciliation and an international conference could help to preserve the peace. Fauriste anxieties about the Franco-Soviet pact, so evident at the time of the Montrouge Congress, had been partly allayed by the British undertaking to Poland, which had reduced the possibility that the *front de la paix* would consist only of France and the Soviet Union.[25] Furthermore, President Roosevelt's message of 14 April to Hitler and Mussolini, asking for assurances that they would not attack or invade specified countries and holding out the possibility of talks on disarmament and free trade, encouraged the Fauristes to hope that an international conference might still take place.

The convergence of the two sides had made it easier for a group known as the synthesists to press their case for the restoration of a close working relationship between Léon Blum and Paul Faure and for the formulation of a unity motion to which all delegates could subscribe. Headed by Albert Rivière, a prominent member of the parliamentary group and the secretary of the Creuse Federation, the synthesists had issued an appeal for unity on 14 May, well in advance of the round of federal congresses and had generated considerable support for their campaign.[26] At the Nantes conference, they came into their own during the debate on general policy as the air of confrontation faded and the spokesmen for the rival groups began to state their views with moderation. Even those who were strongly committed to one or other of the opposed ideas about foreign policy now accepted that a compromise was unavoidable. Camille Planche reminded the congress that at Montrouge he had been one of those who

se sont élevés avec force contre toute idée de synthèse. Je pensais que le Congrès de Montrouge avait été fait pour départager des opinions précises sur la politique extérieure.

Après plusieurs mois d'expérience, je dois reconnaître que celle-ci est concluante, que l'expérience que nous voulions faire est impossible. Il n'est malheureusement pas possible de dégager à l'heure actuelle, dans le Parti, une majorité stable sur la politique extérieure, car celle-ci se heurte à d'autres majorités sur le plan intérieur, qui se contrarient et on arrive au résultat assez lamentable, dont nous constatons, aujourd'hui, ensemble les conséquences.

Dès lors, je crois qu'aujourd'hui, une synthèse s'imposera, non pas certes pour clarifier la situation: je crois qu'on ne peut pas la clarifier, mais pour permettre au Parti de vivre.[27]

[25] On this point, see the comment by Robert Vielle, ibid., pp. 595–6.
[26] See the statement and appeal in *Le Populaire*, 14 May 1939, p. 4, and a clarification by Rivière in ibid., 17 May 1939, p. 4.
[27] Parti Socialiste (SFIO), 36ᵉ Congrès National, Nantes, 27–30 mai 1939, *Compte rendu sténographique*, 29 May 1939, pp. 726–7.

Talks behind the scenes paved the way for an agreement. Léon Blum was unwell during the congress and on Monday 29th he stayed in his hotel room, where he was visited by Paul Faure. The two men considered the possibility of settling the matter themselves but decided on reflection that it would be better to have a small committee draft a unity resolution, thus avoiding the need to resort to the less flexible Resolutions Committee. On the afternoon of Tuesday 30th, Rivière put this proposal to the congress, which appointed a nine-member team consisting of Blum, Marx Dormoy and Jean Zyromski from the Blumiste – Bataille Socialiste alliance, Paul Faure, Justin Arnol and Charles Spinasse from the Fauristes, Rivière and Charles Lussy from the synthesist group, and Maurice Deixonne from the Redressement *tendance*.[28] The team worked throughout the night to produce a motion which Rivière read out to the delegates at 4.15 a.m. on Wednesday 31st. The text was tightly organized and well argued: its foreign policy section endorsed the principle of national defence, recognized the need for a coalition of peaceful powers against the axis governments, praised Roosevelt's message to the dictators and expressed confidence in the value of an international conference, while its statements regarding domestic policy attacked the fiscal and social policies of the Daladier government and condemned what it saw as the injustice of its decree laws, declaring that the Socialist Party was ready, as in 1936, to participate in the formation of a government based on a republican majority and to facilitate a *rassemblement* of all who wished to defend republican institutions.[29] As this latter formulation implied that the leaders should have considerable latitude in deciding the terms under which the party would participate in any future government or political alliance, it is surprising to find Zyromski attacking the Rivière motion and insisting that the original Blumiste text should be put to the vote. His main objection was that the proposed resolution did not embody the idea of a *rassemblement national anti-fasciste*, by which he meant something resembling the original Popular Front movement built around the organized working class.[30] Deixonne thereupon requested that the Redressement text should be kept in play. Zyromski may have hoped to precipitate a division by *tendance* in which the synthesists would have been forced to choose sides or abstain, as had happened at the Royan Congress, but first Marx Dormoy and then Paul Faure asked their supporters to vote for the Rivière motion. The division produced a

[28] Ibid., 30 May 1939, pp. 839–918.
[29] *La Vie du Parti*, no. 84, May 1939, pp. 8–9.
[30] Parti Socialiste (SFIO), 36ᵉ Congrès National, Nantes, 27–30 mai 1939, *Compte rendu sténographique*, 30 May 1939, pp. 979–86.

Table 25. *SFIO, 36th National Congress, Nantes, 30 May 1939: division on motions concerning general policy*

Motion	Mandates	% of total
Albert Rivière	6,395	84.4
Jean Zyromski	565	7.5
Maurice Deixonne	401	5.3
Nadia Gukowski	45	0.6
Abstentions	153	2.0
Absent	21	0.3
Total	7,580	

Source: *La Vie du Parti* (Paris), no. 84, May 1939, p. 13.

convincing victory for the reunited leadership and a crushing defeat for Zyromski. The details of the vote are shown in Table 25.

After eight months of conflict, the party had regained a semblance of order. Blum and Paul Faure were reconciled; the CAP elected at Royan in June 1938 was simply confirmed in office; as were the other executive bodies and agencies; the unity of the loyalist majority had been restored; and Zyromski had once again become the leader of a dissident *tendance*. However, the congress did agree to increase the membership of the CAP from 33 members to 35 as an exceptional measure, and Georges Soulès and Ludovic Zoretti, representing the Redressement group, were chosen to fill the new posts.[31] A renewal of the conflict was always a possibility as long as the core groups associated with Blum and Paul Faure remained in being but, despite a measure of continued animosity, each side observed the settlement which had been negotiated at Nantes.

The signature of the Russo-German Pact on 23 August put an end to any hopes of binding the Soviet Union into an alliance with Britain and France and, for that reason, removed one of the points at issue between the Blumistes and the Fauristes. It also settled the question of whether or not the Socialists should maintain close relations with the Communists; at its meeting on 29 August, the CAP condemned this pact and called on the SFIO's branches and federations to end relations with those who supported the new Soviet policy, in other words, with the French Communist Party.[32] Then, on 1 September the German army

[31] *La Vie du Parti*, no. 84, May 1939, pp. 9–10.
[32] See the circular of 1 September 1939 from Paul Faure to federal secretaries, in *La Vie du Parti*, no. 87, August–November 1939, pp. 3–4.

invaded Poland and on the 2nd the two houses of the French Parliament approved the demand for war credits. After the vote in the Chamber of Deputies everyone was in sombre mood, knowing that there could be no going back. Both Blum and Jules Moch, who had cast their votes for these credits, had sons liable for military service, and Blum, seeing Moch sitting there in tears, approached and put his hand on his shoulder. 'Mon pauvre Jules,' he said, 'Vous avez André et Raymond . . . Moi, j'ai Robert. J'ai voté, moi aussi. C'était notre devoir.'[33] On the following day, France declared herself to be at war with Germany.

The Socialists and the fall of France in 1940

Throughout the winter of the first year of the war the Socialist parliamentary group remained in opposition but it was given a further opportunity to take part in government when, on 20 March 1940, Daladier resigned as Premier. Paul Reynaud, who succeeded him, based his administration firmly on the centre and the centre right of the party spectrum, choosing Daladier to serve as Minister of National Defence, Chautemps as Deputy Premier and Lucien Lamoureux as Minister of Finance. The Socialists agreed to join the government and were represented by Georges Monnet as Minister of Blockade, Albert Sérol as Minister of Justice, Albert Rivière as Minister of Returned Servicemen and Pensioners, François Blancho as Under-Secretary of State for Armaments, André Février as Under-Secretary of State for Information and Fabien Albertin as Under-Secretary of State for Public Works. Though all the Socialists were from the party's second rank of *ministrables*, their presence in Reynaud's team signified the SFIO's willingness to contribute more directly to the war effort.

The great battle for France began on 10 May 1940 when German troops invaded the Low Countries and the French and British units of Army Group I moved into Belgium to meet them. Three days later, German Panzer divisions crossed the River Meuse near the French town of Sedan and drove westwards towards the Channel coast, placing a wedge between the Allied armies to the north and those to the south. To strengthen his own position, Reynaud reorganized his government on 18 May: he took over the Defence portfolio from Daladier, whom he appointed Minister of Foreign Affairs, he brought Marshal Pétain into the Cabinet as Minister of State, and he gave the post of the Interior to Georges Mandel. He also made a change in the supreme command of the armed forces, appointing General Maxime Weygand

---

[33] Moch, *Rencontres avec . . . Léon Blum*, p. 256.

as Commander-in-Chief in place of General Maurice Gamelin. However, the military situation continued to deteriorate. After Belgium had surrendered to the Germans the northern front became untenable, and more than 300,000 British and Allied troops were evacuated from beaches near Dunkirk between 26 May and 4 June. To the south, the remaining armies took up positions along the Somme and Aisne rivers. On 5 June Reynaud further reshaped his administration, taking over the Foreign Affairs portfolio from Daladier and appointing Yves Bouthillier as Minister of Finance and General Charles de Gaulle as Under-Secretary of State for Defence. On the same day, the German armies began their attack on the Somme-Aisne line. Paris was now in imminent danger and the French government, its Socialist ministers included, left the capital and moved southwards by stages to Bordeaux. With them moved elements of the administration, but it was quite impossible to arrange an organized transfer in the time available. Like other political units, the Socialists moved away from the city as individuals or in small groups, trying to interpret as best they could the fragments of information which came their way. Nothing in their experience had prepared them for this ordeal and as the scale of France's military defeat became apparent, they desperately tried to discover a means whereby the state could be preserved as an independent entity, even if this were to mean moving the government to North Africa and continuing the fight from there.

As they witnessed the departure of the government from Paris, the political events in Bordeaux and the final meetings of the Third Republican parliament at Vichy, Léon Blum and his colleagues were trying to live up to an ideal of civic virtue at the same time as they engaged in discussions as to how the government might best preserve French interests in such tragic circumstances. It was no easy task: the determination to be virtuous often conflicted with the need to take pragmatic action to deal with emergencies, even if this meant choosing the lesser of two evils. Feelings of confusion and even of guilt were easily generated in such circumstances for it was difficult for an individual to be sure of his own motivation and intentions, let alone those of others. The distance between this kind of disorientation and the tendency to reduce the chaos of events to a simple drama in which the choice is between good and evil is a short one, and distrust and suspicion damaged all but the closest relationships. As the personal ties between its members were broken, the Socialist group lost not only its capacity for collective action but also its sense of moral certainty.

The fall of Paris to the Germans on 14 June marked the beginning of this process. For those like Blum who had lived and worked in the capital thoughout their political careers, the fact of having to abandon the city in an atmosphere of panic and confusion was deeply demoralizing. Not only was Paris the fixed site of the central government, in which the Council of Ministers and the two houses of parliament lived in symbiosis with a complex structure of administrative divisions and agencies, it was also the sacred grove of France, the very heart of its intellectual and cultural life, where the great scenes of the republican tradition and the drama of the Popular Front had taken place. Several members of the SFIO have described their movements during those last days in the city, and their accounts reveal how shocked and distressed they were by the turn of events; even in early June, no one had been able to believe that the city was in real danger. On Saturday 8th, Blum was still convinced that the government would hold to its decision to defend the city. He had been told that, although the ministries were moving to châteaux in the Touraine region, the ministers themselves were to stay until they received further orders. Throughout Sunday 9th, several Socialist ministers tried to persuade him to leave and when he said that he must stay until after a meeting of the Council of Ministers that evening, they advised him at least to have his car packed and ready for departure. In the afternoon he did take the precaution of sending his daughter-in-law and his granddaughter to stay with Marx Dormoy in Montluçon, and when Georges Monnet (who with his wife Germaine had been for many years close friends of Blum and his late wife Thérèse) telephoned once more to press him to leave, Blum again considered his decision:

le départ ne me blessait pas seulement dans mes sentiments les plus chers; il avait un sens symbolique à mes yeux. Quitter ma maison, quitter Paris; mais quand reverrais-je ma maison et ma ville?[34]

Towards 11 p.m. he received a further telephone call from Monnet during which Germaine also spoke to him and, having finally given her his word that he would go, he set off into the night in his car.

He, too, made for Montluçon, which he was able to reach by daybreak, and he settled his family into a small house which had been made available for them. However, that evening, 10 June, Italy entered the war and Blum was taken with a desire to return to Paris. Dormoy felt the same way, so the two of them drove back from Montluçon on Tuesday the 11th to find the city deserted. They telephoned the Premier's office, the Ministry of War, the Ministry of the Interior and Reynaud's private residence without getting a reply but at last made

[34] Blum, 'Mémoires', in Blum, *L'Oeuvre de Léon Blum, 1940–1945* (Albin Michel, Paris, 1955), p. 23.

contact with the Prefect, with William Bullitt, the American Ambassador, and with the general in charge of the armies defending the city, General Hening. Having spoken to Hening of the need to form a defensive ring around Paris so that it might become the pivot of the French defences, Blum went on with Dormoy to the Palais-Bourbon where an attendant directed them to the solitary clerk who was working on the second floor. Dormoy then set off for the suburb of Belleville on an errand while Blum paid a last visit to his flat. Their return journey to Montluçon took them along the main road south of Fontainebleau in a solid, slowly moving mass of vehicles but at 10 p.m. they left this for a quieter route; instructed by gendarmes to travel without lights, they crossed the Loire towards 2 a.m. and reached Montluçon on the morning of Wednesday 12th.[35]

Paul Faure, who was living in a village in the Vexin district, in the south-western part of the Oise Department, also spent some time in Paris on Sunday, 9 June, and found that his telephone calls for information went unanswered. On his journey home, having had to wait at the bridge across the Seine at Poissy until a column of soldiers had crossed from the north, he made his way against a southward-flowing stream of refugees and took ten hours to cover the 50 km back to his house. He tried to return to Paris the next day but gave up the attempt when the advance guards of the German army made their appearance.[36] Jules Moch, who was serving with the French navy, was in the city on official business on Monday 10th and noticed that a cloud from burning oil depots had blotted out the horizon. At the Navy Office, having destroyed papers and codes, he considered the possibility of mining the bridges downstream, but he was warned by Admiral Darlan that the capital was now an open city and that he should proceed to Toulon.[37] Louis Lévy, a member of the CAP and a war correspondent, also returned to Paris on the evening of Sunday the 9th, and on the following day saw that the ministries were emptying and the newspaper offices were moving out. Only a few people remained in the centre of the city and around the Gare St Lazare he found exhausted refugees. By Tuesday, aware that almost all the official services, including the press service of the general staff, were leaving Paris, he too set off for the south.[38]

---

[35] Ibid., pp. 20–32.
[36] Paul Faure, *De Munich à la Vme République* (Éditions de l'Élan, Paris, [1948]), pp. 70–3.
[37] Jules Moch, *Une si longue vie* (Robert Laffont, Paris, 1976), p. 160. See also Moch, *Rencontres avec . . . Léon Blum*, p. 261.
[38] Louis Lévy, *Vérités sur la France* (Penguin, Harmondsworth, 1941), pp. 149–51.

By Saturday, 15 June, when the German armies, having moved beyond the Seine, were advancing into western, central and eastern France, the French government was installing itself in Bordeaux. Travelling there together, Léon Blum and Marx Dormoy reached the city early that morning and later joined Georges Mandel and some of his fellow ministers in a discussion of events. It was then that Blum first became aware of the fact that serious consideration was being given to an armistice, a prospect which appalled him; he agreed with the others present that the fight must be continued, even if this were to mean moving the government to North Africa. He and Dormoy conferred early in the afternoon with two of the Socialist ministers, Georges Monnet and Albert Sérol, who also agreed that the right course of action would be to continue the battle from outside metropolitan France; at this discussion, Jules Moch, who was still on service with the navy, was also present.[39] The Cabinet met that evening and decided to ask the British government to consent to its making an approach to Germany and Italy in order to discover what armistice terms they would be prepared to offer. In reply, the British government sent two telegrams on Sunday 16th, giving its consent on condition that the French fleet sailed for British ports; then, later that day, it proposed a union between the two countries. When Reynaud took the latter proposal to the Cabinet in the early evening, the idea of a Franco-British union was greeted with little enthusiasm and after an inconclusive discussion the meeting was adjourned until 10 p.m. In the interval, however, Reynaud submitted his resignation to President Lebrun, who promptly asked Marshal Pétain to form a new government.[40]

When the members of the Reynaud Cabinet arrived at the President's headquarters in the Prefecture, rue Vital-Carles, at 10 p.m. and heard the news, no one had any doubt that Pétain would press for an armistice. Working to a prepared list, the Marshal immediately set about selecting a ministry[41] and the question which Blum and the Socialists now had to consider was whether the party should agree to join it if invited to do so, or whether it should revert to its opposition role. The various accounts of how the Socialists were drawn into Pétain's ministry

[39] See Blum, 'Mémoires', in Blum, *L'Oeuvre de Léon Blum, 1940–1945*, pp. 33–9; Blum's testimony in *Rapport fait au nom de la commission chargée d'enquêter sur les événements survenus en France de 1933 à 1945* (Assemblée Nationale, Première Législature, Session de 1947, Annexe au procès-verbal de la 2e séance du vendredi 8 août 1947, no. 2344) (Paris, 1951), Annexes, I, p. 260 (30 July 1947); Moch, *Rencontres avec . . . Léon Blum*, pp. 261–8.
[40] William L. Shirer, *The Collapse of the Third Republic: An Inquiry into the Fall of France in 1940* (Heinemann and Secker and Warburg, London, 1970), pp. 795–815.
[41] Ibid., pp. 814–16.

cannot be reconciled exactly but the following summary of events seems to be the most plausible.[42] It appears that Pétain envisaged including two Socialists in his government and made separate offers to Albert Rivière and Albert Sérol. The latter, who was opposed to the idea of an armistice, simply turned down the offer of a place and went off to his hotel to sleep.[43] Albert Rivière's response was more considered: when he received the invitation to join the ministry, he decided to go to Jean-Fernand Audeguil's house to consult Blum, who was then staying there, and having done so he returned to the Prefecture and refused the offer. However, when the Minister of Finance designate, Yves Bouthillier, pointed out to him that the Marshal was prepared to allocate two portfolios to the Socialists, he had second thoughts. Making his way to Sérol's hotel, he roused him from sleep and drove with him back to Audeguil's house, where the two of them conferred with Blum, Georges Monnet and Audeguil. According to Sérol's account, he (Sérol) told Blum that he was not prepared to join a government which intended to sign an armistice; Blum, however, persuaded by Rivière's argument that it would be desirable to have two Socialists in the Ministry ('ne serait-ce que pour vous défendre, Blum') then urged Rivière to go to see André Février, who was another possible candidate.[44] For his part, Blum later claimed that it was not he but Georges Monnet who had induced Rivière to accept a portfolio and that Rivière had taken it upon himself to enlist Février.[45] In reviewing these events, Monnet accepted Blum's account, but he also pointed out that Blum had not spoken out against the arguments in favour of participation.[46]

[42] For a survey of the evidence, see 'Histoire du Parti Socialiste S.F.I.O.', Part 22, 'Juin–août 1940', Part 1, *Cahier et Revue de l'OURS*, no. 135 (November 1982), pp. 5–10, which refers to material in the Archives de l'OURS; the André Rivière dossier in these archives contains a typed six-page letter (undated, but probably early 1945) from Rivière to Daniel Mayer and others which includes a detailed account of the events of the night of 16–17 June 1940. See also Louis Guitard, *Mon Léon Blum ou les défauts de la statue* (Régirex-France, Paris, 1983), pp. 117–26. Blum gave an account of these events in the memoirs which he wrote in 1940 and which were published in *Le Populaire* in 1945. The relevant section appeared in *Le Populaire*, 21 September 1945, pp. 1 and 2, but the major portion of that section was omitted from the text given in *L'Oeuvre de Léon Blum, 1940–1945* (cf. ibid., pp. 41–2). See also André Février, *Expliquons-nous* (A. Wast, Aspremont, Hautes-Alpes, 1946); a record of an interview with Albert Sérol on 4 April 1953, in Louis Guitard, *Lettre sans malice à François Mauriac sur la mort du Général Weygand et quelques autres sujets* (Aubanel, Avignon, 1966), pp. 284–5; records of interviews with Georges and Germaine Monnet on 6 February and 3 March 1980, in Guitard, *Mon Léon Blum*, pp. 277–93.
[43] From an interview with Sérol on 4 April 1953, in Guitard, *Lettre sans malice à François Mauriac*, p. 284.
[44] Ibid., pp. 284–5. See also letter from Rivière to Daniel Mayer and others [1945], p. 2 (in André Rivière dossier, Archives de l'OURS).
[45] *Le Populaire*, 21 September 1945, p. 2.
[46] See record of interview, in Guitard, *Mon Léon Blum*, p. 287.

Whatever the truth of the matter, Rivière carried out the plan which he thought had been agreed: he sent a message to Février, who had been preparing to leave for Lyon, asking him to go to the Prefecture and, when they met there, told him that both of them had been authorized by Blum, Sérol, Monnet and Audeguil to join the government.[47] In consequence, Rivière agreed to become Minister of Colonies and Février Minister of Labour in the Pétain Cabinet.

Not only at that time but later also, these events were judged by quite different moral criteria. For those who were appalled at the idea of an armistice and could not understand why Reynaud had resigned or why the President had asked Pétain to form a government, the new administration lacked full legitimacy and to that extent foreshadowed the Vichy regime which was soon to succeed it. Seen from this perspective, the participation of Février and Rivière in the ministry was an error. On the evening of 16 June, however, other factors weighed with those involved in the decisions. According to Léon Blum, Rivière had the impression that Chautemps would become the real political leader of the ministry and that he needed the support of the Socialists

pour freiner les tentatives d'extrême réaction qu'il fallait redouter ou même pour s'opposer à certaines représailles personnelles.[48]

In the conference at Audeguil's house, Monnet claims to have taken the line that those of his comrades who favoured an armistice should join the Cabinet because he did not want to see it composed only of reactionary elements who would make sure that the Popular Front was put on trial and that the Socialists were held responsible for the military defeat.[49] There were certainly reasons for such anxieties and this may explain why the participation of Rivière and Février in the ministry was accepted as a justifiable arrangement in the days which followed. As Février was later to complain, they were not disowned nor were they advised to leave the government at any time during their brief tenure of office.[50]

The new government having requested and received the terms of an armistice from Germany and having deemed them to be acceptable, a convention was signed and on 25 June the armistice came into force. Under its provisions all hostilities were to end, the French forces were to be disarmed and demobilized, and the Atlantic coast and northern France came under German occupation. The government left Bordeaux on 29 June and eventually took up residence in Vichy, which became the capital of those regions of southern and south-eastern France which

[47] Février, *Expliquons-nous*, p. 13.
[48] *Le Populaire*, 21 September 1945, p. 2.
[49] See record of interview, in Guitard, *Mon Léon Blum*, p. 287.
[50] Février, *Expliquons-nous*, p. 19.

remained outside German control; it then called on the Chamber of Deputies and the Senate to meet separately at Vichy on 9 July to decide whether there were grounds for amending the Constitutional Laws of 1875, and to meet together as a National Assembly on the 10th to consider a proposal that the ministry, under the authority of Pétain, should have full powers to promulgate a new constitution. Those parliamentarians who had already travelled from Bordeaux to Casablanca aboard the steamer *Massilia* on the assumption that the government would move to North Africa had no means of returning to France but many of the deputies and senators who had remained in the country now made their way to Vichy for the closing drama of the Third Republic.

For those who had been in their constituencies during the battle of France, hearing confusing and often misleading accounts of what was at issue, the decision which now faced them was a very difficult personal one. One such Socialist deputy was Augustin Malroux, of the Tarn Department. On the evening when he received the summons to Vichy he had invited Edouard Depreux, who had just been demobilized from the army, and André Blumel to dine with his family and when the telephone call came through, he took an immediate stand on principle.

Il n'y a pas de question. On me demande de choisir entre la république et le fascisme. Je choisirai la république. Je voterai contre Pétain.[51]

Malroux's wife, Paule, and his two daughters went with him to Vichy and his daughter Anny has given an account of the journey. According to her, on Sunday, 7 July, they drove northwards in their car along the quiet roads of the Massif Central and when they arrived at Vichy they settled into a small hotel. Augustin immediately went out in search of news, and when he returned late in the evening Anny overheard him saying something to her mother about a revolver, and that Jacques Doriot's men (right-wing activists of the Parti Populaire Français) were out on the streets and the word was that those who voted against Pétain's being granted full powers would not get away unscathed. On the morning of the following day, Monday 8 July, when he met his close friend, François Camel, a Socialist deputy for Ariège, he discovered that he too had decided not to vote for Pétain.[52]

Rivière, as Minister of Colonies, had requisitioned the Hôtel d'Angleterre for his staff, and Blum arranged for an informal meeting of the Socialist parliamentary group to take place there on that Monday at

[51] Édouard Depreux, *Souvenirs d'un militant: cinquante ans de lutte: de la social-démocratie au socialisme: (1918–1968)* (Fayard, Paris, 1972), p. 136.
[52] Anny Malroux, *Avec mon père, Augustin Malroux* (Rives du Temps, Albi, 1991), pp. 152–3.

4 p.m. Although Blum was president of the group, it was Félix Gouin who acted as chairman on this occasion. According to Jules Moch, about sixty deputies and senators attended and decided that members of the group should be free to vote as they wished in the parliamentary divisions which lay ahead.[53] Blum had at first favoured taking a stand against the government's proposals for changing the constitution at the separate meetings of the Chamber and the Senate to take place on the following day, when it would be open to both houses to dispute that there were grounds for reviewing the Constitutional Laws of 1875, but he acquiesced in the general conclusion that it would be better to offer resistance at the National Assembly meeting on the 10th.[54] Rivière has claimed that Roucayrol and others who were present said that they had attended merely to obtain information and did not intend to be bound by any decision that might be taken. He has also recalled that, after most of the gathering had dispersed, Blum and those close to him remained behind and that when he, Rivière, had suggested that he might resign from the government, he had been dissuaded from doing so.[55]

By this stage, the Socialist Party had virtually lost its coherence. The former loyalist majority, its solidarity already strained by the controversy over foreign policy in the wake of the Munich agreement, had now become fragmented and consisted of small groups of people bound together by ties of friendship and personal loyalty. The normal processes by which political groups maintain a common outlook and an agreed strategy had ceased to function; accounts of crucial events which had taken place – the fall of the Reynaud government, the conclusion of the armistice, the decision to hold a meeting of the National Assembly – had been passed on by word of mouth rather than by the regular, careful reporting of party officers; the Socialist ministers in Pétain's Cabinet were being treated as men on a defensive mission rather than as the duly approved representatives of their group. The staff of the party's central secretariat and treasury had moved to Limoges but neither Paul Faure nor Jean-Baptiste Séverac had joined them there; and *Le Populaire*, now based at Clermont-Ferrand, had, for a number of reasons including government censorship and transport difficulties, not appeared since 18 June.[56]

---

[53] See Moch, *Rencontres avec . . . Léon Blum*, pp. 271–3. See also Vincent Auriol, *Hier demain*, I (Charlot, Paris, 1945), pp. 116–19, but note that this source incorrectly places the meeting on the 9th.

[54] Blum, 'Mémoires', in Blum, *L'Oeuvre de Léon Blum, 1940–1945*, pp. 75–82.

[55] See letter from Rivière to Daniel Mayer and others [1945], pp. 3–4 (in André Rivière dossier, Archives de l'OURS).

[56] On the arrangements affecting the party organization and the staff of *Le Populaire* in the period from mid-June to 11 July 1940, see the René Hug correspondence contained in 'Histoire du Parti Socialiste S.F.I.O.', Part 22, 'Juin–août 1940', Part 1 (*Cahier et Revue de l'OURS*, no. 135 (November 1982), pp. 21–8), and Part 2 (ibid., no. 138

On Tuesday, 9 July, first the Chamber and then the Senate approved the resolution calling for a reform of the Constitution. The way was then clear for the members of both houses to meet as a National Assembly on Wednesday the 10th, in secret session in the morning and publicly, for the formal proceedings, in the afternoon. These were to be conducted under the watchful eye of Pierre Laval, who had been appointed Vice-President of the Council of Ministers on 23 June and had played a leading role in shaping the plan for changing the Constitution. The venue for the meetings was the town's casino, which was surrounded by police and by *gardes mobiles*. On those participating, the pressures were immense; even friends' capacity for tolerance was placed under strain by the stresses of that Wednesday. The circumstances which led to the final break in relations between Blum and Georges Monnet, for example, reveal how easy it was for misunderstandings to arise. We have already seen how close Monnet and his wife, Germaine, were to Blum but Monnet also felt a loyalty to Paul Reynaud, in whose administration he had served during the battle of France and the move to Bordeaux. On 28 June Reynaud had been badly injured in a motor accident in which his mistress had been killed and he had arrived at Vichy with his head swathed in bandages. There he had talked to Monnet and his former ministers and urged them not to get mixed up in the controversy over the bill but to abstain when it was put to the vote,[57] and Monnet, telling Auriol that Reynaud had spoken to him, said that he intended to abstain.[58] As he knew that a group of his Socialist colleagues associated with Rivière were inclined to vote in favour of the bill, he decided to lunch with them before the final session of the National Assembly in the hope that he could persuade them to abstain also. Germaine knew of this and when she received a telephone call from Blum asking whether she and Georges could meet him for lunch at that same time, she explained why they would not be free to do so. However, when she told Monnet of Blum's invitation, he said that they must be at Blum's side at such a time, and the pair of them set off for the restaurant with the intention of meeting Blum there.[59] For his part, Blum, who was convinced that the only honourable course was to vote against the bill, must have seen Monnet's decision as evidence of a lack of resolution. According to Monnet's own account,

(February 1983), pp. 5–22). Also on *Le Populaire*, see Blum, 'Mémoires', in Blum, *L'Oeuvre de Léon Blum, 1940–1945*, pp. 63–9, and on Paul Faure's movements during this period, see Faure, *De Munich à la Vme République*, pp. 75–6.

[57] See record of interview, in Guitard, *Mon Léon Blum*, p. 288.
[58] See Auriol, *Hier demain*, I, pp. 135–7. Reynaud later told Auriol that he had not given any advice whatever to anyone (ibid., p. 136, n.).
[59] See record of interview, in Guitard, *Mon Léon Blum*, pp. 288–9.

when Blum arrived at the restaurant with Marx Dormoy and Joseph Thivrier,

il a eu, en nous voyant, l'impression que ma femme, au téléphone, avait cherché à se dérober et que, au fond, nous ne tenions pas à nous montrer avec lui. Tout au moins c'est l'impression que ses deux compagnons chercheront à lui donner.[60]

Louis Noguères later reported that during the adjournment of the National Assembly's final session that afternoon, Blum asked him whether he had seen Monnet, adding that it appeared that he wanted to abstain. Noguères himself had then sought out Monnet and had learned that he and Albert Sérol were intending to keep their promise to Reynaud.[61] When the session resumed, the deputies and senators proceeded to vote on the Constitution Bill, which was adopted by 569 votes to 80. Of the Socialists, 89 including Février and Rivière voted with the majority; 36 including Léon Blum, Vincent Auriol, Marx Dormoy, François Camel, Augustin Malroux, Jules Moch, Louis Noguères, André Philip, François Tanguy-Prigent and Joseph Thivrier voted in the minority; while Georges Monnet and Albert Sérol were listed amongst those who had voluntarily abstained.[62] In November 1944, Monnet was among those parliamentarians who were expelled from the party because of their part in this division of 10 July 1940, and although he and Germaine made several attempts to meet Blum and

---

[60] From ibid., p. 289.
[61] See Parti Socialiste (SFIO), 37ᵉ Congrès National, Paris, 11–15 août 1945, *Compte rendu sténographique* (Conservation film of original typescript, Bibliothèque de Documentation Internationale Contemporaine, Universités de Paris), 11 August 1945, p. 18.
[62] For the division list, see *JO, Déb.*, 10 July 1940, pp. 826–8. The members of the Socialist parliamentary group are distributed as follows in the record of the division:

	Senators	Deputies	Totals
For the granting of full powers	3	86	89
Against the granting of full powers	7	29	36
Did not take part	3	25	28
Unable to be at the session	1	6	7
Voluntarily abstained	0	6	6
Totals	14	152	166

The membership list of the group was compiled from the following sources:
(1) for deputies, the group list of 25 May 1939 (*JO (CD), Déb.*, 25 May 1939, p. 1421, as amended by a notification in *ibid.*, 9 July 1940, p. 818); and
(2) for senators, the group list given in *Liste par ordre alphabétique et par départements de messieurs les sénateurs* . . . (Imprimerie du Sénat, Palais du Luxembourg, Paris, 1939), p. 78. The following members of the group were not taken into account: Achille Fèvre (senator, died on 21 January 1940); Charles Valentin (deputy, died on 22 September 1939); and Léo Lagrange (deputy, killed in action on 9 June 1940 but listed amongst those who did not take part in the vote).

set matters straight before the old man died in 1950, they were never able to do so.[63]

The Socialists during the Resistance, 1940–4

Within weeks of these events, the Socialist Party had virtually ceased to exist: the Senate and Chamber of Deputies had been adjourned indefinitely and the members of the parliamentary group had dispersed. The party organization could no longer function effectively; activity at the level of the branches and federations was coming to a standstill and the leaders were scattered and isolated from the rank-and-file. On 15 September 1940, Blum was arrested on the grounds that he was a danger to the security of the state and was imprisoned, first at Chazeron and later at Bourassol. By the early months of 1941, however, there were signs that a Socialist underground was taking shape. Daniel Mayer, who had been active in the ranks of the *anti-munichois* before the war, had set about the task of reconstructing the party in the southern (or Vichy) zone and, on 30 March 1941, he and some colleagues met in Nîmes to establish a Comité d'Action Socialiste (CAS), a meeting which was followed by others in Lyon and Toulouse. In the northern (or occupied) zone, a CAS had been formed by a small group of Parisian activists as early as January 1941, but in that part of the country many Socialists and trade unionists were being drawn into Libération Nord, which soon became a major force in the Resistance movement. Underground networks were also building up in those areas where the party's federations had been strongest before the war, such as those in the Nord, Pas-de-Calais, Allier and Bouches-du-Rhône Departments.[64]

The task of reconstructing the party was falling very largely upon a new generation of leaders and a central figure among these was Daniel Mayer. Born in 1909, he had joined the SFIO in 1927 and had played

[63] Guitard, *Mon Léon Blum*, pp. 289–92.
[64] The earliest published account of the Socialists' resistance record is Robert Verdier, *La Vie clandestine du Parti Socialiste* (Éditions de la Liberté, Paris, 1944). For a fuller treatment, see Daniel Mayer, *Les Socialistes dans la Résistance: souvenirs et documents* (Presses Universitaires de France, Paris, 1968). See also Marc Sadoun. *Les Socialistes sous l'Occupation: résistance et collaboration* (Presses de la Fondation Nationale des Sciences Politiques, Paris, 1982), pp. 109–49; H. R. Kedward, *Resistance in Vichy France: A Study of Ideas and Motivation in the Southern Zone 1940–1942* (Oxford University Press, Oxford, 1978), pp. 95–104; Henri Noguères, in collaboration with M. Degliame-Fouché and J.-L. Vigier, *Histoire de la Résistance en France de 1940 à 1945*, I, *La Première Année juin 1940–juin 1941* (Robert Laffont, Paris, 1967), pp. 339 and 412–13.

a full part not only in the affairs of the Jeunesses Socialistes of the Seine Federation but also in those of the local branch of the 20th *arrondissement* of Paris. Becoming a journalist for *Le Populaire* in 1933, he had seen at first hand the events leading up to the Popular Front and the election victory of 1936, and two years later he had been with the Bataille Socialiste during the crisis of the Seine Federation, and had signed the synthesis motion submitted to the Federal Congress of the reconstructed federation in May. Intelligent and quick-witted, his considerable organizational ability quickly showed itself in a capacity to improvise effective responses to the difficult problems posed by underground politics.[65]

Mayer and his colleagues identified the Socialist *résistants* strongly with the *anti-munichois* of the 1938–9 period rather than with the pre-war pacifists. At a very early stage in their work, they sought to give the party a fresh outlook and a new sense of purpose and to this end they encouraged their followers to think of themselves as members of a persecuted sect, bound at all times to preserve their inner commitment to socialism. They aimed to purge the party of all those parliamentarians who had supported the granting of full powers to Marshal Pétain or who had abstained from voting on 10 July 1940. One of the major problems which they faced lay in the greatly increased activity of the French Communist Party which followed the German invasion of the Soviet Union on 22 June 1941. From the time of the signing of the Russo-German Pact on 23 August 1939, the Communists had been progressively excluded from public politics; the party had been dissolved on 26 September 1939 and its representatives expelled from the Chamber of Deputies on 20 January 1940. However, even before June 1941, some elements of the PCF had taken part in the Resistance and after that date the party organization and its associated groups, the Front National and the Francs-Tireurs et Partisans Français, became a very energetic sector of the underground movement. In one sense, the Communists had thus returned to the arena of party politics, reduced though this now was to inter-party co-operation in the Resistance and in planning for the post-war period. Questions concerning the relationship between the Communists and the Socialists had therefore to be faced once again.

In its struggle to revive the party, the new leadership looked to Léon Blum as an inspirational figure and readily accepted him as its intellectual and moral preceptor. His influence within the party was even fur-

---

[65] See Claude Juin, *Liberté . . . Justice . . . : le combat de Daniel Mayer* (Éditions Anthropos, Paris, 1982), pp. 1–115. See also Charles Pivert, *Le Parti Socialiste et ses hommes: souvenirs d'un militant* (France-Éditions, Paris, 1950), pp. 62–3.

ther strengthened by his success in converting his trial at the Supreme Court of Justice in Riom into a magnificent declaration of faith in the republican tradition and the achievements of the Popular Front. Along with Edouard Daladier, Guy La Chambre who had been Minister of the Air Force from 1938 to 1940, Robert Jacomet, the General Secretary of Defence from 1936 to 1940, and General Maurice Gamelin, he was required to defend himself against the charge that he shared with them the responsibility for the country's lack of preparation for war. Pleading his case at the court's hearings on 10 and 11 March 1942, he not only justified the actions of his administration but also stated his firm belief in civic virtue and democratic values. The Socialist underground ensured that his speeches were widely circulated throughout France, and effectively endorsed the liberal humanism and the faith in parliamentary government which lay behind his words.

When, in November 1942 after the Allied landings in North Africa, the German army moved into the Vichy zone, the Socialist underground had to adapt itself rapidly to the changed circumstances of the Resistance in the southern regions of the country. By this time increasing weight was being attached to the partisan benefits of resistance activity and although many Socialists continued to belong to groups such as Libération Nord and Libération Sud, the need to compete as a political force with the Communists impelled them to strengthen their party organization. In June 1943, therefore, they established a unified executive committee and a bureau under the control of Daniel Mayer as General Secretary. At the same time, the metropolitan Resistance was also becoming more integrated and its principal units, including the Socialists, were represented on the Conseil National de la Résistance (CNR), which had been formed in May 1943.[66]

Once America and the Soviet Union had been drawn into the war, it became possible to nourish the hope that the country might be liberated within two or three years and the political Resistance now began to turn its thoughts to the kind of regime which would be most appropriate for post-war France. There were many different views, but the Socialist underground favoured the establishment of a new and more democratic republic and the implementation of far-reaching economic and social reforms. Although many others in the Resistance agreed with them, they could not ignore the possibility that some groups might see

[66] Regarding the Socialist executive, see Mayer, *Les Socialistes dans la Résistance*, pp. 109–10, and regarding the formation of the CNR, see Noguères in collaboration with Degliame-Fouché, *Histoire de la Résistance en France de 1940 à 1945*, III, *Et du nord au midi . . . novembre 1942 – septembre 1943* (Robert Laffont, Paris, 1972), pp. 395–404.

a return to the Third Republic as being the best means of achieving political and economic stability. If such a plan were to receive wide-spread support, the Socialists would have to decide whether to continue to press for a political revolution, a course which might encourage social unrest and involve them in an alliance with the Communist Party. Given such uncertainties, the left-wing Resistance groups reached the conclusion that the best means of minimizing disorder and conflict during the liberation period would be to form an interim administration to deal with the immediate tasks of post-war reconstruction. As this administration would also have the task of regulating the transition from the Vichy to the Republican state, whatever form the latter might take, they turned to General Charles de Gaulle as being by far the best person to head it.

Although on his arrival in London in June 1940 de Gaulle's aim had been simply to overthrow the Vichy regime and re-establish the Third Republic, he soon formed the view that a fresh start was needed and that France's future must be decided by a freely elected National Assembly. The Socialists quickly decided to give him their backing and in November 1942 Blum sent him a note, for onward transmission to the American President and the British Prime Minister, in which he made the case that a provisional government under de Gaulle's leadership would be the best means of effecting the political transition in liberated France.[67] The Americans were reluctant to accept this idea and recognized, first, Admiral Darlan and, after his death, General Henri Giraud as the French civilian head in Algeria after the occupation of this territory by the Allies. In June 1943, Giraud's Council and de Gaulle's Comité National Français were amalgamated to form the Comité Français de la Libération Nationale (CFLN) and for a brief period the two generals, Giraud and de Gaulle, were co-presidents of this body but on 3 October 1943 de Gaulle became its sole head. Three Socialists – André Le Troquer, André Philip and Adrien Tixier – were included in the reconstituted CFLN, which took office in Algiers on 9 November 1943 and a number of Socialists were also appointed to the Provisional Consultative Assembly, which was formed under an ordinance of 17 September 1943 to represent both the overseas and metropolitan Resistance as well as departmental general councils. Finally, on 3 June 1944 just before the Normandy landings, the CFLN was given the title of the Provisional Government of the French Republic.

[67] Blum. 'Note adressée au Général de Gaulle pour le Président Roosevelt et M. W. Churchill', in Blum, *L'Oeuvre de Léon Blum, 1940–1945*, pp. 382–4, enclosed with letter from Blum to de Gaulle, from Bourassol, November 1942 (ibid., pp. 379–81).

During this same period, the underground Socialists had also been considering what form their own party should take once democratic politics had been restored. Blum, who favoured changes in structure and in organization but not in doctrine, had written in August 1942:

si nous pouvons et devons apporter des amendements profonds à notre organis-ation de parti, à notre tactique politique, à l'inspiration de notre propagande, en revanche – et c'est là le point capital – *nous n'avons absolument rien à changer à notre doctrine socialiste.* Là, rien à 'repenser', rien à réviser. La doctrine socialiste sort de l'épreuve, immuable, intacte.[68]

Again, in March 1943, he had suggested that both the party and the Republic needed new forms of constitutional organization.

Le problème est identique dans les deux cas: trouver les formes d'organisation qui assurent l'autorité et l'unité d'action dans la Démocratie. Le Parti, par exemple, n'a jamais eu de véritable organe directeur, de véritable pouvoir executif – pas plus que la République.[69]

However, Blum was aware that the party's pre-war difficulties could not be blamed on its organizational deficiencies alone, and that it was necessary for it to discover why it had not been able to attract more support. If Socialist doctrine was sound, if it answered to the basic needs of the French people, why had the party been ignored when the nation was threatened in 1939 and 1940? What reasons were there for thinking that, even with a reformed organization, it would come into its own after the war? This problem was the main subject of *A l'échelle humaine*, the book which Blum wrote during his internment. The answer he gave was that, when in 1940 the SFIO should have offered the French people a way forward, it had failed to do so:

Ce qui séparait le Socialisme du peuple, à l'heure de la défaite, ce n'était . . . pas sa vieille doctrine et sa propagande de toujours; non, c'était quelque chose de plus simple et de plus prochaine; c'était l'attitude contrainte et équivoque qu'il avait conservée depuis Munich vis-à-vis du problème de la guerre. Le peuple des travailleurs avait attendu vainement de lui un mot d'ordre clair, entraînant; il n'avait su prendre franchement parti et position ni dans un sens ni dans l'autre.[70]

Blum considered that, while the documents produced by the party's assemblies and parliamentary group before the war had consistently upheld the doctrine of collective security and the principle that workers

---

[68] Blum, ' "Schéma d'une sorte d'instruction pour mes amis", Paris–Londres', 28 August 1942, in ibid., p.364.
[69] Blum, 'Note au Parti', from Bourassol, 1 March 1943, in ibid., p. 392.
[70] Blum, *A l'échelle humaine* (Gallimard, Paris, 1945), pp. 101–2.

should defend the independence of their country, the position which the party had taken in public had seemed ambivalent.

Aux textes qui avaient fixé officiellement la position du Parti, s'était opposée en effet une minorité, importante par les hommes qui la dirigeaient encore plus que par son nombre, redoutable par les arguments qu'elle recélait encore plus que par les arguments qu'elle formulait. A la vérité, depuis Munich, le Socialisme français était partagé en deux fractions foncièrement opposées sur le problème capital de la vie publique et dont la force relative variait avec les circonstances; c'est ce partage interne qui l'avait condamné à l'impuissance et presque au silence.[71]

The Socialists of the Resistance were now persuading themselves that the party which they had reconstructed really did reflect the national will much more fully than the pre-war SFIO had done, and that it would provide the spiritual core of the new Republic. Writing in Algiers, André Philip outlined constitutional proposals which he was confident would meet with general approval.

Le parti socialiste va donc avoir l'occasion de faire triompher ses principes, de réaliser autour de lui un rassemblement général de la démocratie. Cela à condition de procéder préalablement non seulement à une épuration radicale de tous les éléments compromis par une collaboration avec Vichy ou par un lâche attentisme, mais à une modification de ses méthodes, une réorganisation de sa structure, un rajeunissement complet enfin de ses cadres par l'appel aux forces neuves issues des mouvements de résistance.[72]

The period of reflection which the German occupation and the Vichy regime had forced the French Socialists to undergo had resulted in their believing that the future would be theirs. The underground leaders had persuaded themselves that the party's loss of power in 1938 and 1939 had been an aberration; for them, the true measure of its standing in French public life had been its acceptance, during the days of the Popular Front, as the incarnation of the people's will and the defender of the Republic against fascism. Their attachment to this historical myth and their rejection of the principles of Vichy's National Revolution conditioned their acceptance of the romantic republican and liberal humanistic elements in the Socialist tradition. Such a reorientation in outlook had taken them away from Guesdisme, with its idea that the republican regime was in reality a bourgeois creation and that only a revolutionary transformation of society, culminating in the dictatorship of the proletariat, could create the conditions for a truly democratic

[71] Ibid., p. 102.
[72] Philip, *Pour la rénovation de la République: les réformes de structure* (Fraternité, Algiers, n.d.), p. 25.

state. While their ideas about the nature of democracy and the form of the state might have been fresh and innovative, however, their proposals for economic and social reform were influenced more by the traditional doctrines of state socialism than by the theories of economic management which had gained ground in the late 1930s. By 1943, they were recommending the nationalization of such concerns as banks, insurance companies and key industries, the creation of commodity boards for agricultural produce, and a substantial measure of state control to be exercised by powerful central agencies.[73] In minimizing the importance of competition and private enterprise, the underground Socialists were committing themselves to a view of political economy which entailed

la confusion du socialisme et de l'anti-capitalisme, [et] la conviction que le socialisme réaliserait les valeurs au nom desquelles on condamnait le capitalisme.[74]

It was as though the experience gained during the two Blum ministries of 1936–7 and 1938 had been entirely discounted, as if the imaginative reasoning which had informed Blum's proposals of April 1938 had belonged to some other group of people or some other dimension. Here the break in continuity between the Socialist Party of the late 1930s and that of the Resistance had resulted in a crucial loss of economic know-how, so painfully acquired.

The renewal of party activity, August 1944–May 1945

France was freed from German control in the late summer of 1944. After the long battle for Normandy, the armies which had landed there drove swiftly towards the north and east, while those which had come ashore in Provence on 15 August swept up the Rhône valley. On 25 August, de Gaulle returned to Paris and immediately set about reorganizing his provisional government. The reconstructed team, announced on 9 September, contained ten members (including de Gaulle) who were either not identified with political parties or groups or were representatives of the resistance movement in general, and twelve who were

[73] See, for example, the programme dated January 1943 which was published in the underground *Le Populaire*, 16 January and 1 February 1943, in Verdier, *La Vie clandestine du Parti Socialiste*, pp. 48–56, especially pp. 53–5. See also the programme dated 11 December 1943 which the party proposed to the Resistance movement as a whole, in *Le Parti Socialiste et l'unité française* (Éditions de la Liberté, Paris, 1944), pp. 5–24, especially pp. 9–17.
[74] Raymond Aron, 'L'avenir des religions séculières – II', *La France Libre* (London), 8, 46 (15 August 1944), p. 272.

party members – two Communists, three Socialists, three Christian Democrats, three Radicals and one Left Republican. As Provisional President, de Gaulle himself had considerable powers and he had assigned the key portfolios of Finance and War to two non-party ministers, Aimé Lepercq and André Diethelm respectively. The Socialists' representatives were Adrien Tixier (Interior), François Tanguy-Prigent (Agriculture) and Augustin Laurent (Posts and Telegraphs), while associated with them was Robert Lacoste (Production), who had developed close ties with the party during the Resistance. The government later enlarged the membership of the Consultative Assembly but ensured that the powers of this body remained limited. The provisional regime, therefore, had two rather different aspects. In one light, it resembled a presidential system with de Gaulle as an all-powerful chief executive; in another, it conformed to the pattern of a parliamentary system, given that the majority of the groups in the Consultative Assembly considered that the government, however remote it might be, was responsible to them. As a result, the Socialists found themselves in a dilemma for, while they were willing to work with de Gaulle in his efforts to provide the conditions for a material recovery, they also wanted to believe that the restoration of democratic politics was already under way, for they saw themselves as forming the centre of a new governing alliance in France.

As during the Resistance, so now the Socialist leadership was confident that the party could reconstruct its organization while remaining true to its traditional ideas. Addressing the first meeting of the Seine Federation to be held after the liberation of Paris, Daniel Mayer spoke as if the old practices, and they alone, had been responsible for the party's past failings.

Le Parti nouveau n'admettra plus les tendances organisées, les journaux de sectes (*Vifs appl.*). La démocratie n'en régnera pas moins, et si des camarades se concertent pour faire prévaloir leur point de vue, c'est le Secrétariat du Parti qui, impartialement, distribuera partout leurs textes et leurs propositions. Mais, dès le Congrès fini, la discipline absolue sera exigée de tous (*Vifs appl.*).

Par la doctrine, le Parti est le parti ancien. Et ce n'est pas au moment où nos idées, nos solutions se trouvent justifiées par les faits, que nous les abandonnerons.[75]

The exact nature of the reconstructed SFIO became clearer in the course of an extraordinary congress held in Paris between 9 and 12 November 1944. By this stage, 96 of the party's 101 departmental federations (as of 1940) had been re-established and of these, 91 were

[75] On 10 September 1944 (*Le Populaire*, 11 September 1944, p. 1).

represented by a total of 210 delegates. Also present were 36 members of the central bodies of the underground party and three members of the Groupe Jean-Jaurès, which had represented the party in London.[76] The decisions which they took showed that not only were they in general agreement with the views that had been expressed by the central leaders during the Resistance but that they were prepared to put them into practice. In the field of economic policy, the congress adopted a proposal that the Corporation Nationale Paysanne which had been set up under the Vichy regime should be replaced by a Confédération Générale de l'Agriculture (CGA), and it went on to approve a manifesto which, in keeping with the doctrinal fundamentalism of the Resistance period, called for the socialization of all the main branches of the economy.[77] The congress readily accepted the justice of the underground party's demands for a purge of all those deemed to have fallen short of its standards, and expelled 84 Socialist parliamentarians, including Paul Faure, André Février, Georges Monnet, Albert Rivière and Albert Sérol, who had either voted on 10 July 1940 for giving full powers to Pétain or who had, without what it considered to be a valid reason, been absent or failed to cast a vote.[78] As for the party's constitution, the congress, agreeing with the view that organizational weakness had been the basic cause of the failings of the pre-war party, ruled that the CAP and the National Council should be replaced with a single executive body, the Comité Directeur, and it amended Article 19 to restrict the use of proportional representation to the appointment of branch delegates to federal congresses and the appointment of federal delegates to a national congress. The revised article provided that all executive bodies were to be elected by a secret ballot of the members of the relevant assembly (the branch executive by branch meeting, and so on). Moreover, it laid down that, under the terms of the party's constitution, 'groupements d'études ou d'affinités' could not legally exist nor could they be allowed to take the place of the regular bodies of the party.[79]

The new provisions for executive elections were put into immediate effect to choose the twenty-five members of the first Comité Directeur. The names of all the candidates having been placed on a single alphabetical list, published under the authority of the party secretariat, a copy was issued to each delegate to serve as a voting paper for what was

[76] Parti Socialiste (SFIO), *Les Décisions du Congrès National extraordinaire des cadres des fédérations socialistes reconstituées dans la Résistance, 9, 10, 11, 12 novembre 1944* . . . [Paris, 1944], p. 4.
[77] Ibid., pp. 13–15 and 17–19.
[78] Ibid., p. 16.
[79] Ibid., pp. 5–6.

in effect an open-list, simple-majority method of election. This ballot resulted in the return of the following candidates:

Vincent Auriol	Salomon Grumbach	Jules Moch
Elie Bloncourt	Gérard Jaquet	Emilienne Moreau
Gaston Defferre	Pierre Lambert	Marcel-Edmond
Edouard Depreux	Augustin Laurent	Naegelen
Charles Dumas	André Le Troquer	André Philip
Just Evrard	Andrée Marty-	Roger Priou-Valjean
Paul Favier	Capgras	Henri Ribière
Edouard Froment	Daniel Mayer	François Tanguy-
Félix Gouin	Roger Mistral	Prigent
		Robert Verdier

In addition, a special place had been assigned to Renée Blum, the daughter-in-law of Léon Blum who had by this time been deported to Germany.[80] The pre-war party was represented by three full members of the 1938–40 CAP, Grumbach, Favier and Laurent; by six survivors of the parliamentary group now in the Consultative Assembly, Auriol, Froment, Gouin, Le Troquer, Moch and Philip; and by a few activists such as Depreux and Marty-Capgras, who had been prominent in organizational affairs. A significant number of those on the executive, however, had come forward during the Resistance period. Subsequently, the Comité Directeur elected Daniel Mayer as its General Secretary, Robert Verdier as his deputy, Gérard Jaquet as Treasurer, and it established a small standing committee (Délégation Permanente) which consisted of Mayer, Verdier, Renée Blum, Vincent Auriol and André Le Troquer.[81] Robert Verdier was to make an important contribution to the work of the new team. Born into a republican family in 1910, he had embarked on a career in teaching when, like so many of his generation, he was disturbed by the events of 6 February 1934. Moved by them to renew an earlier attachment to the Socialist Party, he campaigned on its behalf in the 1936 general elections and attended its Marseille Congress in July 1937 as a delegate for the Hérault Federation. During the war he took part in the Resistance movement and, after the arrest of one of its original members, joined the executive committee of the underground party.[82] A cultivated, thoughtful man, he was to play a crucial stabilizing role in the days which lay ahead.

---

[80] Ibid., pp. 16–17.
[81] Bulletin Intérieur du Parti Socialiste (S.F.I.O.) (Paris), no. 1, January 1945, p. 1.
[82] Interview with Robert Verdier, Paris, 23 March 1990; Mayer, Les Socialistes dans la Résistance, p. 110.

While the SFIO had come away from the November 1944 Congress with the sense that it had been given a new orientation by the underground movement, it soon became evident that the leadership had overestimated the extent to which the party's departmental and local organization had been changed by the Resistance experience. Many of the members at branch level were still attached to their old ways of thinking and behaving, a state of affairs reflecting the fact that the process of *épuration*, of excluding those considered to have collaborated with the Vichy and the German authorities, had been much more drastic at the upper than at the middle and lower layers of the party.[83] Daniel Mayer and those who had worked with him on the executive committee of the underground party had been given virtual control of the Comité Directeur, but at the crucial departmental-federation level the changes in leadership were more apparent than real. Although very few of the federal secretaries who had held office in September 1939 were restored to their posts after the Liberation, their places had, in general, been taken not by new recruits but by party workers with well-established credentials who had simply moved a rung or two up the ladder of the party hierarchy.[84] At branch level where social ties were strongest, only outright collaborators had been in danger of exclusion. On the question of eligibility for party membership, one commentator was to warn of the need to take account of 'le militant moyen'.

Celui-là n'a pas connu les contacts étendus de la clandestinité. Parfois, il fut un 'résistant non fonctionnel', plein de bonne volonté, mais ne trouvant pas l'occasion de la manifester. Souvent, il a appartenu à un groupe de résistance constitué justement par ses amis, ses camarades politiques d'avant guerre. Rien ne l'a donc sorti de ses façons de penser et de parler. Il y a la droite, et il y a la gauche; il y a les républicains et il y a la réaction: il ne veut pas en démordre.[85]

However, there had been sufficient changes in personnel, especially within the party hierarchy, to prevent a simple reversion to the internal arrangements of pre-war days. Within the General Secretariat, Daniel Mayer and Robert Verdier were still adjusting themselves to the conditions of open politics, neither having had any direct experience of how their office had functioned before 1940. Paul Faure, having been excluded from the party, was now associated with an organization

[83] On this question, see Sadoun, *Les Socialistes sous l'Occupation*, pp. 227–76. See also Jérôme Jaffré, 'La crise du Parti Socialiste et l'avènement de Guy Mollet (1944–1946)' (Mémoire présenté à l'Institut d'Etudes Politiques de l'Université de Paris, Paris, 1971), pp. 19–20.
[84] See Sadoun, *Les Socialistes sous l'Occupation*, pp. 233–7.
[85] BOCA, 'Au Parti Socialiste: les jeux de la tactique et de la doctrine', *Esprit*, 13, 5 (April 1945), p. 755.

known as the Vieux Parti Socialiste S.F.I.O., along with J.-B. Séverac, Théo Bretin and several others of his former lieutenants.[86] Léon Blum was still in captivity in Germany and though Vincent Auriol had stepped into his role as the party's counsellor, it was by no means clear how the SFIO's parliamentary leadership would develop or what relationship it would establish with the organizational élite. The former *chefs de tendance* had also vanished from the scene: Marceau Pivert, who had been in the USA at the outbreak of war had, on being expelled from that country in July 1940, moved to Mexico, where he was still living at the end of 1944 and he had not yet been readmitted to the SFIO; Jean Zyromski had moved from Paris to the Lot-et-Garonne Department and was to join the Communist Party in September 1945; a few of his former colleagues, such as Andrée Marty-Capgras and Pierre Commin, were to establish themselves in the reconstructed party but they had made no public move to revive the Bataille Socialiste. In short, the highly differentiated informal structure of the pre-war SFIO had been largely eroded, and the party of 1944 had emerged from the Resistance as a relatively generalized association, with considerable freedom to change its policies and its strategies as it saw fit. The revival of the old networks of personal connections in the branches and federations meant that there was a possibility that the attitudes and expectations which had sustained the former *jeu de tendances* might in future, under particular circumstances, give rise to some form of internal opposition but, for the moment, they lacked expression.

With so many factors working in its favour, the SFIO now had a major opportunity to broaden its social base by appealing beyond its pre-war clientele of industrial workers and white-collar workers to the ranks of the urban middle classes, including their Catholic components, and to the ranks of small farmers. However, such a change in social strategy would have involved the party in questioning many assumptions about its political strategy; in particular, it would have been forced to accept a different view of its representative function. Instead of defining itself as a party which defended the general interests of the working class, it would have had to accept specific obligations to particular sectional constituencies and to have been prepared to speak on their behalf in parliament and government. No longer would it have been able to retire into opposition to preserve its revolutionary purity – it would have had to signify its unequivocal acceptance of the parliamentary system of government and of its own willingness to take part in coalition

---

[86] See Vieux Parti Socialiste S.F.I.O., *La 'Vieille Maison' se redresse contre les usurpateurs et les scissionnistes: appel de la direction provisoire du Parti* (Paris, n.d.).

ministries in which it was not the dominant group. Finally, if it were to appeal to the Catholic elements in society, it would have had to abandon its anticlericalism. The reasons why the SFIO did not move in this direction are many and complex but perhaps the major obstacle to change was the reluctance of its leaders to contemplate any course of action which would open up an unbridgeable gap between their party and the Communists. They were still inclined to believe that the SFIO and the PCF might one day come together to reconstitute the party which had been divided at the Tours Congress in 1920, a reunification which would restore to the working class its political cohesion and sense of purpose. It was in this spirit that the SFIO's November congress had renewed the offer of unity which the underground Socialist Party had made to the Communist Party during the Resistance period,[87] as a result of which representatives of both parties had been appointed to a Comité d'Entente. This body, which held its first meeting on 19 December 1944, established three subcommittees, one concerned with unity of action, a second with the prospects for union between the two parties, and a third to deal with any disputes that might arise.[88] However, its formation, while welcomed by the Socialists at a sentimental level, also caused them some anxiety, for at a more practical level they were well aware that the Communists were possessed of a highly centralized organization that was quite capable of out-manoeuvring them in the competition for mass support. For this reason, the SFIO's General Secretariat proceeded with caution in putting the new arrangements into operation, instructing federal secretaries that there were to be no Comités d'Entente formed at regional, departmental or local levels.[89]

Such a wary approach to boundary maintenance betrayed the Socialists' general concern about the solidity and integrity of their organization in the departments and the localities. It had been one thing to persuade the units of the underground party to conform to the model of a reconstructed, centralized and morally reborn party but it was quite another matter to ensure that the revived federations and branches accepted the new order. This was especially the case if the new order was perceived as involving the rejection of their pre-war parliamentary representatives and the repudiation of Guesdiste nostrums regarding the party's non-participation in bourgeois governments. However, it

[87] Parti Socialiste (SFIO), *Les Décisions du Congrès National extraordinaire . . . 9, 10, 11, 12 novembre 1944*, p. 10.
[88] See Parti Socialiste (SFIO), 37ᵉ Congrès National, Paris, 11–15 août 1945, *Rapports* (Librairie du Parti, Paris, [1945]), pp. 62–3.
[89] See Circular no. 14, [9] December 1944, in ibid., pp. 61–2; and Circular no. 25, 24 February 1945, in *Bulletin Intérieur*, no. 3, March 1945, pp. 2–3.

was obvious than any drastic attempt to purge local units and fill them with untried, if enthusiastic, recruits from the Resistance generation could end in disaster and was likely to be rejected by the party's electoral clientele. In any case, the imminence of the municipal elections left no time for experimentation. The leadership had to ensure that the SFIO held its own in the competition for control of the town halls in order to provide the party with a solid starting-point in the much more demanding electoral contests to come.

The first ballot for the municipal elections was set for 29 April and the second for 13 May 1945. On the first ballot, the Socialists achieved good results and successfully maintained the integrity of their lists of candidates despite the efforts of the Communists to promote amorphous and all-encompassing joint lists, described as Unions Patriotiques, Républicaines et Antifascistes. On the second ballot, the SFIO's departmental federations were permitted either to withdraw their candidates or to allow them to form joint lists with other groups or parties.[90] Once again, the outcome was satisfactory from the Socialists' point of view: despite some confusion regarding labels and affiliations, the party was credited with majorities in 4,133 of the 35,838 municipalities, a considerable improvement on the position it had been in after the previous elections of May 1935, when it had had majorities in only 1,376 municipalities.[91] This hurdle behind them, the new leaders could now make final preparations for the party's 37th National Congress, due to meet in Paris in August 1945. There, for the first time, they would encounter the local survivors of the old order with their nostalgia for the excitement of the pre-war *luttes de tendance*, for the emotional rhetoric of the Guesdistes, for the grand debates of principle, and for the baroque architecture of the CAP and its subcommittees. Much would depend on how this element interacted with those delegates who represented federations where the experiences of the Resistance had produced new attitudes and aspirations. What the outcome of such an encounter would be was still not clear: already the party's relations with other political groups and its policies for the future were being subjected to scrutiny and debate. The simple certainties of the Resistance movement were being replaced by the complexity and ambiguity of post-war politics. The period of grace was coming to an end.

[90] *Le Populaire*, 3 May 1945, p. 1.
[91] See *L'Année politique 1944–45* (Editions du Grand Siècle, Paris, [1946]), p. 491.

6   The succession crisis of 1946

During the immediate post-war period the SFIO found itself under increasing stress as the combined task of restoring the national economy and constructing a constitutional settlement imposed heavy demands on successive governments. All of these rested on the alliance of three parties, the Communists, the Socialists and the Christian Democrats (the Mouvement Républicain Populaire, MRP), and as the Socialist Party possessed the greatest degree of internal democracy of the three, its rank-and-file members were the first to express their discontent at the disadvantages of being part of a governing coalition. By degrees their sense of grievance brought them to the verge of revolt and the task of this chapter is to describe this change of mood within the SFIO and to analyze the organizational crisis which it brought about at the party's 38th National Congress of August 1946.

The 37th National Congress of August 1945

Early in May 1945 as the war in Europe drew to its close, the French authorities were trying to locate and free those public figures who still remained in German hands. Prominent amongst these was Léon Blum and on 4 May Jules Moch, who was still serving in the navy, was given the task of searching for him. In fact, on that same day, Blum had been liberated in the Tyrol mountains, and on the 14th he was flown in to Orly airport, where Moch was among the crowd waiting to greet him. On 20 May he addressed a conference of the party's federal secretaries and happily returned to his position as Director of *Le Populaire*, but he decided not to accept the place reserved for him on the Comité Directeur. As soon as it was ready, he took up residence in his wife's house in Les Metz, a quiet village in the wooded Jouy-en-Josas area south-west of Paris,[1] where his friends and colleagues could come to talk with him and enjoy his company. He thus made clear his intention

[1] See Jules Moch, *Rencontres avec . . . Léon Blum* (Plon, Paris, 1970), pp. 300–7.

to avoid direct participation in parliamentary and ministerial politics, while offering counsel and, through his column in *Le Populaire*, an enlightened and perceptive commentary on national and international events.

Within a few weeks of his return, the Communist Party launched a major campaign to create a unified party of the left, which it hoped to do largely on its own terms, and immediately placed pressure on Communist-inclined members of the SFIO to persuade their organization to accept a rapid fusion of *les partis frères*. The drive began on 12 June 1945, with the publication in *L'Humanité* of a charter of unity, which envisaged the fusion of the Socialist and Communist Parties to form a Parti Ouvrier Français and which, by borrowing the name of Guesde's original party, and by highlighting the revolutionary aspects of the French Socialist tradition, presented a view of history which was clearly intended to appeal to the Guesdistes within the SFIO. It arranged the gallery of Socialist heroes in such a way as to imply that Guesde was the central figure in the founding period and that Jaurès, while undoubtedly important, was more of a rally leader than a protagonist in the class struggle. Thus it described the proposed party as:

l'héritier de la combativité révolutionnaire d'Auguste BLANQUI. Il se réclame de Paul LAFARGUE qui a tant contribué à faire connaître le marxisme en France, de la politique de classe intransigeante de Jules GUESDE, de la politique de rassemblement des masses populaires contre la réaction symbolisée par Jean JAURES.[2]

Regarding doctrine, it emphasized the singular importance of Marxism, claiming that the Parti Ouvrier Français would

défend et propage le matérialisme dialectique de Marx et d'Engels enrichi par Lénine et Staline.[3]

The charter advocated a dictatorship of the proletariat to destroy capitalism and prepare the way for a communist society and recommended that the unified party should be based on the principles of democratic centralism. In a related move, the 10th National Congress of the Communist Party, held between 26 and 30 June, made a number of proposals for joint action, including combined meetings twice a month of the central executives of the two parties, meetings between their regional executives and between their local branches, the adoption of identical

---

[2] *L'Humanité* (Paris), 12 June 1945, p. 2. Paul Lafargue (1842–1911) was a son-in-law of Karl Marx and a prominent writer and activist in the early years of the Third Republic.
[3] Ibid.

positions by their representatives in the government, co-operation in assemblies, *unité de candidature* in the next elections and collaboration where propaganda and the party press were concerned.[4]

The publication of the charter presented the members of the SFIO's Comité Directeur with a serious problem. At a meeting of the Comité d'Entente on 31 May, the Socialist delegation had complained of several recent instances in which the Communists had attacked their party and had declared that, although unity of action should be continued, all discussions on fusion should be suspended. In any case, it had previously been agreed that each party would submit its draft proposals for achieving fusion to the relevant subcommittee of the Comité d'Entente before there was any public presentation of them and the Socialists considered the printing of the charter in *L'Humanité* to have been a breach of that understanding. They were now faced with a dilemma: were they to do nothing, they risked seeing a wave of support similar to that which had swept through the party in 1919 and 1920 breaking upon the SFIO's next national congress, due to take place in Paris between 11 and 15 August 1945; on the other hand, were they to publish a counter-proposal in *Le Populaire*, they risked being drawn into a debate in which the initiative lay with the Communists, who could claim that the Socialist leadership constituted the chief obstacle to fusion. After some hesitation, the Comité Directeur decided to place the question of fusion on the agenda for the National Congress, to send out to federal and branch secretaries a brochure containing the Communist Party's proposals, and to publish a document on the question which had already been prepared by Auriol.[5] Without actually saying so, the Socialist leaders were acting on the assumption that they were dealing with a pro-Communist opposition within their own organization and that the loyalists, faced with their first post-war challenge, needed both guidance and support.

Auriol's document served this purpose well; while it welcomed the idea of fusion, it clearly distinguished the Socialist from the Communist idea of the dictatorship of the proletariat. For the Socialists, this would be merely a transitional arrangement leading to the establishment of full democratic legality – on no account should it become a regular

---

[4] Ibid., 29 June 1945, p. 1.

[5] *Le Populaire* (Paris), 15 June 1945, p. 1; Parti Socialiste (SFIO), *Minutes of Meetings of the Comité Directeur* (hereafter *CD Minutes*), I, 14 June 1945, pp. 122–5; 18 June 1945, p. 127; 'Histoire du Parti Socialiste S.F.I.O.', Part 24, 'Août 1944–juin 1945', *Cahier et Revue de l'OURS* (Paris), no. 170 (July–August 1986), p. 22. The charter and the Communists' proposals for joint action were placed in a special brochure (Parti Socialiste (SFIO), 37e Congrès National, Paris, 11–15 août 1945, *Propositions du Parti Communiste concernant l'unité de la classe ouvrière en France* [Paris, 1945]).

system of government based on systematic methods of constraint – and the document went on to present the case for a social democratic as distinct from a democratic centralist organization of party life.[6] Léon Blum was also drawn into the fray. In a series of articles published in *Le Populaire* between 5 July and 7 August he argued that it would be impossible for Communists and Socialists to work together if they were asked to consider fusion before their differences had been resolved, and he therefore recommended a period of co-operation to prepare the way for union. The main theme in his articles was the likelihood that future international events might strain relations between the two parties in France. While he conceded that the French Communist Party had achieved a measure of independence from the Soviet Union, he nevertheless suggested that it had still not regained its freedom of judgement.[7]

Blum's implicit advice was that the loyalists should not reject the idea of union out of hand, but that they should aim for the middle ground of party opinion by advocating unity of action as a necessary prelude to fusion. The federal congresses which met in late July and early August in preparation for the National Congress saw numerous contests between groups which took this line and pro-Communist groups which argued that discussions with a view to union should be resumed as soon as possible. In the Seine Federation, which had been reconstructed after the Liberation under the leadership of a new federal secretary, Gérard Jaquet, the debate resulted in the formulation of rival motions and a formal vote by mandates at branch level, which produced an absolute majority for the principle of continuing unity of action with the Communists and a defeat for those who would have preferred the resumption of talks about a union of the two parties (for details, see Table 26).

Commenting on the outcome, Gérard Jaquet described the opposed groups as 'courants' and noted that, from the outset, a certain number 'de camarades . . . s'opposèrent en effet à tout effort de conciliation'.[8] The Seine-et-Oise Congress adopted a resolution which favoured measured steps towards fusion[9] as did the congress of the Pas-de-Calais

[6] For the text, see *Bulletin Intérieur du Parti Socialiste (S.F.I.O.)* (Paris), no. 5, June 1945, pp. 4–8.
[7] Blum, *L'Oeuvre de Léon Blum, 1945–1947* (Albin Michel, Paris, 1958), pp. 36–64.
[8] Jaquet, 'Réflexions sur un congrès', Parti Socialiste (SFIO), Fédération de la Seine, *Bulletin Hebdomadaire Fédéral* (Paris), no. 42, 26 August 1945, p. 1.
[9] See Parti Socialiste (SFIO), 37ᵉ Congrès National, Paris, 11–15 août 1945, *Compte rendu sténographique* (Conservation film of original typescript, Bibliothèque de Documentation Internationale Contemporaine, Universités de Paris), 14 August 1945, pp. 610–13.

Table 26. *Seine Federation, Federal Congress, 22 and 29 July 1945: division on the Charter of Unity (10 August 1945)*

Motions	Mandates	% of total
For immediate resumption of work by the Commission d'Unification	3,791	39.1
For continuing unity of action	5,787	59.6
Abstentions	130	1.3
Total	9,708	

Source: *Le Populaire* (Paris), 11 August 1945, p. 2.

Federation, which envisaged the Socialists producing their own version of a charter for a united party after the forthcoming general elections.[10] Whereas the Gironde and Vaucluse Congresses asked their national delegates to press for the formation of a new unity committee,[11] the Rhône Congress divided on the issue, allocating 86 mandates for a motion recommending the formation of a unified party with a federal and democratic structure, 26 for the Communists' proposal and 6 for a provisional rejection of any unity at all.[12]

During this same summer, the Socialist leaders had taken further steps to broaden the party's appeal to the centre-left range of public opinion. On his return to Paris, Blum had been asked to prepare a declaration of principles to replace the Charter of 1905 and to revise the new party rules which had been sent forward by the extraordinary National Congress of November 1944. Drafts of both the declaration and the rules were approved by the Comité Directeur on 27 June 1945[13] and dispatched to branches and federations for consideration. Both documents indicated a clear intention to break with the past. In preparing the declaration, Blum had emphasized the humanistic and utopian rather than the revolutionary aspect of the party's ideals; instead of suggesting, as the Charter of 1905 had done, that the party could neither work within the existing state nor co-operate regularly with other parties, his text implied that socialism could be achieved without resort to class warfare and violence. It portrayed the SFIO as a party representing not only workers but people in every walk of life.

L'action propre du Parti Socialiste est de grouper sans distinction de croyances philosophiques ou religieuses la masse des travailleurs de tous ordres – tra-

[10] *L'Espoir* (Lens), no. 48, 12 August 1945, p. 3.
[11] *Le Monde* (Paris), 8 August 1945, p. 5.
[12] Ibid., 31 July 1945, p. 5.
[13] *CD Minutes*, I, 27 June 1945, pp. 133–4.

vailleurs intellectuels ou manuels, travailleurs de l'atelier, de la terre, du bureau ou de la boutique – sur le terrain politique, économique et doctrinal . . . [14]

The change in property relations from capitalism to collectivism was no longer justified as an end in itself but as a means of liberating the human spirit:

> La transformation sociale consiste dans la substitution au régime de la propriété capitaliste d'un régime où les richesses naturelles comme les moyens de production et d'échange deviendront propriété collective et où par conséquent les classes seront abolies. Cette transformation accomplie dans l'intérêt de tous les hommes, ne peut être l'œuvre que des travailleurs eux-mêmes. Quels que soient les moyens par lesquels elle sera accomplie, elle constitue par elle-même la Révolution Sociale.
>
> C'est en ce sens que le Parti Socialiste a toujours été et continue d'être un parti d'action de classe et de révolution.[15]

Presumably for the sake of consistency, Blum had proposed the deletion of the creed-like statement which had formed the first article of the old rules.

The draft declaration had been written with such skill that only someone with a detailed knowledge of the doctrinal background to the Charter of 1905 could possibly have challenged Blum regarding the substance of his text, but it was open to fundamentalists to complain not only about the deletion of Article 1 of the rules but also about the obvious changes in wording that could be blamed on a revisionist approach. Most obviously, Blum's substitution of 'un parti d'action de classe et de révolution' for 'un parti de lutte de classe et de révolution' could be thus characterized, but there were other hostages to fortune, such as his use of the term 'propriété collective' instead of the original expression 'une société collectiviste ou communiste' when describing the transformation of social relations. With such examples to hand, it could be argued that Blum's draft reflected an evolutionary rather than a revolutionary view of the future.

Although reworked in a number of places, the draft text of the new rules still presupposed the general organizational structure which had been recommended by the extraordinary National Congress of November 1944; the central position of the Comité Directeur (with a proposed membership of 31 rather than 25) had been preserved, there was

---

[14] Parti Socialiste (SFIO), 37ᵉ Congrès National, Paris, 11–15 août 1945, *Projet de déclaration de principes et de statuts* [Paris, 1945], p. 3. Note that the phrase 'sans distinction de croyances philosophiques ou religieuses' was added to the text by the Comité Directeur on Auriol's suggestion (*CD Minutes*, I, 27 June 1945, p. 133).

[15] Parti Socialiste (SFIO), 37ᵉ Congrès National, Paris, 11–15 août 1945, *Projet de déclaration de principes et de statuts*, p. 3.

still no provision for a National Council, and proportional representation was still restricted to the appointment of delegates, members of the Comité Directeur being elected by the open-list, simple majority system. In short, the basic pattern remained that of a centralized framework in which decisions at the National Congress were to be made as a result of open debate on the merits of each case, rather than on the basis of prior commitments and preconceived opinions. Compared with the first draft of November 1944, this version of the new rules contained a number of revisions and amendments supporting the general aim of inhibiting the *lutte de tendances*. Indeed, Article 18 came very close to imposing a ban on this form of competition:

La liberté de discussion est entière au sein du Parti. Mais nul groupement permanent d'affinités ne saurait y être toléré.[16]

In the same spirit, the article specifying the right of delegates to ask for a vote by mandates at a meeting of the National Congress had been expanded to give delegates the right to exercise their own judgement and to refuse to be bound by the decisions of their federal congresses:

Dans les délibérations du Congrès National, le vote par mandat est de droit, s'il est réclamé par le dixième des délégués.

Toutefois, ce vote par mandat ne peut intervenir que sur des textes présentés par la Commission des résolutions.

Les mandats donnés aux délégués ne peuvent être des mandats impératifs, les délégués devant interpréter la volonté de leurs Fédérations en tenant compte des informations qui ont été apportées au Congrès et des débats qui ont suivi.[17]

Although these drafts showed that the leaders were agreed on the need to strengthen the party's organization, to bring its doctrine up to date, and to broaden its social base, it was difficult for them to follow the logic of their strategy by recruiting large numbers of people from the non-Communist Resistance movements, given the reluctance of the established members to incur political and social obligations which might strengthen the party's social-democratic orientation. However, it was possible to envisage alliances with such movements; earlier the Socialists had been interested in ties with the Mouvement de Libération Nationale (MLN) and when the majority of this organization joined with other groups in June 1945 to form the Union Démocratique et Socialiste de la Résistance (UDSR), the Comité Directeur set out to form a connection with this body. Those in the SFIO who were by this time pressing for a fusion with the Communist Party were against any

[16] Ibid., p. 6.
[17] Ibid. (Article 25).

ties with the UDSR and proposed an alternative alliance with the Mouvement Unifié de la Renaissance Française (MURF), which had absorbed the Front National and was virtually a Communist satellite. The result was a stalemate between the loyalists and dissidents within the SFIO and a further narrowing of the party's window to the centre.

Reduced to its essentials, the task of the party's leadership at the 37th National Congress at Paris on 11–15 August 1945 was to ensure, first, that the pro-Communist movement was kept within acceptable bounds and, secondly, that other sources of conflict, such as opposition to the party's continued participation in the de Gaulle government and objections to the new declaration of principles and the revised rules, were dealt with separately rather than as components of a general schedule of grievances. The congress was held in the Palais de la Mutualité in the 5th *arrondissement* and was attended by 602 delegates representing 97 federations and bearing a total of 10,633 mandates. The latter had been allocated on the basis of enrolment figures for the end of June 1945, with six monthly stamps being accepted as the measure of membership in most departments and three in those which had only recently been liberated.[18] The resultant distribution of mandates by federation had produced a ranking order which bore some resemblance to the pre-war pattern, with Pas-de-Calais (829 mandates), Nord (741), Seine (481), Seine-et-Oise (361), Gironde (331) and Gard (321) at the top of the hierarchy and with 10 federations in the 201–300 mandates range, 15 in the 101–200 range, 37 in the 51–100 range and 29 in the 1–50 range.

The congress began on Saturday 11 August 1945 and, having considered and approved the standard reports, the delegates then turned to the drafts of the revised party rules and the declaration of principles. As the discussion showed, these documents had met with a mixed reception at the federal congresses. Although the declaration was generally well received, some delegates spoke in favour of restoring the Charter of 1905 and the brief creed contained in Article 1 of the former rules; others argued that the document should acknowledge the party's commitment to *laïcité*. Many aspects of the new rules were also criticized: there were isolated calls for the restoration of proportional representation at all levels of the organization and for the retention of *le mandat impératif*; a number of speakers pressed either for the restoration of the National Council or for regular meetings between the Comité Directeur and the federal secretaries in order to prevent the central leaders from losing touch with opinion in the provinces; surprisingly

---

[18] *Bulletin Intérieur*, no. 6, July–August 1945, p. 1.

few speakers, however, questioned the wisdom of the policy of discouraging the *jeu de tendances* or discussed the possibility that, in the absence of *tendances*, other forms of organized opposition might develop within the party, and it was left to Victor Fay of the Rhône Federation to warn that unless dissenting movements were allowed to participate in the running of the party they could behave irresponsibly.

Si les camarades de la minorité ne sont pas associés aux responsabilités de la direction du parti, aux tâches quotidiennes, aux fonctions ingrates, ils seront inéluctablement poussés à faire de la démagogie, puisqu'aucune responsabilité n'est liée à leur situation, et nous aurons, au lieu d'un groupe épars de tendances, une opposition systématique et irresponsable qui fera de la surenchère à l'égard de la direction du parti.[19]

This was the nub of the matter, but Fay's intervention came too late in the debate to concentrate attention on the essential issue – how the party should manage internal conflict. A special committee was asked to consider the draft rules and to report back later in the congress, but it was already clear that the diversity of views which had been expressed would prevent it from producing a generally acceptable proposal.

When Blum addressed the conference immediately after the close of this debate, he warned the delegates that the party could no longer afford to live in the past.

Une tradition, ce n'est pas l'attachement à une lettre; c'est l'attachement à une idée qui vit, et, par conséquent, qui change.

La tradition, cela ne consiste pas à marcher dans la trace exacte de nos aînés; cela consiste à marcher dans leur direction, et en avançant, si nous le pouvons, plus loin qu'ils s'étaient avancés eux-mêmes.[20]

Claiming that the draft declaration embodied 'une fidélité parfaite à tous les principes essentiels du marxisme', he justified his use of the phrase *action de classe* in preference to *lutte de classe* on the grounds that, in the Marxist tradition, the term *action de classe* signified that the workers themselves would achieve their own liberation. However, while thus defending the Marxist content of his text, he refused to lend his support to the Guesdiste principle that a Socialist party could and

---

[19] Parti Socialiste (SFIO), 37e Congrès National, Paris, 11–15 août 1945, *Compte rendu sténographique*, 12 August 1945, p. 236.
[20] Ibid., pp. 256–7. I have preferred the text of his speech contained in this source (ibid., pp. 256–75) to that published at the time in pamphlet form (Blum, *Le Socialisme maître de l'heure* (Éditions de la Liberté, Paris, [1945])) and to that contained in Blum, *L'Oeuvre de Léon Blum, 1945–1947*, pp. 65–78. There are minor variations in wording between the three, but the stenographic record represents the best account of what Blum actually said to his audience on this occasion.

should stand apart from the political system and concentrate on revolutionary objectives.

Il n'y a plus aujourd'hui, dans le monde prolétarien, dans le monde ouvrier ou dans le monde socialiste ou communiste, dans le monde syndicaliste, il n'y a plus personne pour prétendre que l'évolution capitaliste ou que l'évolution des partis ouvriers et prolétariens soit indépendante des formes de politique de la société dans laquelle nous agissons.[21]

He went on to stress the unbreakable connection between socialism and democracy and to criticize the old distinction between reform and revolution:

je ne connaissais pas deux espèces de socialisme, dont l'un serait révolutionnaire et dont l'autre ne le serait pas. Il n'y a qu'un socialisme, et ce socialisme, par lui-même et par essence, est révolutionnaire.[22]

The committee which had been entrusted with the task of considering the draft rules reported back to the congress on two occasions, first on the afternoon of Monday 13th and again on the afternoon of the 14th. On its recommendation, the delegates agreed that the Comité Directeur should retain the powers which it had been given by the November 1944 Congress, that its membership should be increased from 25 to 31 and that those members should be elected by the congress delegates from an alphabetical list of candidates rather than, as a minority on the committee proposed, by proportional representation. The federations were then invited to submit to the incoming executive any recommendations which they might wish to make for amending the draft declaration and rules in order that an agreed version, or alternative versions, could be submitted to an extraordinary national assembly to be held before 1 March 1946.[23]

The next item on the agenda was the political situation. Under this heading, the delegates were invited to discuss, first, the forthcoming elections to a constituent assembly and the proposals for the new French constitution, and secondly, the party's relations with other parties and Resistance movements. The questions concerning elections and constitution-making were introduced on the afternoon of Sunday 12 August by Vincent Auriol. He complained that de Gaulle's Provisional Government had turned down a scheme for *représentation proportionnelle intégrale* for elections to the assembly, had adopted a less satisfactory

[21] Parti Socialiste (SFIO), 37ᵉ Congrès National, Paris, 11–15 août 1945, *Compte rendu sténographique*, 12 August 1945, p. 260.
[22] Ibid., pp. 261/2.
[23] Ibid., 13 August 1945, pp. 514–21; 14 August 1945, pp. 739–41; *Bulletin Intérieur*, no. 6, July–August 1945, p. 2.

system, and had also rejected the Socialists' demand that the cantonal elections for the General Councils should be held after rather than before the assembly elections; in a populist gesture, he suggested to the delegates that the government should be asked to reverse those decisions.[24] As the debate developed, other speakers took up this question – and some even suggested that the Socialist members should withdraw from the government – but it looked as if the outcome would be a strongly worded resolution proposing a change in policy, though not threatening any action which would oblige the Socialist ministers to resign were nothing to be done. At this stage, a new actor stepped out from the wings and transformed a routine exercise in strengthening party solidarity into a serious challenge to the government's authority. The call for robust action came from one of the delegates from the Pas-de-Calais Federation, Guy Mollet.

Then 39 years old, Mollet, with his thick spectacles, his impassive features and his dry, trenchant manner of speaking, gave the impression of being an austere activist. Born on 31 December 1905 in the Normandy town of Flers, the son of a textile worker and a dressmaker, he joined the SFIO in 1923 as a member of the Calvados Federation. There he came under the influence of Ludovic Zoretti, who encouraged him to take an interest in teachers' trade unions and when, in November 1925, he took up a post at a school in Arras, he helped to found the Fédération Générale de l'Enseignement (FGE). Within the SFIO's Pas-de-Calais Federation, which was then under the firm hand of Raoul Evrard, Mollet usually adopted a radical stance. By 1934 he was associated with the Bataille Socialiste; he then joined the Révolution Constructive group during its most active phase; and finally, in 1938 and 1939, the small Redressement group. Mobilized at the outbreak of war, he was wounded and taken prisoner by the Germans in May 1940 and repatriated in January 1941. After his return to France he joined the Organisation Civile et Militaire (OCM) of the Resistance and became secretary of the Departmental Liberation Committee of Pas-de-Calais in December 1944. In the municipal elections of 29 April and 13 May 1945 he was elected to the Municipal Board of Arras and on 19 May he became the city's Mayor.[25]

---

[24] Parti Socialiste (SFIO), 37ᵉ Congrès National, Paris, 11–15 août 1945, *Compte rendu sténographique*, 12 August 1945, pp. 326–7.

[25] On Mollet's life to this point, see Denis Lefebvre, *Guy Mollet: le mal aimé* (Plon, Paris, 1992), pp. 15–76. See also Lefebvre, 'Du pacifisme à la Résistance', in Bernard Ménager *et al.*, *Guy Mollet: un camarade en République* (Presses Universitaires de Lille, Lille, 1987), pp. 197–217; the obituary article by André Laurens and Thierry Pfister in *Le Monde*, 4 October 1975, p. 8; and a letter from Georges Lefranc in ibid., 15 October 1975, p. 6.

When, at about 11 p.m. on Sunday 12 August 1945, he came to the platform at the Paris Congress to speak in the constitutional debate, the audience had already begun to thin out. Nevertheless, he delivered a pungent speech which he concluded by saying that certain things must be impressed upon de Gaulle – the cantonal elections should be held after rather than before the general elections, the electoral system should provide for true proportional representation, and unless de Gaulle met these demands the Socialist ministers would withdraw from his government.[26] From one of the other members of the Pas-de-Calais Federation, we have a first-hand account of the response to his intervention.

Notre camarade G. MOLLET s'avance au micro. Sur le ton incisif, direct, précis, qui lui est particulier, il critique la politique du gouvernement. Les congressistes écoutent plus attentivement, ceux qui étaient dehors sont rentrés. GUY termine son intervention, il demande au comité directeur d'en tirer avec lui la seule conclusion possible: démission des ministres socialistes. Le congrès s'est dressé et acclame notre camarade. La table de notre délégation est entourée par les délégués d'autres fédérations qui viennent se solidariser à la motion que nous avions voté au congrès de Béthune.[27]

Mollet was taking his first step towards becoming the leader of the anti-participationist sentiment within the party. At the congress of his own federation at Béthune on 5 August 1945, he had presented his executive's report on the political situation and had even then suggested that the Socialist ministers should leave de Gaulle's government if it did not honour its promises.[28] Those delegates who were now gathering round the Pas-de-Calais table were not only getting acquainted with Mollet, they were also discussing the possibility of promoting a motion stating his demands. From the point of view of the central leaders, he was a dangerous man. To a large extent he was beyond their control because he was so independent, so untouched by the sympathies which bound them together. His Resistance record was impeccable but he had worked within the OCM network rather than with Libération-Nord to which so many northern Socialists had belonged. He had been actively engaged in the local party before the war but always as a member of minorities – he was neither a Blumiste nor a Fauriste and, unlike Jules Moch, André Philip and Daniel Mayer, he had had no direct contact with de Gaulle and was not inhibited by any personal attachment to

---

[26] Parti Socialiste (SFIO), 37ᵉ Congrès National, Paris, 11–15 août 1945, *Compte rendu sténographique*, 12 August 1945, pp. 373–5.

[27] Jacques Leblond, 'Impressions de congrès d'un jeune', *L'Espoir*, no. 53, 16 September 1945, p. 3.

[28] See ibid., no. 48, 12 August 1945, p. 1.

the Provisional President. He could appeal as easily to the old-style activists with his home-spun Guesdisme as to the new-style men and women of the Resistance with his gestures of impatience at the government's apparent reluctance to establish a new economic and political order.

Perhaps in order to avoid an outflanking move by Mollet, the central leaders decided to take the initiative. Late on the morning of Monday 13 August, Jules Moch asked the congress to vote for a motion which not only condemned the electoral system favoured by the government but also authorized the Socialist ministers to press the case for *représentation proportionnelle intégrale* and for a reversal of the order of the cantonal and general elections. This was an unusual procedure: normally such a policy motion would have been referred first to the Resolutions Committee and then, on the last day of the congress (the 15th), to the delegates as a whole, but Moch claimed that the adoption of his text at this stage would enable it to be considered by the Council of Ministers, which was to meet for its regular session on Tuesday 14th. If he and his fellow signatories – Vincent Auriol, Daniel Mayer and Félix Gouin – were in this way hoping to wrest the initiative from the Mollet camp they were unsuccessful for, just as the chairman was trying to put Moch's text to the vote, Mollet intervened:

au cours de la séance de nuit, hier, j'ai déjà été amené à aborder cette situation et cette discussion, et le succès que le Congrès a fait, non pas à l'homme, mais aux idées qu'il a défendues, m'autorise à dire que j'avais la conviction que cela représentait la volonté unanime du Parti.[29]

He then read out his federation's motion, which threatened the withdrawal of the Socialist ministers from the government. However, when Moch made an impassioned appeal for unanimity (which would give the text more force when it came before the Council of Ministers on the following day), Mollet, having made his point, agreed to accept Moch's motion, which was adopted after a brief debate.[30]

Earlier that day, the congress had taken up the subject of the party's relations with the Resistance movements, when the main issue had been whether or not the party should work with the UDSR. Opposed to the idea were those delegates who wished to support a resolution put forward by the Sarthe Federation recommending a fusion of the pro-Communist MURF and the UDSR. What concerned the Sarthe Federation was that if the SFIO were to form an association with the UDSR,

---

[29] Parti Socialiste (SFIO), 37ᵉ Congrès National, Paris, 11–15 août 1945, *Compte rendu sténographique*, 13 August 1945, pp. 485–6.
[30] Ibid., pp. 483–94/505.

leaving the MURF and the PCF in isolation, the result would be a conflict between a Communist and an anti-Communist bloc at the expense of left-wing unity. However, the Comité Directeur was attached to the principle of working with the UDSR and Daniel Mayer tabled a motion proposing that his executive be given authority to maintain unity of action with its Resistance ally.[31] When put to the vote, this motion was approved by 57.4 per cent of the mandates while 25.6 per cent were cast for the Sarthe text. The details of the division are given in Table 27.

This division provided the first clear indication of the size and extent of a body of opinion which favoured good relations with the Communist Party in the name of working-class unity very similar to that represented by the pre-war Bataille Socialiste. In the event, of the 96 delegations which took part in the ballot, only 51 had given all or a majority of their mandates for the Mayer motion. It had been the support of the large delegations which had ensured that it had obtained a respectable total, despite the large number of abstentions and the mandates given to the Sarthe motion by a significant number of provincial federations; without the bloc votes it had received from the large Bouches-du-Rhône, Nord, Pas-de-Calais, Haute-Vienne, Landes and Haute-Garonne Federations and without the substantial majorities given it by the Seine and Gard Federations, it might not have obtained an absolute majority of the mandates. Over this matter, Mollet was in no position to take up the cause of the minority, for not only was his federation in favour of closer ties with the UDSR but he himself was still associated with the OCM group, one of the components of that body.

Having managed to carry the day on this issue, the leadership was in a better position to confront the more coherent opposition which favoured the taking of immediate steps to prepare for the fusion of the Socialist and Communist Parties. The debate about this proposal began on the afternoon of Monday 13th and concluded on the following morning. In his introductory report, Daniel Mayer rehearsed the case for accepting unity of action as the best means of fostering the mutual trust needed to ensure that any fusion of the two parties would be stable and lasting, an argument which was developed by later speakers such as Augustin Laurent (Nord) and André Philip (Rhône). On the other hand, the reasoning behind the demand for immediate moves towards fusion, or organic unity, was explained by, amongst others, Jean Minjoz (Doubs) and Foulon (Ille-et-Vilaine).[32] There had always been a

---

[31] Ibid., pp. 425–83.
[32] Ibid., pp. 521–90/607; 14 August 1945, pp. 610–74.

Table 27. *SFIO, 37th National Congress, Paris, 13 August 1945: division on motions concerning relations with Resistance organizations*

| | Mandates for the motions of: | | | | | | | | Totals |
Federations	Daniel Mayer (loyalist) no.	%	Sarthe Federation (dissident) no.	%	Abstentions no.	%	Absent no.	%	no.
Bouches-du-Rhône	201	100							201
Gironde					331	100.0			331
Meurthe-et-Moselle	87	89.7	10	10.3					97
Nord	741	100.0							741
Pas-de-Calais	829	100.0							829
Seine	381	79.2	100	20.8					481
Seine-et-Oise					[361]	100.0			[361]
Haute-Vienne	229	100.0							229
Others	3,636	49.4	[2,608]	35.4	[1,114]	15.1	5	0.1	[7,363]
Totals	6,104	57.4	2,718	25.6	1,806	17.0	5	0.1	10,633

Source: Bulletin Intérieur (Paris), no. 6, July–August 1945, p. 6. For details of adjustments, see the appendix (pp. 401–2, n. 9).

possibility that the congress would divide on this issue and also that a poorly expressed motion against the resumption of unity talks could be defeated, so the Resolutions Committee entrusted the drafting of a compromise text to a small subcommittee which included Jules Moch and Mollet. Working to a draft which Moch had prepared, the subcommittee came up with a text which was approved by the Resolutions Committee and, on 15 August, by the congress as a whole.[33]

This left the party with a defensible position in any further talks with the Communist Party. The opening section of the text specified the conditions considered necessary to create a climate of unity between the two parties: each should be open about its doctrines, should defend democracy within itself, the nation and the world, and should avoid being linked to or influenced by any foreign government. Maintaining that these conditions were far from being met by the Communist Party and therefore that the time was still not ripe for organic union, the resolution proposed merely that the Comité d'Entente should meet to ensure that there was co-operation between the two parties during the coming election campaign. After that was over, discussions about fusion could be resumed, in the light of which, parallel congresses of each party could decide whether a joint congress should be convened.[34]

The congress then agreed its policy regarding candidatures for the cantonal and the general elections, and returned to the question of the party's relationship with de Gaulle's government. On the afternoon of the 13th, Vincent Auriol, Jules Moch and Daniel Mayer had met with the General's *directeur de cabinet* to discuss the resolution of the congress favouring *représentation proportionnelle intégrale* and the reversal of the order of the cantonal and general elections, but on Tuesday 14th, the Socialist minister, Adrien Tixier, found that he could not persuade de Gaulle to place the question on the agenda for the meeting of the Council of Ministers which was to take place that day. Later, at the meeting itself, he again tried unsuccessfully to raise the matter.[35] The problem of deciding what should now be done was discussed by the Resolutions Committee of the congress during the night of 14–15 August and it decided, with Mollet dissenting, that the rebuff did not warrant the withdrawal of the Socialist ministers from the government. Making a virtue of his intransigence, Mollet then insisted on presenting

[33] On the drafting of the resolution, see Jules Moch's statement to the congress (ibid., 15 August 1945, pp. 837–40).
[34] *Bulletin Intérieur*, no. 6, July–August 1945, pp. 2–3.
[35] See Daniel Mayer's account to the congress (Parti Socialiste (SFIO), 37ᵉ Congrès National, Paris, 11–15 août 1945, *Compte rendu sténographique*, 15 August 1945, pp. 867–9).

a modified version of his original motion in favour of withdrawal during the closing session of the congress on 15 August.

J'ai déjà eu l'occasion de dire que c'était mon premier congrès national, malgré mes vingt-deux ans de Parti, et j'ai appris ici des choses que j'ignorais. J'ai été amené à constater qu'à côté des débats, nous avons à tenir compte des avis qui peuvent nous être donnés dans les couloirs par différents camarades. C'est ainsi que j'ai été, dans ces quelques jours, impressionné par la quantité et je dirai par la qualité des divers camarades qui sont venus m'affirmer et essayer de me démontrer que je me trompais.[36]

In response, Daniel Mayer tabled the resolution which had been adopted by the majority of the Resolutions Committee. This, while listing the party's grievances and conceding that they would have justified ending its participation in government, nevertheless advised against such a course on the grounds that it would confuse the forthcoming election campaign and weaken de Gaulle's position on the eve of his visit to the United States. Léon Blum then intervened to take the same line and in the subsequent division 71.7 per cent of the mandates were cast for Daniel Mayer's motion and 27.4 per cent for the Mollet text.[37] The detailed result is shown in Table 28.

In the earlier vote on relations with the Resistance organizations there had been a significant number of abstentions but in this ballot there was a simple two-way division. The support for the official position was strong, with the Mayer motion receiving bloc or majority support from 74 of the 95 federal delegations which were present. If one compares the composition of the vote for the Mollet motion on this occasion with that of the vote for the Sarthe motion in the earlier division, it is evident that the two 'oppositions' were by no means identical. Whereas the Sarthe motion had drawn mandates from 52 federations and the Mollet motion from 36, only 22 federations had given mandates to both motions and in only 6 of these were the numbers identical. We have here the fragmentary expression of two different pre-war positions; whereas the vote for the Sarthe motion reflects the preference of the former Bataille Socialiste for a close alliance with the Communists, including, if possible, co-operation in government, the vote for the Mollet motion indicates the survival of a much older Guesdiste antipathy to any participation by the party in the management of the bourgeois state. There is little geographical pattern to the Mollet vote (the bloc votes came from a scattering of rural federations including Seine-et-Marne, Vosges, Côte-d'Or, Ardèche and Gard, and majorities from

[36] Ibid., p. 865.
[37] Ibid., pp. 864–82.

Table 28. *SFIO, 37th National Congress, Paris, 15 August 1945: division on motions concerning the national political situation*

| Federations | Mandates for the motions of: | | | | | | | | Totals |
| | Daniel Mayer (loyalist) | | Guy Mollet (dissident) | | Abstentions | | Absent | | |
	no.	%	no.	%	no.	%	no.	%	no.
Bouches-du-Rhône	201	100.0							201
Gironde	331	100.0							331
Meurthe-et-Moselle	97	100.0							97
Nord	741	100.0							741
Pas-de-Calais	300	36.2	529	63.8					829
Seine	351	73.0	130	27.0					481
Seine-et-Oise	249	69.0	112	31.0					361
Haute-Vienne	229	100.0							229
Others	5,126	69.6	2,145	29.1	64	0.9	28	0.4	7,363
Totals	7,625	71.7	2,916	27.4	64	0.6	28	0.3	10,633

Source: Bulletin Intérieur (Paris), no. 6, July–August 1945, p. 7.

another group, including the important federations of Pas-de-Calais and Rhône) but the significant point is that it had been put together, not by the old methods of working the federal congresses and building up a body of committed delegates with mandates in hand, but by last-minute negotiations at the congress itself and by delegates under heavy moral pressure not to cause difficulties. The revolt which Mollet was to lead to a successful conclusion in 1946 had already begun.

At this stage, however, none of the small opposition groups was in any position to threaten the existing leadership in the elections to the new 31-member Comité Directeur. The ballot produced the following membership for this body:[38]

Vincent Auriol	Salomon Grumbach	Marcel-Edmond
Jean Biondi*	Gérard Jaquet	Naegelen
Elie Bloncourt	Augustin Laurent	Louis Noguères*
Renée Blum	André Le Troquer	André Philip
Gaston Defferre	Andrée Marty-Capgras	Roger Priou-Valjean
Edouard Depreux	Daniel Mayer	Victor Provo*
Charles Dumas	Roger Mistral	Henri Ribière
Just Evrard	Jules Moch	Paul Rivet*
Paul Favier	Emilienne Moreau	François Tanguy-Prigent
Edouard Froment	Marius Moutet*	Eugène Thomas*
Félix Gouin		Robert Verdier

* = new member

All but one of the 26 members (including Renée Blum) of the retiring executive had been re-elected despite the fact that several of them, including Defferre, Jaquet, Mayer and Tanguy-Prigent, had not been well-known figures at the national level of the party before the war. When it met for the first time on 21 August, the new Comité Directeur appointed the following to constitute its Bureau:

Secretary General	Daniel Mayer
Deputy Secretary General	Robert Verdier
Deputy Secretary General in charge of administration	Gérard Jaquet
Treasurer General	Victor Provo

It also formed a Standing Committee (Délégation Permanente) of eight members, consisting of Daniel Mayer, Robert Verdier, Vincent Auriol,

[38] *Bulletin Intérieur*, no. 6, July–August 1945, p. 5.

Renée Blum, André Le Troquer, Eugène Thomas, Marius Moutet and Jules Moch.[39]

The new Socialist leaders felt that they had cause for satisfaction with the outcome of their party's first post-war national congress: the main strands of their general strategy – participation in the de Gaulle government, the maintenance of the Resistance front, alliance with the UDSR, and the avoidance of too close a relationship with the Communist Party – had survived intact and they had been left in complete charge of the party's executive. Although the revised party rules and the declaration of principles had still not been approved, the centralized organizational structure which had been established at the end of 1944 was still in place. On the other hand, the signs of discontent at the branch level of the party were now unmistakable; the charter-of-unity campaign had stimulated the formation of a pro-Communist movement reminiscent of the Bataille Socialiste of pre-war days; the publication of the draft declaration of principles had prompted doctrinal revivalists to defend the Charter of 1905; and the attempt to increase central control through new rules had sparked off demands for the restoration of the National Council, for proportional representation in elections to executive bodies, and for a return to *le mandat impératif*, the practice of issuing binding instructions to delegates. These expressions of dissent were relatively formless and evanescent, much as the *tendances* were reputed to have been in the early Socialist parties, but their number and variety showed that the leadership's control was beginning to weaken.

It was now possible for a determined opposition leader to provide a focus for such scattered discontents, presenting them as symptoms of a much deeper disorder which only a concerted campaign to restore the party to its original form could remedy. This was Mollet's opportunity. He had already shown that he could not be subdued by the party's notables, that he was an independent person and that he belonged to the Guesdiste tradition. He was now in a good position to criticize the leadership as it tried to adjust the party organization to the conditions of post-war politics. By late 1945 the party was still trying to recapture the spaces it had occupied in the French political scene in the 1930s and to discover whether its freedom of manoeuvre had been narrowed by the expansion of other parties and groups. Its improvised campaign of membership recruitment was still in progress; it was still attempting to consolidate its position in cities such as Lille, Marseille, Bordeaux and Toulouse; and its electoral organization had not yet been fully tested. While the party was making this effort to regain its former standing,

[39] *CD Minutes*, II, 21 August 1945, pp. 1–2.

the new leaders could only hope that their methods of regulation and control would be as effective as those which Paul Faure and his team had employed before the war.

The Mollet revolt gathers force, September 1945–June 1946

The elections for the first Constituent Assembly were held on 21 October 1945 under a version of proportional representation which involved a list system within departments or subdivisions of departments and a method of electoral quotients and highest averages for allocating seats. These arrangements favoured parties which were well organized at both the national and regional levels and the campaign for this poll was in fact dominated by three large parties, the Communists, the Socialists and the Mouvement Républicain Populaire (MRP), a Christian Democratic party which had been formed in November 1944. In this election they obtained more or less equal shares of the total valid vote in metropolitan France (25.99 per cent for the Communists, 23.59 per cent for the Socialists and 24.40 per cent for the MRP)[40] and returned similar proportions of deputies to the assembly, the initial strengths of their parliamentary groups being Communists 151, Socialists 139 and MRP 150 in a house of 586.[41] With varying degrees of reluctance, the three parties accepted the necessity of forming an alliance; although a Communist–Socialist or a Socialist–MRP combination would have been numerically possible, all of them were forced to acknowledge that *tripartisme* would provide the most secure basis for government and for constitution-making.

The first test of the new alliance was whether the three parties could reach agreement with each other and with Charles de Gaulle about the form and composition of the new provisional government, which would be responsible to the assembly. Once the negotiations started, the Socialists found themselves serving as a hinge, holding steady while each of their allies swung to and fro in efforts to win attention and influence decisions. Eventually it was agreed that de Gaulle should continue as President and that the lion's share of the posts should be allocated to representatives of the three main parties, the remainder being given to technocrats and to personalities from minor parties. Of

---

[40] These percentages are for aggregate party votes derived from an analysis of constituency returns in *JO (ANC I)*, *Déb.*, 6 November 1945, pp. 7–41; 7 November 1945, pp. 47–9; 8 November 1945, p. 53; 2 December 1945, p. 192; these returns were checked and corrected against those given in Raoul Husson, *Elections et référendums des 21 octobre 1945, 5 mai et 2 juin 1946* (*Le Monde*, Paris, 1946).

[41] From a list of group memberships published in *JO, LD,* 29 November 1945, pp. 7898–9.

the Socialists, Vincent Auriol became a Minister of State, Adrien Tixier Minister of the Interior, François Tanguy-Prigent Minister of Agriculture and Food, Jules Moch Minister of Public Works and Transport, and Eugène Thomas Minister of Posts and Telegraphs. The government took office on 21 November 1945.

The Socialists had expected to be in a much stronger position. They had earlier persuaded themselves that the Resistance movement had given the French people a new faith in the future and that the socialist philosophy was at the heart of that faith. They had seen the SFIO as the potential core of a large *rassemblement populaire* and had hoped that it would emerge from the October elections as the dominant party in the assembly. Instead, they now found themselves trapped in the middle of a stressful alliance, with an aggressive and greatly enlarged Communist Party on one flank and a clerical party, representing a Catholic social movement as well as Resistance reformism, on the other. The Popular Front pattern, in which the Communist Party had known its place and the Radicals had been a predictable centre party, was now a thing of the past.

Experiencing at first hand the frustrations and conflicts entailed in committee work and the passage of the assembly's crowded legislative programme, the members of the Socialist parliamentary group reacted with increasing impatience to the restrictions imposed by *tripartisme*. Many of the deputies lacked experience of parliamentary work and may have been inclined to exaggerate its limitations: only 32 of the original 139 had been members of parliament when war broke out and only 27 (who included 16 of these pre-war veterans) had belonged to the Consultative Assembly of 1943–5. Their constitutional ideas were tinged with Jacobinism; although they were in favour of a parliamentary regime, they also wanted a strong assembly, with a weaker system of checks and balances than the MRP was known to prefer. As far as policy was concerned, they resented having to support the government's measures whether they agreed with them or not.

Among these newcomers was Guy Mollet, who had been returned to the Constituent Assembly from the second Pas-de-Calais constituency in the elections of 21 October 1945 and soon made his way to the front rank of the Socialist parliamentary group in the Palais-Bourbon. He was chosen as a member of the group's Executive Delegation and subsequently nominated as one of the Socialist representatives on the assembly's influential Constitutional Committee. In meetings of the parliamentary group he had already adopted the stern, uncompromising manner which was to distinguish him in later years: Germaine Degrond has recalled his challenging of Gaston Defferre.

Un nouveau député du Pas-de-Calais, jeune, mince, s'opposait à lui [Gaston Defferre] avec ardeur. Sa sincérité était évidente, la simplicité de ses propos était telle que j'arrivai à partager l'opinion fortement structurée qui l'opposait à Defferre. Je ne le connaissais pas encore, sinon de vue, mais ses arguments ne me laissaient aucun doute: c'était un guesdiste comme je l'étais moi-même depuis tant d'années déjà.[42]

The most serious clash between the Socialists and de Gaulle occurred during the Constituent Assembly's consideration of the annual budget, when the Socialist parliamentary group demanded a reduction in defence expenditure. For the first three months of 1946, the government had proposed a spending plan of 40,000 million francs, composed of separate provisions for the armed forces (22,000 million francs), armaments (15,000 million) and military requirements in the colonies (3,000 million). The assembly's Finance Committee had rejected an amendment moved by one of its Socialist members to cut the armed forces budget by 20 per cent but another Socialist revived the proposal when the budget came before the assembly itself. Although under considerable pressure to do so, the Socialist parliamentary group refused to withdraw the motion for amendment and effectively challenged the government to explain why, when France faced economic and financial difficulties, military expenses should not be reduced. At first the Socialists had stood alone but then the Communists indicated that they would also support the amendment and the crisis, which had begun on 31 December 1945, had not been resolved by the morning of 1 January 1946 when Vincent Auriol arrived with a message from de Gaulle to the effect that the adoption of the amendment would make the government's task impossible. Speaking for the Socialists, André Philip treated de Gaulle's communication as a request for a vote of confidence, and he presented his refusal to withdraw the amendment as a defence of the assembly's rights:

nous ne voudrions pas que la question de confiance, posée à tout et hors de tout propos, aboutit à réduire l'Assemblée nationale constituante à n'être plus qu'une chambre d'enregistrement abandonnant toute prérogative.[43]

In the late afternoon, de Gaulle informed the deputies that:

à aucun moment le Gouvernement ne considérerait qu'il a le droit de rester dans ses fonctions et de porter sur ses épaules la charge qu'il assume s'il n'était pas assuré d'avoir la confiance de l'Assemblée nationale constituante.[44]

---

[42] 'Souvenir . . . ', *Bulletin de la Fondation Guy Mollet*, no. 3, January–June 1982, inside front cover.
[43] *JO (ANC I)*, *Déb.*, 31 December 1945, p. 725.
[44] Ibid., p. 730.

The pattern of group alignments continued to build up around the original division between a Marxist majority on one side, based on the Communist and Socialist groups, and a substantial minority, including the MRP and UDSR deputies, which was prepared to vote against the amendment; only the position of the Radicals remained in doubt. Finally a compromise was reached. A modifying amendment credited to two members of the UDSR was carried unanimously; this provided that the proposed reduction should take effect only if the government had not brought forward a measure for the reorganization of the armed forces by 15 February 1946 but that, in any case, the armed forces budget should be cut by 5 per cent.[45]

The Socialist parliamentary group had come very close to precipitating a serious ministerial crisis. Although many Socialists considered that it had shown courage in acting as it had done, the gesture was in reality a blind protest against the inescapable constraints of *tripartisme*. Given the existing distribution of power in the party system and in the Constituent Assembly itself, the SFIO had the choice of three basic strategies, each of which had disadvantages. It could join with the Communists to construct a purely Marxist alliance, which would separate it from the middle classes and threaten it with absorption by its stronger neighbour; it could form a centre alliance with the MRP, the UDSR and the Radicals, which would further weaken its ability to win back working-class support; or it could continue with *tripartisme*, which so limited its freedom of manoeuvre and expression. Of these three possible alliances, *tripartisme* was the only combination capable of carrying through a coherent programme of economic reform and producing a securely based constitutional settlement, but it was evident that neither the parliamentary group nor the Comité Directeur could reconcile itself to this fact. In its desire to protest against constraints, the parliamentary group had demonstrated a disturbing capacity to act to gain a tactical advantage without sufficient regard for the consequences.

Meanwhile, the dissidents within the Seine Federation were threatening to become a centre of resistance to the central leadership. They already constituted a generalized assemblage of individuals and networks, *un courant d'opinion* rather than a *tendance* in the pre-war sense, and their self-styled avant-garde was a mixture of ex-Trotskyists, ex-Communists, Pivertistes and stray personalities from various backgrounds. Amongst the former Trotskyists, the most

---

[45] Ibid., pp. 735–6. See also *L'Année politique 1944–45* (Éditions du Grand Siècle, Paris, [1946]), pp. 417–18; Charles de Gaulle, *Mémoires de guerre*, III, *Le Salut 1944–1946* (Plon, Paris, 1959), pp. 278–81; Jean Lacouture, *De Gaulle*. II, *Le Politique 1944–1959* (Seuil, Paris, 1985), pp. 228–32.

articulate was Jean Rous, who had joined Marceau Pivert's PSOP in 1939 and had been a member of Mouvement National Révolutionnaire and later of Libérer et Fédérer in the Resistance movement. He had helped to rebuild the SFIO's Rhône Federation after Liberation before moving back to Paris.[46] In an article written immediately before the SFIO's National Congress of August 1945 he had argued that the Provisional Government's programme of nationalizing certain industries showed that the French economy was moving towards a form of state capitalism, and that it was incumbent on political parties and trade unions to ensure that, while this was taking place, democratic freedoms were maintained. For this reason, he considered that the SFIO had to be reshaped:

Nous avons dépassé l'étape de l'électoralisme et de la propagande pour entrer dans celle de l'expérience du socialisme, soit par la réalisation positive au pouvoir, soit par la gestion préparatoire. C'est pourquoi il est nécessaire d'opérer une réforme de structure profonde.[47]

He was therefore convinced of the need to oppose the party's

courant libéral, en réalité néo-radical qui, sous prétexte 'd'humanisme', voulait édulcorer le caractère révolutionnaire du marxisme et transformer le parti S.F.I.O. en une sorte de parti de centre, qui aurait été l'aile laïque du fameux 'travaillisme sans travailleurs'.[48]

Closely associated with Jean Rous was Yves Dechézelles, a young lawyer who had been a pre-war member of the SFIO but had left it in 1937 because he disagreed with the National Council's apparent endorsement of the policy of non-intervention in the Spanish Civil War. As he was then living in Calvados, he joined the Communist Party there and was for a short period the secretary of its Caen branch before resigning from the party in 1938. He served in the army at the beginning of the war, was demobilized in Algeria in 1940, and went on to play a leading role in his local Resistance movement. In 1943 he was placed

---

[46] For his own account of his political life to this point, see Rous, 'Carnet de route d'un militant' in Rous, *Itinéraire d'un militant* (Jeune Afrique, Paris, 1968), pp. 15–33; 'De la crise du socialisme au renouveau démocratique et révolutionnaire', *Esprit* (Paris), 17, 2 (February 1949), pp. 306–20; 'Notes d'un militant: vingt-cinq ans d'essais et de combats', ibid., 24, 5 (May 1956), pp. 791–811. See also Fred Zeller, *Trois points, c'est tout* (Robert Laffont, Paris, 1976), pp. 201–16; Jean-Paul Joubert, *Marceau Pivert et le pivertisme: révolutionnaires de la S.F.I.O.* (Presses de la Fondation Nationale des Sciences Politiques, Paris, 1977), pp. 224–5; L. Lequertier, 'Militants et responsables', *La Pensée Socialiste* (Paris), no. 3, April 1946, pp. 19–20.

[47] Rous, 'Le socialisme et les nouvelles perspectives', *Esprit*, 13, 9 (August 1945), pp. 385–97, quotation from p. 393.

[48] Rous, 'De la crise du socialisme au renouveau démocratique et révolutionnaire', p. 308.

in charge of the *cabinet* of Adrien Tixier, the Commissioner for Labour and Social Security in the CFLN, and after the Liberation returned to Paris, but when Tixier became Minister of the Interior in the Provisional Government, Dechézelles gave up his administrative post and resumed his legal career. At that time he was living in the 7th *arrondissement*, where he made contact with other like-minded activists in the SFIO's Seine Federation.[49]

The Parisian branches of the party now contained many shades of Marxist intellectuals who were organizing informal groups aimed at preventing the party from assuming what, in their eyes, would have been a reformist – and in doctrinal terms a revisionist – orientation. They included Pierre Rimbert, a printer and former Communist who had in 1940 formed a Resistance group known as Libertés and founded a journal with the same title, which continued to be published after the liberation of Paris when Rimbert joined the staff of the *Franc-Tireur* newspaper;[50] Léon Boutbien, a doctor who had been a member of Rimbert's Resistance group and who was one of the contributors to *Libertés* after the war; and Suzanne Charpy, who was one of the permanent officials employed by the party to build up a network of Groupes Socialistes d'Entreprises and thus to strengthen its links with industrial workers in the way that the Amicales Socialistes had done before the war.

Within the Seine Federation, the pre-war Pivertistes were also re-gathering their forces. Marceau Pivert himself did not return to France until March 1946 but his former colleagues Charles Lancelle, Henri Barré and Lucien Vaillant (all of whom had been members of the Commission Politique of the rebel federation in 1938) and some of his long-standing lieutenants such as Lucien Weitz and Jacques Enock had rejoined the federation. Alongside them was a new generation of activists, who included Jacques Clément and Lucie Colliard.[51] The Pivertistes' opportunity to bid for the control of the federation came when its first post-Liberation secretary, Gérard Jaquet, was persuaded to accept a post as one of the party's Deputy Secretaries on the Bureau of the central Comité Directeur in August 1945. He had wanted to resign as Federal Secretary on taking up this new position, but the federation's Comité Executif persuaded him to remain in office until

---

[49] Interview with Yves Dechézelles, Paris, 8 July 1992.

[50] See the obituary of Pierre Rimbert published in *L'OURS* (Paris), no. 225, December 1991, pp. 8–9. See also Yvan Craipeau, *Les révolutionnaires pendant la seconde guerre mondiale. II, La Libération confisquée 1944–1947* (Savelli/Syros, Paris, 1978), pp. 98–100; André Thirion, *Révolutionnaires sans révolution* (Robert Laffont, Paris, 1972), p. 485.

[51] On the contacts between Marceau Pivert and his supporters in Paris and Lyon at this time, see Joubert, *Révolutionnaires de la S.F.I.O.*, pp. 237–40.

the federation's annual administrative congress.[52] By the time that this congress was held on 2 December 1945, the Pivertistes and their allies had gained considerable strength, as the divisions on that occasion showed; the annual report of the outgoing executive was approved by a small majority of 6,697 mandates to 4,724 with 890 abstentions, and the administrative report by 5,978 mandates to 5,469 with 864 abstentions.[53] The subsequent election of the federation's Executive Committee appears to have gone in favour of the opposition because the Bureau appointed on 26 December was dominated by Pivertistes, with Charles Lancelle as Federal Secretary, Jacques Clément as his deputy, Lucie Colliard as Administrative Secretary, Suzanne Charpy as Treasurer and Fritscher as Archivist.[54]

There is an obvious parallel between this coup and the capture of the federation by the Gauche Révolutionnaire in February 1938: the national leadership had lost control of one of its strongest regional units. The setback was all the more serious because the equally important Rhône Federation, based in the city of Lyon, had been taken over by a left-wing leadership immediately after the liberation of the region in September 1944. Its leading figures were André Ferrat, a former Communist who had joined the SFIO before the war, and Victor Fay, another former Communist. In Fay's words, they had reconstructed the federation 'après une épuration . . . assez brutale', with the result that André Philip, who represented the first Rhône constituency in the Constituent Assembly, now found himself in the loyalist minority within his local party. Fay and Ferrat had established an evening newspaper, *Lyon Libre*, and were hoping to put their ideas across not only to the workers in the industrial suburbs but also to the lower-middle class in the centre of Lyon.[55]

It was at about this time that the pro-Communist and anti-participationist movements further increased their levels of support throughout the provincial federations. To activists alarmed by the success of the MRP in the elections of 21 October 1945, a closer alliance with the Communists seemed to be the most obvious defensive

---

[52] See Gérard Jaquet, 'Rapport moral', in Parti Socialiste (SFIO), Fédération de la Seine, Congrès Administratif des 2 et 9 décembre 1945, *Rapports, statuts fédéraux* [Paris, 1945], p. 2.

[53] *Le Populaire*, 4 December 1945, p. 2.

[54] Ibid., 27 December 1945, p. 2. For the membership of the federation's Executive Committee, see ibid,. 23–24 December 1945, p. 2.

[55] See Victor Fay, *La Flamme et la cendre: histoire d'une vie militante*, prepared with the assistance of Evelyne Malnic (Presses Universitaires de Vincennes, Paris, 1989), pp. 193–6. See also the obituary article on André Ferrat written by Pierre Rimbert, in *L'OURS*, no. 189, April 1988, p. 11.

arrangement, especially in those regions such as Brittany and Normandy where the SFIO represented anticlerical sentiment. More generally, members were disconcerted by the party's participation in a government which so restricted its ability to develop its own lines of policy and which, under de Gaulle's leadership, attached so much importance to the armed forces. Such negative reactions are understandable; the party had been drawn into *tripartisme*, first by its sentimental attachment to the Resistance front in which Christian Democrats rather than Radicals had been accepted as a non-Socialist but progressive ally, and secondly by the inexorable political logic which had been set in motion by the election results. However, the SFIO had never come to terms with the resultant strategy. Its participation in *tripartisme* had been justified as a means of avoiding less desirable alternatives rather than as a course of action which would give the party good opportunities for enlarging its social base, acquiring a social-democratic reputation and entering coalition governments with a wide variety of partners and policy objectives. This being the case, firm and clear guidance from the party's executive was essential, but the Comité Directeur at this stage was far too embroiled in the affairs of the parliamentary group to take an independent stand. Many members of the newly appointed Comité Directeur had been elected to the Constituent Assembly, with the result that deputies now numbered 22 on the 31-member executive, compared with the maximum of 12 parliamentarians which had been allowed on the 33-member CAP before the war. Not surprisingly, discussions on the Comité Directeur were often dominated by the specific problems which the parliamentary group was encountering in the legislative and constitution-making work of the assembly; it was given few opportunities to put aside immediate concerns and consider questions of long-term strategy.

It was not until 9 January 1946 that the Comité Directeur paid serious attention to the growth of dissent within the party. Gérard Jaquet, after reporting on a meeting of the Comité d'Entente, went on to give an account of the political situation:

Il estime qu'il y a un malaise dans le Parti et un malaise dans le pays, dont l'opinion publique rend responsable les Trois Grands, mais surtout notre Parti. Notre situation est en effet plus délicate que celle du M.R.P. qui se déclare être un parti gaulliste et décidé à soutenir le Général de Gaulle jusqu'au bout. Le Parti communiste a lui aussi une position plus facile que la nôtre, car il déclare qu'il ne voulait pas d'un gouvernement tripartite, mais d'un gouvernement PS–PC. C'est donc notre Parti qui a une position plus difficile pour avoir voulu le gouvernement tripartite qui a échoué devant l'opinion.[56]

[56] *CD Minutes*, II, 9 January 1946, p. 119.

Jaquet took pride in the stand which the parliamentary group had taken in the discussion of the defence budget and showed a surprising readiness to believe that the party had sufficient power to change the political balance in its favour:

> Il estime que de Gaulle conduit le pays et le Parti à un désastre et qu'il faut trouver un terrain de chute qui nous soit favorable; ce pourrait être delui [*sic*] de la réorganisation de l'Armée. Il envisage ensuite quelle pourrait être la formule gouvernementale appelée à succéder à de Gaulle et estime que ce pourrait être soit une formation tripartite à direction socialiste, soit un gouvernement socialiste–communiste, avec des républicains appartenant à d'autres groupes.[57]

André Philip was also inclined to romance about the significance of the defence budget affair and to speculate about how the strategic deadlock could be broken:

> Il estime que les répercussions de notre offensive du 1er janvier ont été excellentes dans le pays. Il indique notamment qu'il a fait à Lyon un meeting qui groupait plus de 5.000 auditeurs. Le Parti a donné une impression de réveil, il faut qu'il se prépare à la bataille sur le terrain des crédits militaires. Il voit deux problèmes à lier: l'organisation de l'Armée et des crédits militaires et le problème constitutionnel.
>
> Il faut dès maintenant désigner les camarades qui interviendront dans le débat sur l'organisation de l'Armée et qui auront à faire des exposés solides et constructifs. De cette façon: ou les autres partis nous suivront et nous aurons l'avantage de l'initiative, ou bien la question de confiance sera posée et il faut envisager alors l'hypothèse de la chute du Gouvernement.[58]

Like Jaquet, he was inclined to see such a crisis as an opportunity for the party to improve its position; while ruling out a Socialist–Communist government, he was willing to envisage another tripartite ministry or, should the MRP refuse to take part, a purely Socialist administration.[59] When his turn came to speak, Vincent Auriol advised caution, reminding the meeting that the parliamentary group had given way over the defence budget to avoid bringing down the government and causing a succession crisis; he warned that they should not contemplate bringing down the ministry if it could be avoided.[60] After two other deputies, Paul Rivet and Marcel-Edmond Naegelen, had resumed speculation about post-crisis possibilities, including that of forming a Socialist–Communist administration, Jules Moch returned to Auriol's point that a succession crisis would be against the interests of the party. He warned

---

[57] Ibid., p. 120.
[58] Ibid.
[59] Ibid.
[60] Ibid., p. 121.

that the MRP would stand by de Gaulle in the event of his resignation and predicted that the SFIO would suffer losses were it to enter the next elections as part of a Communist–Socialist ministry under Maurice Thorez; it was essential, he claimed, to go to the polls with de Gaulle as the head of a tripartite government.[61] The most surprising thing about this exchange was the romanticism which inspired so many of the interventions. It was as though the members of the Comité Directeur were reluctant to concentrate on the basic issues of strategy and to admit that the desperate state of the French economy precluded the abandonment of *tripartisme*.

Within days of this meeting, a governmental crisis of the first magnitude showed that this was indeed the case. On Sunday 20 January 1946 de Gaulle announced that he was resigning as President of the Provisional Government and left the three large parties to decide whether their alliance should continue and, if so, which of their leaders should take his place. As Moch had predicted, the MRP was disposed to move into opposition but it was persuaded to remain in the coalition and to accept Félix Gouin, a Socialist, as being suitable to head the next ministry. The Constituent Assembly elected Gouin as President on 23 January and the members of his government took office on 26 January. Besides Gouin, the Socialists in the new administration were André Le Troquer as Minister of the Interior, André Philip as Minister of National Economy and Finance, François Tanguy-Prigent as Minister of Agriculture, Marcel-Edmond Naegelen as Minister of Education, Jules Moch as Minister of Public Works and Transport and Marius Moutet as Minister of Colonies. In the house, Vincent Auriol took over from Gouin as President of the Assembly and Guy Mollet succeeded André Philip as President of the Constitutional Committee.

Mollet now felt sufficiently confident of his standing within the party to come forward as spokesman for the elements of dissent and opposition within it. He was the chief signatory of a declaration entitled *Appel au Parti* which was published in the SFIO's *Bulletin Intérieur* in February 1946,[62] ostensibly as a document to be considered during preparations for an extraordinary national congress which the Comité Directeur had decided should be held at the end of March. This piece, the first part of which had been written before de Gaulle's resignation, was published after the formation of the Gouin government. Its logic rested on the assumption that the masses had voted for the Socialist and Communist Parties on 21 October 1945 to express their wish for a complete

[61] Ibid., p. 122.
[62] *Bulletin Intérieur*, special number, February 1946, pp. 5–7.

change of methods, men and aims, but that their hopes had been deceived and the country now ran the risk of being taken over either by so-called new-left revolutionaries or by an autocratic ruler. Claiming that the Socialist Party could play a decisive role in saving democracy from this danger and in leading *les classes laborieuses* to victory, the signatories of the *Appel* called upon all activists

à coopérer au redressement rapide du Parti, à la fois dans sa ligne politique et dans sa structure.[63]

This play on the word *redressement*, in the sense of a return to fundamentals, was sustained through a series of paragraphs and served to imply criticism of the party's existing policies:

En vérité notre parti s'est engagé dans une impasse. La cause essentielle est . . . dans l'abandon partiel par le parti de ses positions doctrinales de toujours. Mais une autre cause est dans la position qu'il a prise en face des problèmes de l'unité ouvrière et par là même de la lutte de classes.[64]

The *Appel* touched on the proposals for a fusion of the Socialist and Communist Parties and claimed that even the existence of deep differences between them could not justify

la révision des postulats fondamentaux du socialisme. Loin de nous conseiller d'effacer de nos statuts le mot de 'lutte de classes' l'expérience actuelle nous prouve que cette lutte est plus réelle que jamais, comme moyen pour constituer une société sans classe.

Loin de laisser penser que les remèdes actuellement proposés sont suffisants pour résoudre les difficultés engendrées par le capitalisme agonisant, notre parti se doit d'affirmer avec plus de force que jamais que la *seule* solution est dans la révolution économique et sociale qui portera les travailleurs au pouvoir.[65]

This plea for a *redressement idéologique* was linked to a call for a change in the party's organization by using the network of Groupes Socialistes d'Entreprises to strengthen ties with the working class; by improving contacts with youth, working women and colonial peoples; and by employing better methods of training and propaganda. The *Appel*'s signatories claimed that *les partis ouvriers* had won their first victory in the recent elections and argued that the representatives of those parties should demonstrate the sovereign power of the Constituent Assembly:

Déjà nous avons salué avec joie l'attitude ferme qu'ont pris nos camarades députés lors du débat sur le budget des armées.[66]

[63] Ibid., p. 5.
[64] Ibid., pp. 5–6.
[65] Ibid., p. 6.
[66] Ibid.

The list of the 65 people who had signed this text provides a good indication of the sources of Mollet's support at this stage in his revolt. His basic group was the following he had built up within the party's 141-member parliamentary group; 47 of the signatories were Socialist deputies, although the list did not include any of the party's 7 deputies from the Nord Department, any of the 4 from Gironde, any of the 3 from Haute-Vienne, only one of the 5 from Bouches-du-Rhône and only 2 of the 7 from the Seine. The category of deputies overlaps with other categories; for example, the signatories include 4 members of the Comité Directeur (Elie Bloncourt, Just Evrard and Paul Rivet amongst the deputies and Andrée Marty-Capgras amongst the non-deputies), some survivors from the pre-war *tendances* (Lucien Weitz and Jacques Enock of the Gauche Révolutionnaire and Pierre Commin and Germaine Degrond of the Bataille) and some of the Parisian intellectuals (including Henri Barré, Yves Dechézelles, Jean-Maurice Hermann, Charles Lancelle, Jean Rous and Lucien Vaillant). The composition of the list enables us to draw some conclusions about the origins of the Mollet revolt: first, his following amongst the Socialist deputies gave him potential access to a large number of provincial federations; secondly, he was already in touch with the Parisian intellectuals (a crucial intermediary in this connection was Yves Dechézelles, who had been Administrative Secretary of the parliamentary group in the Consultative Assembly and now held the same post for the group in the Constituent Assembly);[67] and, thirdly, he had established links with several members of the Comité Directeur itself.

The style and themes of the text were reminiscent of those of the Bataille Socialiste motions of the pre-war period, and indeed Mollet was appealing at this time to the pro-Communist rather than the anti-participationist movement in the party. Stripped of its rhetoric, the *Appel* stands out as an attempt to shift attention from the issue of fusion to the issue of doctrine and to censure the implied revisionism in the draft declaration of principles. This line of attack had given the Mollet group the appearance of a *tendance* but in fact its networks of support were less extensive and its normative themes less coherent than those of either the Bataille or the Gauche Révolutionnaire of the late 1930s. At this stage it had the capacity to evolve in any one of several directions: it could concentrate on sectarian issues and strengthen those of its characteristics which made it look like a *tendance* or it could extend its range of protest and become a faction, building up diverse bases of support while emphasizing Mollet's qualities as a leader.

[67] Interview with Yves Dechézelles, Paris, 8 July 1992.

The group appeared to acquire a *journal de tendance* when Jean Rous and his colleagues in Paris decided to launch a new periodical entitled *La Pensée Socialiste*, the first issue of which appeared in February 1946. The journal's governing body consisted of Jean Rous, the director, Henri Barré, Yves Dechézelles, Jean-Maurice Hermann, Charles Lancelle, René Lhuillier, Guy Mollet and Lucien Vaillant.[68] The first issue published an article by Mollet on the subject of democracy and revolution. It contained some material which had already appeared in the *Appel*, including a revised version of the paragraph which had first stated the *redressement* theme and which now read as follows:

C'est parce qu'ils ont conscience du très grave danger que court actuellement la démocratie et parce qu'ils ont la conviction que le Parti pourrait jouer un rôle décisif pour la sauver et pour mener les classes laborieuses à la victoire, que depuis plusieurs mois certains militants ont lancé un cri d'alarme et obtenu peu à peu, un véritable redressement – ou pour mieux dire un raidissement – du Parti, raidissement qu'ils voudraient voir sanctionner et affirmer à l'occasion du prochain congrès.[69]

By using such terms, Mollet was representing himself as the leader of a crusade to restore the party's doctrinal integrity which had, by implication, been compromised by the policies of Daniel Mayer and Léon Blum.

The SFIO's National Assembly of 24 February 1946 offered the first opportunity of testing whether this essentially sectarian conflict, conducted at the highest levels of the party, could be related to similar divisions of opinion at the levels of the branches and federations. In keeping with the instructions given by the National Congress of August 1945, this assembly had been convened to consider and approve the final versions of the new rules and the declaration of principles, which had been further revised by a committee of 16 members, including Léon Blum, Daniel Mayer and Robert Verdier. In the light of suggestions which had been submitted by the federations, the committee had amended the draft declaration to strengthen its reference to secularism (the third paragraph now began with the words, 'Fermement attaché à la liberté de conscience et à la laïcité de l'Etat et de l'école publique, le Parti socialiste') and to the party's revolutionary purpose (it was now described in paragraph four as 'un parti essentiellement révolutionnaire' and as 'un parti de lutte et d'action de classe, fondé sur l'organisation du monde du travail' instead of 'un parti d'action de classe et de révolution' as in Blum's original text). Where the draft rules were concerned,

[68] See the inside cover of *La Pensée Socialiste*, no. 1, February 1946.
[69] Ibid., pp. 22–3, quotation from p. 22.

the committee considered that, as the few suggestions which it had received from the federations had been mainly about points of detail, it was justified in taking the existing draft as a satisfactory basis for its work. It therefore concentrated on tightening up the expression of individual articles rather than attempting a wholesale revision of the text. It retained the provision for a powerful Comité Directeur while stipulating that this body should convene, at least every three months, a conference attended by one delegate from each federation. It sharpened up the article concerning the formation of groups of sympathizers such as the Groupes Socialistes d'Entreprises and it rejected the idea of retaining the creed-like Article 1 of the former rules, on the grounds that this was merely a repetition of certain paragraphs in the declaration of principles. The rules still specified that the votes at the disposal of delegates could not be *mandats impératifs*. The committee also noted that the decision to dispense with proportional representation in the appointments to executive bodies still remained in force. Its abolition

avait pour but, on le sait, de prévenir le retour aux luttes de tendances dont l'âpreté avait compromis la vie même du Parti avant la guerre.[70]

The revised drafts of the rules and the declaration were duly published in the *Bulletin Intérieur*[71] and considered at the local level. The most radical response to the committee's recommendations came from the Seine Federation, which produced a set of counter-proposals. On Sunday 17 February its Federal Council demanded that the pre-war rules should form the basis of the discussion at the forthcoming National Assembly, that the National Council should be restored, that proportional representation should be used for the appointment of executive bodies, and that its own specially prepared text, rather than the draft declaration, should be considered as a statement of doctrine.[72]

Following a conference of federal secretaries on 23 February, the National Assembly met on Sunday 24th. Representation at this meeting had been restricted to one delegate from each federation and the total number of mandates for all 97 federations had been established as 4,460 on the basis of one mandate per 50 members, rather than one mandate per 25 members as provided for by Article 22 of the rules.[73] The draft

---

[70] 'Projet de déclaration de principes et de statuts', the report by Robert Verdier on behalf of the Commission des Statuts, *Bulletin Intérieur*, no. 9, December 1945, pp. 9–10, quotation from p. 10.

[71] Ibid., pp. 11–14.

[72] *Le Populaire*, 19 February 1946, p. 2; *Libertés* (Paris), no. 117, 22 February 1946, p. 2.

[73] For a brief account of the National Assembly, including the details of divisions, see *Bulletin Intérieur*, no. 11, February–March 1946, pp. 3–4.

declaration was the first subject for consideration. It was open to the delegates to reject the proposed text in favour of the Charter of 1905 or an alternative formulation, but in the event they decided by 3,077 mandates to 768 (with 639 mandates attributed to absent federations) to take the committee's draft as the basis for discussion. The actual terms of the document then came under scrutiny but were successfully defended; a proposal by Mollet to delete the words 'action de classe' from the key sentence in the fourth paragraph was accepted without division[74] and a hostile amendment tabled by Roger Veillard, a deputy for Seine-et-Marne and a pre-war supporter of the Bataille Socialiste, was rejected by 2,549 mandates to 1,597, with 73 abstentions and 241 absent.

With some minor changes of wording, the declaration of principles was then approved. It remained very largely the text which Léon Blum had prepared in the summer of 1945, balanced and humanistic in its statement of the party's traditions. None of the amendments had diminished the force of the opening sentence, affirming that the party's aim was to liberate

la personne humaine de toutes les servitudes qui l'oppriment, et, par conséquent, d'assurer à l'homme, à la femme, à l'enfant, dans une société fondée sur l'égalité et la fraternité, le libre exercice de leurs droits et de leurs facultés naturelles.

This statement was amplified by the second paragraph, where it was claimed that the distinctive character of the party

est de faire dépendre la libération humaine de l'abolition du régime de la propriété capitaliste qui a divisé la société en classes nécessairement antagonistes . . .

However, various amendments had sharpened expressions of hostility in the latter part of the text. Thus, the third paragraph now juxtaposed a profession of tolerance with a commitment to secularism, with its anticlerical connotation:

Fermement attaché à la liberté de conscience et à la laïcité de l'Etat et de l'école, le Parti socialiste a pour action propre de grouper sans distinction de croyances philosophiques ou religieuses la masse des travailleurs de tous genres . . .

Similarly, the fourth paragraph, about the party's revolutionary mission, now concluded with the uncompromising statement that the party

[74] Jérôme Jaffré, 'La crise du Parti Socialiste et l'avènement de Guy Mollet (1944–1946)' (Mémoire présenté à l'Institut d'Etudes Politiques de l'Université de Paris, Paris, 1971), p. 208.

a toujours été et continue d'être un parti de lutte de classe, fondé sur l'organisation du monde du travail.[75]

From the perspective of Blum, Mayer and their colleagues, the main
battle had been won; the 1905 Charter, with its references to the earlier
resolutions of the Second International, had been replaced by a much
more confident and optimistic document which, for all its statements
about revolution, accepted that the party's essential mission was to
realize socialism within the framework of existing political institutions.

It was in the afternoon session that Mollet demonstrated his ability
to rally and direct the dissidents amongst the delegates. At his suggestion, the assembly agreed to reinstate, in a slightly amended form,
Article 1 of the pre-war rules,[76] which now read as follows:

Le Parti Socialiste est fondé sur les principes suivants: 'Entente et action
nationales et internationales des travailleurs, organisation politique et économique du prolétariat et du monde du travail en parti de classe pour la conquête
du pouvoir et la socialisation des moyens de production et d'échange, c'est-à-
dire la transformation de la société capitaliste en une société collectiviste ou
communiste.'

Blum had not included this article in his draft and the review committee
had not restored it but, when Mollet raised the matter, the loyalists
did nothing to prevent its reinstatement. Although they challenged the
retention of the word 'communiste' in the final clause of the article, a
motion to retain it was carried by 2,287 mandates to 1,848 with 57
abstentions and 268 absent.

This clash had been much more an aftermath of the earlier debate
on doctrine than an indication of the balance of opinion about the new
rules, and once the specific institutional arrangements proposed in the
latter came under scrutiny, it became clear that the extreme opposition
position epitomized by the demands of the Seine Federation would not
find favour. The set of rules which this session finally approved did not
differ essentially from that which had been approved by the extraordinary National Congress of November 1944. The National Council was
re-established but the Comité Directeur was left with more power than
the CAP had possessed. The National Council was to consist of one
delegate from each federation, as it had done under the 1929 rules; the
members of the Comité Directeur and of the Executive Delegation of
the parliamentary group were to be able to attend its meetings in a
consultative capacity; and it was to be convened by the Comité

---

[75] For the approved text, see *Bulletin Intérieur*, no. 11, February–March 1946, p. 4.
[76] See Jaffré, 'La crise du Parti Socialiste et l'avènement de Guy Mollet', p. 208.

Directeur every three months or whenever necessary. Its general powers were defined in the following terms:

Il assure les contacts entre le Comité directeur et l'ensemble du Parti. Il veille au respect des principes du Parti et des règles statutaires ainsi qu'à l'exécution des décisions des Congrès.

According to Jaffré, this apparent compromise – the restoration of the National Council but the retention of executive powers by the Comité Directeur – was the result of an agreement between Daniel Mayer and Guy Mollet, whereby the latter accepted that the National Council should simply have a monitoring role and that an extraordinary national congress should arbitrate in the case of conflict.[77] Another important change to the draft rules was the removal of the prohibition on the use of *le mandat impératif*, which therefore restored the right of federal congresses to bind their delegates. This was a setback for the leadership. On the other hand, an essential part of their administrative scheme was preserved when a move to restore proportional representation for the election of the party's central bodies was defeated by 3,044 mandates to 1,071 with 345 absent.[78]

The assembly had been faced with a very complex set of questions and it is quite clear that the line of division between the loyalists and the dissidents had varied considerably from issue to issue. The declaration had come under fire from revivalists who wanted to preserve the orthodoxy of the 1905 Charter, from revolutionary Marxists who disliked its humanistic and reformist overtones, and from néo-Guesdistes who were chiefly concerned to substitute the formula *lutte de classe* for the anodyne *de lutte et d'action de classe*. The draft rules had been attacked not only by libertarians, anxious to restore proportional representation for internal elections and to reduce the power of the Comité Directeur, but also by independent-minded federations which wanted to retain control over their delegates through *le mandat impératif* and to re-establish the National Council. Although, with so many fronts to defend, the central leaders had done well to preserve the essential features of both the declaration and the rules, the fluidity of the situation had enabled Mollet to enjoy considerable freedom of manoeuvre and to show clearly that he could represent a diverse opposition.

The extraordinary National Congress which was due to take place at Montrouge between 29 and 31 March was bound to produce another confrontation between the party's leaders and their critics. *Tripartisme*

---

[77] Ibid., p. 188.
[78] For the rules as finally approved, see *Bulletin Intérieur*, no. 11, February–March 1946, pp. 4–7.

304 B. D. Graham

had become a great burden for the party. The hope that the Gouin government, with Socialists in key positions, could somehow transform the terms of domestic politics had been disappointed; when he had taken office in January as Minister of National Economy and Finance, André Philip had found that the deficit on the 1946 budget would be about 319,000 million francs instead of the 198,000 million which had been predicted earlier[79] and his subsequent measures to increase taxes, remove subsidies and reduce spending had not remedied the situation. The French government was now relying upon the United States to supply financial aid and Léon Blum and Jean Monnet had been sent to Washington to explore the prospects for a loan. Thus, instead of becoming one of the great reforming administrations, comparable to the Blum government of 1936–7, the Gouin ministry had been forced to nurse a severely damaged economy and to bear all the unpopularity which that entailed. Anti-participationists in the SFIO could now claim with even more conviction than before that the party should not be involved in government under such circumstances.

Tripartisme had also been blamed by many in the party for restricting their representatives' freedom of action in the debates about the details of the draft Constitution Bill, which was still being considered by the Constituent Assembly and its Constitutional Committee at the end of March. Although the Communists, the Socialists and the MRP had reached broad agreement on the basic institutional structure of the proposed constitution, in which a national assembly, advised by an economic council and a council of the French union, would be capped by a council of ministers and a president, the MRP would have preferred more checks and balances within this framework than the other two parties were prepared to accept. Many of the public debates about the bill had centred on the draft declaration of rights which it was to include; when the Constituent Assembly had discussed the draft between 7 and 21 March, MRP speakers had argued that, as well as recognizing the rights of individuals, there should also be recognition of the rights of collectivities such as families and regional and professional groupings. MRP proposals intended to give the head of a family the right to choose a school for his children were pressed to a division and were amongst a group of amendments to the draft which were rejected by 321 votes to 222, with the MRP voting in the minority alongside conservative

[79] See *La Politique économique et financière d'André Philip et Albert Gazier, 26 janvier–2 juin 1946* (Éditions de la Liberté, Paris, 1946), p. 22. See also André Philip's report to the Finance Committee of the Constituent Assembly (*Le Monde*, 2 February 1946, p. 8) and an article by the Paris correspondent of the *Times* ('France facing hard facts', *The Times* (London), 19 February 1946, p. 5).

groups.[80] It was such incidents which continued to fuel anticlerical sentiment within the SFIO, which held firmly to the belief that the state should control the education of children.

By March 1946, therefore, the Socialist leaders faced a crisis of confidence within their party which was similar to that which their predecessors had encountered in the spring of 1938, before the Royan Congress. In the latter instance, the leaders had adopted a policy of *attentisme* in the hope that dissent and opposition would eventually subside to manageable levels, but the constraints of the political calendar prevented Daniel Mayer and his colleagues from adopting a similar approach in the spring of 1946. Under the law of 2 November 1945 which regulated the Constituent Assembly, the new constitution had to come into force within seven months of the first meeting of the assembly after approval by a referendum, and by March 1946 a complicated timetable had built up within these limits. First, a law to govern the elections to the new National Assembly would have to be formulated by the Committee of the Interior and approved by the Constituent Assembly; next, the Constituent Assembly would have to approve the Constitution Bill, which would then be submitted to referendum; and finally there would be elections to a new assembly, a National Assembly if the proposed constitution had been approved or a second Constituent Assembly elected under the Electoral Law of 17 August 1945, if the first Constitution Bill had been defeated at the referendum. At first the dates for these events had been provisional, but by 19 March 1946 the Cabinet had decided to aim at holding a referendum on 5 May and the elections on 2 June.[81]

The Comité Directeur's decision to hold the Montrouge Congress had been taken on 9 January 1946, at which time the intention had been to invite delegates to discuss the Constitution Bill, the party programme and electoral tactics as part of an orderly preparation for eventual elections to a National Assembly, but by March the whole schedule of events was being treated as a kind of escape route by which the party could break away from the entanglements of *tripartisme* and regain its freedom of expression and movement. It was easier for the leadership to tolerate this optimism than to ask the federations and their delegates to consider seriously the basic questions of strategy. However, the reluctance on the part of the federations to explore the full range of possible circumstances in which the party might find itself after the constitutional referendum and the elections left the General Secretary

[80] *JO* (*ANC I*), *Déb.*, 14 March 1946, pp. 775–80; 15 March 1946, pp. 808–26 and 841–2 (division).
[81] *Le Monde*, 20 March 1946, p. 4.

in a very difficult position. There were so many questions which had not been answered satisfactorily: if *tripartisme*, which implied a strategy of maintaining the Resistance front of Communists, Socialists and the MRP, was no longer acceptable to the party's membership, which of the alternative strategies (a popular front in association with the Communists, a centre alliance with the UDSR and the newly formed Rassemblement des Gauches Républicaines (RGR), and complete independence) was he to regard as the one best suited to the party's long-term interests? It was now clear that the Mollet group was aiming at the first of these alternatives, a Communist–Socialist alliance within a popular front, but it was difficult for Mayer to force that group to justify its preference openly when the loyalist forces themselves were so unsure of the merits of the existing policy.

In the absence of a searching debate about objectives, the question of general strategy was reduced to the much simpler question of electoral tactics. On 30 January, a majority of the members of the Comité Directeur had decided to recommend that in the elections the party should put forward purely Socialist lists in all departments, rather than joint lists with allied parties or groups,[82] and this policy was taken to represent the first step towards a strategy of independent action; it allowed members of quite different views to share the hope that an electoral surge would lift their party well clear of all its rivals. At the same time, Léon Blum was taking the line that

il sera nécessaire que nous ayons une position qui cette fois se distingue claire-ment, se distingue nettement, sans confusion possible, et des communistes d'un côté, et du M.R.P. de l'autre. Nous représentons, nous, le socialisme démo-cratique, et nous avons à nous montrer au pays comme étant par excellence le Parti qui incarne à la fois le socialisme et la démocratie.[83]

The Montrouge Congress opened on Friday 29 March with 370 delegates in attendance, representing 97 federations and bearing 4,485 mandates. The first main item on the agenda was the question of electoral strategy, and this should have provided the leadership with an opportunity to obtain virtual unanimity around a proposal to prepare exclusively Socialist lists for the general elections. However, Yves Dechézelles, present as one of the delegates of the Seine Federation, moved that the subject should be deferred until after the discussion of the party's programme and of the draft Constitution Bill. Daniel Mayer spoke against the motion but when it was put to the vote it was carried

---

[82] *Bulletin Intérieur*, special number, February 1946, p. 2.
[83] 'Communication de Léon Blum au Comité Directeur et au groupe parlementaire réunis le 5 février 1946', in Blum, *L'Oeuvre de Léon Blum, 1945–1947*, p. 266.

by a comfortable majority.[84] The details of the division are given in Table 29.

Although the motion had been justified on procedural grounds, the main object of the manoeuvre had been to demonstrate that the party's leadership lacked support, and in this it succeeded: of the 95 federal delegations which were present for the division, 64 had voted for the proposal (63 *en bloc* and one by a majority) and only 26 against it (25 *en bloc* and one by a majority), there being five bloc abstentions. The leaders had been supported by about half of the largest federations, including Nord, Bouches-du-Rhône, Gironde, Dordogne, Gard and Haute-Vienne, but they had been deserted by the majority of the smaller provincial units. The Pas-de-Calais, Seine and Seine-et-Oise Federations now formed the vanguard of what was becoming a formidable opposition movement.

The fuel for this movement was an intense anti-bureaucratic sentiment directed chiefly against the Comité Directeur; for example, the resolution submitted to the congress by the Haute-Garonne Federation had claimed that the party

a été dirigé par un Comité Directeur qui, en dehors des erreurs qu'il a pu commettre sur le plan politique, en dehors des méthodes qu'il a employées et qui n'ont pas toujours été inspirées par le respect de la règle démocratique, a été incapable, sur le plan administratif, de gérer le Parti d'une manière satisfaisante et d'en faire un redoutable instrument de combat.[85]

In the debate which now ensued, these complaints were linked with insinuations that alternative strategies had not been explored and that failure was due to human error rather than circumstances. According to Jean-Pierre Bloch (Aisne), the choice was a simple one:

Si nous voulons regrouper le pays, c'est en affirmant cette volonté que le gouvernement ne sera plus un gouvernement tripartite, mais que le parti est décidé à tout faire pour que le gouvernement de demain soit un gouvernement de la classe ouvrière.[86]

Guy Mollet made the familiar charge that the party should not be helping to govern the bourgeois state:

Il faut que nos représentants et que nos ministres ne soient pas simplement de bons administrateurs, ce qu'ils sont généralement, et nous devons nous féliciter presque dans tous les cas, du choix des hommes et de leur compétence.

[84] See *Le Populaire*, 30 March 1946, p. 2; *Le Monde*, 30 March 1946, p. 8.
[85] Motion on general policy from the Haute-Garonne Federation, in documents relating to the extraordinary National Congress, Montrouge, 29–31 March 1946 (consulted at SFIO headquarters, 12 Cité Malesherbes, 1960).
[86] Minutes of the extraordinary National Congress, Montrouge, 29–31 March 1946, p. 106 (consulted at SFIO headquarters, 12 Cité Malesherbes, 1960).

Table 29. *SFIO, extraordinary National Congress, Montrouge, 29 March 1946: division on proposal by the Seine Federation to hold the discussion on electoral tactics after the discussion of the party programme and the draft Constitution Bill*

Federations	Mandates: For proposal no.	%	Against proposal no.	%	Abstentions no.	%	Absent no.	%	Totals no.
Bouches-du-Rhône			177	100.0					177
Gironde			130	100.0					130
Meurthe-et-Moselle			43	100.0					43
Nord			327	100.0					327
Pas-de-Calais	309	100.0							309
Seine	216	100.0							216
Seine-et-Oise	166	100.0							166
Haute-Vienne			76	100.0					76
Others	[2,191]	72.0	686	22.6	[133]	4.4	31	1.0	[3,041]
Totals	2,882	64.3	1,439	32.1	133	3.0	31	0.7	4,485

Source: Bulletin Intérieur (Paris), no. 12, April 1946, p. 3. For details of adjustments, see the appendix (pp. 402–3, n. 10).

Il ne suffit pas qu'ils soient de bons administrateurs; il est nécessaire qu'ils soient en même temps des militants socialistes agissant dans le gouvernement, s'entourant de militants socialistes (*Appl.*) de telle façon qu'ils ne soient pas simplement les administrateurs d'un régime capitaliste qui crève, mais les préparateurs d'un régime socialiste qui va naître.[87]

Mollet's prestige in the party was now considerable; one commentator observed that the congress, had it had the power to do so, would have made him a member of the Comité Directeur, if not General Secretary, then and there.[88] In the event, the congress adopted the principle of having exclusively Socialist lists in the next elections,[89] and there the matter of general strategy was allowed to rest.

The SFIO thus entered the potentially dangerous period of April–May 1946 without a clear understanding between leaders and members about what should be done in the event of certain contingencies, and this weakness was soon exposed in the final stages of the constitution-making process. In the end, the MRP decided that the institutional arrangements specified in the Constitution Bill had left too much power at the disposal of the National Assembly, and that the countervailing bodies (the President, the Council of the French Union, the Economic Council and the High Court) would be unable to check its actions sufficiently. On 19 April, when the Constituent Assembly adopted the bill by 309 votes to 249, the MRP voted with the Radicals, the UDSR and the right in the minority while the Socialists and the Communists formed the bulk of the majority.[90] The bill was immediately seen by many people as a document which reflected the views of the Socialists and the Communists, and an indication of their intention to convert the French state into a *régime d'assemblée*.

The SFIO's General Secretary was forced to absorb the strain of this apparent change in the alliance pattern. On the evening of 19 April, after the division on the bill, some Socialist deputies from the provinces had informed Daniel Mayer that their federations or branches intended to organize joint meetings with the Communist Party. Acting on his own authority, he had sent a telegram to all federations asking them to begin the campaign immediately for the constitutional referendum on 5 May but placing an absolute ban on joint campaigning with the Communist Party.[91] On 23 April his action was approved by the Comité

---

[87] Ibid., p. 123.
[88] Jacques Fauvet, 'Indépendance et rigueur du Parti Socialiste', *Le Monde*, 31 March–1 April 1946, p. 2.
[89] *Bulletin Intérieur*, no. 12, April 1946, p. 3.
[90] *JO (ANC I), Déb.*, 19 April 1946, pp. 2081–2.
[91] *CD Minutes*, II, 23 April 1946, p. 195.

Directeur, which also turned down an invitation from the Central Committee of the Communist Party to participate in a common referendum campaign.[92] Approval of the Constitution Bill would at least have freed the SFIO from this uncomfortable position, but the referendum on 5 May resulted in the rejection of the bill by a majority of 52.82 per cent of the valid votes. Constitution-making had now to begin all over again.

The general elections, already scheduled for 2 June 1946, became a means of electing the members for a second constituent assembly. The Socialist leaders used the campaign period to separate themselves from the Communists and to indicate that they were now willing to accept many of the MRP's ideas about constitutional arrangements. Writing in *Le Populaire*, Daniel Mayer maintained that the nation did not want Maurice Thorez to be the next President of the Provisional Government and implied that a Communist-led administration was out of the question:

on ne gouverne pas un pays contre la moitié de la nation; l'hégémonie bolchevique dans un gouvernement donnerait cette impression . . . [93]

André Le Troquer was more blunt: at Moulins on 23 May he claimed that Thorez had indeed deserted when he went to the Soviet Union at the end of 1939 and that to call for him to take power was to serve the cause of Russia.[94] Regarding the constitutional issues, Félix Gouin spoke of the need for an effective upper house, for a president with prestige and authority, and for an independent judiciary,[95] all of which were in accord with the views of the MRP.

The results of the elections of 2 June came as a great disappointment to the Socialists. Whereas the MRP had expanded its share of the valid votes in metropolitan France from 24.40 to 28.11 per cent and the Communists had increased theirs marginally from 25.99 to 26.15, the Socialists' percentage had fallen from 23.59 to 21.06 between the elections of 21 October 1945 and this poll.[96] The SFIO had in fact lost ground in all the regions of metropolitan France except Normandy and

[92] Ibid., pp. 195–9: on the background, see *Le Monde*, 23 April 1946, p. 2.
[93] Mayer, 'Et d'abord, mises au point!', *Le Populaire*, 16 May 1946, p. 1.
[94] *L'Année politique 1946* (Editions du Grand Siècle, Paris, 1947), p. 142. See also *Le Monde*, 24 May 1946, p. 2; *Le Populaire*, 24 May 1946, p. 2.
[95] Speech on 27 May 1946 (*Le Populaire*, 28 May 1946, p. 1).
[96] These percentages are for aggregate party votes derived from analyses of constituency returns for the elections of 21 October 1945 (see p. 287, fn. 40 above) and for those of 2 June 1946 (*JO* (*ANC II*), *Déb.*, 12 June 1946, pp. 2497–528: 13 June 1946, pp. 2533–5; 19 June 1946, p. 2549; 26 June 1946, pp. 2574–6; 11 July 1946, pp. 2666–7. These returns were checked and corrected against those given in Husson, *Elections et référendums des 21 octobre 1945, 5 mai et 2 juin 1946*).

Brittany, where increases may have been due to its revived reputation for anticlericalism. One reason for the loss of support may have been the shift from the policy (which had been applied in several constituencies for the elections of 21 October 1945) of joint lists with the UDSR, to the policy of independent Socialist lists wherever possible. Indeed, Jacques Fauvet has suggested that where joint lists had been tried in the earlier poll and abandoned on this occasion, electors had switched their allegiance from the Socialists to the lists of the MRP or, less often, to those of the RGR.

Le socialisme de 1946 ne leur a plus paru être celui qu'ils espéraient avoir découvert en 1945. Sa rupture avec les éléments socialisants de la Résistance semble bien avoir été une lourde faute du point de vue électoral. Et l'affirmation un peu tardive de son originalité à l'égard du communisme n'a pu, dans le même temps, compenser les déceptions et finalement la désaffection des électeurs nouvellement venus au socialisme en 1945 soit par la Résistance, soit par l'attrait que pouvait exercer un socialisme apparemment plus attaché aux valeurs humaines, voire spirituelles.[97]

The SFIO responded cautiously to the situation created by the election result. Meeting on 9 June, the National Council rejected a motion against participation in the next government. However, while authorizing the Comité Directeur and the parliamentary group to take part in negotiations with other parties, it stated that the new government should adjust wages, salaries, and retirement and other pensions to take account of essential needs, and should convene a conference to consider basic economic issues.[98] It also approved a note of guidance for the Comité Directeur and the parliamentary group which proposed that members of parties other than the SFIO should take charge of the Presidency, the Ministries of National Economy, Finance, Food, and Labour, and of any agency responsible for fixing prices but stipulated that the Minister of Education should be a Socialist, or at least a secularist (*un laïque*). The same note called for prior agreement on a government programme, for the rapid adoption of a constitution, and for the holding of a general election by October 1946 at the latest.[99]

Despite such efforts to limit its responsibilities, the Socialist Party accepted the continuation of *tripartisme*, at least for the term of the second Constituent Assembly. The parliamentary groups of the three

---

[97] Jacques Fauvet, *Les Partis politiques dans la France actuelle* (Editions du 'Monde', Paris, 1947), p. 74. See also François Goguel, 'Géographie du référendum et des élections de mai–juin 1946', *Esprit*, 14, 7 (July 1946), pp. 27–54.

[98] *Bulletin Intérieur*, no. 13, April–May 1946, p. 12.

[99] Ibid., no. 14, June 1946, p. 2.

allies numbered Communists 143, Socialists 127 (not including one *apparenté*) and MRP 165 in a house of 586 members[100] and their combined total of 435 deputies still constituted by far the largest and most stable majority for the tasks ahead. The MRP took the initiative in forming a new government and one of its leaders, Georges Bidault, was elected as President of the Provisional Government on 19 June. He then formed a ministry which took office on 23 June, in which he retained the Foreign Affairs portfolio for himself and allocated the main economic posts to members of his party: Robert Schuman became Minister of Finance and François de Menthon Minister of National Economy. The Socialist ministers in the new administration were Félix Gouin (a Vice-President), Edouard Depreux (Interior), François Tanguy-Prigent (Agriculture), Marcel-Edmond Naegelen (Education), Jules Moch (Public Works and Transport) and Marius Moutet (Colonies).

The Socialists, who considered that they had been unfairly blamed for past failures of policy, had settled for fewer posts of importance than they had held in either of the two preceding governments and this loss of power, coupled with the electoral setback of 2 June, increased the unrest felt by members of the party's branches and federations. The disenchantment was all the greater because their historical mythology had persuaded them that their potential constituency was, if not the majority of the population, at least a substantial portion of it. Where history was concerned, they were fixed on the idea that the Popular Front had been checked, both in 1937 and again in 1938, by the Senate, aided and abetted by the machinations of financial and business interests, when the reality was that the refusal of the Radicals to accept further reforms had been a reasonably faithful reflection of the individualism and economic conservatism of the mass of the peasantry and the middle classes. The Socialists were equally prone to believe that the Resistance movement, as an expression of social and economic aspirations rather than as an anti-German or anti-Vichy phenomenon, had been socialist in nature and widely supported throughout the country. These potent myths were at one with their theory that it was from unified social movements that electoral and parliamentary majorities of the left would arise, a theory which prevented them from appreciating fully the value of cultivating specific sectional interests amongst the workers, the peasants and the middle classes.

Instead of asking hard questions about why the MRP had been able to consolidate and extend its electoral support and why the Communists

---

[100] From a list of group memberships, as on 16 June 1946, in *JO, LD*, 16 June 1946, pp. 5338–9.

were continuing to flourish in both working-class and peasant areas, the Socialists explained their predicament as a function of *tripartisme*, complaining that they had been obliged, by a sense of responsibility, to accept duties which were thankless. They felt that they had been forced to effect a compromise to meet other parties' views about the constitution and that, during the period of the Gouin government, they had been placed in the unenviable position of having to oppose wage and salary increases without being able to freeze prices. Consequently, they had had to confront rather than represent the discontent of workers and civil servants. Such a line of reasoning enabled them to believe that once the adoption of a constitution had put an end to *tripartisme* they would find the long-awaited electoral support which had eluded them and that they would then once more be in a position to control the making and unmaking of governments.

Sadly, they failed to realize that an alternative and realistic strategy was within the party's grasp. The notion of a planned and mixed economy could have been developed into a coherent and systematic programme by leaders as able as André Philip and Jules Moch. Instead, the SFIO remained bound to doctrinaire schemes for widespread nationalization, justified as a prefiguration of a collectivized economy, and to inflationary and redistributionist ideas in the field of public finance. In its original form, the declaration of principles drafted by Blum had invited the party to become more inclusive in its social attachments, and more open to influences which would have driven it in a social-democratic direction, a possibility identified at the time (usually pejoratively) as movement towards the model of a *parti travailliste*. The inhibitions against such a change were strong; the SFIO's loyalty to the CNR's programme of 15 March 1944, which despite its collectivist bias was expressed in very general terms, tied the hands of those in the party who were inclined to develop a range of policies to deal with the postwar situation; and at all levels of the organization there was a strong belief that the party's purpose was to represent the working class as a whole rather than a broad span of interests extending through the peasantry and the urban middle classes.

The idea that the SFIO could somehow escape from the constraints of *tripartisme* was exploited in several ways. First, it allowed the anti-participationist lobby to argue that the party's best means of freeing itself from the alliance was by returning to opposition and gathering its strength for a subsequent drive for power. On the other hand, this notion of escape permitted the revolutionary left to claim that the way forward was not independence but a shift in allegiance, to be achieved by doctrinal *redressement*, a break with the MRP and closer collaboration with the Communist Party. Both these proposals were néo-Guesdiste in inspiration, but they emphasized different themes in the Guesdiste tradition. Even so, the challenge which they posed to the party's leaders was formidable. Unless those leaders could develop a social-democratic strategy and thereby broaden the social range of the party's membership and support, they would find themselves dealing with a powerful and complex wave of néo-Guesdiste opposition within the organization.

That opposition was already gathering force. We have noted the growth of dissent within the parliamentary group, the capture by former Pivertistes of the Seine Federation, the friability of loyalist support at both the National Assembly of 24 February and the extraordinary National Congress of 29–31 March, and the acceptance of Guy Mollet as the spokesman of the discontented. Had the Constitution Bill been approved by the referendum of 5 May, and had the party greatly increased its vote in the general elections of 2 June, the revolt might have dissipated. Now it had to be dealt with by other means. All that the leaders could do in the short term was to offer assurance that this time round a satisfactory constitution bill would be produced, that it would be approved in the subsequent referendum, that the party would do well in the next elections, and that, in the meantime, it would limit to the very minimum its responsibilities within the Bidault government. It was easy for their opponents, scorning this line of reasoning, to argue that to restore the party's fortunes more drastic measures were needed.

The 38th National Congress, Paris, 29 August–1 September 1946

We have now reached the threshold of the dramatic events which occurred at the SFIO's 38th National Congress in Paris between 29 August and 1 September 1946. On the first day of this meeting the *rapport moral* (annual report) submitted by the General Secretary, Daniel Mayer, was rejected by a two-thirds majority. At once Mayer, speaking on behalf of the senior officials involved, said that they recognized the implications of the vote but would continue to deal with routine business until a new bureau had been appointed. Negotiations behind the scenes eventually produced a measure of agreement for a policy resolution and, on 4 September, a newly elected Comité Directeur appointed Guy Mollet as General Secretary. In this section, then, we watch the wave of unrest which finally broke against the Paris Congress.

Inevitably, comparisons will be made between this crisis and the one which preceded the Royan Congress of June 1938. On that occasion

Paul Faure had played a major role in the conflicts which built up around the congress, whereas Daniel Mayer was anxious to preserve the neutrality of his office and not become the protagonist of a particular point of view. Again, while Faure had been prepared to meet trouble in advance and to do battle with his chief opponents before the congress began, Mayer – apart from making one fruitless effort to parley with Mollet and his group – chose to wait until the congress before inviting a confrontation. However, such comparisons are useful only against an understanding of the extent to which the party's organizational structure in 1946 resembled that which had obtained in the early months of 1938. We need, then, to form an impression of the party's membership and the characteristics of its federations in the immediate post-war period.

By December 1945, the SFIO had re-established 97 federations, 90 of which represented metropolitan departments and seven of which represented overseas departments and territories. Membership recruitment and maintenance still depended upon the pre-war methods of issuing both a permanent card and an annual card to which the monthly subscription stamps could be fixed. By 31 December 1945 the number of annual cards dispatched to federations by the central Treasurer totalled 339,005[101] compared with the pre-war peak of 286,604 in the calendar year 1937. These figures may be taken to represent levels of maximum membership – the number of people whose interest in the party extended at least to the act of enrolment or re-enrolment – although allowance must be made for the fact that not all the cards sent out to federations might actually have been assigned to members. The total number of monthly stamps sold in the course of 1945 came to 2,651,630, an average of 7.82 stamps for each annual card, compared with the 1937 figures of 2,476,988 stamp-sales or an average of 8.64 stamps per annual card. These figures provide some indication of the degree of continuing commitment amongst recruits and by the most stringent test, that of dividing stamp-sales totals by 12, we obtain a minimum membership of 220,969 in 1945. The number of national mandates at the disposal of federations was largely determined by this measure; each federation had one mandate by right, but additional mandates were allocated for every 25 units in its minimum membership. Then, in January 1946, in order to reduce the number of delegates eligible to attend national plenary meetings, the Comité Directeur decided to allocate one mandate for every 50 units.[102] By the time of the Paris Congress,

---

[101] Calculated from the figures by federation presented in 'Tableau comparatif des cartes et timbres 1945–1946', in Parti Socialiste (SFIO), 39ᵉ Congrès National, Lyon, 14–17 août 1947, *Rapports* (Librairie du Parti, Paris, [1947]), pp. 129–30.

[102] *Bulletin Intérieur*, no. 10, January 1946, p. 3

the total number of mandates held by the federations was 4,485, of which sizeable shares were possessed by the six largest units – 327 by Nord, 309 by Pas-de-Calais, 216 by Seine, 177 by Bouches-du-Rhône, 166 by Seine-et-Oise and 130 by Gironde.

As in 1938, so in 1946 the politics of the federations formed the essential context for the National Congress; therefore, before turning to the preparations for the Paris meeting, it will be useful to look at post-war conditions in the eight federations which were reviewed in Chapter 2. Of these eight, it was the Nord Federation which most closely resembled its pre-war counterpart. Its strength at the end of 1945, namely 21,600 annual cards and a minimum membership of 16,333, was only slightly below the level it had reached at the end of 1938, when it had had 23,800 annual cards and a minimum membership of 19,167.[103] In the post-war general elections, Socialist candidates in the constituencies of the Nord Department continued to win significant shares of the valid votes – 29.04 per cent in the poll of 21 October 1945 and 28.78 per cent in that of 2 June 1946; on both occasions seven Socialist deputies were returned to the Constituent Assembly from the department.[104] The federation's pre-war leader, Jean Lebas, had played a major part in the Resistance movement in the Nord and had founded an underground newspaper, L'Homme Libre, before being arrested by the Gestapo in May 1941 and sentenced to three years' hard labour in Sonnenburg, where he died in March 1944.[105] He was succeeded as leader of the federation by his former lieutenant, Augustin Laurent, who was ably supported by Victor Provo, the Mayor of Roubaix. Under Laurent's direction the federation continued to embody the values which it had represented in the pre-war party – social democracy, anti-bolshevism, discipline, and loyalty to the central leadership; without its consistent support, Léon Blum and Daniel Mayer would have been in a much weaker position in the summer of 1946.

On the other hand, the Pas-de-Calais Federation, whose course had conformed so closely to that of the Nord Federation in the 1930s, had now moved in a different direction under the stewardship of Guy Mollet. The unit's pre-war leader, Raoul Evrard, who had been Treasurer of the underground Socialist Party, had died shortly after his arrest

[103] In this and the following studies of federations, membership figures are minima (the number of stamps sold divided by 12) and are taken from the following sources: for 1938 data, Parti Socialiste (SFIO), 36ᵉ Congrès National, Nantes, 27–30 mai 1939, Rapports (Librairie Populaire, Paris, 1939), pp. 142–3; and for 1945 data, Parti Socialiste (SFIO), 39ᵉ Congrès National, Lyon, 14–17 août 1947, Rapports, pp. 129–30.
[104] In this and the following studies of federations, the electoral data have been compiled from constituency returns given in JO (ANC I), Déb. and JO (ANC II), Déb. (for details see fn. 40 and fn. 96 above).
[105] Jean Piat, Jean Lebas (Parti Socialiste (SFIO), Paris, 1964), pp. 20–2.

by the Gestapo[106] and its former secretary, André Pantigny, had also died after being deported to Germany.[107] The break in the succession had made it easy for Mollet to assert himself after the Liberation; we have seen how quickly he was able to establish himself as the spokesman for dissident elements within the party's parliamentary group and he was equally successful at building up support within his own federation. Although he belonged to its leadership group and was a member of its Executive Committee, he tended to act as a free agent beyond the direct control of its bureaucracy, which was headed in 1946 by Camille Delabre, the federal secretary. At times he behaved as though he were still an activist, at others as a sober member of the leadership. At the Federal Congress at Béthune on 17 February 1946, he called for 'le raidissement de la politique du Parti et une réforme des organismes centraux', spoke of the gap which separated the Socialists from the MRP, and emphasized the need for *l'unité ouvrière*, that is, for a fusion of the Socialist and Communist Parties, subject to certain conditions, his motion being carried by 9,626 mandates as against the 3,169 for a rival text proposed by Marcel Dupuich.[108] By contrast, at the next federal congress, which was held on 24 March 1946 to deal with administrative matters, he gave a well-considered account of the progress of the Constitution Bill.[109] As Mayor of Arras, Mollet was in a position to appeal to a large and diverse urban audience, as was his ally and fellow deputy, Henri Henneguelle, the Mayor of Boulogne, and together they were involved in shifting the party's social base away from its former dependence on the mining basin and drawing in other sections of local society. The Pas-de-Calais Federation in 1945 remained one of the strongest units in the party, with 24,150 annual cards and a minimum membership of 15,417, compared with the 1938 figures of 13,600 annual cards and a minimum membership of 9,583. In elections in the department, the Socialists' share of the vote in the poll of 21 October 1945, 37.04 per cent, was well above that of 1936, but it declined in the elections of 2 June 1946 to 31.35 per cent of the valid votes. On both occasions, five Socialist deputies were returned from the department.

The Bouches-du-Rhône Federation had also undergone changes between the Royan and the Paris Congresses, largely because of events which had taken place in the city of Marseille before and during the

---

[106] Daniel Mayer, *Les Socialistes dans la Résistance: souvenirs et documents* (Presses Universitaires de France, Paris, 1968), pp. 109 and 144.

[107] Marc Sadoun, *Les Socialistes sous l'Occupation: résistance et collaboration* (Presses de la Fondation Nationale des Sciences Politiques, Paris, 1982), p. 234.

[108] *L'Espoir* (Lens), no. 76, 24 February 1946, pp. 1 and 2.

[109] Ibid., no. 81, 31 March 1946, pp. 1 and 3. See also Jean Vavasseur-Desperriers, 'Guy Mollet et les militants socialistes du Pas-de-Calais de 1944 à 1958', in Ménager *et al.*, *Guy Mollet: un camarade en République*, pp. 33–58, especially pp. 34–7.

war. After there had been reports of serious failings in the management of its affairs, the city had been placed under the control of a specially appointed administrator by a presidential decree of 20 March 1939[110] and the Socialist leader, Henri Tasso, had seen his office reduced from that of Mayor to President of the Municipal Council. Having been elected to the Senate in October 1938, he had voted in favour of the granting of full powers to Marshal Pétain at the National Assembly on 10 July 1940, and had then virtually retired from public life until his death in 1944. His lieutenant, Pierre Ferri-Pisani, had been arrested in April 1943 and deported to Buchenwald,[111] where he was still being held at the end of the war. The collapse of the Tasso regime had provided an opportunity for new leaders to come forward, and after Liberation Gaston Defferre tried to take charge of the party's units in Marseille.

Defferre soon showed himself to be a political manager who was both energetic and resourceful. Born in 1910 into a Protestant family, he had become a lawyer in Marseille in the 1930s, joining the SFIO in 1933 and becoming the secretary of its branch in the city's 10th canton in 1935. During the war he played an active part in the Resistance as one of the main figures in the Brutus network and was a member of the executive of the underground Socialist Party from 1943 until Liberation. Returning to Marseille as President of its Municipal Delegation, he took over the *Mairie* on 23 August 1944, shortly after the departure of the Germans, and, with the help of Francis Leenhardt and Horace Manicacci, steadily consolidated his position. One of his first moves was to appropriate the premises of the *Petit Provençal*, the owners of which were alleged to have been collaborators, and to bring out his own newspaper, *Le Provençal*, with *Le Soir* as its evening companion. After heading a successful list of candidates in the municipal elections of April–May 1945, he became President of the Municipal Council, and he continued to keep up his contacts in Paris through his membership of the Provisional Consultative Assembly and of the SFIO's Comité Directeur.[112]

The first setback for Defferre occurred in the cantonal elections of 23 and 30 September 1945, in which the Socialists polled well in the Bouches-du-Rhône Department as a whole but poorly in Marseille itself, where the Communists won 10 of the 12 seats. Defferre then sent

[110] *JO, LD*, 21 March 1939, pp. 3671–3.
[111] See Georges Marion, *Gaston Defferre* (Albin Michel, Paris, 1989), pp. 130–2.
[112] See ibid., pp. 21–123; David S. Bell, 'Politics in Marseilles since World War II with special reference to the political role of Gaston Defferre' (D. Phil. thesis, University of Oxford, 1978), pp. 1–21; obituary article on Defferre by Jean-Marie Colombani and Patrick Jarreau, *Le Monde*, 8 May 1986, p. 9.

an open letter to the Prefect of the department offering to resign both as President of the Municipal Council and as a member of that body, expressing his concern to respect the wishes of the people of Marseille. Neither offer of resignation was taken up immediately but 17 Socialist members of the Municipal Council refused to follow his example by offering theirs; another resigned from the party altogether.[113] By this stage, Ferri-Pisani had returned from Buchenwald and had begun to rebuild his support within the party. He came into direct conflict with Defferre over the composition of the joint SFIO–UDSR list which the federation had decided to enter for the elections of 21 October 1945 in the first Bouches-du-Rhône constituency. The dispute concerned the ranking of candidates in the joint list and when the national committee for liaison between the SFIO and the UDSR decided that it should be headed by Defferre (SFIO), Leenhardt (UDSR) and Ferri-Pisani (SFIO) in that order, Ferri-Pisani and his supporters complained that the second placing should have been his. The question then came before the unit's Federal Council, which decided that the sequence should be Defferre, Ferri-Pisani and Leenhardt, whereupon Defferre requested that the situation in the federation be considered at an extraordinary meeting of the SFIO's Comité Directeur. This was held in Paris on the afternoon of Thursday 4 October 1945; at it, Daniel Mayer gave an account of the conflict and Defferre sketched in the background, drawing attention to what had happened in Marseille since 1939. Saying that he had consulted both Léon Blum and the secretary of the federation, Félix Gouin, who were agreed that the federation should be dissolved, Defferre recommended that this should be done

pour éviter des critiques de la population qui, dans le cas contraire, verrait un retour aux mœurs politiques d'avant-guerre.

Deciding that the federation would best be reconstructed, the Comité Directeur authorized Félix Gouin to carry out the task; it also approved lists of candidates for both the constituencies in the department, specifying that the first three places in the list for the first constituency should go to Defferre, Leenhardt and Irène Laure. Ferri-Pisani's name had now been dropped altogether.[114]

According to a press report, 10 of the 12 Socialist branches in Marseille then refused to ratify the official list for the first constituency, approving instead a dissident list headed by Ferri-Pisani.[115] Defferre,

---

[113] *Le Monde*, 20 October 1945, p. 3.
[114] *CD Minutes*, II, 4 October 1945, pp. 26–9, quotation from p. 27.
[115] *Le Monde*, 12 October 1945, p. 4.

openly stating that the central issue was one of political morality, referred to:

Quelques éléments qui essayaient de rétablir à Marseille les mœurs politiques d'avant guerre, que je m'étais moi-même efforcé de bannir de la ville depuis la Libération, se sont élevés contre la décision du comité directeur et ont fait une liste dissidente.

He claimed that the Comité Directeur had dissolved the federation

non pas en raison de l'existence de tendances opposées, mais parce que notre parti rénové et rajeuni entend ne pas laisser refleurir dans nos sections et dans notre fédération les mœurs dissolues d'avant guerre.[116]

The elections of 21 October 1945 in the first Bouches-du-Rhône constituency were at once a victory and a defeat for Defferre. He had the satisfaction of seeing the SFIO–UDSR list poll 25.37 per cent of the votes and win three of the nine seats at stake while Ferri-Pisani's dissident list secured only 6.08 per cent of the votes and won no seats, but he was also faced with the fact that the Communists had obtained 41.72 per cent of the votes and four seats.[117]

Whereas at the Liberation Defferre had been an unknown quantity, this complicated crisis had revealed his intentions clearly. By his offer to resign from the municipal presidency, he had shown that he was prepared to fight the Communists in Marseille and would not accept a local popular front; thus, he placed himself outside the boundaries of the Mollet group as far as general strategies were concerned. Moreover, his depiction of the conflict with Ferri-Pisani as being part of a larger struggle against the revival of pre-war political values was evidence of his determination to avoid clientelism and to adopt an open, public-spirited style of municipal politics. He had the advantage of support from the central leadership, and his control of the *Provençal* gave him the means of reaching beyond the narrow audience of the party faithful, despite the efforts of his opponents to suggest that he and Horace Manicacci were simply building up their own organization under the pretext of reconstructing the federation.[118] There is no doubt that the results he achieved were impressive; by the end of 1945, the reconstructed federation had distributed 9,100 annual cards and had recruited a minimum membership of 8,800.

Defferre did not withdraw his letter of resignation as President of the Municipal Council and his Communist rival, Jean Cristofol, suc-

---

[116] Letter from Defferre, ibid., 17 October 1945, p. 7. On the background, see Marion, *Gaston Defferre*, pp. 125–47.

[117] *JO (ANC I)*, *Déb.*, 6 November 1945, p. 11.

[118] See the text of a pamphlet reproduced as an appendix to Bell, 'Politics in Marseilles since World War II', pp. 403–4.

ceeded to that post on 28 January 1946. Meanwhile, Félix Gouin had become President of the Provisional Government in Paris, and Defferre was appointed to serve under him as a Secretary of State. In this capacity he experienced at first hand the failure of the Gouin government to restore the economy and to persuade the Constituent Assembly to produce a constitutional settlement which would satisfy the MRP as well as the Communists and Socialists. In the elections of 2 June 1946, the Socialist vote in the Bouches-du-Rhône fell in keeping with the general decline, from 25.37 to 24.33 per cent in the first constituency and from 41.40 to 37.28 per cent in the second, Defferre being returned to the Constituent Assembly from the former and Gouin from the latter. Of the two men, Gouin was closer to the central leaders while Defferre remained relatively uncommitted, not likely to associate himself with the Mollet group but by no means an uncritical loyalist.

As for the Gironde Department, after the Liberation the Socialists there tried to win control of Bordeaux by building upon the goodwill derived from their work in the Resistance. As in Marseille, they were faced with the need to establish a new leadership. The federation's pre-war guide, Robert Vielle, had thrown in his lot with Paul Faure but some continuity with the federation of the 1930s was provided by two former Bordeaux deputies, Jean-Fernand Audeguil and Gaston Cabannes. Audeguil, who was a member of the Provisional Consultative Assembly, had been chosen to head the administration of Bordeaux after Liberation, and he became Mayor of the city after leading a broadly based list of candidates to victory in the municipal elections of April–May 1945. The party's position in the region was further strengthened when it won 35.76 per cent of the votes in the Gironde constituency in the elections of 21 October 1945 and returned four deputies (who included Audeguil and Cabannes) to the first Constituent Assembly. It was at about this time that Defferre embarked on the strategy of defying the Communists and bidding for the centre support which was ultimately to ensure his dominance of the political system in Marseille, but in Bordeaux Audeguil made the mistake of trying to hold together a very wide front extending from the Communists to the conservatives. He soon found himself in difficulty; the Communists began to attack the employers, the latter took exception to the action of the tripartite governments in Paris, and there were clashes over various aspects of municipal policy.[119] Local support for the SFIO now began to weaken and in the elections of 2 June 1946 its share of the vote in

---

[119] See Jacques Lagroye, *Société et politique: J. Chaban-Delmas à Bordeaux* (Pedone, Paris, 1973), pp. 52–5.

the Gironde constituency fell sharply to 27.98 per cent and its representation in the second Constituent Assembly was reduced to three deputies.

Although none of the Socialist deputies from Gironde had signed Mollet's February *Appel*, their federation was also showing signs of frustration and at the National Council meeting of 9 June 1946 it joined with the Alpes-Maritimes Federation in putting forward a motion against participation in future governments.[120] There was a real danger that the Gironde unit, one of the most powerful in the party organization and one which had registered a distribution of 8,200 annual cards and achieved a minimum membership of 6,458 by the end of 1945, would drift into dissidence, blaming its local setbacks on the policy compromises involved in *tripartisme* and the lack of firm guidance from the Comité Directeur.

We come now to the Seine Federation which, while it had always been one of the largest in the pre-war SFIO, had been unable before the war to establish itself as the dominant force in the local politics of the capital and its outer suburbs. Not only had it lost support in the working-class areas of Paris, but the rancour of its internal disputes had frightened away many lower-middle-class people; except in one or two outer municipalities such as Sceaux, it had shown little ambition to cultivate broad support and offer itself as a party of local government. After Liberation, therefore, with Gérard Jaquet as its federal secretary, it made a determined effort to show that it could compete on even terms with the Communists, that it was interested in taking power at the local level, and that it wanted to win the allegiance of those members of the middle class who had been attracted to social-democratic ideals during the Resistance. Jaquet gave an assurance to the extraordinary National Congress of November 1944 that his federation had decided to do away with the *luttes de tendance*:

> Le Parti socialiste est et doit rester un parti démocratique. Chaque opinion doit pouvoir s'exprimer librement. C'est justement pour cela que nous avons combattu pendant quatre ans. Mais, nous ne voulons pas que, sous le couvert de cette indispensable liberté de pensée et de parole, nos militants puissent s'entredéchirer et négliger ce qui doit rester notre but commun: l'instauration d'un monde plus juste et plus humain.[121]

The federation's most important test as far as local politics were concerned was whether the Socialists could gain a commanding position on

[120] See *Bulletin Intérieur*, no. 13, April–May 1946, pp. 12–13.
[121] Parti Socialiste (SFIO), Congrès National extraordinaire, Paris, 9–12 novembre 1944, *Compte rendu sténographique* (Conservation film of original typescript, Bibliothèque

the two overarching institutions in the Seine Department, the Paris Municipal Council consisting of 90 members, and the General Council consisting of these 90 and another 60 representatives of the suburban cantons. The first signs were auspicious: on 20 March 1945 the Socialist leader, André Le Troquer, was appointed to the Presidency of the Provisional Municipal Council,[122] but the Communists nevertheless emerged from the Paris municipal elections of 29 April as the largest party. Under a system of proportional representation, they polled 29.6 per cent of the votes and won 27 of the seats in the council while the Socialists gained only 11 per cent of the votes and 12 seats.[123] Le Troquer was subsequently re-elected as President of the Council but only as the representative of a broad temporary front which included the Communists.[124] Even an alliance with the newly formed UDSR did not enable the SFIO to do much better in the cantonal elections of 23 September, when the suburban members of the General Council were elected, also by proportional representation; only 9 Socialist candidates were returned while the Communists won 25 of the 60 seats in contention. The combined results of the two elections produced a 150-member house which contained 52 Communists, 21 Socialists, 28 representatives of the MRP and 49 of other groups.[125] This outcome left the Socialists with fewer seats than they had hoped to gain, but, as in *tripartisme* at the national level, they had the advantage of holding the balance of power between the Communists and the MRP.

In the general elections of 21 October 1945, the Socialists, working in tandem with the UDSR, gained a surprisingly high level of votes, however. The Seine Department had been divided into six constituencies for this poll and joint SFIO–UDSR lists were nominated in all of them. In Paris itself, these lists attracted 21.06, 18.40 and 23.51 per cent of the votes in the first, second and third constituencies respectively, and in the outer areas they secured 22.40 per cent in the fourth (southern) constituency, 23.04 per cent in the fifth (western), and 19.49 in the sixth (north-eastern) constituency, winning the parties 12 of the 53 seats. This remarkable advance was undoubtedly due to the improved efficiency of the SFIO's alliance with the UDSR and, more generally, justified its policy of looking beyond its traditional clientele for the support of the middle classes. Meanwhile, the federation had succeeded in rebuilding

de Documentation Internationale Contemporaine, Universités de Paris), 9 November 1944, p. 254.
[122] *Le Monde*, 22 March 1945, p. 2.
[123] *L'Année politique 1944–45*, p. 201; *Le Populaire*, 1 May 1945, p. 1.
[124] *Le Monde*, 21 June 1945, p. 5.
[125] *L'Année politique 1944–45*, p. 293.

its organizational strength to some extent and by December 1945 had distributed 14,103 annual cards and recruited a minimum membership of 10,762.

It was at this point that the federation began to revert to its pre-war character. As we have already seen, in December 1945 a group of former Pivertistes led by Charles Lancelle took control of the unit and they now began to form a point of determined opposition to the policies of the party's central leadership.[126] The return of Marceau Pivert himself in the spring of 1946 increased the likelihood that the federation would move even further towards the position once occupied by the Gauche Révolutionnaire. Pivert did not wait long before applying for readmission to the party and when his request came before the Comité Directeur on 22 May, anxiety was expressed that he might cause trouble. According to the minutes of the meeting, Andrée Marty-Capgras said that she considered it to be a political question and

qu'il ne faut pas introduire un élément trouble dans le Parti, car PIVERT est l'homme de toutes les déviations, il a la folie d'être un chef.[127]

In the end, the Comité decided that his application should be referred to the forthcoming National Congress and that, in the meantime, no branch or federation should admit him to party membership.[128] The matter was then taken up by his former branch in the 15th *arrondissement* which, while noting that it was for the National Congress to make the final decision, urged the party's central authorities to agree to his readmission.[129]

Having neglected their alliance with the UDSR and seen their relations with the Communists worsen in the weeks preceding the poll after criticism of the latter by Daniel Mayer and André Le Troquer, Parisian Socialists went badly prepared into the campaign for the elections of 2 June 1946. The results revealed that their support had fallen in Paris itself to 18.44, 16.61 and 19.55 per cent of the votes in the first, second and third constituencies respectively, and in the outer suburbs to 21.65, 21.31 and 19.24 per cent in the southern, western and north-eastern constituencies, but they were still able to return eleven deputies to the Second Constituent Assembly. It was as if the party in the capital had been once more divided into rival groups. Under Lancelle, the federa-

---

[126] See the reports of the Seine Federation's Federal Congresses of 17 February 1946 (*Le Populaire*, 19 February 1946, p. 2) and 24 March 1946 (ibid., 26 March 1946, p. 3; *Le Monde*, 26 March 1946, p. 4).

[127] *CD Minutes*, II, 22 May 1946, p. 216.

[128] Ibid., pp. 215–16.

[129] See *À propos d'une demande de réintégration* [Paris, 1946], 2 pp. (Bibliothèque Nationale).

tion's leadership was strongly committed to the campaign to bring Marceau Pivert back into the party, and three of the Parisian deputies, Henri Barré, Roger Deniau and Paul Rivet, were inclined to support the Molletistes. On the other hand, the majority of the deputies, including Daniel Mayer, Robert Verdier, André Le Troquer, Edouard Depreux and Gérard Jaquet were on the loyalist side. Once more, the intensity of the party's internal conflicts and the sectarianism of its left wing were condemning it to minority status in the most important metropolitan area in the French political system.

Unlike the Seine Federation, whose organizational continuity had been interrupted by the 1938 crisis and the post-war reconstruction, the Seine-et-Oise Federation had survived the occupation with many of its pre-war leaders still in place and, in several cases, still imbued with the sentiment which had drawn them in the 1930s to the Bataille Socialiste. Although the secretary of the underground federation, André Kleinpeter, had died in Buchenwald, Pierre Métayer, one of the most prominent of the unit's pre-war activists, had taken over as Federal Secretary after Liberation. At the end of 1945 the federation was credited with 10,330 card-holders compared with the 11,300 it had had in 1938, and its minimum membership was 8,250. The level of the Socialist vote in the department, which contained two constituencies, was comparable to that in the Seine and fell from 21.00 to 19.99 per cent between the elections of 21 October 1945 and those of 2 June 1946. Of the department's four Socialist deputies in the first Constituent Assembly, three – Germaine Degrond, Pierre Commin and Guillaume Detraves – had signed Mollet's *Appel* and only Métayer had not done so.

The vulnerability of the SFIO's provincial federations to competition from a greatly strengthened Communist Party is well illustrated by the case of the Haute-Vienne unit, which before the war had almost completely dominated the politics of its department but had seen its position seriously undermined between 1940 and 1944. During the occupation the Communists and the local units of the Francs-Tireurs et Partisans Français, the military wing of the Front National, had built up considerable strength in Haute-Vienne and at Liberation they virtually took control of the department and of its administrative centre, Limoges.[130] The prefect appointed under the authority of the Provisional

---

[130] See Guy Decouty, 'Introduction à l'étude de l'évolution de l'opinion politique dans le Département de la Haute-Vienne' (thesis, Institut d'Etudes Politiques de l'Université de Paris, Paris, [1950]), pp. 233–8. See also passing references to the post-Liberation situation in Haute-Vienne in 'Rapport adressé au général de Gaulle par un haut fonctionnaire envoyé en mission dans le Midi', Toulouse, 6 September 1944, in de Gaulle, *Mémoires de Guerre*, III, *Le Salut 1944–1946*, pp. 297–9.

Government to take charge of the department was Jean Chaintron, who belonged to the Communist Party and was a member of its Central Committee.[131] Certainly the ability of the SFIO's federation to recover lost ground was impaired by the loss of its pre-war parliamentarians; at the extraordinary National Congress of November 1944 the two Socialist senators and four of the five Socialist deputies from the department were expelled from the party, either for having voted at the National Assembly of 10 July 1940 in favour of full powers being given to Marshal Pétain or, in one case, for not having taken part in the division. The fifth deputy, Léon Roche, who had voted against full powers, had died in June 1944. The federation's hopes now rested on two men, Adrien Tixier and Jean Le Bail. Tixier, born in 1898 in Haute-Vienne, had served with the International Labour Organization during the inter-war years, had represented the Free French in Washington between September 1941 and May 1943, had joined the CFLN in Algiers in June 1943, and after the return to Paris had been given the important post of Minister of the Interior in the Provisional Government.[132] Jean Le Bail, a relatively minor figure in the pre-war federation, now became its federal secretary.

The first confrontation between the parties in the municipal elections of 29 April and 13 May 1945 ended badly for the Socialists. In the crucial contest for Limoges, the pro-Communist list was successful in both ballots and enabled the Communists to take power, thus ending a period of Socialist control of the town hall which had begun thirty-three years earlier, in 1912. In the department as a whole, the Communists took control of 88 of the 209 municipalities and the Socialists of 66, the remaining 55 being controlled by majorities whose affiliations were unclear.[133] By contrast, the cantonal elections of 30 September 1945 (only one ballot was held in Haute-Vienne) saw the Socialists polling much more strongly than the Communists; they secured 25 of the 29 seats on the General Council, the Communists won only 3, and the remaining one was taken by an independent.[134]

Working now in alliance with the UDSR, the Socialists went on to win an outstanding victory in the elections of 21 October 1945, when the joint SFIO–UDSR (MLN) list took 49.53 per cent of the votes and

[131] Decouty, 'Introduction à l'étude de l'évolution de l'opinion politique dans le Département de la Haute-Vienne', p. 238.
[132] See *Le Populaire*, 21 September 1944, p. 1; 19 February 1946, p. 1; *Le Monde*, 20 February 1946, p. 2.
[133] Jean Lenoble, 'L'évolution politique du socialisme en Haute-Vienne sous la IIIme République' (thesis, Institut d'Etudes Politiques à l'Université de Paris, Paris, [1950]), pp. 172–3.
[134] Ibid., pp. 173–4.

captured three of the department's five seats for Tixier, Gaston Charlet and André Foussat, a result which compared well with that which the party had obtained in the 1936 elections, when it had gained 46.94 per cent of the votes and had won all five seats under the *scrutin d'arrondissement* voting method. However, the Communists had managed to increase their share of the vote from 17.12 to 33.28 per cent between 1936 and 1945 and, in the 1945 elections, returned two deputies to the Constituent Assembly, one of whom, Marcel Paul, was appointed Minister of Industrial Production in the government which de Gaulle formed on 21 November 1945. The death of Tixier on 18 February 1946 deprived the federation of one of its most popular figures. It decided to go ahead with a purely Socialist list in the elections of 2 June 1946, choosing Le Bail rather than Charlet to lead its team of candidates, and on this occasion the Socialists lost a good deal of support. Their share of the vote fell steeply to 36.49 per cent while the Communists' share rose to 38.13 per cent, both parties gaining two of the five seats assigned to the constituency. Within the subdivisions of the department, the Communist vote exceeded that of the SFIO in the three rural areas of Brellac, Rochechouart and Saint-Yrieix and in one of the two Limoges districts.[135] One explanation offered for the Socialists' reverse was that Le Bail lacked 'voter-appeal', being

plus un doctrinaire qu'un militant, de tempérament peu expansif, froid, il n'a rien du meneur de foules.[136]

On the other hand, some in the Socialist federation clearly felt that the Communists were using patronage as a means of building up a clientele in the department, and they made significant moves to check this process both before and after these elections. In May 1946, the Socialist majority of the General Council decided to send a delegation to the Minister of the Interior, André Le Troquer, to make the allegation that Jean Chaintron, who was still prefect of the department, was pursuing a partisan policy.[137] Then, in June, *Le Populaire du Centre* began accusing Marcel Paul, still Minister of Industrial Production, of having supplied Communist activists in the department with coupons for several thousands of motor-tyres, an allegation which Paul denied in an official communiqué.[138]

---

[135] See Husson, *Elections et référendums des 21 octobre 1945, 5 mai et 2 juin 1946*, p. 229. See also Decouty, 'Introduction à l'étude de l'évolution de l'opinion politique dans le Département de la Haute-Vienne', pp. 245–6 and 357.

[136] Decouty, 'Introduction à l'étude de l'évolution de l'opinion politique dans le Département de la Haute-Vienne', p. 358.

[137] *Le Monde*, 9 May 1946, p. 3.

[138] Ibid., 21 June 1946, p. 2. See also ibid., 29 June 1946, p. 3.

The pre-war Haute-Vienne Federation had been inclined to take an anti-participationist position in debates about strategy and this period of adversity revived the old yearning for independence and the purity of opposition. Early in June 1946, we find a member of the federation's executive offering the following advice:

Nous devons passer dans l'opposition, . . . pas de compromission avec les autres partis; pas d'unité d'action avec le parti communiste si nous voulons encore sauver quelques 'plumes', pas de direction ou de participation au gouvernement de demain.[139]

Despite the federation's size (in December 1945 its number of card-holders was 6,300 and its minimum membership 3,792), it obviously felt insecure in the face of an aggressive and resourceful Communist opponent. In this case, too, patience was wearing thin both with *tripartisme* and with the leadership which had taken the party into that alliance.

The Meurthe-et-Moselle Federation, once the main provincial stronghold of the Gauche Révolutionnaire, had changed its character since pre-war days. Although its organizational strength had fallen from a minimum membership of 3,167 in 1938 to 2,108 at the end of 1945 (when the number of card-holders was placed at 2,750), its electoral following had increased from 18.26 per cent at the first-ballot vote in 1932 and the unusually low share of 9.25 per cent in 1936 to 21.82 per cent in the elections of 21 October 1945 and 22.18 per cent in those of 2 June 1946. Its most important assets were its two parliamentary representatives, René Peeters and Pierre-Olivier Lapie; both were returned to the first Constituent Assembly but only Peeters was elected to the second. Peeters was a metal-worker and a trade unionist who had been a member of the Executive Committee of the pre-war federation between 1932 and 1939 and its Deputy Treasurer between 1933 and 1935;[140] during the war, he had belonged to Libération-Nord and he became secretary of the federation in November 1945, when it was formally re-established after a period of provisional organization.[141] Pierre-Olivier Lapie had represented the third Nancy constituency as a member of the small USR group in the Chamber of Deputies during the 1936–40 legislature; mobilized at the outbreak of war, he had served on the Maginot Line and in the Norwegian campaign before joining de Gaulle in London in June 1940; after a period as Governor of Tchad,

---

[139] From an account by the federation's Propaganda Delegate which had been published in *Le Populaire du Centre* (cited by Jacques Fauvet, *Le Monde*, 13 June 1946, p. 1).

[140] From the biography given in Jean-Marie Moine, 'Le mouvement socialiste en Meurthe-et-Moselle sous la Troisième République' (Mémoire de maîtrise présentée à l'Université de Nancy, Nancy, 1973), p. 232.

[141] Jean-Paul Chagnollaud, 'La Fédération Socialiste de Meurthe-et-Moselle (1944–1977)', *Annales de l'Est* (Nancy), 5th Series, 30th Year (1978), no. 2, p. 139.

he was with the Foreign Legion in the Libyan and Tunisian campaigns and served in the Provisional Consultative Assembly as a member of the Parliamentary Resistance Group.[142] Both were independent in their views and neither had signed Mollet's *Appel*.

These eight cases provide some indication of why support for the central leadership was so limited and fragile in the summer of 1946. In every instance, the break in organizational continuity and experience had been severe; except in the Nord and Seine-et-Oise Federations, units had come under the control of relatively untried leaders who soon found themselves in difficulty. In several cases, as in the Seine, Bouches-du-Rhône and Gironde Departments, the SFIO had been given important positions of authority immediately following the end of Vichy rule but had then lost ground as rival parties re-established themselves. In addition, the SFIO's local workers adapted their style of operation slowly and imperfectly to the new conditions of electoral campaigning and propaganda-work created by the introduction of the system of proportional representation within large multi-member constituencies. Under the *scrutin d'arrondissement* employed in the 1928, 1932 and 1936 elections, the Socialists had become accustomed to competing with the Radicals and with conservative groups in an amateurish and genteel style of electoral politics in which sporadic press publicity and a sequence of speeches in different localities were accepted as the normal methods of presenting candidates and policies. They were therefore disconcerted by the scale and efficiency of the campaign techniques employed by the Communist Party and the MRP in the post-war period; the Communists covered the new constituencies with teams of workers, sponsored front organizations and used their newspapers for aggressive propaganda, while the MRP was backed by the clergy in many regions and was assisted by strong youth organizations, such as the Jeunesse Agricole Chrétienne (JAC) and the Jeunesse Ouvrière Chrétienne (JOC). Writing in March 1946, a Socialist activist in Isère complained that

nos militants ont le sentiment d'être désarmés et impuissants devant la propagande formidablement orchestrée des autres grands partis.

Having outlined the methods and resources available to the Communists and the MRP, he concluded:

Sans argent, sans permanents, ne disposant, le plus souvent, que d'une presse politique hebdomadaire à faible tirage et à faible rayonnement, notre parti est considérablement handicapé par rapport à ses 'concurrents'.[143]

---

[142] Mayer, *Les Socialistes dans la Résistance*, pp. 50–1.
[143] Alix Berthet, *Ripostes* . . . (Parti Socialiste (S.F.I.O.), Fédération de l'Isère, Grenoble, 1946), p. 3. See also the comment by Jaffré, 'La crise du Parti Socialiste et l'avènement de Guy Mollet', p. 152.

Caught in often desperate local circumstances, the SFIO's activists were prone to blame the Comité Directeur and the central secretariat for having encumbered them with the heavy burden of co-operation with the Communists and the MRP. As a result, Daniel Mayer and his colleagues found themselves dealing not only with a strongly motivated opposition, of the kind presented by the majority of the leaders of the Pas-de-Calais, Seine and Seine-et-Oise Federations, but also with the growing lack of confidence which a combination of the frustrations of *tripartisme* and annoyance at local setbacks had generated in the Bouches-du-Rhône, Gironde and Haute-Vienne units. The kind of uncritical loyalty which Paul Faure had enjoyed in the pre-war organization was now to be found in only a few of the federations such as the Nord.

The decision to hold the 38th National Congress in Paris between Thursday 29 August and Sunday 1 September was taken by the Comité Directeur on 4 June 1946[144] and the formal procedures for this meeting were set in train. The party's officers had then to prepare the final version of their accounts of the year's activities and in the *rapport moral* which he had to submit on behalf of the Comité Directeur, Mayer coupled a review of the work of the outgoing administration with a statement about future objectives, claiming that the most urgent task facing the party was the education of its activists and the creation of new cadres. He suggested that the success of this task would depend on its being undertaken methodically and based solidly on doctrine:

Lorsque nous parlons de doctrine, nous n'avons pas l'intention de demander à nos militants et propagandistes de traiter dans les réunions de propagande des points de doctrine qui demeureraient abstraits pour les auditoires de travailleurs et de faire de nos réunions des séances de l'Académie des Sciences Morales et Politiques. La doctrine socialiste est toujours vivant, car elle s'appuie essentiellement sur les faits économiques.

He pointed out that it was doctrine

qui permettra au militant d'asseoir ses convictions, qui lui donnera cette *Assurance* et, qu'on me permette le mot, cette foi socialiste, vertus nécessaires dans cet apostolat qu'est la propagande.[145]

Although expressed in general terms, this characterization of doctrine embodied a contrast between a common-sense view of socialism, with

---

[144] *CD Minutes*, II, 4 June 1946, p. 218.
[145] Parti Socialiste (SFIO), 38e Congrès National, Paris, 29 août–1 septembre 1946, *Rapports* (Librairie du Parti, Paris, [1946]), p. 5.

an emphasis on considering immediate and concrete issues in the light of basic notions of fairness, and the abstract theorizing employed, for example, by contributors to *La Pensée Socialiste*. Carefully phrased, it was essentially an invitation to the Comité Directeur to place its authority behind a particular view of the function of doctrine in party life and, implicitly, to reject that which had been stated in Mollet's February *Appel*.

The Comité Directeur considered the *rapport moral* at its meeting on 27 June 1946. Copies of the draft had been sent to each member beforehand and only Elie Bloncourt complained that he had not had time to study it; however, he agreed to send a message by telephone within twenty-four hours of the meeting to indicate how he would vote. Once the text had been adopted, Mayer insisted that his colleagues should defend it before their federations.[146] Throughout, this business had been conducted as though the Comité Directeur had accepted responsibility for the *rapport moral* and for the account which had been given of its stewardship since the 37th National Congress of August 1945.

The leaders of the Mollet group then decided to issue a general policy statement calling on the National Congress to reject the *rapport moral* and to affirm the need for doctrinal *redressement*. The tactical considerations behind this decision were not only that the scrutiny of the annual reports, with the *rapport moral* first in line, would be the initial item on the congress agenda and therefore the best point at which to register dissent before informal discussions had taken the edge off grievances, but also that an attack on the *rapport moral* could serve as a means of pulling together the diverse range of anti-bureaucratic complaints which were coming in from the federations. Although the institution of the *rapport moral* had been revived after the war to permit the Comité Directeur to account for its activities, there was no doubt that the effective responsibility for it remained with the General Secretary. The Mollet group's proposal to reject the 1946 report was therefore aimed much more at Daniel Mayer than at his executive.

Early versions of the Mollet motion had been circulated amongst party members in July 1946 with the obvious intention of attracting as many signatories as possible before the text was dispatched to federations and branches. The original signatories were Mollet himself, five of the people associated with *La Pensée Socialiste* and *Libertés* – Yves Dechézelles, Henri Barré, Léon Boutbien, Jean Rous and Pierre Rimbert – and, surprisingly, François Tanguy-Prigent, the Minister for

---

[146] *CD Minutes*, II, 27 June 1946, pp. 236–7 and 239.

Agriculture and a member of the Comité Directeur.[147] In a separate
development, Daniel Mayer had asked 'quelques camarades avec les-
quels il a constaté certaines divergences de vues' to prepare a statement
which was to be published, along with a text submitted by the party's
branch in the 6th *arrondissement* of Paris, in a special issue of the
Bulletin Intérieur.[148] The first of these two documents had been signed
by fourteen deputies, three of whom – André Philip, Augustin Laurent
and Gaston Defferre – were members of the Comité Directeur. The
text from the branch of the 6th *arrondissement* had no signatories but
its main protagonist, Roger Priou-Valjean, was also a member of the
Comité Directeur. By commissioning one text and accepting the other,
Mayer had allowed important members of the party's executive to criticize, albeit mildly, strategies and policies for which they were collectively responsible and thus to dissociate themselves to some extent from
the report which was going to the National Congress in their name.

By the time that the Comité Directeur met on 31 July, Mayer had
learnt about the Mollet motion and reported to his colleagues that it

[147] There exist four successive versions of the Mollet motion, the cumulative amendments
to which affect only a small proportion of the text. These versions are:

Version A, in *Congrès National S.F.I.O. (août 1946): Résolution sur le rapport moral
et sur la politique générale* (Entreprise de Presse, 100 rue Réaumur, Paris) (no
signatories). Hereafter Tract I.

Version B, in *Résolution sur le rapport moral et la politique générale du Parti en vue
du Congrès National d'août 1946* (Entreprise de Presse, 100 rue Réaumur, Paris) (48
signatories: the names of the principal signatories – Guy Mollet, François Tanguy-
Prigent, Yves Dechézelles, Henri Barré, Léon Boutbien, Jean Rous and Pierre Rimbert – are given in an initial list and the names of the other 41 signatories are provided
in a separate list). Hereafter Tract II.

Version C, in *Résolution sur le rapport moral . . . Congrès National d'août 1946* (no
printing details) (60 signatories: in the list of signatories, the names of six of the
principals – Mollet, Barré, Dechézelles, Boutbien, Rous and Rimbert – are followed
by an alphabetical list of 53 other names and a short paragraph reporting Tanguy-
Prigent's approval of the text except for the recommendation to reject the *rapport
moral*). Hereafter Tract III.

Version D, in *Bulletin Intérieur*, no. 15, 1 August 1946, pp. 1–3 (with the names of
the seven principal signatories and a note regarding Tanguy-Prigent's qualified
approval), and in two tracts: (i) *Résolution sur le rapport moral . . . Congrès National
d'août 1946* (Arras – I.N.S.A.P. – 46) (60 signatories, presented as in Tract III).
Hereafter Tract IV; and (ii) *Résolution sur le rapport moral . . . Congrès National
d'août 1946* (no printing details) (60 signatories: 59 names, including those of all the
principals other than Tanguy-Prigent, are listed alphabetically and there is the usual
reference to the latter's qualified approval of the text). Hereafter Tract V.

For details of provenance, see the Bibliography, p. 409. The Archives Léon Blum
(Archives d'Histoire Contemporaine de la Fondation Nationale des Sciences Politiques, Paris) include a typescript MS of Version A with the names of the seven
principal signatories (4 BL 2 Dr 5 sdr a). This version was edited and published, minus
the list of signatories, in Blum, *L'Oeuvre de Léon Blum, 1945–1947*, pp. 289–93.

[148] *CD Minutes*, II, 31 July 1946, p. 256.

had been signed by Tanguy-Prigent and by twenty or so members of the parliamentary group. Noting that the text of the motion contained a paragraph recommending that the national congress should reject the *rapport moral*, he objected to the attitude which Tanguy-Prigent had taken and offered to resign as General Secretary on the grounds that he could not defend the report before congress unless he could speak on behalf of the Comité Directeur as a whole. Defending his actions, Tanguy-Prigent

déclare avoir assisté aux conversations qui ont précédé la rédaction du texte qui, pour lui, constitue le moyen de créer un choc psychologique. Il souligne qu'il est depuis longtemps hostile à la politique menée par le Parti, aussi bien vis à vis du M.R.P. que du Parti communiste. Il voudrait une affirmation plus nette de la position du Parti et c'est pour cela qu'il a accepté cette motion. Il a bien adopté le rapport moral du Comité directeur, mais c'était avant la rédaction du texte.[149]

Paul Rivet expressed agreement with what Tanguy-Prigent had said about policy, revealing incidentally that he too had been asked to sign the Mollet motion but that he had refused to do so because he considered himself to be collectively responsible with other members of the committee for the *rapport moral*. This implicit distinction between responsibility for the report as a symbol of authority and support for the ideas which it represented was a fine one, but other speakers accepted it without hesitation; Salomon Grumbach expressed the view that:

il doit y avoir entre les membres du Comité directeur une solidarité dans l'action publique, tout en estimant que chaque Membre a le droit d'avoir son opinion et de l'exprimer.

He also observed that:

nous touchons à la fin d'une expérience, celle qui avait trait à la suppression des tendances dont nous allons retrouver la cristallisation.[150]

Later in the discussion, Louis Noguères said that, had he been present at the meeting of the Comité Directeur which had dealt with the *rapport moral*, he would have repeated the criticism which he had made in the past but that, since the report had been adopted, he would defend it when it came before his federation.[151] In another intervention, Tanguy-Prigent pointed out that he had given his assent to the ideas in the Mollet motion without having read the actual text, and he agreed to issue a statement to the effect that, as a member of the Comité

---

[149] Ibid.
[150] Ibid., p. 257.
[151] Ibid., pp. 257–8.

Directeur, he could not associate himself with that passage in the resolution which recommended a vote against the *rapport moral*.[152]

Given such a reaction by his executive to the news about the Mollet motion, all that Mayer could do, short of resigning from office, was to endeavour to regulate the situation and he wisely proposed that before the National Congress there should be a meeting between some members of the Comité Directeur and the signatories of this document. This meeting took place at the office of *Le Populaire* at 8.30 a.m. on Friday, 2 August,[153] and at it Mayer, conferring with fifteen or so signatories of the motion, pressed them to remove from the text some of the phrases which he considered would merely give ammunition to the party's opponents. He also told them that he realized that, in voting against the *rapport moral* they were trying to bring about 'le départ et par conséquent le changement du secrétaire général du parti' and he said that, in order to maintain unity, he was prepared to announce publicly that he would not continue as General Secretary provided that they dropped their opposition to the report. He then left the room so that they could consider the matter and when he returned forty-five minutes later they turned down his proposal.[154] He subsequently learned that, although Mollet had been in favour of accepting it, he had been persuaded by some of his friends that Mayer's departure would not guarantee a change of policy, whereas the rejection of the *rapport moral*, or its approval by no more than a narrow majority, would serve that end.[155]

The three texts were duly published by the central secretariat in a special issue of the *Bulletin Intérieur* for the benefit of the party's branches and federations.[156] They were presented without critical comment and the secretariat made no attempt to counter the arguments which they contained or to add to the material which had already been

---

[152] Ibid., pp. 258 and 259.

[153] Ibid., p. 259.

[154] See statement by Mayer, Parti Socialiste (SFIO), 38ᵉ Congrès National, Paris, 29 août–1 septembre 1946, *Compte rendu sténographique* (Original typescript, Centre de Documentation du Mouvement Ouvrier et du Travail, Nantes), 29 August 1946, pp. 123–5.

[155] See Daniel Mayer, *Pour une histoire de la gauche* (Plon, Paris, 1969), pp. 310–12; Claude Juin, *Liberté . . . Justice . . . : Le combat de Daniel Mayer* (Editions Anthropos, Paris, 1982), pp. 189–90. See also Jaffré, 'La crise du Parti Socialiste et l'avènement de Guy Mollet', p. 252, citing an interview with Mayer on 29 December 1970.

[156] See *Bulletin Intérieur*, no. 15, 1 August 1946, pp. 1–15.
    The edition of this issue held in the Library of the Fondation Nationale des Sciences Politiques differs in minor respects (typesetting. layout and some details of spelling and punctuation) from that held in the Library of the Office Universitaire de Recherche Socialiste (OURS). All quotations below are from the OURS edition.

issued in the bound volume of annual reports. Daniel Mayer restricted himself to a personal statement in which he said that some of his friends had proposed that he should either join with them in producing a text or at least sign one 'qui aurait pour but . . . de grouper par avance un certain nombre de mandats' but that he had refused and would continue to do so.

J'ai la ferme conviction que c'est un texte unique qui sortira de nos délibérations. Et le secrétaire général du Parti doit se sentir entouré de la confiance de tous et être l'interprète de l'ensemble du Parti. Il ne saurait être le 'leader' provisoire d'une fraction contre une autre.[157]

Let us now consider each of the texts which were sent at this point to the branches and federations. The Mollet text was by far the most trenchant and uncompromising of the three; its authors claimed that the basic cause of the party's malaise was doctrinal in nature and that

nous estimons que doivent être condamnées toutes les tentatives révisionnistes, notamment celles qui, se fondant sur une conception erronée de l'humanisme, ont pu laisser croire à nos adversaires que le Parti oubliait cette réalité fondamentale qu'est la lutte des classes.
C'est cet affaiblissement de la pensée marxiste dans le Parti qui l'a conduit à négliger les tâches essentielles d'organisation, de propagande et de pénétration dans les masses populaires pour se cantonner dans l'action parlementaire et ministérielle . . .

From this moral failing had stemmed other mistakes, and they therefore asked the congress to break with this political line by refusing to adopt the *rapport moral*. They then offered their *politique de redressement* as a means of restoring moral certainty:

Non seulement les expériences historiques récentes ne contredisent point les données essentielles du socialisme scientifique, mais elles démontrent que seule l'action offensive de la classe ouvrière peut promouvoir le progrès social et sauvegarder les libertés.

The resolution also contained proposals for new domestic and international policies, advocating more firmness in dealing with the party's political neighbours. Although it did not go to the length of rejecting *tripartisme* and proposing an alternative alliance, it nevertheless insisted that the party

doit affirmer ses conceptions en toute indépendance et ne plus apparaître comme un parti-charnière situé à mi-chemin du Parti communiste et du M.R.P.

[157] Ibid., p. 11.

It recommended that the party reveal 'le fonds paternaliste et réactionnaire de la doctrine du M.R.P.' and mobilize republican opinion for the defence of secular schooling. Where relations with the Communist Party were concerned, it proposed that the SFIO should reaffirm its interest in bringing about the political unity of the working class. However, it acknowledged that this could not be done so long as the national Communist Parties

ne se seront pas libérés de leur assujettissement politique et intellectuel vis-à-vis de l'Etat russe et tant qu'ils ne pratiqueront pas une véritable démocratie ouvrière.

Although the resolution approved of unity of action with the Communists at the national level, it warned against giving the impression either that the party was being towed along behind the Communist Party or that it was systematically rejecting that party's proposals. Finally, it recommended organizational reform:

Dans la rude compétition où sont engagés les partis, l'insuffisance de notre appareil administratif, de nos moyens de propagande, de notre presse, s'est révélée trop manifeste pour qu'il soit nécessaire de la souligner.[158]

The basic motif in this text was what its protagonists called *le redressement socialiste*. At one level, they used it as a synonym for *raidissement*, for a hardening of the party's structure:

nous sommes obligés de constater qu'une épuration politique s'avère de plus en plus nécessaire, si le parti doit jouer son rôle. Il y a maintenant le problème des hommes qui le dirigent qui doit être posé, avec fermeté.

Le problème véritable de redressement socialiste, il faut le chercher dans le renouvellement de ses cadres et de ses dirigeants.[159]

'Redressement' also suggested the action of a group of travellers taking stock of their whereabouts and returning to the right path for their journey. In an article in *La Pensée Socialiste*, Jean Rous explained why the use of the word was appropriate:

Parce que les militants avaient le sentiment qu'il fallait arrêter le parti socialiste sur une pente qui le menait vers un nouveau parti radical ou vers un 'travaillisme' sans travailleurs qui demeure le grand dessein de la coalition capitaliste et chrétienne.

Il fallait donc redresser un cours dangereux.[160]

---

[158] Ibid., pp. 1–3.
[159] Léon Boutbien, 'Redressement socialiste', *Libertés*, no. 141, 8 August 1946, p. 6.
[160] Jean Rous, 'Le congrès du redressement socialiste', *La Pensée Socialiste*, nos. 7–8, August–September 1946, p. 3.

In both senses, the term provided a doctrinal focus for an otherwise aimless anti-bureaucratic movement at the level of the federations.

This motion was eventually signed by 59 members of the party and supported by Tanguy-Prigent, who had stated that he would not associate himself with that passage of the resolution which recommended voting against the *rapport moral*[161] but whose approval of the remainder of the document was not in doubt.[162] This list of names provides valuable information about the extent of the Mollet group's influence at this stage in its revolt against the central leadership. Of the 60 names listed, 39 were members of the party's 128-strong parliamentary group and another 5 had been deputies in the first but not in the second Constituent Assembly. Overlapping with this set of names was a smaller one of those associated with *La Pensée Socialiste* and *Libertés*, including Henri Barré, Yves Dechézelles, Jean Rous, Pierre Rimbert, Charles Lancelle, René Lhuillier and Lucien Vaillant, and the Pivertistes were represented not only by Lancelle and Vaillant but also by Lucien Weitz and Jacques Enock. Like Mollet's February *Appel* (39 names were common to both lists) this roll-call of supporters offered several quite different forms of testimony – that a substantial minority of the parliamentary group was willing to defy the Comité Directeur and the General Secretary, that the Parisian intellectuals approved of Mollet's doctrinal position, and that important figures in the provinces (Jean Pierre-Bloch and Elie Bloncourt in Aisne, Jacques Arrès-Lapoque and Maurice Deixonne in the South-West, Jean Minjoz in Doubs and Tanguy-Prigent in Brittany) could serve as rallying points for regional dissent.

The Philip resolution was not so much a counterblast to the Mollet motion as another attack on the policies of the central leadership, but from a radical republican rather than a néo-Guesdiste perspective. When Mayer had become aware of 'certaines divergences de vues' with some of his colleagues, he had invited them to prepare a statement for publication in the *Bulletin Intérieur*[163] and they appear to have prepared

---

[161] *Bulletin Intérieur*, no. 15, 1 August 1946, p. 3.

[162] As noted above (n. 147), the complete list of signatories was first published in Tract III, p. [4]. This tract, which must have been published after the meeting of the Comité Directeur on 31 July, described Tanguy-Prigent's position in the following terms:
notre camarade TANGUY-PRIGENT qui est un des promoteurs de la résolution, donne son accord à tout notre texte, à l'exception des mots qui recommandent le rejet du rapport moral. il ne peut s'associer à ce passage pour une raison de discipline et de correction, étant donné qu'il ne s'est pas opposé au vote du rapport moral au sein du Comité Directeur, lors d'une réunion tenue antérieurement à la rédaction de notre résolution.

[163] See *CD Minutes*, II, 31 July 1946, p. 256, and above p. 332. Although the relevant passage in these minutes does not refer to Philip and his colleagues by name, it seems clear from the context that it is to them rather than to the authors of the Mollet motion that Mayer was referring.

their text without being fully aware of the line which would be taken by the Mollet group in their motion. The Philip resolution was essentially directed against the orthodox case which the Comité Directeur had accepted and which Mayer and Verdier, as the SFIO's chief officers, were therefore obliged to justify, namely, that there was no alternative to *tripartisme* under existing circumstances, that the party had no choice other than to work with the Communists and the MRP to produce a constitutional settlement and to implement an agreed programme of social and economic reforms, that the Radicals would not have been suitable allies for either purpose, and that the party's commitment to collectivist principles and to the ideal of a centrally directed economy would eventually win the support of a majority of the voters. The authors of the Philip motion asserted that most people were simply interested in the restoration of acceptable living conditions, mainly in respect of food and housing, and that, while the Communists and the MRP had understood this and acted accordingly, the Socialists had given the impression that they were not responding 'assez directement aux aspirations concrètes du peuple'. Too many of the party's activists 'se sont tenus dans des discours généraux et vagues' and preached incessantly about the need for a revolution which in fact had already begun.

Au lieu d'apparaître comme un parti moderne préoccupé de tous les aspects de la vie des citoyens, on a, dans trop de départements et de circonstances, évoqué l'idée d'un parti de type périmé, confiné dans la déclaration révolutionnaire impuissante ou uniquement spécialisé comme les radicaux d'antan dans les affaires électorales.

The text stressed the need to identify the issues of principle which distinguished the SFIO from the Communist Party and the MRP:

en face du socialisme verbal du M.R.P. et du socialisme totalitaire du Parti Communiste, il n'est que d'affirmer notre socialisme à la fois humain et révolutionnaire.

The authors then attempted to explain why the party, the sole expression of the dominant idea of democratic socialism, had suffered such a heavy loss of votes, and they placed most of the blame on errors of judgement and policy on the part of the central administration, particularly in the field of publicity and propaganda. Implicitly criticizing Blum's management of the party's main journal, they claimed that the newspapers of the Communist Party and the MRP had shown

une vivacité de réaction à tout ce qui peut servir leur parti, qui fait totalement défaut au 'Populaire' et à la plupart des journaux socialistes.

The motion also had a constructive side, discussing the role of economic planning within the framework of a mixed economy and the scope for Socialists to shape and guide such an economy. Philip and his colleagues assumed without question that the party should participate in government, and that it had a responsibility to make clear the need

de dresser pour un avenir proche le grand plan de la reconstruction de nos ruines, de la modernisation de notre outillage public, industriel et agricole, . . .

They outlined an economic structure in which a sector of nationalized industries would coexist with a free enterprise sector and in which a system of factory committees would prepare the way for workers' control of the whole of production.[164]

This motion was essentially a message to the radical republicans within the party to have the courage of their convictions, to dispense with romanticism about the Resistance movement and the party's revolutionary heritage, and to strike out in a social-democratic direction. The fourteen signatories of the text were all respected members of the parliamentary group and three also belonged to the Comité Directeur; their names and constituencies were as follows:[165]

> Georges Archidice (Lot)
> Jean Charlot (Var)
> Gaston Defferre (Bouches-du-Rhône I)*
> Albert Gazier (Seine V)
> Robert Lacoste (Dordogne)
> Augustin Laurent (Nord II)*
> Francis Leenhardt (Bouches-du-Rhône I)
> Pierre Métayer (Seine-et-Oise II)
> Jean Meunier (Indre-et-Loire)
> René Peeters (Meurthe-et-Moselle)
> André Philip (Rhône I)*
> Christian Pineau (Sarthe)
> Paul Ramadier (Aveyron)
> Alexandre Roubert (Alpes-Maritimes)

*member of Comité Directeur

Some of this group, such as Peeters and Leenhardt, were newcomers to parliamentary life but the majority were experienced; five – Philip, Lacoste, Laurent, Pineau and Ramadier – had held office in post-

---

[164] *Bulletin Intérieur*, no. 15, 1 August 1946, pp. 11–15.
[165] Ibid., p. 15. The list on this page in the edition held at the Library of the Fondation National des Sciences Politiques includes an additional name, that of Gérard Ouradou, a Socialist deputy for Seine II.

Liberation governments and others such as Gazier and Meunier were effectively *ministrables*. Although they were by no means rebels, they had placed themselves apart from the praetorian guard which now stood ready to defend the General Secretary and which included men such as Vincent Auriol, Edouard Depreux, Félix Gouin, André Le Troquer, Jules Moch and Marius Moutet.

For all that they differed in content, the Mollet and Philip motions nevertheless implied a very similar attitude towards party organization. Both represented the SFIO as something of an army preparing for battle and the occupation of territory, and as something of a corporation, to be judged by the effectiveness with which it defined and realized its goals. The third motion, from the party's branch in the 6th *arrondissement* of Paris, was based on the very different premise that the party was essentially a missionary body, the aim of whose members should be to renew their faith and bear witness to their ideals. It stressed the need to state clearly the differences between Socialists and Communists and urged the party to recreate

la mystique révolutionnaire qui soulève les militants et leur donne la force; pour 'gonfler' ses militants, il ne peut plus rester centriste, aux solutions moyennes et médiocres des compromis.

It was highly critical of the party's methods of recruitment and organization and harsh in its judgement of how *Le Populaire* was being run. Like the Mollet motion, it advocated *redressement* but it did not call for the rejection of the *rapport moral*.[166]

The federal congresses preparatory to the National Congress took place throughout August. Although the networks associated with the Mollet and Philip groups must have been much weaker and less reliable than those connected with the major *tendances* of the pre-war period, many federations treated the motions as though they were *textes de tendance* and the federal congresses, in voting upon them, easily reverted to the convention of *le mandat impératif*. The tide was now running strongly against the central leadership; although the Nord Federation voted for the *rapport moral*, the Bouches-du-Rhône, Gironde, Pas-de-Calais and Seine Federations voted against it, as did a number of provincial federations including Alpes-Maritimes, Aube, Cantal, Gard, Hérault, Jura, Loiret, Maine-et-Loire, Puy-de-Dôme, Sarthe and Somme.[167] Where separate divisions were taken on whether or not to

[166] Ibid., pp. 4–10.
[167] See *Le Populaire*, 13 August 1946, p. 3; 20 August 1946, p. 3: 22 August 1946, p. 4; 27 August 1946, p. 3; 28 August 1946, p. 3; *L'Espoir*, no. 102, 25 August 1946, pp. 1 and 2 (for the Pas-de-Calais congress); *L'Espoir du Cantal* (Aurillac), 31 August 1946, p. 1 (for the Cantal Congress).

approve the *rapport moral* and on which of the three texts to support, the results indicated a tendency for more votes to be cast against the *rapport* than for the Mollet motion and, conversely, for more votes to be cast for the Philip motion than for the *rapport*.[168] Much depended on how the issues were addressed, and there was at least one case, the congress of the Landes Federation, in which the delegates voted not only against the *rapport moral* but also against the motions themselves, on the grounds that they did not wish to see a return to the *jeu de tendances*.[169] Although the relative support for the two principal motions on general policy was difficult to estimate, it was quite clear that the Mollet group had a good chance of achieving its first objective, the defeat of the Comité Directeur's annual report on the opening day of the National Congress.

The central leaders had kept track of the results of the federal congresses and were therefore aware of the seriousness of the situation which they now faced. On his return to Paris after presiding over the congress of the Corrèze Federation on Sunday 25 August, Robert Verdier encountered Léon Blum in the office of *Le Populaire* in the Boulevard Poissonnière; Blum acknowledged that 'la bataille est perdue' and Verdier recalls that Daniel Mayer also knew that this was so. However, he and his friends were also aware that events could still work in their favour and that various factors, such as the prestige which still attached to the team which had led the underground party, personal considerations, ties of friendship, and memories of the recent past, could influence the choice of General Secretary by the incoming Comité Directeur.[170] The Mollet group's ability to maintain sufficient coherence to dominate proceedings beyond the first day of the National Congress was already in doubt, but the crucial question was whether the existing leadership, now in full retreat, could regroup its own forces in time to stage a decisive counter-attack.

The 38th National Congress of the SFIO opened on Thursday 29 August in the Maison de la Mutualité in the 5th *arrondissement* of Paris and was attended by 380 delegates bearing between them 4,485 mandates on behalf of the party's 97 federations. The first item on the agenda was the consideration of the annual reports, and almost immediately the *rapport moral* itself came under discussion. During the morning and afternoon sessions the scope of the debate was broadened

---

[168] See the details of divisions at the congress of the Côte-d'Or, Nièvre and Saône-et-Loire Federations (*Le Populaire*, 27 August 1946, p. 3).

[169] Pierre Lamarque-Cando (Landes), Parti Socialiste (SFIO), 38ᵉ Congrès National, Paris, 29 août–1 septembre 1946, *Compte rendu sténographique*, 29 August 1946, p. 49.

[170] Interview with Robert Verdier, Paris, 23 March 1990.

to take in a whole range of issues: the case for a radical change in the party's strategy and methods of organization was forcefully presented by Jean Rous and Pierre Rimbert of the Seine Federation and Victor Fay of the Rhône Federation, while other speakers directed criticism against the central secretariat and Daniel Mayer. One delegate declared bluntly:

Nous devons nous dire que ce qui importe, c'est de changer, non pas la doctrine, qui n'en a pas besoin, mais le secrétariat du parti, mais l'esprit qui y règne et les méthodes de ce parti.[171]

Another listed a series of alleged failings and concluded:

quel doit être, à notre sens, le secrétariat de demain? Le secrétaire du parti de demain, ce ne doit pas être forcément un orateur, un orateur éloquent, allant, de soireé en soireé, battre les estrades à travers le pays. Le parti a peut-être tort de vivre sur des habitudes qu'avant la guerre lui a données Paul Faure. Il faudrait peut-être penser qu'il y a eu d'autres secrétaires du parti dans l'histoire du parti. Un homme comme Dubreuil, avant 1914, était secrétaire du parti.[172]

Having made these historical comparisons, he went on to describe what he and others wanted the General Secretary to be.

Nous pensons qu'il est nécessaire d'avoir quelqu'un qui veille sur le parti, qui connaisse sa carte des fédérations, sa carte de la presse socialiste, qui connaisse les points faibles et sache y porter remède au jour le jour, heure par heure. Il n'est pas nécessaire non plus d'avoir un secrétaire du parti qui intervienne sans cesse dans les discussions politiques du parti, dans la marche du groupe parlementaire, dans la marche du Comité Directeur, ou d'une C.A.P., ou d'une commission exécutive, comme vous voulez.[173]

Augustin Laurent was clearly swimming against the current when he tried to defend the decision of the Nord Federation to support the *rapport moral* and by so doing, to express confidence in the Comité Directeur.

In the evening session, Guy Mollet returned to the attack, recommending that the party should improve the organization of the secretariat while giving each member of the Comité Directeur specific tasks. He implied that the SFIO had been too passive within the framework of *tripartisme*:

trop souvent, au cours des délibérations, au cours des prises de position, notre Parti ou les représentants de notre Parti ont fait figure de médiateur alors que, dans la situation politique même, nous aurions pu faire figure d'arbitre . . .

---

[171] Pierre Lamarque-Cando (Landes), Parti Socialiste (SFIO), 38ᵉ Congrès National, Paris, 29 août–1 septembre 1946, *Compte rendu sténographique*, 29 August 1946, p. 54.
[172] Max Lejeune (Somme), ibid., p. 76. Louis Dubreuilh was the first General Secretary of the SFIO.
[173] Ibid., p. 77.

Cette position de médiateur nous a amené parfois à des positions tellement indéfendables, tellement incompréhensibles qu'une partie de l'opinion publique en est arrivée à savoir ce que sur certains problèmes pensent les militants des partis de son pays, se dit à notre gauche et se trouve à notre droite et que la situation du Parti socialiste se situe entre les deux.[174]

He therefore proposed that the general lines of the party's policy be formulated more precisely. Turning pointedly to the issue of class alliances, he said:

À ceux qui nous disent que nous risquons d'éloigner de nous une partie des classes moyennes je réponds: si les classes moyennes sont en train de se prolétariser, c'est à elles qu'il appartient de venir au socialisme et nous ne devons permettre à aucun moment que ce soit le socialisme qui aille à elles.[175]

When his turn came to speak, Daniel Mayer identified the different complaints against existing policies and dealt with each in turn. He claimed that those who sought the revival of the party were in fact indulging in nostalgia for the past, and that those who objected to *tripartisme* had ignored the lack of any real alternative, whether in the form of a Communist-Socialist government or of an alliance with the Radicals instead of with the MRP. As if to counter Mollet's reference to the middle classes, he inserted into his remarks about the impracticality of a Communist-Socialist government the observation that the defeat of the first Constitution Bill had shown that the two parties' combined forces had failed to win the support of even one half of the country

et, on ne saurait, surtout en période de reconstruction et de reconversion économique, gouverner sans l'assentiment ou sans la bienveillante neutralité de ces larges couches de la population que l'on appelle les classes moyennes, mais qui sont en France, la majorité sociale de la Nation.[176]

Reminding his audience that reform prepares the way for revolution, he denied that the party had changed its fundamental doctrines or principles, and dismissed the notion that there was a conflict between Marxism and humanism – 'quelle condamnation de toute la merveilleuse synthèse du socialisme français!'[177] He argued that Guy Mollet, were he to become General Secretary, would in a matter of weeks be forced to defend the party against an intrusive Bolshevism and to restrict unity of action with the Communist Party.

---

[174] Ibid., p. 95.
[175] Ibid., p. 96.
[176] Ibid., p. 108.
[177] *Le Populaire*, 30 August 1946, p. 3.

Mais, même s'il le fait, il aura donné en France et dans le monde, l'impression que la victoire de ses amis sur les miens aura été la victoire des éléments unitaires du parti, et par conséquent la victoire du Parti Communiste sur le Parti Socialiste, et de Pierre HERVE sur Léon BLUM.[178]

Léon Blum then came to the platform and constructed the first part of his speech around two rhetorical questions about the causes of the conflict within the party.[179] First, was the conflict a reflection of doctrinal differences? Secondly, was it an expression of disagreement over the party's general strategy? Where doctrine was concerned, he challenged the distinction between revolutionary and non-revolutionary socialism, asserting that what really mattered was whether a revolutionary trans-formation of the social structure could or could not be achieved.

Si nous luttons pour cette transformation, ce n'est pas seulement parce qu'elle est dans le sens d'une loi de l'histoire, parce qu'elle traduit le [progrès] des forces de production et des rapports sociaux que ces forces de production déter-minent, c'est aussi parce qu'elle est conforme à la justice.[180]

Turning to the second question, about strategy, he pointed out that the difficulties attaching to the exercise of power by the Socialist Party were inescapable and that when it took power in a capitalist society it 'devient par là même, en tout ou en partie, le représentant, le gérant d'affaires de cette même société capitaliste qu'il condamne, qu'il veut détruire et qu'il veut remplacer'. Whereas the Communists would use the exercise of power to destroy the organization which they were managing, it was otherwise for the Socialists.

Quand nous exerçons le [pouvoir] dans le cadre de la société capitaliste, nous le faisons de bonne foi, nous le faisons dans l'intérêt de la classe ouvrière, mais aussi dans l'intérêt général de la Nation.[181]

Addressing the delegates directly, he accused them of being afraid.

Je crois que dans son ensemble, le parti a peur, il a peur des communistes, il a peur du qu'en dira-t-on communiste. C'est avec une espèce d'anxiété timorée

---

[178] Parti Socialiste (SFIO), 38ᵉ Congrès National, Paris, 29 août–1 septembre 1946, *Compte rendu sténographique*, 29 August 1946, p. 123. Pierre Hervé was a Communist journalist who had also been a Resistance leader. At the time of this congress, he was a Communist deputy in the second Constituent Assembly, representing the Finistère constituency.

[179] I have based my account of Blum's speech on the text given in ibid., pp. 132–47. However, this contains certain stenographical and typographical errors which were corrected when the text was published in *Gavroche* (Paris), no. 106, 5 September 1946, p. 5 and I have taken account of these in the quotations which follow.

[180] Parti Socialiste (SFIO), 38ᵉ Congrès National, Paris, 29 août–1 septembre 1946, *Compte rendu sténographique*, 29 August 1946, p. 135.

[181] Ibid., p. 141.

qu'il se demande: 'comment vont voter les communistes, que dira le journal communiste si j'agis de telle ou telle façon?' La polémique et le dénigrement communistes agissent sur vous, vous gagnent à votre insu et vous découragent car la force intérieure vous manque pour lui résister. Vous avez la peur électorale, vous avez peur que vos camarades qui vous désigneront ou ne vous désigneront pas comme candidats ne vous placeront pas sur la liste en ordre utile.[182]

By this stage, Blum had come close to asserting that the proposal to reject the *rapport moral* was evidence of a general failure of will, of an essentially neurotic attempt to recreate the scattered forms of a past existence.

Vous avez . . . la peur du nouveau, bien que vous invoquez sans cesse la nécessité d'un renouvellement. Vous avez la nostalgie de tout ce qui peut vous écarter du passé tel que vous l'avez connu et pratiqué. Vous ne voulez pas de nouveauté dans l'organisation du parti.

Vous avez rétabli le conseil national, vous rétablirez en tous ces jours la représentation proportionnelle, vous avez commencé de rétablir le jeu des tendances et nous voyons revenir le mandat impératif.[183]

Where political alliances were concerned, Blum scolded the delegates for their inability to imagine a combination other than those which they had known in the past.

Il est probable que nous aboutirons demain à cet incroyable paradoxe: une campagne entreprise dans le parti au nom du renouvellement d'une part, au nom du redressement doctrinal de l'autre va aboutir à quoi? car ce sera probablement son unique résultat positif en dehors du Parti, un rebroussement des alliances, une coalition du type bloc des gauches sur le plan de la laïcité et le cas échéant sur le plan de l'anti-cléricalisme.[184]

Blum's frustration shows in this speech. Before the war he could have relied on his fellow leaders to have thwarted any attempt to stage an open-ended policy debate on the first day of a congress, before the chemistry of informal discussions and negotiations had had any effect. Now, faced with the certainty that a majority of the mandates would be cast against the *rapport moral*, he could only shame his opponents:

Le mal est en vous, c'est le manque d'ardeur, de dévouement, le manque de foi, le manque de courage, et le vote de la motion Guy MOLLET contre le vote du rapport moral, ça été une espèce d'alibi moral pour apaiser leur mauvaise conscience.[185]

[182] Ibid., pp. 143–4.
[183] Ibid., p. 145.
[184] Ibid., pp. 145–6.
[185] Ibid., p. 146.

The last part of this sentence appears to refer to votes for the Mollet motion at many of the preceding federal congresses, but Blum's draft notes for the speech show that he had taken it from his original hand-written draft, in which he had passed judgement on the motion itself; before amendment, this draft had read:

La motion G.M. . . . savez-vs ce qu'elle est. Elle est une *espèce d'alibi* par lequel vs avez cherché à abuser votre mauvaise conscience.[186]

Usually so sensitive in his discussion of such matters, Blum had, in this instance, come close to accusing Mollet and his colleagues of trying to ease the sense of their own inadequacy at having failed to serve the cause of revolution.

When the division came, the *rapport moral* was rejected by 2,975 mandates against 1,365 with 145 abstentions, according to figures published at the time.[187] However, an addition of the votes by federation produces a slightly different set of totals, which are set out, with other details of the result, in Table 30. The scale of the defeat was overwhelming; only 20 of the 97 federal delegations had given over 50 per cent of their mandates for the approval of the report and only Nord of the six largest federations had done so. However, the federations voting against the proposal varied a good deal in their political characteristics, from those which were strongly attached to the Mollet revolt for doctrinal reasons, such as the Pas-de-Calais, Seine and Seine-et-Oise units, to those which were anti-Communist and yet critical of the central leadership, such as the Bouches-du-Rhône and Haute-Vienne units.

In his own explanation of this reverse, Mayer has identified a series of factors which worked against him, such as the members' disappointment at the results of the general elections of 21 October 1945 and 2 June 1946 and the tendency for people to attack him as a means of indirectly threatening Léon Blum, with whom he was so closely identified. His administrative actions were criticized: some complained that he was too often absent from Paris, others that he did not visit departments frequently enough and others that he was censorious, as in the action he had taken to draw the attention of federal secretaries to the absence of deputies from meetings of the parliamentary group. There were also objections from different interests regarding alliances and policies; thus, Max Lejeune (Somme) and Pierre Lamarque-Cando (Landes) were against working with the Communists, others wanted an

---

[186] From p. 28 of handwritten draft of speech contained in file 4BL 2 Dr 5 sdr a of *Le 38ème Congrès* in the Archives Léon Blum (Archives d'Histoire Contemporaine de la Fondation National des Sciences Politiques, Paris).

[187] *Bulletin Intérieur*, no. 18, August–September 1946, p. 1.

Table 30. *SFIO, 38th National Congress, Paris, 29 August 1946: division on proposal to approve the rapport moral*

Federations	Mandates For proposal no.	%	Against proposal no.	%	Abstentions no.	%	Absent no.	%	Totals no.
Bouches-du-Rhône	43	24.3	128	72.3	6	3.4			177
Gironde			130	100.0					130
Meurthe-et-Moselle	28	65.1	14	32.6	1	2.3			43
Nord	297	90.8	30	9.2					327
Pas-de-Calais	18	5.8	291	94.2					309
Seine	43	19.9	160	74.1	13	6.0			216
Seine-et-Oise	25	15.1	141	84.9					166
Haute-Vienne			76	100.0					76
Others	916	30.1	1,999	65.7	126	4.1			3,041
Totals	[1,370]	30.5	[2,969]	66.2	[146]	3.3	0	0.0	4,485

Source: Bulletin Intérieur (Paris), no. 18, August – September 1946, p. 6. For details of adjustments, see appendix (p. 403, n. 11).

agreement with them, and others again wanted the problem of *laïcité* given absolute priority. Anti-Semitism also played its part; although it was not presented as an argument, it was used 'comme le surplus entraînant l'adhésion'.[188] In some federations, moreover, there was sympathy for those parliamentarians who had been expelled from the party by the extraordinary National Congress of November 1944 for actions they had taken or failed to take when the National Assembly of 10 July 1940 had voted in favour of full powers for Marshal Pétain.[189]

Such a variety of often contradictory complaints against the central secretariat had been quite common before the war, but the large *tendances* had been able to integrate them into their own anti-bureaucratic campaigns and to provide them with doctrinal justification. After the war, in the absence of *tendances*, such grievances were nursed in isolation and generated a vague resentment which often resulted in defections from the loyalist camp. As Jaffré has observed:

L'interdiction des tendances rend plus aisée les reclassements dans la mesure où les positions des militants ne sont plus cristallisées.[190]

In one respect, the Mollet revolt was an aggregate of diverse and specific protests. By the time of the National Congress, Mollet was presenting himself not so much as a latter-day *chef-de-tendance* as a General-Secretary-in-waiting with the political and administrative skills needed to right a whole series of wrongs; although his team of backers was still intact and still intent on doctrinal objectives, the essential characteristics of the coalition which he had assembled to reject the *rapport moral* were those of a faction, a group of diverse interests which had grown up around a claim to leadership.

The factional aspect of the conflict became much clearer once the *rapport moral* had been dealt with. Until the actual division had taken place, the attention of the delegates had been largely concentrated on the articulation of grievances and the censuring of the central secretariat, but after the vote the issue of leadership became paramount. Once the result of the division was known, Mayer came to the platform and announced that he and the other members of the Bureau (Robert Verdier and Gérard Jaquet, the Deputy Secretaries, and Victor Provo, the Treasurer) were already drawing conclusions from the vote, but that they would deal with current business until the incoming Comité

---

[188] Mayer, *Pour une histoire de la gauche*, pp. 307–10, quotation from p. 310. Cf. Juin, *Le Combat de Daniel Mayer*, pp. 186–9.
[189] See Juin, *Le Combat de Daniel Mayer*, pp. 168–70.
[190] Jaffré, 'La crise du Parti Socialiste et l'avènement de Guy Mollet', p. 189.

Directeur had appointed a new Bureau.[191] What had begun as an attack on administration and policy had become a succession crisis: the delegates were now being forced to consider who should take Mayer's place as General Secretary. Was it to be Guy Mollet or a member of the established leadership, such as Augustin Laurent? The final choice would lie with the new Comité Directeur, whose 31 members were to be chosen towards the end of the congress, and everything now depended on whether the Mollet group could dominate that election as it had dominated the battle over the *rapport moral*.

On the second day of the congress, Friday 30 August, the consideration of the various annual reports continued. The first real test of whether the Mollet revolt had retained its force came in the afternoon, when the report on *Le Populaire* offered an opportunity for the critics of its style of news presentation and of its defence of party interests to have their say. Léon Blum, who as the Political Director of *Le Populaire* had to accept some responsibility for its editorial policy, responded in a dignified manner to the points which had been made; nevertheless, the report was rejected by a clear majority.[192] The details of this division are shown in Table 31. The loyalists gained a better result from this division than from the earlier one on the *rapport moral*; the number of federal delegations giving them over 50 per cent of the mandates had risen from 20 to 38, and the aggregate vote in the affirmative had risen from 1,370 (or 30.5 per cent of the total) to 1,745 (38.9 per cent), a net gain of 375 mandates which had been produced by 755 gains as against 380 losses. Beyond these broad measures, what do these divisions tell us about the intensity of the internal conflict between the loyalists and their opponents? In particular, does a comparison of the votes by federal delegation in the two ballots indicate that the reports were being approved or rejected on general grounds, as a means of defending or attacking the established leadership, rather than as specific and separate accounts, each to be judged on its merits? There are two patterns of voting which point to the existence of a generalized and tactical response by some of the federations; first, in 25 instances federations distributed their mandates identically in both ballots; and, secondly, another 25 federations converted absolute majorities for approval or rejection of the *rapport moral* into bloc votes for the same preference with regard to the report on *Le Populaire*. Both types of behaviour are consistent with a conflict between hostile groups, each treating the

---

[191] Parti Socialiste (SFIO), 38ᵉ Congrès National, Paris, 29 août–1 septembre 1946, *Compte rendu sténographique*, 29 August 1946, p. 148.
[192] Ibid., 30 August 1946, pp. 198–225.

Table 31. *SFIO, 38th National Congress, Paris, 30 August 1946: Division on proposal to approve the report on Le Populaire*

Federations	Mandates:								Totals
	For proposal		Against proposal		Abstentions		Absent		
	no.	%	no.	%	no.	%	no.	%	no.
Bouches-du-Rhône	43	24.3	128	72.3	6	3.4			177
Gironde	34	26.2	83	63.9	13	10.0			130
Meurthe-et-Moselle			43	100.0					43
Nord	327	100.0							327
Pas-de-Calais			309	100.0					309
Seine			216	100.0					216
Seine-et-Oise			166	100.0					166
Haute-Vienne			76	100.0					76
Others	1,341	44.1	1,470	48.3	188	6.2	42	1.4	3,041
Totals	1,745	38.9	2,491	55.5	207	4.6	[42]	0.9	4,485

Source: Bulletin Intérieur (Paris), no. 18, August – September 1946, pp. 6–7. For details of adjustments, see the appendix (p. 403, n. 12).

reports as matters of organizational confidence. On the other hand, a large number of federations reacted in quite different ways to the reports: in many cases a delegation which had voted against the *rapport moral* in the first division voted for the *Le Populaire* report in the second, while in some cases the reverse occurred. These are the patterns we should expect to find where opposition to central policies had remained unsystematic and selective, and where the conflict between loyalists and Molletistes had not become all-consuming. We may conclude, therefore, that only a proportion of the federations – perhaps no more than half of the total – had been strongly influenced by the Mollet revolt.

The debate on general policy, which began on the evening of the 30th, directed the attention of the delegates to the questions which had been raised by the Mollet and Philip motions before the congress. The main speakers approached the central issues from different angles, but each was trying to reassure the moderate delegates and to allay the anxieties which had been aroused by the debate on the *rapport moral*. When he addressed the congress on the morning of Saturday 31st, Philip suggested that the question of whether or not the party should participate in government was no longer relevant in the context of modern economic and social conditions.

Le capitalisme, tout au moins sous la forme où nous l'avons connu, est incapable de se reconstituer. Nous sommes dans un régime de transition qui aboutira à autre chose et ce sera soit le socialisme démocratique, soit une sorte de collectivisme autoritaire et technocratique qui prendra la forme d'un national-socialisme ou d'un national-communisme. C'est la même chose.[193]

He argued that the main danger facing them was not capitalism but the possibility of totalitarian rule and for that reason the party could no longer shirk the responsibility of government. Defending the formula of *tripartisme*, he said that the MRP had been a more suitable partner than the Radical Party which, in economic and social terms, he considered to be more reactionary than many other parties. He spoke against continuing arrangements with the Communists for unity of action, holding out the hope that after the next general elections the Socialist Party would be able to take power in its own right on the basis of a three-party alliance in parliament.[194]

Confronted by such arguments, spokesmen for the Mollet motion then sought to convince the congress delegates that they could be trusted to take a responsible attitude both towards the question of

[193] Ibid., 31 August 1946, p. 354.
[194] Ibid., pp. 353–61.

coalition ministries and in relations with the Communist Party. Yves Dechézelles maintained that he and the motion's other signatories were not absolutely opposed to participation in government; what they did require was that the government in question should meet the demands of the working class and carry out reforms which would make it easier for that class to take power. Although conceding that the bureaucratic and totalitarian Stalinism of the Communist Party was repugnant to Socialists, he questioned the wisdom of dissolving the Comité d'Entente on the grounds that a section of the working class was still influenced by the Communists.[195] Jean Courtois went further, suggesting that the Socialists' refusal to keep the Comité in being would enable Communist activists to represent the SFIO as turning to the bourgeoisie, but even he denied any interest in the organic unity of the two parties.[196] Mollet, in a speech delivered at the end of the debate on Saturday evening, first directed the delegates' attention to Blum's defence of socialist humanism and suggested that laying emphasis on this aspect of the party's doctrine could give a misleading impression of it.

En laissant supposer à ceux qui, sur le plan moral ou intellectuel, se rapprochent de nous par une conception commune de l'humanisme qu'ils sont devenus socialistes, on oublierait l'essentiel qui est de leur faire acquérir une conscience de classe et de les préparer à la lutte de classe.[197]

In terms similar to those which Philip had used earlier in the day, he argued that society was involved in a transition from capitalism to socialism and that the party's participation in power within this process should take a particular form.

Au pouvoir, nous restons les représentants de la classe ouvrière. Au pouvoir, nous n'avons pas à corriger le système capitaliste, mais à fournir à la classe ouvrière les tremplins de son action de demain.

Dans l'action ministérielle, nous voudrions que nos représentants ne soient pas seulement les bons gérants qu'ils sont toujours, mais qu'ils soient toujours aussi des militants qui préparent dans les faits et par l'établissement des hommes qui contrôlent ces faits, l'avènement du socialisme.[198]

On the subject of the party's relations with the Communists, he kept closely to the wording of his motion, saying that organic unity would not be possible so long as Communist Parties remained politically and intellectually subject to the Russian state and lacked real working-class democracy. As for unity of action with the PCF, he envisaged this

[195] Ibid., pp. 411–13.
[196] Ibid., pp. 424–8.
[197] Ibid., p. 450.
[198] Ibid., p. 452.

happening only in well-defined circumstances, after the SFIO had taken a decision at the national level.[199]

By this stage, the Mollet revolt was losing its momentum. Its early successes – the rejection of the *rapport moral* and of the report on *Le Populaire* – had been the end result of the wave of protest which it had set in motion earlier, during the season of the federal congresses, but this had not produced anything resembling a large and disciplined group of delegates at the National Congress. To carry out a palace revolution there, and then to defend the centres of party authority against those whom he had ousted, Mollet would have needed many more experienced henchmen than he in fact possessed. It had therefore been in his best interest to adopt a conciliatory tone in the general policy debate, presenting himself and the members of his team as responsible people capable of developing sensible policies while carrying out their programme of *redressement*. His immediate tasks were to prepare for the work of the Resolutions Committee, which would shortly be convened to consider the texts of certain motions, and to take part in the elections to the Comité Directeur, the polling for which was to be held between 8.45 and 10.00 o'clock on that Saturday evening.

The outcome of the congress now depended on the Resolutions Committee, which began its meeting at midnight. Its main problem was how to bridge the gap between the Mollet and the Philip motions; either it would solve this and produce a motion on general policy which would preserve the unity of the party, or it would have to ask the final plenary session to choose between alternative texts, one based on the Philip motion and the orthodox view of party policy, and the other on the Mollet motion. The committee contained 32 members, 14 of whom represented the Mollet motion, 4 the Philip motion, and 14 various other sectors of opinion within the party.[200] It was too large and heterogeneous a body to deal efficiently with the problem of drafting a joint resolution on general policy, so it sensibly assigned this task to a small subcommittee consisting of André Philip and Jules Moch on one side and Guy Mollet and Yves Dechézelles on the other. According to Dechézelles, there were certain points, particularly the issues relating to unity of action with the Communists and to colonial policy, on which agreement could not be reached. The subcommittee stuck to its task until 10 a.m. on the morning of Sunday, 1 September, and then broke up with matters still in dispute.[201] Dechézelles went off to snatch a few

[199] Ibid., pp. 453–4.
[200] Ibid., pp. 476–7.
[201] Juin, *Le Combat de Daniel Mayer*, p. 214. See also Jérôme Jaffré, 'Guy Mollet et la conquête de la SFIO en 1946', in Ménager *et al.*, *Guy Mollet: un camarade en*

hours' rest but the full committee remained in session until 1.30 p.m. and succeeded in narrowing the differences between the various motions. Mollet and the representatives of the Nord Federation were then deputed to draft alternative paragraphs between which the delegates were to choose, but in the end they agreed that a mutually acceptable text could be inserted into the motion.[202]

On Sunday afternoon, Jules Moch presented the final resolution to the plenary session and it was adopted almost unanimously. The first section of the text, concerned with principles, acknowledged the need for the party to play an essential role in affairs; the second section, on domestic problems, touched on a number of policy issues such as the need for further reforms of structure; the third discussed relations with other parties; and the fourth dealt with international problems. Of these, the third section was the most sensitive because it came to grips with the difficult issues of strategy which had distinguished the Mollet from the Philip motion; it avoided any retrospective justification of *tripartisme*, referred critically to the MRP and the Radicals, and took a hard line on future relations with the Communists. The relevant subsection on the latter question began with a paragraph which followed closely the passage in the Mollet motion to the effect that political unity could not be achieved so long as the Communist Parties remained tied to the Russian state and were undemocratic. It then went on:

Désormais, le Comité Directeur du Parti sera seul habilité pour prendre contact, et uniquement dans des circonstances exceptionnelles, avec les organisations politiques, syndicales ou philosophiques voisines en vue d'actions communes ayant des buts précis, limités dans leur objet et dans le temps.[203]

In other words, notice had been served that the party was no longer interested in maintaining previous arrangements for joint discussions with the Communists. This paragraph was the one which Mollet and the representatives from Nord had agreed should be inserted in the resolution – though with the understanding than in the event of an important division within the incoming Comité Directeur concerning this policy, the point at issue should be referred to a meeting of the National Council.[204] Less contentious was the statement regarding strat-

République, p. 29; and Alain Bergounioux, 'Guy Mollet et la rupture du tripartisme', in ibid., p. 383.

[202] See Jules Moch's account of the work of the Resolutions Committee, Parti Socialiste (SFIO), 38ᵉ Congrès National, Paris, 29 août–1 septembre 1946, *Compte rendu sténographique*, 1 September 1946, pp. 526–7.

[203] *Bulletin Intérieur*, no. 18, August–September 1946, pp. 3–5, quotation from p. 4.

[204] See the references to this undertaking given by Jules Moch, Parti Socialiste (SFIO), 38ᵉ Congrès National, Paris, 29 août–1 septembre 1946, *Compte rendu sténographique*, 1 September 1946, p. 527, and by Eugène Thomas, ibid., p. 535.

egy, which simply noted that the composition of the Constituent Assembly had necessitated a coalition government and that, failing the formation of a purely Socialist ministry, the SFIO would take part in a future coalition only

à la condition que ses associés au pouvoir acceptent au préalable un programme minimum de réalisations précises répondant aux aspirations de la classe ouvrière.[205]

Finally, this was the day on which the congress approved the readmission of Marceau Pivert to party membership.[206]

The results of the election to the Comité Directeur were now known but the group affiliations of the successful candidates were far from clear, mainly because the voting method employed had produced a complicated outcome. In accordance with the rules, the Comité Directeur had to consist of 31 members, of whom not more than 10 were to be members of the second Constituent Assembly. Each delegate had been given a ballot paper containing an alphabetical list of nominees and had been required to cross out all but the names of those candidates for whom he or she wished to vote, any completed ballot paper containing more than the prescribed limits (31 candidates and 10 parliamentarians) being treated as invalid.[207] The procedure for allocating seats was governed by the simple-majority principle: candidates were ranked in the descending order of their total votes and the first 31 on the list declared elected. Such a method can produce two main patterns of vote distribution: in a political system in which parties have widespread backing, each party usually draws up a list of candidates and asks its supporters to vote for that list; by contrast, in a system in which parties are weak, electors tend to vote either for candidates known to them locally, or for those with high standing at the centre of the system. Whereas the reliance on lists generally produces a series of plateaux, open competition (or free voting) tends to produce a wide range of votes by candidate, with central notables obtaining very high totals and local notables very low ones. As we shall see, both patterns were present in the August 1946 election for the Comité Directeur, but the open competition pattern was the stronger of the two.

The nomination process for such polls engaged the energies both of the federations, always anxious to provide local champions with an

---

[205] *Bulletin Intérieur*, no. 18, August–September 1946, p. 5.
[206] See Parti Socialiste (SFIO), 38ᵉ Congrès National, Paris, 29 août–1 septembre 1946, *Compte rendu sténographique*, 1 September 1946, pp. 497–506.
[207] See Daniel Mayer's explanation of the voting procedures, ibid., 31 August 1946, p. 456.

356   B. D. Graham

opportunity to run for office, and of the centrally organized groups
(such as the loyalists and the Molletistes on this occasion), concerned
to build up a full list of candidates and one which included the names
of people capable of serving as top party officials should they be needed.
Each of the central groups faced special problems in 1946: the chief
handicap for the Molletistes was that many of their most reliable candidates lacked national standing; for the loyalists, it was that the new
requirement that the number of parliamentarians on the Comité should
not exceed ten had forced them to search out relatively unknown candidates. (The outgoing Comité Directeur contained 21 deputies, the
great majority of whom were loyalists.) Daniel Mayer also faced the
problem that Gérard Jaquet, one of his two deputy secretaries, had said
that he would not stand for re-election,[208] so he approached Georges
Rougeron, from the Allier Federation, and asked him to be a candidate
for the post. Rougeron was at first reluctant to agree, but was persuaded
to do so by Léon Blum, who met him at the house of his son, Robert
Blum.[209]

By the time polling took place on the evening of 31 August, the
register of candidates contained the names of 95 people,[210] including
those of 23 members of the outgoing Comité Directeur (Mayer had
formally announced that none of the remaining eight members – Vincent Auriol, Just Evrard, Edouard Froment, Félix Gouin, Gérard
Jaquet, André Le Troquer, Jules Moch and Roger Mistral – were
standing for re-election).[211]

Lists of loyalist and Molletiste candidates were being distributed[212]
and delegates were under pressure to vote for a ticket as well as for
individual candidates. The register of nominees contains the names of
25 deputies, some of whom (notably Jean Biondi, Gaston Defferre,
Marius Moutet, Marcel-Edmond Naegelen, André Philip, Eugène
Thomas and Robert Verdier) probably belonged to a loyalist sub-list,
and some (including Raymond Badiou, Henri Barré, Alexandre Baurens, Jean Courtois, Roger Deniau, Guy Mollet, François Tanguy-
Prigent, Maurice Rabier and Germain Rincent, all of whom had signed
the Mollet motion) to a Molletiste sub-list. It is more difficult to distin-

---

[208] Interview with Gérard Jaquet, Paris, 23 July 1992.
[209] Letter from Georges Rougeron to the author, from Bézenet, 24 February 1993.
[210] See the list of candidates' names given in the election result in *Bulletin Intérieur*, no.
18, August–September 1946, p. 5. By some error, the name of the candidate ranked
89th was omitted from this list.
[211] Parti Socialiste (SFIO), 38ᵉ Congrès National, Paris, 29 août–1 septembre 1946,
Compte rendu sténographique, 31 August 1946, p. 456.
[212] Interview with Gérard Jaquet, Paris, 23 July 1992.

guish the two sub-lists of non-deputies, but the loyalist ranks probably contained Salomon Grumbach, Renée Blum, Roger Priou-Valjean, Victor Provo, Jean Texcier, Charles Dumas and Georges Rougeron, while the Molletiste ranks probably included Jacques Arrès-Lapoque, Elie Bloncourt, Léon Boutbien, Yves Dechézelles, Camille Delabre, Charles Lancelle, Jean Pierre-Bloch, Pierre Rimbert, Jean Rous, Pierre Stibbe and Lucien Vaillant (all of whom had signed the Mollet motion) as well as Oreste Capocci, Suzanne Charpy, Victor Fay, André Ferrat and Jacques Piette (who had not). Several of the candidates mentioned above were strongly supported by their federations and thus formed an intermediate layer between those who were dependent on the backing which they received from their respective camps and those, such as Henri Malacrida (Hautes-Alpes), Pierre Lamarque-Cando (Landes) and Max Lejeune (Somme), who were essentially the representatives of their local party organization.

The electorate consisted of all those delegates who had been appointed to attend the congress by their federations, each federation being entitled to have two delegates plus an additional delegate for every 15 mandates (or remainder of 8 or more) above the first 15. This produced a total of 395 delegates for this congress, of which 23 came from Nord, 22 from Pas-de-Calais, 15 from Seine, 13 from Bouches-du-Rhône, 12 from Seine-et-Oise and 10 from Gironde. Of the 97 federations represented, three – Moselle, Hautes-Pyrénées and Vendée – were absent at the time of the vote and one – Maine-et-Loire – abstained, with the result that 385 ballot papers were lodged with the returning office; 29 of these were declared to be invalid, so the contest was decided on the basis of 356 votes.[213] The names of those elected and the number of votes each obtained are set out in Table 32. Of the successful candidates, 18 were newcomers to the Comité Directeur; 23 members of the retiring team had stood for re-election but only 13 were returned. Where the competition between the two groups was concerned, fortunes had been mixed; although the loyalists could take heart from the strong support registered for Philip and Mayer and the return of Grumbach, Renée Blum, Depreux, Naegelen, Provo, Laurent and Verdier, they had also seen the defeat of Jean Biondi, Gaston Defferre, Marius Moutet, Louis Noguères and Eugène Thomas. The Molletistes could be pleased by the election of several of their champions and sympathizers, including Capocci, Tanguy-Prigent, Mollet

[213] See the announcement of the results by Daniel Mayer, Parti Socialiste (SFIO), 38ᵉ Congrès National, Paris, 29 août–1 septembre 1946, *Compte rendu sténographique*, 1 September 1946, p. 525.

Table 32. *SFIO, 38th National Congress, Paris, 1 September 1946: ranked list of members elected to the Comité Directeur*

Rank	Name	New member	Deputy	Vote	% of total valid vote
1	André Philip		*	272	76.4
2	Oreste Capocci	*		270	75.8
3	Daniel Mayer		*	263	73.9
4	Salomon Grumbach			248	69.7
5	François Tanguy-Prigent		*	246	69.1
6	Renée Blum			243	68.3
7	Guy Mollet	*	*	240	67.4
8	Emilienne Moreau			237	66.6
9	Roger Priou-Valjean			234	65.7
10	Edouard Depreux		*	227	63.8
11	Marcel-Edmond Naegelen		*	225	63.2
12	Léon Boutbien	*		207	58.1
13	Jacques Arrès-Lapoque	*		203	57.0
14	André Ferrat	*		203	57.0
15	Victor Provo			200	56.2
16	Jean Texcier	*		192	53.9
17	Georges Brutelle	*		191	53.7
18	Irène Laure	*		190	53.4
19	Augustin Laurent		*	186	52.2
20	Amadou Lamine-Gueye	*	*	183	51.4
21	Jean Courtois	*	*	183	51.4
22	Yves Dechézelles	*		180	50.6
23	Suzanne Charpy	*		178	50.0
24	Charles Dumas			173	48.6
25	Robert Verdier		*	169	47.5
26	Pierre Commin	*		160	44.9
27	Jean Pierre-Bloch	*		147	41.3
28	Charles Lancelle	*		143	40.2
29	Henri Malacrida	*		139	39.0
30	Jean Rous	*		139	39.0
31	Georges Rougeron	*		138	38.8

Source: Parti Socialiste (SFIO), 38ᵉ Congrès National, Paris, 29 août–1 septembre 1946, *Compte rendu sténographique*, (Original typescript, Nantes), 1 September 1946, p. 525.

himself, Boutbien, Arrès-Lapoque, Ferrat, Dechézelles, Lancelle and Rous, but they had nevertheless failed to secure the election of Barré, Fay, Rimbert, Stibbe and Vaillant.

It is difficult to judge the extent to which free and directed voting contributed respectively to this outcome. Some federations would not have bound their delegates to make a joint decision, but in other cases, most notably the Nord Federation, delegates would have been expected to vote for the same candidates,[214] and such discipline would have facilitated the practice of organizing lists. The range in magnitude of the 31 highest votes (from 272 to 138) suggests that free voting was the norm and that the results were strongly influenced by particular preferences for individual candidates. However, had the election been wholly shaped by this type of voting behaviour, the votes for the party's leading personalities, of whatever persuasion, would have been much higher than the levels actually reached by well-known and generally respected candidates such as Philip, Mayer, Grumbach, Tanguy-Prigent, Renée Blum and Mollet, which suggests that those delegates who did vote for a list were deleting the names of notables associated with the opposing list (for example, a delegate intending to vote for Mollet and his colleagues would probably have crossed out the names of Philip, Mayer and other candidates known to be loyalist in outlook). If this were the case, the shortfall between the total number of votes and the leading votes of one group would provide an approximate measure of the extent of list-voting for the opposing group; this method of calculation indicates that between 84 and 93 delegates voted for a Mollet list or lists (if the votes for Philip and Mayer are taken as markers) and that between 110 and 116 delegates voted for a loyalist list or lists (using the votes for Tanguy-Prigent and Mollet as markers). Both levels are well below the vote of the lowest ranked of the successful candidates which may help to explain why neither group swept the board in this election. Whatever the reason, the main point for our analysis is that this crucial election produced an ambiguous outcome so far as the overall conflict was concerned; both the loyalists and the Molletistes could claim the allegiance of some members of the new Comité Directeur but there were other successful candidates whose positions on the central issues facing the party were still relatively unknown.

The prospect that Guy Mollet might be elected to the post of General Secretary by the incoming Comité Directeur had spread alarm amongst the loyalists from the opening day of the congress, after the rejection of the *rapport moral* had been seen as an indirect censure of Mayer and his fellow officers. According to Edouard Depreux, the outgoing team of leaders held several meetings to explore the possibility of finding a candidate who might be successfully put forward against Mollet; Depreux says that his own name was mentioned but that he refused to stand, that some thought was given to Naegelen, and that in the end it was Augustin Laurent, the secretary of the Nord Federation, who was

---

[214] Speaking in general terms, Robert Verdier has pointed out that the delegates of Nord Federation 'décident comment elle [i.e. la Fédération] vote et tous les délégués votent de la même manière' (Interview, Paris, 23 March 1990).

chosen.[215] However, because of the confusion surrounding the elections to the Comité Directeur, it was difficult for anyone to predict whether the Molletistes or the loyalists would carry the day if the choice of General Secretary were pressed to a division. The informal structure of the Comité was complex: its most stable elements were the core groups of the opposing sides; surrounding each of these were their various sympathizers; and in the middle were two members whose preferences were unclear. The core of the Molletistes consisted of Mollet himself, Tanguy-Prigent, Dechézelles, Boutbien and Jean Rous, with Arrès-Lapoque, Capocci, Charpy, Commin, Courtois, Ferrat, Lamine-Gueye, Lancelle, Laure, Moreau and Pierre-Bloch as associates. On the loyalist side, the core group included Renée Blum, Depreux, Laurent, Mayer, Naegelen, Philip, Priou-Valjean, Rougeron and Verdier, with Dumas, Grumbach and Texcier (the director of the literary review, *Gavroche*) as associates. Two uncommitted members are left: Brutelle, a former member of the Resistance from the Seine-Inférieure Federation; and Malacrida, who had an outstanding Resistance record and had stood unsuccessfully as a candidate in the Hautes-Alpes constituency in the elections of 2 June 1946.[216]

Such was the body which met on the evening of Wednesday 4 September 1946 to elect its officers. Tanguy-Prigent was unable to attend but all thirty other members were present. During the first item of business, the consideration of the rules which were to govern the committee's proceedings, there was a significant clash when Ferrat, Mollet, Capocci, Boutbien and Courtois argued that votes should be taken by a roll-call or by raising of hands, while Depreux, Malacrida, Verdier and Mayer said that, on occasions, it was necessary to be able to maintain confidentiality of voting. The principle of a secret ballot, which was approved by 17 votes to 11 with 2 abstentions,[217] must count as a defeat for Mollet and his colleagues, for whom open ballots would have served to prevent wavering sympathizers from breaking ranks. The meeting

---

[215] Edouard Depreux, *Souvenirs d'un militant: cinquante ans de lutte: de la social-démocratie au socialisme: (1918–1968)* (Fayard, Paris, 1972), p. 377. See also Georgette Elgey, *La République des illusions 1945–1951, ou la vie secrète de la IVᵉ République* (Fayard, Paris, 1965), p. 219.

[216] See the breakdown of these members presented in Table 18 in Jaffré, 'La crise du Parti Socialiste et l'avènement de Guy Mollet', p. 234. My own classification is based on a number of sources including interviews with Robert Verdier (7 July 1992), Daniel Mayer (7 July 1992), Yves Dechézelles (8 July 1992), Gérard Jaquet (23 July 1992), correspondence with Georges Rougeron (February 1993), the signatory lists of the Mollet and Philip motions, the positions taken by speakers in the debates at the party's 38th National Congress, and indications in contemporary press reports.

[217] For the record of this meeting, see *CD Minutes*, III, 4 September 1946, pp. 1–6; the account of the above division is given in ibid., p. 1.

then began to deal with the appointment of the Bureau and the various delegations of the Comité Directeur. Philip, who was in the chair, called for nominations for the post of General Secretary. The name of Augustin Laurent was proposed by Priou-Valjean and that of Mollet by Courtois. There then followed an exchange in which Mollet's supporters showed they thought that he had already established a prior claim to the office. The original typescript of the minutes records the sequence of statements as follows:

BOUTBIEN souligne qu'il y a eu au Congrès un très gros courant en faveur de Guy MOLLET.

Jean TEXCIER rappelle que la démocratie se traduit par le vote, et que la discipline est l'obéissance aux décisions prises.

Pour FERRAT, le Parti doit prouver à ses adhérents qu'il entend tirer la substance du vote des fédérations sur le rapport moral.

CAPOCCI: On doit donner satisfaction à la majorité qui s'est exprimée au Congrès.

GRUMBACH estime que l'on ne peut pas tirer de conclusions logiques de l'ensemble du Congrès. [handwritten addition omitted here]

DEPREUX: Le rapport moral a été repoussé ce qui constitue un blâme collectif à l'ancien Comité directeur, mais la motion du Congrès sur les relations avec le Parti communiste était contraire aux thèses soutenues par Guy MOLLET.

CAPOCCI: Les votes des fédérations ont donné une indication très nette pour Guy MOLLET.

When this record was approved at the subsequent meeting, on 11 September, a statement by Grumbach was rectified, and this must be the reason for the addition to the above text of the following handwritten amendment:

Il ne serait pas sage de refuser aux camarades qui ont eu la majorité au congrès l'appui le plus entier.[218]

The obvious concern of Mollet's close supporters to place moral pressure on those whose allegiance was uncertain is evidence that his core group was not confident of winning the division. The cut and thrust of the arguments is revealing. Boutbien refers in general terms to the support for Mollet among the congress delegates and implies that his appointment should simply be accepted; Texcier asserts a contrary view, that the democratic ethic requires a vote to decide the issue and a disciplined acceptance of the outcome. Ferrat and Capocci then repeat the argument that the rejection of the *rapport moral* was in essence an

---

[218] Ibid., p. 3. For the reference to rectification to the minutes of 4 September, see Minutes of the meeting of 11 September 1946, in *Cahiers Léon Blum* (Paris), nos. 6–8 (December 1979–July 1980), p. 123.

endorsement of Mollet's candidature and should therefore be respected. According to the typed record, Grumbach denies that the National Congress has produced a simple outcome, implying that the rejection of the *rapport moral* has to be set against Mollet's acceptance of the joint policy resolution. Depreux makes two telling points, first that the rejection of the *rapport moral* was formally directed against the Comité Directeur rather than against the General Secretary and secondly that the passage concerning relations with the Communist Party contained in the policy resolution was contrary to Mollet's ideas on this subject. Finally, Capocci returns to the point that the support which had been given to Mollet's motion in the federal congresses was an indication of support for the man himself.

In the ballot which followed, Guy Mollet was elected as General Secretary by 16 votes to the 14 given to Augustin Laurent.[219] The details of the division were secret so we cannot know for certain how the votes were cast, but there is general agreement that Salomon Grumbach tipped the balance by voting for Mollet. According to Depreux:

Contre toute attente Salomon Grumbach, tout en se déclarant favorable à Augustin Laurent, vota pour Guy Mollet, en disant: 'Après le rejet du rapport moral, le parti attend ce dernier. Il ne faut pas le heurter.' Si Grumbach n'avait voté pour Guy Mollet, il y aurait eu 15 voix contre 15, conformément aux pronostics des 'pointeurs', et Augustin Laurent aurait été proclamé élu au bénéfice de l'âge, à moins qu'on ait recherché un troisième homme; je ne vois pas bien lequel, mais plusieurs stratèges y ont pensé.[220]

Quilliot considers that two members who were not favourably disposed to Mollet's policy positions nevertheless voted for him, and that these two were probably Grumbach and Brutelle, 'soucieux de respecter ce qu'ils considèrent comme la volonté majoritaire'.[221] Daniel Mayer also considers that Mollet was elected because of the vote by Grumbach,

qui était pour nous, pour l'ancienne majorité, qui avait voté pour le rapport moral et le soutenait, mais qui a eu le sentiment que le Parti attendait quelque chose de nouveau. Il s'est prononcé pour que Guy Mollet soit Secrétaire.

'Si moi, Salomon Grumbach, je votais comme je le souhaite, le Comité Directeur donnerait l'impression de brusquer le Parti, qu'il ne suit pas la nouvelle majorité du Congrès.'[222]

Finally, Robert Verdier recalls Grumbach taking the view that, given the vote against the *rapport moral* and that for the general resolution

---

[219] *CD Minutes*, III, 4 September 1946, p. 3.
[220] Depreux, *Souvenirs d'un militant*, p. 378.
[221] Roger Quilliot, *La S.F.I.O. et l'exercice du pouvoir, 1944–1958* (Fayard, Paris, 1972), p. 182. On the position of Brutelle, see Lefebvre, *Guy Mollet: le mal aimé*, p. 110.
[222] Juin, *Le Combat de Daniel Mayer*, p. 190.

(which he considered had taken account of the weight of the Mollet motion), they would have an unhealthy situation were they to have a General Secretary other than Guy Mollet because of 'une espèce de vote de surprise'.[223]

After his election, Mollet called on all the members of the Comité Directeur to work together. However, first Laurent and then Verdier refused his invitation to become a Deputy Secretary and when Mayer, in the interest of party unity, asked that the three places for *délégués permanents* on the Délégation Permanente du Comité Directeur (a body composed of the General Secretary, the Deputy Secretary and representatives (*délégués permanents*) of the Comité, which dealt with contingencies) should be given to his supporters, his move prompted Ferrat to remark, 'Alors vous nous imposez trois contrôleurs.'[224] In fact, though, Mayer's proposal had cleared the way for Mollet to propose the appointment of his own supporters as Deputy Secretaries, in the knowledge that the loyalists would be satisfied with having three of their number on the Délégation Permanente. Dechézelles was appointed as Deputy Secretary (Administration) by 16 votes to 14 abstentions, Arrès-Lapoque as Deputy Secretary (Propaganda) by an identical vote, and Laurent, Mayer and Verdier became *délégués permanents*. Finally, Provo and Boutbien were elected unanimously to the posts of Treasurer and Deputy Treasurer respectively.[225]

There was left the problem of reconciling Blum to the new settlement. His one remaining official position within the party was the directorship of *Le Populaire* and, at its meeting on 4 September, the new Comité Directeur had agreed that he should be reappointed but that the decision should not be made public until he had been informed.[226] Then on Friday 6 September Blum wrote to Mollet to tell him that he had, in fact, decided before the National Congress that he could not accept a renewal of his appointment but that he now felt that his retirement would lead to false and troublesome interpretations.[227] Therefore, at its meeting on 11 September, the Comité Directeur was told that Blum had agreed to the Bureau's request that he should continue as Director of the newspaper, and it appointed Robert Verdier to serve as his deputy.[228]

[223] Interview with Robert Verdier, Paris, 23 March 1990.
[224] *CD Minutes*, III, 4 September 1946, p. 4. For the composition of this body after the previous National Congress, see ibid., II, 21 August 1945, p. 2.
[225] Ibid., III, 4 September 1946, pp. 4–5; *Bulletin Intérieur*, no. 19, October 1946, p. 1.
[226] *CD Minutes*, III, 4 September 1946, p. 5.
[227] Letter from Blum to Mollet (on *Le Populaire* notepaper, dated 'vendredi'), in 4 BL 2 Dr 5 sdr a of Archives Léon Blum (Archives d'Histoire Contemporaine de la Fondation Nationale de Sciences Politiques, Paris).
[228] Minutes of meeting of 11 September 1946, in *Cahiers Léon Blum*, nos. 6–8 (December 1979–July 1980), p. 126.

By such steps a measure of order was restored to the party's central institutions and organizational unity was preserved, but private reflection on the causes of the crisis continued. Blum's speech to the National Congress on 29 August had shown that even then he had been trying to identify and understand the intangible factors which were creating such widespread disaffection within the party. One such factor was leadership style, and this was the subject of a letter which Gaston Defferre had written to him on 3 September:

Une des choses qui, à mon avis, a provoqué le mécontentement des camarades du parti c'est le sentiment confus d'ailleurs, qu'ils ont eu que le parti n'était pas véritablement dirigé.

Autrefois quand vous étiez dans l'action toutes les décisions étaient prises courageusement, nettement – les difficultés n'étaient pas évitées elles étaient résolues.

En même temps que sur le terrain des principes vous preniez toutes vos responsabilités vous avez toujours su agir de telle façon qu'à aucun moment les militants n'avaient l'impression que leur volonté n'etait pas respectée.

En bref vous étiez ferme sur le terrain des principes et libéral et compréhensif avec les hommes alors que depuis quelques temps on a souvent, peut-être à tort, eu l'impression contraire.[229]

This was a well-meaning letter in which Defferre tried to warn Blum that Mayer's style had been judged to be indecisive and that Mayer himself had not been sufficiently understanding in his dealings with people. Nevertheless, it ignored the basic point that the relationship between Blum and Mayer was very different from that which had obtained between Blum and Faure in the pre-war period. After his return to Paris in 1945, Blum had accepted responsibility for the revision of the party's statement of doctrine and had resumed his work with *Le Populaire*; apart from that, he had avoided direct involvement in organizational affairs and in the business of the parliamentary group. Vincent Auriol might conceivably have filled the place which Blum had left had he not, for a crucial period, been almost wholly absorbed in his duties as President of the Constituent Assembly and a senior minister. The result was that Daniel Mayer had found himself burdened with extremely demanding responsibilities – mustering support for a new declaration of principles and party rules, managing an executive which was heavily weighted with representatives from the parliamentary group, and attempting to apply a strategy which took insufficient account of realities and assumed that, somehow, the party could escape

---

[229] Letter from Defferre to Blum, from Marseille, 3 September 1946, in 4 BL 2 Dr 6 sdr b of Archives Léon Blum (Archives d'Histoire Contemporaine de la Fondation Nationale de Sciences Politiques, Paris).

from its alliance with the Communists and the MRP. It is greatly to his credit that he was able to carry out his duties with such dignity.

Whatever truth there may have been in Defferre's assessment of the situation, there was far more to be considered than the skill and temperament of someone such as Mayer. As we have seen, the revolt against the central leadership was by no means as well organized as had appeared to be the case; had it been so, it could have swept through the debate on general policy at the National Congress, dominated the elections to the Comité Directeur, and placed Mollet in an unassailable position as General Secretary. As it was, the crucial meeting of the executive on 4 September was a confused affair which could easily have resulted in the choice of Augustin Laurent as General Secretary. In the days which followed, while memories were fresh and judgements still tentative, it might have been possible to analyse the fine detail of these events but for that there was no time. Instead, the currents of speculation began to flow around them, forming them into patterns of opposed myths, in one of which Blum and Mayer were seen as wronged heroes while in another Mollet was hailed as the preserver of an endangered party. Both myths still hinder our understanding of this crisis, which was a much more complicated and impersonal process than its main actors were to allow.

7   Epilogue: the Socialists and the advent of the Third Force

Within a few months of its 38th National Congress, the SFIO was embroiled in the complicated politics which accompanied the establishment of the Fourth Republic. The constitutional framework developed by the second Constituent Assembly was approved by 53 per cent of the votes in the referendum of 13 October 1946 and arrangements were then set in hand for elections to the two houses of parliament, the National Assembly and the Council of the Republic, the members of which would elect the first President of the Republic for a seven-year term. The President's first task would be to choose a Premier who, once in office, would be expected to obtain the approval of the National Assembly for the government which he intended to form. At last the period of provisional government was coming to an end and there was intense competition between the parties for a secure place within the permanent system.

The Socialists had hopes that they would emerge from the National Assembly elections of 10 November as the largest party in the new house and thus be in a position to form a purely Socialist government based on a broad parliamentary alliance with other parties[1] so the results of the poll were a great disappointment to them. In metropolitan France, the Communists' share of the vote rose from 26.15 per cent in the elections of 2 June 1946 to 28.38 per cent, that of the MRP fell slightly from 28.11 to 26.24 per cent, and that of the SFIO sharply from 21.06 to 17.87 per cent.[2] When group strengths were registered a few weeks later, the numbers of deputies in the main units (excluding *apparentés*, or associate members) were: Communists 169, MRP 163, Socialists 101, Radical Socialists 43, UDSR 23, Inde-

---

[1] See Blum's editorial on this theme ('Coalitions et soutien') in *Le Populaire* (Paris), 24 October 1946, in Blum, *L'Oeuvre de Léon Blum 1945–1947* (Albin Michel, Paris, 1958), pp. 324–6.
[2] The percentage shares of the vote for the election of 10 November 1946 are based on an analysis of the constituency returns given in *JO (AN)*, *Déb.*, 28 November 1946, pp. 7–36; 29 November 1946, pp. 42–3; 30 January 1947, p. 103.

pendent Republicans 27, and the right-wing Parti Républicain de la Liberté (PRL) 35 in a house of 619 members.[3] In arithmetical terms, the old tripartite alliance of the Communists, the Socialists and the MRP could have had a base of more than 430 members, well above the 'constitutional' or absolute majority of 310, but it was also possible for interested groups to think in terms either of a Popular Front alliance of Communists, Socialists and Radicals with more than 310 seats, or a centre alliance of Socialists, the MRP, the Radicals and the UDSR with about 330 seats. These alternatives were soon under discussion, and once more the Socialists found themselves at the centre of a field of contrary forces, pulled one way by the Communists and another by the increasingly confident groups at the centre and centre right of the party system.

Both the Communist Party and the MRP wanted to break away from *tripartisme*, the former in pursuit of a new Popular Front and the latter in quest of a centre alliance; each put its leader forward as a candidate for the presidency of the provisional government which was needed to provide a bridge between the outgoing Bidault ministry and the first regular administration of the Fourth Republic. For this election, the constituency was the membership of the newly appointed National Assembly. First Maurice Thorez and then Bidault failed to obtain the absolute majority (310) of the votes required and finally, in the third ballot on 12 December, Léon Blum was elected to the post. Having tried without success to arrange a coalition government, Blum decided to form a purely Socialist administration, which took office on 16 December. The negotiations surrounding the candidatures of Thorez and Bidault had already compelled the Socialists to consider once again the question of alliances and this had been the subject of debate at a specially convened meeting of the party's National Council on 3 and 4 December. The first session of this gathering had recommended that the members of the Socialist parliamentary group should vote for Thorez when his nomination was put to the vote: the second, held after his name had been rejected, involved the delegates in a choice between two policy motions. In one, the Sarthe Federation proposed that the party should neither support nor participate in any government, nor should it join any parliamentary majority which did not include the Communists; in the second, the Vaucluse Federation recommended that, while the party should not participate in any government, it should give its support to any administration which was prepared to implement acceptable measures and policies. Both motions were loaded with

---

[3] Ibid., 29 November 1946, pp. 40–2.

implications. Whereas the Sarthe text had been framed to try to pre-serve the principle that the Socialists should not break with the Com-munists in order to join a centre alliance, the Vaucluse text had been written to appeal not only to anti-participationist sentiment but also to those among the delegates who were prepared to explore new parlia-mentary strategies, including that of providing conditional support to a centre government. For his part, Mollet recommended the acceptance of the Sarthe proposal, and this was the one eventually approved by 2,242 mandates against 2,125 for the Vaucluse motion, with 55 absten-tions and 63 mandates credited to absent delegates.[4] This vote had been designed as a tactical response to a particular situation, but Mollet and his supporters on the Comité Directeur came to attach considerable significance to the Sarthe formula, despite the possibility that the parlia-mentary group might find it unduly restrictive and that it could, there-fore, become a point of contention between that group and the General Secretary.

Meanwhile, the elections for the Council of the Republic having been completed, the final stages in the establishment of the new regime were being set in train. On 16 January 1947, the members of both houses of parliament elected Vincent Auriol as the first President of the Fourth Republic; having consulted the party leaders, he appointed Paul Ram-adier, a fellow Socialist, to be Premier. Ramadier's government, which took office on 22 January, included representatives from an unusually wide range of party groups – from the Communists on the left to the Radicals, the UDSR and the Independent Republicans on the centre right – but the distribution of the key portfolios showed Ramadier's intention to retain the essential control in the hands of the Socialists and the MRP. Within the Socialist contingent, Félix Gouin had been given charge of the economic plan which was being developed by Jean Monnet and his colleagues, Edouard Depreux had been entrusted with the Ministry of the Interior, André Philip with National Economy, Jules Moch with Public Works and Transport, François Tanguy-Prigent with Agriculture, Robert Lacoste with Industrial Production, Marcel-Edmond Naegelen with Education and Marius Moutet with Colonies, while amongst the MRP ministers Georges Bidault had been assigned the Foreign Affairs and Robert Schuman the Finance portfolios. The underlying strategy was quite clear: with a Socialist President, a Socialist Premier and with Socialist control of most of the key domestic port-folios, the SFIO was looking to occupy the centre of Fourth Republican

[4] *Bulletin Intérieur du Parti Socialiste (S.F.I.O.)* (Paris), no. 21, December 1946, pp. 3–4; *Le Populaire*, 4 December 1946, pp. 1 and 4; 5 December 1946, pp. 1 and 4; *Le Monde* (Paris) 5 December 1946, p. 1; 6 December 1946, p. 1.

politics, much as the Radicals had provided the effective centre of the politics of the Third Republic except for certain brief interludes. At its disposal the party now had a sizeable body of *ministrables* who were in a good position to dominate the parliamentary group and to challenge the authority of the Comité Directeur.

The area in which a clash between Guy Mollet and the parliamentary group was most likely to occur was over the problem of deciding whether or not the party should side with the Premier if he came into conflict with the Communists over a major question of policy. The problem was first posed during the National Council meeting of 19 and 20 March 1947, which coincided with a major parliamentary crisis over the government's Indo-China policy. In December 1946, fighting had broken out in Tonkin China between the French military forces and the Viet Minh guerrillas and by March 1947 the point at issue was the best means of restoring peace and order; should the French authorities negotiate directly with Ho Chi Minh, the head of the Vietnamese government associated with the Vietminh, or should they encourage the formation of an alternative government which would accept integration in an Indo-Chinese federation within the French Union? The Ramadier government had tried to pursue a compromise policy by retaining French troops in Tonkin China while at the same time holding open the possibility that a new administration could be established in that province. In the days preceding the meeting of the National Council there had been a debate on Indo-China in the National Assembly, during which the government had come under attack not only from right-wing deputies but also from the Communists, who were pressing for direct negotiations with Ho Chi Minh and his government. When, on 18 March, a motion of confidence had been put to the vote and adopted, the Communist ministers had voted for it but the remaining Communist deputies had abstained. There was talk of a crisis, and the first session of the National Council on the 19th concluded with a debate on the Indo-China question. Tension increased on the 20th, when the Communists said that they would vote against a request for additional funds for the defence budget, a move which obliged Ramadier to put a question of confidence to the Assembly, thus challenging the Communist ministers, and indirectly the Communist parliamentary group, to make up their minds as to whether or not they wished to remain within the parliamentary majority. The second session of the National Council was disturbed by these events but in the end the delegates simply adopted a resolution which called on the Comité Directeur and the parliamentary group, in the event of a ministerial crisis, to avoid any action which might drive the two parties into opposed blocs; where

Indo-China was concerned, it specified a policy which generally conformed to the government's position. Had the crisis not been resolved, the Comité Directeur might have been forced to adopt a stronger line, but once again the Communist ministers observed the convention of collective responsibility, voting for the extra defence funds while the rest of their group registered abstentions.[5]

The Socialist connection with the Communists was again placed under strain in the last few days of April 1947, when a strike at the Renault works in Paris spread rapidly to other factories in the region and first the CGT and then the Communist Party came out in support of the widespread demand for wage increases. In his declaration to the National Assembly on 21 January, Ramadier had committed himself to continue the policy of bringing down prices while at the same time resisting pressure for higher wages and he saw no sound reason for modifying his position. At a Cabinet meeting on Thursday 1 May, Auriol told Maurice Thorez and other Communist ministers that he expected Ramadier to go before the National Assembly to obtain renewed backing for his policies and he made it clear to them that, even were the Communist ministers to leave office, he would not accept the government's resignation.[6] On Friday 2 May, Ramadier put a question of confidence to the National Assembly but, because under Article 49 of the Constitution one full day had to lapse before the vote could be taken, it was deferred until 10 a.m. on Sunday the 4th. The Assembly duly met at that hour and at 12.50 p.m., after a brief debate, adopted an order of the day expressing confidence in the general policy of the government by 360 votes to 186. All the members of the Communist group, ministers included, voted with the opposition, but Thorez and his colleagues made no move to resign from the government.[7]

At 3 p.m. Auriol, Ramadier and Blum conferred briefly at the Pavillon de Marly, the former hunting-lodge near Paris reserved for official figures, and Blum expressed the view that Ramadier should remain at the head of the government.[8] He and Ramadier then left to attend a meeting of the Comité Directeur, where Ramadier argued that it was now necessary for him to drop the Communist ministers from his Cabinet. However, Mollet insisted that Ramadier himself should resign from office, a view which was endorsed by 12 votes to 9. Voting with

[5] For the relevant National Council resolutions, see *Bulletin Intérieur*, no. 24, March 1947, pp. 2 and 3. On the background, see B. D. Graham, *The French Socialists and Tripartisme 1944–1947* (Weidenfeld and Nicolson, London, 1965), pp. 252–7.

[6] See Vincent Auriol, *Journal du septennat 1947–1954*, I, *1947*, ed. Pierre Nora (Armand Colin, Paris, 1970), 1 May 1947, pp. 205–10.

[7] See *L'Année politique 1947* (Éditions du Grand Siècle, Paris, 1948), pp. 92–3.

[8] Auriol, *Journal du septennat 1947–1954*, I, *1947*, 4 May 1947, pp. 215–16.

Mollet in the majority were Jacques Arrès-Lapoque, Léon Boutbien, Georges Brutelle, Suzanne Charpy, Pierre Commin, Yves Dechézelles, André Ferrat, Charles Lancelle, Emilienne Moreau, Jean Pierre-Bloch and Jean Rous, and the minority consisted of Jean Courtois (who had supported Mollet at the 38th National Congress), Edouard Depreux, Salomon Grumbach, Amadou Lamine-Gueye, Daniel Mayer, André Philip, François Tanguy-Prigent, Jean Texcier and Renée Blum.[9] This debate had raised the question of whether the organization should control the activities of the party's parliamentary group and it is significant that the majority contained no parliamentarians other than Mollet, who was a deputy, whereas the minority included five deputies (Depreux, Lamine-Gueye, Mayer, Philip and Tanguy-Prigent) and one member of the Council of the Republic (Grumbach). The members of the Comité Directeur then attended a meeting of the parliamentary group, but this body decided by 69 votes to 9 that Ramadier should be advised to dismiss the Communist ministers and assign their portfolios to others until the National Council, which was due to meet on the following Tuesday, could consider the matter.[10] The Comité Directeur then met again at 7 p.m. to reconsider its position and this time the division produced 10 votes in favour of the continuation of the government and 9 votes for its resignation; the reversal of the balance between the two sides had been caused by the decision of Emilienne Moreau to vote with the Blumistes on this occasion, the abstention of Jean Pierre-Bloch and the absence of Charles Lancelle.[11]

A special decree published on the morning of Monday 5 May put an end to the tenure of office of four of the five Communist ministers and the fifth resigned that afternoon. Although their departure was not taken to signify a definite break in party alignments, Mollet and his supporters kept up their opposition to the policy of the parliamentary group and tried to persuade the National Council, which began its session on Tuesday 6 May, that the Ramadier government should resign. In the final division, 2,125 mandates were cast for resignation and a majority of 2,529 for continuation, with 2 abstentions. However, the National Council also adopted a policy resolution stating that the party could neither lend itself to a coalition which, through anti-communism, would result in the formation of opposed blocs and divide the workers, nor participate in a government supported by a reactionary majority.[12]

---

[9] Parti Socialiste (SFIO), *Minutes of Meetings of the Comité Directeur* (hereafter *CD Minutes*), III, 4 May 1947 (first meeting), pp. 348–53.
[10] Auriol, *Journal du septennat 1947–1954*, I, *1947*, p. 759, n. 13.
[11] *CD Minutes*, III, 4 May 1947 (second meeting), p. 354.
[12] *Bulletin Intérieur*, no. 25, April–May 1947, pp. 1–2.

Mollet's group had suffered its first tactical defeat but its resources were still considerable. Despite the fact that bloc votes from the Nord and Haute-Vienne Federations and a solid majority vote from the Bouches-du-Rhône Federation had been cast in favour of keeping the Ramadier government in office, the option of resignation had been backed by the Gironde, Seine and Seine-et-Oise Federations and, of course, by the Pas-de-Calais Federation. Mollet, by sticking to the principle that Socialists should never break with that section of the working class connected with the Communist Party, had adopted a position very similar to that which Paul Faure had exploited so effectively in the late 1920s and early 1930s during the expansive early period of the Bataille Socialiste, when he had stressed the need to avoid involvement in government and to preserve the doctrinal integrity of the party. Unlike Faure, he lacked the important backing of the parliamentary group and the Communist Party which he faced was a larger and more complex one than that which Faure had encountered in the inter-war period; nevertheless, his hostility towards the parliamentary group and his suspicion of the motivation of the *ministrables* were very reminiscent of the attitudes of his predecessor.

In his confrontation with the parliamentary group, Mollet had been backed by a solid group within the Comité Directeur but in June 1947 one of his two deputies, Yves Dechézelles, resigned from his post. In a letter to Mollet he explained that the gap between the general orientation which had been determined by the 38th National Congress and the actual policy of the majority of the party's representatives at the level of government and parliament had become so wide that he no longer felt able to carry out the duties assigned to him by the Comité Directeur. He went on to complain about the government's policies regarding Indo-China and Madagascar, the Comité Directeur's decision of 4 June to dissolve the Bureau National of the Jeunesses Socialistes, and the situation which had been created by the National Council's approval of the continuation of the Ramadier government.[13] He was replaced as Deputy Secretary by Georges Brutelle, but his departure from the party's Bureau deprived Mollet of a valuable source of information about French colonial affairs, and particularly about the worsening situation in Indo-China.

At the 39th National Congress held at Lyon between 14 and 17 August 1947, however, Mollet gained further support for his basic strategy. His *rapport moral* was approved by 3,068 mandates to 1,111 with

---

[13] Letter from Dechézelles to Mollet, from Paris, 12 June 1947, ibid., no. 26, May–June 1947, p. 7.

606 abstentions, and his motion on general policy received 2,423 mandates, compared with 2,002 given to a motion from the Nord Federation, 274 to a text sponsored by Dechézelles, and 85 abstentions. Whereas at the 1946 Congress, Mollet had allowed his motion to fall away in the Resolutions Committee, on this occasion he insisted on putting his text to the vote and avoided a compromise or synthesis motion. His 1947 resolution envisaged the Comité Directeur's taking control of the party press, its parliamentary representatives and its ministers, repeated the familiar argument that participation in government could be justified only if it enabled the party to implement a truly socialist programme, criticized the Ramadier government's policies and set out a heavily *dirigiste* case for state intervention in the economy. Besides forcing through this motion, the Mollet group also improved its position on the Comité Directeur. In the elections for this body, Mollet himself and most of the members of his group were returned, along with others of his supporters such as Pierre Rimbert, Camille Delabre and Jacques Piette. Several Blumistes, including Daniel Mayer, Robert Verdier and Gérard Jaquet, also secured places but they were now quite definitely in a minority.[14] At its first meeting on 27 August 1947, the new Comité unanimously elected Mollet for his second term as General Secretary, and Brutelle and Pierre Commin as his deputies.[15] Not only was the parliamentary group now on the defensive; Ramadier had been so shaken by the decisions which had been taken at this congress that he asked Auriol if he could resign as Premier, an eventuality which the President refused to contemplate.[16]

A few weeks later, two events were dramatically to alter the conditions affecting French party politics. In October 1947, the French Communist Party decided to adopt a position of outright opposition to the government, and Charles de Gaulle's new organization, the Rassemblement du Peuple Français (RPF), had a remarkable success in the municipal elections. The first sign that the PCF was hardening its views came on 5 October with the news that, at a meeting towards the end of September, nine European Communist Parties, including those of France and Italy, had established an information bureau, subsequently known as the Cominform, and had claimed that the world was now divided into opposed blocs, one imperialist and anti-democratic and the other anti-imperialist and democratic.[17] The changed mood of the PCF was made clear on 30 October at a meeting of its Central Committee,

[14] Ibid., no. 27, August 1947, pp. 1–9.
[15] Ibid., p. 10.
[16] Auriol, *Journal du septennat 1947–1954*, I, *1947*, 18 August 1947, pp. 397–8.
[17] Ibid., p. 804, n. 17; *L'Année politique 1947*, p. 192.

when it adopted a resolution to the effect that the collaboration which had taken place between the Communists and other parties during the period of the Popular Front, the Resistance and *tripartisme* was at an end and that it would no longer participate in government.[18] Almost as disturbing for the non-Communist parties had been the rapid growth of the RPF, which de Gaulle had founded in April 1947 with the aim of bringing about a revision of the Constitution and rallying the French people to support this venture. In the municipal elections of 19 and 26 October 1947, the RPF had won more than 38 per cent of the votes in the large towns, mainly at the expense of the MRP, and de Gaulle, heartened by this result, had issued a statement on 27 October calling for the dissolution of the National Assembly, the holding of fresh elections within a majority voting system, and a revision of the Constitution by the incoming Assembly.[19] Faced with two such determined and aggressive opponents, those parties which were committed to the principle of parliamentary democracy were forced to combine to defend the Fourth Republic and its underlying regime.

Awareness of these issues influenced the way in which the various parties responded to the ministerial crisis which developed in November 1947. For their part, the Socialists showed an unusual willingness to work towards a general settlement with the MRP. Although Ramadier's personal qualities were admired, the MRP considered that a new and more stable government was required and a search for a suitable successor was already under way when, on 19 November, the Ramadier ministry resigned from office. Léon Blum was then asked to form an administration but as he obtained only 300 votes in the investiture ballot on the 21st (9 short of the constitutional majority), Auriol had to turn to other possible candidates. He eventually persuaded Robert Schuman of the MRP to undertake the task and Schuman formed a broad-based ministry in which the Socialists were given the important portfolios of the Interior (Jules Moch), Industry and Commerce (Robert Lacoste), National Education (Marcel-Edmond Naegelen), Public Works and Transport (Christian Pineau) and Labour and Social Security (Daniel Mayer).[20] The movement for the creation of a Third Force, that is, for a broad alliance of those parties which were prepared to defend the parliamentary regime, now had wide support and a meeting of the SFIO's National Council on 16 and 17 December authorized the party's Comité Directeur to proceed with negotiations to organize such an

[18] *L'Année politique 1947*, p. 215
[19] Ibid., pp. 193–6.
[20] Ibid., pp. 216–22.

arrangement.[21] On 2 January 1948, the Comité National d'Initiative of the Third Force reached broad agreement on the principles of the alliance and decided to form an executive bureau and, at a later stage, a National Committee.[22]

The Third Force also had an international dimension and by joining it the Socialists signified their willingness to accept the value of the Marshall Plan in aiding the economic recovery of western Europe, and to take a stand against the Communist take-over of Czechoslovakia in February 1948. Mollet was in Vienna when the Czech crisis was brewing and he actually took the opportunity to visit Prague, where the Czech Socialists sought to reassure him about the wisdom of sharing power with the Communists. Although they made light of Mollet's expressions of anxiety, he learned soon after his return to Paris that the Communists had seized power in their country.[23] However, rather than accept that France should simply align itself with the United States in what was to become the Cold War, Mollet and his fellow Socialists insisted on the need for a united Europe as a kind of middle ground between the Soviet Union and the USA. The acceptance of the Third Force meant that Mollet faced a major adjustment of strategy and the necessity of managing a realignment of groups within the SFIO. The pattern which had held at the time of the 39th National Congress had been one where the majority of the Comité Directeur had been set against the ministers and most of the members of the parliamentary group, but Mollet and some of his original supporters now had to come to terms with recent opponents such as Augustin Laurent, Edouard Depreux and Gérard Jaquet, and thus a new ruling group was established within the party.[24] As this realignment was taking place, many of his supporters on the left of the SFIO tried unsuccessfully to develop various forms of opposition to the new strategy. Yves Dechézelles formed a group known as the Action Socialiste Révolutionnaire; Elie Bloncourt, Andrée Marty-Capgras, Jean-Maurice Hermann and Pierre Stibbe became involved in the Mouvement Socialiste Unitaire et Démocratique and were amongst those whose activities on behalf of this organization caused their expulsion from the party in January 1948 on charges of indiscipline;[25] and

---

[21] *Bulletin Intérieur*, no. 29, January 1948, p. 18.

[22] Ibid., pp. 3–4.

[23] Denis Lefebvre, *Guy Mollet: le mal aimé* (Plon, Paris, 1992), pp. 126–7.

[24] On this point, see Gilles Morin, 'La S.F.I.O. et la Troisième Force, octobre 1947–juillet 1948, une expérience peu connue, le bureau exécutif de la Troisième Force', *Cahier et Revue de l'OURS* (Paris), no. 175 (May–June 1987), pp. 28–37, especially p. 35.

[25] See *Bulletin Intérieur*, no. 29, January 1948, p. 26.

Jean Rous, Léon Boutbien, Pierre Rimbert, Raymond Badiou, Amadou Lamine-Gueye, Maurice Rabier and Jacques Arrès-Lapoque were drawn into the Rassemblement Démocratique Révolutionnaire (RDR), which had been formed as a rallying-point for the non-Communist left.[26] For a period, the Comité Directeur tolerated a situation in which individuals could belong to both the RDR and the SFIO but it eventually decided that from 7 May 1948 no Socialist could be a member of the RDR at the local, departmental or national level without also belonging to the equivalent unit of the Third Force.[27]

The change in strategy was confirmed at the party's 40th National Congress held in Paris between 1 and 4 July 1948, when a motion supported by a majority of the Resolutions Committee recommended the continued acceptance of the rally behind the Third Force. This text, which went on to express approval for secularism, the social security system, nationalizations, the maintenance of the Resistance press and increased purchasing power for the workers, was given 3,652 mandates as against 955 for a motion defended by Jean Rous, with 119 abstentions. The division list showed that the large federations of Bouches-du-Rhône, Nord, Pas-de-Calais, Seine-et-Oise and Haute-Vienne had given the bulk or all of their mandates in favour of the official motion, and the weakness of the left-wing opposition was demonstrated by the size of the majority (3,675 mandates against 733 with 138 abstentions) for the rejection of a proposal to allow individual members of the party to take part in the activities of the RDR. The new ruling group was able to dominate the elections to the Comité Directeur, which now contained very few members of the praetorian guard which had surrounded Mollet on the committee elected at the 38th National Congress: Léon Boutbien, Jean Courtois and André Ferrat still had places but Jacques Arrès-Lapoque, Yves Dechézelles, Jean Rous, Charles Lancelle and Suzanne Charpy were no longer there.[28] Yet Mollet's position as General Secretary was still secure. On 7th July he was re-elected to that office by the new committee, which also reappointed Georges Brutelle and Pierre Commin as his deputies.[29]

A long period of ministerial instability in the months following this congress placed the Third Force alliance and its constituent units under

[26] On these three organizations, see Gilles Martinet, 'La gauche non conformiste', *La Nef* (April–May 1951), pp. 50–1; Jean Rous, 'De la crise du socialisme au renouveau démocratique et révolutionnaire', *Esprit*, 17, 2 (February 1949), pp. 312–15; Roger Quilliot, *La S.F.I.O. et l'exercice du pouvoir 1944–1958* (Fayard, Paris, 1972), pp. 281–90.
[27] See *Bulletin Intérieur*, no. 34, June 1948, p. 6.
[28] Ibid., no. 35, July 1948, pp. 3–15.
[29] Ibid., no. 37, November–December 1948, p. 5.

considerable strain. The difficulties began on 19 July 1948 when, as a result of the National Assembly's decision to adopt a motion to reduce defence expenditure proposed by a Socialist deputy, the Schuman government resigned. André Marie, a Radical leader, then formed an administration which included Léon Blum as one of two Vice-Premiers, Paul Reynaud, an Independent, as Minister of Finance and Economic Affairs, and a number of Socialists, among them Jules Moch as Minister of the Interior and Daniel Mayer as Minister of Labour and Social Security. Things did not go smoothly, as Reynaud's determination to overhaul the economic and financial policies of the government in order to prepare France for the ending of American aid under the Marshall Plan in 1952 met with severe criticism from the Socialist ministers, who were concerned that the levels of real wages should not be depressed by price increases.[30] Unable to reconcile the opposed points of view, André Marie decided on 27 August to submit the resignation of the ministry, and Robert Schuman was asked to form another administration. His first attempt failed when first the Socialists and then the Radicals refused to accept places in his Cabinet, but he succeeded in his second attempt and on 5 September took office with a government which included Christian Pineau, a Socialist, as Minister of Finance. This appointment earned him the hostility of most of the Conservative and Radical deputies and led to the fall of his ministry when a vote of confidence was rejected by the National Assembly on 7 September.[31] Auriol was coming to the conclusion that the Third Force formula was no longer working; however, the experienced Radical leader, Henri Queuille, was persuaded to continue the search for a stable administration. On 11 September he formed a broad-based ministry extending from the Socialists to the PRL and wisely decided to keep the portfolio of Finance and Economic Affairs in his own hands; most of the other important posts were allocated either to the Socialists or the MRP, the former being given the portfolios of the Interior (Jules Moch), National Defence (Paul Ramadier), Public Works (Christian Pineau), Industry and Commerce (Robert Lacoste) and Labour and Social Security (Daniel Mayer).[32]

The French economy, boosted by the inflow of American aid under the Marshall Plan, was now well on the way to recovery. Measured against bases of 100 for the year 1938, the index of French industrial production had risen from 84 in 1946 to 113 in 1948 and that of national

[30] See Auriol, *Journal du septennat 1947–1954*, II, *1948*, ed. Jean-Pierre Azéma (Armand Colin, Paris, 1974), 5 August 1948, pp. 352–8; 27 August 1948, pp. 372–87.
[31] See ibid., 5 and 7 September 1948, pp. 426 and 676, nn. 27–8.
[32] Ibid., p. 678, n. 54.

income from 83 in 1946 to 96 in 1948.[33] However, the Socialists were well aware that the long years of austerity and shortages had made their supporters impatient for an improvement in their living standards, and they resented having to share the responsibility for government policies while the CGT and the Communists were able to encourage their members to make demands without having to consider whether there were resources to meet them. Moreover, each Socialist minister found himself with heavy administrative duties; Jules Moch, for example, had, as Minister of the Interior, to bear the strain of dealing with the strikes which spread through France in the autumn of 1948, strikes which the Communist Party and its allies in the CGT encouraged as a means of challenging the government's authority.[34] As during *tripartisme*, it looked as though the SFIO had sacrificed the material interests of its supporting groups in order to carry out public duties for the good of the Republic. It was difficult for the party organization, under these circumstances, to maintain the enthusiasm of its activists and there were indications that membership numbers were declining.[35]

By the time that the party's 41st National Congress was held in Paris between 15 and 18 July 1949, the large ruling majority which Mollet had assembled in 1948 was beginning to crumble. On the left of the party, Léon Boutbien, Jacques Arrès-Lapoque and Suzanne Charpy had come forward with a motion calling for an end to participation in government and withdrawal from the Queuille ministry while also arguing that the concept of the dictatorship of the proletariat still deserved serious consideration.[36] A more substantial challenge to Mollet's position was set out in a discussion paper which became known as the Depreux–Philip motion, after its principal signatories. This suggested that the party needed to be reformed substantially if it were to deal effectively with the choice between participation in government, conditional support for a government, and opposition. Besides Edouard Depreux and André Philip, its initial signatories included Gaston Defferre, Gérard Jaquet, Marceau Pivert and Jacques Piette.[37] They were, in effect, employing the same adversarial method which Mollet himself had used in framing his *redressement* motion in 1946; there was the same suggestion that the party's organization had been neglected by its bureaucracy; that this state of affairs was impairing its ability to

---

[33] See Table I in Jean-Pierre Rioux, *La France de la IVe République*, I, *L'Ardeur et la nécessité 1944–1952* (Seuil, Paris, 1980), p. 245.
[34] See ibid., pp. 211–13.
[35] See Quilliot, *La S.F.I.O. et l'exercice du pouvoir 1944–1958*, pp. 290–2.
[36] 'Être et rester socialiste', *Bulletin Intérieur*, no. 43, June 1949, pp. 9–12.
[37] *D'abord refaire le Parti!* (no printing details) (author's collection).

promote its policies and to act effectively at the levels of parliament and government; and that they, the critics, possessed the vision and skills required to improve its management. It seemed likely that, were the SFIO to suffer setbacks of the kind which had affected it in the summer of 1946, the balance of advantage could swing their way.

At the 41st National Congress, the majority of the Resolutions Committee again approved a short policy statement which simply affirmed the need for the party to take steps to define and advance its own policies; while opposing both the idea of permanent participation in government and that of systematic non-participation, it argued that the question was one to be determined not by doctrine but by circumstances. This text obtained 1,663 mandates, the Depreux–Philip motion 852, the Boutbien motion 423 mandates, and there were 14 abstentions. The division list revealed that the Nord, Seine-et-Oise and Haute-Vienne Federations were still aligned with the Pas-de-Calais Federation in the majority, but that the Depreux–Philip motion had been backed by bloc votes from the Bouches-du-Rhône and Gironde and a majority of the mandates from the Seine Federation.[38] These were the only signs of serious dissent. The elections to the Comité Directeur did not produce a significant change of membership[39] and Mollet, Brutelle and Commin were all returned to their posts in the secretariat when the incoming Comité Directeur held its first meeting on 20 July.[40]

Mollet's place in the party's internal political system was now secure; he had completed his transition from his initial position on the left of party opinion to his new place at the centre and had secured the backing of the powerful Nord Federation; he had strengthened the role of the Comité Directeur in relation to the parliamentary group and had established his right, as General Secretary, to play a full part in discussions as to whether or not the SFIO should join a coalition government. To a much greater extent than Paul Faure, he had taken a direct interest in national and international affairs and his reports to the party in the late 1940s show an intelligent and increasingly sophisticated grasp of the basic policy issues. In the process, he had himself become one of the party's *ministrables* and much better prepared to deal with a major portfolio than he had been when he had served as a Minister of State in Blum's short-lived ministry between 16 December 1946 and 16 January 1947. He had also become skilled at dealing with the constant flow of low-level conflicts within the party's leadership group, and had

---

[38] *Bulletin Intérieur*, no. 44, November 1949, pp. 5–6 and 13.
[39] Ibid., p. 12.
[40] Parti Socialiste (SFIO), 42ᵉ Congrès National, Paris, 26–29 Mai 1950, *Rapports* (no publication details), p. 164.

avoided the mistake of representing his critics as forming a bloc or standing for a fixed attitude. When he denied, in October 1948, that the Comité Directeur contained *tendances clichées*, he incidentally provided a revealing glimpse of his own idea of how to avoid lasting confrontations.

Quant à l'accusation portée contre certains camarades du Comité Directeur de ne plus être des hommes libres et de ne plus avoir le courage de prendre de positions personnelles différentes des miennes, je veux simplement rappeler qu'il n'y a pas, dans le Comité Directeur, de position permanente. Lorsqu'on a élu l'actuel bureau, certains ont voté pour le Secrétaire général, d'autres contre. Mais quinze jours après, dès le premier débat politique, les votes se confondaient, la moitié de ceux qui avaient voté contre moi se trouvaient d'accord avec mes impressions et inversement. Il n'est pas de minorité constituée que représenteraient les uns ou les autres; pas davantage de majorité fidèle. Il n'est que des hommes qui réfléchissent et prennent librement leurs responsabilités.[41]

By the autumn of 1949, the party was losing patience with its coalition partners. Contrary to expectations, the SFIO had not become the Radical Party of the Fourth Republic; even in the Third Force coalitions it had been treated as a party on the left margin of acceptability, especially where financial and economic policies were concerned, and the clash between its ministers and Paul Reynaud during the period of the André Marie government had shown it the futility of pursuing goals which were incompatible with those of its coalition partners. It had agreed with its allies about the basic strategy of the Third Force, but by 1949 both the PCF and the RPF had become known quantities; the time of rapid movement which had created so much uncertainty in 1947 and 1948 had given way to a form of trench warfare in which the need to maintain the Third Force in a state of immediate readiness was no longer so pressing. Unless the SFIO were willing to modify its ideas, its most sensible course seemed to be to move back into opposition and to take its case to a general audience. As Minister for Labour and Social Security, Daniel Mayer was especially concerned about a number of issues affecting industrial relations. In particular, he considered that the time had come to provide for free wage bargaining (the state had been determining wage levels since 1946), with a system of collective agreements between employers and employees, and for legislation to deal with conciliation and arbitration procedures in labour negotiations. Added weight was given to his arguments by the devaluation of the franc on 19 September 1949, which threatened to increase prices and

[41] From a speech by Mollet at an information session of the National Council, 9 October 1948 (*Bulletin Intérieur*, no. 36, October 1948, p. 42).

thus to decrease real wages. Mayer also favoured interim allowances for low-paid workers, but met with resistance from Maurice Petsche, who had taken over the Finance and Economic Affairs portfolio from Queuille, and from others in the Cabinet.[42] Although a communiqué regarding the government's intentions in this area of policy was agreed at a Cabinet meeting on 1 October 1949, Mayer said that he could not accept several of the points made, especially a phrase which simply referred to the issue of special assistance for low-paid workers by indicating that arrangements would be made to meet the exceptional situation affecting certain wage-earners; he therefore reserved the right not to observe the principle of collective ministerial responsibility within the institutions of his party where such points were concerned (in other words, he was claiming the right to discuss these matters with members of the SFIO's Comité Directeur),[43] and he further stated these views in a letter of 3 October to the Premier.[44] Queuille had now reached the limit of his patience, and on 5 October he handed his resignation to Auriol, complaining of the action of the SFIO's Comité Directeur in supporting Mayer, which provoked the President to express his regret that this body had broken yet another government.[45]

The subsequent ministerial crisis proved very difficult to resolve. Jules Moch was given a chance to form a government but, though he obtained the necessary majority in an investiture vote, he failed in his efforts to put together a team of ministers which would have been acceptable to all the parties of the Third Force. René Mayer, a Radical, also tried to assemble a ministry and actually persuaded the Socialist parliamentary group to accept his terms, but this body later reversed its decision following the rejection of the same terms by the SFIO's Comité Directeur.[46] Finally, a new government was installed under Georges Bidault, the MRP leader, with Socialists holding the portfolios of the Interior (Jules Moch), Public Works (Christian Pineau), Industry and Commerce (Robert Lacoste), Labour and Social Security (Pierre Segelle) and Posts and Telegraphs (Eugène Thomas). However, the

---

[42] See Auriol, *Journal du septennat 1947–1954*, III, *1949*, ed. Pierre Kerleroux (Armand Colin, Paris, 1977), 28 September 1949, pp. 338–40. See also the account of these policy differences in Guy Mollet's report to the National Council on 6 November 1949, in *Bulletin Intérieur*, no. 45, December 1949, pp. 5–6.

[43] See Auriol, *Journal du septennat 1947–1954*, III, *1949*, 1 October 1949, pp. 345–8.

[44] For the text of this letter, see 'Histoire du Parti Socialiste S.F.I.O.', Part 27, '1948–1951', *Cahier et Revue de l'OURS*, no. 177 (September–October 1987), pp. 9–10. See also Georgette Elgey, *La République des illusions 1945–1951, ou la vie secrète de la IVᵉ République* (Fayard, Paris, 1965), pp. 410–11.

[45] See Auriol, *Journal du septennat 1947–1954*, III, *1949*, 5 October 1949, pp. 348–9.

[46] See 'Histoire du Parti Socialiste S.F.I.O.', Part 27, '1948–1951', *Cahier et Revue de l'OURS*, no. 177 (September–October 1987), p. 10.

task of maintaining a consistent negotiating position throughout this period of crisis had strained relations between the Comité Directeur and the party's parliamentary group. In consequence, the Comité Directeur proposed that all decisions regarding the adoption of a government's programme, the acceptance or refusal of participation in or support for a government, and related matters such as the resignation of a Socialist Premier or the withdrawal of Socialist ministers from a coalition, should be taken by a committee consisting of the 31 members of the Comité Directeur and 15 members elected by the Socialist parliamentarians.[47] The formation of such a body, which became known the Comité de 46, was approved by an extraordinary National Congress of 13–14 December 1949. The same congress also adopted a resolution which accepted the SFIO's participation in the Bidault ministry by 1,933 mandates to 957, with 54 abstentions.[48] It was perfectly clear, however, that the party was attaching itself to this administration with certain misgivings.

These were to increase in January 1950 when Bidault, experiencing difficulty in securing approval for his government's budget, was not in a position to make concessions to the Socialist ministers when they returned to the question of special allowances for low-paid workers. An initial allowance had been made in November 1949 and its renewal had been proposed by the National Assembly on 26 January 1950, but the terms of the payment, and in particular the upper salary limit of those eligible for it, had still to be determined. After the matter had been discussed by the Comité de 46 on the evening of 1 February, the Socialist ministers decided to press for the acceptance of their proposals and, meeting with a refusal, on 4 February they resigned from the government.[49] At once, Bidault reorganized his Cabinet and carried on without them.

The SFIO had discussed the philosophy of participation almost continuously since 1945 and there was now general agreement that it was no longer a matter of high principle but rather one of convenience. However, there remained the central problem of whether the parliamentary group, released from the responsibilities of power, should simply revert to a position of outright opposition or whether, following Blum's advice, it should provide constructive support for Bidault's gov-

---

[47] For the proposal as presented by Mollet, see *Bulletin Intérieur*, no. 45, December 1949, pp. 20–1.

[48] Ibid., no. 46, January 1950, pp. 31–2.

[49] See Auriol, *Mon septennat 1947–1954*, ed. Pierre Nora and Jacques Ozouf (Gallimard, Paris, 1970), pp. 250–4. See also Jules Moch, *Rencontres avec . . . Léon Blum* (Plon, Paris, 1970), pp. 332–4.

ernment.[50] It was the latter approach which was decided on at a meeting of the National Council held on 25–26 February 1950.[51] Blum's advice still carried weight on other than policy matters too. Jules Moch, who, freed from ministerial duties, was revising a book on doctrine which he had written during the war, had decided not to write the final draft until he had had an opportunity to discuss his ideas with the old man, and he had arranged to see Blum at his house in Jouy-en-Josas on Wednesday 29 March. When he reached there, however, he found that Blum was already engaged in animated conversation with Félix Gouin, who had arrived unexpectedly to unburden himself of his worries about a scandal involving wine-trading to which his name had been unjustifiably linked. Blum had not fully recovered from an operation which he had had in November 1948 and, obviously tired, he asked Moch to come back in two days' time.[52] The meeting was not to take place, for the following day, while writing some letters, he suffered a coronary thrombosis and died a little before 4 p.m. That evening, the National Assembly decided that he should have a state funeral and the ceremony was held on 2 April in the Place de la Concorde as hail showers swept across Paris.[53] In the Socialist delegation, Guy Mollet and Daniel Mayer walked side by side, flanked by others of the party's national leadership. Each of them would miss Blum for personal reasons, and as a group they now had only his writings and their shared memories to remind them of a person of great humanity whose experience had been one of their most important links with the early days of French Socialism.

[50] Blum, 'Les solutions intermédiaires', *Le Populaire*, 16 February 1950, in Blum, *L'Oeuvre de Léon Blum 1947–1950* (Albin Michel, Paris, 1963), pp. 274–6.
[51] See *Bulletin Intérieur*, no. 47, March 1950, pp. 6–7.
[52] Moch, *Rencontres avec . . . Léon Blum*, pp. 334–5. See also Jean Lacouture, *Léon Blum* (Seuil, Paris, 1977), p. 555. On the wine-trading scandal, see Auriol, *Journal du septennat 1947–1954*, III, *1949*, p. 545, n. 190.
[53] Lacouture, *Léon Blum*, pp. 556–7.

8 Conclusion

We have now completed our review of the crises which affected the Socialist Party in 1938 and 1946. All that remains is to compare their general features and to draw some conclusions from the comparison.

As we have seen, the crisis of 1938 occurred because of the reluctance of the SFIO's leaders to abandon the Popular Front or, more precisely, to end the alliance with the Radicals and have the party return to the role of qualified opposition which it had assumed before 1936. They took this position first because they wished to protect the reform legislation of 1936, which they feared might be repealed or watered down by a conservative government; secondly, because some of them, especially Léon Blum, were concerned about the deterioration of the international situation and the need to ensure an adequate measure of continuity and stability in French domestic politics; and finally, because they still hoped that the Popular Front could be given a new lease of life and a further programme of reforms carried through parliament. Their difficulty lay in justifying this policy to the party's ordinary members, who were still wedded to the view that, ideally, the party should avoid participation in the government of a bourgeois state and that, rather than compromise its principles by attempting to sustain an alliance which no longer served its purpose, it should retreat once more to the well-known ground of opposition.

In the late 1930s, the two dissident *tendances* exploited this rank-and-file sentiment in different ways. Whereas the aim of the Bataille Socialiste was to revive the Popular Front by means of mass action and a greater involvement with the Communist Party, that of the Gauche Révolutionnaire was to make an appeal to tradition and, claiming that the Socialist Party was not acting in accordance with its founding Charter of 1905, to call for a much more determined revolutionary movement, a *front populaire de combat*. The combined strength of these two groups reduced the loyalists to a minority in the first division on general policy at the National Council of 17 January 1938, thereby virtually

384

forcing the parliamentary group to support the Chautemps government from the outside rather than accept places in a new administration. The formation of Blum's second ministry, in March 1938, raised briefly the possibility of a return to the unanimity and confidence of 1936 but when it fell, after only four weeks in office, the party had once more to come to terms with a Popular Front which had lost its momentum. The National Council of 9 April 1938 took the view that the Socialist Party should restrict itself to providing support for another minority government under Radical leadership.

At this stage, when the *lutte de tendances* was entering a phase of particular intensity, the dissolution of the party's Seine Federation both weakened and distracted the forces of opposition within the organization. At the Royan Congress in June 1938 the leaders were able to secure approval for two crucial decisions – that endorsing the disciplinary action which had been taken against the Seine Federation and another confirming the strategy of 'support without participation' in the party's dealings with the Daladier government, still at that time serving as a Popular Front administration. A break in the alliance had thus been avoided, but only by a narrow margin; the party could have faced a much more serious crisis had the leadership not agreed to accept 'support without participation' as a compromise strategy. That choice having been made, however, it was possible for Paul Faure to use his influence amongst the federal secretaries and the large federations to pull together the elements of a loyalist majority around a limited number of clear objectives. Blum then employed his considerable rhetorical skills to rally waverers to his banner at the Royan Congress.

Eight years later, in 1946, the rival merits of opposition and participation were to be discussed in very similar terms, but on this occasion it was the continuation of *tripartisme* which was at issue. Once again the established leaders of the party believed that the SFIO had to take part in government to give new form and purpose to French republicanism; once again, the traditionalists amongst the rank-and-file pressed for a return to the healing isolation of opposition. Now, however, with the pre-war *tendances* no longer in existence, the various currents of dissent converged within a broad and heterogeneous protest movement headed by Guy Mollet. Although amorphous and weakly organized, this movement could identify itself with Mollet's claim that the party's strategies were based on a faulty analysis of the political, social and economic trends in post-war France and that the party itself was being badly managed. A motion expressing these views attracted widespread support amongst the party's departmental federations in the weeks preceding the 38th National Congress in Paris and, on 29 August 1946, the first day of this gathering, delegates influenced by this motion voted in a majority against the approval of the executive's annual report, whereupon Daniel Mayer announced that he and his fellow officers would draw the appropriate conclusion from the vote. However, the Mollet group lacked the strength and cohesion needed to dominate the subsequent formulation of general policy and the elections to the incoming executive, and although Mollet succeeded Mayer as General Secretary on 4 September 1946, he was obliged to share power with members of the former leadership group.

How did the internal opposition to the SFIO's central leadership vary in form and style between the crisis of 1938 and that of 1946? In the pre-war conflict, the attack on the leaders and their loyalist majority came from the two *tendances*, which appealed to doctrinal and philosophical principles to justify their policy positions; in the post-war confrontation, the Mollet group was essentially a faction, an assemblage of diverse interests built around its leader's bid for power, despite its use of doctrinal themes at certain stages in its development.

Why were the *tendances* so sectarian in their behaviour? Part of the answer lies in the nature of the party's beliefs in the 1930s. Its myths about its own origins were very complex, embodying images of the 1789, 1831 and 1848 revolutions as increasingly articulate expressions of collectivist ideas, and particular interpretations of the Paris Commune, the foundation of the Third Republic, the Dreyfus affair and, above all, of its own formation in 1905. This was treated as a time of revelation when the purpose of socialism became completely clear for the first time and responsibility for a revolutionary mission was fully accepted. The Charter of 1905 was respected as the written testimony to that revelation. Although Jules Guesde and Jean Jaurès were given their due place in the founding event, neither was treated as the architect of the organization or the author of the Charter: it was as though the party's genesis had been the result of a deep underlying movement of ideas rather than the work of ordinary men and women. In the 1920s, the leaders of the reconstructed SFIO had kept that myth alive by treating the Tours Congress of 1920, when the Socialists parted company with the Communists, as marking a temporary separation of two natural allies. The central moral theme of the myth was that the party had acquired a sense of vocation in 1905, that the Charter was a statement of that vocation, and that the actions of the party's leaders must be governed by its principles.

In the context of 1938, the attachment of Léon Blum and Paul Faure to the ideals of 1905 was never questioned. It was the party faithful as a whole who, in the eyes of the Gauche Révolutionnaire, had become too worldly, too preoccupied with day-to-day activities. It felt that the SFIO was losing its vision and, rather like some medieval religious order, it saw its own task as being to set an example by living up to the original principles of the Charter, keeping that vision fresh and alive. It refused to accept that the party's doctrine was the product of experience and treated the body of ideas which Blum had developed over the years – ideas regarding the distinction between the exercise and the conquest of power, and the philosophical differences between Communism, Socialism and Radicalism – as no more than a series of responses to tactical exigencies. Whenever matters of basic principle arose at party congresses, it was always the 1905 Charter and its short companion piece, the first article of the party's rules, that were treated as the basis of doctrine.

The reluctance of the party's leaders to challenge the scope and content of the 1905 Charter had several consequences for the party's internal politics. First, strategy, in the sense of an integrated set of principles and aims about activity in elections, parliament and government, was often developed in the heat of events and justified on pragmatic and utilitarian grounds. Secondly, reflections on particular experiences, such as the lessons learned during the creation of the Wheat Office in 1936, were left floating in the air and were not assimilated into a systematic body of ideas. It remains a paradox that a party which contained some of the most intelligent and perceptive people in French politics could effectively fail to organize its ideas about policy, and contingent ideas about the nature of the state, into a rounded and coherent body of doctrine capable of informing strategy. It should have been possible, even in the turbulent circumstances of 1938, for the party's leadership to have pointed to the inadequacy of the Charter as a means of providing a demarcation, for all time, of the moral boundaries to action but this they did not do. As a result, the Gauche Révolutionnaire was able to exploit the opportunities for revivalism while the leaders were justifying participation in or support for government on grounds of expediency rather than of principle. Although the Bataille Socialiste was more inclined than the Gauche Révolutionnaire to make an issue of current policies in its confrontations with the central leadership and to justify its stand from its own version of Marxism rather than the Charter, it too was deeply embroiled in the *jeu de tendances* and the business of formulating lengthy resolutions for national plenums, of sustaining groups of committed supporters at branch and federation level, and of bidding for places on the national executive.

After the war, the party's leaders sought to prevent the revival of *tendances* by a mixture of moral pressure and changes to the rules. In particular, the abandonment of proportional representation for elections to the national executive removed the incentive for groups to mobilize support for policy resolutions which could then be used to secure places on the executive for representatives of their views. Attempts to do away with other practices which had favoured the activities of *tendances* were less successful. At the National Assembly of 24 February 1946, the opponents of reform were able to re-establish the National Council and to restore the use of the *mandat impératif*; the restitution of the National Council ensured that federal delegates could once more be assembled every three months, instead of annually for the national congress, thus reviving the closely spaced cycles of activity so conducive to generating expressions of dissent, while the return of the *mandat impératif* gave back to group leaders in the federations the crucial power of controlling delegates who might otherwise be swayed by rhetoric or moral pressure at national meetings.

With these conditions restored, it should have been possible for determined leaders to revive the system of *tendances*. Although the principal figures of the pre-war groups were absent – Zyromski had joined the Communist Party and Marceau Pivert did not return to Paris until the spring of 1946 – a number of their former lieutenants were still in the party and (as we saw in the case of the Seine Federation) had begun to resort to their former methods of operation. The Mollet group itself, when it was first formed, virtually mimicked the behaviour of the pre-war *tendances* by associating itself with *La Pensée Socialiste* and *Libertés* (which resembled *journaux de tendance* in some respects) and by touching upon grand issues of doctrine and strategy in its February *Appel* but its example did not inspire other groups to form and follow suit.

Much more important than the changes in the rules were the steps taken by the post-Liberation leadership to replace the Charter of 1905 with a new statement of doctrine. On his return to Paris at the end of the war, Blum had been asked to prepare a Declaration of Principles for this purpose but his draft, which was circulated before the Paris Congress of August 1945, met with sufficient objections to delay its approval until after further consideration. However, when it was adopted at the party's National Assembly of 24 February 1946, it still resembled in basic outline the document which Blum had originally prepared. The readiness of the majority of the members to accept its substitution for the Charter was due to several factors – their respect for Blum, whose testament it was felt to be; the belief that the years of occupation and the Vichy regime constituted a break in the continuity of French history and that both republicanism and socialism had to be rebuilt on new foundations; and a greater aggressiveness on the part of the Communist Party, which had justified its attempt to form a united

Marxist party in 1945 by reference to democratic centralism and Marxism–Leninism rather than to the democratic-socialist heritage of the SFIO. Wary of such a powerful neighbour, many Socialists felt that it had become more important to demonstrate the distinctiveness and relevance of modern French socialism than to revive the past for sentimental reasons.

In spite of this, the liberal humanism of the Declaration provoked Mollet and other néo-Guesdistes to attack Blum's text with arguments drawn from their own version of Marxist orthodoxy, built around beliefs in the primacy of the class struggle, in the strength of the bond between the proletariat and socialism, and in the inevitability of some form of political revolution. In the words of the Mollet motion:

nous ne considérons pas le marxisme comme un dogme. Il est une méthode de prospection des faits économiques et sociaux, une doctrine d'action qui permet de progresser dans la lutte pour l'émancipation des travailleurs, à la condition d'être constamment confrontée avec le réel et enrichie par les leçons de l'expérience.[1]

Although Mollet and his colleagues were critical of the way in which the party had acted within the alliance and governments of *tripartisme*, they did not go so far as to say that the SFIO should take no part in the business of running the country; in this way they avoided the difficult questions contained in the Charter about whether Socialists should remain completely separate from the bourgeois state. Their Trotskyist allies such as Jean Rous, too, grounded their doctrinal arguments on contemporary rather than historical material, stressing the point that modern capitalism was changing into a kind of corporatism, thus setting quite new problems for Socialist action.

For all these reasons, the Declaration of Principles was at least tolerated where it was not fully approved, and the Charter of 1905 was allowed to pass into history. The acceptance of the Declaration greatly reduced the scope for revivalism which the Gauche Révolutionnaire had exploited so effectively in 1938 and removed one of the basic conditions needed for the formation of *tendances*. Moreover, the sectarianism of the Mollet group rested on its claim that the existing leaders had not been sufficiently rigorous in their analysis of social and economic developments – a very different matter from suggesting that they had broken with tradition and abandoned their allegiance to the party's founding principles. Daniel Mayer was criticized for the way in which he was running the party and he, and indirectly Blum, were taken to task for having allowed their humanistic philosophy and their belief in individual

---

[1] *Bulletin Intérieur du Parti Socialiste (S.F.I.O.)* (Paris), no. 15, 1 August 1946, pp. 1–2.

as well as collective rights to affect their judgement; according to the Molletistes, they had virtually accepted the heresy that it was possible for a Socialist party to achieve its objectives within the framework of the bourgeois state. The term *redressement*, the motif for the Mollet revolt, signified not a wish to revive the intellectual schema of 1905 but a determination to correct the party's course and steer it towards revolutionary objectives in the current circumstances.

This point brings into focus an aspect of the Mollet group to which we shall return, namely, its resemblance to the Bataille Socialiste. Both organizations were prepared to envisage close co-operation with the Communist Party, and both were primarily concerned with the analysis of the situation which faced them in their own era rather than with the preservation of a time-bound morality. However, whereas the Bataille Socialiste had always to compete with the Gauche Révolutionnaire and its revivalism, the Mollet group was alone in its combat with the leadership and was not obliged to make half-hearted appeals for a return to past purity. With a monopoly over dissidence, it was able to fashion itself as a vehicle for a generalized protest and to claim that a change in strategy, allied with a change in leadership, would remedy a whole series of alleged deficiencies within the party, from doctrinal weakness to unhappy alliances and administrative and organizational failings. In the pre-war setting, the pressures of having to compete with the Gauche Révolutionnaire had forced the Bataille Socialiste to retain the form of a *tendance*, and to accept the constraints and the specialization of function which that form entailed, but after the war its virtual successor, the Mollet group, could develop a form and a generalized method of appeal which brought it a heterogeneous and widely dispersed support. This enabled Mollet to attract a following by means of direct personal ties to a much greater extent than Zyromski had been able to do. With the weakening of revivalism, the culture of *tendances* had been undermined. The renewal of opposition within the party in 1946 found expression in a single group whose mode of operation and internal structure made it more like a faction and less like a sect than its pre-war counterparts.

With these differences in mind, let us look more closely at the processes of action and reaction which accompanied the two crises. In the 1938 conflict, a potentially disruptive challenge from the Gauche Révolutionnaire was met forcefully at an early stage (with the dissolution of the Seine Federation), checked and controlled in the middle stage (during the congresses of the federations) and finally repulsed at the Royan Congress itself. In the 1946 crisis, by contrast, the challenge posed by the Mollet group was practically ignored until the very last moment. Although Daniel Mayer tried unsuccessfully to prevent the leaders of the group from attacking the executive's *rapport moral* and the Philip text was used during the federal congresses to serve as an alternative to the Mollet motion, no concerted attempt was made to stop the revolt in its tracks. As a result, it continued to gather momentum and obtained a majority in the first division of the Paris Congress on 29 August 1946. It is true that Mollet subsequently accepted a single policy resolution and that his group failed to dominate the elections to the Comité Directeur, but the scale and impact of his initial campaign had been considerable.

The contrast between the vigorous leadership response in 1938 and the virtual absence of reaction in 1946 becomes more intelligible when we consider how the basic leadership roles (those of organizational manager, party head, principal strategist and chief doctrinaire) were disposed on the two occasions. In 1938 Paul Faure as General Secretary was cast in the role of organizational manager, while Léon Blum combined the roles of party head and principal strategist with that of chief doctrinaire. These two men formed a flexible and effective duumvirate; as organizational head, Paul Faure was able to deal with the protests and anxieties caused by the dissolution of the Seine Federation and to set the conditions for the subsequent round of federal congresses, where his apparent refusal to circulate the texts of *motions de tendance* by means of a special issue of *La Vie du Parti* was of crucial importance. While Faure was thus engaged, Blum remained in the background, free to intervene as arbiter should the conflict spin out of control or to offer his own influential interpretation of the immediate problems facing the party in the parliamentary arena. This division of labour continued at the Royan Congress, with Faure bearing the brunt of the challenges in the fields of discipline and procedure and Blum justifying policy decisions and placing the issues of strategy in a general context.

In 1946, the very different disposition of the leadership roles produced structural weaknesses which the Mollet group were able to exploit to maximum effect. As Paul Faure had been, so Daniel Mayer was organizational manager by virtue of his office as General Secretary. However, with so many of the party's notables busily occupied in public positions – Félix Gouin was President of the Provisional Government from January to June, Vincent Auriol was President of both the first (from 31 January 1946) and the second Constituent Assemblies, and several others served as ministers for various periods – Mayer was forced to assume, to a very large extent, the roles of party head and chief strategist as well. Blum, whose role was now restricted to that of chief doctrinaire, was away in the United States between the middle of

March and the end of May and was therefore unable to give Mayer direct support during the intense debates about strategy which took place as the first Constitution Bill received its final consideration before being rejected in the referendum of 5 May. Besides, Mayer had so identified himself with Blum's views that he was often regarded, unfairly, as being something of an amanuensis rather than as an independent judge of doctrinal questions. By having had to assume so many of the central leadership functions, Mayer was exposed to attack from several quarters: not only was he criticized for his alleged shortcomings as an organizational manager but for errors of judgement as a strategist – he was blamed for the break with the Communists which occurred during the campaign for the elections of 2 June, for example, and for excessive reliance on the connection with the MRP. The range of his responsibilities also reduced his freedom of action in the organizational field, where he was most vulnerable. As the Mollet revolt began to affect the federations, he adopted a policy of remaining above the fray; for this reason, he not only refused to lend his name to any of the texts but tolerated the publication in the *Bulletin Intérieur* of the Mollet motion and other texts which were to be considered at the federal congresses. Blum, even after his return from the United States, had very little opportunity to intervene in the dispute; it was only on the first day of the Paris Congress, with the die already cast, that he was able to make a stand, challenging the concept of *redressement* and the reasoning which lay behind it.

The contrast between the two crises also reflected a difference in the leaders' understanding of the form of the conflict. In 1938 they were generally familiar with the character of the *jeu de tendances*, which had evolved from a similar pattern of conflict in the very early days of the SFIO. They also knew that the main aim of the Gauche Révolutionnaire was to bring about something resembling a religious revival amongst the membership, a revival capable of spreading through the federations like a forest fire. To frustrate this aim they had tried to restrain the Seine Federation and had appealed to the sense of discipline of the majority of the party's members, Faure having acted on the principle that revolt must be checked at once and prevented from spreading outward from its point of origin. After the war, apparently supposing that dissent within the party would almost inevitably take that form, the party's new leaders did everything in their power to discourage the formation of *tendances*. The Mollet revolt surprised them by gaining such a hold within the parliamentary group, by drawing to itself such a diversity of interests, and by concentrating its attack on strategies and personalities. Unlike the Gauche Révolutionnaire which had hoped for a sudden and wholesale conversion of the membership to its cause, the Molletistes threatened to wear away the leadership's support by a process of piecemeal subversion and attrition. Only at the annual congress could they be confronted and brought to battle.

In general, the arrangement of leadership roles at the centre of power in a political party will bear as much relation to the exigencies of internal conflict as to those of external pressures. In 1938 Faure and Blum, in meeting their obligations, were as closely attuned to the requirements of the *jeu de tendances* as were Marceau Pivert and Zyromski themselves, not only because they were conversant with the pragmatic and normative rules, to use Bailey's terms,[2] but also because they had trained themselves to respond in a precise and timely way to initiatives from their opponents. At no point in his long and involved struggle with the Gauche Révolutionnaire did Faure fail to seize an advantage and at no point did he overreact. Blum was equally adept at identifying half-formed objections to existing policies or strategies and then meeting them with a mixture of pragmatic and doctrinal reasoning which would conform to the common-sense judgements and prejudices of the rank-and-file. Each man had reliable lieutenants – Séverac in the case of Faure and Dormoy in that of Blum – who understood exactly what was at issue and could help to absorb the strain of particularly difficult situations. This pattern was partly a product of individual experience, but it was also partly a structural response to the existence of a particular mode of internal conflict, somewhat analogous to the resistance an organism will develop over time to a recurrent disease. In these terms, the steps taken to inhibit the formation of *tendances* in the post-war SFIO constituted an organizational prophylaxis, but the party had no immunity from the form of internal opposition represented by the Mollet revolt. Paradoxically, the lessons learned from that confrontation were later applied by Mollet himself; because he had used the same techniques, he knew how to prevent dissident leaders from building up support in the parliamentary group, from using national plenums to exploit grievances against the party's bureaucracy, or from presenting issues of strategy as issues of doctrine.

Measured against the notional gradations between a pure sect and a pure faction, the Gauche Révolutionnaire can be placed near the sectarian point of the scale and the Mollet group near the factional point, with the Bataille Socialiste occupying a position in the middle. However, in

---

[2] See, for example, F. G. Bailey, *Stratagems and Spoils: A Social Anthropology of Politics* (Basil Blackwell, Oxford, 1969), pp. 68–9 and 76.

the two crises which we have studied, the characteristics of each group and of the conflicts in which they took part varied considerably from one period of time to another. In 1946, as we have seen, the Mollet group at first resembled a *tendance*, but as the revolt gathered strength its factional characteristics became more and more pronounced. In the 1938 crisis, the sectarian aspect of the competition between the two *tendances*, and between each of them and the established leadership, was most marked in February 1938, when a National Council meeting projected for 27 March was the focus of activity; both the Gauche Révolutionnaire and the Bataille Socialiste were vying with each other to heighten the revolutionary aspect of their texts, and even the *Socialiste* had reached the point of trying to justify its strategic preferences by appeals to doctrinal principles. However, after the dissolution of the Seine Federation in April, the Gauche Révolutionnaire shifted the weight of its challenge towards an anti-bureaucratic campaign directed against the General Secretary and his colleagues. From that point onwards, with the conflict centred increasingly on personalities, the contest became more and more a factional confrontation: the personal qualities of Marceau Pivert and Paul Faure were the subject of comparison, and the Gauche Révolutionnaire, intent on winning the debate over discipline, accepted support wherever it was offered. The federal congresses did something to shift the conflict back towards sectarianism but at the Royan Congress itself there were persistent attacks on the *tendances* as being vehicles for personal ambition: even Zyromski was forced to defend his status as a *chef de tendance*, less concerned with mandates than with affirmations of belief.

At their most factional, the three groups resembled each other: each presented its leader as someone deserving of support on personal grounds, each diversified its support, and each found difficulty in maintaining its position under stress. If we restrict observation to the sectarian characteristics of the three groups, however, we find that we are dealing with very different styles of rhetoric, of doctrinal enquiry and of inspirational leadership. The revivalism of the Gauche Révolutionnaire was used to exploit the resources of the party's romantic revolutionary tradition. It claimed to express faith in a vision, as embodied in the Charter of 1905, and it relied on conversion to create a party committed to its outlook. Advocating voluntarism as the revolutionary ethic, it declared that activists should work with the mass of the people, creating revolutionary opportunities rather than waiting for these to be supplied by the laws of history. On the other hand, the Mollet group and the Bataille Socialiste drew upon Guesdiste tradition and thus stressed the importance of systematic analysis in ensuring that the revolutionary party could predict the flow of events and work with them. The Molletistes' appeal for *redressement* was essentially a call for disciplined action, for working to an agreed framework of precepts in the belief that social change could be studied scientifically.

In both the 1938 and 1946 crises, the dissident groups directed their criticism against the radical republicanism of Léon Blum, Vincent Auriol and other prominent figures in the party's central leadership. In the pre-war conflict, Blum had on two occasions (in June 1937 and in April 1938) rejected their demands that he should condone popular demonstrations against the Senate for its resistance to his financial policies. He was not, however, prepared to take the further step of declaring that the SFIO should accept that it was an integral part of the parliamentary system and that participation in government should be treated as a routine responsibility. His reluctance to acknowledge the extent of the party's republican obligation enabled both the Gauche Révolutionnaire and the Bataille Socialiste to make moral capital out of the party's dilemma, the former dwelling on its departure from the view of revolutionary politics embodied in the Charter of 1905, the latter playing on the leaders' alleged reluctance to break with the Radicals and join with the CGT and the Communists in creating a more advanced version of the Popular Front. After the war, the SFIO's full involvement in the constitution-making process meant that it could no longer claim that the institutions of government in the French state were instruments of bourgeois rule, and this made it easier for the radical republicans in the party to reveal their true colours. However, they were still suspected of favouring a more extended system of social and political alliances for the party, even if this entailed greater reliance on middle-class electoral support and a toning down of the party's anticlericalism. Mollet and his colleagues made great capital out of their claim that the party needed to strengthen its ties with the proletariat and renew its attachment to *laïcité*.

One of the less obvious consequences of the Mollet revolt was that it strengthened the position of néo-Guesdisme in the SFIO and reduced the chances that the radical republicans would be able to produce a revised programme and a new body of social theory for the party. As he took over as General Secretary, Guy Mollet's instinct was to encourage activists to accept that the analytic methods derived from historical materialism were still an effective means of understanding society and that class relations remained the basic elements of social structure. On 7 March 1947, at the opening day of a Socialist study programme in

Paris, he explained his own view of what the learning process involved:

d'abord, réétudier les principes, c'est-à-dire dans l'œuvre, mais plus encore dans la vie de nos grands précurseurs, rechercher ces lois explicatives qui peuvent nous permettre d'apprécier exactement la situation présente. Il ne s'agit pas d'apprendre je ne sais quel catéchisme d'action affirmée, mais d'étudier la pensée de nos grands anciens et alors, librement, – car on ne choisit comme on ne crée que dans la liberté – après confrontation des points de vue, après questions, . . . choisir soi-même.

Il ne s'agit pas davantage d'ailleurs de réviser, de réajuster une doctrine ou une méthode longuement éprouvée, mais de la confronter avec les faits.

Et puis, ces principes ainsi établis, être capable d'analyser scientifiquement la situation de l'heure, de juger de la véritable importance et de l'exacte signification des différents événements.

C'est ainsi, et seulement ainsi, qu'il deviendra possible aux militants du Parti de juger avec exactitude dans quelle étape actuelle de la Société nous nous trouvons, comment, dans cette étape, doivent être résolus les grands problèmes de la stratégie socialiste: participation gouvernementale, programme de transition, modalités d'action.[3]

Not only was Mollet asking Socialists to believe that historical change is determined and therefore predictable, that societies evolve by stages, that man through reason can discover the nature of a given stage, and that the foundation of rational thought lies in the knowledge of principles and of explanatory laws, but he was also exhorting them to make choices, to relate doctrines and methods of enquiry to the facts, and to judge the true significance of individual events in order to resolve problems of strategy. Each activist was being called on to be both a true believer and a pragmatist, forever condemned to consider the rival claims of inherited wisdom, *la pensée de nos grands anciens*, and actual experience.

This was a tall order, and when the tension snapped, as it was bound to do, the activist found himself veering towards dissident groups which claimed to have solved the basic dilemma, either through a voluntarist approach of the kind offered by the romantic revolutionaries or through the rigid determinism of Guesdisme. Seen in this light, the Gauche Révolutionnaire and the Bataille Socialiste of 1938 and the Mollet group of 1946 were all trading on the same insecurity at the core of the party's organizational ethic and, paradoxically, the intensity with which they expressed their own versions of doctrinal truth served to strengthen and maintain that ethic. Whatever their private doubts, both dissidents and loyalists continued publicly to portray French society as a structure of opposed classes, with the proletariat on one side and the bourgeoisie

[3] Parti Socialiste (SFIO), *Etudes Socialistes* (Paris), nos. 1–2, 1 April 1947, p. 11.

on the other. Both groups reduced sectional interests within the working class, within the peasantry, and within the middle classes, to crude notions of collective interest and revolutionary potential. As a result, both weakened the SFIO's ability to come to terms with an increasingly differentiated and complex social structure and, consequently, to play a major role in the politics of the Fourth Republic.

Appendix

National Council and National Congress Divisions
The research for this book has entailed an analysis of many of the divisions by mandate at meetings of the National Congress and the National Council of the SFIO between June 1937 and September 1946. During that period the results of these divisions were recorded both as aggregate votes and as lists of the distribution of mandates by federation and were presented in the party's journal (*La Vie du Parti* until 1940 and the *Bulletin Intérieur du Parti Socialiste (S.F.I.O.)* after 1945) and for the 34th (1937) and 35th (1938) National Congresses in the published *Comptes rendus sténographiques*.

In order to obtain reliable and comparable division lists, the records of votes by federation were checked for any errors of transcription and addition which might have been made when the original data were prepared and printed. Two basic checking techniques were employed: first, the addition of the mandates attaching to each federal delegation, to make sure that the total matched the number of national mandates allocated to that federation, and, secondly, the addition of the mandates recorded under the different headings of a division in order to compare the results with the official returns published in the party journal. If a discrepancy was detected, the necessary adjustment has been made. When errors in the calculation of the total votes appear to have occurred, the result published in the party journal has been referred to in the text and the adjusted figures have been given in the table setting out the details of the division. Square brackets have been used in the tables to indicate adjusted figures and I have used the adjusted rather than the published results in the comparison of divisions and in the analysis of changes in voting patterns over time.

The following is a list of those divisions cited in the text or in tables where figures have been adjusted to some extent:
1 National Council, 22 June 1937, vote on motion for approval of participation in the Chautemps government (source: *La Vie du Parti*, no. 75, 5 August 1937, p. 300). See p. 16.

(a) The name of the Saône-et-Loire Federation is given in the list of votes for the motion but the number of mandates has been omitted; the number has been assumed to be 70, the total of mandates allocated to this unit.

(b) The Haute-Vienne Federation was recorded as having given 138 mandates for the motion but this figure exceeds the total number of mandates assigned to the federation, namely, 136. The vote has been assumed to correspond to the latter figure. For the adjusted total votes, see p. 16, n. 12.

2   34th National Congress, 13 July 1937, vote on motion approving the decision of the National Council of 22 June 1937 (sources: *La Vie du Parti*, no. 75, 5 August 1937, p. 299; Parti Socialiste (SFIO), 34ᵉ Congrès National, Marseille, 10–13 juillet 1937, *Compte rendu sténographique*, pp. 604–5). See p. 17.

(a) The Aude Federation has been credited with 5 abstentions in keeping with the record in *La Vie du Parti* and the attribution of the same number of abstentions to the Aube Federation in the *Compte rendu* has been treated as an error.

(b) The Seine-et-Marne Federation has been recorded in *La Vie du Parti* as having cast 52 votes against the motion but this vote has not been reported in the *Compte rendu*.

(c) Both *La Vie du Parti*, no. 76, 25 November 1937, p. 303, and the *Compte rendu*, p. 608, report a request from the Commission Executive of the Savoie Federation to change the vote cast by its delegation in this division, but, although the message must have been received before printing, the original vote was not altered in either source.

3   34th National Congress, 13 July 1937, division on motions on general policy (sources: *La Vie du Parti*, no. 75, 5 August 1937, pp. 299–300; Parti Socialiste (SFIO), 34ᵉ Congrès National, Marseille, 10–13 juillet 1937, *Compte rendu sténographique*, pp. 606–7). See Table 4, p. 69.

Both sources record the Hautes-Pyrénées Federation as having allocated 10 mandates for the Blum–Faure motion, 19 for the Bracke–Zyromski motion and 8 for the Marceau Pivert motion, whereas the total number of mandates assigned to the federation was only 33. It has been assumed that the first of these votes, that for the Blum–Faure text, was 6 rather than 10, because this change would mean that the total of votes by federation for this motion would be 2,949, which corresponds to the published figure.

4   National Council, 7 November 1937, division on motions on general policy (source: *La Vie du Parti*, no. 76, 25 November 1937, p. 302). See p. 19.

(a) The Haute-Vienne Federation was recorded as having given 68 of its 136 mandates to the Séverac motion and only 8 to this motion as amended by Zyromski. It has been assumed that the latter figure should also be 68.

(b) According to the votes by federation, the total number of absent votes for this division was 47 rather than the published figure of 27.

5　National Council, 17 January 1938, first division on general policy (sources: *La Vie du Parti*, no. 77, 15 February 1938, pp. 305–6; no. [78], 10 March 1938, p. 312, for a request to rectify the Nièvre vote). See Table 5, p. 87.

(a) The distribution of mandates for the Nièvre Federation given in the original list was 4 for the Sérol motion, 28 for the Zyromski motion and 16 for the Marceau Pivert motion, but the Nièvre Federation asked for this to be rectified to 16 for the Sérol, 28 for the Zyromski and 4 for the Marceau Pivert text. This has been treated as a request to correct a recording error and the second set of figures has been used in calculations.

(b) Even without these changes, the totals of the votes by federation do not correspond with the total votes published at the time and addition errors have been assumed. The total votes given in Table 5 are therefore adjusted figures.

6　National Council, 17 January 1938, second division on general policy (source: *La Vie du Parti*, no. 77, 15 February 1938, p. 306). See Table 6, p. 90.

The distribution of mandates for the Seine-et-Oise Federation was given as 24 for the Graziani motion and 127 for the Marceau Pivert motion. It has been assumed that the first figure should have been 224; this produces the correct total of 351 mandates for the federation and a total for the Graziani motion which corresponds with the published total.

7　35th National Congress, Royan, 7 June 1938, division on general policy (sources: *La Vie du Parti*, no. 80, 28 June 1938, p. 319; Parti Socialiste (SFIO), 35ᵉ Congrès National, Royan, 4–7 juin 1938, *Compte rendu sténographique*, pp. 612–14). See Table 19, p. 213.

(a) The Charente-Inférieure Federation had been allocated 119 mandates for use at this National Congress, but both sources gave its distribution of mandates in this division as 82 for the Blum motion, and 29 for the Hérard motion, making a total of 111, 8 short of its full quota of mandates. The votes by federation in the Hérard column add up to the published total of 1,430 for his motion if the 29 mandates from the Charente-Inférieure Federation are included in the set, whereas those in the Blum column add up to only 4,864, 8 short of the published total of 4,872, if the Charente-Inférieure vote for the Blum text is taken to be 82; I have therefore assumed that the number of mandates given to the latter text by the Charente-Inférieure delegation was 90 rather than 82.

(b) Although the *Compte rendu* did not record the number of mandates allocated by the Morbihan Federation to the Zyromski motion, *La Vie du Parti* gave it as 7.

8 National Council, 4–5 March 1939, division on motions concerning foreign policy (source: *La Vie du Parti*, no. 82, March 1939, p. 15). See Table 22, p. 232.

(a) The distribution of mandates for the Cantal Federation was recorded as 8 for the Lebas motion, 18 for the Spinasse motion and 1 abstention, producing a total of 27 compared with the unit's quota of 25 mandates. It has been assumed that the vote for the Spinasse motion was 16, which produces the correct total for the federation and for the motion itself.

(b) The Constantine Federation claimed that its delegate had made an error in assigning all 53 of its mandates to the Spinasse motion and that 48 should have been given to the Lebas and 5 to the Spinasse text (see *La Vie du Parti*, no. 83, April 1939, p. 4). However, this cannot be taken as a correction of the record of the actual division and the figures have not been adjusted to take this proposed change into account.

9 37th National Congress, Paris, 13 August 1945, division on motions concerning relations with Resistance organizations (source: *Bulletin Intérieur*, no. 6, July–August 1945, p. 6). See Table 27, p. 281.

(a) The distribution of mandates for the Doubs Federation was reported in this source to be 23 for the Mayer motion, 50 for the Sarthe motion and 73 abstentions, although it had been allocated only 73 mandates for this National Congress. In contrast, the Drôme Federation (next to Doubs in alphabetical order) was not mentioned in the record, although its allocation was also 73 mandates. It has been assumed that the 73 abstentions assigned to the Doubs unit should have been attributed to the Drôme unit.

(b) The Haute-Savoie Federation had been allocated 67 mandates for this National Congress, but the only vote attributed to it was 76 for the Sarthe motion. It has been assumed that this is a printing error and that the correct figure should be 67.

(c) The distribution of mandates for the Seine-et-Marne Federation was recorded as having been 4 mandates for the Mayer motion,

63 for the Sarthe motion and 361 for the abstentions column but no votes were reported for the Seine-et-Oise Federation. These federations had been allocated 67 and 361 mandates respectively for this National Congress and it has been assumed that the 361 abstentions credited to Seine-et-Marne in fact belong to the Seine-et-Oise unit.

(d) Even with the above adjustments, the totals produced by an addition of the votes by federation vary markedly from the published results, producing 2,617 instead of 2,718 for the Sarthe motion and 1,907 instead of 1,806 for the number of abstentions. It has therefore been assumed that the 101 mandates attaching to the Pyrénées-Orientales Federation should have been recorded in the list of votes for the Sarthe motion and not included amongst the list of abstentions.

10   Extraordinary National Congress, Montrouge, 29 March 1946, division on the proposal by the Seine Federation to hold the discussion on electoral tactics after the discussion of the party programme and the draft Constitution Bill (source: *Bulletin Intérieur*, no. 12, April 1946, p. 3). See Table 29, p. 308.

(a) The Ain Federation is recorded as having given 21 mandates for the motion. This number has been changed to 22, which corresponds to the total number of mandates given to the unit for this National Congress.

(b) The votes by the Charente, Isère, Jura, Landes, Loir-et-Cher and Haute-Loire Federations were not recorded in the *Bulletin Intérieur* and were presumably omitted at some stage in the transcription process. The numbers of mandates allocated to these federations for this National Congress were Charente 21, Isère 80, Jura 21, Landes 86, Loir-et-Cher 35 and Haute-Loire 12, producing a total of 255 mandates. An addition of the printed votes by federation (including the adjustment to the Ain vote) produces totals which fall short of the published totals by 234 mandates in the case of the total for the motion and by 21 in the total of abstentions, which indicates (given the high frequency of bloc voting at this time) that either the Charente or the Jura unit gave its mandates to the abstention column and that the remainder gave their mandates for the motion. Assuming that at some stage, possibly in the printing of the returns, a group of votes for the motion extending in an alphabetical list from Isère to Haute-Loire was omitted in error I have placed all the mandates of the Isère, Jura, Landes, Loir-et-Cher and Haute-Loire Federations in the set of votes for the motion and assigned the 21 mandates of the Charente Federation to the abstentions column.

11 38th National Congress, Paris, 29 August 1946, division on the proposal to approve the *rapport moral* (source: *Bulletin Intérieur*, no. 18, August–September 1946, p. 6). See Table 30, p. 347.

In this case there are no obvious indications of errors in the record of votes by federation but these produce totals which differ slightly from those published at the time. The former totals have been preferred for inclusion in Table 30 and for purposes of comparison with the data presented in Table 31 on p. 350.

12 38th National Congress, Paris, 30 August 1946, division on proposal to approve the report of *Le Populaire* (source: *Bulletin Intérieur*, no. 18, August–September 1946, pp. 6–7). See Table 31, p. 350.

In this case also there are no obvious indications of errors in the record of votes by federation, in which the total number of mandates attributed to federations whose delegates were absent at the time of the division is 42. This figure has been preferred to the published total of 142 absences.

Finally, it should be noted that the results cited in Chapter 7 for the late 1940s have been taken directly from the summary returns given in party publications and have not been checked by a recalculation of the results by federation.

Bibliography

In working on the details of the SFIO's internal politics in the period from 1937 to 1950, I was greatly assisted by the following monographs, whose interpretations of the material and bibliographical guidance were invaluable.

For the late 1930s
Nathanael Greene, *Crisis and Decline: The French Socialist Party in the Popular Front Era* (Cornell University Press, New York, 1969);
Daniel Guérin, *Front populaire: révolution manquée: témoignage militant* (François Maspero, Paris, 1976); and
Jean-Paul Joubert, *Marceau Pivert et le pivertisme: révolutionnaires de la S.F.I.O.* (Presses de la Fondation Nationale des Sciences Politiques, Paris, 1977).

For the period of the Resistance
Daniel Mayer, *Les Socialistes dans la Résistance: souvenirs et documents* (Presses Universitaires de France, Paris, 1968); and
Marc Sadoun, *Les Socialistes sous l'Occupation: résistance et collaboration* (Presses de la Fondation Nationale des Sciences Politiques, Paris, 1982).

For the immediate post-war period
Jérôme Jaffré, 'La crise du Parti Socialiste et l'avènement de Guy Mollet (1944–1946)' (Mémoire présenté à l'Institut d'Etudes Politiques de l'Université de Paris, Paris, 1971).

PRIMARY SOURCES

ABBREVIATIONS OF NAMES OF INSTITUTIONS

BDIC   Bibliothèque de Documentation Internationale Contemporaine, Nanterre
BN   Bibliothèque Nationale, Paris
BNDP   Bibliothèque Nationale, Département des Périodiques, Annexe de Versailles
OURS   Office Universitaire de Recherche Socialiste, Paris
SFIO   Section Française de l'Internationale Ouvrière

ARCHIVES

Archives Léon Blum (Archives d'Histoire Contemporaine de la Fondation
  Nationale des Sciences Politiques, Paris)
Archives Maurice Deixonne (OURS, Paris)
Papiers des Amis de Marceau Pivert (22 AS 1–3, Archives Economiques et
  Sociales, Archives Nationales, Paris)
Archives de la Fédération du Nord (SFIO), Lille
Archives de l'OURS

ORAL INTERVIEWS

Dechézelles, Yves: Paris, 8 July 1992
Jaquet, Gérard: Paris, 23 July 1992
Mayer, Daniel: Paris, 7 July 1992
Rimbert, Pierre: Paris, 17 April 1980
Verdier, Robert: (i) Paris, 23 March 1990
  (ii) Paris, 7 July 1992

PARTI SOCIALISTE (SFIO): SERIES OF UNPUBLISHED AND PUBLISHED
DOCUMENTS, REPORTS AND PROCEEDINGS OF PARTY INSTITUTIONS

1 Executive institutions
Commission Administrative Permanente. Procès-verbaux (manuscript, OURS),
12 April 1939–6 June 1940
Comité Directeur. Procès-verbaux (manuscript, OURS)
  i 13 November 1944–10 August 1945
  ii 21 August 1945–21 August 1946
  iii 4 September 1946–30 July 1947
'Réunions du Comité Directeur de la S.F.I.O., de novembre 1944 à août 1946'
(including introduction by Jean-Pierre Rioux and extracts from meetings of the
Comité Directeur from 13 November 1944 to 11 September 1946), in 'La SFIO
face aux défis de l'après-guerre (1944–1947)', *Cahiers Léon Blum* (Paris), nos.
6, 7 and 8 (December 1979–July 1980), pp. 3–132.

2 National Congresses
31st, Toulouse, 20–23 May 1934
  i *Rapports* (Librairie Populaire, Paris, 1934)
  ii *Compte rendu sténographique* (Librairie Populaire, Paris, n.d.)
32nd, Mulhouse, 9–12 June 1935
  i *Rapports* (Librairie Populaire, Paris, 1935)
  ii *Compte rendu sténographique* (Librairie Populaire, Paris, n.d.)
33rd, Paris, 30 May – 1 June 1936
  i *Rapport* (dated 30 May – 2 June 1936) (Librairie Populaire, Paris, 1936)
  ii *Compte rendu sténographique* (Librairie Populaire, Paris, n.d.)
34th, Marseille, 10–13 July 1937
  i *Rapports* (dated 15–18 May 1937) (Librairie Populaire, Paris, 1937)
  ii *Compte rendu sténographique* (Librairie Populaire, Paris, n.d.)

35th, Royan, 4–7 June 1938
  i *Rapports* (Librairie Populaire, Paris, 1938)
  ii *Compte rendu sténographique* (Librairie Populaire, Paris, n.d.)
36th, Nantes, 27–30 May 1939
  i *Rapports* (Librairie Populaire, Paris, 1939)
  ii *Compte rendu sténographique* (Conservation film of original typescript, BDIC)
Extraordinary, Paris, 9–12 November 1944
  i *Compte rendu sténographique* (Conservation film of original typescript, BDIC)
  ii *Les Décisions du Congrès National extraordinaire des cadres des fédérations socialistes reconstituées dans la Résistance 9, 10, 11, 12 novembre 1944* (Paris, n.d.)
37th, Paris, 11–15 August 1945
  i *Projet de déclaration de principes et de statuts* (n.d.)
  ii *Propositions du Parti Communiste concernant l'unité de la classe ouvrière en France* (n.d.)
  iii *Rapports* (Librairie du Parti, Paris, n.d.)
  iv *Compte rendu sténographique* (Conservation film of original typescript, BDIC)
Extraordinary, Montrouge, 29–31 March 1946
Compte rendu sténographique (Original typescript consulted at head office of SFIO, 12 Cité Malesherbes, Paris, in 1960)
38th, Paris, 29 August – 1 September 1946
  i *Rapports* (Librairie du Parti, Paris, n.d.)
  ii *Compte rendu sténographique* (Original typescript, Centre de Documentation du Mouvement Ouvrier et du Travail, Nantes)
39th, Lyon, 14–17 August 1947
  i *Rapports* (Librairie du Parti, Paris, n.d.)
  ii *Compte rendu sténographique* (Original typescript consulted at head office of SFIO, 12 Cité Malesherbes, Paris, in 1960)
40th, Paris, 1–4 July 1948
Rapports (Librairie du Parti, Paris, n.d.)
41st, Paris, 15–18 July 1949
Rapports (Paris, n.d.)
42nd, Paris, 26–29 May 1950
Rapports (Société d'Editions du Pas-de-Calais, Arras, n.d.)

3 Commission Nationale des Conflits
Séance du 11 Avril 1938. Extrait du procès-verbal (OURS)

4 Records of federations
Fédération du Nord
40th Federal Congress, 1934
  i *Rapports* (for session of 13 May 1934) (Lille, 1934)
  ii *Comptes rendus* (for sessions of 4 February and 13 May 1934) (Lille, 1934)

43rd Federal Congress, 1937
  i *Rapports* (for session of 28 November 1937, dated 21 November 1937)
    (Lille, n.d.)
  ii *Compte rendu* (for session of 25 April 1937) (Lille, 1937)
  iii *Compte rendu* (for session of 28 November 1937) (Lille, 1938)
44th Federal Congress, 1938
  Compte rendu (for session of 18 December 1938) (Lille, 1938)
45th Federal Congress, 1939
  i *Rapports* (for session of 21 May 1939) (Lille, 1939)
  ii *Compte rendu* (for session of 21 May 1939) (Lille, 1939)
46th Federal Congress, 1945
  Rapports et compte rendu (for the session of 5–6 August 1945) (OURS)
47th Federal Congress, 1946
  Rapports (for the session of 23–24 March 1946) (Lille, n.d.)
48th Federal Congress, 1947
  Rapports (for session of 25 January 1948) (Lille, n.d.)
Fédération de la Seine
Congrès Fédéral administratif, 12 juin 1937 (Paris, n.d.) (BDIC)
Commission des Résolutions émanée du Congrès Fédéral du 23 janvier 1938
    (BDIC)
Commission des Résolutions émanée du Congrès Fédéral du 15 mai 1938 (BDIC)
Congrès Administratif des 2 et 9 décembre 1945, Rapports, statuts fédéraux
    (OURS)
Branch publication
Quinzième Section de la Fédération de la Seine
*La Gauche révolutionnaire du Parti Socialiste S.F.I.O. et le groupe bolchevick –
    léniniste (trotskyste), controverse entre Trotsky et Marceau Pivert* (Library
    of the London School of Economics and Political Science)

PARTI SOCIALISTE (SFIO): JOURNALS OF RECORD AND INTERNAL
PERIODICALS (ALL PUBLISHED IN PARIS)

1 Journals of record
For the national party
La vie du Parti (until 1940) (BDIC, BNDP, OURS)
Bulletin Intérieur du Parti Socialiste (S.F.I.O.) (from 1945) (Fondation
    Nationale des Sciences Politiques, OURS)
Bulletin Socialiste (pre-war) (BN)
Etudes Socialistes: Hebdomadaire de l'Ecole Socialiste S.F.I.O. (1947) (author's
    collection)
For the federations
Seine: *Juin 36* (pre-war) (BDIC, BNDP)
Seine: *Bulletin Hebdomadaire Fédéral* (post-war) (OURS)
Seine-et-Oise: *Fédération Socialiste de S.-et-O.* (post-war) (OURS)

2 Internal periodicals
Pre-war
La Bataille Socialiste (BDIC, OURS)

Les Cahiers Rouges (BN, OURS, Papiers des Amis de Marceau Pivert in Archives nationales)
Le Socialiste (BDIC, BNDP, OURS)
Post-war
La Pensée Socialiste (OURS)

3 Records of internal groups
Bulletin Intérieur de la Gauche Révolutionnaire (22 AS 1–3, Papiers des Amis de Marceau Pivert, Archives Nationales; Archives Maurice Deixonne, OURS)

PARTI SOCIALISTE (SFIO): TRACTS, MOTIONS AND MISCELLANEOUS
INTERNAL DOCUMENTS (BY SETS IN CHRONOLOGICAL ORDER)

1 Set of documents held at OURS regarding the Federal Congress of the Seine Federation, 23 January and 7 February 1938
Cyclostyled letters from *Le Socialiste* i 14 January 1938
ii 26 January 1938
Le Socialiste, Motion du 'Socialiste': schéma
Motion du 'Socialiste' pour le redressement du Parti dans la région parisienne
Le Socialiste, Pour le redressement du Parti dans la région parisienne

2 Brochure held at BDIC relating to the above congress
La Bataille Socialiste, *Pour le Congrès du 23 janvier 1938*

3 Tracts and cyclostyled documents in the Archives Maurice Deixonne (OURS) relating to events between March and May 1938
Parti Socialiste S.F.I.O. (Tendance Gauche Révolutionnaire), *Après le Conseil National du 12 mars 1938, à bas l'Union Nationale! La déclaration de la minorité*
Alerte! . . . Le Parti est en danger! (Parti Socialiste (S.F.I.O.), Fédération de la Seine, Paris, March 1938)
Aux camarades de la Tendance G. R., Paris, le 24 mars 1938
Parti Socialiste S.F.I.O. – Fédération de la Seine, Amicales Socialistes de la Seine, *Aux côtés des métallos*
Dernière heure – 28 mars minuit. Alerte.
Parti Socialiste S.F.I.O., Tendance Gauche Révolutionnaire, *Assez de ruses, assez de mensonges, qui trompe-t-on? et pourquoi?*
L[ucien] Hérard, *Aux secrétaires de section de la Côte d'Or: aux membres du Parti* (Dijon)
La Fédération Socialiste de la Seine aux camarades de province
L[a] Fédération de la Seine à toutes les fédérations du Parti S.F.I.O.
Déclaration: la minorité de la C.A.P. (tendance G. R.)
Appel aux militants du Parti Socialiste

4 The files of the Papiers des Amis de Marceau Pivert (in the Archives Nationales) contain a number of tracts, including duplicates of certain of those in the Archives Maurice Deixonne, and also:

Fédération Socialiste de la Seine, Amicales Socialistes de la Seine, *Grèves de la métallurgie mars 1938*, Dossier 28, 22 AS 1

5 The BN has a file entitled '**Parti Socialiste S.F.I.O., tracts du Parti Socialiste S.F.I.O. 1944–1946**', which includes:
À propos d'une demande de réintégration [*c.* May 1946], regarding the campaign for the readmission of Marceau Pivert to the SFIO

6 Several versions of **Guy Mollet's** *redressement* **motion for the 38th National Congress** were published in the form of tracts (see p. 332, n. 147), namely:
Congrès National S.F.I.O. (Août 1946): résolution sur le rapport moral et sur la politique générale (Entreprise de Presse, 100 rue Réaumur, Paris). No signatories (OURS). Referred to as Tract I
Résolution sur le rapport moral et la politique générale du Parti en vue du Congrès National d'août 1946 (Entreprise de Presse, 100 rue Réaumur, Paris). 48 signatories (included in 'Parti Socialiste S.F.I.O., Tracts du Parti Socialiste S.F.I.O. 1944–1946', BN). Referred to as Tract II
Résolution sur le rapport moral . . . Congrès National d'août 1946 (No printing details). 60 signatories (BDIC). Referred to as Tract III
Résolution sur le rapport moral . . . Congrès National d'août 1946 (Arras – I.N.S.A.P. – 46). 60 signatories (OURS). Referred to as Tract IV
Résolution sur le rapport moral . . . Congrès National d'août 1946 (no printing details). 60 signatories (OURS). Referred to as Tract V

7 Motion relating to the 41st National Congress (July 1949)
D'abord refaire le Parti! (no printing details) (xerox copy in author's collection)

OFFICIAL PUBLICATIONS

1 *Journal Officiel de la République Française*, comprising records of parliamentary debates, records of bills introduced and other papers (*Documents*), and records of legislation (*Lois et décrets* under the Third Republic, the post-war Constituent Assemblies, and the Fourth Repubic; and *Ordonnances et décrets* under the Provisional Government until 21 November 1945)

2 *Rapport fait au nom de la commission chargée d'enquêter sur les événements survenus en France de 1933 à 1945* (Assemblée Nationale, Première Législature, Session de 1947, Annexe au procès-verbal de la séance du vendredi 8 août 1947, No. 2344) (Paris, 1951)

Select list of newspapers and periodicals
L'Année politique (Paris)
La Bataille (Lille)
Bulletin de la Fondation Guy Mollet (Paris)
Cahier et Revue de l'OURS (Paris)
Cahiers Léon Blum (Paris)
Le Combat Social (Montluçon)

410   Bibliography

L'Espoir (Lens)
L'Espoir du Cantal (Aurillac)
Esprit (Paris)
Le Figaro (Paris)
La France Libre (London)
Gavroche (Paris)
L'Humanité (Paris)
Libertés (Paris)
Le Monde (Paris)
L'OURS (Paris)
Le Populaire (Paris)
Le Populaire Girondin (Bordeaux)
Le Populaire du Rhône (Lyon)
La Revue Socialiste (Paris)
Le Socialiste Aveyronnais (Rodez)
Le Socialiste Côte-d'Orien (Dijon)
Ce Soir (Paris)
Le Temps (Paris)
The Times (London)

SECONDARY SOURCES

Abellio, Raymond [Georges Soulès], *Ma dernière mémoire*, I, *Un faubourg de Toulouse 1907–1927*. Paris, Gallimard, 1971.
Ma dernière mémoire, II, *Les Militants 1927–1939*. Paris, Gallimard, 1975.
Adamthwaite, Anthony, 'Reactions to the Munich crisis', in Neville Waites (ed.), *Troubled Neighbours: Franco-British Relations in the Twentieth Century*. London, Weidenfeld and Nicolson, 1971, 170–99.
France and the Coming of the Second World War 1936–1939. London, Frank Cass, 1977.
Alexander, Martin S. and Graham, Helen (eds.), *The French and Spanish Popular Fronts: Comparative Perspectives*. Cambridge, Cambridge University Press, 1989.
Aron, Raymond, 'L'avenir des religions séculières – II', *La France Libre*, 8, 46 (15 August 1944), 269–77.
Audry, Colette, *Léon Blum ou la politique du Juste*. Paris, René Julliard, 1955.
'Tombeau de Léon Blum', *Les Temps Modernes*, 112 and 113 (1955), 1753–1802.
Auriol, Vincent, *Pour les candidats aux élections cantonales de 1937: la vérité sur la gestion socialiste*. Paris, Librairie Populaire, 1937.
Hier . . . demain, 2 vols. Paris, Charlot, 1945
Mon septennat 1947–1954, ed. Pierre Nora and Jacques Ozouf. Paris, Gallimard, 1970.
Journal du septennat 1947–1954, I, *1947*, ed. Pierre Nora. Paris, Armand Colin, 1970.
Journal du septennat 1947–1954, II, *1948*, ed. Jean-Pierre Azéma. Paris, Armand Colin, 1974.
Journal du septennat 1947–1954, III, *1949*, ed. Pierre Kerleroux. Paris, Armand Colin, 1977.

Azéma, Jean-Pierre, *De Munich à la Libération 1938–1944*. Paris, Seuil, 1979.

Bailey, F. G., *Stratagems and Spoils: A Social Anthropology of Politics*. Oxford, Blackwell, 1969.

Baker, Donald Noel, 'Revolutionism in the French Socialist Party between the World Wars: the revolutionary *tendances*'. Ph.D. dissertation, Stanford University, 1965.

'The politics of Socialist protest in France: the left wing of the Socialist Party, 1921–39', *The Journal of Modern History*, 43, 1 (March 1971), 2–41.

'The Socialists and the workers of Paris: the Amicales Socialistes 1936–40', *International Review of Social History*, 24 (1979), 1–33.

Baker, Robert P., 'Socialism in the Nord, 1880–1914', *International Review of Social History*, 12 (1967), 357–89.

Bauchard, Philippe, *Léon Blum: le pouvoir pour quoi faire?* Paris, Arthaud, 1976.

Bazal, Jean, *Le Clan des Marseillais: des nervis aux caïds 1900–1974*. [Paris], Authier, 1974.

Bell, David S., 'Politics in Marseilles since World War II with special reference to the political role of Gaston Defferre'. Ph.D. dissertation, University of Oxford, 1978.

Belloni, Frank P. and Beller, Dennis C., 'The study of party factions as competitive political organizations', *The Western Political Quarterly*, 29, 4 (December 1976), 531–49.

(eds.), *Faction Politics: Political Parties and Factionalism in Comparative Perspective*. Santa Barbara, Calif., ABC-Clio, 1978.

Berthet, Alix, *Ripostes. . . .* Grenoble, Parti Socialiste (S.F.I.O.), Fédération de l'Isère, 1946.

Bilis, Michel, *Socialistes et pacifistes: l'intenable dilemme des socialistes français (1933–1939)*. Paris, Syros, n.d.

Blum, Léon, *Lettres sur la réforme gouvernementale*. Paris, Bernard Grasset, 1918.

La Réforme gouvernementale. Paris, Bernard Grasset, 1936.

Bolchevisme et socialisme, 8th edn. Paris, Librairie Populaire, 1936.

L'Exercice du pouvoir: discours prononcés de mai 1936 à janvier 1937, 4th edn. Paris, Gallimard, 1937.

Jean Jaurès: conférence donnée le 16 février 1933 au Théâtre des Ambassadeurs. Paris, Editions de la Liberté, 1944.

À l'échelle humaine. Paris, Gallimard, 1945.

L'Histoire jugera. Montreal, Editions de l'Arbre, 1945.

Le Socialisme maître de l'heure. Paris, Editions de la Liberté, [1945].

'Notes sur la doctrine', *La Revue Socialiste*, 3 (July 1946), 257–61.

L'Oeuvre de Léon Blum, 9 vols. Paris, Albin Michel, 1954–72.

BOCA, 'Au Parti Socialiste: les jeux de la tactique et de la doctrine', *Esprit*, 13, 5 (April 1945), 754–6.

Bonnet, Georges, *Défense de la paix: de Washington au Quai d'Orsay*. Geneva, Constant Bourquin, 1946.

Le Quai d'Orsay sous trois Républiques 1870–1961. Paris, Fayard, 1961.

Vingt ans de vie politique 1918–1938: de Clemenceau à Daladier. Paris, Fayard, 1969.

Borne, Dominique and Dubief, Henri, *La Crise des années 30: 1929–1938*. Paris, Seuil, 1989.

Bourdé, Guy, *La Défaite du Front Populaire*. Paris, François Maspero, 1977.

Broué, Pierre and Dorey, Nicole, 'Critiques de gauche et opposition révolutionnaire au Front Populaire (1936–1938)', *Le Mouvement Social*, 54 (January–March 1966), 91–133.

Brunet, Jean-Paul, *Histoire du socialisme en France (de 1871 à nos jours)*. Paris, Presses Universitaires de France, 1989.

Bullock, Alan, *Hitler: A Study in Tyranny*, revised edn. London, Penguin, 1962, reprinted 1990.

Candar, Gilles (ed.), *Jean Longuet, la conscience et l'action*. Paris, Revue Politique et Parlementaire, 1988.

Chagnollaud, Jean-Paul, 'La Fédération Socialiste de Meurthe-et-Moselle (1944–1977)', *Annales de l'Est*, 5th Series, 30th year (1978), no. 2, 137–66.

Chautemps, Camille, *Cahiers secrets de l'Armistice (1939–1940)*. Paris, Plon, 1963.

Chevallier, Pierre, *Histoire de la franc-maçonnerie française*, 3 vols. Paris, Fayard, 1974–5.

Clouet, Stéphane, *De la rénovation à l'utopie socialistes: révolution constructive, un groupe d'intellectuels socialistes des années 1930*. Nancy, Presses Universitaires de Nancy, 1991.

Colton, Joel, 'Léon Blum and the French Socialists as a government party', *The Journal of Politics*, 15, 4 (November 1953), 517–43.

'The French Socialist Party: a case study of the non-Communist left', *The Yale Review*, 43 (Spring 1954), 402–13.

Léon Blum: Humanist in Politics. New York, Alfred A. Knopf, 1966.

Combes, Annie, 'Monographie de la Fédération Socialiste de la Sarthe'. Thesis, Institut d'Etudes Politiques de Paris, 1953.

Compère-Morel, A., *Grand dictionnaire socialiste du mouvement politique et économique national et international*. Paris, Publications Sociales, 1924.

Copfermann, Emile, *David Rousset: une vie dans le siècle: fragments d'autobiographie*. Paris, Plon, 1991.

Craipeau, Yvan, *Les Révolutionnaires pendant la seconde guerre mondiale*, I, *Contre vents et marées (1938–1945)*. Paris, Savelli, 1977.

Les Révolutionnaires pendant la seconde guerre mondiale, II, *La Libération confisquée 1944–1947*. Paris, Savelli/Syros, 1978.

Dalby, Louise Elliott, *Léon Blum: Evolution of a Socialist*. New York, Thomas Yoseloff, 1963.

Decouty, Guy, 'Introduction à l'étude de l'évolution de l'opinion politique dans le Département de la Haute-Vienne'. Thesis, Institut d'Etudes Politiques de Paris, [1950].

Deixonne, Maurice, *La Vérité sur la scission de Royan*. Aurillac, Imprimerie du Cantal, 1938.

Depreux, Edouard, *Souvenirs d'un militant: cinquante ans de lutte: de la social-démocratie au socialisme: (1918–1968)*. Paris, Fayard, 1972.

Devillers, Philippe, *Histoire du Viêt-Nam de 1940 à 1952*. Paris, Seuil, 1952.

Dupeux, Georges, *Le Front Populaire et les élections de 1936*. Paris, Armand Colin, 1959.

'L'échec du premier gouvernement Léon Blum', *Revue d'Histoire Moderne et Contemporaine*, 10 (1963), 35–44.

Edelman, Maurice, *France: The Birth of the Fourth Republic*. Harmondsworth, Middlesex, Penguin, 1944.

Elgey, Georgette, *La République des illusions 1945–1951, ou la vie secrète de la IVᵉ République*. Paris, Fayard, 1965.

Ensor, R. C. K., *Modern Socialism as Set forth by Socialists in their Speeches, Writings, and Programmes*, 3rd edn. London, Harper, 1910.

Faure, Paul, *De Munich à la Vᵐᵉ République*. Paris, Editions de l'Elan, [1948].

Fauvet, Jacques, *Les Partis politiques dans la France actuelle*. Paris, Editions du 'Monde', 1947.

La IVᵉ République. Paris, Fayard, 1959.

Fay, Victor, *La Flamme et la cendre: histoire d'une vie militante*. Saint-Denis, Presses Universitaires de Vincennes, 1989.

Ferretti, J., *Ce qu'est le Parti Socialiste*. Paris, Librairie Populaire, 1928.

Feuer, Lewis S. (ed.), *Basic Writings on Politics and Philosophy: Karl Marx and Friedrich Engels*. New York, Anchor Books, 1959.

Février, André, *Expliquons-nous*. Aspremont, Hautes-Alpes, A. Wast, 1946.

Flandin, Pierre-Etienne, *Politique française 1919–1940*. Paris, Editions Nouvelles, 1947.

Fraser, Geoffrey and Natanson, Thadée, *Léon Blum, Man and Statesman*. London, Victor Gollancz, 1937.

Frossard, L.-O., *De Jaurès à Léon Blum: souvenirs d'un militant*. Paris, Flammarion, 1943.

Gamelin, Maurice. *Servir*, II, *Le Prologue du drame (1930–août 1939)*. Paris, Plon, 1946.

Gaulle, Charles de, *Mémoires de guerre*, 3 vols. Paris, Plon, 1954–9.

Gay, Peter, *The Dilemma of Democratic Socialism: Eduard Bernstein's Challenge to Marx*. New York, Collier Books by arrangement with Columbia University Press, 1962.

Gillet, Marcel and Hilaire, Yves-Marie (eds.), *De Blum à Daladier: Le Nord/Pas-de-Calais 1936–1939*. Lille, Presses Universitaires de Lille, 1979.

Goguel, François, 'Géographie des élections du 21 octobre 1945', *Esprit*, 13, 13 (December 1945), 935–56.

'Géographie du référendum et des élections de mai–juin 1946', *Esprit*, 14, 7 (July 1946), 27–54.

'Géographie du référendum du 13 octobre et des élections du 10 novembre 1946', *Esprit*, 15, 2 (February 1947), 237–64.

La Politique des partis sous la IIIᵉ République, 2 vols. Paris, Seuil, 1946.

Géographie des élections françaises, de 1870 à 1951. Paris, Armand Colin, 1951.

Goguel, François and Dupeux, Georges, *Sociologie électorale*. Paris, Armand Colin, 1951.

Gombin, Richard, *Les Socialistes et la guerre: la S.F.I.O. et la politique étrangère française entre les deux guerres mondiales*. Paris, Mouton, 1970.

'Socialisme français et politique étrangère', *Etudes Internationales*, 2, 3 (September 1971), 395–409.

Graham, B. D., *The French Socialists and Tripartisme 1944–1947*. London, Weidenfeld and Nicolson, 1965.

'The play of tendencies: internal politics in the SFIO before and after the Second World War', in David S. Bell (ed.), *Contemporary French Political Parties*. London, Croom Helm, 1982, 138–64.

Representation and Party Politics. Oxford, Blackwell, 1993.

Greene, Nathanael, *Crisis and Decline: The French Socialist Party in the Popular Front Era*. Ithaca, N.Y., Cornell University Press, 1969.

Guérin, Daniel, *Front Populaire: révolution manquée: témoignage militant*, new edn. Paris, François Maspero, 1976.

Guesde, Jules and Lafargue, Paul, *Pourquoi l'avenir est au socialisme*, 3rd edn. Paris, Librairie Populaire, 1933.

Guitard, Louis, *Lettre sans malice à François Mauriac sur la mort du Général Weygand et quelques autres sujets*. Avignon, Aubanel, 1966.

Mon Léon Blum ou les défauts de la statue. Paris, Régirex-france, 1983.

Halperin, S. William, 'Léon Blum and contemporary French socialism', *Journal of Modern History*, 18, 3 (September 1946), 241–50.

Hérard, Madeleine, Pivert, Marceau and Hérard, Lucien, *Rupture nécessaire: réponse à Maurice Deixonne*. Dijon, Editions du Parti Socialiste Ouvrier et Paysan, 1938.

Hine, David, 'Factionalism in West European parties: a framework for analysis', *West European Politics*, 5, 1 (January 1982), 36–53.

Hostache, René, *Le Conseil National de la Résistance*. Paris, Presses Universitaires de France, 1958.

Husson, Raoul, *Elections et référendums des 21 octobre 1945, 5 mai et 2 juin 1946: résultats par département et par canton*. Paris, Le Monde, 1946.

Ingram, Norman, *The Politics of Dissent: Pacifism in France 1919–1939*. Oxford, Clarendon Press, 1991.

Jackson, Julian, *The Popular Front in France: Defending Democracy, 1934–38*. Cambridge, Cambridge University Press, 1988.

Jaffré, Jérôme, 'La crise du Parti Socialiste et l'avènement de Guy Mollet (1944–1946)'. Mémoire, Institut d'Etudes Politiques de Paris, 1971.

'Guy Mollet et la conquête de la SFIO en 1946', in Bernard Ménager *et al.* (eds.), *Guy Mollet: un camarade en République*. Lille, Presses Universitaires de Lille, 1987, 17–32.

Jankowski, Paul, *Communism and Collaboration: Simon Sabiani and Politics in Marseille, 1919–1944*. New Haven, Yale University Press, 1989.

Jaquier, Maurice, *Simple militant*. Paris, Denoël, 1974.

Joll, James (ed.), *The Decline of the Third Republic*. St Antony's Papers, no. 5. London, Chatto and Windus, 1959.

Jolly, Jean (ed.), *Dictionnaire des parlementaires français: notices biographiques sur les ministres, députés et sénateurs français de 1889 à 1940*, 8 vols. Paris, Presses Universitaires de France, 1960–77.

Joubert, Jean-Paul, 'A contre courant: le Pivertisme: de la "vieille maison" au "parti révolutionnaire" (Etude d'un courant socialiste révolutionnaire entre la S.F.I.O. et le P.C.F.)', 2 vols. Thesis, Institut d'Etudes Politiques, Université des Sciences Sociales de Grenoble, 1972.

Marceau Pivert et le Pivertisme: révolutionnaires de la S.F.I.O.. Paris, Presses de la Fondation Nationale des Sciences Politiques, 1977.

'De l' "unité d'action" aux tentatives de "rassemblement national" autour du Front populaire (1934–1938)', in *L'Identité du socialisme français: Léon Blum et les 'révolutionnaires' du Parti Socialiste*. Paris, *Cahiers Léon Blum*, nos. 17–18 (1985), 21–52.

Judt, Tony, *La Reconstruction du Parti Socialiste 1921–1926*. Paris, Presses de la Fondation Nationale des Sciences Politiques, 1976.

Marxism and the French Left: Studies in Labour and Politics in France, 1830–1981. Oxford, Clarendon Press, 1986.

Juin, Claude, *Liberté . . . Justice . . . le combat de Daniel Mayer*. Paris, Editions Anthropos, 1982.

Kedward, H. R., *Resistance in Vichy France: A Study of Ideas and Motivation in the Southern Zone 1940–1942*. Oxford, Oxford University Press, 1978.

Kramer, Steven Philip, 'La stratégie socialiste à la Libération', *Revue d'Histoire de la Deuxième Guerre Mondiale*, no. 98 (April 1975), 77–90.

Lachapelle, Georges, *Elections législatives: 1ᵉʳ et 8 mai 1932: résultats officiels*. Paris, *Le Temps*, 1932.

Elections législatives: 26 avril et 3 mai 1936: résultats officiels. Paris, *Le Temps*, 1936.

Lacouture, Jean, *Léon Blum*. Paris, Seuil, 1977.

De Gaulle, II, Le Politique 1944–1959. Paris, Seuil, 1985.

Lagroye, Jacques, *Société et politique: J. Chaban-Delmas à Bordeaux*. Paris, Pedone, 1973.

Lapie, Pierre-Olivier, *De Léon Blum à de Gaulle: le caractère et le pouvoir*. Paris, Fayard, 1971.

Lefebvre, Denis, *Guy Mollet: le mal aimé*. Paris, Plon, 1992.

Lefranc, Georges, 'Histoire d'un groupe du Parti Socialiste S.F.I.O.: révolution constructive (1930–1938)', in *Mélanges d'histoire économique et sociale en hommage au professeur Antony Babel à l'occasion de son soixante-quinzième anniversaire*, II. Geneva, 1963, 401–25.

Le Mouvement socialiste sous la Troisième République (1875–1940). Paris, Payot, 1963.

'Le courant planiste dans le mouvement ouvrier français de 1933 à 1936', *Le Mouvement Social*, 54 (January – March 1966), 69–89.

Histoire du Front Populaire (1934–1938), 2nd edn. Paris, Payot, 1974.

'Le socialisme français dans l'entre-deux guerres', *Information Historique*, 40 (1978), 128–36.

Lenoble, Jean, 'L'évolution politique du socialisme en Haute-Vienne sous la IIIᵐᵉ République'. Thesis, Institut d'Etudes Politiques de Paris, (1950).

Léon Blum, chef de gouvernement, 1936–1937. Paris, Armand Colin, 1967.

Levy, D. A. L., 'The Marseilles working-class movement, 1936–1938'. Ph.D. dissertation, University of Oxford, 1982.

'From clientelism to communism: the Marseille working class and the Popular Front', in Martin S. Alexander and Helen Graham (eds.), *The French and Spanish Popular Fronts: Comparative Perspectives*. Cambridge, Cambridge University Press, 1989, 201–12.

Lévy, Louis, *Vérités sur la France*. Harmondsworth, Middlesex, Penguin, 1941.

416   *Bibliography*

Ligou, Daniel, *Histoire du socialisme en France (1871–1961)*. Paris, Presses Universitaires de France, 1962.

Logue, William, *Léon Blum: The Formative Years 1872–1914*. DeKalb, Ill., Northern Illinois University Press, 1973.

MacRae, Duncan, *Parliament, Parties, and Society in France 1946–1958*. New York, St Martin's Press, 1967.

Maitron, Jean, *Dictionnaire biographique du mouvement ouvrier français*, XIII, Part 3, *1871–1914*. Paris, Editions Ouvrières, 1975.

Malroux, Anny, *Avec mon père, Augustin Malroux*. Albi, Collection Rives du Temps, 1991.

Marcus, John T., *French Socialism in the Crisis Years 1933–1936: Fascism and the French Left*. New York, Praeger, 1958.

Marion, Georges, *Gaston Defferre*. Paris, Albin Michel, 1989.

Martinet, Gilles, 'La gauche non conformiste', *La Nef* (April–May 1951), 46–56.

Mayer, Daniel, *Les Socialistes dans la Résistance: souvenirs et documents*. Paris, Presses Universitaires de France, 1968.

Pour une histoire de la gauche. Paris, Plon, 1969.

Ménager, Bernard, et al. (eds.), *Guy Mollet: un camarade en République*. Lille, Presses Universitaires de Lille, 1987.

Michel, Henri, *Histoire de la Résistance (1940–1944)*. Paris, Presses Universitaires de France, 1958.

Mirkine-Guetzévitch, Boris, 'La République parlementaire dans la pensée politique de Léon Blum', *La Revue Socialiste* (NS), no 43 (January 1951), 10–24.

Moch, Jules, *Arguments socialistes*. Paris, Editions de la Liberté, 1945.

Le Parti Socialiste au peuple de France. Paris, Editions de la Liberté, 1945.

Rencontres avec . . . Léon Blum. Paris, Plon, 1970.

Le Front Populaire, grande espérance . . . Paris, Librairie Académique Perrin, 1971.

Une si longue vie. Paris, Robert Laffont, 1976.

Moine, Jean-Marie, 'Le mouvement socialiste en Meurthe-et-Moselle sous la Troisième République'. Mémoire de maîtrise, Université de Nancy, 1973.

Nicolaï, Jean-Baptiste, *Simon Sabiani*. Paris, Olivier Orban, 1991.

Nicolitch, Suzanne, *Front Populaire, Socialisme, Franc-Maçonnerie*. Paris, Groupe Fraternel Spartacus, 1938.

Nicholson, Norman K., 'The factional model and the study of politics', *Comparative Political Studies*, 5, 3 (October 1972), 291–314.

Noguères, Henri, et al., *Histoire de la Résistance en France de 1940 à 1945*, 5 vols. Paris, Robert Laffont, 1967–81.

Noland, Aaron, *The Founding of the French Socialist Party (1893–1905)*. Cambridge, Mass., Harvard University Press, 1956.

Panebianco, Angelo, *Political Parties: Organization and Power*, trans. Marc Silver. Cambridge, Cambridge University Press, 1988.

Parti Socialiste (SFIO), *Le Parti Socialiste et l'unité française*. Paris, Editions de la Liberté, 1944.

La Politique économique et financière d'André Philip et Albert Gazier. Paris, Editions de la Liberté, 1946.

Paul-Boncour, Joseph, *Entre deux guerres: souvenirs sur la III* République*, III, *Sur les chemins de la défaite 1935–1940*. Paris, Plon, 1946.

Philip, André, *Pour la rénovation de la République: les réformes de structure*. Alger, Fraternité, [*c*. 1944].

Les Socialistes. Paris, Seuil, 1967.

Piat, Jean, *Jean Lebas*. Paris, Parti Socialiste SFIO, 1964.

Pivert, Charles, *Le Parti Socialiste et ses hommes: souvenirs d'un militant*. Paris, France-Editions, [1950].

Pivert, Marceau, *Révolution d'abord! La révolution avant la guerre*. Paris, Editions 'Nouveau Prométhée', [1935].

Tendre la main aux Catholiques? Réponse et réflexions d'un socialiste, 2nd ed. Paris, Librairie Populaire, 1937.

'Juin 36', *La Revue Socialiste* (NS), no.62 (December 1952), 532–9.

'Juin 1936 et les défaillances du mouvement ouvrier', *La Revue Socialiste* (NS), no. 98 (1956), 2–33.

Pivert, Marceau, Hérard, Lucien and Modiano, René, *4 discours et un programme: de l'exercice à la conquête du pouvoir*. Paris, Supplément au no. 1 des *Cahiers Rouges*, 1937.

Quilliot, Roger, *La S.F.I.O. et l'exercice du pouvoir 1944–1958*. Paris, Fayard, 1972.

Rabaut, Jean, *Tout est possible! Les 'gauchistes' français 1929–1944*. Paris, Denoël/Gonthier, 1974.

Rebérioux, Madeleine, 'Les tendances hostiles à l'état dans la S.F.I.O. (1905–1914)', *Le Mouvement Social*, 65 (October–December 1968), 21–37.

Reynaud, Paul, *La France a sauvé l'Europe*, 2 vols. Paris, Flammarion, 1947.

Rioux, Jean-Pierre (ed.), *Révolutionnaires du Front Populaire: choix de documents 1935–1938*. Paris, Union Générale d'Editions, 1973.

'Les socialistes dans l'entreprise au temps du Front Populaire: quelques remarques sur les Amicales Socialistes (1936–1939)', *Le Mouvement Social*, 106 (January–March 1979), 3–24.

La France de la IV République*, I, *L'Ardeur et la nécessité 1944–1952*. Paris, Seuil, 1980.

Rose, Richard, 'Parties, factions and tendencies in Britain', *Political Studies*, 12, 1 (1964), 33–46.

Rous, Jean, 'Le socialisme et les nouvelles perspectives', *Esprit*, 13, 9 (August 1945), 385–97.

'De la crise du socialisme au renouveau démocratique et révolutionnaire', *Esprit*, 17, 2 (February 1949), 306–20.

'Notes d'un militant: vingt-cinq ans d'essais et de combats', *Esprit*, 24, 5 (May 1956), 791–811.

Itinéraire d'un militant. Paris, Jeune Afrique Edition, 1968.

Sadoun, Marc, *Les Socialistes sous l'Occupation: résistance et collaboration*. Paris, Presses de la Fondation Nationale des Sciences Politiques, 1982.

'Sociologie des militants et sociologie du Parti: le cas de la SFIO sous Guy Mollet', *Revue Française de Science Politique*, 38, 3 (June 1988), 348–69.

Sarazin, James, *Dossier M . . . comme milieu*. Paris, Alain Moreau, 1977.

Séverac, J.-B., *Le Parti Socialiste: ses principes et ses tâches: lettres à Brigitte*. Paris, Editions de la Bataille Socialiste, 1933.

Shirer, William L., *The Collapse of the Third Repul.·ic: An Inquiry into the Fall of France in 1940*. London, Heinemann and Secker and Warburg, 1970.

Soulier, A., *L'Instabilité ministérielle sous la Troisième République (1871–1938)*. Paris, Sirey, 1939.

Thirion, André, *Révolutionnaires sans révolution*. Paris, Robert Laffont, 1972.

Touchard, Jean, *La Gauche en France depuis 1900*. Paris, Seuil, 1977.

Verdier, Robert, *La Vie clandestine du Parti Socialiste*. Paris, Editions de la Liberté, 1944.

P.S./P.C.: une lutte pour l'entente. Paris, Seghers, 1976.

Vieux Parti Socialiste S.F.I.O., *La 'Vieille Maison' se redresse contre les usurpateurs et les scissionnistes: appel de la direction provisoire du Parti*. Paris, [1945].

Wall, Irwin Myron, 'French socialism and the Popular Front'. Ph.D. dissertation, Columbia University, 1968.

'French socialism and the Popular Front', *Journal of Contemporary History*, 5, 3 (1970), 3–20.

'The resignation of the first Popular Front government of Léon Blum, June 1937', *French Historical Studies*, 6, 4 (Fall 1970), 538–54.

Weill-Raynal, Etienne, 'Marceau Pivert', *La Revue Socialiste* (NS), no. 118, (June 1958), 561–6.

Werth, Alexander, 'After the Popular Front', *Foreign Affairs*, 17, 1 (October 1938), 13–26.

France 1940–1955. London, Readers Union/Robert Hale, 1957.

Willard, Claude, *Le Mouvement socialiste en France (1893–1905): les Guesdistes*. Paris, Editions Sociales, 1965.

Williams, Philip M., *Crisis and Compromise: Politics in the Fourth Republic*. London, Longmans, 1964.

Wright, Gordon, *The Reshaping of French Democracy*. London, Methuen, 1950.

Zariski, Raphael, 'Party factions and comparative politics: some preliminary observations', *Midwest Journal of Political Science*, 4, 1 (February 1960), 27–51.

Zeller, Fred, *Trois points: c'est tout*. Paris, Robert Laffont, 1976.

Ziebura, Gilbert, *Léon Blum et le Parti Socialiste 1872–1934*, trans. Jean Duplex. Paris, Armand Colin, 1967.

Zyromski, Jean, *Sur le chemin de l'unité*. Paris, Editions 'Nouveau Prométhée', 1936.

Index

Abellio, Raymond (*see* Soulès, Georges)
Action Socialiste Révolutionnaire, 375
Albertin, Fabien, 242
Albertini, Georges, 176
Allemane, Gaston, member of CAP,
  Political Secretary of the Seine
  Federation (1938), 162, 185, 215
Allemane, Jean, 27
Amicales Socialistes, 95, 98, 99, 102, 103,
  137–8, 292
anschluss, 117–18, 120, 122, 123, 130,
  153, 226
anti-clericalism, 42–3, 265, 294, 301,
  304–5
Archidice, Georges, 339
Arnol, Justin, member of CAP, 215, 225,
  231, 232, 240
Arrès-Lapoque, Jacques, member of
  Comité Directeur, Deputy Secretary of
  SFIO 1946–7, 357, 358, 360, 363, 371,
  376, 378
Audeguil, Jean-Fernand, 247, 248, 321
Auriol, Vincent, Minister of Finance in
  Blum government (1936–7), 15;
  Minister of Justice in Chautemps
  government (1937–8), 17; biography,
  36–7; pre-war role in internal politics of
  SFIO, 40, 83–4, 119, 130, 157, 200,
  226, 395; member of second Blum
  government (1938), 126; at National
  Assembly (July 1940), 251, 252;
  member of Comité Directeur, 262, 285,
  295, 356; post-Liberation role in
  internal politics of SFIO, 264, 269–70,
  276–7, 279, 282, 340, 364, 395; Minister
  of State in second de Gaulle
  government (1945–6), 288, 289;
  President of first and second
  Constituent Assemblies (1945–6), 296,
  391; first President of the Fourth
  Republic, 368, 370, 373, 374, 377,
  381

Badiou, Raymond, 356, 376
Barré, Henri, 292, 298, 299, 325, 331,
  337, 356, 358
Bataille Socialiste, 1, 12, 14, 17–19, 23,
  40, 51–2, 53, 54, 60, 61, 65–71, 77, 80,
  83–94, 96–103, 106–11, 120–5, 127–30,
  133, 140, 141–2, 144–5, 147, 157–60,
  161, 163, 172–5, 177, 182, 184–6, 187,
  188, 189, 191, 194–214, 217–18, 221,
  226–7, 230, 231, 235, 237–8, 240, 241,
  254, 264, 277, 280, 283, 286, 298, 301,
  325, 372, 384–5, 387, 390, 394–7
Baurens, Alexandre, 356
Bedouce, Albert, Minister of Public
  Works in first Blum government
  (1936–7), 36, 40
Bernstein, Eduard, 21–2
Benoit, ——, pre-war Federal Secretary
  of Vosges Federation, 125
Bidault, Georges, President of
  Provisional Government (1946) and
  Premier (1949–50), 312, 314, 367, 368,
  381, 382
Biondi, Jean, member of Comité
  Directeur, 285, 356, 357
Blancho, François, 242
Blanqui, Louis Auguste, 27
Bloch, Jean-Pierre, 307, 337, 371
Bloch, Marcel, 185
Bloncourt, Elic, member of Comité
  Directeur, 262, 285, 298, 331, 337, 357,
  375
Blum, Léon, secretary and later president
  of the pre-war Socialist parliamentary
  group, 9, 33; Premier (1936–7), 13–16,
  23; pre-war views on foreign policy, 14,
  119–20, 123, 130, 153, 161, 185, 198,
  201, 225–6, 227–8, 232–3, 384; member
  of Chautemps government (1937–8),
  16; and *Le Populaire*, 23, 33;
  biography, 32–3; political philosophy,
  33–6, 67, 222–3, 386–7, 395; proposes

419

DATE DUE